For Joyce

Contents

Pelican Books

The Ancien Régime in Europe
Government and Society in the
Major States 1648–1789

E. N. Williams was born in Leicester, educated at Pembroke College, Cambridge, and served in the Royal Artillery during the war. Having taught History and English in three Grammar Schools, he has, since 1957, been Head of the History Department at Dulwich College. He is the author of *The Eighteenth-Century Constitution* and the very successful *Life in Georgian England* as well as the Pelican *Documentary History of England*, vol. 2.

E. N. Williams

The Ancien Régime in Europe

Government and Society in the
Major States 1648-1789

Penguin Books

Books Ltd, Harmondsworth, Middlesex, England
Penguin Books Australia Ltd, Ringwood, Victoria, Australia

—

First published by The Bodley Head 1970
Published in Pelican Books 1972

—

Copyright © E. N. Williams, 1970

—

Made and printed in Great Britain
by Richard Clay (The Chaucer Press) Ltd,
Bungay, Suffolk
Set in Linotype Plantin

8. FRANCE: THE COLLAPSE OF THE ANCIEN RÉGIME

9. RUSSIA: FROM GRAND DUCHY TO WORLD EMPIRE

10. RUSSIA: THE GROWTH OF AUTOCRACY

14. PRUSSIA: FREDERICK I AND FREDERICK WILLIAM I

15. PRUSSIA: ABSOLUTISM AND PRUSSIANISM

16. PRUSSIA: FREDERICK THE GREAT

17. AUSTRIA: THE RISE OF THE AUSTRIAN MONARCHY, 1620–1740

18. AUSTRIA: MARIA THERESA, 1740–80

19. AUSTRIA: JOSEPH II, 1780–90

20. BRITAIN: MIXED MONARCHY

21. BRITAIN: SOCIAL EVOLUTION
AND WORLD POWER

22. CONCLUSION

Preface

It is pleasant to record my gratitude here for the help that a number of friends have generously given. I have benefited greatly from the incredulity of my pupils, one of whom, Paul Dukes, has now become my mentor. I have also picked the brains of several long-suffering colleagues, including Michael Gross, Brian Howes, and David King, to whom I am very grateful. And once more I take pleasure in thanking Michael Langley-Webb, who has gone implacably through the manuscript. During the Ancien Régime, Pope recommended authors to 'get your enemies to read your works in order to mend them'. I am fortunate enough to get the same service from a friend.

Dulwich, May 1969   E. N. W.

Introduction

The Old Order and the New

In 1789 a Swiss traveller named Ludwig Meyer von Knonau made the following entry in the diary he was keeping of a journey from Zürich. 'As we got to the other side of Bözberg near Hornussen and entered Austrian territory,' he wrote, 'we were struck by the sight of the house-numbers, which seemed like a kind of shower, and appeared to us as a symbol of the hand of the sovereign, inexorably extending over the property of the private person.'[1] These little white plaques with their street-names and house-numbers, which the Emperor Joseph II imposed on his subjects, also indicate that the Swiss traveller had entered the historical epoch in which we live today: the era of the nation-state. This phenomenon was one of the chief products of the Ancien Régime, comprising the apparatus of bureaucracy on the one hand and the citizen-masses on the other, all equal in their subjection to it. But this period also produced another invention, likewise typical of the times in which we live. In 1792 the Prussian officer, Christian von Massenbach, complained of the 'new French method of attack, not with sword or cannon, but with far more dangerous weapons, by which they tried to inspire the common soldier with Republican sentiments'.[2] But democracy was not a concept which had to wait for the French Revolution to be forged. It was an ideal generated under the Ancien Régime, like most of the aims for which the French people fought.

This is not to imply, however, that Europe at the end of the eighteenth century consisted of nation-states each controlled by their citizens. Far from it. It will be evident in every chapter, in fact, that the drag of traditional modes of living, thinking, and governing was overwhelmingly too heavy for the efforts of the modernizers; and that eighteenth-century Europe was still in the thrall of institutions and states of mind which had been brought to life during the Middle Ages. France in 1789, for example, was not yet fully a state, but still a federation of provinces. And the French were not yet a nation of citizens, but still an association of communities: the three Estates, for example – the Clergy, the Nobility, and the Third Estate – and within these the smaller groupings, the religious orders, the universities, the nobility of the sword, the nobility of the robe, the gilds and fraternities, each with their own status and privileges legally and socially recognized. The noble house of Laval, for instance, was governed by its own body of customary law, recognized by the *Parlement* of Paris (the supreme judicial body), which differed from the customs of Anjou, Brittany, and Maine – the provinces in which the family properties were situated. Before they were Frenchmen, the inhabitants of the lands belonging to the King of France were Bretons, or Normans, and so on. They were also citizens of Rennes or Rouen, mayors or town councillors, Jesuits or Capuchins, judges, treasurers, goldsmiths, shoemakers, freeholders, share-croppers – even serfs. Indeed, the best way to understand this period is to forget the existence of states, and nations, and citizens as we know them, and to bear in mind that all three had to be slowly and painfully created by human effort. Under the Ancien Régime, all that can be affirmed is that concepts of all three had been formulated, that the techniques for bringing them into existence had been invented, and that here and there a good start had been made in putting them into practice. In other words, the history of this century and a half covers the conception and birthpangs of the new order in which we now live, but the familiarity of this must not be allowed to blind us to the peculiarities of the old order which gave the period its name.

International Relations

With the bulk of the ensuing chapters devoted to the traditional ways of life, and to the efforts of innovators to change them – in other words, to the internal histories of the main European states – there is room only to sketch their external relations one with another. This is not to say that diplomacy and war were unimportant. On the contrary, it was precisely the need to raise men and money for foreign aggression (or defence against it) that drove kings to modernize their states so as to modernize their societies. The relation between foreign affairs and home affairs was always intimate, and the fortunes of each vitally affected the other. The more efficiently a king exploited his home resources, the more successful he was abroad; and the more victorious his foreign policy, the more powerful he became at home. And this feed-back was present in the converse cases also, for it was the inactive states (mainly aristocratic oligarchies such as Poland, Holland, Belgium, or Venice) that got left behind in the eighteenth century. A peaceful foreign policy, that is, usually went with stagnation at home, where innovations would have been too disturbing. 'It is dangerous', wrote Paolo Renier, a reforming Venetian aristocrat, in 1767, 'to introduce into military or civil bodies anything which smacks of novelty, and particularly in those countries which are at peace; for tranquillity outside, in the ordinary way, makes them unquiet inside.'[3]

In international relations the Ancien Régime carried over much that was traditional: for example, the practice of forming alliances by means of royal marriages, or going to war over a disputed succession, or on behalf of a certain Christian denomination, or even crusading against the 'infidel Turk'. At the same time, however, this period also introduced Europe into the era in which we now find ourselves – that of the modern states system. Before the eighteenth century, Europe was thought of as a collection of communities arranged vertically in a hierarchy, at the head of which reigned the temporal power of the Emperor and the spiritual power of the Pope. Such a concept, for example, was basic to the plan for perpetual peace which Leibniz published in 1677. 'All the Christian kings and princes', he wrote, 'are subject to the orders of the Universal Church, of which the Emperor is the director and temporal head.'[4] And the same thinking underlay the life's work of the opponent of the Emperor, Louis XIV of France. His foreign aims were, of course, firstly, to round off the territories of France in order to give the state defensible frontiers; but, secondly, he planned to substitute himself for the Emperor as the chief ruler in Europe. He did not hope to rule all Europe directly himself, but to force all the other rulers to recognize him as the head of the hierarchy. In other words, he was acting in the tradition of Charles V and Philip II, while his opponents – England, Holland, and Austria – followed *their* opponents by forming alliances to restore the balance of power.

After Louis XIV's defeat the diplomats of Europe learned to live with the concept which has prevailed ever since: the idea of Europe as a horizontal system of autonomous powers constantly jostling for position in a restless process of adjustment and readjustment, aimed again at preserving a rough equilibrium. Britain, the most powerful state in the eighteenth century, did not imitate Spain or France and aim at a European hegemony. She instead used her weight to maintain the balance in Europe so as to be free to concentrate on her empire overseas. Voltaire, writing in 1751, said that the states of Europe were 'at one in the wise policy of maintaining among themselves as far as possible an equal balance of power'.[5] This does not mean that governments were driven by any other motive than pure self-interest. 'Their fundamental principle', said Frederick the Great, 'has constantly been to grasp at everything in order to increase their territory continually; and their wisdom has consisted in forestalling the tricks of their enemies, and playing the subtler game.'[6] Egotism still reigned supreme in eighteenth-century international relations, but it was an educated egotism, worldly-wise, calculating, and restrained. By this time there were so many near-equal states in Europe that they all (in the words of a modern student) 'exhibited a kind of schizophrenia, the outcome of the conflict between their urge to expand and their need to be careful'.[7] This helps to explain the inhibited stateliness of late-eighteenth-century warfare. It was a time when clear-headed calculation had ceased to be swayed by religious emotion, but had not yet become swamped by ideological ardour. Reason was in charge, and reason told rulers to restrain their ambitions. 'Arms and military discipline being much the same throughout Europe,' wrote Frederick the Great in 1775, 'and alliances as a rule producing an equality of force between the belligerent parties, all that princes can expect from the greatest advantages at present is to acquire, by accumulation of successes, either some small city on the frontier or some territory which will not pay the expenses of war.'[8]

By this stage the great powers of Europe, according to Frederick, were France, England, Austria, and Russia in the first rank, followed by Spain, Holland, and Prussia; and these are the states considered in the following chapters. One or two previously powerful rulers had fallen low. The Holy Roman Emperor, for example, was only of account in so far as he was also the head of the Austrian Monarchy. Even before the Thirty Years' War (1618–48), Sully had compared the Empire to a wrestler with the muscles of a giant whose heart had grown weak; and this war proved that the muscles were not all that powerful either. It was the last attempt till the nineteenth century to unite the numerous German principalities into a centralized state, and it failed. Starting as a double effort by the Habsburgs to crush the independence of the German princes and stamp out Protestantism, it drew in, one after another, nearly all the states of Europe, from Sweden down to Italy, and from Spain across to Muscovy. Finally, the Treaties of Westphalia (1648) gave international recognition to the fact that Germany was not a state, but a miniature Europe.

In addition to the Emperor, three other formerly powerful states – Sweden, Poland-Lithuania, and Turkey – had fallen behind with the rise of three new ones – Austria, Russia, and Prussia. Of the still great powers, Spain had declined from the leading position she had enjoyed in the sixteenth century; while Holland, having rocketed to world-power status in the first half of the seventeenth century, just managed to maintain this position during the rest of the period. Between 1648 and 1713 France was the most powerful state, but already the ultimate victor, England, was drawing level. During the War of the League of Augsburg (1688–97), when English and Dutch resources were pooled under the rule of William III, Louis XIV was forced to suspend building operations at Versailles, while William went ahead with *het Loo* in Holland, and Kensington and Hampton Court in England. Moreover, the predominance of Holland in the early seventeenth century and of England in the eighteenth century fittingly demonstrates the dependence of military power on financial strength. And that in turn depended, not only upon the size of the human and material resources provided for a country by nature, but also upon the extent to which these were exploited and brought to bear by effort and ingenuity. In other words, the strength of a state depended on the character of its society and the performance of its organs of government: the two chief subjects of this book.

Main Types of State

One broad difference that can be distinguished between the great powers of the Ancien Régime was that between those, on the one hand, where an energetic state was trying to goad a sluggish society into motion, and those, on the other, in which the state was trying to ride a stampeding society. (Communities in which both state and society grazed peacefully through traditional pastures did not become great powers.) Holland and England belong in the second category; Russia, Prussia, Austria, seventeenth-century France and eighteenth-century Spain belong to the first. Seventeenth-century Spain declined because the drag of a reluctant society was too much for a feeble state. Eighteenth-century France displayed the efforts of a too-powerful state trying incompetently to damp down the energies of a too-ebullient society. The French Revolution was the result.

The societies of Europe were strung out along a road leading from primitive agrarian life based on lord and serf, at one end, to industrial capitalism with its richly diverse social structure, at the other. Broadly speaking, this road ran East–West across Europe. Travelling eastwards from the Elbe was like travelling backwards in economic history. The East was more thinly populated than the West, and the cultivable area was brought fully under exploitation much later. Parts of Poland, Hungary, and South Russia became settled and farmed only in the seventeenth and eighteenth centuries. Some Balkan communities were only emerging from their forests at the moment when

Lancashire workers were entering their factories. For one reason or another, the mass of the cultivators of the soil had been reduced to serfdom during the late Middle Ages and early modern times. The owners of the soil, the nobles, were often at one and the same time the landlords, seigneurs, and employers of those who worked it. In other words, they did not lease out their estates to tenant-farmers and then live on the rents like western aristocrats. Instead, those within reach of ports exploited their estates as large-scale agricultural entrepreneurs, using their serfs as their labour-force, and selling their grain, timber, beer, and other products, to the merchants of the West. Other commercial activity had either failed to develop at all, or, where it had flourished during the Middle Ages, it had succumbed to the competition of the West. Towns, where they existed, had been brought under control of the monarch or the nobility; and trade was in the hands of foreigners – principally the Dutch. Social mobility was restricted by the stark simplicity of the social structure. In places where the landlords belonged to a different nationality and religion from their serfs, it was extremely difficult to rise in the world. But even in areas where lord and serf were brothers, they were often separated by a layer of aliens – Germans, Greeks, Jews, perhaps – who performed the elementary industrial, commercial, and professional tasks, and effectively acted as a damp-course on social aspirations.

In contrast, the societies of the West had been transformed by economic and political growth into complex social hierarchies bubbling with activity. In the medieval period they had achieved a head start, and then they had had the good fortune to be first in on the geographical discoveries and the subsequent trading boom with the Americas and the Indies. Maritime trade, bringing its stimulating flow of precious metals and other goods produced by the sweat of the non-European masses, had acted like magic on western Europe. Every kind of economic activity had been set in rapid motion, and by the mid seventeenth century western Europe was well on the way to the economic, political, and intellectual predominance she has enjoyed in the world down to the twentieth century.

The Corporative Society

Inside the societies of western Europe, and to a lesser extent in central Europe and parts of the East, the effects of economic growth and political development were making the division of communities into Estates – usually three or four – a hopelessly crude method of social description. This corporative system, in which men formed groups linked to other groups in vertical hierarchies, was being undermined by the class system which divides societies into horizontal layers. Since, however, the corporative method of classifying mankind still filled the minds of most Europeans in this period, and was still the basis of social status, legal privilege and political power – was, in fact, the Ancien Régime – its manifestations must be examined here. It was felt by many, for example – especially the most privileged – that the world would come to an end if men attempted to move out of the condition of life to which God had called them. 'If marriages intermingle the Estates', wrote the Marquis de Mirabeau in the middle of the eighteenth century, 'they will poison and destroy everything.'[9] Even in the most devout aristocratic households, adultery with a member of the Third Estate was much to be preferred to marriage. Of course, economic growth and absolute monarchy were gradually replacing these divisions with new ones, but a history of the Ancien Régime must look hard at Estates as well as classes.

Estates derived from feudal Europe, when the First Estate, who prayed, the Second Estate, who fought, and the Third Estate, who worked, added up to an adequate description of social reality. During the Middle Ages, as commerce developed and monarchies crystallized out of the international order, this simple arrangement grew more complex with the emergence within each Estate of sub-groups of various kinds, consisting of men joining together for common action in various walks of life. Trade and industry produced members of the Third Estate who were not peasants, and who did not live on manors. These urban groups – merchants and craftsmen – formed companies and gilds. Groups of companies and gilds joined together to form

municipal boroughs. Lawyers, doctors, and so on, joined together to form their professional organizations, too. At that
time, when the individual was helpless by himself, joint action
could wrest status and privilege from the community and from
the rulers – as trade unionists have discovered since. In a
similar way the texture of the First and Second Estates also
grew more complex, as their members too joined forces in ever
more varied units. Members of the First Estate became enrolled into monasteries, cathedral chapters, charitable institutions, universities and schools – each with its common property,
its charter of liberties, its legally defined privileges, its body
of law, its internal hierarchy, and so on. Similarly, members of
the Second Estate formed their noble houses, their orders of
chivalry, their associations of knights. In all three Estates,
groups joined other groups to form larger associations, gaining
recognition and exercising authority over wider territorial areas.
Territories then joined together to form provinces. Often, at
the instigation of the monarch, who needed their help, whole
Estates would come together in a Diet, or a Parliament, or a
Zemsky Sobor, or a Cortes, or a Reichstag, which as time went
on developed their own corporate authority and privileges. And
as kings joined province to province, so Estates joined Estates,
forming larger units – like the Estates-General of France,
which brought down the Ancien Régime.

The kings of the Ancien Régime, then, did not inherit feudal
monarchies, but structures far less crude. They did inherit the
remnants of the feudal system, but this was thickly overlaid by
the corporative system just described. Every state was thus a
corporative state – an *état d'ordres*, a *Ständestaat* – that is, a
collection of manors and boroughs, gilds and companies,
Estates, races, territories, and provinces, even monarchies, in
which the ruler acted on his subjects not directly, but through
intermediaries. Between the king and the individual stood, not
merely feudal lords, but also a multitude of intermediate authorities, each with legislative, judicial, and executive powers,
which rivalled the authority of the king's own bureaucrats. It
should always be borne in mind that the states with which we
are familiar today – France, Spain, Holland, Austria, and so on

– did not then exist, but were still only being painfully created. In the seventeenth and eighteenth centuries these states were assemblages of provinces which had been added one to another at different times and in different circumstances – by marriage, by conquest, by inheritance, by treaty – and, except in Russia, rulers had made little attempt to penetrate into them as far as internal government was concerned. They had simply, as a rule, sworn solemn oaths to protect their new subjects in their traditional rights and liberties – thus creating awkward limitations on the powers of the would-be absolutist kings of the Ancien Régime.

In Styria, for example, a province of the Austrian monarchy, the office run by the permanent committee of the Provincial Estates at Graz (their traditional executive organ) was larger than the office of a French Intendant (the pioneering agents of absolute monarchy). It was these officers (and not the men from Vienna) who organized the military establishments on the Turkish border, provided chemists and midwives and other medical services, ran the customs, maintained the forests, appointed university professors, and so on. In France the province of Languedoc was also still largely self-governing on the very eve of the French Revolution. De Tocqueville, who devoted a special supplement to it at the end of his *Ancien Régime*, picked out three peculiarities which made it 'an object of envy' to the other provinces. First, it had 'an assembly composed of men of substance, esteemed by the population, respected by the royal power ... in which every year the special interests of the province were freely and seriously discussed'. Secondly, there was the fact that 'most of the public works were executed at the expense of the province alone'. And, thirdly, 'the province had the right of levying itself, and by the method which it preferred, some of the royal taxes and all those which it was authorized to raise to satisfy its own needs'.[10] Among their public works was a system of roads admired by Arthur Young, the draining of the marshes of Aigues-Mortes in the Camargue, the construction of the great canal joining the Rhône at Beaucaire with the Mediterranean at Sète, and the creation of Sète as an international port. They also went half-shares with Louis

XIV in the cutting of the Canal du Midi which linked the Mediterranean with the river Garonne near Toulouse.

At one end of the monarchy of Brandenburg-Prussia (to take another case) the County of Cleves conducted its own foreign policy when this period opened; and at the other, East Prussia was a feudal vassal of the King of Poland. In the Spanish monarchy, the so-called King of Spain ruled a galaxy of kingdoms and provinces: Castile, Navarre, the three Basque provinces, the kingdom of Aragon (itself consisting of Majorca, Aragon, Valencia, and Catalonia). And within Catalonia, the City of Barcelona, of which the King of Spain was Count, was a special case. The same king was also the Duke of Burgundy (Belgium); and here he had ten separate provinces to deal with, each with its own liberties engraved in ancient charters, and guaranteed countless times by his predecessors. In England – the most unified and the most uniform of the great powers – the City of London was practically an independent, self-governing community. Moreover, in the rest of the country most of the appointments to office in the central and local administration were in private hands. But there was no provincial separatism in England to compare with that on the Continent, and though the Estates (that is, the Houses of Parliament) limited the crown more than elsewhere, they were central Estates, and there was no danger, as in many Continental countries, that their victory would lead to the break-up of the kingdom into provinces. On the other hand, the King of England also ruled Scotland and Ireland, as well as colonies overseas, and there was always the possibility of their breaking away – as, indeed, the American Colonies successfully did in 1776.

There is one further element to be added to this account of the bodies making up the corporative state: and that is those royal bureaucrats who had managed to become independent of the crown. The French *officiers* are the best-documented example of this phenomenon, but it was found everywhere in Europe. From the high Middle Ages onwards, kings everywhere had created officers of various kinds to take power away from the members of the Estates. These royal servants had worked mainly in the royal courts of justice (set up to provide appeals from feudal and municipal justice) and on the boards for assessing and collecting royal taxes. With the passage of time, as is the tendency of bureaucracies, these officers grew independent of their royal masters. Whether their posts had been given to them by warm-hearted kings, or sold to them by impecunious ones, or simply let slip by lazy ones, they became private property, capable of being bought and sold, and passed on from father to son. At that time, public office was not yet looked upon as a public duty. It was a status symbol with privileges attached, which one purchased or inherited or had conferred upon one for reasons unconnected with one's competence, training, or assiduity. It was what Loyseau, the French social student, called in 1613: 'an ordinary dignity with public functions' (as opposed to a revocable one, like that of an Intendant).[11] Or it was, as Sir William Blackstone, the English jurist, described it: 'a *right* to exercise a public or private employment and to take the fees and emoluments thereunto belonging'.[12] One made as much profit out of it as possible. Moreover, office-holders often secured exemption from taxation and military service, and sometimes even secured ennoblement. At the end of the seventeenth century, a third of all the households in Dijon (to take a French example) enjoyed the privileges of office-holders, or nobility, or both. As Montesquieu said in the following century, the King of France did not own gold-mines like the King of Spain, but he was nevertheless richer. The vanity of his subjects was more inexhaustible than any mine whatever.[13] The kings may have gained their subjects' money by the sale of offices, but they lost more in return. They lost the right to appoint, promote, or dismiss their own servants; but their servants still had the right to exploit the public. Thus the *officiers* of France, and their equivalents in other states, formed one more component of the corporative state – and one more obstacle in the way of centralizing absolutism.

In 1776 the French nation was thus described to Louis XVI by the *Avocat-Général* Séguier as:

The clergy, the nobility, the sovereign courts, the lower tribunals, the officers attached to these tribunals, the universities, the academies, the financial companies, the commercial companies, all present, and in all parts of the State, bodies in being which one can regard as the links of a great chain of which the first is in the hands of Your Majesty, as head and sovereign administrator of all that constitutes the body of the nation.[14]

The Absolute State

In that speech Séguier gives a formidable summary (if not a complete list) of all the opponents of the crown in the late part of this period. If he is right to call them a chain, then it was a chain which tied the royal hands all through the Ancien Régime, and prevented the full formation of absolute monarchy. The creation of the absolute state, which Jaime Vicens Vives, the great Spanish historian, has called a 'fundamental phenomenon in the history of the last five centuries',[15] took on a new intensity from the middle of the seventeenth century onwards. It is from this point that we can date the effective rise of the modern bureaucratic state which governs the nations of the world today, even though the Ancien Régime was only one stage on a long road of monarchical growth reaching far back into the Middle Ages. The years on either side of 1648 were important in the history of monarchy, for a series of revolutions and rebellions broke out which, though partly provoked by assertive monarchies, demonstrated to all Europe the anarchy which could result from the very weakness of governments. These disturbances included the English Civil War and the execution of Charles I (1642–49), the French Frondes (1648–53), the revolts of Catalonia and Portugal against Madrid (1640), the revolutions in Naples and Sicily (1647–48), peasant revolts in Austria (1648), Sweden (1650–53), Switzerland (1653), Poland (1648–51), the Ukraine (1648–54), and Muscovy (1648–50). Adler Salvius, the Swedish representative at the peace congress in Westphalia, reported back to his government in 1648: 'One would call it a great miracle that everywhere in the world one hears tell of revolts of people against sovereigns, for example, in France, England, Germany, Poland, Muscovy, Turkey.... Whether this can be explained by a certain general disposition of the stars in the sky or by something like a general agreement of people against bad governments, God alone can know.'[16]

For our purposes, the causative role of the heavenly bodies in history is a question that must be left on one side, as must the much more interesting debate over whether these disturbances were all part of a 'general crisis' and what sort of a crisis it was. The point here is that fear of anarchy underlay the drive to absolutism: it motivated Hobbes's *Leviathan*, the great text-book of strong government, and assisted the great practitioners of it, Richelieu, Mazarin, and Louis XIV. After this, there were no further general revolutionary movements till 1789, and the years of the Ancien Régime were characterized by the steady accumulation of monarchical power. They were also marked by greater material prosperity, and, it seems, human happiness.

The misery of our ancestors has been more common under weak government than under strong, and in this period it was the monarchies which were the main agents of progress. 'The Estates proved to be a drag on public welfare', as Gerhard Oestreich has said, 'and the princes certainly were also egotistical, but also the element which promoted the general interest.'[17] Wherever the monarchs tried to enlarge their control, they encountered the entrenched interests of the corporative state, each pleading its ancient rights and liberties against the innovations of absolutism. At the present time, we prize our rights and liberties, and invest them with an aura of sanctity. So did the Estates under the Ancien Régime – those who were fortunate enough to possess them; but in their age 'rights and liberties' tended to signify only advantages which their owners enjoyed over the rest of the community. The liberties in whose defence the European nobilities fought a running battle with their rulers mostly amounted to the privilege of maintaining the lower orders in a servile condition – to the privilege to behave, perhaps, like a certain Russian princess who said to her guests as they arrived at her country house: 'I am delighted you have come, I was so bored that I was going to have my Negroes beaten to pass the time.'[18] As Bernardo Tanucci, a key adviser to Charles III of Spain both in Naples and Madrid, said in 1746, 'feudal tyranny is the most shameful political invention that the human race has ever chosen'.[19] For the only hope for the suffering masses of Europe was the success of a better invention, the modern state; and the only route to that in most countries of the Ancien Régime was *via* absolute monarchy. And by 'absolute monarchy' is meant, in the first place, a government which took decisions without going cap in hand to the Estates (that is, irresponsible government); and, in the second place, a government whose decisions were really carried out (that is, an effective government).

'Politics', said Prince Kaunitz, the Enlightened first minister of both Maria Theresa and Joseph II of Austria, 'is the art of sheltering the rights of the crown from the incursions of the Estates, and of extending their limits without encroaching on the privileges of the nation.'[20] The lead in this process was given by Louis XIV of France, and his methods were followed first by Russia and Prussia, and then by Austria and Spain. Success depended on the personal effort and ability of the monarch, working, not with the judicial and administrative councils and colleges inherited from the past, but alone, except for a handful of hand-picked secretaries and ministers at the centre, and in the provinces represented by a new generation of royal bureaucrats, who were appointed, promoted, dismissed, posted, and paid by the monarch, and responsible to him. In France these latter were the Intendants, but they appeared all over the Continent in various guises. Their tasks were partly the traditional ones of extending the protection of the royal courts of justice, and of extracting as much revenue as possible from the public; and partly some new activities, henceforth characteristic of the modern state. These new tasks nearly all derived from what a modern historian has called the 'military revolution'.

As has been mentioned already, two seventeenth-century dangers were increasing the importance of the armed forces: firstly, the external ones resulting from the greater scope of international war, and exemplified by the Thirty Years' War – the first European war; and, secondly, the internal threat from civil discord, shown in the so-called 'general crisis'. Both dangers eased the task of centralizing absolutists, for their subjects, even members of the First and Second Estates, were prepared to make sacrifices in the interests of security.

But the 'military revolution' made absolutism not merely possible, but also essential. During the century before 1648, developments in the use of fire-arms and changes in military tactics led to the formation for the first time of standing armies, since warfare now called for much higher levels of training and drill than had been necessary hitherto. The days of the feudal retinue of the barons, or the trained bands of the cities, or of the gangs of ruffians hired for a campaign by the Estates, and other forms of private military enterprise, were numbered. Armies became professional, very much larger (as a comparison between Philip II's 40,000 and Louis XIV's 400,000 will make clear), and permanent (since this was cheaper than disbanding them for the winter). Navies developed similarly. And both became beyond the resources of a noble, or even a province. 'Only the state, now', as Michael Roberts has said, 'could supply the administrative, technical and financial resources required for large-scale hostilities. And the State was concerned to make its military monopoly absolute.'[21] And in so doing, it made the power of the crown absolute as a consequence.

In the first place, the Intendants of France, and their equivalents elsewhere, had the task, not only of driving a good bargain with the contracting captains and colonels who raised the mercenaries, but also of staying with them, in peace and in war, to make sure that the contracts were observed, that the troops were properly trained and kitted-out – that the regiments, in other words, really were royal units, and not private armies still. This work involved a proliferation of civil servants; but this was only the start. Other officials, in the second place, were required to organize food and fodder, uniforms and boots, masts and rigging, billets and transport, and so on. Thirdly, to pay for all this, a vast increase in royal revenues was required, involving new taxes and new functionaries to invent and collect them. And, fourthly, in order to raise the tax-paying capacity of the citizens, monarchs made all those interventions into economic and social life known to historians as mercantilism and Enlightened absolutism. In state after state on the

Continent, bureaucrats drained marshes, dug canals, constructed ports, sank mines, built roads, opened factories, founded banks, dissolved monasteries, abolished holy days, took over universities, schools, and poor-houses. Whether economic policies were mercantilist, as they were till the middle of the eighteenth century, or Physiocratic, as they tended to become thenceforth, governments all required more civil servants. Mercantilists of the earlier absolutist states required government intervention in the economy in order to jerk it into life. Physiocrats of the Enlightened absolutist states required government intervention in order to clear away institutional debris such as gilds or internal customs duties which interfered with the natural working of the economy. In either case, the State was putting an invalid-carriage under a supine society in the hope that it would move in the same direction that the Dutch and English societies were marching on their own two feet.

On the whole, they succeeded. Bureaucracy, that is, managed to produce a passable substitute for private enterprise. But it did so at a cost which can never be properly calculated. Confining ourselves to the purely economic costs, how much wastage must there have been in a system which soaked up so much of private savings through the taxation and office-selling mechanisms only to spend it on display and war? And how could a dynamic bourgeoisie be expected to flourish, or even emerge at all, when the State acted as a magnet for all the talent and ambition at work in society at large? According to Ivan Pososhkov, the Russian critic in Peter the Great's time, fifty to sixty thousand parasites lived on the salt monopoly who could very well have been used in industry.[22] And in France, Roland Mousnier has suggested that absolute monarchy in fact delayed economic growth, that the French desire for office to a great extent explains why 'France has remained above all an agrarian country whose industry made only very slow progress and preserved old characteristics, while the first industrial revolution was taking place in England'.[23]

To summarize, then, absolute monarchy arose out of the need for internal and external security which made a standing army as a royal monopoly essential. This army required higher revenues; the revenues required economic growth; they all required the formation of a royal bureaucracy to eliminate, or push aside, the manifestations of the corporative state. But the theorists of strong government such as Hobbes or Bossuet must not lead us into exaggerating the practical effects of absolutism in that era. The size of the state apparatus, for one thing, was small compared with today's. Prussia under Frederick the Great – the most intensely bureaucratized state in Europe – had one civil servant for every 450 inhabitants. Germany in 1925 had one for every forty-six.[24] Frederick was not even able to find out the annual consumption of coffee in his dominions, for example. Prince Kaunitz once made the remark, typical of the sometimes ingenuous (and perhaps pathetic) optimism of the Enlightenment, that 'to construct a good building it is necessary to demolish the old one'.[25] But with social and political institutions it is impossible to start afresh. The old lives on alongside the new and limits it. The absolute state did not abolish the corporative state: it added to it. The functionaries of the kings worked alongside the functionaries of the Estates, even employing them at times, as in France where the Intendants put *officiers* on their pay-roll as *sous-délégués*. In other words, a student of absolute government under the Ancien Régime must bear in mind the remark of Jaime Vicens Vives, who pointed out that there was 'an abyss between the apologetics of the prince and the institutional arrangements in a state, as well as between these arrangements and the everyday practice of the government'.[26]

Taking into account the differences, then, between political theory, constitutional law, and day-to-day administration, one can divide the European states into three kinds, at the risk of a certain amount of over-simplification. There were, firstly, Russia, which had absolutism without corporative institutions; secondly, Holland and England, which had corporative institutions without absolutism; and thirdly, France, Spain, Austria, and Prussia, which had both. In Russia (except on the western borders) the corporative organs of resistance to absolutism were weak or non-existent. There had been no sub-infeudation, and every noble was the direct vassal of the tsar. The Church was other-worldly and non-political; urban growth was slow. As new provinces were annexed to the Muscovite nucleus, they were fully geared into the machinery of government. The Russian people – even the nobles – had little legal protection against such ruthless autocrats as Ivan the Terrible or Peter the Great. All were equal in their obligations to serve the tsar. 'It is no longer one's lineage which brings honour,' wrote Prince Michael Shcherbatov, in the reign of Catherine the Great, 'but one's function, merit, and seniority in the service.'[27] The very fact that careers were more open to talent among the Russian nobility than anywhere in the West – except in the U.S.A. – is itself a sign of the absence of corporate power there in the face of the autocracy. And it was not until the reign of Catherine the Great that the nobles were allowed to form themselves into Estates on western lines; and it was only then that the crown guaranteed them in the possession of certain privileges which were the birthright of most citizens of Holland or England. And just as the nobles were subservient to the tsar, so were the serfs helplessly in the power of their lords. As late as the very end of the eighteenth century, Count A. A. Arakcheev could write: 'Every woman on my estate must give birth every year, preferably a son to a daughter. If someone ·gives birth to a daughter, I exact a fine; if a dead child is born, or a miscarriage – a fine also; and if there is a year the woman does not deliver a child, then she is to present eight yards of linen.'[28]

In Holland and England, by contrast, the rights and liberties of the corporative state were deeply rooted growths. There was, however, an important difference between them. The Dutch Republic was a group of seven separate provinces, whose corporative institutions prevented unity from being achieved. England was a united kingdom, by contrast, which had even passed through a phase of absolutism under the Tudors. From the mid seventeenth century onwards, the corporative institutions were running the absolutist institutions – in an absolutist manner or not, according as it suited their interests. But, whatever the differences, the Estates in Holland and England were in charge; and they also differed in another respect from their counterparts in the rest of Europe. The men who controlled the English and Dutch corporative bodies were dynamic and innovating, especially in economic and intellectual fields. Their cousins elsewhere were steeped in reaction.

Finally, France, Spain, Prussia, and Austria presented the spectacle of continuous struggle between innovating monarchies and strongly entrenched, and conservative, corporative institutions. In these circumstances, absolutism could not become autocracy. Theorists such as Bossuet, and practitioners such as Louis XIV, recognized that the power of the Monarchy, though deriving from God, was limited by divine law, natural law, and the rights of their subjects from earlier grants by monarchs. Even Bodin, the great theorist of sovereignty, said: 'If you do away with the corporations and communes, you will ruin the state, and turn it into a barbaric tyranny.'[29] Thus absolutism grew there, but so did the means to prevent it from becoming an Asiatic tyranny. And broadly speaking, the Continental states fostered the one, and Holland and England encouraged the other.

The Enlightenment

Both trends, the absolutist and the liberal, found intellectual support in the Enlightenment. This body of ideas was put together like a rocket by the British and Dutch in the first half of the period, and then launched by the French in the second half, when it burst over Europe in a shower of brilliant concepts. The main ingredients were, firstly, the body of ideas recovered from classical Greece and Rome during the Renaissance and after. 'The Greeks were the teachers of the Romans,' said Diderot to Catherine the Great, 'the Greeks and the Romans have been ours.'[30] The ancients taught the moderns to rely on reason and observation, and to use both in criticizing baseless superstitions, myths, and dogmas. This attitude led them, secondly, to despise what they regarded as the barbaric intellectual darkness of the Middle Ages, to refuse to accept the unproved pontifications of the Churches or the Scriptures, and to oppose wherever they found them all attempts by kings and priests to stifle free speculation. David Hume remarked on the havoc that a close inspection of libraries would cause. 'If we take in our hand any volume', he said, 'of divinity or school metaphysics, for instance; let us ask, *Does it contain any abstract reasoning concerning quantity or number?* No. *Does it contain any experimental reasoning concerning matter of fact and existence?* No. Commit it then to the flames: For it can contain nothing but sophistry and illusion.'[31]

In the third place, the men of the Enlightenment liberated their minds in a revolutionary way from thraldom to both classical and medieval authorities, and had the confidence to rely on the logic of their own mental processes working on the facts which they themselves had observed. In other words, they applied to human life the methods of Bacon, Descartes, and Newton, which had brought about the Scientific Revolution of the seventeenth century. Like them they abandoned the attempt to explain the mysteries of the purpose of things, and concentrated on describing how things behaved here and now. 'Interest was directed', as a modern authority has put it, 'to the *how*, the manner of causation, not the *why*, its final cause.' There was a 'general transference of interest from metaphysics to physics, from the contemplation of Being to the observation of Becoming'.[32] Like the scientists, the *philosophes* (as the publicists of the Enlightenment were called) believed that nature obeyed universal laws which could be discovered by patient collection of facts and logical reflection on them. Just as Newton had discovered the laws governing the physical world, so men would soon discover the laws governing the human world. And these would include not only explanations of how, in fact, human beings behaved individually and in societies, but also recommendations about how they ought to behave; that is to say, they confidently expected to provide for mankind definitive systems of ethics and politics, as well as the sciences of history, geography, psychology, economics, sociology, and so on.

Following on from this, as the fourth broad characteristic of the Enlightenment, was the general secularization of life characteristic of Europe after 1648. Men paid more attention to the question of how to bring about earthly happiness than of how to achieve eternal salvation. And in this trend, the predilections of philosophers were backed by events in the real world. The Thirty Years' War had taught men the vanity of force as a method of reconverting Europe to the Catholicism of the Counter-Reformation; while ideological exhaustion had shown them the sanity of toleration. This development did not lead to atheism or irreligion, however, but men more and more adopted the attitude expressed in the eighteenth century by the English country gentleman, George Shiffner, to take a typical example. 'Men of different opinions worship God in their own way,' he wrote, 'we are to respect them in their different manner of worship ... the existence of an Omnipotent God whose Providence over-rules all events is the universal belief of all People of whatever Denomination.'[33] Given this attitude, it is not surprising that religious warfare effectively came to an end in 1648, and that the religious map drawn up by the Treaties of Westphalia has remained essentially the same down to this day.

The quest for earthly happiness brings us to the fifth characteristic of the Enlightenment: its optimistic belief in the possibilities of improving the human condition by political action, its confidence in the essential goodness of men, and in the possibility of improving them by providing a favourable political, economic, and social environment. Hence the attempts of the *philosophes* to catch the ear of kings, and the willingness of kings to listen to the advice of *philosophes*, if not, like Joseph II of Austria, to become *philosophes* themselves. Hence also the schemes so common in the eighteenth century for reforming the law, abolishing torture and capital punishment, stopping persecution, freeing the press, founding orphanages and poor-houses, reforming schools and universities, emancipating serfs, abolishing privileges, creating prosperity. 'Public instruction is the common means of procuring the prosperity of nations', wrote Jovellanos in a report for Charles III of Spain; 'and they are thus powerful or weak, happy or unfortunate according to whether they are enlightened or ignorant.'[34]

With this we have reached politics again, for there could be no reform which did not hurt some individual or group who profited from things as they were. In political ideas, the sixth characteristic of the Enlightenment, both the kings who wished to be absolute and the Estates who resisted them based themselves on the theory that political power is a trust from the community. Attempts to justify political conduct by appealing to divine right or long-established tradition no longer rang convincingly in eighteenth-century ears, and supporters of absolutism, oligarchy, and democracy, all managed to deduce their position from the premise that the people were the source of all power. From this derives in part the paradoxical nature of many of the political struggles of the Ancien Régime: between absolutists, on the one hand, enforcing justice, toleration, humanitarianism, and material progress, and liberals on the other defending privileges, superstition, cruelty, and reaction. Or the later paradox of French-revolutionary civil servants putting through measures planned by the ministers of Louis XVI; or the later one still of nineteenth-century liberals constructing their programmes out of the ideals of Joseph II and Charles III. For the Ancien Régime, to conclude, produced both the bureaucratic state and also the means whereby it could be subordinated to the wishes of society.

Holland: From the Golden Age to the Periwig Period

The Uniqueness of Holland

No other state of the Ancien Régime could compare with the Dutch Republic, or the United Netherlands, or Holland, as it is variously called. During the eighty years preceding the Treaties of Westphalia (1648) she had been hastily assembled from seven separate provinces, and had rocketed upwards to a moment of world dominance in the arts and sciences, business and colonization, diplomacy and war. Her blast-off during the Revolt of the Netherlands (1568–1609) pointed her on a vertical trajectory till 1648, when Spain was forced to recognize her independence. After that, she levelled off till the end of the seventeenth century, and then spent the rest of the Ancien Régime coasting round in orbit. Her form of government went right against the trend of the times. In a world of expanding monarchies, she was a republic. Surrounded by unitary states, she remained a federation. Resisting the vogue for centralization and absolutism, she retained provincial sovereignty and local self-government. Eschewing the services of career-bureaucrats, she was governed by bevies of amateurs taking time off from their businesses; and far from becoming stream-lined and modern, her administration stayed cluttered up with rights and liberties dating from a bygone age.

Her economy, on the other hand, was the most advanced to be found. It flourished on private enterprise, not, as elsewhere, on State prodding. In a Europe where agriculture still predominated, the Dutch Republic was overwhelmingly commercial. When most of Europe lived in the country, Dutchmen concentrated in towns. Instead of courtly nobles or rustic barons, her élite derived from bourgeois merchants, manufacturers, bankers, and shippers; and her typical rank and file were not peasants, but shopkeepers and craftsmen, sailors and mechanics. Moreover, their way of life and frame of mind were unique. In place of the pretensions of princely baroque, her art and architecture showed the honesty of middle-class simplicity. Where others persecuted, she left people alone. Where others enforced intellectual uniformity, she encouraged diversity. And when others drove out religious minorities or dissenting intellectuals, she welcomed them, and put their talents to work.

One of these was Jean-Nicolas Parival, a citizen of France, a country which was in nearly every respect at the opposite end of the spectrum from Holland. After retiring from his Chair in French at Leyden University, he declared in 1669 that he 'never tired of admiring the happiness of the subjects of the States of Holland and could not help envying their condition'.[1] While France and other nations were aggressive, the Dutch were defensive. While they amassed armies, she relied on her fleets. While they could not advance without war, she could not flourish without peace. Unfortunately, they were giants, and she was a pigmy. During the eighteenth century, her two millions could not compete with the five, ten, or twenty millions of her rivals; and while they progressed, she stagnated. Even so, as the Ancien Régime ended, she was still not to be outclassed. Her radical movement was threatening revolution several years before 1789; and if it was in France that the bitter social rivalries were first fought out, the contenders' names – 'democrats' and 'aristocrats' – had been invented in Holland.

The Economic Miracle

The Golden Age of the Dutch Republic was the result of what would today be termed an 'economic miracle'. The speed with which the Dutch mastered their natural element, the sea, astonished the world. 'The prodigious increase of the Netherlands in their domestic and foreign trade, riches and multitude of shipping', wrote Sir Josiah Child in 1669, 'is the envy of the present and may be the wonder of future generations.'[2] 'The people that we call Red-hairs or Red Barbarians', wrote a

Chinese chronicler, 'are identical with the Hollanders and they live in the Western Ocean. They are covetous and cunning, are very knowledgeable concerning valuable merchandise, and are very clever in the pursuit of gain. They will risk their lives in search of profit, and no place is too remote for them to frequent.'[3] The people of the United Provinces – or rather of Holland and Zeeland, since the other five were mainly agrarian provinces – took inspired advantage of a geographical position that was for a time extremely favourable. These two provinces controlled the mouths of the Rhine, the Maas, and the Scheldt, and lay at the point where routes from the Baltic, the North Sea, the Channel, and the Atlantic crossed. Their essential role had long been to organize the exchange of Baltic grain, timber, and naval stores with North Sea and Arctic fish, and Spanish and Portuguese salt, wine, and textiles. When our period began, writes Charles Wilson,

by extraordinary enterprise and efficiency, they had managed to capture something like three-quarters of the traffic in Baltic grain, between half and three-quarters of the traffic in timber, and between a third and a half of that in Swedish metals. Three-quarters of the salt from France and Portugal that went to the Baltic was carried in Dutch bottoms. More than half the cloth imported to the Baltic area was made or finished in Holland.[4]

When the Spanish and Portuguese colonial empires were formed, the Dutch added to their repertoire all the exotic wares that now piled up in the warehouses of Seville and Lisbon: tobacco and sugar and dye-stuffs from across the Atlantic; pepper and nutmeg and cinnamon from the Far East. Later, during the Revolt against Spain, they moved forward from this medium-haul commerce on the seas of Europe to the long-haul trade over the oceans of the world. Even as they were defending their watery homeland against the attacks of the Duke of Parma, they were thrusting into Spanish possessions in the Caribbean and in South America, and taking over from the Portuguese in Africa, India, and Indonesia. The Dutch East India Company was founded in 1602, and the Dutch West India Company in 1621. During the course of the seventeenth

century, Dutch shipping was plying the Arctic route to Russia
and the Mediterranean route to the Middle East. Dutchmen
set up a depot in Canton. They discovered Australia. They
signed a trade treaty with the Shah of Persia. And between
1639 and 1854 they were the only Europeans allowed to trade
with Japan by that 'bold, haughty and exacting nation', as the
East India Company called them.[5]

In 1644, when Catalonia in her turn was in revolt against
Spain, her representative at the peace conference in Westphalia
wrote, with some envy after passing through Holland: 'The
Dutch at the beginning of the war were much poorer and more
broken down than us, but in a short time by means of trade
they have made themselves the richest and most powerful
people in the world.'[6] In the early eighteenth century, Daniel
Defoe wrote: 'The Dutch must be understood as they really
are, the Middle Persons in Trade, the Factors and Brokers of
Europe ... they *buy* to *sell* again, *take* in to *send* out, and the
greatest Part of their vast Commerce consists in being supply'd
from All Parts of the World, that they may supply All the
World again.'[7] No people in the world were so dependent upon
overseas trade. And this did not apply only to their exchange
activities. Their industries, too, relied on imported raw materials or semi-finished articles, whether it was brewing beer,
refining sugar, milling oil, packing fish, cutting tobacco, distilling gin, building ships, finishing cloth, or forging cannons.
Their very bread was baked from imported grain.

As well as being an *entrepôt* and a shipping centre, the
Dutch Republic was also the financial hub of the world. In
1628 Admiral Piet Heyn captured the Mexican silver fleet,
enabling the West India Company to distribute a dividend of
seventy-five per cent. But very soon the market forces replaced
brute force, and ships laden with silver regularly sailed up the
Channel into Dutch harbours of their own free will – to pay
for the goods which Spain had bought from Holland. Amsterdam, with its Bourse, Exchange Bank, and Loan Bank, became
the headquarters of banking, loan-raising, and insurance. The
Exchange Bank, as Sir William Temple the English diplomat
wrote, was 'the greatest Treasure either real or imaginary that

is known anywhere in the World'. Its 'Stocks and Revenues', he added, are 'equal to that of some Kingdoms'.[8]

Not content with being at the centre of things at Amsterdam, Dutchmen took their ingenuity and enterprise to all parts of the world. Dutch capital floated the Bank of England. Dutch carpenters built the locks of the Canal du Midi in the south of France. Dutch engineers drained the Lincolnshire and Cambridgeshire Fens, as well as the marshes of Tuscany. Dutch merchants in Nantes monopolized the wine-trade of the river Loire. In the war between Sweden and Denmark in 1645, the fleets of each side were furnished by Dutch firms. The Van Robais family from Middelburg became the biggest textile manufacturers in Abbeville. Dutchmen monopolized the export of marble from Italy and caviare from Russia, ran the Polish Mint and the copper mines of Hungary, taught the Townshends and Walpoles how to rotate their crops, owned much of Swedish iron and copper, and held perhaps a quarter of the British National Debt.

The traffic was not all one-way, however; and one of the secrets of Dutch greatness was their willingness to give shelter to refugees from religious and racial persecution. Amsterdam was unique as a cosmopolitan centre, where foreigners of every description lent character to the scene like garlic in a stew. Freedom, as Baruch Spinoza – himself a member of an immigrant family – wrote, made Amsterdam 'great and admired by the whole world. In this flourishing state, this city without a peer, men of every race and sect live in the greatest harmony.'[9] The most powerful stimulant of all to Dutch growth was probably the flight of Protestant traders and craftsmen from the Southern Netherlands during the Revolt. They made Leyden, for instance, the biggest manufacturer of the New Draperies in seventeenth-century Europe. In addition, at the start of our period there were about a thousand Sephardic Jews in Amsterdam – refugees from the Inquisition in Spain and Portugal – who made their mark in business and scholarship. Again, after 1685 Holland benefited greatly from the revocation of the Edict of Nantes which drove thousands of Huguenots into the Republic, a blood-transfusion greatly stimulating to industrial and intellectual activity. Frenchmen introduced the manufacture of brocades, taffetas, and velvets, for example, hitherto a French monopoly; and they helped to make Holland the centre of European publishing. 'The French language', wrote Pierre Bayle, a refugee from France, 'is so well known in this country that more French books are sold here than others.'[10] Thus Holland became the most suitable platform for any radical who wished to spread heterodox views, firstly, because of the convenience of French, the universal language of the Ancien Régime; secondly, because of Dutch tolerance; and thirdly, because of the size of the Dutch publishing industry. 'In the whole world', said a report of 1699, 'there are not more than ten or a dozen cities where books are printed on any considerable scale. In England, there are London and Oxford; in France, Paris and Lyons; in Holland, Amsterdam, Leyden, Rotterdam, The Hague, and Utrecht; in Germany, Leipzig; and that is about the sum of it.'[11] It is not surprising that Holland attracted such free spirits as Descartes, Spinoza, and Locke.

Society

Descartes was thus exaggerating when he called Amsterdam a 'great town where apart from myself there dwells no one who is not engaged in trade'.[12] On the other hand, it was peculiarly trade and traders that gave Dutch society its special flavour. Some of the provinces, such as Friesland, Groningen, or Overijssel, may have preserved a semi-manorial way of life; but the province of Holland – which provided over half the total revenue and was almost entirely responsible for Dutch economic, intellectual, and artistic greatness – was overwhelmingly urban, as any community with an economy based on fishing and trade was bound to be. Nowhere in Europe was such a concentration of towns to be found. Famous centres such as Dordrecht and Rotterdam, Delft and The Hague, Leyden and Utrecht and Amsterdam were only five, ten, or twenty miles from one another. In such a province there was little room for nobles and peasants; and what nobles there were lived modestly, but exclusively, and were of little weight in political life. In contrast with all the other states in this book, Holland was dominated by the bourgeoisie.

The typically middle-class virtues of simplicity, frugality, hard work, and cleanliness impressed all foreigners. It was a general custom 'to spend less than one earns', wrote Pallavicino, a Papal Nuncio in 1676, 'and it is considered a shameful extravagance and indeed loose living to do otherwise'.[13] And Lady Mary Wortley Montagu thus described Rotterdam in a letter from there in 1716: 'All the streets are pav'd with broad stones, and before the meanest artificers' doors, seats of various colour'd marbles, and so neatly kept that I'll assure you I walk'd allmost all over the Town Yesterday, incognito, in my slippers without receiving one spot of Dirt, and you may see the Dutch maids washing the Pavement of the street with more application than ours do bed chambers.'[14]

Life in Rotterdam, and in all the other towns of the United Provinces, was dominated by an élite of the most successful businessmen. This patrician group, whose social and economic origins lie back in the Middle Ages, had grasped the opportunities offered by the Revolt to seize political power in the borough corporations, in the Provincial Estates, and in the States-General of the Republic itself. In the late seventeenth century it was rapidly converting itself into a closed oligarchy. Known as the Regents, these men monopolized the seats on the boards of the banks and the trading companies, and were gradually transforming their public offices into hereditary private property. At the same time, they began to withdraw their capital from active business and become rentiers, in order to spend all their time in politics and administration. By the eighteenth century it was not easy for an outsider to break into this little oligarchy of about 10,000 persons. According to Sir William Temple who knew them well in the 1670s, they were

a people differently bred and mannered from the traders, though like them in their modesty of garb and habit, and the parsimony of living. Their youth are generally bred up at schools, and at the Universities of Leyden or Utrecht, in the common studies of humane learning, but chiefly of the civil law, which is that of their country.... Where these families are rich, their youths, after the course of their studies at home, travel for some years, as the sons of our gentry use to do; but their journeys are chiefly into England and France, not much into Italy, seldom into Spain, nor often into the more Northern countries unless in company or train of their public ministers. The chief end of their breeding is to make them fit for the service of their country in the magistracy of their towns, their provinces, and their State. And of these kind of men are the civil officers of this government generally composed, being descended of families who have many times been constantly in the magistracy of their native towns for many years, and some for several ages.[15]

They stayed in the magistracy for the rest of the Ancien Régime, in general performing very valuable public service. Pieter Geyl has called them 'the most remarkable social phenomenon in the Netherlands during the seventeenth century'. 'Sober and dignified,' he added, 'level-headed and lucid, not amiable but bold and steady, such were the burgher regents at their best.'[16]

Below the level of the Regent families, Dutch society broadened out in a pyramid of classes such as was found in most centres of commerce and industry. In this respect, the towns of the Dutch Republic were not so very different from London, or Paris, or Barcelona. Immediately outside the charmed circle lived what Temple called the 'Merchants and traders, whose application lies wholly that way, and who are the better content to have so little share in the government, desiring only security in what they possess'.[17] The more fortunate of these would educate their sons and marry off their daughters in such a way that in the next generation, perhaps, they would become Regents, thereby introducing their families, as Temple said, 'into the way of government and honour, which consists not here in titles, but in public employment'. Further down the scale lived the main body of middle-class and lower-middle-class burghers, who had no hope of entry into the Regent class. These middling merchants and manufacturers, lawyers and managers, preachers and doctors, shopkeepers and artisans, master-mariners and farmers no longer had political power. The organizations to which they belonged exercised little lever-

age in normal times. Their gilds were no longer consulted by
the Regents; while their Civic Guard units, which policed the
towns, were officered by Regents – as Rembrandt showed in
his group portrait *The Company of Capt. Frans Banning Cocq*
(better known as *The Night Watch*), which dates from 1642.
Normally, the Regents were so skilful in their management of
affairs that the burghers were no political problem; but, as we
shall see, there were moments – usually in times of international
danger – when they could be brought out onto the streets by
firebrand Calvinist preachers during the seventeenth and eighteenth centuries, and by radical politicians during the 1780s.
During these moments of crisis (though not in the 1780s) the
burghers usually demanded that power should be handed over
to the only serious alternative to the Regents which Holland
possessed – the Stadholder, the Prince of Orange.

Also on these occasions, the middle-class and lower-middle-
class burghers usually mobilized the workers, the vast body of
skilled and unskilled labourers who manned the ships, the
docks, the workshops and the farms. They were perhaps the
most educated, spirited, and outspoken working men in Europe.
Temple mentioned 'the strange freedom that all men took in
boats and inns, and all other common places, of talking openly
whatever they thought upon all the public affairs, both of their
State, and their neighbours'.[18] Ever ready to suspect the Regent
class of graft, inefficiency, irreligion, and selling out to the
enemy, they too could be roused to a very ugly mood by the
sulphurous phraseology favoured by the preachers – called
predikants. The murder of the De Witt brothers in 1672 is only
one instance of this. Such revolutionary situations taught the
Regents and the more respectable burghers to have no truck
with the practice of democracy, however much they were forced
to use its language at times as a counter-weight to the monarchical claims of the Princes of Orange. Moreover, rioting also
stirred up the murky lower depths of Dutch society: the unemployed and unemployable, the casual labourers and tramps,
the thieves and drifters, beggars and rag-pickers, ballad-sellers,
louts and thugs – all the *grauw*, or rabble, which was a permanent reproach and threat to Holland, and to all states.

Indeed, this social layer thickened, as the graph of Dutch prosperity passed its peak just after mid century, and it increasingly haunted the minds of the ruling élite. Pieter de la Court's book, *The Interest of Holland* (1662) – which expressed what might be termed the philosophy of the Regent class – referred to the *grauw* as 'the sottish ill-natured rabble, who ever hate and are ready to impeach the aristocratical rulers of their republic'.[19]

Religion

Conflicts between the Regent families, on the one hand, and the middle and lower classes, on the other, were usually embittered by the gall of religious feeling. Though the Revolt of the Netherlands had issued in a Protestant victory, Dutch society was far from being theologically all of a piece. In the first place, just over half the population were still Roman Catholics in 1650, and forty per cent still were at the end of the eighteenth century. Theoretically, they were not permitted to worship, but owing to the tolerant attitude of the Regents, and the bribable posture of the officials, they managed to hear Mass regularly, often in buildings which looked like dwelling houses without, but which had been converted into chapels within. Thus the Revolt had not been a Protestant, let alone a Calvinist, monopoly; and, though the Calvinists had supplied most of the anti-Spanish fighting spirit, they were a minority movement (more typical of the Flemish industrial towns of the South) which had foisted itself onto the broader-minded Regents of the Northern provinces. The latter's sympathies were more in tune with the humanism of Erasmus than the harsh doctrines of Calvin; and they acquiesced in the forms of Calvinist worship, without swallowing its spirit.

In the seventeenth century, then, there were two kinds of Calvinism: the moderate, which the Regents supported, and the militant, which was rampant among the middle and lower classes. The moderates adopted the liberal views of Arminius, who played down the differences between Protestants and

Catholics; while the militants demanded the literal acceptance of Calvin's teachings. On predestination, for example, the militants held rigidly to Calvin's drastic doctrine that God has destined some men for eternal bliss and the rest for damnation; while the moderates could not bring themselves to believe that a God of love could be so inhumane. On Church–State relations, another controversial issue, the militants believed that the Church should be free from interference from the State – strictly, in fact, should rule the State. The moderates, for their part, were determined to see that the wild *predikants* did not run amok, but were fully supervised by the town councils. On the question of toleration, another sore point, the militants wished to wipe out the enemies of God forthwith, whether they were Spaniards abroad or Dutchmen at home. The Regents, for their part, took a liberal attitude, partly because Erasmian reasonableness and moderation were still their creed, and partly because persecution was bad for trade.

These and other questions were debated at the famous Synod of Dort (Dordrecht) in 1619, which ended by drawing up a new confession of faith. The line which was now laid down for Calvinists to toe was that of militant puritanism. The *predikants* and the rank-and-file burghers, in other words, tasted doctrinal victory; but the Regents showed no weakness over the organizational issue, and the State remained firmly in charge of the Church. Thus a paradoxical situation resulted in which the Reformed Church based on strict Calvinism became the official Church of a State which was still run by the moderates. The State paid the stipends of the *predikants*, and public office was restricted to those who accepted the dictates of Dort; yet the State was in the hands of moderates who refused to allow the Reformed Church to force its views on the rest of the community. Of course, Calvinism helped to shape the Dutch character. There is no doubt, as Huizinga has said, 'that the life of the people was cast in a Calvinist mould'.[20] But it was moderate, not fanatical, Calvinism which influenced the leaders of Dutch life in politics, philosophy, science, and the arts. Neither can Dutch history be used to exemplify any theory depicting Calvinism as the ideology of capitalism. In Holland the capitalists were moderates; militant Calvinism was for the herd.

Besides Roman Catholics, Arminians, and militant Calvinists, other religious groups flourished in this oasis of tolerance: Baptists, Mennonites, Lutherans, and other Christian sects; besides the Sephardic Jews of Amsterdam, and the Ashkenazic Jews from Eastern Europe, who settled in Amsterdam and the eastern provinces. The policy of the Regents, however motivated, was an important factor behind Holland's intellectual and material success, and it furnished an example from which the persecuting states of Europe later drew lessons. 'Toleration and freedom of religion', wrote Peter de la Court, 'is not only exceedingly beneficial for our country in general but particularly for the reformed religion, which may and ought to depend on its own evidence and veracity.'[21] The Regents 'countenance only Calvinism', wrote Gerard Brandt, the moderate Calvinist minister and historian, 'but for Trade's sake they *Tolerate* all others except the Papists: which is the reason why the treasure and stock of most Nations is transported thither, where there is full Liberty of Conscience: you may be what Devil you will there, so you be but peaceable'.[22]

Civil peace, however, would have been impossible in Holland if the ruling class had not damped down the crusading fire of the *predikants*; and the fact that all the other religious groups looked to the Regents for protection from the militants was, as will be shown, an important element in the political situation right through the Ancien Régime. Deep feelings were, of course, involved. When a moderate Regent of Amsterdam invited a colleague who happened to be strict to attend an Arminian service, he replied that he would rather sit in a brothel with seven whores.[23] And it was thanks to the Regents that the peevish *predikants* were restrained from burning witches, closing dance-halls, or taking the joy out of Christmas. When the Synod of the province of Holland resolved in 1655 'that public and free residence of all Romish Mass priests and other such clerics should without exception be terminated, forbidden and if need be forcibly prevented', the civil authorities refused.[24]

And when the shrill-voiced consistory of Amsterdam demanded the closing of the Town Theatre in 1664 because it 'cannot be regarded otherwise than as designing to spit into God's face', the burgomasters turned a deaf ear.[25] What would have become of the celebrated Golden Age of literature, art, and science had the puritans been free to do their worst is a question. As it was, the elementary schools of the villages, the Latin schools of the towns, and the five universities, while officially teaching the orthodoxies of Dort, were in practice enabled by the broad-mindedness of the Regent class, and the cosmopolitan nature of Dutch society, to make their contribution to an intellectual advance which astounded Europe. It was fortunate that the universities at Leyden, Franeker, Harderwijk, Groningen, and Utrecht were modern foundations, and thus better able to tackle modern subjects such as anatomy, astronomy, botany, physics, and chemistry than institutions of medieval origin in other countries. Judging by the thousands of foreigners who flocked there every term, they offered the finest education in Europe. And judging by the amount of genius produced by the Dutch people in the seventeenth century, it was they who were most fitted to benefit from it.

Art and Science

On account of the language difficulty, Holland's greatest poet, Joost van den Vondel (1587–1679), and his fellow writers are hardly known outside Dutch-speaking communities. Her scientists and painters, on the other hand, are world famous. Christiaan Huygens (1628–95) greatly improved the telescope, and among other things discovered the rings of Saturn. He also invented the micrometer, improved the air-pump and pendulum-clock, and made theoretical contributions to science of Newtonian importance in the laws on the collision of elastic bodies, the wave theory of light, and theory of the polarization of light. Anthonie Leeuwenhoek (1632–1723) made important discoveries with the microscope in the field of blood corpuscles, spermatozoa, and microbes. Hermann Boerhaave (1669–1738) was professor of Medicine, Botany, and Chemistry at Leyden

University, and so widely renowned that he was said to have safely received a letter simply addressed 'Boerhaave–Europe'.

The extreme Calvinists were thus unable to prevent the extension of scientific knowledge. Neither could they weaken the extraordinary partiality of the Dutch people for pictures – or the efforts of the painters to satisfy the great demand. The traveller Peter Mundy wrote in 1640:

As for the art of painting and the affection of the people to pictures, I think none other go beyond them, there having been in this country many excellent men in that faculty, [and] some at present, as Rembrandt, etc. All in general striving to adorn their houses, especially the outer or street room with costly pieces; butchers and bakers not much inferior in their shops, which are fairly set forth, yea many times blacksmiths, cobblers, etc., will have some pictures or other by their forge and in their stall. Such is the general notion, inclination and delight that these country natives have to paintings.[26]

Every town had its group of artists, and they were accepted by everyone as part of ordinary life, as men to be traded with like butchers and bakers, not worshipped as idols as in other communities. The concentration of artistic talent in such a tiny community in one century was so heavy that it would be a hopeless task to do them justice here. Only a few can be mentioned: Cuyp, Ruysdael, and Hobbema for landscapes; Steen, de Hooch, and Vermeer for urban scenes and interiors; the van de Veldes for seascapes; Frans Hals for portraits; and of course Rembrandt, one of the greatest artists in European history. The Dutch painters were distinguished in that century of the baroque by their lack of pompous, theatrical, or monumental effects, and by their penchant for the realistic depiction of the everyday activities of life. This naturalism was perhaps a visible sign of the effects of Calvinist education on the Dutch character. It certainly distinguished Dutch art from the more effusive manner of Rubens and his like in the still-Catholic Southern Netherlands. On the other hand, it may have been due to the market. In the Dutch Republic painters were not asked to design great altar-pieces for baroque churches, or to cover whole ceilings with symbolism flattering to princes.

Those who commissioned works there were private citizens, gilds, and town-councils; and their pictures were meant to be hung in parlours, orphanages, and town-halls. And the fact that taste was formed by patrons of this kind, and not by monarchs and nobles and bishops, was the result of Holland's peculiar form of government.

Government

All Dutchmen agreed that their federal republic was the chief safeguard of their religion and whole way of life. 'The reformed religion will be surer and better preserved', wrote Pieter de la Court, 'by the prudent, immortal and almost immutable sovereign Assembly of the States of Holland and other Colleges subordinate to them than by those voluptuous, lavish, transitory and fickle monarchs and princes, or their favourites, who alter the outward form and practice of religion as may be most consistent with their pleasures and profits.'[27] In the 'Disunited Provinces' (as Temple called them) sovereignty lay with the components: that is, the seven provinces of Holland, Zeeland, Utrecht, Friesland, Gelderland, Groningen, and Overijssel. In each of these, power was vested in the Estates, which were variously composed, and which, unlike the representative institutions of the rest of Europe, usually gave overwhelming weight to the delegates from the towns. The Estates of Holland, for example – their Noble Great Mightinesses, as they were styled – consisted of nineteen delegations with one vote each: eighteen represented towns and one the nobility. Their Noble Mightinesses of the Estates of Zeeland similarly included only one representative of the nobility. Gelderland and Overijssel, on the other hand, gave them more votes. Since all bodies normally required a unanimous vote before action could be taken, however, and since disputes frequently arose in the Estates, delegates often had to go back to consult the borough corporations who had sent them. Thus, in practice, power was exercised by the towns.

The towns were governed by corporations, between twenty and forty strong, which had long since emancipated themselves from the control of the citizenry at large, and which now formed self-contained little oligarchies enjoying membership for life, and fixing the replacement of deceased colleagues by co-optation. Amsterdam had a corporation of thirty-six members who chose nine Aldermen as the judicial arm, and four Burgomasters as the executive, apart from other subordinate officials. Dordrecht had a corporation of forty, and a magistracy of eight. In the more rural provinces of Friesland and Groningen (which had never been feudalized) the property-owning peasants, grouped in self-governing associations, had a voice in the corporations. All the towns of the Republic were islands of autonomy, whose internal affairs were their own concern, except in those periods when the Stadholder (whose office will shortly be described) managed to swing appointments and sway votes – whether by legal authority or corrupt influence. Moreover, the chief towns in a province controlled its government, for it was their delegates who sat on the Provincial Estates.

Similarly, the Provincial Estates controlled the Republic as a whole through their membership of the chief all-Dutch institution, the States-General, which met daily at the Hague. Their High Mightinesses were essentially a committee of ambassadors from the Provincial Estates. They controlled foreign policy and defence, and levied the taxes required for these purposes. Here again unanimity was required, and the United Provinces were notorious for the dilatoriness with which they arrived at decisions of peace or war. Deadlock at the Hague sent the ambassadors home to consult the Provincial Estates; and, as we have seen, back beyond them to the town councils. And all-Dutch policy-making would have been more desultory than it actually was had not two officials built up something in the nature of a party-system. These were, in the first place, the Stipendiary Councillor (or chief legal officer of the Estates of Holland), and, in the second, the Stadholder, the nearest approach the Dutch had to a king under the Ancien Régime.

The power of the Stipendiary Councillor derived from the might and wealth of the province of Holland, which placed in the common pool by far the biggest share of taxation and talent, sea-power and economic strength. He headed the delegation from Holland at the States-General, and presided over the debates. The fact that Holland paid the piper enabled him to call the tune by brow-beating, or persuading, or corrupting enough delegates from the other provinces. The Stadholder gerrymandered in a similar manner, though his power was differently based. This office dated from the days when the provinces owed allegiance to the Dukes of Burgundy. The Stadholder of each province was the viceroy of the Duke there. Since the Revolt, however, the Princes of Orange, descendants of William the Silent, had usually been Stadholder in the five provinces of Holland, Zeeland, Utrecht, Overijssel, and Gelderland, while the Nassau branch of the family – descendants of his brother – had held it in the other two, Friesland and Groningen. In addition, the posts of Captain-General and Admiral-General – that is, the command of the armed forces – were usually given by the States-General to the Princes of Orange. Even in those periods when the Nassaus took an independent line, the Princes of Orange exercised a powerful leverage in Dutch politics. Their strength derived, in the first place, from their landed estates inside and outside the Netherlands, including Orange in the south of France, where they were sovereign princes. In wealth and prestige they were well above many of the princes of Germany, let alone the capitalists of Amsterdam. William III, for example, was the great-grandson of Henry IV of France; he was also grandson of Charles I of England, while his aunt married the Great Elector of Brandenburg-Prussia, and he himself became King of England (1688). Secondly, they inherited the glory which William the Silent and his sons, Maurice and Frederick Henry, had won in the heroic struggle of the Eighty Years' War (1568–1648). Moreover, in the third place, a Prince of Orange, when in office as Stadholder and Captain-General and Admiral-General, could form a political connection capable of swaying the debates at the Hague, not unlike that of the Stipendiary Councillor. The nucleus of the Orange party was formed from the posts which the Prince could offer on the Orange estates themselves, together with the patronage in the armed forces, and the role which they often shared with the corporations in the appointment of burgomasters and other urban officials.

Politics

Dutch politics were thus polarized between the Prince of Orange, on the one hand, and the Regents of the 100,000-strong city of Amsterdam, on the other. And when they were at loggerheads Holland cut a dithering figure in European politics. As Sir George Downing said in a compliment to the British Monarchy in 1664: 'You have infinite advantages upon the account of the form of the government of this country which is such a shattered and divided thing.'[28] On the one side, the Regents of Amsterdam, with their eyes on the sea, favoured peace, because it fostered trade and kept taxes down. But if war had to be waged, then they put their faith and money into the fleet and not the army, and would much rather convoy merchantmen than man citadels. On the other side, the Orange party, with their eyes on the land, wanted an army to fend off the attacks of Spain, in the first half of the century, and France, in the second. Moreover, they had to think about the Principality of Orange and all their other non-Dutch properties; and during the English Civil War they wished to intervene on behalf of their relatives, the Stuarts. All of this was highly suspect in Amsterdam, where the Regents were haunted by the fear that the Orangists would use the army to destroy the provincial liberties that had been so carefully preserved from medieval times, set up a modern monarchy, pursue the interests of the dynasty rather than those of the nation, and squander the profits of trade in useless territorial aggression. War, it was thought, was peculiarly the trade of monarchs, who were, as one Amsterdammer said, 'a gang of crowned fools, who cry nothing but fire and blood, and destruction'. 'A monarchical government', said Pieter de la Court in the *Interest of Holland,* was the equivalent to 'a death from which there would be no resurrection'.[29]

Early in the century, the struggle between the Stipendiary Councillor, Johan van Oldenbarneveldt, and the Stadholder,

Maurice of Orange, had led to the crisis of 1618. In the event, the Orangists locked up the leading Amsterdammers in the castle of Loevestein, judicially murdered Oldenbarneveldt, and in 1621 renewed Holland's struggle with Spain by joining in the Thirty Years' War. In 1647, when the next Stadholder, Frederick Henry, died, the Loevestein party (as they were now called) took charge and made peace with Spain in the Treaty of Münster (1648), much to the disgust of the heir, William II. This overfed young man, who would have been a real menace to the Loevesteiners had he not been so workshy, engaged in secret negotiations designed to provide Dutch military aid to the exiled Stuarts and to fight a joint war with Mazarin against the Southern Netherlands. In the meantime, led by Amsterdam, the province of Holland began unilaterally to disband its share of the federal army, while William II embarked on a scheme of replacing Loevestein men with creatures of his own in all the towns of Holland. The fears of the Loevesteiners, both for their liberties and their peace, were thus explained by one of their pamphleteers in 1650, who said that William 'had resolved to remove in all the towns of Holland, and also in some other provinces, several magistrates who had scorned to look up to him like slaves, and to fill their places with others of a slavish disposition. And if he had succeeded therein we should have been dragged into two wars at once, to wit against the Parliament of England to help the King of Scotland, and against the King of Spain in order to please the frivolous Frenchies, to whom he had wholly lost his heart.'[30] The critical year was 1650, when William II clapped six leading Loevesteiners (including the father of Johan de Witt) into Loevestein Castle, and then attempted to seize Amsterdam by force. He bungled the attempt, however, and died towards the end of the year. The Regents expressed their relief in a medal which they caused to be struck. Its text ran: 'The last hour of the prince is the beginning of freedom.'[31] And this freedom lasted from 1650 to 1672, when the Loevesteiners governed the Republic under the leadership of the new Stipendiary Councillor, Johan de Witt. 1672, as will be seen, was another year of crisis, which brought a further swing of the pendulum. The Orange party took over, and governed Holland for most of the rest of the century.

Thus, although the Dutch Republic was 'a shattered and divided thing', and was constantly plagued by the Orange–Amsterdam power-struggle, the result was not permanent deadlock, but a periodic swing from one side to the other. When foreign danger threatened, and when decisiveness was urgently necessary, then one party would defeat the other, or both would work together in temporary harmony. And what saved the day on those critical occasions was the fact that politics in Holland did not consist only of the crude Orange–Amsterdam rivalry, but was complicated by the pressures of other groups with ideals to accomplish or interests to push.

These complicating elements on the Dutch political scene were in outline as follows. In the first place, there was a struggle within the Regent class itself between the Ins and Outs. There were never enough places to go round in the Dutch administration, and under a period of Loevestein domination disappointed and despairing aspirants to office became Orangists in the hope of sharing the spoils at the next swing of the pendulum. In the second place, there was the polarity between the maritime provinces, Holland and Zeeland, on the one hand, and the landward provinces, on the other. The rivalry between town and country was also involved here; as well as that between commerce and agriculture, bourgeois and noble, navy and army. These dissensions led to disputes over economic policy, as well as over foreign policy and defence arrangements. Thirdly, and often coinciding, was the division between the masterful province of Holland, on the one hand, and the remaining provinces, on the other, which envied her wealth and resented her preponderance. Fourthly, there was the rivalry between the Regent class, on the one hand, and the middle and lower classes, on the other. An economic crisis bringing bankruptcies, unemployment, and hunger (such as occurred during the Anglo-Dutch War of 1652–54, for example) was sufficient to set fire to the resentment which the masses always kept stoked up against the patrician oligarchy. Indeed, all times of international danger or defeat were perilous for the

Regents, as the murder of de Witt in 1672 illustrates. The snobbish burghers were always ready to believe that the Regents were corrupt, and to doubt whether experience in the counting-house was an adequate preparation for the aristocratic arts of diplomacy and war: prejudices which the House of Orange knew well how to exploit till very late in the Ancien Régime. 'The people as a whole', wrote the Marquis de Saint-Evremond, 'are disposed to submit more readily to the authority of a chief than to that of the magistrates, who are in reality but their equals.'[32]

The alliance between Prince and people against the oligarchs was always strong when, as de Witt once said, the country was in 'a desperate condition, it being as it were blockaded and besieged'. At such a moment, he added, the impression gains ground 'that a chief is what is needed, or else matters will never prosper, an opinion which is so deeply rooted in the general mind, that of the common rabble hardly one in a thousand is free of it'.[33] Moreover, the sympathy between the chief and the common rabble was fortified by the religious feelings which were aroused by the fifth of these rivalries which cut across Dutch politics: that between the Church and the State.

The *predikants* and their fanatical followers in the Dutch Reformed Church were principally drawn from the middle and lower classes, as has been said. They opposed the Regents who refused to let them turn Holland into a theocracy, or wipe out the Protestant and Catholic dissenters, or embark on a crusade against Spain. The Orangists, for their part, knew how to profit from this religious odium – for their enemies were the *predikants'* enemies: the Regents and the Spanish. In 1618, for example, during the controversies of the Synod of Dort, Maurice supported the strict Calvinists against the moderates, not because he was a religious fanatic, but because he needed all the support he could muster against Oldenbarneveldt. He forged a friendship which succeeding Princes of Orange always took care to keep sweet. This, in its turn, led to the complementary alliance between the Regents and the other religious groups, and reveals the sixth of the struggles we have been considering: that between the Reformed Church, on one side, and the Arminians, Lutherans, Baptists, Mennonites, Roman Catholics, Jews, and free-thinkers, on the other. All these latter looked to the tolerant Regents for protection from the literal implementation of the decisions of the Synod of Dort.

This mesh of rivalries held Dutch politics together, and prevented the rifts between Orange and Amsterdam from tearing the nation in two. For the lines of division rarely all coincided. Instead they criss-crossed one another to form a safety net. As a result, extremes were avoided, and a balance maintained between the monarchical and the republican movements, between the centralizing and the separatist tendencies. Violence there may have been, but not revolution. Dutchmen could change their rulers without destroying the régime; and they could accomplish the various changes of direction that were required in an increasingly hostile world.

Foreign Affairs

The international scene during the Stadholderless régime (which lasted from 1650 to 1672) was temporarily vacated by the really great powers of Europe, and Holland was free to play the lead in diplomacy and war. This was the hiatus between the decline of Spain and the rise of France, when Germany was exhausted by the Thirty Years' War, and France, Spain, and England were crippled by civil war. It was a temporary lull, during which modest powers such as Holland, England, Denmark, and Sweden could indulge their commercial squabbles, before the age when they all became absorbed in the much grander world struggle between Louis XIV, on the one side, and most of the rest of Europe, on the other. When our period begins, the end of Dutch commercial predominance was already in sight, as envious rivals made their warlike preparations. As Rijkloff van Goens, a high official of the Dutch East India Company, reported in 1655 on arrival from the Far East: 'There is nobody who wishes us well in all the Indies, yea we are deadly hated by all nations.'[34]

The Dutch Republic required every bit of its diplomatic guile, naval skill, military heroism, and financial strength, merely to survive. Between 1658 and 1660 she successfully fought for Denmark against Sweden and helped to prevent Swedish domination over the Baltic, and in particular stopped Sweden gaining both banks of the Sound, the entrance to the Baltic. In maintaining the balance in this area, Holland was preserving her mastery of Baltic commerce, the basis of her whole economic success. The three wars with an increasingly aggressive Britain (1652–54, 1665–67, 1672–74) were also principally commercial. They were of a piece with the English Navigation Acts (1651 and 1660) and the British lust after 'more of the trade the Dutch now have' (see p. 523). Similarly, the French attack of 1672 was big with commercial motives as well as the desire to pursue the greater glory of Louis XIV. It was of a piece with Colbert's protective tariff of 1667, and his general desire to prise off Dutch enterprise, skill, capital, and shipping, all of which had fastened themselves on to the French economy like leeches. 'If the King subjected all the united provinces of the Netherlands, their commerce becoming the commerce of His Majesty's subjects', reported Colbert in 1672, 'there would be nothing to desire more.'[35] War, however, went right against the grain of the Dutch patricians, who simply wished to get on with their commerce. 'Special attention must be paid', ran an instruction of the East India Company to its staff in 1650, 'to driving a peaceful trade throughout Asia, which is what keeps the cooking going in the kitchens of the fatherland.'[36]

Johan de Witt

During these dangerous years, when for the last time Dutch diplomatic activity was spotlighted in the centre of the world's stage, the United Netherlands were governed by Regents of Holland under the leadership of their Stipendiary Councillor, Johan de Witt. This cultivated patrician was the son of one of the six leaders that William II had imprisoned in the castle of Loevestein; and in the period of anti-Orange reaction after the Stadholder's death, he and his Loevesteiners led the

Republic in the direction of greater federalism. In 1651 the
provinces were given increased powers over the military units
in their care, with the result that the Dutch forces were almost split into seven separate armies. In this way, it was felt,
the privileges of the Regents would be safe from attack by any
future Stadholder and Captain-General. As de Witt's predecessor, Jacob Cats, once contended – using an argument that
was typical of the time and place – the Regents favoured 'a
form of military government after the example of the oldest
republic the world has ever known, namely, that of the He-
brews, that is to say God's own people who from the time they
were led out of Egypt until the time of the Kings, being about
450 years, never appointed a regular Captain-General, notwithstanding that they were continually engaged in warfare, but
chose a head or general for each separate campaign'.[37] And in
accordance with the same thinking, the town councils voted
to appoint their officials themselves, and not in accordance
with the wishes of any outsider (that is, the Stadholder). A
further blow at the Orange family came in 1654, when the
Estates of Holland passed the Act of Seclusion, declaring that
no Prince of Orange could be appointed Stadholder or Captain-
General. The other provinces protested, but Oliver Cromwell insisted – and this became the only way for de Witt to
end the Anglo-Dutch War (1652–54).

With the Stuart Restoration in England (1660), Holland
could repeal this Act, but de Witt blocked all further moves in
favour of the Prince of Orange. In 1666, when William III
was sixteen years old, the Estates of Holland declared him a
'Child of State' and began to supervise his education. In 1667,
by the Perpetual Edict, the Estates abolished the Stadholdership of their province, and declared that the office of Stadholder in any province was incompatible with the post of
Captain-General of the Union. After a long struggle, the other
provinces accepted the latter point in the Act of Harmony
(1670); and William was then admitted to the Council of
State.

By this date, the situation was turning against de Witt at
home and abroad. In the Republic, a formidable opposition

was building up to the power of the Loevestein party. Against
them were arrayed the landward provinces and the pro-Orange
nobility, the middle and lower classes everywhere (especially
during the slumps caused by the Anglo-Dutch wars), the
predikants (whom the Regents restrained from persecuting the
other religious groups), the Outs among the Regent families
(who were deciding that they stood a better chance of office
under an Orange restoration), and all those who saw that de
Witt was jeopardizing the Republic's external security. Abroad
the United Provinces were virtually isolated, while France and
Britain were planning a joint onslaught (Treaty of Dover, 1670).
De Witt was driven by motives of the highest patriotism, but
he was also bemused by the deep Regent desire for peace.
'Above all things', Pieter de la Court had written, 'war, and
chiefly by sea, is most prejudicial, and peace very beneficial,
for Holland.'[38] De Witt's appreciation of the situation owed
more to wish-fulfilment than statesmanship, for the true
interest of Holland required a call to arms, not an olive branch.

Similarly, with William III, he misjudged his man. He
assumed that he would frustrate the peaceful pursuits of the
Dutch people, by supporting the warlike ambitions of the Orange
family; and that he would endanger the liberties of the
towns and provinces by introducing the machinery of centralized absolutism. It was a tragic mistake; but, as Pieter Geyl has
said, 'the tradition of the Orange party *had* for a generation
been lacking in national purpose. How could De Witt have
foreseen that the young William would have the strength of
mind to break with that tradition?'[39]

De Witt's delusions about Louis XIV and William III led
straight to the terrible events of 1672, which issued in the
overthrow of the first Stadholderless régime by violence instead
of by a peaceful transition. Louis ordered 100,000 men across
the Rhine and then westwards into the heart of the Republic.
He forced the small Dutch army to take cover in the province
of Holland behind the water-barrier which they created by
opening the dykes. And as Louis entered the town of Utrecht
in early July, the panicking Dutch people precipitated the
change of régime. In Zeeland, then Holland, they forced their

Regents to forget the Perpetual Edict and make William Stadholder. At the Hague the States-General appointed him Captain-General and Admiral-General for life. In August, de Witt
resigned as Stipendiary Councillor, and shortly after met his
end at the Hague where he had gone to visit his brother who
was in prison in the gaol in the main square. The hysterical
mob dragged them both out into the square, filled them with
musket-shot, strung them up head-down and naked on the
gallows, and then hacked them to pieces for subsequent sale.
It was a tragic vengeance to wreak on the man who had led
the Republic during the period of its greatest economic, intellectual, and artistic achievements.

William III

Meanwhile, William had the urgent task of ending the Republic's diplomatic isolation, securing the defeat of Louis XIV,
forcing the enemy to evacuate Dutch territory, and establishing his control over the sprawling Dutch system of government. Only twenty-one in 1672, and slight, pale and stooping,
with a perpetual cough and a delicate appetite, he nevertheless
displayed at once the grim patience, iron will, and high vision,
which fitted him to lead Holland, then Britain, and, indeed, all
Europe through decades of extreme danger. He was immediately presented with an opportunity of selling his country
to the enemy. This was a Franco-British peace plan whereby
they would receive slices of Holland, and he would be recognized as sovereign (not merely Stadholder) of what was left. He
replied that he and the States 'would rather die a thousand
deaths than submit to such conditions. He liked better', he
told the British representatives, 'the condition of Stadholder
which they had given him, and ... he believed himself obliged
in conscience and honour not to prefer his interest before his
obligation.'[40] It was a maxim to which he remained faithful for
the rest of his life. By 1674, instead of sacrificing the country
to the dynasty, in the tradition of his immediate predecessors,
he had revived the spirits of the nation, formed an alliance
with Spain and the Emperor and others, signed a favourable

peace with England, and secured the evacuation of French troops.

All this depended on securing effective rule inside the Republic. The end of the first Stadholderless period has some- times been called 'the revolution of 1672', but neither of the two possible meanings of the phrase really applies. William gained office by a perfectly legal process; and he made no basic changes in the methods of government: the rule of the Regents went on as before. What was new in William's thirty years of Stadholdership was the assuaging of the rivalries which had criss-crossed the Dutch political scene, and the civilizing of the methods of settling differences between them. On the one hand, William's foreign policy eventually narrowed the gap between Orange and Amsterdam by his organization of the long-term, world-wide defence of Europe against Louis XIV, and by his ultimate success in convincing the Regents that this was good for trade and Protestantism as well as for the United Provinces as a whole. On the other hand, the internal disposi- tions he made between 1672 and 1675, and the appointments policy he pursued thereafter, lubricated the whole political machine with the oil of influence and patronage. Though he had been thrust into office on the backs of the mob, William had no intention of pushing Dutch government in the direction of democracy. Naturally, the Regents saw eye to eye with him in this, though something had to be done to satisfy the popular execration of the Loevesteiners. The Estates of Holland asked William to 'change the government' so that 'the citizenry should not take it upon itself to restore order'.[41] The changes that William made were far from revolutionary. Out of about 500 hereditary town councillors in the eighteen towns which were represented on the Estates of Holland, he replaced about 160. Pro-Orange families took the places of pro-Loevesteiners. Outs replaced Ins, but there was no social difference between them. The Regents were still in command. The new council- lors were called 'Yes-Men' by the Loevesteiner pamphleteers, which is exactly what William wanted them to be. Similar changes took place in the other provinces; but in Utrecht, Gelderland, and Overijssel, which had been conquered by the

French, the Stadholder achieved almost monarchical power. As these provinces were evacuated by the French troops and asked to rejoin the Union (1673–74), William made them agree to a 'Government Regulation', which gave him control of all chief appointments on the town councils and the Estates. In the same years, Holland and Zeeland converted the Stadholdership into an hereditary office (1674), and the States-General did the same with the offices of Captain-General and Admiral-General (1675).

Before very long, William had the best of both worlds. The Regent oligarchy still governed the Republic, but in the Orange interest, not against it. William appointed a noble in each province to look after the patronage. They in turn had an agent in each town. In Rotterdam, for example, the sheriff and the burgomaster performed this function; and on one occasion when two members of the Groeninx family wished to be chosen by the Stadholder as members of the council, the sheriff and the burgomaster made them pledge a bond of 4,000 guilders and put their hand to an agreement that 'in matters of competition for or assignation to places on the Town Council, offices or commissions depending upon the same', they would 'follow blindly and without any contradiction the gentlemen afore-mentioned and ... vote as these would require of them'.[42] In Zierikzee, in Zeeland, the leaders of two rival cliques were persuaded by William's agent in 1684 to work together in future. 'We contracting parties', they agreed, 'undertake not only to maintain each other in those offices that we at this moment fill or shall fill in future, but also to favour each other's families, children and friends and help them obtain whatever is possible; promising to help in the promotion of the children not only in their parents' lifetime but also after their demise.'[43] Quite clearly, William III was no novice in the gentle arts of parliamentary management when he accepted the British crown in 1689, and found himself surrounded by Whigs and Tories.

His influence was not all-powerful, of course, and at first he had fierce struggles with Holland and Amsterdam over his life's work – the frustration of French ambitions. Once the French had evacuated Dutch territory (1674), and the war had moved away elsewhere, the Regents of Holland lost interest in it, however European in scale it had now become. William was never at this stage able to make them accept his policy, that the safety of the Republic depended solely upon the formation of a grand alliance with Britain, the Empire, and other states, which would stop Louis XIV in his tracks wherever he struck – not simply when he raided Holland. It was against his wishes that they brought this war to an end in the Treaty of Nijmegen (1678). And it was against their wishes that he tried to organize opposition to Louis' cynical aggressions in Alsace and elsewhere in the early 1680s, known as the 'Reunions'. The Regents of Amsterdam (one of the rare municipalities in history to place foreign policy regularly on its agenda) objected to being 'a fertile milch cow' paying, as a pamphlet said, 'a larger quota than all the other towns of the province of Holland together and as much as one third of all that the seven provinces together have to raise'.[44] Businessmen regarded war as an out-dated, aristocratic indulgence, typical of the Stadholder and his noble courtiers, who under the Stadholderless régime (said another pamphlet) 'were not sufficiently well off to keep a horse or a lackey at their own expense'.

What brought Amsterdam eventually round to William's way of thinking were the excesses of Louis XIV: his increasingly vain-glorious aggressiveness abroad, and his revocation of the Edict of Nantes at home (1685). His claim on the Spanish inheritance was a threat to Holland's dominant position in Spain's economy, while his attack on the Huguenots filled the Republic with religious refugees. The French were revealed at last – even to Amsterdammers wishing to mind their own business – as a danger to profit and Protestantism. From this point on William received encouragement in his tireless diplomacy aimed at creating the so-called League of Augsburg. In 1688 the Regents had sufficient vision to vote him the use of their army and navy to bring off the Glorious Revolution. And they followed up this investment by exhausting themselves in two long anti-French wars: the War of the League of Augsburg (1688–97) and the War of the Spanish Succession (1702–13). Co-operation between the Stadholder and the Regents had never been so cordial, but already the Republic had in effect entered the second Stadholderless period. From 1689 onwards William concentrated on his role as King of England, and Dutch affairs were managed by Anthonie Heinsius, who became the Stipendiary Councillor of Holland the same year. During the 1690s William lost control of Dutch policy. As Stephen Baxter has said, William's 'advice was treated with respect and his support, as King of England, was essential to the Dutch government; but his position as Stadholder had by now almost completely disappeared.... The firm of William and Heinsius had gradually and amicably changed its name to become the firm of Heinsius and William.'[45] And when William died in 1702 without issue, his heir was a member of the Nassau branch of the family, traditional Stadholders of Friesland and Groningen. The Regents refused to appoint him Stadholder, and thus the second Stadholderless period began officially in 1702. It lasted till 1747, when, as will be seen, it was brought to end once more by a French invasion, just as in 1672.

William III and Heinsius between them had led the United Provinces through a heroic period at the head of European affairs. The fact that the three great peace conferences of the era took place on Dutch soil – at Nijmegen (1678), Rijswijk (1697), and Utrecht (1713) – testifies to the central role the Republic played in world diplomacy and war. But she had already passed her peak, and in the eighteenth century cannot be regarded as a major power. Already in the War of Spanish Succession she managed to fulfil only one of her two chief war aims: the preservation of the Southern Netherlands as a barrier between herself and France. 'My concern above all other things', William wrote to Heinsius in 1700, 'is to prevent the Spanish Netherlands from falling into the hands of France.'[46] In 1701, when French troops occupied the area, he wrote: 'It is now more than twenty-eight years that I have worked without interruption to save that barrier for the Republic, sparing neither my pains nor my person, and you can easily imagine how angry I am to see it lost now in a single day without firing a shot.'[47] Thanks to the support of her British ally, however,

Holland gained her point in the end, and by the Barrier Treaty of 1715 she was allowed to man seven fortresses in what was by then the Austrian Netherlands. On the other hand, it was also Britain which caused her to miss her second main objective: the safeguarding of her commercial predominance in the Spanish Empire. True, the trade was kept out of French hands as she wanted – but it was the British, not the Dutch, who gained Minorca and Gibraltar and the domination of the Mediterranean, along with the *navio de permiso* and the *asiento* and the monopoly of the Atlantic. (See pp. 124, 526.)

Eighteenth-Century Decline

Signs of Dutch decline in many fields of activity were evident before the seventeenth century ended. The arrangements for Anglo-Dutch naval co-operation in the War of the League of Augsburg, for example, showed that maritime superiority had passed to Britain. Britain was to supply five ships to Holland's three, and in any joint action the British Admiral was to be in command. But this was only the beginning. During the war, Holland sent to sea each year about 100 ships manned by about 24,000 men – not counting the enormous merchant fleet. A century later, during the fourth Anglo-Dutch War (1780–84), the Regents could muster only seventeen ships and 3,000 men for the battle of Dogger Bank (1781). The ship-building industry tells the same story. In the Zaan shipyards near Amsterdam, 306 vessels were under construction in 1707, whereas in 1770 only twenty-five to thirty were built, and the years 1790–93 averaged only five a year. Fishing also declined. Between the late seventeenth century and the late eighteenth, the herring fleet fell to half, the Dogger Bank cod-fishing fleet to below half, while the Arctic whalers fell from about 260 to about fifty. At the same time, the Dutch were ousted from their exclusive role as world carriers, as the merchant fleets of Britain, Hamburg, and the Scandinavian countries caught up with them and passed them. Moreover, the Republic suffered the inevitable fate of the go-between whose customers make direct contact with one another. Nor did she keep abreast

technically; and if the Tsar of Russia had wanted to learn ship-
building in 1797, instead of a hundred years earlier, he would
not have gone to Zaandam to learn the latest methods. Holland's charts were out of date, her equipment old-fashioned.
Dutch whalers were throwing harpoons by hand long after the
job had become mechanized. Her merchantmen had lost that
advantage which perhaps more than any other had put the
Republic ahead in the seventeenth century: cheap freights.
'The Dutch have also occasion for a greater number of men
to work their ships than other nations', wrote a Swedish
observer in the 1770s, 'as their rigging is made after the old
fashion with large blocks and thick cordage, heavy and clumsy
in every respect.'[48] 'We are no longer innate inventors,' wrote
a Dutchman in 1775, 'and originality is becoming increasingly
rare with us here. Nowadays we only make copies, whereas
formerly we only made originals.'[49]

The eighteenth-century record of the Dutch on their native
element, the sea, is thus a mixture of decline and stagnation.
On land, the picture is similar. In agriculture the peasants
were slow to adopt techniques pioneered in Britain and France;
though progress was achieved in dairy-production, cattle-rais-
ing, market-gardening, and arable-farming. In industry the
Republic suffered severely from foreign competition, as rival
states, following mercantilist principles, raised tariffs against
Dutch products and put bounties on their own. Moreover,
the sophisticated crafts in which Holland had once enjoyed
a virtual monopoly – textile-finishing, paper-making, sugar-
refining, glass-blowing, and so on – had now been learned by
other nations, often under Dutch tuition. The effect on Holland was catastrophic. 'Most of their principal towns are sadly
decayed', wrote James Boswell from Utrecht in 1764, 'and instead of finding every mortal employed, you meet with multitudes of poor creatures who are starving in idleness. Utrecht
is remarkably ruined.'[50] Textiles were badly hit. Leyden's
annual production of 139,000 pieces in 1671 (the peak year)
fell to 84,000 in 1700, 54,000 in 1750, and 29,000 in 1795. Decline was also evident in another field of production – artistic
and intellectual output – though here it was a matter of

quality, not quantity, and for this statistics will never be available. For the Dutch historian, Johan Huizinga, 'the general collapse of Dutch culture in the eighteenth century' was 'an agonizing fact'.[51]

Dutch stagnation or decline in the eighteenth century was undeniable, but it does not seem so agonizing when one recalls the extraordinary heights of Holland's seventeenth-century achievements. In the eighteenth century the Dutch people simply became ordinary again. Theirs was the case, as Charles Wilson has said, 'of a small and far from well-endowed people which had, by an earlier opportunism of genius, created a position for itself higher than was warranted in terms of crude power, and was now overtaken by the nemesis of normality'.[52] But if the decline is undeniable, the causes are less clear, and here we enter the realm of speculation. As has been suggested, much of the explanation lies outside the Republic itself. The rise of France and Britain, Russia and Prussia, created a world in which Holland was outmatched. While these heavy-weights even increased their population during the eighteenth century, the Dutch – for reasons which are not clear – steadily maintained their two million. Holland could no longer compete in such a class, and had to rely on Britain for defence. She also had to suffer the consequences of the War of the Spanish Succession (1702–13), which set Britain on the road to world domination, but which left Holland with a depleted navy and a crippling debt. This load – which rose from thirty million guilders in 1688 to 148 million in 1713 – had a numbing effect on Dutch life because of the level of taxation it necessitated. Already in 1696 Gregory King showed that Dutchmen were paying nearly three times as much per head as Frenchmen or Englishmen, and in 1785 they were still in the lead. One result was the neglect of the armed forces, and the consequent weakening of Dutch force in the world. 'They became more wedded than before', as C. R. Boxer has said, 'to a peace at any price policy.'[53] Holland and Zeeland would not vote taxes for the army, while the landward provinces refused to vote any more for the navy, and so both suffered. Another consequence of high taxation was to reduce the spending power of the Dutch public, and thus constrict an economy already handicapped (in comparison with rivals) by a minuscule home market. A further result was to raise Dutch wages above the European level, and thus lower the competitiveness of Dutch products – especially in such a labour-intensive industry as textiles.

Holland was not, however, simply the victim of adverse circumstances, for part of the explanation lies in conditions inside the Republic. The system of government and the social structure – that is, the oligarchy of Regents – must bear some share of the blame. During the second Stadholderless period (1702–47), the patrician families strengthened their grip on all the organs of state. 'So intimate was this union between business and government', Walter L. Dorn has said, 'that in the course of its evolution the Dutch state has assumed more and more the character of a comprehensive commercial corporation.'[54] As a result, Holland 'sank into a sweet slumber', as Johan Huizinga put it, 'to enjoy her dreams of durable peace and the clinking of ducats'.[55] Her timid foreign policy, and her lack of resources to back it, became accepted norms of European diplomacy. In the War of the Austrian Succession (1740–48), the French broke the famous Barrier and conquered the Austrian Netherlands (Belgium). In 1747, when they invaded the Dutch Republic itself, they provoked the same reaction as in 1672: a pro-Orange revolution. William IV was chosen as Captain-General and Admiral-General, and also made Stadholder of all seven provinces – the first of his line to achieve this distinction – though it made no essential difference to the way Holland was governed. The Orange régime now lasted as long as the Ancien Régime. After William IV's death there was a regency till William V came of age in 1766. He brought no changes either, saying that he was 'no friend to novelties'.[56] He had the misfortune to look, according to Sir Joshua Reynolds, 'very like King George [III], but not so handsome'.[57] 'I wish I were dead,' he wrote in 1781, 'that my father had never been Stadholder.'

With or without a Stadholder, the Regents floated higher and higher above the businessmen from whom they sprang with each generation that passed. As early as 1688 the English consul at Amsterdam noted that 'the older severe and frugal way of living is now almost quite out of date in Holland; there is very little to be seen of that sober modesty in apparel, diet, and habitations as formerly'.[58] Instead, the Regents became frenchified in dress and style of life, more exclusive than ever in their methods of recruitment, and less enterprising than before in their economic activity. Many withdrew from the fatigues of active commerce and industry to become rentiers, drawing their five per cent interest from practically every ruling house in Europe. And so, with talent and capital shying away from active enterprise, Holland fell further and further behind in the race for economic growth. And with banking, money-lending, insurance, and such-like refined activities rating so high in the Dutch scale of values, and mere manufacturing rating so low, an industrial revolution was out of the question – quite apart from the lack of coal and iron. In that case, there was no hope for the thickening layer of permanently unemployed at the bottom of Dutch society so long as Holland remained a loose federation of closed oligarchies with no other ambition than that of sitting tight.

The End of the Golden Age

The beginning of the end of the Ancien Régime was the outbreak of the American Revolution, which gave new ideological intensity to the traditional political rivalries which had marked Dutch life since the Revolt. The Enlightenment similarly sharpened opposition thinking. And passions were further aroused by the fourth Anglo-Dutch War (1780–84), in which the performance of the Republic was nothing to boast about. It arose when the British declared war on Holland because the Regents could not resist the temptation to trade with the American revolutionaries. William V and the Orange party, on the other hand, were pro-British. Out of the acrimonious debates of these years emerged a new party, the Patriots, made up of the chief enemies of the existing régime, the religious and political Outs. Taking their place in it were anti-Orange

Regents, Roman Catholics, Lutherans and other sects outside the Reformed Church as well as middle and lower-middle-class burghers in the provinces of Holland and Zeeland, and nobles from the landward provinces. Uniting them all was a desire to break the Regent and Orange monopoly of power and influence, and to modernize Dutch institutions on the latest lines. In other words, to turn the Republic into a nation and a state.

Between the humiliating peace with Britain in 1784 and the crisis year of 1787 the Patriots made rapid gains. They also sprouted a radical wing, known as the Free Corps, a semimilitary organization. Broadly speaking, the Patriots wanted to reduce or eliminate the role of the Stadholder in government, and to open the oligarchies to a wider circle of burghers; while the Free Corps aimed at democracy. In the provinces of Holland, where the Patriots were strong, the Estates voted William V out of his offices as Stadholder and Captain-General. In the town of Utrecht, where the Free Corps was strong, the corporation was dissolved, and a new one created by a general election. By 1787 the country was on the brink of civil war when the Free Corps began to clash with the troops of the Stadholder. On the urgent representations of the British, the King of Prussia (William V's brother-in-law) despatched 20,000 men and put the Patriot movement down. 'I could not keep my eyes from watering', said the British ambassador, at the gratitude of the Prince and 'of those who compose the uppermost class of the people.'[59]

The Patriots were not finished, however. Some went underground, while others found refuge in France. And when the French Revolutionary armies marched into Holland in 1793, the former rose to support the latter who marched in with them. Two years later, the Dutch Ancien Régime ended. The Stadholder William V was deposed, and the Regent oligarchy was replaced by the much more representative Batavian Republic. It had needed the French Revolution to create a state out of the 'disunited provinces', and a nation out of their people.

Spain: Seventeenth-Century Decline

BY the mid seventeenth century Spain was in full decline. As failure followed failure, both rulers and ruled were haunted by the question of what had gone wrong since the Golden Century. The Conde Duque de Olivares (as Philip IV's chief minister was usually called) wrote as follows of the year 1640: 'This year can undoubtedly be considered the most unfortunate that this Monarchy has ever experienced.'[1] But Olivares was to know only the half of it, and there was much worse to come. 'Never have such great preparations been made in all theatres of war', he went on, 'and yet the results have been far worse than could ever have been imagined.' Perhaps if Spaniards had allowed themselves to imagine the full possibilities of their collapse, they might have taken realistic steps to forestall it; but they looked the other way, and disasters accumulated for the remainder of the seventeenth century. For their part, the monarchy and the aristocracy continued to act as if Spain were still the richest and most powerful empire in the world. In 1649, for example, when the new queen, Mariana of Austria, arrived in Madrid, the streets and squares were decorated more gorgeously than ever before, and at the many feasts and receptions the dresses, the jewelry, and the ceremony reached new heights of ostentation. Such extravagance in the midst of poverty was unfortunately only too characteristic of the Spanish upper class; and their behaviour was as escapist and fraudulent as the baroque palaces and churches they were building, in which sumptuous decoration disguised walls made of brick and rubble.

Signs of Decay

If the underlying causes of Spanish decay remain a matter for argument, the outward signs of it were plain for all to see. Indeed, they were visible in the last years of the reign of Philip II

(1556–98). The defeat of the Invincible Armada by England (1588) was only one setback in his scheme to stem the tide of Protestantism with Spanish blood and treasure, and to make Spain the lord of all Europe. After that came peace with France (1598) and England (1604); followed by the twelve-year truce with Holland (1609) which made the shameful acknowledgement that the Monarchy was incapable, at least for the time being, of reconquering its rebellious subjects. During the years of peace which marked the reign of Philip III (1598–1621), France, Holland, and England continued their youthful rise as military, naval, and commercial powers, while Spanish governments confined themselves to ransacking their country's wealth to satiate the appetites of Court favourites. Under Philip IV (1621–65), when serious economic decline really set in, Spain again set out on a policy of ill-advised aggression, in a crazy attempt to prove to the world, and to convince herself, that she was not the sick man of Europe. It is true that the new Favourite, the Count-Duke Olivares, who was in effect the prime minister of Spain till his fall in 1643, worked selflessly in the interests of the Monarchy, and did his utmost to support his warlike designs abroad with fundamental reform at home. Unfortunately, like others after him, he found Spanish society and institutions peculiarly resistant to change, even change for the better; but, even had his reforms gone through, he would probably still have failed abroad, since he rashly led Spain into adventures for which she no longer had the strength or the spirit. In 1621 he refused to renew the truce with Holland, now fully refreshed since 1609, and much invigorated after swallowing up large portions of Spanish commerce. From this it was only a step to full participation in the Thirty Years' War, a crusade in which Spain tried to relive the past as the sword of the Counter-Reformation and the head of the Habsburg alliance against France. She entered the disastrous Mantuan War (1626–31) in a fruitless attempt to head off a French presence in north Italy. In 1628 the Dutch sea-captain Piet Heyn captured the New Spain silver fleet – all except three vessels – and in the 1630s the Dutch took possession of Portuguese colonies in the Far East and in Brazil. In 1634 they conquered the Spanish base of Curaçao. Even the one military victory – over the Swedish army at Nördlingen (1634) – brought disaster in its train. It forced Richelieu at last into full and open participation in the Thirty Years' War (1635). A Spanish drive on Paris from Flanders was foiled at Corbie (1636). Spanish troops surrendered Breda to the Dutch in 1637. The French captured Breisach on the Rhine in 1638, thus cutting Spain's line of communication with Flanders via north Italy. The other line, via the English Channel, was cut when Admiral Tromp beat the Spanish squadron at the battle of the Downs, off the French coast, in 1639.

The next year was Olivares' 'most unfortunate' year. The French thrust into Spain at both ends of the Pyrenees; and the monarchy itself began to break up as Catalonia and Portugal came out in open rebellion, with French encouragement. Disintegration went further in 1641, when two Andalusian aristocrats were caught conspiring to take Andalusia out of the monarchy and turn it into an independent kingdom. And, by 1643, the antipathy of all the great noble landowners was so sharp that Olivares fell from power. The débâcle still continued, however. The second front, in Spain, in the war against France necessarily weakened Spain's main effort in Flanders, where the Spanish infantry lost its reputation for valour in the battle of Rocroi (1643). In 1647 the Monarchy declared itself bankrupt; Naples and Sicily rebelled; the Spanish infantry suffered another French defeat at Lens. In 1648 a plot was unearthed to make the Duke of Hijar king of an independent Aragon. Chastened at last by a little realism, Spain took part in the negotiations at Westphalia which ended the Thirty Years' War, and even accepted the unkindest cut of all by recognizing the independence of Holland in the Treaty of Münster in 1648. And not only that: Spain also handed over some of her strong-points along the Dutch frontier, and gave the Dutch the right to close the river Scheldt, in other words, to bottle up Antwerp, ruin the commerce of the Spanish Netherlands (Belgium), and accelerate the economic collapse of Spain herself.

Spain hoped by these sacrifices to concentrate with more success on her chief problems: the war with France, and the revolutions in Catalonia and Portugal. Only with Catalonia did she make any headway. Here, Spain was helped by the outbreak of the Frondes in France (forcing Mazarin to withdraw French aid from Catalonia), and by the divisions among the Catalans themselves. The wealthy bourgeoisie of Barcelona and the noble landowners of the hinterland had initiated rebellion to preserve their constitutional rights against the centralizing programme of Olivares in Madrid. In so doing, unfortunately for them, they had let loose revolutionary forces they had no wish to encourage: mountain brigands, as well as oppressed workers and peasants. Besides this unwelcome development, they discovered that the France of Richelieu and Mazarin was even more oppressive (because more efficient) than the Castile of Olivares. In other words, Madrid's very weakness was an attraction. In these circumstances, Catalan resistance was gradually broken down even by the demoralized Castilian troops, and Barcelona surrendered in 1652. Philip IV recognized all Catalonia's laws and liberties (1653), and she became once more part of the Spanish Monarchy. Here, then, there had been no loss. On the other hand, there had been no gain: for Olivares' centralizing programme had now to be abandoned for as long as the house of Habsburg ruled in Madrid.

With France and Portugal, Spain was less fortunate. The war with Mazarin dragged on till 1659, partly because the French received English help. In 1655 Cromwell's forces captured Jamaica. In 1656 and 1657 Admiral Blake destroyed silver fleets from New Spain; and in 1657 an Anglo-French army beat the Spanish at the battle of the Dunes. At the peace of the Pyrenees (1659), Spain had to sign away Artois in Flanders, and Roussillon and part of Cerdagne, which had been part of Catalonia since 1493. At the same time, the fateful marriage of Philip IV's daughter to Louis XIV was contracted: a union which ultimately led to the War of the Spanish Succession (1701–14), when practically the whole of Europe fought over the inert and disintegrating body of Spain, and when the crown of Spain passed from the Habsburgs to the Bourbons. In the meantime, all attempts to bring the Portuguese to heel were fruitless. Portugal, unlike Catalonia, was united against Castile, and moreover ably led. She had her own overseas empire, and played a part in world commerce similar to that of Holland, France, and England. Her ruling classes were dynamic and forward-looking, unlike the Catalan aristocracy whose horizon was still limited to the careful preservation of a way of life achieved in the late Middle Ages. Spain was forced at last to sign the Treaty of Lisbon (1668), recognizing Portugal as a sovereign state.

Philip IV

Philip IV, who was king of Spain during this landslide in her international reputation, was only sixteen when he succeeded in 1621, and so can hardly be held responsible for the warlike decisions that were taken at that time. 'Woe to the land whose king is a child', wrote a discontented Catalan in 1626, as the new king was about to honour the Principality with his first visit.[2] But matters failed to improve as he matured, and, by the time he was a man, Spain was too deeply committed to aggression for withdrawal to be possible without an unthinkable loss of face. Besides, though Philip was conscientious and able, he had no force of character and only limited managerial talent. He was, from the start, putty in the hands of his Favourite, the Count-Duke Olivares. He was one of the many victims of the Habsburg family's policy of consanguineous marriages, and his four grandparents were each direct descendants of Juana *la Loca*: not a healthy endowment. His official face, a motionless mask, is perhaps the most widely known of all the monarchs mentioned in this book, thanks to the many revealing portraits that Velázquez painted of the royal family and Court, as well as its attendant dogs, jesters, and dwarfs. Behind those impassive eyes raged a never-ending war between the appetites of a sexuality which was unquenchably demanding and the imperatives of a conscience which was penitent to the point of saintliness. He was happier in the company of painters and writers than councillors and secretaries; and thanks to Olivares, even as a boy, he was more familiar with the underworld of Madrid prostitutes and actresses (in so far as these are distinguishable) than with any other corner of his empire. Here, in Madrid, was to be found, in Martin Hume's phrase, 'the phosphorescent focus of a great nation's decay'.[3] For his pleasure, a network of agents covered the kingdom spotting talented actresses; and he proved to be, as the contemporary letter-writer, Jeronimo Barrionuevo, once said, 'a fine hand at bastards, but with very poor luck as regards legitimate children'.[4] Over thirty illegitimate children have been counted, though only one, Don John of Austria (son of the sweet-voiced Maria Calderon) achieved official recognition. As for legitimate heirs, he managed to produce only the sick and sorry creature, Charles II, with whom this stream of the Habsburg family finally ran into the sand.

Nor did Philip improve as he grew older. He dismissed Olivares only to succumb to other grandees: Don Luis de Haro (1643–61), and the discordant pair, the Count of Castrillo and the Duke of Medina de las Torres (1661–65).

Philip's journeys from brothel to confessional and back again were a treadmill which left him insufficient time or vigour to give public affairs the consideration they desperately required. And the more exacting grew his lechery, the more maudlin became his remorse. In 1643, he met Sor Maria, the abbess of the convent of the Immaculate Conception at Ágreda, and began a correspondence with her which ended only with his death. His letters reveal the tragic mental confusion under which the king and so many of his subjects laboured in the seventeenth century. He was convinced, for example, that the decline of Spain was God's punishment for his own sins. 'The greatest favour that I can receive from His holy hands', he wrote in 1655, 'is that the punishment He lays upon these realms may be laid upon me; for it is I, and not they, who really deserve the punishment, for they have always been true and firm Catholics.'[5] This breath-taking piece of conceit was also a glaringly mistaken appreciation of the situation in which Spain found itself at that time, leading to mistakes of policy. In addition, the Spanish Church encouraged an attitude of resignation before the divine will; and too many Spaniards considered that taking the sacraments, or visiting a shrine, or hiring a flagellant to do vicarious penance, were appropriate ways of managing their worldly affairs. It is not surprising that bad decisions were taken at the Council board of

Philip IV when his homework consisted, not of mastering the documents his secretaries placed before him, but of spending the evening backstage at a Madrid theatre or on his knees at the Escorial before the corpse of his great forebear, the Emperor Charles V.

Government

As has been mentioned already, the fatal decisions were taken when he was still a boy. At that time he informed his first Cortes (parliament) that the first duty of a Spanish sovereign was 'with holy zeal befitting so Catholic a Prince to undertake the defence and exaltation of our Holy Catholic faith; ... to aid the Emperor in Bohemia; to fight the rebel Hollanders again, and to defend everywhere our sacred faith and the authority of the Holy See'.[6] This was a re-hash of the crusading programme of the sixteenth century, an aping of the policies of Charles V and Philip II, a misguided attempt to extend Habsburg land-power in Germany and Italy, while neglecting Spain's true maritime and commercial interests. And the armies marched just at the moment when Spain, along with the rest of Europe, was entering upon her long economic depression. Thus the Monarchy over-taxed its strength abroad and was forced into two principal measures at home, one of which would have been advantageous had it not utterly failed in the execution, while the other was the more pernicious the more it succeeded. The first of these policies was the centralization programme of Olivares, which, as has been shown, led to the Catalan and Portuguese revolutions and had to be abandoned. The second was the policy of financial juggling, to which we must now turn.

The financial policy of Philip IV's Treasury consisted of a series of disastrous, short-term expedients to extract more money out of a shrinking economy. The Spanish crown had long since learned to make ends meet by anticipating the revenue. Each year, Genoese bankers signed contracts (*asientos*) with the Treasury to supply the necessary funds in Italy or Flanders (or wherever they were required) on the security of the revenue about to come in from the Spanish American silver fleets and the taxes on the Spanish people. It was a method of financing the extravagances of the present out of the privations of the future. Unfortunately, under Philip IV the income plummeted. In the five-year period 1656–60, for example, the fleets brought in only about one tenth of what they had imported in the period 1616–20. It thus became necessary to extract more money from the Spanish nation; and the chief methods used by Philip IV for doing this followed precedents of the previous reign, and were as follows.

In the first place, the value of the new copper coinage (*vellon*) was tampered with, causing surges of inflation interspersed with sudden jerks of deflation. As a sample of these financial twists and turns (which naturally tore the economy in shreds) let us take the 1640s and 1650s. In 1641 the Treasury doubled the value of all four-*maravedi* coins minted before 1603, and trebled the value of all two-*maravedi* and four-*maravedi* pieces minted since that year. This may have helped to finance Olivares' wars, but it caused such a steep rise in prices that in 1642 the Treasury called in the various *maravedi* coins and reissued them at half their previous value. The needs of the war could not be denied, however, and in 1651 inflation began again. All pieces of two-*maravedis* were restamped at four times their old value, and 100,000 ducats' worth of new two-*maravedi* coins were issued weighing only a quarter the weight of the previous ones. In 1652 deflation was necessary once more: the eight-*maravedi* pieces became two-*maravedis*, the two-*maravedis* of 1651 became one-*maravedi*, and so on. Disappointed holders of the coinage were compensated with government bonds (*juros*) backed by the tobacco monopoly.

This insidious method of raising increased revenue from the people without imposing new taxes continued right through the reign of Philip IV and into that of Charles II (1665–1700). It flooded Spain with worthless copper coins, the falling value of which is indicated by premiums on silver in terms of *vellon* which rose to 120 per cent in 1665, 180 per cent in 1669, and 275 per cent in 1680. This last year saw the worst financial crisis of the century, necessitating a brutal deflation which brought wholesale prices crashing down by forty-five per cent – a figure which, if compared with the fall of thirty-eight per cent which the United States experienced in the depression of 1929, gives a vivid idea of the deadly effect this policy had on Spanish business.

The year 1680 also saw employed the second financial device resorted to by seventeenth-century Spanish governments: bankruptcy. This was the first time Charles II had used it, but Philip IV fell back on this form of financial treachery in 1627, 1647, and 1653. On these occasions, creditors of the crown were fobbed off with *juros* of doubtful value instead of their rightful dues. Government bonds were not good to hold because of the third type of money-raising common in this period: reducing the interest on them by fifty per cent – even from 1658 onwards cutting it down by sixty and seventy per cent. A fourth money-raising device was to increase the tax-load. The *millones*, a purchase-tax levied on articles of everyday consumption – on meat, wine, oil, and vinegar – was extended to fish, paper, soap, tallow candles, pepper, and so on. Fifthly, the crown sold its own property – a seductive device to a hard-pressed executive because it did not require the consent of the Cortes. Philip IV sold crown lands, government offices, patents of nobility, and seigniorial rights over town and villages (*señorios*). Sixthly, forced loans and free gifts were extorted from the wealthy (who had ample means of recouping on the poor) and special grants were levied on the clergy.

The disastrous effect which these measures (and others like them) had on the Spanish economy and society will be described later. They amounted to a series of savage blows at a nation already brought to its knees by social and economic evils of a deeper nature. This financial policy, which was nothing more than a sophisticated form of plunder, so pauperized the mass of the people that they were in no condition to withstand the famine and plagues and other natural disasters that beset them as well. In 1679, for example, the city of Antequera reported that in their third year of dearth most families were 'eating bread made of beans, barley, and other seeds of low quality, and many here, out of extreme poverty, have had to keep themselves alive on weeds, spending their savings to keep alive; and now disease has supervened so powerfully ... that there are more than 1,200 people in hospital, and the greater part are dying, while through the streets a cart tirelessly passes, picking up the dead'.[7]

Madrid was by then accustomed to receiving such sombre reports, just as it was used to hearing of lost battles and unfavourable treaties. Repeated defeat seemed to unhinge the Court's judgement, and that of the whole upper class. They alternated between bouts of black religious mysticism and periods of wild extravagance. Philip IV himself, a sombre statue tormented within, typified them well. Now and then he would attempt to fend off the divine wrath by clearing the streets of Madrid of prostitutes. At other times he would indulge himself. In 1657 he and the queen were entertained by the Marquis of Heliche, the eldest son of the chief minister, Don Luis de Haro. The banquet wrote Barrionuevo,

cost 16,000 ducats.... There was a dinner served of 1000 dishes; and there was one monstrous stew in a huge jar sunk in the ground with a fire beneath it.... It contained a three-year-old calf, four sheep, 100 pairs of pigeons, 100 partridges, 100 rabbits, 1000 pigs' trotters, and 1000 tongues, 200 fowls, 30 hams, 500 sausages, and 100,000 other trifles.... There were three or four thousand persons present, and there was plenty for everybody, and to spare. So much was left, indeed, that it was brought back to Madrid in baskets, and I got some relieves and scraps. And all this was in addition to tarts and puffs and pasties, sweet cakes, preserves, fruits, and enormous quantities of wine and sweet drinks.[8]

The disastrous reign came to an end in 1665. 'Of all his Majesty's household,' wrote an eye-witness, 'the Marquis of Aytona and two other servants alone wept for the death of their King and master; and in all the rest of the capital there was not one person who shed a tear.'[9] It would be over-simplifying the Spanish predicament, however, to place the blame exclusively on the inadequacies of Philip IV and his ministers. They made serious errors, of which the two worst were the European adventures they embarked on and the monetary chaos they created to pay for them; but there is a good deal more to the decline of Spain than this. And Louis XIV's patronizing remark, that 'it would appear as if the monarchs of Spain since Charles V had tried by their bad conduct to destroy their realm rather than to preserve it',[10] is not the whole story. For Philip IV inherited a system of government, a social structure, an economic crisis, and a national psychology, on which Richelieu himself would have had difficulty in making an impact.

Although in the sixteenth century, Spain had pioneered the building of the 'Renaissance monarchy', by the mid seventeenth century she had fallen far behind in constitutional creativity. The Venetian ambassador reported in 1653 that she was the most poorly governed country in the world. Essentially, she suffered from the malady – endemic in Europe in the so-called age of absolutism – which rendered her kings too weak to govern with the force required in the dangerous international world of the Ancien Régime. Spain was only a loose confederation of kingdoms, principalities, and provinces, which happened to owe allegiance to the same man as sovereign. Leaving aside Portugal as by now effectively independent, the House of Habsburg ruled over Castile, Navarre, the Basque provinces, and the Kingdom of Aragon. Only in Castile did the crown have any pretensions to effective power, for each of the other territories was still at the corporative-state (or *Ständestaat*) stage of development. In Navarre, the king was represented by his Viceroy residing at Pamplona – but he was a mere constitutional monarch. The people had their own institutions of government, and were well entrenched behind constitutional rights and privileges which could not be abated one jot without the consent of the Cortes of Navarre. The common people here did not have to pay taxes to Madrid as the Castilians did, neither could they be conscripted for the royal army. The Basques had similar privileges. Here the Habsburgs were *señors* of the three provinces of Viscaya, Guipúzcoa, and Álava. In the first of these (to take it as an example) the executive power of Madrid was hamstrung by the Vizcayan representative body, known as the *Junta General*, whose ninety-three members met every two years under a certain oak tree at Guernica, when fine, and in the church of *Nuestra Señora de la Antigua*, if wet. They were extremely sensitive about their traditional privileges, recognized by a long line of Spanish kings; and when Olivares tried to collect a salt tax and raise troops there in 1632, they rose in rebellion.

In the Kingdom of Aragon the members of the Cortes were similarly jealous of their ancient rights, as may be gathered from the oath of allegiance they took to the crown. 'We, who are as good as you are,' they promised, 'take an oath to you who are no better than we, as prince and heir of our kingdom, on condition that you preserve our *fueros* and liberties, and if you do not, we do not' (the *fueros* being their traditional constitutional rights).[11] In this kingdom the king was faced by four distinct units: Aragon, Valencia, Catalonia, and Majorca. The *fueros*, and the spirit with which they were defended, were broadly similar, and so Catalonia may be taken as an example, perhaps slightly extreme, of them all. Here, the Habsburg monarch was a contractual prince who could not expect obedience unless he also kept his side of the bargain. A pamphleteer wrote in 1622:

In Catalonia the supreme power and jurisdiction over the province belongs not to His Majesty alone, but to His Majesty and the three estates of the province, which together possess supreme and absolute power to make and unmake laws, and to alter the machinery and government of the province... These laws we have in Catalonia are laws compacted between the king and the land, and the prince can no more exempt himself from them than he can exempt himself from a contract.[12]

The Catalan Cortes consisted of three Estates: the clergy, the nobility, and the representatives of thirty-one towns. Without its consent, the King of Spain could not touch a single law or institution. It could meet only in his presence, and always refused to consider royal requests for financial aid till its own grievances had been redressed. In between meetings of the Cortes its six-member standing committee, the *Diputació*, was in day-to-day charge of protecting Catalan *fueros* from violation by the agents of Madrid, of collecting, and spending, Catalan taxes, and of raising any subsidy which the Cortes may have voted for the crown. It goes without saying that only a tiny proportion of the taxation paid by Catalans was intended for the crown. Moreover, the royal domain in Catalonia was small:

another sign of royal weakness. The income from the royal patrimony was less than a quarter of the revenue spent by the *Diputació*, and less than half that enjoyed by the Barcelona city council. Barcelona itself, represented in the Cortes by five syndics (one of whom was President of the Third Estate), was almost an independent republic. It was the only city of Spain to reserve a permanent box in the Plaza Mayor at Madrid, at a minimum cost of eight ducats a bullfight. Its vast wealth had enabled the ruling oligarchy to purchase extensive privileges from the Count of Barcelona (who happened to be King of Spain) and they now had little need to pay much attention to the crown. Altogether, the headstrong Catalans were an intractable problem to the Habsburgs: comparable in ungovernability to the Hungarians or the Irish. 'Forgive my language, which is the most restrained I can manage', wrote Olivares in understandable irritation in 1640, 'but no king in the world has a province like Catalonia.'[13]

The King of Spain, then, had serious limitations on his power as ruler of the various provinces of the Iberian peninsula. But these were only part of his responsibilities. He was also Count of Flanders, Duke of Milan, King of Naples and Sicily and Sardinia. Space forbids any description of the internal government of these dependencies except to say that the crown had its fill of *fueros* to swallow in each of them. The institutional links between the Iberian and the extra-Iberian territories will be referred to in the section devoted to the government of Castile. The government of the Indies will likewise be touched on there, for it must not be forgotten that the King of Spain was also ruler of a vast colonial empire.

In Spain itself the king was incapable of putting into effect any serious reforms, however idealistic he might be. Any minister who really meant business, as Olivares did, found himself with a revolt on his hands. The centrifugal forces were too strong. The Spaniard's first loyalty was to his own village and then to his province; and an all-Spanish patriotism hardly existed. Besides, the Spanish people did not feel themselves tied to any monarch by unbreakable bonds. The rights of succession in the Iberian provinces had always been rather confused. They had been fought over frequently from Visigothic times onwards, and were to be much disputed further, during the Ancien Régime and after. On the other hand, the tension between Madrid and the provinces was not so fierce as to break up the Monarchy into its component parts. For one thing, the provinces never aided one another against Madrid. Valencia in 1520, Aragon in 1591, and Catalonia in 1640 each had to fight its own battles, and could expect no help from the other egocentric provinces. Thus Madrid was never overwhelmed, and, under the Habsburgs, was never really predominant. A rough equilibrium existed which the ruling nobles in each province preferred to any other solution. The arm of Madrid was long enough to help them smash ambitious moves on the part of the peasants or workers, but not long enough to disturb their own monopoly of social, economic, and political power.

The chief links between Madrid and the dependent provinces were, on the one hand, a series of Viceroys resident there – in Naples, Sicily, Navarre, Catalonia, Peru, New Spain, and so on – and, on the other, Councils attendant upon the King in Madrid – such as the Council of Aragon, the Council of Italy, the Council of Flanders, the Council of the Indies, and so on. 'As the king is represented in different ways,' wrote Olivares, 'being king of different kingdoms which have been incorporated into the Crown while preserving their separate identities, it is necessary to have in the Court a Council for each one. Your Majesty is thus considered to be present in each kingdom.'[14] These Councils received reports from the appropriate Viceroys, advised the king on general policy for the provinces concerned, and then issued his instructions back to the Viceroys. And above these territorial Councils were a number of others with responsibility for the Monarchy as a whole: for example, the Council of the Inquisition, the Council of Finance, the Council of War, and the Council of State, where decisions of high policy were taken.

It remains to mention the Council of Castile, the chief organ for the government of Castile, and to the disgust of non-Castilians well on the way to being the chief committee of the whole empire. Here was one chief source of the tension between the

centre and the periphery which plagued Spain throughout the
Ancien Régime and after. For though the non-Castilian viewed
the Monarchy as a confederation of equals, the capital, Madrid,
was in the centre of Castile, while the chief Court appointments
and government posts were given to Castilians, and the energies
of the Monarchy were concentrated on Castilian (in so far as
they were not purely Habsburg) interests. On the other hand (to
look at the Castilian point of view), it had been Castilian men,
money, and enterprise that had created the Golden Age in the
first place; and now that decline had set in (and it was principally Castilian decline), the general opinion in Castile was that
it was high time the other parts of the Monarchy bore their fare
share of the burden. This was the crux of Olivares' policy which
ultimately led to the rebellions of 1640. 'The most important
thing in Your Majesty's Monarchy,' he wrote in his famous
memorandum for Philip IV, 'is for you to become king of
Spain: by this I mean, Sir, that Your Majesty should not be
content with being king of Portugal, of Aragon, of Valencia
and count of Barcelona, but should secretly plan and work to
reduce these kingdoms of which Spain is composed to the style
and laws of Castile, with no difference whatsoever. And if Your
Majesty achieves this you will be the most powerful prince in
the world.'[15] Unfortunately, Philip IV did not achieve it, and
became instead one of the weakest. For after 1640 the policy of
Castilianization was placed in cold-storage for the rest of the
seventeenth century.

Even without military failure abroad and rebellion at home,
the policy of Olivares could not have been imposed without a
thorough overhaul of the conciliar system of government. At the
start, under Charles V and Philip II, the Councils had been a
dynamic force in the acquisition and government of a vast empire; but serious deficiences had become manifest by the middle
of the seventeenth century. The bureaucracy was top-heavy,
over-manned, cluttered with paper, inefficient where it was not
actually corrupt, and far too unwieldy for anyone other than a
managerial genius to run. Problems were passed from hand to
hand up the hierarchy in such a stately fashion that by the time
a decision had been taken by one of the councils, and this had

been drafted into a recommendation (*consulta*) to the king – any consequent action tended to be too late to be relevant. Levers were pulled hard in Madrid, but in the localities at the other end of the bureaucratic machine hardly anything stirred. The civil service, in other words, had turned into the opposite of what it had been intended for. It now acted as a barrier between king and people, preventing the government doing anything effective on behalf of the nation.

If the grip of Madrid on the peripheral regions was feeble, its power in the Kingdom of Castile itself had been only too strong – strong enough, for example, to plunder it to exhaustion in the interests of Habsburg ambitions abroad. It had been in Castile that the King of Spain had acted as a 'Renaissance monarch'. The nobility had been subdued and domesticated (at the peasantry's expense); the only representative organ, the Cortes, had been reduced to the level of a tax-voting machine; while over the whole kingdom had been flung a network of officials under orders from the Council of Castile in Madrid. In each important town – usually the capital of a province – was posted a royal official, the *corregidor*, who was armed with a broad range of powers appropriate to the chief provincial agent of the Council of Castile. He supervised the municipal councils (*municipios*) and other local institutions in their day-to-day working; he acted as military governor of his area; he was the chief agent of the Treasury there; and he was also the district judge to whom appeal could lie from the surrounding town and village courts. From him, there was appeal to a small number of regional courts called *Audiencias* or *Chancillerías*, which were roughly equivalent to the *Parlements* of France. From them there was a further appeal possible – to the supreme court in Madrid, the Council of Castile.

On paper this looks as sinewy a system of centralized absolutism as the Ancien Régime could devise. The nobility, the chief enemies of the crown, had no representative institutions either national or regional, for they had long been eliminated as an Estate from the Cortes. This body consisted of only thirty-six representatives of eighteen important towns, and most of these were appointed *corregidors* or *oidors* (judges), or given other rewards, for their patriotism in voting such new taxation as the crown demanded. It was a constitution which appears at first glance to be as wieldy as anything Charles I of England could have desired; but the last three Habsburgs did not think so. The power of the landed nobility was not so easily pushed aside, and by the mid seventeenth century it had flowed back in full tide into all the channels of government. It overwhelmed Philip III and Charles II, and was only kept at bay under Philip IV during the rule of Olivares, who cut out a lot of dead wood and re-formed the Councils. Otherwise, the aristocracy (that is to say, the Grandees of Spain and the Titled Nobility of Castile) filled all the important posts at Court, on the Councils, in the Vice-royalties, in the embassies, and in the armed forces; while they and the larger middle groups of nobles (the *caballeros*) manned the lesser posts at Madrid, and also became *corregidors* in the provinces, judges in the *Audiencias*, and deputies to the Cortes.

Another feature of the administration which reduced its amenability to royal discipline was the fact that it was worm-eaten from top to bottom with the sale of offices. The job of high sheriff (*alguacil mayor*) in the Council of Castile went for 136,000 ducats; that of Chancellor in the Treasury for 282,000 ducats. In 1640 Velázquez was given the office of clerk in the weight-office, so that he could sell it to a third person. Its price was 6,000 ducats. But to appreciate the full extent of this corruption, and thus the full measure of the weakness of the crown over its own officials, it is necessary to dig below the level of the central government in Madrid, and below that of the *corregidors* in the provinces, in order to examine the administration as it was carried on in the cities, towns, and villages.

In most municipalities (*municipios*) the original democratic form of government had long since given way to control by local nobility, or in some cases by bourgeois patricians. This domination had come about in various ways: by corruption or sheer banditry, in some cases; in others, it had been the fault of the crown. Needy Habsburg kings had sold municipal offices, such as that of magistrate (*regidor*) on the town-council (*ayuntamiento*) for ready cash. And by the mid seventeenth century, most towns in Castile were run by nobles who owned their offices and could pass them on to their children. (In the provinces of the Crown of Aragon, and in Navarre and the Basque provinces, this degeneration had not gone so far, since these areas were protected by their *fueros* from such a commercialization of their local government by the crown. In the city of Valencia, for example, nobles succeeded in acquiring municipal offices for the first time only in 1652.) In the larger cities of Castile the office of *regidor* would cost perhaps 20,000 ducats. Olivares had found it useful to acquire the office of *regidor* in each of the cities which sent deputies to the Cortes – and his widow continued to enjoy their possession after his death. In small towns, by the middle of the seventeenth century, an arrangement had been arrived at by which offices were divided equally between nobles and commoners (*la mitad de oficios*). The majority of towns had this compromise, but in the larger towns the monopoly of offices had been acquired by the nobility – who were town-dwellers in Spain, along with their tenants and farm-labourers. What had happened was that the nobility had secured royal permission to turn their cities into nobles' cities (*ciudados de estatuto*) on payment of a substantial fee. In such places, would-be office-holders had to go through the often elaborate business of *probanzas*: that is, giving proofs of nobility, of *limpieza de sangre* (purity of blood – from non-Spanish taints), and of abstention from manual labour (*oficios viles y mecanicos*). Madrid, Seville, Ciudad Real, Ávila, and Córdoba were such cities. Jerez managed to acquire this status in 1724. In Toledo, another of them, the Duke of Maqueda was appeal judge (*alcalde de las alzadas*); the Count of Cifuentes was mayor (*alcalde mayor*); the Marquis of Montemayor was magistrate (*alcalde*) of the Mesta; and the Count of Fuensalida was chief constable (*alguacil mayor*). Of course, these high aristocrats did not perform these humble duties in person. They employed substitutes, or if the posts were profitable they farmed them out.

It did not matter whether it was nobles or commoners who exercised these functions, however. The point was that they were not agents of the crown. Moreover, their power was not limited by the city boundaries, for it was a peculiarity of

Spanish local government that such cities ruled areas as big as
English counties and more, and thus held many of the surrounding towns and villages in a kind of lord-vassal relationship.
The village of Artiega, for example, paid the town of Salmas de
Anana a loaf and two eggs per inhabitant at Easter; as well as
a certain quantity of white bread and thirty-nine *reales* for the
refreshment of the notables. Such villages, if they could afford
the expenses of pushing their case through the courts, could
acquire the privilege of being an independent community (*privilegios de villazgo*). Artiega did not succeed in escaping from
subjection till 1830.

In urbanized Spain, then, local power had not only been
snatched from the people: it had also been alienated from the
king. The situation was similar in the countryside. Only a
minority of the land-surface of Spain was administered by royal
officials. The greater part had passed under the control of the
nobility and the Church. In earlier centuries, monarchs had
been forced by financial necessity, or in some cases swayed by
piety, to grant to private individuals, or to institutions, the
rights of jurisdiction over large areas of land. In Catalonia, for
instance, over seventy per cent of the towns and villages were
under non-royal jurisdiction. The Duke of Cardona owned, or
shared the jurisdiction in more than 230 towns and villages. The
biggest abbey, Ripoll, possessed more than 6,000 vassals. These
seigneurial rights of jurisdiction (*señorios*) went usually to
nobles, or monasteries, or bishoprics, or Military Orders –
and these usually owned the land concerned as well, though
not necessarily, as the land and the *señorio* over it could be
separately owned. As well as possessing the control over first-
instance civil and criminal jurisdiction, the holders of *señorios*
enjoyed some or all of the following rights: the monopoly of
the oven, the mill, the oil-mill, the wine-press, the slaughter-
house, the tavern, and so on, as well as rights over hunting
and fishing. In addition, they might own public offices, such
as clerkships, and public sources of income, such as tolls over
bridges and ferries: all of which they could farm out for
income. Out of every thousand head of livestock that crossed
the bridge at Alconetar, for example, the Count of Alba de

Liste collected three as *señor* of the district, a privilege which brought him into numerous conflicts with the great sheep-owning ring, the Mesta.

Sometimes the lord also owned the tithes, or part of them, monopolized the firewood on the village waste, and took the lion's share of the rights of common pasture. Often he pocketed the ten per cent purchase-tax called the *alcabala*: a privilege which symbolized vividly the ability of the clergy and nobility to profit from the crown's weakness. Most communities (or their lords) had at some distant date made a contract with the crown to pay a fixed sum each year (the *encabezamiento*), collecting the *alcabala* themselves. With the rise in prices that had characterized modern history, the king's share, the *encabezamiento*, had shrunk till it was worthless, while the villages (that is, the lords) continued to collect their full ten per cent. More than 3,000 villages in Castile paid the *alcabala* to their *señors* instead of to the king. One lord in this category was the Marquis de Astorga, whose *señorio* of Villamañán included thirty towns and villages. At Villamañán itself, as well as drawing a large income from rights such as those already mentioned, he also named the mayor and eight *regidores* (four nobles and four commoners) from the sixteen names proposed to him. All the other places owed him similar dues. One village of forty inhabitants called Villivañe paid him twenty-four *reales* and the value of eight hens at St Martin's, as well as 1,000 *maravedis*, a load of wheat and a load of rye and the produce of the *alcabalas*. The Abbey of Santa María de Belmonte in Asturias (to take an ecclesiastical example) owned the land as well as the civil and criminal jurisdictions. Each inhabitant gave the monks, among other dues, a sow, a lamb, a basket of bread, and a bundle of firewood. The monks appointed councillors, judges, and clerks, kept a prison, and collected fines. One year, the tenants tried to pay four *reales* instead of the usual sow they gave on St Martin's day, and thus profit from the rising prices. The monks refused, and many villagers were gaoled. Later they compromised on six *reales* in lieu of the sow. The monks of another monastery, at Osera, were said to have two measures: one which they used when they were selling grain, and a bigger one which they used when they were receiving their dues.

This has inevitably been a much over-simplified account of the non-royal *señorios* of the Ancien Régime. The reality was much more complicated, and to give a clear account of it would have taxed the talents of a seventeenth-century lawyer, let alone a twentieth-century historian. It was a chaos in which the ownership of land was intertwined with the possession of police powers, civil and criminal jurisdiction, ecclesiastical jurisdiction, public office, the cure of souls, and the collection of taxes – the owners being monasteries, or bishops, or chapters, or one of the Military Orders, or nobles, or town-councils. The oppressiveness of the rule of the *señors* varied from place to place and time to time. Broadly speaking, the nobility were harder task-masters than the clergy; and both were freer to fleece their vassals in the provinces which were still protected by *fueros* than they were in Castile, where the *corregidores* and *Audiencias* acted as some restraint on baronial tyranny. In the Kingdom of Aragon, especially in Aragon and Valencia, where the vassals had inherited the inferior situation of their Morisco predecessors, the *señors* could be very exacting. In Aragon they still had the power of life and death; and many a baron erected a gallows on his estates to keep this right fresh in the minds of his vassals, though few actually exercised it in the seventeenth century. On the other hand, these landlords sometimes had to pay dear for their tyranny. When they rebelled against Madrid (as they did in 1640, for example, and again in the War of the Spanish Succession) the lower classes failed to identify with them, and even rebelled against them. Practically everywhere in Spain (as in most of Europe) tenants preferred royal to noble land on which to be vassals. They would rather be under the authority of royal officials, as a writer said in 1643, than of 'little lords and barons who usually tyrannize them and gnaw them right down to the bone with unjust taxes'.[16] The town of Montilla, for instance, began a court case in 1622 to escape from the clutches of its *señors*, the Dukes of Medinaceli, who used their monopoly of the

mills and oil-presses extortionately. It was not till 1771 that they
managed to get a favourable verdict. At that point, the Duke
immediately lodged an appeal.

Thus the nobles (the *hidalgos*) – or, to be more exact, the
upper ranks of them, the grandees, the titled nobility, and the
caballeros – had been amply compensated with local power for
the amount of central power they had lost to the Monarchy.
Together with their relatives and friends, clients and vassals,
they ruled little kingdoms of their own. At one end of the
scale, their mode of life might be that of the cattle-raiding
brigands in the Pyrenees. At the other, as on one of the vast
landed estates (*latifundios*) of Andalusia, a grandee would maintain a semi-royal court, proceed on State visits to his towns
and cities, administer his territories with *corregidores* and
Audiencias of his own, and take policy decisions at the top in
a miniature Council of Castile. A fugitive from royal justice
was as safe in the castle of one of these aristocrats as he
would be in sanctuary. And this tradition of the private ownership of public powers – at its worst in the second half of the
seventeenth century – did incalculable damage to the social
and economic health of Spain, and contributed greatly to its
decline. The *señorios* and *municipios* formed yet another
barrier between king and people, further cushioning the impact of the State upon society. Together with the bureaucracy,
they hastened Spanish decline, and hindered what little attempts
the crown made to arrest it. Royal decrees gathered dust on the
shelves of town-council offices, or got buried in the family
archives of powerful lords. The very fact that some of them
were repeated so often is a proof of their ineffectiveness. The
Habsburgs were in the position of weak schoolmasters
repeatedly calling for order.

Society

Apart from political considerations, however, apart from the
human and structural weaknesses of the Spanish State, the
make-up and mentality of society itself seemed to predestine
the Monarchy to shipwreck. There was an undertow of
decadence in the people which was perhaps too strong for any

ruler, however gifted, or any political system, however efficient, to navigate. Spanish society seemed haunted with an economic death-wish. Its structure was still that of medieval times, with its horizontal division into Estates – clergy, nobility, and commoners – only slightly modified by the dissolvent of wealth, if to a large extent cut across by the vertical patterns of clientage. Social mobility existed, of course, though not to the detriment of the old order – rather the opposite. A commoner who saved a little would imitate his betters by entailing his property, and then spend much of his time, and not a little of his money, acquiring recognition as a noble (*hidalgo*). This step would involve the abandonment of business, and purchase of a country estate, and perhaps a *señorio*. His children and grandchildren in their turn would try to rise through the ranks of the *hidalgos*: to become a *caballero*, a titled noble, or even a grandee.

This kind of osmosis simply reinforced the traditional social structure, and prevented the formation of a powerful middle class. In this sense, social mobility in Spain was too easy. Unlike most of their European counterparts, the Castilian peasants had not been enserfed – a blessing they owed to the 700-year struggle with the Moors, which had kept all Castilians equal in the common danger. Said Dorotea to Fernando in *Don Quixote*: 'Although a peasant and labouring girl, I consider myself the equal of you who are a lord and a knight.'[17] There was thus no insurmountable barrier in the way of social ascent once *limpieza de sangre* had been proved. This same circumstance also encouraged social emulation by the way in which (owing to the lack of barriers) the values of the *hidalgos* filtered right down to the bottom of the social scale. 'The natives of these kingdoms', wrote one of Philip IV's ministers, 'each one in his own sphere and estate desire honour and esteem more than anything else, and each one strives to get ahead.... Scarcely a son follows his father's trade; the son of a cobbler hates that trade; the son of a merchant wants to be a *caballero*, and so on.'[18]

Living on one another's doorsteps in Madrid and the provincial cities and towns, the *hidalgos* and commoners achieved a rude egalitarianism in their pride in their pure Spanish blood, and in their sensitivity over questions of honour. Foreigners noted how difficult it was to distinguish lords and commoners as they mingled familiarly at *fiestas* and bull-fights. One even addressed beggars with proper respect, and, if refusing alms, one did it with due ceremony. The British ambassador's wife, Lady Fanshawe, remarked on the respect which the nobility showed to all other ranks. 'I have seen a grandee and a duke', she wrote in 1664, 'stop his horse, when an ordinary woman passeth over a gutter, because he would not spoil her clothes, and put off his hat to the meanest woman that makes reverence, though it be to their footmen's wives.'[19] This respect was mutual, and sumptuary laws had to be repeated again and again in an effort to keep the different orders of society outwardly distinguishable. Police officers, clerks, notaries, estate-agents, merchants, silversmiths, and so on, were not supposed to keep a coach; while another law, often reissued up to 1691, forbade 'artisans in manual trades, tailors, shoemakers, carpenters, blacksmiths, weavers, tanners, shearers . . . and workers and ploughmen and labourers to wear any silk whatever, except caps, hoods or bonnets of silk'.[20] Similar rules were laid down for their wives. Such rules, however, were self-stultifying. By officially recognizing that silks and coaches conferred social distinction they made commoners all the more frantic to get into them. And so all classes joined in their disdain for business, as fit only for Jews, Arabs, and other foreigners; and in their fastidious attitude towards manual occupations, which they regarded as suitable only for slaves or Frenchmen. This *hidalgo* prejudice reinforced a social process which the economy itself was causing: the anaemia of the Spanish bourgeoisie, and the polarization of society into two groups – the handful of the rich and the masses of the poor.

The rich belonged to the highest ranks of the nobility: the grandees of Spain and the titled nobility of Castile; in other words, about 100 dukes, marquises, counts, and viscounts at the start of the seventeenth century, and about 530 at the end. Below this cream came the larger middle layer of nobles who called themselves *caballeros*. All so far mentioned were *hidalgos*, of course, but at the base of the noble hierarchy was the multitude of mere *hidalgos*, some so poor, in the North, that the term had acquired a pejorative connotation. And below the *hidalgos* were the majority of the Spanish people: the *estado general*.

Hidalgos had the right to be called 'Don'. They also enjoyed the privileges of not paying direct taxes, of not being tortured (except in very serious cases), of not suffering humiliating punishments (such as being whipped or sent to the galleys), and of not being hanged, but of being decapitated instead. They were exempt from conscription and billeting. They could not be imprisoned for debt (except to the crown), and had the right to be locked up separately from commoners. Moreover, their children passed the school-leaving examination (*bachillerato*) after three years, while commoner children had to work for four. On top of these status-symbols, the grandees enjoyed additional privileges. They could remain covered in the royal presence. They could sit down in the royal chapel. They could go before archbishops. Moreover, they had free entry into royal palaces to within two rooms of the spot where the monarch dressed; and they went to war only with the pay and rank of general. It required a special royal decree before they could be arrested; and when they were in residence on their estates, troops were not stationed in the area. Some families had special marks of favour in addition. The Counts of Salinas y Ribadeo had the right to dine at the royal table on Twelfth Night, after which the clothes worn by His Majesty on that day were sent on to them.

There were, of course, regional and local variations on this basic pattern. In Barcelona and Valencia (where business was no disgrace) there was a powerful class of ennobled bourgeoisie: the *ciudadanos honrades*. Or, to take another example, in Roa a commoner woman who suckled a *hidalgo* child acquired the privileges of nobility for life, and so did her husband. As time went on, the grandees and titled nobility increasingly came to be thought of as the only really noble ranks. They were more abundant in Catalonia and Valencia and southern and central Castile than in the North, where mere *hidalgos* were such a high proportion of the population that their rank became devalued. In the Basque province of Guipúzcoa, even at the end of the eighteenth century, every inhabitant was a *hidalgo*; half those of Vizcaya were also, as well as a sixth of those in Asturias, and a twelfth of those in Àlava and Navarre. In these parts, they were the equivalent of the English lower gentry and yeomanry.

The middle ranks of the nobility were the *caballeros*: that is, *hidalgos* with a certain amount of wealth. All over provincial Spain they lived in the towns and cities on the income from their estates and from their investments in urban property and in government and other bonds (*juros* and *censos*). Their chief aim in life (at least, that of the top three or four thousand of them) was to secure the robes of knighthood (*habito*) in one of the four Military Orders: Santiago, Alcántara, Calatrava in Castile, and Montesa in the Kingdom of Aragon. These Orders had been created during the Middle Ages to take part in the Reconquest; but the crown had taken over the Masterships of each of them in the early modern era, and they had formed one of the chief means whereby the 'new monarchy' had domesticated the nobility. To Spaniards, the *habito* was a prize worthy of a lifetime's endeavour, because the Orders enshrined those military and religious virtues which the Reconquest had taught Spaniards to value as the highest. Entry was most difficult, and the *probanzas* were exhaustive in the search for any hint of plebeian, or Jewish, or Moorish origin, or any smell of the workshop in the family cupboard. But this was another of its attractions. The possession of a *habito* was the most cast-iron guarantee available in Spain of nobility and *limpieza*. Its achievement was a gratifying deliverance for a family from doubts about its blood, a neurosis which made the life of many a Spaniard a nightmare, thanks to the vicious effect of the Inquisition, which was still hard at work under the Ancien Régime. And, finally, another attraction of the Orders were the *encomiendas* which were available to the lucky few. These were lordships over lands which the Orders had acquired during the Reconquest, and on them they ruled over a million subjects. At the start of the seventeenth century, the Order of Santiago owned ninety-four *encomiendas*: Calatrava – fifty-one; Alcántara – thirty-eight, and Montesa – thirteen. The income which they brought to their temporary lords (*comendadores*) averaged 1,500 to 3,000 ducats per annum, though some were really valuable prizes, fit for princes (who usually got them in any case). The *encomienda* of Socuellamos, for example, was worth 14,000 ducats a year in the eighteenth century.

It is not surprising that the existing *comendadores* and *caballeros* were indignant when Philip IV, in his desperate search for funds, even sold *habitos*. Though commoners were not supposed to receive them, the government invented a formula whereby they could reward rich merchants who had assisted the Treasury. This was to make the distinction between retail and wholesale trade, between keeping a shop and not keeping a shop. A papal bull allowing the second was secured in 1622, and during the wars of Olivares against France and Holland a quite unseemly horde of bourgeois secured admission to the Orders. In the case of Velázquez they thought up another fiction: that he did not work with his hands as a professional painter, but only to please the king. After 1650 the Orders began to revert to their original purity (except in the case of great military leaders), and in the eighteenth century it was exceptional for a non-*hidalgo* to receive a *habito*.

Like the nobility, the clergy formed a privileged Estate. The two were much intertwined, since the top positions in the Church went to the younger sons of aristocrats, though it was possible for plebeians of talent to become bishops. Because of its size, wealth, and prestige, the Church played a role of the first importance in the Spanish Monarchy. Secular and regular clergy together totalled between 180 and 200 thousand, and the numbers were growing. As the Spanish economy went from bad to worse, and as society became split between the rich and noble few, on the one hand, and the impoverished masses, on the other, the Church increasingly became a haven from the poverty and contempt which were the lot of the *estado general*. There was plenty of room for them. Burgos, with a population of not more than 8,000 at the end of the seventeenth century, had fourteen parish churches and forty-two monasteries and convents. Toledo, with a population of about 20,000, possessed the richest and most numerous cathedral chapter in Christendom after St Peter's in Rome. Besides the Dean (whose income was 30,000 ducats a year), there were forty canons, and twenty others called *extravagantes* because they attended only on certain occasions. This was a lavish provision of personnel since, according to a contemporary, 'a canon neither baptizes, nor marries, nor buries, nor prays, nor teaches, nor administers. His role is strictly decorative.'[21] Thus, in addition to the canons, there were fifty prebendaries, forty-eight chaplains, twenty-four clergy for night duty only, as well as four readers, ten precentors, and forty boys in the choir. The cathedral at Seville, to take a final example, was equipped and manned to say 100,000 masses a year.

An establishment of this size implies great wealth, and the Church was growing richer all the time. Its possessions were inalienable (in mortmain), and were constantly being added to by the gifts of the faithful. A royal survey of the 1740s showed that the Church in Castile owned one seventh of all the pasture and arable land, that is, reckoning by surface-area. Reckoning by income, the Church received a quarter of the total, being in possession of the more productive land. The ownership by the clergy of *señorios* has already been referred to. In addition, the Church owned much urban and rural housing, as well as bonds and mortgages. They owned three quarters of Castile's *censos*. In Salamanca the cathedral chapter owned 400 houses. And besides this capital, of course, the clergy enjoyed a vast income from tithes and other sources. 'With great sorrow I tell you', wrote Fray Benito Feijoo in the early eighteenth century, probably about his own province of Galicia, 'in one of the poorest provinces of Spain, where there are infinite numbers of poor people, not because the natives are lazy, but because the work of their hands is rewarded in such a way that they do not manage to earn their essential sustenance, the luxury of the ecclesiastics I am informed is greater than in other more opulent provinces. What pomp! What adornment! What an abundance of everything!'[22]

It is impossible to generalize about the quality of the role

performed by the Church in Spanish society in return for this
income, for there were sinners and saints and every shade in
between. In view of the methods of recruitment, the standard
was high, for it was not to be expected that all the younger sons
of the aristocracy, for whom the richer benefices were reserved,
and for whom family chapels were endowed, would have a
vocation. Philip IV's brother, for example – Ferdinand, the
Cardinal-Infante who won the battle of Nördlingen – was
made Cardinal-Archbishop of Toledo at the age of ten, without setting foot in his cathedral (1619). Admission to the
Church was easy. Except that women had to put up a sum of
money, the religious orders accepted all comers. And it was
only to be expected that the great influx of commoners into
the Church during the seventeenth century would include many
who entered simply to find food and shelter – or even a cover
for criminal or amorous activities. 'The priests go through these
streets like complete ruffians', wrote an informer to Mariana of
Austria while she was Regent for Charles II, 'flirting with the
wenches, walking along with them and talking to them with a
great deal of impudence and lack of restraint, and boasting of
being great ladies' men.'[23] In 1689 the government asked all
prelates to stop ordinations for the time being. 'The numbers of
those who have been received into minor orders has been so
great these last years that there is scarcely a bachelor boy in
many places who is not in them, and many of a more advanced
age, after losing their wives, manage to become ordained, and
practically all of them do it in order to enjoy the privileges
which go with this state: to live with greater freedom, to be
excused taxes – and from other worldly motives.'[24]

On the other hand, the clergy in general were loved and
respected, sometimes to a superstitious degree. An order that
was issued by the government in 1708 for the billeting of troops,
for example, laid down that soldiers on arrival at a village must
first seek accommodation with commoners. If this was insufficient, they then had to apply to the nobles. If this proved
to be not enough they were then to 'ask the ecclesiastics to
admit them, but nevertheless, if they do not wish to do it,
do not oblige them to'.[25] The clergy lived very close to the

people; and there was hardly a moment when the people were not in church hearing Mass, or the clergy were not parading the streets in celebration of some saint's day or other. Indeed, the Church was so intimately involved with the daily life of the people that it was in danger of succumbing to worldliness itself. Sometimes there were three or four holy days in a week; and these often became holidays, as a result of the dancing in the churchyards and monasteries, and the street-processions with their tabernacles and carnival-giants, hymn-singing children and self-chastising penitents. Critics felt that the Jesuits especially were too indulgent to human weaknesses on these occasions: a reproach which the Enlightened and Jansenist writers amplified in the eighteenth century. Ceremonies which gave consolation to thousands of simple and pious souls could also act as a cover for all manner of hypocrisy, exhibitionism, perversion, and vice. Seventeenth-century Spain was still in the grip of the religious exaltation which had been both a cause and a result of the Reconquest and the Counter-Reformation – but in many minds Christianity easily shaded off into superstition. When the Duke of Arcos visited his mistress, a beautiful actress, in order to make love to her, he used to try to keep his sin a secret from heaven by covering the head of an *Ecce Homo* which she kept in her vestibule. Magic powers were everywhere to be found in Spain. Fray Feijoo blamed the clergy for these excesses. 'When they had a gullible priest who was devoted to exorcism', he wrote, 'then they would have three or four or more women in the parish who would play the role of women possessed by devils (*energumenas*) and give forth horrible howls in church when the sacred host was raised. If a reasonable priest were to take over from this one and finding out about this deception told them to be silent otherwise he would drive out the devils with a big stick, then they would all consider themselves cured.'[26]

The most popular clergy were the friars who went among the people preaching, and teaching, and performing works of mercy. 'I have seen some of them so well patronized', wrote the French vistor, de Vayrac, 'that they had their sleeve all torn and covered with filth from the breath of those who kissed them.'[27] In all the towns and villages of Spain, Franciscans and Capuchins ran the little primary schools, while the Jesuits were responsible for the secondary and higher education. Wealthy families usually kept a friar in the house as a meal-time guest and family counsellor.

The monasteries, on the other hand, did little more than enjoy the income they were able to screw from their tenants. If they were not all actually centres of vice, they were in ripe decay, both spiritually and intellectually. 'In matters of learning', wrote Caspar Sala of the monks, about the middle of the seventeenth century, 'what professorial chairs do they hold in Catalonia? What sermons do they preach? In what controversies do they distinguish themselves? What books and treatises have they written? None. On the contrary, it is almost a matter of pride amongst them that they possess no books and do not talk of the sciences; and if any of them should want to read they abuse him; and it is a miracle if ever an abbot preaches a sermon.'[28] The problem was not simply that the monks never opened a book themselves, but that the clergy were nearly all reactionaries in the world of scholarship, and, as will later be shown, chiefly responsible for the long way that the Spain of the Ancien Régime trailed behind the rest of intellectual Europe.

On the whole, though, the performance of the Spanish Church was creditable by the standards of the time. The bishops resided in their dioceses and worked conscientiously for the most part. They came from the middle ranks of the nobility and were quite unlike the blue-blooded absentees of France. Similarly, the bulk of simple parish priests pulled their weight year in, year out. Whether they were visiting the sick or closing the taverns during Mass, making the village lads learn their Latin grammar or publishing the names of notorious sinners, their impact on society was powerful. And a proportion of the income they took from the people they gave back to them in the form of charity. At mid-day when the Angelus sounded, gates opened in monasteries and bishops' palaces all over Spain, and the throng of waiting mendicants were given their ration of garlic soup and bread. It has been estimated that 150,000 full-time beggars maintained themselves in this way. Doubtless, the Church's over-generous alms-giving exacerbated rather than solved the problems of poverty. By surrounding the giving and taking of alms with a religious aura, the clergy put Spain at an economic disadvantage with the Protestant states of Europe, where the clergy preached the gospel of work.

Below the nobility and clergy stretched the multitudes of the *estado general*, whose destiny was so much in the hands of these privileged minorities. As elsewhere, most of the Third Estate were peasants; and, as in most of Western Europe, this term covered a complex hierarchy of people engaged in agriculture, from landless labourers at the bottom of the scale through to the successful farmers who were beginning to form a kind of rural bourgeoisie at the top – with a diversity in between too rich to describe. Moreover, the picture was further complicated by regional variations dependent on customary and legal traditions, geographical conditions, farming methods, and so on. The most important geographical division was that between, on the one hand, the rainy arc stretching across the North from Galicia through Asturias, the Basque provinces, and those parts of Navarre, Aragon, and Catalonia which lay on the slopes of the Pyrenees; and, on the other, the arid remainder, the Centre and South. Roughly speaking, the wet areas fostered an independent peasantry; while the dry spawned a wretched race of insecure tenants and landless (often workless) labourers. Within these broad areas local variations caused by nature or man contradict these generalizations: for example, the depressed peasantry of Galicia, where the soil was sour, or the market gardens (*huertas*) of the coastal plain of Valencia, where irrigation was bringing prosperity to a dense population.

In the rainy regions the population was scattered over the countryside in tiny hamlets and small family farms on secure hereditary tenures. In the Basque country, for example, where local custom was well protected by provincial *fueros*, and where a high proportion of the population belong to the *hidalgo* Estate, peasant families were secure in the hereditary possession of their ten-acre farms. In Catalonia, to take another example, the prosperous wheat and wine peasants held their land from the lords on a long-term tenure called *censo enfiteútico* which was as secure as the massive farmhouses they lived in. Rather like the English copyholder, this kind of farmer had only to pay small dues on occasion: otherwise, he was free to plant, build, drain, mortgage, bequeath, sublet, sell, and generally behave as if the property were his own.

In the arid Centre and South, the regions of high altitudes and barren soils, the peasant was a very different kind of person. For one thing, it was very difficult there to draw the normal urban-rural distinction, since both lords and tenants (following the Reconquest tradition) lived, not disseminated over the countryside, but concentrated in villages of 300–400 people in the Centre, and in towns of several thousands in Extremadura, La Mancha, and Andalusia. In these regions, the peasants had no chance of improvement because most of the land was inalienably tied to powerful owners: either the Church under mortmain, or the nobility under entail (*mayorazgos*), or the municipalities (whose land was known as their *propios*). In the small number of *municipios* which were still democratically controlled, the peasants were better off, since the *propios* were managed for the benefit of all. But as most *ayuntamientos* were under noble domination, the *propios* were out of peasant reach. Moreover, there was another institution which kept peasants off the land. Large tracts of the Centre and South were controlled by the powerful sheep-raising combine, the Mesta, in which the monasteries and the grandees were big owners. The Mesta enjoyed royal protection, and had secured a virtual entail (called *posesión*) on all the lands on which it fed its migrant flocks. All this compulsory pasture combined with the *propios*, the *mayorazgos*, and the lands under mortmain to produce the chief economic problem of Spain under the Ancien Régime: the existence side by side of so much land inadequately cultivated, if at all, on the one hand, and the multitudes of starving, landless labourers, on the other. For the land in the dry areas was either rented to tenant-farmers at high rents and on short leases (many of which allowed arbitrary eviction); or, as was typical in Andalusia and Extremadura, managed in large *latifundios* worked by armies of landless labourers – 'the most unfortunate men I know in Europe', as they were called by a reforming minister in the eighteenth century.[29] At harvest time, these men – the *braceros* – were hired in the nearby towns or recruited from the seasonal immigrants from poorer provinces such as Galicia. They were brought out to the estate, and housed and fed and watered in the barns of the white-painted *cortijo*, as the headquarters of a large estate was called: a group of buildings which were empty for the rest of the year, except for a handful of permanent staff. The situation of the *braceros* was especially hopeless, since any attempt by a reformer to help them, or any move by the *braceros* to help themselves, could easily be blocked by the aristocracy, who controlled the *municipios*, the bureaucracy, the Cortes, the Court, and the Councils, and provided the prime ministers and Favourites. Similarly, the landowners worked together to keep the *braceros*' daily wages at near starvation level. And at the same time their land-usage – or rather their lack of it – kept down agricultural production. The *latifundios* contradicted the demands of economics and social justice, as a modern expert, C. Viñas Mey, has said. Then, just as today, 'the peasant could not develop his livelihood through lack of land, which was held in excess quantities by people who, owning lands of a size out of all proportion, neither could, nor wanted to, cultivate them'.[30] In good times, the situation of the *bracero* was cheerless; in bad, his plight was tragic. Bad harvests, with their consequent plagues, mowed them down in droves. The seventeenth century was the worst period for disease since the Black Death, and Spain was badly hit in 1598–1602, 1629–31, 1647–52, and 1676–85. No generation escaped. In the mid-century famine, Murcia lost 40,000 dead, Seville 60,000; and at least a quarter of the 600,000 inhabitants of the province of Seville lost their lives. In 1685 a minister described in a report 'the most miserable conditions which exist in the whole Kingdom of Castile, and in particular in Andalusia, where even the most powerful people are without wealth, the middling people very poor, and the workers in all the arts and crafts have become vagabonds in some cases, and most of them begging for alms, the poor beggars dying of hunger (as the Brothers of the Holy Charity, who have been burying them, have discovered) through lack of even what is given at the gates of the monasteries, since they have nothing themselves. The same happens to the women whom dire necessity sends begging from door to door, because the work of their hands does not pay enough to keep them alive; and to others staying in seclusion, not having anything to go out in, not even to Mass; and to others of all ages (and this is a greater shame) who have had to turn to vice to feed themselves.'[31]

The masses of central and southern Spain thus had a destiny as sombre as that of east-European serfs. They faced it at times with oriental resignation, and at others with desperate violence that scared the authorities. 'A people that lies in hopeless poverty is no people, most powerful lord', wrote the satirist, Francisco de Quevedo, 'it is an explosive charge, a danger, a menace, because the starving multitude knows no fear, and is not afraid.'[32]

Spain's greatest social weakness was the absence of an enterprising bourgeoisie to fill the yawning gap between rich and poor. The *hidalgo* mentality with its contempt for business and scorn for manual labour fired everyone involved in either with the desire to escape from it as soon as possible. No matter how often royal decrees were issued, and reissued, ruling that commerce was not incompatible with nobility, so long as the business was wholesale, and so long as the manual work was performed by employees, it was impossible to shift Spaniards from their conviction that consumption was more honourable than production. Alfonso Núñez de Castro wrote in 1675:

Happily let London manufacture the most highly prized cloths; Holland, cambrics; Florence her coarse cloths; India, beavers and vicuñas; Milan, brocades; Italy and Flanders, linen – for the enjoyment of our capital; which hereby only proves that all the nations produce craftsmen for Madrid, and that she is the queen of the Capital Cities, since they all serve her and she serves nobody.[33]

As will be seen later, the lion's share of Spain's foreign and colonial trade, and much of her other big business, had fallen into the hands of foreigners. And such Spanish merchants as did grow rich on the luxury trades of Madrid, or the commerce of Seville or Cádiz, were only too anxious to buy an estate, form an entail, acquire a *señorío*, secure a patent of nobility, and forget their origins. Or, if not, then at least put their sons into the bureaucracy or the army or the Church.

And the contempt for work bit deep into the social structure. The activities of tavern-keepers, tinkers, knife-grinders, black-smiths, butchers, and others, were 'vile' in Spanish eyes – and such work tended to be done by gipsies and foreigners. A southern proletarian would never carry water or sweep the streets – occupations fit only for slaves. He would take to the roads sooner, or hire a pair of crippled children from the Foundling Hospital and beg as a poor widower – or die of hunger, even.

Of course, the towns and cities of Spain, principally peopled though they were so often by nobles and peasants, had to have their contingents of merchants, professional men, shopkeepers, artisans, and labourers, reluctant though these may have been. They tried to compensate for their ignoble manner of life by joining gilds and fraternities whose purpose was as much to maintain the respectability of the trade as to monopolize the market in it. Gild members – even those consisting, say, of half a dozen cobblers – felt superior to those unfortunate enough to be unqualified for admission; and gilds constantly strove for privileges and other tokens that would raise their status in the hierarchy of business. Silversmiths, painters, booksellers, master-builders, and surgeons who were not barbers managed, for example, to gain exemption from the sumptuary laws that forbade rich clothes to manual workers. The tailors of Seville in 1692 tried to get it established that entry into their gild 'required the same qualities of *limpieza* as they require for the honorific public offices'.[34] The silversmiths, painters, and printers tried hard to secure exemption from the *alcabala*, on the grounds that their work was intellectual and artistic, and that they scarcely used their hands at all. Even the praying blind men (*ciegos oracioneros*) were organized. Those in Valencia went through a three-year apprenticeship during which they memorized fifty prayers, to guitar or violin accompaniment.

The Economy

These antiquated notions crippled Spain's economy at a time when her chief rivals, Holland, France, and Britain, were growing fast, and when their businessmen were remaking the world in a new image. Of course, they were not the only cause of Spain's economic collapse. There were other causes, some of which have been argued about since the early seventeenth century; while others have been brought into the debate only recently. One crucial underlying factor was the fall in population. While the population of Europe as a whole rose, and while that of England and Wales probably doubled, the population of Spain dropped from about 8,485,000 in 1600 to about 7,000,000 in 1700. And, what was worse, this fall of nearly one and a half million was concentrated in the Centre, in Castile – in the region, that is, which still bore the brunt in taxation and manpower of Spain's pretensions to the political and religious leadership of Europe. The population in the peripheral regions seems to have remained steady, and even to have begun to rise as the century ended – and this in spite of the loss which the Kingdom of Aragon sustained with the expulsion of the *Moriscos* between 1609 and 1611. This expression of religious, racial, and social prejudice deprived Spain of about 300,000 very productive workers. This loss apart, and the emigration to the Indies, and the movement from the centre to the periphery, it is now considered that the population loss was mainly caused by death by war, famine, and disease. Habsburg ambitions in Europe, in other words, contributed mightily to the haemorrhage from which Spain suffered, especially between 1635 and 1668, when Spain was fighting France, Holland, Catalonia, and Portugal. 'Has not Flanders been an honourable graveyard for Spaniards?' wrote Peñalosa in 1679. 'And has not Germany in many parts been defended and protected by them? All the best part of Italy, the richest and most populous area – is not that governed by Spaniards?'[35]

The strain of these wars left Spain pock-marked with abandoned farmlands and empty villages. The province of

Extremadura suffered especially from the long-drawn-out and hopeless war with Portugal. The town of Valencia de Alcántara, for example, which had 1,500 tax-paying households in 1636, was reduced by 1688 to 401 families, of which only 260 paid taxes. The suburbs had been demolished for defence purposes, and the town contained 934 ruined houses. Bad harvests and epidemics hit every generation in the seventeenth century, and it was these that took the main toll of the Spanish population. A minister wrote to the Queen Regent in 1669:

In carrying out my duties, I visit many places which a few years ago contained a thousand households and now contain only five hundred; and some of five hundred hardly show signs of having a hundred; and in all of them there are innumerable people and families who pass a day or two without breaking their fast, and others who simply eat grasses they collect in the countryside, and other means of sustenance never before used or heard of.[36]

The sacrifice of a million and a half souls inflicted more damage on Spain's morale and economy than the loss of provinces in Flanders or Italy would have done – though it was impossible to convince the Monarchy of this till very late in the Ancien Régime. And the sombre routine of those left alive hardly bears contemplation, as they battled against pitiless weather, thankless soil, and ruthless landlords, while acre upon acre of the most fruitful land was kept out of their reach by mortmain, *mayorazgos*, *municipios*, and the Mesta. A three-fold return on their seed was the normal expectation of the Spanish farmer: a four- or five-fold return indicated a good year. But peasants with a surplus in a good season found their marketing frustrated by bad transport, and by short-sighted price-fixing by governments afraid of urban riots. Peasants without a surplus suffered in good years and bad. In the good years, they had nothing to sell; in the bad years they had nothing to eat. Fray Feijoo, who knew this area well in the late seventeenth and early eighteenth centuries, wrote:

In Galicia, Asturias, and the mountains of Leon, there are no people more famished or less protected than the peasants. A few clothes cover their flesh, or rather I should say, uncover it, in view of all the holes. Their habitations are as full of holes as their clothes, and the wind and rain show themselves in as if it were their own home. Their food is a little black bread accompanied by some cheese or some vile vegetable, but all in such minute quantities that some of them leave the table satisfied scarcely once in a lifetime. Attached to these miseries is continuous bodily labour of a most arduous kind, from the moment when light dawns till the coming of night.[37]

The low output of Spanish agriculture caused empty bellies in the interior, and forced the coastal areas to import grain from abroad – thus adding to the chronic deficit in the overseas balance of payments. Moreover, starving peasants lacked purchasing power and thus could hardly be a market for industry and commerce. Thus the countryside made its contribution to the collapse of Spain's business-life, which is very clearly revealed by the statistics. The population of Burgos, the old co-ordinating centre of Castilian trade, fell from the 20,000 of the Golden Age to 3,000 by the mid seventeenth century. Toledo dropped from 11,000 in 1594 to 5,000 in 1694. Segovia dropped from 5,548 to 1,625 in the same period. In 1721 Cuenca had 1,485 houses in ruins. Shipping told the same story. The trading fleet dwindled, and trade with the American colonies (one of the main sources of Spanish power) dropped by seventy-five per cent. During the five years from 1600 to 1604, fifty-five ships left for the Indies, and fifty-six arrived home from them. During the ten-year period from 1701 to 1710, the corresponding figures were eight and seven. The flow of precious metals in the period 1656-60 was a tenth of what it had been in the period 1616-20. This drop was in part due to the fact that the American mines were producing less silver; and in part due to the decline in American trade. The colonists no longer required their former quantities of Spanish goods: either because they were now producing them themselves, or because Spanish America was passing through its own seventeenth-century economic crisis; or because foreign merchants had snatched the trade out of Spanish hands.

Possibly the chief cause of Spain's inability to compete successfully in an aggressively capitalist world was psychological: the *hidalgo* mentality already referred to. The Reconquest and the Counter-Reformation had produced and maintained a mental outlook which combined knight-errantry with spiritual exaltation. The Spanish mind was filled with contempt for Jews and Moors, *Conversos* and *Moriscos*; not only because they were non-Spanish; nor simply because they were non-Christian; but also because they were non-noble. These persecuted groups had been workers and bourgeois, whose industriousness had planted fear in the hearts of the nobility and clergy, and envy in the minds of the masses. In other words, in Spanish eyes, to be fully Christian and truly Spanish involved abstention from just that way of life which in this period stole the Golden Century away from Madrid, and gave world power to Amsterdam, Paris, and London. The prejudice against work is evident in all the literature, and obvious in the elaborate system of *probanzas* through which every aspirant had to be dragged who wanted to obtain a bride, or a *habito*, or membership of a town fraternity, or a place in the university, or a post in the civil service, or a commission in the armed forces, or an apprenticeship in a gild. The Statutes of 1655 issued by the Order of Santiago, for example, excluded Jews, Moors, and heretics from admission, as well as any 'trader or barterer or one holding vulgar and mechanical employment, such as silversmith, mason, inn-keeper, painter ... or other inferior employment, such as tailors and other such people who live by the work of their hands'.[38]

This attitude of exclusiveness was not only directed at deviants within the borders of Spain, however, but also extended to the ideas and manners of the rest of Europe. The Church and State of the Spanish Counter-Reformation continued to add fuel to the aggressive xenophobia which had fired the Reconquest. They eliminated humanism, stamped out Protestantism, and dragged usurers before the Inquisition at home; while abroad they conquered an empire in the Americas, crusaded against heresy in Europe, and erected barriers against the new philosophy of the Scientific Revolution. Spain in decline was closed and isolated and stubbornly conservative. 'Not only must the Prince refuse to innovate against traditional custom in important matters,' wrote Enríquez de Villegas in 1641, 'but also in the very smallest; and he must believe that the ancient is the most correct, and that change is from good to bad.' And he went on to advise princes 'to avoid the sound of novelty, which is horrible in the ears of the people'.[39] Any change was horrible to contemplate in part because of the sheer success of Spain during the previous century. Like the declining Ottoman Empire, Spaniards refused to throw down the weapons with which their heroic forbears had won such glory in the past; and, also like the Turks, they abased themselves in passive resignation before the inscrutable providence of God. Meanwhile, their outlook increasingly diverged from that of their rivals in Europe. Spaniards became passive, not active; mystical, not empirical; pessimistic rather than optimistic; depending on faith rather than reason; seeking aid in magic rather than science.

And the worse things became, the more abjectly did Spaniards succumb to the most reactionary elements in the Church, who were able to convince them that their defeats abroad and famines at home were God's vengeance on their wickedness. Surrounded by death, and living in imminent fear of destruction, the Spanish fell prey to their imagination. Mysticism or puritanism, superstition or sorcery possessed their minds, ousting common sense. During the terrible mid-century famine years (so the ambassador from Modena reported in 1649), a thousand men of Seville married the women with whom they had hitherto been living in sin. A similar frame of mind placed villagers in the thrall of witches, town-dwellers under the spell of sermonizers, and kings in the power of their confessors. Every aspect of Spanish life was affected, but, to limit ourselves to the economic field, this outlook left Spain a child in a world of businessmen. Thus, the Counter-Reformation held back the growth of capitalism. When the ministers of Philip IV, for example, were thinking of canalizing the Manzanares and Tagus, they referred their plans to a board of theologians who reported back to the king as follows: 'If God had wanted both rivers to be navigable, he could have effected it simply by a "fiat", and it would be an infringement of the rights of Providence to improve that which, for reasons not to be understood, it had wished to remain imperfect.'[40]

In this atmosphere it is not surprising that Portuguese and Genoese bankers and merchants took over in Spain where the Jews and Moors had left off. A similar economic abdication occurred abroad. The Habsburgs' aggressive foreign policy gave Dutch, French, and British interlopers the chance illegally to eat up Spanish colonial trade. Its successive failures led to treaties which allowed them to do so legally. The Treaty of Münster with the Dutch in 1648, the Treaty of the Pyrenees with the French in 1659, the treaty of friendship with the British in 1667 conceded valuable trading privileges in each case. And in the markets of Europe, Spain's wool retreated before the British, her iron before the Swedish, and her silk before the Italian. Moreover, as we have seen, the monetary chaos inside Spain, the violent fluctuations between inflation and deflation caused by the crown's tampering with the coinage, scattered business confidence, and often reduced Spaniards to the level of bartering.

Charles II

Thus we come back full circle to the crown in the search for the causes of Spain's decay. After the death of Philip IV in 1665, the Court exercised an even more malevolent influence on Spanish fortunes; and under Charles II (1665-1700), the last of the Habsburgs, the Monarchy sank to the very bottom of decay. This grotesque end-product of Habsburg selective breeding was just able to stand at the age of six, but could not yet walk by himself. As the poor specimen grew, he became subject to fevers, giddiness, discharges, rashes, and other disorders to such a degree that it became clear to all the courts of Europe that he would probably die before very long. Moreover, he would leave no heir, because, though he married twice, he was widely believed to have been bewitched into impotence. And since such an event would lead to the partitioning of the Spanish empire, and possibly a large-scale war, Charles II's health became one of the main threads in the web of European power politics, and the subject of innumerable diplomatic reports. Stanhope, the British ambassador, wrote in 1696:

They cut his hair off in his sickness, which the decay of nature had almost done before, all his crown being bald. He has a ravenous stomach, and swallows all he eats whole, for his nether jaw stands so much out, that his two rows of teeth cannot meet; to compensate which, he has a prodigious wide throat, so that a gizzard or liver of a hen passes down whole, and his weak stomach not being able to digest it, he voids in the same manner. The King's life being of such importance in this conjecture as to all the affairs of Europe, I thought might excuse these particulars, which otherwise might seem impertinent.[41]

With such a creature at the head of affairs, power in Madrid passed into the hands of Favourites and factions, causing a scramble for office twice punctuated by unprofitable military coups from the Kingdom of Aragon led by the king's bastard brother, Don John of Austria (1669 and 1676). The central government's control over the provinces relaxed completely, as the bureaucrats made what profit they could on the capital they had invested in their jobs, and the Councils purred with the leisured circulation of *consultas*. The peripheral regions were left in full enjoyment of their *fueros*, as the impact of Madrid grew more and more muffled. The only exception to this laxity was the government of the Count of Oropesa, who held chief office from 1685 till 1691. He tried to persuade nobles to take up business by officially declaring once more that it was not ignoble. He tried to use the *Junta de Comercio*, which had been founded in 1679, to prevent the gilds impeding industrial progress. He tried to reduce the *latifundios*, and stop the increase of mortmain. Unfortunately, his modernization programme had little success. He found, like many a reformer since, that it was impossible to shift the entrenched interests with a government machine with so much slack in it.

Throughout the rest of the reign, though, little positive was attempted. The aristocracy either grabbed the levers of power and manipulated them in their own interests, or insolently ignored Madrid altogether. 'All power resides in the Grandees', wrote the Venetian ambassador, Federico Cornaro, in 1683, 'who, bound together by reason of family relationships and private interests, have no thought for the public welfare or the interests of the Crown. So great has grown their power, and so small that of the king, that if he wanted to govern in an absolute and despotic manner he would not succeed in the attempt.'[42] The wealthy owners of the Andalusian *latifundios* could secure practically any royal favour they wanted by giving presents to the current Favourite: especially during the ascendancy of Fernando de Valenzuela, who had Queen Mariana of Austria in his pocket from 1670 to 1676. Another Venetian ambassador, Foscarini, said in 1686 that former kings had called the Grandees to Madrid in order to ruin them, but 'now they were destroying the one who had destroyed them'.[43] The crown was so low in funds that hard cash could buy the rank of Grandee or titled noble. D.Agustín de Villavicencio paid 70,000 pesos in 1668 to become the Marquis de Alcántara del Cuervo; and in 1680, the year of the last financial crash of the seventeenth century, the Court could not afford to set out on its traditional trip to the Escorial till an office of *corregidor* in America, and two places as teller (*contador*) had been sold first. In the same year the king allowed the daughters of the Marquis de Monroy to inherit the 436 escudos a month that he had drawn as Governor of the Castle at Cambrai. When the Treasury informed Charles that the marquis should have been receiving only 150 escudos, and that the rest should have gone for the upkeep of twenty halberdiers and ten soldiers at the fortress, and suggested that since he had enjoyed pay which was not his for so long there was no need to pass it on to his daughters, the King replied: 'Let the resolution be put into effect; and I shall bear in mind what you represent to me for the future.'[44]

Unfortunately, the laws of the market apply to the sale of honours, and there was an all-round drop in value which was in the interests neither of the crown nor of the ancient aristocracy. Finally, in 1692, a royal decree ruled that all those who had received the rank of titled noble since the first of January 1680, for a price less than 30,000 ducats, could consider themselves as nobles only for life. To convert their title into a hereditary one, they had to make up the difference.

The decline in the market value of its wares was only one

sign of the collapse of the authority of the crown. Another scandal was the perversion of justice in the interests of the great. Aristocrats such as the Marquis del Valle, who murdered an official, and the Count de Alcantín, who removed a married woman from a convent, were simply requested by the Council of Castile to retire to their estates. In 1668 the Count de Villalonso was arrested for breaking into his widowed aunt's house and stealing a large sum of money. His friends, the sons of the Admiral of Castile, rescued him from the royal prison at the head of a body of armed men. Their punishment was a fine of 8,000 ducats and six years' exile in Oran; but when the Admiral offered his sons as officers in the new regiment of Guards that was being raised, the Queen Regent told the Council that, in view of their fine gesture, the young men should be relieved of all criminal responsibility. But such pitiable acts of weakness before the importunities of the great only worsened the situation. When the state is too feeble to maintain law and order, men will take steps to look after themselves. Duelling became frequent, and clientage spread its tentacles. Great men in Madrid hired gangs of ruffians to settle a score, while in the provinces lesser men took to the hills as bandits.

Abroad, the catalogue of failures was not yet complete. The Treaty of Commerce of 1667 invited Britain to prey on Spanish economic life. By the Treaty of Aix-la-Chapelle (1668) Spain lost a number of Flemish strongpoints to France, including Lille, Tournai, Charleroi, and Oudenarde. By the Treaty of Nijmegen (1678) Spain had to hand over Franche-Comté and fourteen more Flemish frontier posts to France. In the meantime, the king's health gave increasing cause for alarm. 'His ankles and knees swell again,' reported Stanhope in 1698, 'his eyes bag, the lids are as red as scarlet and the rest of his face a greenish yellow. His tongue is *trabado* as they express it, that is, he has such a fumbling in his speech, those near him hardly understand him.'[45] It is thus not surprising that Austria, France, Holland, and Britain had for some time been considering the possible permutations of a share-out of what was left of the Spanish Empire when Charles II finally ended everyone's suspense, and died. The three claimants were Philip, grandson of Louis XIV, the Archduke Charles, second son of the Emperor, and Prince Joseph Ferdinand of Bavaria. This last was the favourite candidate of the Spanish (who did not want their Empire partitioned) and of the other powers (who could not afford to allow either France or Austria to inherit the whole). Unfortunately, the young prince died in 1699, and the last months of Charles II's existence were spent vacillating between rival French and Austrian agents who gathered round his bed like vultures. In 1700 he signed his will leaving all his possessions to Philip of France. The following month he died; and while those he left behind looked in vain for funds to pay for his funeral, the War of the Spanish Succession opened, and the ultimate degradation of Habsburg Spain was accomplished.

A great empire had been dragged low in a network of interconnected weaknesses. The economic depression, a European-wide phenomenon, had been deepened in Spain by an unfavourable social structure and a peculiar frame of mind. In addition, the seventeenth century inherited the debts which the Golden Century had accumulated, at a time when the flow of bullion had created the illusion of wealth. And now they had to be met just as that flow dried up. Moreover, all attempts at reform in Spain were nullified, on the one hand, by a governmental structure too weak to carry out the royal will, and, on the other, by unwise and unsuccessful aggression in Europe in pursuit of dynastic goals and religious mastery – a policy which resulted in the neglect of the Atlantic and the invasion of the Spanish economy by foreigners. Spain, it is true, was plagued by several generations of kings unfitted for their task; but other countries have successfully survived this occupational hazard of hereditary monarchy. Spain did not, because she was betrayed by those who alone were in a position to stop the rot: the nobility. Her greatest single weakness was not the Habsburg line, but several generations of aristocrats who failed to produce the ability, or find the courage, to address themselves to the problems with which their country was so arduously beset.

Spain: Eighteenth-Century Revival

The New Dynasty

During the eighteenth century, the embers of Spanish greatness were once more – and for the last time – blown into the semblance of a blaze by the new Bourbon dynasty. The period falls naturally into two parts: the first consisting of the reigns of Philip V (1700–46) and Ferdinand VI (1746–59), and the second of the reign of Charles III (1759–88). The first period was characterized by the change from the Habsburg to the Bourbon dynasty (though with little improvement in the personal capacities of the monarchs), together with the introduction of new blood into government circles, and the hesitant and piecemeal (and in some cases only temporary) adoption of policies more in accordance with Spain's real interests and possibilities. The second period saw the balance swing firmly towards the recognition of ability rather than birth as a qualification for public office; towards reforming measures coloured by idealism to a certain degree, and aiming at the general interest rather than that of a privileged minority; and towards foreign policies which gave higher priority to Spain and the Indies than to the family interests of the reigning dynasty.

The War of the Spanish Succession (1700–14) gave to Philip V an advantage denied to the Count-Duke Olivares. It enabled him to obliterate the *fueros* of the Kingdom of Aragon (that is to say, their constitutional liberties) and begin the assimilation of Castile and Aragon into a uniform state – an act of centralization which was the indispensable preliminary to the creation of the Spanish nation. When he arrived in Spain to take over his inheritance, he was in general made welcome in Castile, but in the Kingdom of Aragon many powerful interests opted for the Archduke Charles, the Austrian candidate, who was proclaimed King of Aragon in 1706. It was like a repetition of the Catalan revolution of 1640, only this time France was on the side of Madrid, not Barcelona, and the rebels depended on the support of the British fleet. When this was withdrawn in 1711 – because the Archduke became the Emperor Charles VI on the death of his brother – the rebel provinces of Catalonia, Aragon, and Valencia were, as usual, insufficiently united to hold out against Castile. In 1714 Barcelona was taken and the Principality of Catalonia occupied by Bourbon armies. Philip was now in a position to ignore the *fueros*, and to treat the Catalans as defeated rebels. He could begin with a clean sheet, and give the province a new constitution, known as the *Nueva Planta*. By this, the office of Viceroy was replaced by that of Captain-General-Governor, ruling in co-operation with the *Audiencia*. The Principality was divided into twelve areas for local government, each under a *corregidor*, as in Castile. Moreover, Catalonia now at last had to pay something like its proper share in taxation to the Spanish Monarchy; but, instead of introducing the chaotic Castilian revenue system, Philip gave Catalonia the *catastro* – a uniform tax based on ability to pay. And finally, in order to supervise the workings of the new revenue system, a new office, that of *intendente*, was introduced, modelled on the French office, and later to be extended to Castile as well.

The other sections of the Crown of Aragon received similar treatment. The provinces of Aragon and Valencia, which had been conquered by Philip before Catalonia, received their new form of government from 1707 onwards, while the *fueros* of Majorca were brought to an end in 1715. Furthermore, the Cortes of the Crown of Aragon was incorporated into that of Castile: in other words, they were from now on rendered powerless to block the centralizing will of Madrid. Henceforth, the Spanish crown legislated by decree, while the only central representative institution left to the Spanish people was turned into a docile club of sycophants. 'Lord,' it resolved in 1760, for example, 'the Kingdom is ready not only to swear the oath of fidelity and render the legal homage, but also to carry out whatever Your Majesty proposes, in order to vouch for the love and fidelity with which they desire the greatest attention of Your Majesty.'[1] A comparison of these words with the language used by the Cortes of Aragon under the Habsburgs (see p. 87) will demonstrate what a step forward had now been taken in the direction of centralized absolutism. Even though the Basque provinces and Navarre kept their *fueros* till the nineteenth century – they could hardly be touched, having supported the Bourbon dynasty from the start – Philip V was in a position of unusual strength. Not only did he wield more effective control – and thus enjoy greater revenues – than his predecessors; but, thanks to the Treaties of Utrecht and Rastatt, his responsibilities in Europe were far less than theirs, being limited now to the Spanish peninsula. For, by the treaties of 1713 and 1714, Spain lost her possessions in the Netherlands, Milan, Naples, and Sardinia to Austria, as well as ceding Sicily to Savoy. Secondly, Philip had to renounce all claim to the throne of France; and, thirdly, Spain had to concede to Britain Minorca and Gibraltar as well as important trading concessions in the American colonies, the chief of which were the monopoly of the slave trade (the *asiento*) and the right to send one ship each year to trade with South America (the *navio de permiso*). This dismemberment of Spain marked the lowest point she touched in a century of decline; but it also offered the Monarchy an unprecedented opportunity: the chance to concentrate all its resources (now swelled by the *Nueva Planta*) on Spain and the colonies. It was a chance that could be grasped only by a king prepared to look upon the surgery of Utrecht, not as amputations, but as the removal of malignant growths, and to turn Spanish foreign policy away from its antiquated obsession with military power in Europe towards Spain's proper destiny: naval power on the oceans of the world and the economic exploitation of her colonial possessions.

Philip V

Unfortunately, the melancholy hypochondriac, Philip V, was too much like his Habsburg predecessors in personal qualities and political ambitions ever to make this kind of imaginative leap. Though capable of cutting a dash when a prince, he grew into a stupid, obsessed, and indolent king, who oscillated between lucidity and idiocy, and spent days in bed staring into space, and months in the same clothes stinking to high heaven. Moreover, he was sexually enslaved by his second wife, Elizabeth Farnese, a comely but awesome shrew, who never left his side for a moment. Between the two of them they delayed Spanish recovery by at least a generation, and, as the events proved, till it was too late. For his part, he hankered after the throne of France after the death of his formidable grandfather, and also tried to regain the Italian provinces which Spain had lost to Austria. She at the same time wasted Spanish blood and treasure trying to win the duchies of Parma, Piacenza, and Tuscany to which she had some claim. She wanted these as consolations for her two sons by Philip V, who she assumed would not succeed to the throne of Spain, as the king already had two sons by his first wife.

Under Alberoni, a priest from Parma (1717–19), Spain pursued these ends by attacking Austria, with whom she had not made peace at Utrecht. Spanish forces invaded Sardinia and Sicily in 1717; but the great powers were not prepared for the balance of Utrecht to be upset so soon. A British fleet sank the Spanish squadron off Cape Passaro in 1718, and Philip had to abandon his campaign as well as his minister. Under Ripperdá, a colonel from Holland (1719–28), Spain pursued the same ends by the opposite means: an alliance with Austria (Treaty of Vienna, 1725). Equally unsuccessful, he too was dismissed. From then on, in the era of Patiño, Campillo, and Ensenada (1728–46), the military and diplomatic opportunities available to Spain were used more realistically, and a certain success was achieved. In 1731 Elizabeth Farnese's eldest son, Don Carlos, received Parma and Piacenza. During the War of the Polish Succession (1733–38), Spain supported France (by the first Family Compact, 1733), and occupied Naples and Sicily. (Sicily was by this date Austrian, having been exchanged for Sardinia with Savoy in 1720, after which the latter was usually known by the name of the Kingdom of Sardinia.) At the Treaty of Vienna which ended this war (1738), Spain received

Naples and Sicily for Don Carlos on renouncing Parma and Piacenza. During the War of the Austrian Succession (1740–48), Spain supported France again (second Family Compact, 1743) and by the Treaty of Aix-la-Chapelle (1748) received Parma, Piacenza, and Guastalla for Elizabeth Farnese's second son, Don Philip.

Ferdinand VI

By this date, Philip V was dead, and the shrill voice of his wife was no longer heard in Spanish councils. Under King Ferdinand VI (1746–59), Spanish foreign policy changed direction. The peaceful pursuit of advantages for Spain herself replaced the war-like chase after gratifications for members of the Bourbon family. It was a policy worked out by Patiño before he died, disillusioned by the French alliance; and it was put into practice by Ferdinand's chief ministers, Carvajal and Ensenada (1746–54) – though it is far from clear how so mediocre a king managed to acquire so able a pair of servants. Carvajal believed, in the first place, that Spain should abandon her Italian aspirations, and should concentrate instead on preserving the American empire, now so gravely menaced by the aggressive acts of the British government and her private merchants, who were trying to turn the *asiento* and the *navio de permiso* of 1713 into the thin edge of a vast wedge of economic imperialism. And Carvajal also believed, in the second place, that this should be achieved by peaceful neutrality and diplomatic guile, not war – for France and Spain together were no match for Great Britain, even if France played her full part, which was always doubtful. 'I see this kingdom in the absolute necessity of peace,' he wrote; 'I see that the formidable power of two states [England and Holland] which have an insatiable desire for our Indies is about to join together, and that they and our allies [France] have not swallowed them up between them because each is jealous of what the others acquire.'[2] And while Carvajal steered a neutral course between Britain and France, and tried to settle Anglo-Spanish disputes by friendly negotiation (though with no help from the rapacious British), Ensenada gave Spain her first taste of Enlightened reform, and rebuilt the navy. 'Without a fleet', he wrote in 1747, 'the Spanish Monarchy will not be able to make itself respected, nor preserve her Dominion over her vast States, nor will this peninsula flourish – the centre and heart of all.'[3]

In the final years of the reign (1754–59), when the king was out of his mind, and Spanish policy was in the hands of the Irishman, Bernardo Ward, Spain took peace and neutrality to suicidal extremes which Carvajal would never have countenanced. During the Seven Years' War (1756–63), Spain stood idly by while Britain upset the Atlantic balance of power by defeating France in Canada – so becoming a greater menace than ever to the Spanish empire. The new king, Charles III (1759–88), was too late to restore the balance. He entered the war on the side of France (by the third Family Compact, 1761), but the British were indomitable. Spain not only failed to regain Minorca and Gibraltar, but also had to make further concessions as well. By the Treaty of Paris (1763), Spain received back Manila and Havana (they had been conquered by the British), but had to cede Florida to Britain, and to accept the British point of view of several long-standing Anglo-Spanish disputes. Accordingly, the British were to be allowed to cut logwood in Honduras, while the Spanish were to abandon their claim to fish off Newfoundland and also allow the litigation over Spanish ships captured by the British before the war to be settled in British courts. As compensation, France gave up to Spain the part of Louisiana which she still controlled – for France now badly needed the Spanish alliance. For her part, Spain at last reached the conclusion that her future safety depended upon close Franco-Spanish friendship against the menace of Britain.

Though the foreign policy of the first two Bourbons had initially pursued archaic goals, and had only gradually arrived at a realistic appreciation of the importance of Spain's extra-European and maritime role, it nevertheless was executed with a new vigour and achieved partial success. It at least maintained Spain's status as one of the major powers. Similarly, at home, Habsburg lethargy was thrown aside, and numerous improvements in government and in economic life were set in train, mainly with a view to raising resources to throw behind the foreign activities. The integration of the Kingdom of Aragon into the Castilian administrative system has already been mentioned. Further steps were taken in the direction of centralized absolutism as the reigns progressed. In this respect, Spain benefited from having a king, and, at the start, ministers, from the land of Richelieu, Louis XIV, and Colbert. When he arrived in Spain, Philip V put Jean Orry and other French administrative experts to the task of reforming the royal household, the Treasury, the revenue-collecting machinery, the military and naval administration, and other parts of the civil service. They could do little at first beyond making the existing machinery work more efficiently, but further improvements were brought in during the eighteenth century which, in broad outline, took responsibility away from the councils, and gave it to ministers. During the seventeenth century, the councils had been dominated by the great nobles, and these now had to be ousted in the interests of royal power and sheer efficiency. 'Preserve all the external prerogatives of their rank', advised Louis XIV in 1705, 'and at the same time exclude them from a knowledge of all matters which might add to their credit.'[4] But the councils had other faults in addition. They were bogged down in routine, and moved at a snail's pace. The Council of Castile (the chief committee in the kingdom) dealt with every single aspect of government, and was far too distracted by detail. 'I will not hold myself up talking about the origin of the Council of Castile and the powers it had in antiquity', wrote Ensenada in 1751, '... but I will say that whatever one learns of the tasks that, directly or indirectly, were entrusted to it ... one will find that to carry them out in the proper interests of the kingdom, its ministers had to be well versed in all the sciences and arts and mechanics – a knowledge which, without a special grace from God, no human creature could ever acquire.'[5]

Under the Bourbons the councils were left to chew over their administrative and judicial detail, while effective policy-making became the job of secretaries (later called ministers), drawn from the lower ranks of the nobility, or even from outside, and often originating not in Castile, but in the peripheral provinces or abroad. Only one secretary had been inherited from Habsburg times: the *Secretario de Despacho Universale*. This office was split first into two (1702), then four (1714), and then five (1754), which were the Secretaryships of State, of Ecclesiastical Affairs and Justice, of War, of the Navy and the Indies, and of the Treasury. It was in such posts as these, sometimes holding more than one at a time, that Patiño, Campillo, Carvajal, Ensenada, and so on, made their mark on Spanish life. They could travel over Spain to see things at first hand, they could have personal contact with the monarch (and not on their knees, as in Habsburg days), and they were in a position to impart a vigour to government that Spain had not known for over a century.

A third move towards tightening the grip of the central government was the imposition of a small number of *intendentes* to supervise the *corregidors* (1749), and the general rationalizing of the whole system of provincial government. Each *intendente* was responsible to Madrid for financial, military, judicial, and police affairs in his region. He also acted as *corregidor* of the provincial capital in which he was based. Below him, the *corregidors* exercised similar functions in their districts, being assisted in judicial matters by chief magistrates (*alcaldes mayores* or *tenientes*). In areas of military importance, the functions of *corregidor* were performed by military governors (*gobernadores*). Appointments to all these posts were made by the crown, and to a large extent merit and effort replaced purchase and even birth as criteria of recruitment and promotion. Something like a proper career structure evolved, and the Spanish bureaucracy gradually became a fitter instrument for bringing under central control the *señorios*, *municipios*, and other enclaves of privilege, self-government, and popular oppression – if ever this was to be seriously attempted.

A fourth improvement under the Bourbons was the creation of an army, an essential organ of government under the Ancien Régime, but not to be found under the last Habsburgs. A decree of Charles II in 1691, for example, had announced that the monarchy was 'threatened by the most powerful enemies from the East to the North; without means of defence; the ports, cities, and castles on the coasts of both seas without fortifications; the towns and cities of all the rest of the kingdom wide open, their walls demolished ... and that in most places scarcely a musket, arquebus, or pike will be found'.[6] Yet by the mid eighteenth century, Spain had an army worth the name, in which the regiments of the line were manned by volunteers, foreigners, and vagabonds, while the militia was recruited from native conscripts chosen by lot. The officers were provided by the nobility, who now rediscovered their military vocation, and who flocked in to enjoy the social cachet and high pay which the military career increasingly provided.

Although these reforms in the civil and military administration were aimed at tightening Madrid's grip on the localities, there is not a great deal of progress to record under the first two Bourbons. Several attempts were made to recover royal rights, offices, and other sources of income which had been so wantonly sold or given away in the seventeenth century, but the Treasury found itself in a painful quandary. It could not afford to buy them back without an increase in its revenue, and it could not increase its revenue without buying them back. The general result was that the nobility increased its power in the localities. Jerez became a noble city – a *ciudado de estatuto* – in 1724, after which date members of the city council had to show proofs of *limpieza*, nobility, and abstention from manual labour (*oficios viles y mecánicos*). Cádiz followed suit in the 1730s. This booming commercial centre insisted that its officials had to be natives of the city, or resident there for twenty years, and prove nobility and *limpieza*. Manual labour, on the other hand, was not a disqualification, for Cádiz was one of those municipalities, rare in Spain, ruled by an ennobled commercial oligarchy. Increased local power also came to the nobility by another legal process. Small towns which were governed by neighbouring cities could buy themselves out of their bondage by paying the crown for the privileges of self-government (*privilegios de villazgo*). In this way, they rescued themselves from the power of the city oligarchies – but in many cases only to fall prey to their own local nobles.

The Economy

In spite of these limitations, the re-invigorated government machinery did enable such ministers as Orry, Patiño, Campillo, and Ensenada to make sufficient impact on the nation to pull the economy out of its seventeenth-century nose-dive, and even, by the 1740s, to achieve business progress. Economic policy was formulated in the Committee of Trade (founded in 1679, and after 1730 called the *Junta de Comercio y Moneda*). The measures taken were Colbertian in the main, though with an increasing tendency towards free-enterprise from mid century onwards. In the first place, the Treasury was reformed, and there was no repetition of the monetary chaos which the Habsburgs had inflicted on business life. In the second place, many improvements were made in overseas commerce. The monopoly of the American trade was transferred in 1717 from Seville to Cádiz, which had by then in any case swallowed up the bigger part of this trade. But the time was past when Castile could enjoy alone the benefits of empire, and merchants from Viscaya, Catalonia, and other provinces were demanding their share. In 1740 the convoy system through which colonial trade was channelled was abolished but restored again in 1754 owing to the outcry of the Cádiz monopolists. But another attack on the monopoly system had more success, and became a model for later commercial policy. In 1728 the Caracas Company was founded in San Sebastián, in the Basque province of Guipúzcoa. Modelled on the trading companies of Holland, Britain and France, it possessed the monopoly of trade with what is now Venezuela, much of whose trade hitherto had been in the hands of Dutch smugglers. Its great success was an important stimulus to the movement for the liberalization of colonial trade which grew in the reign of Charles III.

A third method by which the Bourbons tried to stimulate the economy was the opening up of trade within Spain. In 1716 the customs barriers between Castile and the Kingdom of Aragon were abolished. In 1717 internal customs were abolished in their entirety; but Navarre and the Basque provinces immediately began to flourish their *fueros*. In fact, they made such an outcry that their customs posts were restored, and henceforth they were known as the *Provincias Exentas*. At the same time, the *corregidors* received orders to look to the improvement of roads and bridges, though not a great deal was achieved. The bulk of Spanish internal trade still had to sail round the coast, or move unhurried on the backs of mules.

Fourthly, efforts were made to encourage manufacturing and mining in order to bring an end to Spain's ruinous dependence on foreign goods. In true Colbertian spirit, the early Bourbons favoured the spread of gilds, though these only resulted in freezing manufacturing in its small-artisan stage of development, and were in general only really successful in organizing religious processions. Other mercantilist measures were the placing of restrictions on the export of raw materials and on the import of manufactured goods. Decrees of 1717, 1718, and 1728, for example, prohibited the import of Chinese and other Asian textiles, and had a healthy effect on the nascent cotton industry of Barcelona, a city which was destined in the nineteenth century to grow into the Manchester and Liverpool of Spain combined. Also helpful were the steps taken to encourage the immigration of foreign craftsmen. Less successful, however, was that other typically mercantilist nostrum: the establishment of royal factories.

Some, like the tapestry works in Madrid and the glass works at San Ildefonso, were set up to provide luxury articles for royal palaces. Others, like the silk factory at Talavera de la Reina, the tobacco factory at Seville, and the textile works at Guadalajara, were pilot schemes to show private enterprise the way. In contrast, however, with the vigorous private enterprise of such peripheral centres as Barcelona, Valencia, Cádiz, Bilbao, or San Sebastián, these pampered concerns proved incapable of arresting the industrial decay of the centre. Circumstances were cruelly against them. Demand was kept low by the impoverishment of the peasants and the comparative depopulation of the central provinces; while the scarcity of road and water transport had the same effect by adding to the cost of raw materials and to the expense of marketing the finished articles.

The experience of the cloth factory at Guadalajara was typical. This brain-child of Alberoni was brought into the world by Ripperdá in 1718. It was sited first at Santander, then at El Escorial, and finally at Guadalajara. Fifty Dutch weavers were imported to work in it, and the object was to put an end to the economic disgrace whereby Spaniards bought cloth from Britain made from their own Merino wool. During its first twenty years the factory could not sell its products, and only half its looms were at work; and by 1740 among many recipes which were mooted to stimulate sales was the drastic one of compelling merchants to buy its products. Ferdinand VI made up its losses to the value of two million *reales* a year, as well as providing it with free raw material and directing that the armed forces should be dressed in its cloth – all without success. In 1756 a speculator bought up all the factory's surplus, and then bankrupted himself trying to sell it. Under Charles III, it received further royal blood-transfusions in the region of seven million *reales* a year, and by the 1780s it was employing almost 4,000 weavers, though its products were said to be of lower quality than the worst serge of Barcelona and dearer than the finest stuffs of Abbeville. It never did succeed in making a profit, and was wound up in the early nineteenth century.

Agriculture – the fifth sector of the economy which came in for government attention – made little progress in this period. Little could be done to counter the blows of a malevolent geography, and nothing was done to liberate the acres kept uncultivated by the *municipios*, the *mayorazgos*, the Church, and the Mesta. The *corregidor* of Cáceres calculated that the land required for grazing 1,000 sheep and employing three or four shepherds would feed 150 people if cultivated. It followed that if the wastes of Extremadura were ploughed up (instead of being devoted to three and a half-million sheep and 17,000 shepherds) the population of the province could rise from half a million to two and a half million inhabitants. Under Philip V and Ferdinand VI, however, the Mesta still enjoyed royal protection. Its privileges were extended to the Kingdom of Aragon in 1726, and the general policy of reserving vast pastures at low rents for it was maintained. In these circumstances, agricultural progress was obstructed; and the Spanish masses suffered the dearths of 1709, 1723, 1734, 1750, and 1752, as well as plagues of locusts, which were especially destructive in 1755 and 1756. At the same time the contradiction of the seventeenth century continued: that is, thousands of beggars, thousands of landless labourers, on the one hand, and mile after mile of empty countryside, on the other. The main road through Andalusia went through vast deserts: yet Spain, with her chronic adverse trading balance, had to import foreign grain.

The country was unlikely to climb out of its agrarian misery, however, while it remained a century or so behind the rest of western Europe in intellectual development. The measures which the government of Ferdinand VI had to adopt to deal with the locust plague of 1755 indicate that Spain was still the closed country of the Counter-Reformation. In the middle of the Age of Reason, the Spanish method of fighting locusts was to bring out the venerated image of San Gregorio Ostiense from his church at Mues in Navarre. He was the special protector of crops against locusts and other ills, and his technique of pest-control was not elaborate. He was taken to the stricken fields, where water was ceremoniously poured through a hole in his head. This was collected in containers and applied to the affected crops. In 1755 villagers vied with one another for his ministrations, and to avoid violence the government issued a decree describing his itinerary from Navarre through Valencia and Murcia to Andalusia, Extremadura, and La Mancha, and so back again.

Technical conservatism was not confined to villagers, however, for the whole educated class, with a few exceptions, had been shielded from any contact with the Scientific Revolution by the clergy, who monopolized the schools and universities, and censored the press. 'Literature cannot make any progress in Spain', wrote Feijoo, one of the exceptions, 'while our writers limit their study and their pens to what those living a century and a half ago knew and wrote.'[7] And any chemistry that a student picked up was in the form of medieval alchemy; while his physics was straight Aristotle. 'The ancients enjoyed a better temperament', went the ingenious argument of Father Muñana, who went into print on behalf of tradition, 'because they ate more substantial food, and because human nature, still young, possessed more vigour. At that time, although they were heathens, they could create a Philosophy, and we cannot, even though we are Christians.'[8]

In the first half of the eighteenth century, the Benedictine monk, Fray Feijoo, was the most important publicist of modern knowledge. Between 1726 and 1759 he published essay after essay on every subject under the sun criticizing Spanish intellectual backwardness, trying to drive away the witches and demons from Spanish minds, demonstrating that empirical knowledge was dangerous only to superstition not Christianity, attacking the Spaniards' out-of-date concept of honour. 'If things are looked at in the light of reason', he wrote, 'the most useful to the public is the most honourable.'[9] Although his books sold well, his converts were few. The majority of Spaniards held fast to their *fiestas* and their bull-fights; and nothing was further from aristocratic minds than the acceptance of social utility as a criterion of value. Real change in the direction of the Enlightenment could only come from the pressure of the state; and the state could exert pressure only by becoming more absolute. And these were the tasks that the new king, Charles III, set himself, when he succeeded in 1759.

Charles III

Charles III was one of the more successful of the generation of Enlightened monarchs who ruled Europe in the second half of the eighteenth century. Under his rule, Spain flourished again, without any doubt. The only uncertainty is how to apportion the credit between the king and his very able ministers. When he arrived in Spain, he had already served a useful apprenticeship as Don Carlos, the son of Elizabeth Farnese; then as Duke of Parma, and then as King of Naples and Sicily. Unlike Spain, Italy was open to the new ways of thinking, and Charles III was the complete Catholic, Enlightened absolutist, having been especially influenced by his secretary of state, Bernardo Tanucci. In Madrid he astonished everyone by spending a few hours regularly each day actually working at his job as king. He also pleased the Spaniards with the frugality of his Court, and he distinguished himself among the kings of Europe by the innocence of his long widowhood after Queen Amalia died in 1760. In fact, he found little time for any other pursuit than hunting, and nothing would deflect him from his routine. He rose at five, prayed for half an hour, and then worked at his desk till seven – writing his instructions in his own hand. (He did not wish to forget how to write, he said.) Then he drank chocolate, heard Mass, and dined in public with his family at twelve. He spent the rest of the day hunting, followed by a little more work, then supper at nine and bed at ten. It was almost impossible to persuade him to vary the dishes he ate, or change his clothes, or dismiss palace servants, or replace ministers. He very much liked his own way, could be cruel to opponents, and entertained exalted ideas of the status of kings. 'It is necessary that you should understand', he once wrote to his son, the future Charles IV, 'that the man who criticizes the operations of the Government, even if they are not good, commits a crime, and produces distrust among the vassals which is very prejudicial to the sovereign, because they grow used to criticizing and despising all the rest.'[10]

His life's work, and that of his ministers, was the familiar programme of Enlightened absolutism, put into effect, though, in a rather gingerly fashion, if at all. A recent authority (who regards this generation of administrators as the ancestors of the nineteenth-century Liberals) looks on them as 'architects rather than as builders'.[11] In outline, theirs was a blue-print for the resurgence of Spain in Europe and across the Atlantic, to be effected by stimulating economic growth. In order to achieve this it was necessary to root out traditionalism wherever it was entrenched: in the Church, the universities and schools, in the *municipios* and *señorios*, in the entailed estates of the nobility and the mortmain of the clergy, in the restrictive practices of the gilds and the uncultivated wastes of the Mesta. This programme required government reform in the direction of centralized absolutism, and changes were made in two distinct stages. The first period (1759–66) saw rapid reform under Esquilache, and came to an abrupt end through the Fronde-type uprising named after him: the Mutiny of Esquilache. During the second period (1766–88), reforms were brought about by Aranda, Floridablanca, and Campomanes at a much steadier pace. Many were not carried out at all but remained only magnificently worked out plans.

Esquilache

During the first period, the habit-bound king kept on most of the ministers of Ferdinand VI, though giving first place to an Italian expert he had brought over from Naples, the Marchese di Squillace – known in Spain as the Marqués de Esquilache. He was Secretary of the Treasury, and also, from 1763 onwards, War Minister as well. He set up a new committee – the *Junta del Catastro* – whose task was to reform the Treasury, and rationalize the revenues on the basis of a single tax levied in accordance with ability to pay. One of its members was Ensenada, the most vigorous reformer of the previous reign, who had already worked out as far back as 1749 a single-tax scheme based on the one introduced in Catalonia in 1716. He knew that this was the nub, the central problem of the Spanish Monarchy. 'The Treasury is the axis of the government of a monarchy', he said, 'and because Spain forgot this principle she has had two long centuries of such lamentable decadence.'[12] The nobility, however, and all privileged groups preferred the decadence to the *catastro*, and no serious tax-reform was ever achieved. Esquilache's second measure also angered the high nobility. He reorganized the Council of Castile, and filled vacancies on it with *manteístas* instead of *colegiales*. The former were members of the lower nobility, university graduates trained in the law and making their career through the ranks of the bureaucracy, and called *manteístas* because of their long robes. Patiño and Ensenada were such men. The *colegiales* were aristocrats who had been to one of the *colegios mayores*. These were schools in each university town, originally set up to educate the poor, but now exclusive to the children of the grandees and titled nobility, and the channel through which they passed into the top positions in the administration, the Church, and the armed forces. Rivalry between *colegiales* and *manteistas*, between the upper and lower nobility, was endemic in Charles III's reign, and was to a certain degree a struggle between soldiers and civilians, and, according to some Spanish historians, a struggle between the nobility and the bourgeoisie. Whatever the interpretation, the *colegiales* were an élite in Spanish life impossible to shift, for they hung together like English ex-public-school men – as Charles III's queen, Amalia, noticed on arrival in Madrid. 'The league of the *colegiales*' she wrote, 'is much more solid than that of the freemasons.'[13] It was not long before they were out for Esquilache's blood.

He made further enemies when he crossed swords with the Five Major Gilds (the *Cinco Gremios Mayores*) of Madrid. This was the wealthiest banking and mercantile combine in Spain, which borrowed the savings of the public at two and a half per cent and then lent them to the government at four or four and a half per cent. They also had the monopoly of – and thus the pleasure of fixing their own prices for – jewelry, linens, woollens, cloth of gold and silver, silk, drugs, and spices. When Esquilache began to limit the prices of these articles, he was laying up trouble for himself right in the heart of Madrid.

The third major interest which his reforms antagonized was the Church. Spain already had a long tradition of *regalismo*: of campaigns to increase the power of the crown over the Church at the expense of the papacy. And already in 1737 and 1753, concordats had been negotiated with Rome in which most of the crown's claims over clerical taxation, presentation to bishoprics, prebends, and so on, had been met. Charles III now stepped up the harassment of the clergy again. He sharply increased clerical taxation by refusing to renew the 200-year-old contracts on which it had hitherto been assessed – a system which had given the clergy all the benefit of the fall in the

value of money during that time. Moreover, clergy without
occupations in Madrid were ordered to return home to their
parishes (1759). Church courts were forbidden to detain laymen
or their property without the permission of the ordinary courts
(1760). Papal bulls and briefs could not be published in Spain
without the royal permission – the *exequatur* (1762). Perhaps
the most serious cause of ecclesiastical umbrage was the
government's patent hostility to mortmain, evinced, for example, in the decree of 1760 which ordered that property
henceforth acquired by the Church would pay the same taxes
as lay property.

Finally, Esquilache annoyed the lower orders of Madrid and
other cities by a series of measures designed to remove urban
filth. Vagabonds were rounded up, street-lighting was installed,
refuse was collected at regular hours, and householders were
forbidden to throw it out of their windows. These, and other
similar improvements, irritated the man in the street – as
Vicente Rodríguez Casado has put it – like a boy suffering from
contact with soap and water. It was another such paternalistic
interference in the life of the crowd that was the immediate
cause of the Mutiny of Esquilache (1766). In that year Esquilache forbad the wearing of the customary broad-brimmed hats
and long cloaks, on the ground that these clothes helped
criminals to escape capture.

The rioting that began in Madrid on Palm Sunday, and then
spread to provincial centres, is believed to have been organized
by a conspiracy of *colegiales* and clerics taking advantage of
popular discontent. But the common people would not have
risen had they not been hungry. The drought of the years 1760
to 1766 had pushed up grain prices; and when Esquilache freed
the trade in grain (1765) in an effort to abolish the black market,
bring food on to the open market and thus reduce prices,
unfortunately for him the prices continued to mount. And,
whether as a result of spontaneous public anger or sinister
aristocratic plotting, the mob sacked Esquilache's house and
demanded his death. The following day, a mob of screaming
rioters forced the king to dismiss his minister, withdraw the
dress regulations, and fix lower prices for food.

Aranda, Campomanes, and Floridablanca

Like a mild heart attack, the mutiny of 1766 warned Charles III to take things more steadily in future. For the remainder of his reign (1766–88), he changed his speed – though not his direction. The three chief ministers who dominated this era were all keen reformers. The Count of Aranda, who was President of the Council of Castile from 1766 to 1773, and then French ambassador, may have been an Aragonese aristocrat, but he had fully absorbed the outlook of the French Enlightenment. The other two were *manteistas*, Enlightened, but still Catholic. Campomanes was a *fiscal* of the Council of Castile from 1762 to 1783, and then President of it from 1783 to 1791. Floridablanca was *fiscal* from 1766 onwards, and Secretary of State and Secretary for Ecclesiastical Affairs and Justice from 1776 to 1792. During these years, the Council of Castile emerged from its early-Bourbon obscurity to become the senior organ of government, and the *fiscals* and Presidents (but not the ordinary councillors) played the role of ministers – and a few of them were secretaries at the same time. The king usually took decisions with each minister individually till 1787, when the *Junta de Estado* was formed – a council of chief ministers with the job of co-ordinating the work of the different departments.

Government

At the same time, a steady effort was maintained to improve the efficiency of the central, provincial, and local administration, and raise the level of its personnel. 'It is absolutely essential', said Charles III, 'that Councillors should not simply be lawyers (*letrados*), but *politicos* experienced in the art of governing. It is a good thing if a great part of them have served in the presidencies and regencies of the *Audiencias* and *Chancillerias* both in these Kingdoms and in the Indies.' Similarly, with regard to the choice of presidents and governors of Councils, he believed that 'neither birth nor nobility, nor the military career, nor any other accidental quality of the kind, should be the reason for their selection'.[14] Appointment and promotion, far from being purchased, now came to depend on qualifications, experience, and merit. And improvement in the personnel went hand in hand with the increasing specialization of function that marked the civil service. *Intendentes* ceased to double up as *corregidors*. They dealt only with army and revenue matters, while the *corregidors* concentrated on law and order. In the 1770s regulations were issued fixing the mode of entry into these careers, salaries, duties, and so on. And in 1783 there was a further bout of rationalization in the duties of *corregidors* and *alcaldes mayores*, who exercised constant pressure on the *municipios*, taking over much of their judicial work, supervising their finances, having a say in their appointments, and so on. And this surveillance of local government by the agents of Madrid occurred not only in towns on royal land, but penetrated into the privately-owned towns of nobles, bishops, monasteries, and the four Military Orders.

The military, as well as the civil, arm was improved in quality and size; and to do this Charles III brought recruiting increasingly under the direction of his civil servants, taking it out of the corrupt hands of the *municipios*. The *quintas* – the selection of conscripts by lot – formed one of the most oppressive aspects of the impact of the state on society, and the *municipios* did everything they could, honest or dishonest, to save their sons from its horrors. In 1745 Seville, whose population was about 18,000, claimed that it had only 12,980, and tried to get legal exemption from the *quintas* on various grounds for all but 201 of these, whose case they also took up, but on other grounds. Other towns resorted to hiring vagabonds or visiting harvesters from Galicia in order to produce their quota. As well as using the bureaucracy to make the *municipios* pull their weight, Charles extended the use of conscripts. They were posted to regiments of the line as well as the militia, so that the foreign element could be reduced to a very small proportion. As the reign progressed, the army improved in quality, morale, and prestige. There were usually about 2,000 applications for the 200 officer-cadetships available.

By the end of the Ancien Régime the Spanish army possessed a strong sense of its own identity, and was in a position to intervene in politics as an interest in its own right.

This strengthening of the civil and military arms of the Monarchy, however, did not permit any basic shake-up of local government. Although often discussed, nothing was ever done to take municipal administration out of the hands of the noble oligarchs who had purchased their posts; and the governments of Charles III had to rest content with putting pressure on them, in two directions, from above and from below. From above, the Council of Castile's committee, called the *Contaduría General de Propios y Arbitrios* (1760), supervised the way in which *municipios* managed the income they drew from their common lands (*propios*) and from local taxes (*arbitrios*). Through the *intendentes* and *corregidors*, it tried to prevent communes from wantonly selling their landed capital, and tried to see that they hired out the commons in a fair manner. It even initiated schemes – which were not very successful – for breaking up the commons and sharing them out among the landless labourers. From below, what appeared to be a very democratic scheme of supervision was inaugurated in 1766 by Campomanes immediately after the mutiny of Esquilache. Each commune had to elect four *diputados del comun* (two in places of under 1,000 inhabitants) and a *sindico personero* to sit and vote with the town council (the *ayuntamiento*) on questions of food-supply. In these elections, all lay rate-payers had the vote, and members of the *ayuntamientos* and their relatives were forbidden to take part in the proceedings. Later, the powers of these representatives were extended, and they voted on resolutions to do with the management of the *propios*, the running of the *quintas*, and so on. And in 1768 another improvement was initiated, first of all in Madrid, and then in all cities which had *Audiencias* or *Chancillerías*. Madrid was divided into eight sections, each under an *alcalde de cuartel*, whose job was to put down crime. Each of these sections was divided into eight sub-sections, each under an *alcalde de barrio*, who had to be a resident of the *barrio*, and who was elected (like the *diputados*) by the rate-payers, between December 1 and Christmas, so that he could take office on the first day of the new year. The duties of an *alcalde de barrio* were to supervise law and order, improve the cleanliness of the streets, control the taverns, inspect the weights and measures, relieve the paupers, and so on.

This was magnificent, but it did not turn out to be democracy. The elected officers proved to be no match for the proud nobles who had owned the government of the towns for generations. And, in any case, the Spanish system of values being monolithic, it was not to be expected that the elected element would behave very differently from the hereditary. The perfume of *hidalguía* was too sweet on the nostrils of the commoners, and it was not long before the *diputados* were trying to convert their temporary representation of the people into a life-office. In Palma de Majorca, a weaver, a boiler-maker, a carpenter, and a cooper were elected. They immediately began to wear swords, the sign of nobility, while the cooper took to wearing a wig from that moment on.

Nobility

Thus the attack on the nobility and clergy in their local bastions was mild compared with what happened in France, Austria, Prussia, and other absolutisms. The noble and bourgeois oligarchs who ran the *municipios* did not find it necessary to make great changes in their way of life, even though they were sandwiched in between the *corregidors* above and the *diputados* below. And if this was the case on royal land, there was even more independence on the *señorios*, where the powers of the lord, whether he was a noble, a bishop, a dean and chapter, a monastery, or one of the Military Orders, were not basically touched. The Treasury and the Council of Castile spent many hours on this problem, and Campomanes produced volumes of bold plans for the abolition of the *señorios* and mortmain: plans which may have been useful to nineteenth-century Liberals, but which gathered dust on the shelves of the civil service under the Enlightenment. According to the census of 1797, the nobles at that stage still owned fifteen cities, 2,286 towns, and 6,380 villages and hamlets; while the clergy owned

seven episcopal cities, 395 towns, and 3,494 villages and hamlets. In other words, Spain was still 'a monstrous Republic
formed of little republics', as Olavide, one of Charles III's reforming bureaucrats, described it. It was still 'a body composed
of other and smaller bodies, separated and in opposition to
one another, which oppress and despise each other and are in
a continuous state of war. Each province, each religious house,
each profession is separated from the rest of the nation and
concentrated in itself.'[15]

The resistance to the crown was diffused among innumerable locations, and it no longer swamped the central organs of
government at Madrid as the grandees had done under the last
two Habsburgs. Indeed, the grandees evinced a certain disdain
for the bureaucracy of Madrid, as a career fit only for *mantéis-
tas*. The Spanish aristocracy under Charles III does not seem
to have made up its seventeenth-century lack of civic virtues.
In their ability to ignore the State, the great families resembled
the nobility and gentry of Britain, though they differed sharply
from them in public spirit and creative energy. 'A breed so
degenerate as that of the Grandees of Spain', wrote Molden-
hawer, a foreign traveller, 'perhaps does not have an equal in
the world. There is not a single man of talent among them.
They lack education, they are ignorant, lazy, and frivolous,
stupidly proud and extravagant.... There are exceptions, but
they are few.'[16] Similarly, the opposition to the crown was not
concentrated and institutionalized as it was in the diets and
parliaments of the other parts of Europe. The Spanish Cortes
was the last place to rally resistance to the king. In 1789 – Resistance Year, as it were – the first business discussed by the
Cortes of Spain after being formally opened by the king was
three requests which had been laid before His Majesty in the
name of all members by the deputy from Burgos. One of these
was a petition for good seats at the forthcoming bullfight.

Clergy

In addition to the nobility, Charles III also kept up the pressure
on the Church. He had, after all, spent twenty-four years as

King of Naples, and was naturally a keen *regalista*. For its part, the Church did not put up a very strong resistance because it was weakened by internal divisions: between the upper and lower clergy (though not so sharply as in France), between the seculars and the regulars, and between the Jesuits and most of the remaining orders. The attack on the Jesuits began immediately, for Charles's Enlightened ministers needed to wrest Spanish higher education from their control. Moreover, since the Order had so many enemies, it was a convenient target on which to deflect the hatreds that Esquilache's reforms had aroused. Justly or unjustly, the Jesuits were accused of being mainly responsible for bringing the masses on to the streets in 1766; and in 1767 they were expelled from Spain and the American colonies, and a campaign was set on foot to persuade the Pope to dissolve the Order altogether.

At the same time civil servants had orders to weaken the powers of the Church courts in favour of the magistrates employed by the State; to reduce the amount of money that went to Rome in the form of annates and other Church levies; and to increase the amount of ecclesiastical revenue that went to the State, by cutting out immunities and other methods of evasion. It used to be said in this reign that there was no good *corregidor* who was not under excommunication half the time. Furthermore, reforms were ordered in church life in accordance with the views of what in Spain were called 'Jansenists'. Like the Febronians in Austria and Germany, these reformers favoured a reduction in the power of the Pope, and opposed many of the most popular festivals and ceremonies as superstitious, if not worse. They were especially hostile to the Jesuits, who were indulgent towards these traditional celebrations of the Spanish people. In 1769 the *mayas* and *altares de mayo* were banned – ribald revels of the First of May, in which Spaniards paid court to the *maya*, a maiden dressed in finery. These ceremonies were accompanied by an amount of drinking, singing, dancing, and other indulgences, which Jansenists regarded as shocking. In 1777 dancing was forbidden in churches, churchyards, and cemeteries. *Gigantones* – outsize carnival figures – were outlawed in 1780. Other measures ordered the burial of corpses outside churches instead of inside, for reasons of hygiene; allowed meat to be eaten on Sundays; and limited the right of asylum to two churches only in large towns, and one in smaller places.

Reforms of this kind, of course, aroused the ire of the Inquisition, and anyone preaching or writing in favour of Jansenism was in danger of having his orthodoxy examined by that fearsome tribunal. The archbishop and four bishops who had sat on the royal commission which had decided to expel the Society of Jesus, for example, found themselves subject to their attentions. Campomanes and Floridablanca, in a memorandum of 1768, concluded as follows: 'The tribunals of the Inquisition today compose the most fanatic body in the State and the one most attached to the Jesuits, who have been expelled from the kingdom; the inquisitors profess exactly the same maxims and doctrines; in fine, it is necessary to carry out a reform of the Inquisition.'[17] Charles III brought this rogue institution, which had been too independent of both Rome and Madrid, under royal supervision. During the remainder of the Ancien Régime, its methods became less barbarous, its victims fewer. During the reigns of Charles III and Charles IV, only four people were burnt, but whether this fall in business was due to government pressure, or shortage of heretics after so many centuries of persecution, is a question. Certainly, there was no intention on the part of Charles III to destroy the Inquisition. Even the Enlightened Count of Aranda – decidedly no friend of the Church – agreed that it had to continue in existence, since the mass of Spaniards believed that the safety of Christianity itself was dependent on it. The king even had to sacrifice Pablo Olavide to them: one of his most valuable civil servants, *intendente* of Seville and Andalusia, colonizer of the Sierra Morena, reformer of university syllabuses – but also reader of the *philosophes* and correspondent of Voltaire and Rousseau. He was arrested in 1776, brought out of his confinement in 1778 for his *auto da fé*, sentenced to the loss of his property, eight years re-education in a monastery, and banishment.

The Enlightenment

The fate of Olavide had a chastening effect on the minority of
Spaniards, members of the government often, such as Aranda,
Campomanes and Floridablanca, who were in touch with the
European Enlightenment. For the institution which had
crushed Jews and Arabs, humanists and Protestants, was now
standing guard against the *philosophes*. In 1756, for instance,
Montesquieu's *De L'Espirit des Lois* was banned, and all the
works of Voltaire were placed on the Index in 1762, and those
of Rousseau in 1764. But the Order of Jesus and the Inquisition
were only two of the obstacles in the path of Charles III's reforming ministers. The education system was another. Jovellanos, another of the king's progressive advisers, and a zealous
Catholic who took communion every two weeks, regarded
reform here as the essential precondition of economic advance.
In a report of 1784, he lamented the amount of Latin and 'old
and absurd philosophy' that was taught, which 'only serves to
cause an overproduction of chaplains and friars, doctors, lawyers, clerks, and secretaries, while mule-drivers, sailors, artisans,
and ploughmen are scarce'.[18] Already in 1770 – and following
the lead of Olavide in Seville – the government had launched
a programme of university reform, ordering the universities to
produce plans for teaching moral philosophy, mathematics, and
experimental physics. Some institutions began to make changes,
and before the Ancien Régime was over were introducing a
favoured few to the latest philosophy and science; but before
Spain could become Enlightened there was a dead weight of
traditionalism to shift. The kind of opposition that Charles's
ministers were up against is evident from the first reply which
Salamanca, the leading university, sent in answer to the government's request:

We have heard tell of a man called Obbés [Hobbes], and of the
Englishman Jean Lochio [Locke], whose works comprise four books,
but the first author is very terse; the second, besides being not at
all clear, must be read with extreme caution; and we are right not

to give such a work to our young men, and thus avoid the damage that can arise from such doctrines.[19]

Reforms were also begun in the *Colegios Mayores* and other academies which prepared candidates for the universities and the armed forces. With the Jesuits out of the way, it was easier to reform curricula, and with the funds derived from their confiscated property it was also possible to found new schools at secondary and primary level. More important, perhaps, for their direct effect on the economy were the institutions set up outside the regular educational network by the learned societies which sprang up during the reign with the ardent encouragement of Campomanes. The first of these was the Basque Society of the Friends of the Country (*Amigos del País*), established in 1765 to foster the arts and sciences and all branches of economic activity. Ten years later in Madrid, after prodding by Campomanes, who went to great lengths to persuade the upper classes to take an interest in useful work, the nobility and clergy founded the Royal Economic Society. Others followed all over Spain, and by 1789 they existed in fifty-six towns and cities, and the total reached seventy before the enthusiasm began to wane. They were generally well supported by the merchants, the civil servants, the parish clergy, and the middle ranks of the nobility: the nearest group of people that Spain possessed to an enterprising bourgeoisie. They financed scientific research, published papers, and ran learned journals. They offered prizes and bursaries, founded chairs and lectureships, and even went into business themselves. They provided Spain with a number of primary schools, as well as schools of spinning, weaving, drawing, and other useful arts. At the same time, they campaigned for the liberalization of the economy from its age-long trammels. They wrote against the tolls, the gilds, and the Mesta; and they advocated the construction of roads and the cultivation of the wastes. Moreover, in Barcelona, a similar function was performed by the *Junta de Comercio* (founded in 1758), which encouraged the cotton industry, and also provided nautical and other technical training. In general, these learned bodies provided the knowledge and enthusiasm which was so conspicuously lacking in the regular local authorities.

The old *municipios* had never done their duties in the past, and Campomanes was wise not to rely on them to change under the Ancien Régime.

Practical learning and economic development were also encouraged by Enlightened individuals. Charles III, for instance, ran a model farm at Aranjuez. And not all aristocrats were absentees who performed the economic function of sucking the substance out of their estates to squander it in Madrid and the provincial capitals. The Counts of Fernán Nuñez, for example, were Enlightened Absolutists in miniature. They doubled the population and income of their estates in a century, by importing Flemish weavers, starting cloth manufacture, irrigating the fields, providing markets and fairs, promoting agricultural competitions, and awarding school-prizes. Similarly, not all clerics wasted their wealth in indiscriminate charity. Whereas Fray Francisco de San José, Bishop of Málaga from 1704 to 1713, distributed 732,000 ducats in charity in eight years, including 80,000 in daily alms at his palace gates, 20,000 for medicine for the poor, and 200,000 to finance intercessions for the dead; Don José Molina Lario, Bishop of Málaga from 1776 to 1783, spent two million on an aqueduct to bring water to the city.

The Economy

All these activities helped Spain to enjoy a modest share of the European boom that blessed most of the second half of the eighteenth century. The improvement in the quality of the bureaucrats, and the extension of their powers over *municipios* and *señorios*, nobles and clergy, enabled the state to stimulate economic growth, and thus bring more revenue to Madrid. In the reign of Charles III, the role of the Treasury had become something more sophisticated than the frantic search for ready cash which was all it amounted to under the Habsburgs; and in the king's eyes it was less important to levy and collect taxes than to cultivate the territories that produced them. And 'cultivation', he said in 1787, 'consists of stimulating the population by stimulating agriculture, crafts, industries, and commerce'.[20] It is impossible to say how much Spanish economic growth owed to government help, and how much to other causes, but there is no doubt of its existence under the Bourbons. The population, for instance, rose from the seven million of 1700 to the 10,409,879 of the census of 1786: an increase of fifty per cent which indicated a very different social and economic climate from what it had been in the seventeenth century.

As far as agriculture is concerned, the undoubted increase in output, and the rising prosperity of certain types of peasants, estate-agents, and landowners, were more the result of economic causes than government action or aristocratic paternalism. The grandees and titled nobility did not become improving land-lords. Most of them were only superficially touched by the Enlightenment, and became frenchified only in their dress, or their salon-manners. Father Isla wrote: 'I knew a *marquesa* in Madrid who learned how to sneeze in French.'[21] But further than that they did not go, for any application of the French Enlightenment to the Spanish economic and social field would have meant the end of their way of life, which was parasitical. The efforts of learned civil servants, and the pamphlets of the Economic Societies, had little effect on farming practice. There was no widespread adoption of new crops or rotations; and the increase in output was due to the extension of the cultivated area rather than to improved estate-management on the part of the nobility. On the whole, the aristocrats refused to adopt a proprietorial attitude towards their estates, in which everything was entailed, even the pictures on the wall, the books in the library, the relics in the chapel, and the posts on the municipal council. They felt and behaved, not like owners, but temporary squanderers of the usufruct; and many a noble house was saved from bankruptcy only by the adamant refusal of the crown to break entails, or otherwise indulge the incumbents in their extravagances. 'It is an insufferable and notorious injustice', said Charles III, 'that the most powerful people in the king-dom, full of luxury and abundance, do not pay taxes equivalent to their income, after they have taken it to spend in Madrid and the provincial capitals, where they regularly live, depriving the people who produce it of the advantages of their con-sumption.'[22]

The action of the State, however, was not very effective in controlling the profit-taking, nor mitigating the suffering, that resulted from the rise of food prices in Charles III's reign, though dearth was not so frequent as in the first half of the century, nor so disastrous as under the Habsburgs. The dwarf-peasants in central Spain on short-term tenures from rack-renting owners felt the pinch; and so did the agricultural workers on the southern *latifundios*. The landowners, and the large-scale leaseholders of aristocratic property – already coming to be known as *caciques* – profited greatly. The peasants in the Basque provinces did well, and so did those in the Kingdom of Aragon who had secure tenures and sufficient output to take advantage of the rising market. In Galicia and Asturias, where the lease for three lives, called the *foro*, was widespread, the owners (the *foreros*) – who were usually nobility and clergy – began raising the rents as soon as the three lives were up. The tenants (*foristas*) continually protested to Madrid, and in 1763 the Council of Castile made one of its few effective interventions into agriculture. It froze the rents. From that point on the *foristas* grew rich. Benefiting from the fixed rents, they sub-let their farms in smaller holdings at economic rents to tenants who by the end of the century were sub-letting again in handkerchief-sized plots. The mass of the dwarf-cultivators of the soil in these provinces were as badly hit as any by the price rise.

Another positive government measure was to abandon its special protection of the Mesta now that cultivation was clearly much more profitable than animal husbandry. In 1786 their right of *posesión* – that is, their perpetual grazing rights at fixed rents over vast acreages – was abolished, along with their much abused rights of transit for their migrant flocks. In 1788 landowners were given permission to enclose and plough up the pastures. Unfortunately, the basic agricultural problem was not touched by the State, except for the drawing up of plans, and when Charles III died Spain was still plagued with its land-hungry masses, on the one hand, and, on the other, its vast acreages of uncultivated land artificially kept off the market by mortmain, entail, and the rights of the *municipios*.

Industrial development was mainly limited to the provinces of the periphery, while central Spain stagnated in a pre-capitalist world of small workshops and restricted output. The Golden Age relationship was now completely reversed, and all the vigour and enterprise emanated from the coastal areas, especially on the Mediterranean. The *Nueva Planta*, the abolition of the internal customs, the equitable tax system, and the protection of the cotton industry were all government measures which helped Catalonia to begin its rise to economic dominance; but they do not explain the mysterious psychological revolution which turned that land of lawless brigands, touchy rebels, lazy workers, and faint-hearted gildsmen into what a contemporary journalist, Mariano Nipho, called 'a little England in the heart of Spain'.[23]

With the seas cleared of Barbary pirates from the 1730s onwards, the Catalans came down from the hill-villages where they had been sheltering and began to irrigate and plant the coastal plain. In the same decade Estaban Canals started what was probably the first modern cotton factory in Barcelona. Other enterprising capitalists appeared, and began to reduce the stick-in-the-mud gildsmen to the level of wage-earners. In the 1780s spinning-jennies were imported from England. In 1790 the first steam-engine was installed when Simón Pla y Ca. took out a twenty-year patent on one. Meanwhile, Catalan ships penetrated everywhere: bringing sugar from the West Indies, selling wine and brandy in northern Europe, teaching the Galicians how to fish the ocean, and salt and smoke the results. This was a break with the *hidalgo* spirit, and Castilians resented their thrust and drive, as a man taking a siesta will resent the coming and going of busy neighbours. 'Those who love laziness and wish to get rich with little work at the expense of their neighbours', wrote Larruga in 1792, 'cannot tolerate Catalans establishing themselves outside their principality. But sensible men appreciate their worth and regard them as brother Spaniards.'[24]

Certainly, the Catalans, and the other peoples of the Kingdom of Aragon, regarded themselves as Spaniards by the end of the Ancien Régime, for by that time the Spanish nation had been created, as the War of Independence against Napoleon proved. The population of Aragon, Valencia, and Catalonia had been sulky and unco-operative with Philip V and Ferdinand VI, but they regarded Charles III as their king from the moment he landed in Barcelona on his way from Naples. And his policies helped to make them prosperous. In 1767, for instance, a decree ordered the construction of a network of highways linking Madrid at the centre with the provinces on the circumference: Catalonia, Valencia, Andalusia, Galicia, and the Basque provinces. And between that date and 1778 Floridablanca as Superintendent of Roads was in charge. More important still was the increasing liberalization of colonial trade: that is, the encouragement of peripheral merchants to enjoy the profits which had hitherto been the perquisite of Castilians in Seville and Cádiz. In 1765 the Cádiz monopoly came to an end, when nine Spanish ports (Santander, Gijón, La Coruña, Seville, Cádiz, Málaga, Cartagena, Alicante, and Barcelona) were made free to trade with five American islands (Cuba, Santo Domingo, Puerto Rico, Margarita, and Trinidad). This freedom was extended to Louisiana in 1768, Campeche and Yucatán in 1770, and Santa Marta in 1776. In 1778 a new regulation was issued which, though full of restrictions protecting Spanish industry, established more or less free-trade relations between Spain and her empire; and those places which were still not included nearly all received the concession before the eighteenth century was over.

This loosening up of an old colonial system had a tonic effect on the Spanish economy. It also made a welcome, though belated, break with the blinkered policy of the Habsburgs, who had simply regarded the empire as a source of bullion; and it marked the break-through to a more Enlightened imperial policy which regarded colonies as the economic complement of the mother-country. And along with free trade went measures to improve the effectiveness of the imperial administration. Unfortunately, it was all too late. Increased absolutism only gave the colonists a desire for self-government; and increased Enlightenment gave them better means to achieve it. Moreover, Charles failed to loosen a commercial strangle-hold more constricting than the old Seville-Cádiz monopoly, and that was the favoured trading position which had been acquired over the years, by fair means and foul, by Great Britain. The British threat could not be eliminated by port regulations or customs dues. It was a question of diplomacy and war.

Foreign Affairs

As has been shown, Charles III was too late in entering the Seven Years' War (1756–63) to prevent Britain attaining a dominating position in North America. The subsequent recovery of Spain under his rule, however, allowed her to enjoy again, and for the last time, a brief hey-day of great-power status. She maintained the close friendship with France which was established by the Family Compacts, not for sentimental reasons, but because the facts dictated it. France wished to replace Britain as the exploiter-in-chief of the Spanish empire; and Spain, for her part, was helpless without France against the overwhelming might of the British navy. Opportunity for action re-appeared during the War of American Independence (1776–83). Spain joined in the war against Britain with a view to driving her out of America and reconquering Florida, Minorca, Gibraltar, and Jamaica – though the Secretary of State, Floridablanca, was also well aware of the danger that the British colonies, once free, might prove a greater menace to the Spanish empire than Britain herself. In the outcome Spain's successes in this war (even if counterbalanced by her failure to recapture Gibraltar and by the collapse of the Franco-Spanish attempt to invade England) were rewarded in the Treaty of Versailles (1783), the most favourable treaty signed by Spain since the sixteenth century. By it, she received Florida and Minorca.

Conclusion

Thus, when he died in 1788, Charles III left Spain in a much stronger position that he found her in. But not in a secure one. Wherever one penetrates below the surface, whether at home, abroad, or in the colonies, one finds time-bombs ticking away which could probably not have been dismantled in time, even if circumstances had been favourable: even if, for example, Charles IV had been an able ruler, or the French Revolution had not overturned the world beyond the Pyrenees, or if Napolean had not invaded the country in 1808. Abroad and in the colonies, the War of American Independence may have had a happy outcome for Spain; but it also showed (as did the events of the next two decades) that Spain was too weak politically to control her empire, too backward economically to keep British commerce out, and too feeble at sea to prevent British and Americans entering South America. She could not even prevent the British causing economic havoc at home by blockading the Spanish coast whenever she was so minded. Moreover, the French Revolution blunted Spanish foreign policy by making her dither between two painful courses: joining France, her old ally, but now her ideological foe, or aiding England, her old enemy, but now her ideological friend.

And a glance at the reforms at home also reveals weaknesses. The Enlightened programme was characterized, as Jaime Vicens Vives has said, by the 'amplitude of the objectives proposed and the timidity of the means employed to reach them'.[25] Charles III and his ministers stopped short of tackling the crucial political, social, and economic problems; but proceeded far enough with the planning stages to give their enemies ample time to prepare counter-measures. The country was united, and a nation had been created. There was a national flag in the black and gold of Castile and Aragon; and a traditional tune had been adapted as a Royal March – later to become the national anthem. Men from Navarre, the Basque Provinces, Aragon, Catalonia, and Valencia served alongside Castilians in the new Spanish army. There was thus no question now, as had happened 150 years previously, of the discontented aiming to solve their problems by breaking up the Monarchy into its constituent parts. Instead, it was to be a struggle to capture the centre of a united state. And there was no shortage of discontented Spaniards. The country was littered with social groups clamouring for the removal of crying injustices, or striving to realize cherished ideals. And opposing them were the privileged groups whose interests these threatened. The multitude of mendicants, landless labourers, and dwarf-husbandmen were a menace to the ample domains monopolized by the Mesta, the *municipios*, and the great landlords, clerical and lay. The resentment of the taxpaying masses focused on the privileges of the exempt. The Enlightened intellectuals undermined the authority of the reactionary clergy. The reforming bureaucrats discomforted the nobility and clergy in their *señorios* and *municipios*. The capitalists in their factories injured the craftsmen in their gilds. The *manteístas* piqued the *colegiales*. Moreover, new interests were emerging to exacerbate and complicate the political struggle: middle-class bosses in the countryside, the rising bourgeoisie on the coasts, the industrial working-class in the cities, the professional soldiers in the army. And beneath these dissensions lay the deeper struggle: between the emptying Centre, where political authority resided, and the burgeoning perimeter where economic power was generated.

Whether a peaceful earthing of these tensions would have been possible, if the system of Charles III had had the chance to continue, will never be known: for the French Revolution and the Napoleonic invasion inaugurated an era in which Spaniards accustomed themselves to settling their problems by violence. But this is to go beyond the confines of the Ancien Régime. Charles III may not have created a utopia, but neither, on the other hand, did he provoke a bloody revolution, like Joseph II or Louis XVI. The deluge, when it came, fell a reasonable time after him.

France: The Inheritance of Louis XIV

The Frondes

This period of French history is bounded by two aristocratic rebellions. The success of the one at the end set in train the Revolution which destroyed the Ancien Régime; the failure of the one at the start enabled Louis XIV to complete its construction. For it was the horrors of the Frondes (as the earlier revolts were called) that not only determined the king to crush the nobility by the use of absolute power, but also predisposed the rest of society to let him do it.

The Frondes (1648–53) terrorized Louis XIV's childhood, forcing him on one occasion to be exhibited to the Paris mob which had broken into his apartments, and on others to flee the capital with his family and his government. For a number of reasons it was a period especially favourable to aristocratic insubordination. Firstly, the minority of the king was an ideal moment for his relatives, the Princes of the Blood, to further their own ambitions, whether these were to capture the state for themselves, or to render it incapable of interfering with their own independence. Magnates such as Louis of Condé, the brilliant general of the Thirty Years' War, or his brother Conti, were not content to look on passively, while France was governed by the Queen-Mother as sole regent along with her lover, Cardinal Mazarin, as first minister. Secondly, the structure of French society at that time was such that each of these princes, and others like them, could bring into the field an army of lesser adventurers, nobles, gentlemen, bourgeois, and peasants, who were bound to their leaders by a mixture of semi-feudal vassalage and semi-modern patronage. And, thirdly, the loyalty of such followers to their lords was fortified by the multiple grievances they nursed against the centralizing tendencies of the Monarchy, as they were operated by Mazarin and by his great master and predecessor, Cardinal Richelieu. Local jacks-in-office resented inspection by new men sent from Paris; and the whole nation was restive under the crushing weight of taxation.

The mounting exactions and tightening central control were both due mainly to war, which was the fourth element favourable to the Frondeurs. France was feeling the strain of the long death-struggle with both branches of the House of Habsburg. The year 1648 saw the end of the Thirty Years' War which brought peace with the Austrian branch, but the conflict with Spain was not to end till 1659. Moreover, the war involved the presence on the frontiers of French armies whose commanders could about-face, at appropriate moments, and take leave of fighting the Spanish in order to join one or other of the competing cliques at home. Some actually fought for the Spanish, feudal theory allowing a vassal this choice of a lord; while the Spanish gave what help they could to the Frondeurs, it being part of the war effort of any great power to stimulate revolt among the enemy.

The fifth disturbing element was the economic crisis, which was intense in France during the years 1647–51. For most of the seventeenth century after about 1620, the economic weather over the whole of Europe was disturbed and threatening, when it was not outright stormy. The curve of the price-rise of the previous century flattened out in the 1630s, and for the next hundred years prices oscillated at a lower level (except during famines), economic growth slowed down, confidence evaporated, and slumps were endemic. In some areas the blow fell later. Languedoc, for instance, prospered till the late 1650s; and the peasants really suffered in the last quarter of the century, when the prisons, as Le Roy Ladurie has said, 'were too small to contain all those who went bankrupt'.[1] The causes of these disturbances are still not properly understood, but the reduction in the import of precious metals from the New World was one factor; warfare another; government financial manipulation a third. Probably, the basic economic pattern was set by the harvest; and France was assailed by a succession of five harvest failures in the years 1647 to 1651. In a society dominated by agriculture (as Europe was at that time) a bad harvest caused a recession throughout the economy; in mid century France it caused bankruptcies, unemployment and mass starvation. In the countryside, as many as thirty per cent of some villages died of malnutrition or disease; while many of the remainder had to sell up and take to the roads, crowding into the towns and cities. Agitators' work was easy in such circumstances, and it was the agitators-in-chief, the Parlement of Paris, which constituted the sixth element in the troubled situation which produced the Frondes.

The Parlement of Paris was the only institution in France capable of becoming the legal focus of the discontents of the people and of assuming the leadership of a movement of resistance. In spite of its name, it was significantly different from the body across the Channel which had waged successful war against Charles I and was now about to bring him to the block. Briefly, it was the highest court of appeal in the central area of the kingdom, covering about a third of the territory and serving about half the people; the rest of France being served by about a dozen provincial Parlements or similar courts. In addition, the Parlement of Paris had the right to register royal decrees and to send back remonstrances about any aspect of this legislation it did not like. Right up to the Revolution, their power fluctuated according to the general political situation: sometimes they rubber-stamped the king's wishes, sometimes they blocked his way at every turn. They particularly disliked the centralizing policies of Henry IV, Richelieu, and Mazarin; and in 1648 they grasped the opportunity of a royal minority and a foreign prime minister to refuse to register seven new taxation edicts and to demand the abolition of the Intendants, the chief agents of centralization.

Mazarin was at first conciliatory: France was after all in the middle of a fight to the finish with Spain. But the Parlement had the bit between its teeth. It not only requested the dismantling of the apparatus of central power so painfully erected since Henry IV had brought an end to the Wars of Religion: it also formulated demands which would have made it a separate Estate of the realm and turned France into a limited monarchy, if not a confederation of provinces. It claimed to be heir to the powers of the ancient King's Council, to have the right to assemble, on its own initiative, the Princes of the Blood, the peers of the realm and the officers of the crown, in order to deliberate upon affairs of state and impose their decisions on the king.

Once the crucial battle of Lens had been won against Spain, and France had been saved from invasion and possible dismemberment, Mazarin struck back and arrested Broussel, the leader of the opposition (August, 1648). But the Parlement resisted. They called in the feudal nobility to act as their generals; they brought out the mob on to the streets of Paris; while their colleagues in the provincial Parlements encouraged sedition across France. 'For my part', wrote the Duc d'Epernon from Bordeaux where he was Governor-General of Guyenne and Gascony, 'I shall do everything in my power to keep the people in the respect which they lose easily once they lose fear; and there is more danger that they will lose it at the present time seeing how little consideration the chief officers of the Sovereign Courts have for the wishes of Messieurs the ministers and the authority of the King.'[2] The sight of aristocrats raising the masses against the crown was not unfamiliar under the Ancien Régime – until they tried it once too often in 1789. In 1649 the Court had to release Broussel and slip out of Paris; and for the next five years France suffered the terrors of civil strife in the middle of an international war and an economic crisis. While the King of France besieged his own capital, the citizens of Paris stormed the Bastille.

The Parlementaires soon withdrew from the struggle, however, for they had stirred up forces which soon took the management of the fight against Mazarin out of their hands. Mob rule and feudal anarchy were as damaging to their interests as they were to the crown's, and so in March, 1649, they came to terms with Mazarin, thus bringing to an end the first Fronde – the *Fronde Parlementaire*. But the Princes of the Blood and their vassals had by no means had enough, and the second Fronde (*Fronde Princière*) dragged on from 1650 to 1653. Some of the magnates fought for the Queen-Mother; others fought against her; some, like Condé, for each side in turn. Both sides called in foreign aid, and French society was subjected to a series of nightmarish experiences the memory of which served to facilitate Louis XIV's authoritarian reforms: peasant revolts and urban anarchy, military occupation and religious persecution, treason here and treachery there, baronial bandits at one end of the social scale and looters of city shops at the other. Uncultivated fields, abandoned villages, several burned down, were described by a government agent, Du Bosc, in 1650. 'Longueil ... was burned two or three weeks ago by His Royal Highness's regiment,' he wrote, 'the churches being pillaged and profaned. As we neared the gates of that town, we saw several large flocks of sheep, nothing but skin and bone, going out in search of pasture. Those who drove them, shepherds and peasants, told us that they were dying of hunger, animals and people, and that the sheep had not once been out of the town for four, five, and six weeks, for fear of being picked up by the soldiers.'[3]

All over France restive social groups were encouraged by their betters, who objected so strongly to royal centralization and increased taxation: that is, to Intendants and tax-farmers. In 1651, for example, the Parlement of Toulouse forbade the Intendant to function in Languedoc. It was a post, they declared, 'odious to all the kingdom'.[4] France saw most of the medieval horrors which political strife brings, and some of the modern ones in addition. And so it was with the profoundest relief that the bourgeoisie, the centre of gravity of French society, saw Mazarin put an end at last to gangsterdom above, anarchy below, and humiliation without.

The Parlement of Paris had confiscated Mazarin's property and then sold it to provide funds to reward his assassination, but his resilient cunning triumphed in the end. In October 1652 Louis XIV entered Paris once more – to cries of *Vive le Roi* – and the last serious mutiny before 1789 was over. It may have been hard for a king to unify a country of the size and diversity of France, but it was even harder for his opponents to weld their supporters sufficiently together to overthrow him. Early in 1653 Mazarin followed, and by the autumn of the year Bordeaux, the last stronghold of Frondeur-cum-Spanish resistance, was taken. In 1659, Mazarin brought the long Spanish war to an end with the advantageous Peace of the Pyrenees. And by the time of his death (1661) he had one more achievement to his credit: he had taught Louis to be his own Mazarin.

These are the chief reasons why the French people acquiesced in the erection of an absolutism which became the model for most of Europe: for it was created by a monarch trained in the hard school of the Frondes and able to satisfy the deepest desires of the bourgeoisie – order in château and slum, and security on the frontiers. 'Louis XIV did more good for his country than twenty of his predecessors together', wrote Voltaire in the next century;[5] and that (in more modest terms) is the theme of this section. But for a full appreciation of this achievement in state building, it is necessary first to make a closer inspection of the obstacles lying in the way.

A Corporative State

The French under Louis XIV were not yet a nation, and France hardly a state. 'France would be the mistress of the world', wrote the king himself, 'if the divisions among her children had not too often exposed her to the jealous furies of her enemies.'[6] In Provence, the King of France was the Comte de Provence, and called himself such; in Dauphiné, he was the Dauphin de Viennois. His kingdom was a corporative state, a federation of provinces, districts and cities, which had been steadily assembled, piece by piece, since medieval times; and each unit retained certain rights, liberties, privileges, usages and customs, depending on the particular circumstances in which its instrument of union, its contract, or treaty, or surrender was negotiated. When, after his first conquest of Franche-Comté (1668), Louis XIV signed an agreement with its representatives, the first clause read: 'Everything will remain in Franche-Comté in the same state as it is at present, as regards privileges, franchises and immunities.'[7] Some provinces, such as Artois, Flanders, Burgundy, and Languedoc (amounting in all to about a third of the kingdom), still had their own Estates, with the right of collecting and in part spending their own revenue. John Locke saw two sessions of the Estates of Languedoc at Montpellier in 1676, which had, he wrote, 'all the solemnity and outward appearance of a Parliament. The king proposes and they debate and resolve about it. Here is all the difference that they never do, and some say dare not, refuse whatever the king demands.'[8] But Locke was already making the Whig error of exaggerating French slavery. This was at the height of Louis' power, and provincial estates were by no means always so submissive. They interposed a barrier between the crown and the people which did not exist in the other provinces (the *pays d'élections*); and, as the focus of local patriotism, they were capable of putting up a fierce resistance to royal demands as long as the Ancien Régime existed, especially in Languedoc and Britanny.

Great variations existed in the legal system. In the South, the courts enforced Roman law; in the Centre and North customary law held sway, in all its manifold varieties. Louis XIV's failure to iron out these differences was one of the shortcomings of his reign, according to Voltaire, who wrote 'that what is just or right in Champagne should not be deemed unjust or wrong in Normandy'.[9] But it was worse than that, for the customs did not simply vary from province to province, or even from village to village. In some villages in the Beauvaisis, for example, the law varied from property to property, so that one village might be governed by three different customs.[10]

There was a similar Gothic confusion about the tax-collecting machinery. The customs duties (*traites*) were farmed, and France was far from being a common market. The older provinces were earlier farmed out to five different companies, but from 1661 they were exploited by one large syndicate and henceforth the area was known as the Five Great Farms. Of the remaining provinces, some, such as Brittany, Flanders and Artois, each had their own separate tariff; while Alsace, Franche-Comté, and the Three Bishoprics had a common one. Some cities had tariff walls up against the rest of France, but free trade with the rest of the world.

But customs were only part of the royal revenues, and there was no uniformity about the remainder. Some provinces (Brittany, Artois, and Franche-Comté, for example) paid no salt-tax (*gabelle*); some paid a small *gabelle*, some a large one. Where the *gabelle* was paid, the area was divided into districts called salt-depots (*greniers*) each with its own tribunal – 229 of them at the start of Louis XIV's reign.[11] Unlike the customs and salt-duties, the main direct tax, the *taille*, was not farmed, but collected by state employees, except, as has been mentioned, in the *pays d'états*. For this purpose France was divided into areas called *Généralités*, each consisting of smaller districts called *Élections*. The total amount of *taille* required was fixed by the king's ministers and divided among the *Généralités*. Each *Généralité* apportioned its share among the *Élections*, who thereupon divided their share among the parishes. At each level above the parish there were tribunals of *officiers* who organized this, called *trésoriers-généraux* in the *Généralités*, and *élus* in the *Élections*. Similarly, the collection of the *taille* was carried out by *receveurs-particuliers* in the *Élections* and *receveurs-généraux* in the *Généralités*. At parish level the work was done by the inhabitants in turn.

In case the above description makes the *taille*-collecting machinery seem like an area of rational order in a fiscal chaos, it should be added that there were two sorts of *taille*. In those areas, mainly in the South, where it was levied on the land, it was bearable; but elsewhere it was an onerous, personal impost. Moreover, large numbers of people were exempted from the *taille* : for example, the clergy, the nobility, the royal household, the *officiers* of the courts of justice, the *officiers* of finance themselves, mayors and town councillors and so on. Most of the large cities, such as Paris, Rouen, or Dieppe paid no *taille*. Beauvais, for example, had the privilege from 1472 onwards of paying *subsistances* and *subventions* to the king instead; that is, lump sums which the city authorities collected from the citizens by their own machinery.[12]

In the same way, the Church was a patchwork of differing usages. Those bishoprics which formed part of France in 1516 came under the Concordat of Bologna, which granted the King of France the *régale*: the enjoyment of episcopal revenues during a vacancy, and the patronage of many of the benefices. In provinces added later, the Pope had not surrendered these lucrative rights. Over and above these regional variations there were other differences in doctrine and behaviour which will be dealt with later.

Thus the more one penetrates below the surface unity of the geographical expression called France, the more striking appears the diversity. Some parts of the country, such as Burgundy or Brittany, had been independent duchies well on the way to becoming nation-states; others, such as Lille or Strasbourg, had been little urban republics. Roussillon, which France gained in 1659, was a part of Catalonia; Alsace, acquired in 1648, a part of Germany; Avignon still belonged to the Pope.

Superimposed on these regional variations can be discerned at least three distinct administrative structures for royal control and local government, typical of three different historical periods. In the first place, the medieval network of thousands of baronial courts in the villages and gild-controlled corporations in the towns was still the basic pattern of law and order; and above that level, for his army, the king was embarrassingly dependent upon the retinues which the feudal magnates could bring into the field. Though in theory feudalism no longer existed and each man knew only one lord, the king, feudal attitudes persisted. A man who married the distant cousin of a great lord might become his client: he would work for him, spy for him, go to war with him. In return, the lord protected his client, fed and clothed him, used his influence to get him a job, the captaincy of a fortress if he were a gentleman, a seat in a royal court of justice if he were a bourgeois.

The weaker the crown, the stronger grew these protection associations, for if the king could not defend his subjects they had perforce to turn to the local strong man. And it was one of Louis XIV's most important contributions to French political evolution to make the crown an attractive force powerful enough to neutralize local fealties: the essential preliminary to changing France from a collection of communities into a nation of individuals. In his youth, however, the great lordships were far from subdued. At worst, they could deteriorate into the bands of brigands that from time to time terrorized the fastnesses of the Auvergne mountains; or aim at the throne, as they did in the Frondes. At best, they threw out the king's measures in the provincial Estates at Dijon, Rennes or Montpellier; or, what is worse, made themselves indispensable as governors of the thirty or so military areas into which France was divided. The nobility of the sword, as they were called, never ceased to harry the crown as long as the Ancien Régime existed.

The second administrative layer was that of the *offices* created by late-medieval and Renaissance monarchs in the first wave of centralization. In these early efforts to emasculate feudal separatism, French kings had organized hierarchies of courts for tax-collecting and peace-keeping purposes. These were manned by bourgeois lawyers, and supervised by central courts in Paris, directly under the king and controlled by bourgeois ministers. The *taille* (as has been shown) was levied and collected by some of these *officiers* in the *Généralités* and *Élections*. The king's justice was similarly administered by a network of tribunals laid out on top of the medieval one. Aggrieved Frenchmen could now appeal from manor or municipal courts to the higher courts of the *Baillis*, as they were called in parts of France, or *Sénéchaux*, as they were called in others. Above these were the courts of the *Présidiaux*; and from these again there was an appeal to the provincial *Parlements*, and from these to the *Parlement* of Paris. Police duties were carried out by another hierarchy of *officiers*, called the *maréchaussée*, or constabulary.

This promising bureaucratic machinery, the most elaborate in Europe, had unfortunately by the seventeenth century slipped out of the king's grasp. The top men were no longer bourgeois, but members of a second nobility, the *noblesse de robe*, with political ambitions of their own, as we have seen in the Frondes. There it was clear that the members of the Parlement of Paris were no longer willing servants of the king; but neither were the most humble *officiers* in the local tax-offices. By Louis XIV's time they could cock a snook at the crown, which no longer had the power to discipline them. For by now they all owned their offices, which were bought and sold and handed down from father to son like any other piece of property. The chief offices in provincial capitals such as Aix-en-Provence or Toulouse were worth 100,000 livres apiece. Nicholas Fouquet paid a million to be *procureur-général* to the Parlement of Paris.[13] Louis XIV broke him, but he could not have disciplined the *officier* class as a whole, much as Colbert would have liked, for to buy them all out would have cost the crown about eight times its normal annual revenue. France had become a limited monarchy – 'a monarchy', as Roland Mousnier said, 'limited by the sale of offices'.[14]

The crown had become the prisoner of its servants owing to the chronic shortage of money that all European monarchs encountered in that era. They all resorted to the sale of offices, though the French Kings were ahead in this, as in every other experiment in the art of government. Desperate for ready cash, they created and sold jobs to members of the bourgeoisie who regarded office as a safe investment for the gains of commerce or agriculture. The salary, the perquisites, and, above all, the prestige were the interest on the capital sunk. Further, from 1604, the kings levied an annual tax called the *paulette* on public offices; and in return for paying this the owner was allowed to designate his successor. Thus the *officiers* became an hereditary caste, which the king could never afford to buy out or do without. And not merely for lack of cash: for France could not be governed without the legal and financial expertise which these officers alone possessed – even though they used it to fleece the public. As Richelieu wrote, 'he who buys justice wholesale can sell it retail'.[15] The only remedy was the creation of a third administrative layer, to act as inspectors of the second and first.

This was the band of *commissaires*, the most well-known of whom were the Intendants. Unlike the *officiers*, these hand-picked bureaucrats were appointed and dismissed by the king at will. They had been tried by Henry IV and Richelieu; in the Frondes, the Parlement of Paris had forced Mazarin to dismiss them, but he gradually re-introduced them in his later years. Under Louis XIV they were used extensively: they were the typical and essential agents of the crown in the formation of the Ancien Régime and will be explained more fully in a later place.

Social Structure

France was thus an assemblage of regions and districts, duchies and towns, loosely held together by three overlapping sets of government agents. But that is only part of the story, for Louis and his ministers had far more serious obstacles in their path. The cracks in the structure so far described were criss-crossed by the deeper rifts of class rivalry.

The apex of French society, the *noblesse d'épée* were passing through a critical period. Proud of their lineage, jealous of their privileges and sensitive of their honour, they had long been the chief enemies of the Monarchy. And while kings had been undermining their political power, the middle classes had been eating away at their wealth, and they had been sapping their own strength in warfare and extravagant living. They had exhausted themselves in the Wars of Religion, neglected their estates during the Habsburg conflicts and utterly discredited themselves in the Frondes.

Beneath them in status, but rivalling them in wealth and political weight, were the *noblesse de robe*, the cream of the *officier* class, who sat on the benches of the Parlement of Paris and of the other sovereign courts both in the capital and in the provinces. These *robins*, as they were called, had been brought low in the Frondes, but were too deeply rooted in the indispensable bureaucracy to cease being a threat to the crown. Their minds were divided between envy of the nobility of the sword, hostility to the king and his Intendents and fear of the ambitions of the bourgeoisie.

The bourgeoisie was a miscellaneous collection of social groups and to give them all one name is probably misleading. Highest in status came the main body of the *officiers*: those who had not yet become members of the nobility of the robe. Then came the great bankers and financiers of Paris, the ship-owners and merchants of Nantes, Bordeaux, or Marseilles, the manufacturers of Amiens, Rouen, or Beauvais. Close behind were the members of the professions: the lawyers, the doctors, surgeons, and apothecaries, along with the writers, painters and archi-

tects, not to mention the master-craftsmen of the gilds and corporations. Among them should also be included not only the
greater farmers of the villages who leased estates of three to
four hundred acres from noble or ecclesiastical landlords, but
also the main body of the clergy and the whole gamut of the
petite bourgeoisie: the holders of small offices in local government, the masters of the smaller workshops, employing perhaps
one journeyman and a pair of apprentices. Taken together, the
bourgeoisie was a huge reservoir of talent and industry. Steadily
fed at one end by constant streams of successful peasantry, it
produced at the other the statesmen and businessmen, the philosophers and artists who were to make France the greatest country in Europe. All through the Ancien Régime, they were
France's greatest strength, and at the start they were the king's
firmest support.

At the base of the social pyramid lay the majority of the population: the vast army of artisans, labourers and domestic servants in the towns and cities, and the numberless peasants of the
bourgs and villages. It is not easy to distinguish between these
two groups, for the streets of the towns were often filled with
starving peasants, on the one hand; while, on the other, manufacturers in such centres as Lyons, Rouen, Abbeville, or Lille
were using the putting-out system to turn hordes of small
farmers into a semi-industrial proletariat. Business conditions in
the late seventeenth century fluctuated between stagnation and
slump; thus the State had little to fear from the lower orders as
long as the middle and upper groups remained loyal. The relations of the working masses with their king were of the utmost
simplicity. They sometimes broke out into one of their desperate rebellions, and the king sent his soldiers to shoot them down.
Otherwise, the minds of the peasants and workers were exclusively concerned with the struggle for existence, for they were
chronically in debt, permanently under-nourished and now
and then decimated by famine. The Monarchy of the Ancien
Régime either encouraged, or acquiesced in, or was unable to
prevent, the terrible exploitation which the masses suffered at
the hands of nature or of their social superiors. Its principal
concern, in view of the Frondes, was not that the lower orders

had empty bellies, but that the nobility or bourgeoisie might encourage their mutinous outbreaks.

Religion

Finally, one more feature must be added to this sketch of the divided state of France when Louis XIV took command: ideological struggles were endemic and bitter. They mainly concerned religion, for the Church was beset by old and new rivals without, and bedevilled by divisive factions within. Under the Ancien Régime this was of urgent concern to the State, and could not be regarded as a matter of private opinion, of no interest to politicians. The French Church, for example, enjoyed an income greater than that of the king. It belonged to an international organization whose head, the Pope, was still a factor, though a declining one, in European diplomacy and war. Through its control of the chief means of communication, the schools and universities, the press and the pulpit, it was a major influence on the minds of the vast mass of the people. It was intimately bound up with social and economic life at every turn. It was a principal source of income to the nobility whose sons and daughters were establishing an almost exclusive grip on its richer bishoprics, abbeys, and convents; while the village church was the place where the inhabitants elected their tax-collectors, entered into business-deals, stored timber or grain, or heard government regulations read out by the curé as part of his sermon. Moreover, with the exception of a few free-thinkers at the top of society and an unknown quantity of pagans at the bottom, the French people were still deeply influenced by the religious revival of the Counter–Reformation. As Robert Mandrou has said, 'France did not turn rationalist at the wave of a wand the day after the publication of the *Discourse on Method*'.[16] Salvation was still a matter of such real concern that men were prepared to commit or suffer violence in its cause.

For all these reasons, religion was politics, sectarian disputes caused civil strife, and no monarch could afford to ignore them. Louis XIV was faced with disputes between Protestants and

Catholics, between Jansenists and Jesuits, Gallicans and Ultramontanes, between himself and the Pope, and between the new empirical philosophy and Christianity itself. His solutions to these problems could not help but etch deep lines on the features of the Ancien Régime.

6

France: Louis XIV and the Foundation of the Ancien Régime

The King

When Mazarin died in 1661, Louis XIV, an extremely present-able young prince of twenty-two, was already impatient to put into practice the political lessons he had learned in the hard school of the Frondes and from the admonitions of his wily prime minister. The General Assembly of the Clergy was in session at the time, and when the Archbishop of Paris asked the king to whom they were henceforth to address themselves, Louis replied: 'A moi, Monsieur l'Archevêque.'[1] For he intended to rule as well as reign. Moreover, he was not unqualified to do so. The laws of genetics must now and then endow a hereditary monarch with kingly qualities, and, if Louis was not every inch a king, he was able to put up quite a passable imitation. 'In the midst of other men', wrote the Duc de Saint-Simon, who disliked him, 'his figure, his courage, his grace, his beauty, his grand mien, even the tone of his voice and the majestic and natural charm of all his person distinguished him till his death as the King Bee, and showed that if he had only been born a simple private gentleman, he would equally have excelled in fêtes, pleasures, and gallantry, and would have had the greatest success in love.'[2]

His appetite for the opposite sex was truly royal and typically Bourbon; but he never allowed his procession of mistresses any political power. On this point he had two pieces of advice to offer the Dauphin:

First, that the time allotted to a *liaison* should never prejudice our affairs, since our first object should always be the preservation of our glory and authority, which can only be achieved by steady toil. Secondly – and more difficult to practise – that in giving our heart we must remain absolute master of our mind, separating the endearments of the lover from the resolution of the sovereign.[3]

Business and pleasure were kept steadily apart, and he took the former very seriously indeed. 'The profession of king,' he wrote, 'is great, noble, delightful, when one feels worthy of everything one undertakes.'[4] And he worked regularly and methodically for long hours each day, receiving ministers and ambassadors, with his haughty, reserved and secretive manner, which managed to be charming and awe-inspiring at one and the same time. A general once admitted to him on coming into his presence: 'I never trembled like this before Your Majesty's enemies.'[5]

He ruled France as an absolute monarch. 'A little severity', he told the Dauphin, 'was the greatest kindness I could have for my people.'[6] And he had no intention of sharing his power with Parlements, or Estates, or generals, or any other representatives of his people. In this he would have been supported by practically everyone who reflected upon politics in the second half of the seventeenth century. The rebellions which had run over Europe like a rash, as well as the ceaseless international wars, amply explain the cry for strong government. And France, after the Frondes and the Habsburg wars, with whole provinces depopulated by famine and invasion, required peace and order so that this vast accumulation of human and material resources could be developed to its full potential, secure from foreign raids. In the conditions of the time, this could be provided by no other form of government than absolute monarchy.

Not that Louis XIV justified his conduct with reasoning of this utilitarian kind. For the king, and for most of his subjects, arguments cut little ice still, if they were outside the Christian frame of reference. 'He who gave kings to men', wrote Louis in his *Instructions for the Dauphin*, 'wished them to be respected as his lieutenants, reserving to himself alone the right to examine their conduct.'[7] 'There is something religious in the respect which one renders the prince,' wrote Bossuet, Bishop of Meaux and royal preacher *par excellence* in his *Politics drawn from the actual words of the Holy Scriptures*. 'Service of God and

respect for kings are things united.'[8] 'Kings are absolute lords,'
Louis advised the Dauphin, 'and naturally have the full and free
disposal of all the belongings not only of churchmen, but of
laymen as well.'[9]

In order to play the absolute monarch in the France of the
Ancien Régime, the king had to reduce to obedience or impotence the chief rivals for his power: prime ministers, Princes
of the Blood, the nobility of the sword, the provincial Estates,
the Parlements and the whole of the *officier* class. Louis was
ready for the drudgery involved. 'The King must know everything,' he wrote. 'Empires are only preserved by the same means
by which they are created, namely vigour, vigilance, and hard
work.'[10] After Mazarin there was no prime minister. The king's
mother, Anne of Austria, his brother, Monsieur, and princes
such as Condé were allowed no part in the central government.
His Council of State, which under his chairmanship took the
chief political decisions, was limited to his five or six chief
ministers and was never cluttered up with dignitaries sitting
there because they possessed a certain title or held a certain
post. No one had a right to be in the cabinet: men were sent
for or not, just as the king required.

His Ministers

The king's ministers came almost entirely from the *noblesse
de robe* and the bourgeoisie. After his experiences with the
Frondes, he deliberately resolved not to appoint anyone of
birth, who would already have an exalted position in his own
right. 'It was important for the public to know', he wrote, 'from
the rank of those whom I employed, that I had no plans for
sharing my authority with them.'[11] 'It was a reign of vile bourgeoisie', wrote Saint-Simon, the disgruntled spokesman of the
ousted nobility.

These ministers slaved away morning and night bringing
matters of State to that mature point where high decision could
be taken, either at the Council (which met three or four times a
week) or more commonly in individual consultation with the
king. It is a matter of dispute whether Louis really directed the

destinies of France, or whether he signed on the dotted line after Colbert or Louvois had done the real work. Certainly, he played off one against the other so as to see both sides of a question and at least give the appearance of running affairs, like the god he claimed to be. On the one hand, he could be said to be fortunate to have inherited from Mazarin such able and energetic departmental heads; on the other, it was he who gave them office and kept them there till they dropped. Louis' personal qualities can only be fully appreciated in comparison with the failings of his two successors.

With the exception of Colbert, the son of a merchant-draper in Rheims, Louis' ministers came from *robin* families. The first generation, Hugues de Lionne, the son of a counsellor of the Parlement of Grenoble, Michel Le Tellier, a trained lawyer who handled the generals on Mazarin's behalf during the Spanish War, Nicolas Fouquet, son of a counsellor of state, and Colbert himself were all well-trained by Mazarin and, with one exception, retained by Louis. The exception was Nicolas Fouquet, the Superintendent of Finances, who, like his colleagues, had made a fortune out of politics, but who, unlike them, tactlessly displayed the fact for all to see. He entertained the king too lavishly at his new château of Vaux-le-Vicomte – built by Le Vau, decorated by Le Brun, with gardens landscaped by Le Nôtre. His ostentation was an affront to the sufferings of the people, deep in economic crisis, and an insolence to the young king, who had not yet enlarged Versailles. Such an overmighty subject had no place in Louis' world. He was disgraced, his post was abolished and his builders and decorators filched for Versailles. Otherwise, Mazarin's men laboured on, training another generation in their turn, usually their own relatives.

Michel Le Tellier was Secretary of State for War. His son, the Marquis de Louvois, collaborated with him and then succeeded to the office on his father's death. Louvois was succeeded by *his* son, the Marquis de Barbezieux. Similarly, Jean-Baptiste Colbert's son, the Marquis de Seignelay, succeeded his father as Secretary of State for the Navy; Colbert's brother, Colbert de Croissy, became Secretary of State for Foreign Affairs, till he was succeeded by *his* son, the Marquis de Torcy.

With such servants at his command, Louis was supreme in the executive department of government. His powers were as great in the legislative and judiciary, for the Parlements, which hitherto had claimed to check him here, were ordered by Louis (1673) to register edicts immediately and without alteration. Remonstrances could be presented only afterwards, and then once only. Thus armed, the king could levy taxes and spend revenue as he wanted. On his sole authority he codified the laws in a series of Ordinances which remained the basis of French law till Napoleon's reforms: civil (1667), criminal (1670), and commercial (1673). As well as supreme law-maker, he was also chief justice. By his *lettres de cachet*, he could arrest, imprison or exile any suspect, no questions asked. His Council could 'evoke' cases out of the Parlements and other courts to be dealt with as public policy required.

Intendants

Thus at the centre of affairs, Louis was as absolute as a king could be. And the Sun-King's rays penetrated to the remote corners of the kingdom. His Intendants and other *commissaires* were armed with his executive and judicial authority, and they saw to it that the two older systems of local administration, the feudal lords and the *officier* bureaucrats, either exerted the king's will or were by-passed. These Intendants, like the king's ministers, were taken from *robin* and bourgeois families. They were appointed on merit, promoted rapidly and sent out to the provinces at the age of thirty or thirty-five: young and industrious representatives of a vigorous new monarchy. As tactfully as they could, they supervised the work of those members of the old nobility who were provincial governors and military commandants; they browbeat or cajoled the provincial Estates where they still existed; and everywhere they invigorated the daily work of the *officiers* who ran the police, the law courts, and the tax-offices.

They had begun in the sixteenth century in piecemeal fashion, a small number, often sent out temporarily to do a special job. Between 1635 and 1648, however, they were turned by Richelieu into a wholly new institution. Instead of merely ensuring that the bureaucrats did their jobs, they became bureaucrats themselves. As Roland Mousnier has said, 'from a reforming inspector, the provincial Intendant became an administrator.'[12] As Louis XIV's reign proceeded, they became numerous, permanent, and powerful. Even obstreperous Brittany had a permanent Intendant from 1689, and he, by the end of the reign, had eighty-six assistants (*sous-délégués*) working for him. Other commissaires were added from time to time: Lieutenants-General of Police and Inspectors of Manufactures, who, together with the Intendants, not merely tuned up the administrative machine, but, more important, enforced those new policies by which Louis and his ministers moulded France into a new shape.

Colbert

Economic policy was Colbert's affair, rather than the king's who was bored by such matters, and much preferred to receive the surrender of a Dutch fortress than to visit an armaments factory. Colbert realized that the former depended on the latter; and that the latter depended on French economic growth, only to be achieved by state planning. 'Trading Companies are the armies of the King,' he wrote, 'and the manufactures of France his reserves.'[13] In other words, Mercantilism, as this economic planning was called, was primarily to ensure the power of the state. The prosperity of the people was a happy by-product. It had been the policy of French kings from Henry IV onwards, whenever they had had the political strength to enforce it; but it reached its perfection only under Louis XIV.

Mercantilists were fundamentally concerned with acquiring gold and silver, without which, in the conditions of the seventeenth century, no state could feel independent, let alone strong. It was needed to hire troops, buy armaments, fit out warships. It bought allies in time of war; it bought food in time of dearth. To possess it was to deny it to others; and if the mercantilist theory that a country's wealth was proportional to the poverty of its neighbours is now thought to be somewhat ingenuous, it is nevertheless understandable. There was a fixed amount of gold and silver, and it was in short supply. It had been calculated that Europe in 1660 had only as much gold and silver in circulation as the Bank of France had in metal coinage in 1929. In those circumstances, France's gain was her enemies' loss.

Gold and silver were acquired by a favourable balance of trade, and Colbert's policies were all designed to achieve this. To develop trade, he improved inland transport: rivers, ports, canals and roads were developed, though he had little success in breaking down internal customs barriers. He built a navy and a merchant fleet. To rival the British and Dutch, he founded trading companies, for commerce and colonization in the four corners of the world. Only one, the East India Company, survived him. They failed because of investing habits deep in the French character at that time. In contrast to England and Holland, the nobility and bourgeoisie in France tended to put their money only into land or office or government stock. They wanted security and status rather than profits; and they refused to risk their savings on the waves. As J. Savary said in his popular seventeenth-century manual *Le Parfait Négociant*, 'from the moment a merchant in France acquires great riches in commerce, his children – far from following that profession – on the contrary enter the public offices ... whereas in Holland the children of individual merchants ordinarily follow the profession and trade of their father'.[14] And the minority of Frenchmen who were prepared to take the plunge (and they became millionaires in the eighteenth century) favoured individual, not company, trading. The merchants of Marseilles, for example, whose ships had long been familiar in Genoa, Constantinople, Smyrna, and Alexandria, resisted all attempts by Colbert to dragoon them into a Levant Company.

Thus Colbert's reach was less than his aim, but it was long enough; and he firmly placed France on the map of world commerce. More successful, and equally in the service of a favourable balance of trade, were his measures to encourage industry, with the double object of selling to the foreigner and avoiding buying from him. To ensure a supply of skilled labour, special privileges were granted to Dutch textile workers,

German miners, Italian glass and silk experts. John Locke saw
some of the first at Carcassonne in 1677. 'They have got into
this way of making fine cloth', he wrote, 'by means of eighty
Hollanders which, about five or six years since, Mr Colbert got
hither. They are all now gone but about twelve, but have left
their art behind them.'[15] Training was one of Colbert's chief
preoccupations. Courses were given at the Gobelins 'factory',
a series of workshops which supplied the crown with furniture
and tapestry. Schools were established at the naval dockyards;
French workers were forbidden to emigrate; paupers were
rounded into workhouses where they had to learn a trade.

Similarly, Colbert roped in the capitalists, foreign or French,
and got them to revive old industries or start new ones. Privileges were granted, like monopolies and high tariff walls. Some
firms had an assured market in the state: that of Dalliez de La
Tour, for example, who had made his money as *Receveur-
général* in Dauphiné, and who for many years supplied the
crown with cannon and anchors. The king lent money, or
buildings, or equipment, or raw materials – or sometimes his
name, for several hundred *manufactures royales* were started
in Colbert's time. Other encouragements were to allow the big
cloth manufacturers in centres such as Amiens and Rouen to
be exempt from gild regulations and thus free to employ the
peasants in the surrounding villages by the 'putting-out' system.
In a few cases, particularly in war time, the State actually
nationalized production, as when it took over for a period the
iron works in the Nivernais to be run by engineers of the fleet.

Colbert, austere and tireless himself, tied up the whole of
French industry in the most detailed tutelage, in order to ensure the perfection of its products. His Intendants and Inspectors of Manufactures, and their assistants, visited and revisited
the workshops to see that the standards laid down by the State
were maintained: standards which fixed lengths, breadths,
and weights, qualities of material and types of finish. Shoddy
work was punished by fines, confiscation or burning of the product, and even (after 1670) a nine-foot-high pillory. The authority of the gilds was backed by the State, whose inspectors
encouraged the process whereby the control in each gild was

concentrating in the hands of a few of the richer employers. Colbert also tried to make the free crafts organize themselves into gilds; and he was successful in many of the towns, where the number of the gilds almost doubled by 1700. In Paris they increased from 60 to 114. In the countryside, however, he never succeeded in dragooning the peasant-workers into gilds, and his attempts often provoked riots, as in Flanders in 1670. His ideal would have been to see the whole of French industry minutely regulated by gilds, under the supervision of the State; and his exemption of new industries from gild regulations was meant to be only a temporary privilege, till the industry was on its feet.

Twenty years of Colbert's tyranny revolutionized France's commercial and industrial position in the world. Agriculture tended to be left to its own devices : it did not, after all, increase the country's stock of gold and silver. Though it benefited as the prospering business community bought more of its products, its methods remained antiquated and its productivity low. In contrast, French manufactures began to dominate the world's markets, and French skill and taste started to accumulate that renown which they have never lost since. 'French glass attained a splendour and beauty which have never been surpassed elsewhere', wrote Voltaire in the middle of the next century when French cultural supremacy was unquestioned. 'The carpets of Turkey and Persia were excelled at *La Savonnerie*. The tapestries of Flanders yielded to those of *Les Gobelins*.'[16]

All the arts and crafts felt the impulse of Colbert's drive. He told Charles Errard in Rome to buy up for the king the best works of art that came on the market. 'We must act in such a way', he wrote to him in 1669, 'as to have in France everything there is of beauty in Italy.'[17] This was the period when Paris replaced Rome as the headquarters of European art, a shift symbolized by the failure of Bernini's visit to Paris in 1665. Colbert invited him to design the east front of the Louvre and then rejected his baroque curves in favour of Charles Perrault's classical colonnade. For Colbert was not only *Contrôleur-Général* of Finance and Secretary of State for the Navy, but also Superintendent of Buildings : the only responsibility of his in which Louis took a genuine interest. The king's extensive building programme at residences such as the Louvre, Marly, and Versailles, set to work armies of architects, painters, sculptors, and furniture makers. The strict gravity of this work imposed an aesthetic dictatorship on France, which was reinforced by the precepts of the various academies. The Academy of Painting and Sculpture was nationalized by Colbert in 1663, and here French artists were trained under the guidance of Le Brun, its director, who was first painter to the king. In 1668 the Academy of Rome was founded, where a dozen French painters could study the antique and Renaissance masters on the spot, as Poussin had done. There they would find, to quote the words of an Academy official, André Félibien, 'an inexhaustible source of beauty of design, in well-chosen attitudes, in subtlety of expression, in well-ordered folds of drapery, and in that elevated style to which the ancients raised Nature'.[18]

In 1671 the Academy of Architecture was founded; while in 1672 the Academy of Music gave the Italian, Lully, the monopoly in France of setting verse to music, thus assisting at the birth of French opera. And the first academy of all, the *Académie Française*, which Richelieu had organized as a private society under State protection (1635), was nationalized in 1671. Colbert gave it rooms in the Louvre and funds for its scribes, paper, pens, ink, heating, and so on. 'All the words of the language, all the syllables', wrote Racine, 'seem precious to us, because we look on them as so many instruments which must serve the glory of our August Protector.'[19]

The energy given out by the resurgent Monarchy thus impelled the arts as much as every other aspect of French life. The king galvanized into action all the varied talents of France, which in their turn devoted themselves to elevating his prestige. And at Versailles the system achieved its consummation. Louis decided that neither the Tuileries and the Louvre in Paris nor St Germain and Fontainebleau in the country were magnificent enough for the king of France; and he set to work to transform his father's little hunting lodge at Versailles into a palace worthy of the greatest power in Europe. The genius of Le Vau, Hardouin-Mansart, Le Brun, Le Nôtre, and all the craftsmanship that had been called forth and trained by Colbert's central planning, were concentrated on the creation of a town, a château and a park which would astonish the world. And all the other arts were at the service of Court life there. In 1674, for example, the final conquest of Franche-Comté was celebrated by a fête lasting six days, which included performances of *Fêtes de L'Amour et de Bacchus* by Lully and Quinault; *Alceste* by Quinault; *Le Malade Imaginaire* by Molière; and *Iphigénie* by Racine. And this pageant of music and drama ended with the greatest firework display ever seen.

The instruction given at the academies, and the training provided by the schools of the *manufactures royales*, were based on rules laid down in such works as Francois Blondel's *Cours d'Architecture*, or Nicolas Boileau's *Art Poétique*. Acting on the principle that 'the state knows best', paternal government extended to the whole of French cultural activity. Louis XIV was not only the father of his people but their school-master as well; and he did all he could to ensure that nothing was taught which might undermine authority and tradition. In this he was backed, or rather pushed from behind, by the Church and the Parlements. In 1671 he forbade the teaching of the new philosophy of Descartes at the University of Paris. In 1675 he wrote to the University of Angers to stop the Oratorians from giving a course on Descartes there. Aristotle, St Thomas Aquinas and Ptolemy were the authorities to lecture on, and not the men who were creating the new experimental science. The Faculty of Medicine, for example, had to manage without teaching the circulation of the blood: a restriction upon which Boileau composed a mock decree forbidding 'the blood to be vagabond any more, to wander or circulate in the body, under the penalty of being completely handed over and abandoned to the Faculty of Medicine'.[20]

The press was similarly disciplined. Nothing could be published without first passing the censor and obtaining the *'privilège du roi'*. Even Bossuet himself had to go through this process. But the most ambitious attempt of Louis to keep French thinking in leading strings was his religious policy, whose slogan was *'une foi, une loi, un Roi'*. 'Armies, councils, all human industry would be feeble means of keeping us on the throne', he wrote, 'if each one ... did not revere a superior power, of which ours is a part.'[21]

The Church

Though Christians were menaced by the external danger of empirical thought (the most insidious enemy they had ever had to face) they put most of their effort into internal debates. The issues involved were complicated and often abstruse; the theological distinctions drawn are sometimes invisible to the naked eye of today; and, in the complex politics of the various struggles, the number of variables was such as to render it hazardous to attempt a brief explanation. The chief elements were as follows. First, there was the king, who in religious, as in all matters, wished to be absolute master: to have no truck with heretics inside his kingdom, nor any nonsense from the Pope in Rome. Second, from his confessor Père La Chaize downwards, he was under the influence of the Jesuits. These were the shock-troops of religious orthodoxy and papal power; and Louis' relations with them were complicated by the fact that he loved the former and feared the latter. Third, there was the Pope (or Popes, for their policies varied). Their relations with the king were governed by their desire to retain or extend their power over the Church inside France, on the one hand, and, on the other, by their moves in the constant flux of international power politics. Fourth, religious orthodoxy was threatened in France by the Jansenists, an austere and puritanical reform movement. Jansenists were deeply convinced that only those who had received divine grace were predestined to salvation, and that the Jesuits and all their works were far too indulgent to human frailties. Fifth, there were the Huguenots, whom we shall reserve, as Louis did, for later treatment.

Overlapping the above 'parties' in the French religious quarrels, were two, not so much 'parties', as points of view: Ultramontanism and Gallicanism. The Ultramontanes regarded the Church as an absolute monarchy under the Pope, as the immediate representative of God on earth; and believed that

Frenchmen should submit obediently to papal orders. This point of view was supported by Jesuits, and by the *dévots*, those converts to mysticism and good works which the wave of revivalism washed up on the upper reaches of French society in the late seventeenth century. Gallicanism, on the other hand, stood for the rights of the French Church against papal interference. But there were at least two kinds of Gallicanism. First, 'episcopal' Gallicanism was a set of doctrines (largely worked out by the Sorbonne) that regarded the Church as a constitutional monarchy, in which Councils were superior to the Pope, and in which bishops received their authority direct from God, and not indirectly through the Pope. These Gallicans supported the king against the Pope. Second, the 'parlementary' Gallicans also supported the king against Rome and asserted the superiority of Councils over the Pope; but they differed from the bishops on the situation inside France. The bishops wished to govern the Church independently of the State through the Church courts; the Parlements asserted that the Church must be subordinate to the king's courts, i.e. the Parlements; and, like the English parliamentarians, they supported their arguments with a mass of historical learning of doubtful accuracy.

The king was usually a long-term Gallican, but was capable of being a short-term Ultramontane: it depended on how the religious issue fitted in with his total policy. There were times when he was prepared to use a Papal Bull in order to persecute the Jansenists; there were other times when he said that papal pronouncements had no regal force in France till the Assembly of the Clergy and the Parlements had ratified them. And as his policy twisted and turned so did that of all the other 'parties' involved; and, though Jansenists and Gallicans usually worked together (and were often the same men), there were times when Jansenists supported the Pope.

Broadly speaking, Louis harassed the Jansenists throughout his reign, except for the period of the so-called 'Peace of the Church' from 1668 to 1679. The basic text of Jansenism, Cornelius Jansen's *Augustinus* (1640), had been condemned more than once in Rome: and in 1653 five propositions from it were declared to contain heresy by the Papal Bull *Cum*

Occasione. The Jansenists, using a distinction probably first hit upon by Pascal (whose *Lettres Provinciales* were powerful propaganda for the movement), found a way of obeying the Pope but going on as before. The distinction was between *law* and *fact*: they agreed that they must accept the papal ruling (which was infallible) on the five propositions, but they denied that they were contained in the *Augustinus* – a question of fact, on which the Pope was not infallible.

On his accession, Louis intensified the persecution. In 1661 he got a General Assembly of the Clergy to give the Pope's ruling the force of law in France. The Jansenists resisted, including four bishops and the convents of Port-Royal-des-Champs, not far from Paris, and Port-Royal in the Faubourg St Jacques in the capital itself. Louis expelled their boarders and novices (1661); three years later the twelve chief nuns were expelled and the rest excommunicated; in 1665 the convent was placed under military guard and cut off from the outside world. In 1668, however, the pressure was relaxed. Royal diplomats got the recalcitrant martyrs to sign a form of words, which by not saying very much appeared to be a compromise. This 'Peace of the Church' was necessary because of Louis' war with the Pope; but in the 1680s the king began to give further turns to the screw. Port-Royal was forbidden to accept any more nuns, and its leaders were exiled. In 1709 the nuns were arrested and redistributed in brutal fashion among anti-Jansenist convents. In 1710 Port-Royal-des-Champs was destroyed, the dead dug up from the cemetery and the area ploughed over.

In the meantime, Louis' intermittent sniping at the papacy over such matters as the privileges of French diplomats in Rome rose almost to the level of an international war and religious crusade when financial stringency forced him to demand the extension of his right of *régale* to those fifty-nine dioceses where he still did not enjoy it. Louis would only promote bishops of Gallican sympathies; the Pope would only institute Ultramontanes. By 1688 there were thirty-five dioceses without a bishop. But already before this, the issue had levitated itself, as bread-and-butter matters do, into a question of principle. In 1682 the Assembly of the Clergy issued the Declaration of the Four

Articles, drawn up by Bossuet. First, it recalled the doctrine of the two powers and said that, in temporal matters, kings were not subject to the Church. Second, it affirmed (or implied, since the wording was imprecise) the superiority of General Councils over the Pope. Third, it affirmed that the Pope must not infringe the ancient national customs of the French Church. And, fourth, it declared that in matters of faith the Pope's rulings could be amended by the Church if it did not agree with them.

This was the worst year of the quarrel; but before the dispute was settled French troops occupied Avignon, the French Church seemed likely to break away from Rome, Louis was in imminent danger of being excommunicated, while his ambassador to Rome actually was. At home Louis was at the height of his power, buoyed up by the patriotic sentiments which the struggle called forth in the French people, and strengthened by the backing, not only of the Parlements, but of the bishops as well. His policy of choosing his higher clergy from *robin* families now stood him in good stead, and the General Assembly of the Clergy, filled with the families of Colbert, Le Tellier and their like, was ready to eat out of his hand. 'We are so closely attached to Your Majesty', they wrote to the king in 1680 (after expressing their 'extreme displeasure' with papal policy) 'that nothing is capable of separating us from you.'[22] Louis' was a precarious eminence, however, for it was a dangerous game for a king to encourage such insubordinate thoughts in the minds of his subjects. In the 1690s the quarrel was called off, for Louis had bigger problems to solve: the War of the League of Augsburg (1688–97) and the economic crisis of 1693–94. In 1693 a vaguely worded compromise was arrived at with a new Pope. Louis got his way, more or less, over the *régale*, and he agreed to soft-pedal the Four Articles.

In the cut and thrust of his struggles with the Jansenists and the papacy, Louis was fighting, it could be said, a necessary war against enemies who were real threats to his absolute power. This was far from being true of his persecution of the Huguenots. The million and a half or so French Protestants had long been content with the religious toleration and civil equality guaranteed them by Henry IV's Edict of Nantes (1598); and with their business acumen and technical skill they were an asset to French life. They were strong in the west and south, in towns such as Caen, La Rochelle, Saumur, Montauban, Montpellier, and Nîmes or in the fastness of the Cevennes; and whether peasants or craftsmen, merchants or *officiers*, they worked industriously and worshipped regularly, as minorities do. But, to the king, they seemed a blot on his sovereignty and, to the Church, a slur on their evangelism.

In the early part of the reign intermittent harassing of the Protestants went hand in hand with desultory attempts to absorb them. Turenne, himself a Huguenot till 1688, took a leading part in the latter, which, however, came to grief as the persecution was intensified. Why Louis took the unwise decision to wipe out the Protestants is not entirely clear. He was certainly pressed to do so by the General Assembly of the Clergy in 1675 and again in 1680; and probably he felt that concessions to the evangelical zeal of his bishops were a necessary *quid pro quo* for the support they were giving him in his quarrel with the Pope. Moreover, to wipe out heresy in France would show the world that he was the Most Christian King, in spite of his struggle with the Pope, who would thus appear in a bad light.

He became increasingly susceptible to arguments of this nature in his maturer years when he became a *dévot*. His conversion was brought about by Père La Chaize, his confessor, and Madame de Maintenon, his confidante – formerly the governess of the royal bastards, and from 1683, his secret wife. 'Perhaps the king is not so far away from thinking of his salvation as the Court thinks', she wrote in 1679;[23] and during the following year Louis began to take his devotions seriously, and to be more influenced by the *dévots* who surrounded him, not only the genuine ones, but also the servile kind who fitted La Bruyère's definition: 'A *dévot* is one who under an atheist king would be an atheist.'[24] In this new frame of mind, the king was anxious to atone for the sins of his youth and for his attacks on the head of the Church. As Spanheim, the envoy from Berlin, put it, he was in a state of 'blind resignation to the

directors of his conscience';[25] and the persecution of the Huguenots gave him, as the more cynical Saint-Simon put it, 'the
pleasure of easy penance at someone else's expense'.

Whatever the explanation, the Huguenots were increasingly
harassed. The wording of the Edict of Nantes was narrowly
interpreted by the magistrates in order to keep Protestants out
of public office. Every attempt was made to convert them:
terrorism, on the one hand, and bribery, on the other. From
1674 the Historiographer Royal, Pellisson, ran a *Caisse des Conversions*, offering cash payments to converts which 'prepared
their hearts for the work of grace'. In 1681 the Intendant of
Poitou hit upon the idea of the Dragonnades, which later became general, and Huguenots were subjected to the worst
social persecution that the seventeenth century could devise:
they had troops forcibly billeted on them. Finally, in 1685, on
the grounds that the large numbers of conversions had rendered
it redundant, the Edict of Nantes itself was revoked. A month
before, the king had written: 'I cannot doubt but that it is the
divine will which wishes to use me to bring back to his ways all
those submitted to my orders.'[26] And after it was over, Bossuet
called it 'the miracle of our day', which 'God alone could
perform'.[27]

After 1685 it was illegal to be a Protestant. In Angers, where
the gates of the Huguenot cemetery had for long been used as a
garbage dump, a crowd of 5,000 or so stood in the pouring rain
singing the *Te Deum* while the Protestant church was demolished by workmen and boys.[28] Elsewhere, torture, rape, and
whipping drove untold numbers illegally to seek refuge abroad,
possibly as many as 800,000. The damage to French commerce
and industry was intensified by the gains that accrued to countries such as Britain, Brandenburg, and the Netherlands which
took the refugees in. Saint-Simon later called the revocation 'an
immense internal wound'. 'It depopulated the kingdom', he
wrote, 'and transported our manufactures and nearly all our
commerce to our neighbours and further beyond; made other
States flourish, at the expense of ours, filled their countries
with new towns and other habitations, and gave to all Europe
the frightful spectacle of such a prodigious people proscribed,

fugitive, naked, wandering about without any crime, looking for refuge far from their home-land.'[29]

But the Huguenots were not obliterated nor the Jansenists silenced; and their complaints swelled the streams of criticism which began to spring up in the second half of the reign. Louis' system of government was effective over men's actions, but not over their thoughts. It could call into being roads and canals, châteaux and port-installations; it could organize law and order and economic growth; but it could not prevent Frenchmen from admiring Descartes or hating Jesuits. In fact, its very success in the one sphere was the cause of its failure in the other.

Armed Forces

The account of Louis' successes, however, is not yet complete; and mention must be made of what was, perhaps, his most crucial victory over the past: the subordination of the armed forces to the State. This development, which Le Tellier, the Secretary of State for War, set in motion after the Peace of the Pyrenees (1659), and which his son, Louvois, continued in more brutal fashion till his death in 1691, was another aspect of the victory of the crown over the nobility. In the past, the king's army, raised by a mixture of feudal clientage and commercial contracting, was hardly a State institution at all. The important commands were in the patronage of three great noble magnates, the colonel-general of the infantry, the grand-master of the artillery, and the colonel-general of the cavalry. Under Louis XIV these were subordinated to the Secretary of State for War and their powers extinguished. Henceforth, the two Le Telliers with their staff of civilian Intendants controlled appointments, promotions, recruitment, discipline and provisioning. Much of the old system remained. Recruits, for example, were still raised by colonels and captains by their own methods on payment of a lump sum by the state; but the Intendants were now on the spot to see that they fulfilled their contract and that all concerned were present and ready for action. In line with this policy, the old military governorships in the provinces and in the border fortresses were gradually shorn of their tendency to become centres of revolt against the crown. These posts were still given to great nobles, but only on a three-year tenure; and, in any case, their holders were encouraged to live in Versailles, leaving the real military-governing to be carried out by lieutenant-generals appointed by the king.

By methods such as these Louis XIV and his bourgeois ministers subjected to the will of the State its chief opponents, the nobility of the sword. Their origin, their purpose and their pleasure was armed combat. 'At the first rumour of the war in Flanders', wrote the king, 'my court swelled in an instant with an infinity of gentlemen asking me for employment.'[30] Throughout his reign he provided them with plenty of work, but, under him, they fought as and when he required; in other words, they drew their swords, not against one another, nor against the king, but against his enemies, whether peasants at home taxed to the point of insurrection, or states abroad that lay in the path of French aggression.

Foreign Policy

The place of France in the jungle of international power-politics was intimately bound up with the process of centralization just described. Without this stiffening of the administrative framework the king would have been unable to raise the money or the men, or to impose common action on his diverse provinces and classes, in order to repel the enemies that lurked on every frontier. Absolute monarchy made those foreign victories possible, which in their turn strengthened the prestige of the crown: thus dictatorship and defence stimulated one another till the one turned into the tyranny from which the Ancien Régime could never recover and the other into that aggressiveness against which the rest of Europe soon kept itself permanently on guard.

Attack is often the best form of defence, and when a French king launched an attack on a neighbour the motive could have been either to anticipate an intended invasion, by securing a more defensible frontier, or to satisfy old-fashioned territorial greed. It is not possible to pin-point the moment of change, but the former motive operated before the Thirty Years' War and certainly the latter held the field throughout most of Louis XIV's reign. The Treaties of Westphalia (1648) and the Pyrenees (1659) mark the end of a century or so of the encirclement, invasion, and possible dismemberment of France by the powerful Habsburg houses of Austria and Spain. From now on, France had the initiative, and Louis used it, at first, to round off his frontiers, by occupying the gateways on the great military roads into France, so as to deny them to the enemy and to use them as bases from which to launch attacks abroad. In 1648 France strengthened her eastern border by gaining the sovereignty of the three bishoprics of Metz, Toul, and Verdun (occupied by the French for almost a century already) and of all the property that the Habsburgs owned in Alsace, either as Emperor or head of the house of Austria. In 1659 Louis plugged a gap in his southern frontier by securing Roussillon and Cerdagne in the Pyrenees; he advanced his north-eastern border by gaining Artois; and he strengthened the east by adding a few more fortresses in the Lorraine area.

There followed eight years of peace during which Colbert and Le Tellier laid the foundations of French reconstruction – so long frustrated by war and revolution. But Louis' ambitions soared higher than mere frontier gains. Like his contemporaries, he saw Europe as an ordered hierarchy of kingdoms under a head; but unlike them he saw himself, not the Emperor, as the head. 'The Kings of France', he said, 'hereditary Kings ... can boast that, without exception, there is not in the world today a better house than theirs, nor a more ancient monarchy, nor a greater power, nor a more absolute authority.'[31] His mouth began to water at the prospect of the declining kingdom of Spain. Philip IV died in 1665, leaving everything to his already moribund heir, Charles II, the son of his second wife. Louis' queen was the eldest daughter of Philip's first wife, and certain clauses in the Treaty of the Pyrenees had been so skilfully drawn up by Mazarin's men, that Louis' lawyers were able to concoct quite a reasonable claim, first of all to sections of the Spanish inheritance (such as the Netherlands and Franche-Comté), and eventually to the entire kingdom itself. Louis' foreign policy from 1667 to practically the end of his reign is the story of the glories, and then the miseries, of perpetual diplomacy and war in pursuit of these lands.

Louis was no soldier, but he was well served by a magnificent army led by generals of the calibre of Turenne, Condé, Luxembourg, and Vauban. He loved to project the image of the great captain, to 'show the whole earth' as he once put it, 'that there is still a king in the world'.[32] Nothing pleased him more than making his solemn entry into an enemy fortress once it had been safely reduced by his troops, as, for example, in 1667, when he appeared before Lille, surrounded by his court (which included the queen and his two mistresses in the same coach) and received the keys of the city from the chief magistrate, to the sound of tolling bells. 'Warfare', he wrote later, 'is the most worthy and the most agreeable occupation of sovereigns';[33] and, beginning in 1667, he gave France thirty-three years of warfare out of the forty-eight that remained of his reign. But at the end of that period he admitted to his great-grandson: 'I have loved war too much.'[33]

The earlier years, when French diplomats and generals called the tune of European politics, saw glory indeed as France swallowed up slices of the Spanish Netherlands (Treaty of Aix la Chapelle, 1668), grasped Franche-Comté (Treaty of Nijmegen, 1678), and absorbed the remainder of Alsace, including the independent city of Strasbourg (1681). But already the other great powers were steadily making the counter-moves in what was becoming the regular European ritual: the formation of a coalition to 'preserve the balance of Europe' whenever any one power seemed to be aiming at 'universal monarchy'. As early as 1667, Europe was affronted by a French publication called *The just claims of the King to the Empire*, which declared that Louis XIV had the right to take most of Germany, which was the 'patrimony and former heritage of French princes and had been possessed by Charlemagne as King of France'.[34] But Louis' actions spoke louder than these words. 'Such conduct', wrote Archbishop Fénelon in his famous *Lettre au Roi* (probably 1694), 'has reunited and aroused all Europe against you.'[35] In 1688 William of Orange became also King of

England, and the massive coalitions he organized to fight the two long wars (the War of the League of Augsburg, 1688–97 and the War of the Spanish Succession, 1702–14) proved that Louis had over-extended himself. The financial resources of London and Amsterdam, combined with the Anglo-Dutch fleets and the troops of such powers as the Emperor, Savoy, Brandenburg, and other German princes, ultimately wore down, though they did not overwhelm, French military prowess. At the treaties of Utrecht (1713) and Rastatt (1714), Louis retained his conquests in Franche-Comté and Alsace, and got his grandson accepted as Philip V of Spain.

On the face of it, Louis left France bigger and safer than he had found her, but at a certain price, the exorbitance of which gradually became clear during the remainder of the Ancien Régime. Abroad, Great Britain already possessed those two sources of strength which enabled her in the end to bring France to her knees: the mixed monarchy of the Hanoverian succession and a firm foot in the door of world commerce. At home the damage is more difficult to compute, but the two chief items in the account were the chronic indebtedness of the crown and the early trickles of a flood of criticism which together overwhelmed the Monarchy in 1789.

Criticisms

This criticism was one of the important aspects of French life which foiled the effects of absolutism under the Ancien Régime. However firm grew the grasp of the French administration (the most sophisticated in Europe), ideas constantly slipped through its fingers and percolated downwards from a handful of intellectuals to the educated classes in general. This critical attitude was fed from a number of sources. The *Parlementaires* had not abandoned their Frondeur belief that royal centralization was uprooting ancient liberties embedded in the fundamental law of the nation. The Jansenists had not ceased to regard the king's Jesuit advisers as the agents of anti-Christ, and, in the lower orders of the clergy, were increasingly adopting the view, known as *Richérisme*, that God had given authority in the Church, not to the Pope alone, nor even to all the bishops, but to the body of the clergy equally.

Such complaints against established authority were particular cases of a more general shift of outlook which affected the thinking of a sufficient number of Louis' subjects as to amount to an intellectual revolution. Broadly speaking, following in the wake of the scientific discoveries of the seventeenth century, of Descartes' provisional doubt, and of Locke's reliance on observation, a habit gradually formed of subjecting old ideas to searching examination and rejecting those that were not in accordance with reason and experience. And experience was steadily being enlarged, not only in observatories and laboratories, but also by the historical investigation of past non-Christian civilizations and by the geographical exploration of contemporary non-European societies. 'Doubt is the beginning of science', wrote Jean Chardin, who published a travel book on Persia in 1686, 'he who doubts nothing, examines nothing; he who examines nothing, discovers nothing.'[36] Scepticism about the past combined with optimism about the future; relativism gained on absolutism; nature replaced divine providence as the motive force of the universe; and social utility replaced ancient tradition as the criterion of moral judgement. The destructive powers of these ideas were not fully exploited till the Enlightenment of Louis XV's reign, but, under Louis XIV, complaints circulated in sufficient profusion, whether in print, in manuscript or by word of mouth, to make it impossible for the authorities to suppress them.

The work of the censors increased in difficulty as more and more printed matter was smuggled in from the freer presses of Holland. Pierre Bayle, a native of Foix but a resident of Rotterdam, published his *Dictionnaire Critique* there in 1692. It was an explosive list of the intellectual errors of mankind, whose fall-out contaminated orthodoxy for many years to come. 'There was not a single line of it that was a clear blasphemy,' wrote Voltaire, who knew about this kind of thing, 'and which, however, did not lead to unbelief.'[37]

'It is the purest delusion', wrote Bayle, 'to suppose that because an idea has been handed down from time immemorial to succeeding generations, it may not be entirely false.'[38] This was the frame of mind in which critics now began to cast a cool eye on French society and government, undazzled by the fading rays of the Sun King. Jean de La Bruyère, whose *Les Caractères ou les moeurs de ce siècle* (1688) went through nine editions in as many years, was a member of the Condé household, and thus close to the centre of high society. He subjected the French way of life to merciless criticism which was all the more effective for being only implied. His description of the perfect sovereign, for example, was on the surface a eulogy of Louis XIV, and only as an afterthought did readers see how far below the ideal their king fell. La Bruyère was one of the first to show a genuine concern for the sufferings of the lower classes; and he asked the seditious question: 'Was the flock made for the shepherd or the shepherd for the flock?'[39]

Less ambiguous were the criticisms of Archibishop Fénelon, though it is doubtful if the king ever saw the *Lettre au Roi*, which he wrote in Cambrai, in retirement from court intrigues. His censures gained in force from his well-known religious zeal, intellectual distinction, and noble character. 'This prelate', wrote Saint-Simon, 'was tall and thin, well proportioned, with a big nose, eyes from which fire and intelligence poured like a torrent, and a face unlike any I ever saw and which, once seen, could never be forgotten.... His whole personality breathed thought, intelligence, grace, measure, above all nobility. It was difficult to turn one's eyes away.'[40] Fénelon was unsparing in his exposure of the evils of France:

For about thirty years your principal ministers have shaken and overthrown all the former maxims of the State in order to heap up to its height your authority, which had become theirs because it was in their hands. They have talked no longer about the State or about laws, they have talked only of the King and his good pleasure. ... You have destroyed half the real power inside your State in order to make and defend vain conquests outside. Instead of drawing money from these poor people, you should give them alms and nourish them. The whole of France is nothing more than a great poorhouse, desolated and provisionless.[41]

The complaints became louder as the crisis of the War of

Spanish Succession deepened, bringing slaughter and devastation, famine and disease, when the army had to be employed to
shoot restive peasants as well as to hold back Marlborough. In
that worst year of 1709 a song was heard sung in the streets of
Dijon, whose translation goes: 'The grandad is a braggart, the
son an imbecile, the grandson is a mighty coward, oh! what a
lovely family. How I pity you, you French, to be under such a
rule. Take my tip and do as the English have done.'[42]

Sufferings of the People

'In Paris', wrote the Duchess of Orléans, 'the dearth is frightful; everywhere one sees people sink to the ground, literally
dead from famine; ... everywhere one hears nothing but complaints and groans, from the greatest to the feeblest.'[43] In
Cambrai, close to the fighting, Fénelon wrote to the Duc de
Chevreuse: 'If the king came to the frontier ... he would see
the discouragement of the army, the disgust of the officers, the
relaxation of discipline, the contempt for the government, the
ascendancy of the enemies, the secret revolt of the people, and
the irresolution of the generals when it is a question of striking
a great blow.'[44] There was talk of calling the Estates-General;
in Paris, the people began a march on Versailles, but were
barred by troops at the bridge at Sèvres.

The sufferings caused by war and slump were exacerbated by
the mounting tyranny of the régime, as military necessities
forced the king to give a few extra turns to the screw of
despotism. The constant need at Versailles was more and
more revenue to compete with the seemingly inexhaustible
supplies possessed by the governments of Great Britain and
Holland. French financiers, unlike their British counterparts
after 1688, had insufficient control over, and thus insufficient
confidence in, the government to permit the formation of a
Bank of France. Thus French ministers had to use their
ingenuity in getting more out of the existing taxes and invent-
ing new ones as well. The *taille* and the *gabelle* were collected
with increasing ferocity, sometimes with the use of dragoons;
the General Assembly of the Clergy and the provincial estates

were browbeaten into voting larger *dons gratuits*; provincial nobles and bourgeois were urged to buy newly created offices in the administration as presents for their children; even letters of nobility were offered for sale. Two new taxes were introduced, the *capitation* (1695) and the *dixième* (1710), which were ultimately foisted off on to the non-privileged as an addition to the *taille*, though their object had been to equalize the tax burden. Even the registration of births, marriages, and deaths was taxed – though not without resistance, in Périgord and Quercy, for instance. There, according to Saint-Simon, 'the poor and many other humble people baptized their children themselves without taking them to church, and got married secretly by mutual consent before witnesses'.[45]

This burden of taxation thrust the lower classes permanently down to the borders of starvation; and in years of bad harvest desperation drove them to insurrection. The year 1709 was especially bad, and the Intendant of Montauban feared for his own safety. He reported to Versailles that he knew the names of the leaders of the revolts in Quercy, but they were so numerous that it would have been dangerous to make examples. 'There were nine of the most guilty', he wrote, 'whom I hanged on the spot. That had its effect. I cannot think without trembling that I saw thirty thousand armed men in Quercy, Cahors besieged for ten days, and myself surrounded in my carriage by a detachment of that good company, from whom I extricated myself by a miracle.'[45]

Thus did the French people encounter the machinery of absolutism. The Intendants increased in numbers and powers; and they stayed longer in the areas, where, for good or ill, instead of merely supervising the work of the *officiers*, they actively deployed the full powers of the crown. Except in Paris and Lyons, they controlled (after 1683) the election of mayors, whose real importance in running municipal affairs was in any case brought to practically nothing in 1692, when the position of mayor was made into an *office*, capable of being purchased by socially ambitious bourgeois. The towns lost their independence and in all important matters were drawn into the Intendant's administrative net. John Law, coming from

laissez-faire Great Britain, was astonished at their powers, and
called them 'vice-roys'. As bureaucrats will, they enlarged their
staffs of *sous-délégués*, paradoxically often taking into their pay
the very *officiers* whose duties they were supposed to supervise.
Similarly, the Intendants-General of Police and the Inspectors
of Manufactures spawned assistants; while, at the centre, the
expanding bureaucracy occupied the two long buildings on
either side of the fore-court at Versailles when the Court
established itself there from 1682 onwards.

And the more complex grew the machinery of government,
the more difficult it was to control from the centre, where, in
any case, the quality of the leadership deteriorated in the second
half of the reign. After the deaths of Colbert (1683) and
Louvois (1691), the impulse slackened. Even though the
ministers were often the sons and nephews of the first great
generation, they had not the same force. Nor had they the
same power. The king himself in his declining years took a
greater part in policy-making; and thus the Monarchy became
in practice what it was supposed to be in theory – to use the
words of Bossuet 'this immense people united in a single person, a secret intelligence locked up in a single head and
governing the whole body of the State'.[46]

Unfortunately, Louis was no longer the man he had once
been, either in wisdom, judgement, or patience; and France
was now governed by an irascible old man, increasingly
influenced by Madame de Maintenon and her party of *dévots*
and Jesuits, who goaded him into the unwisdom of persecuting
the Jansenists once more. He got the Pope to publish the Bull
Unigenitus (1713) which condemned 101 propositions contained
in *Moral Reflections on the Testament*, a popular, Jansenist
devotional work, published by Pasquier Quesnel as long ago
as 1671. This stirred up Gallican sentiment once more, most
strongly expressed by Noailles, the Archbishop of Paris. And
what was more serious, it stimulated the Parlement of Paris to
oppose the royal will for the first time since Louis' personal
rule began. They declared themselves unable to receive the
Bull in France. Louis summoned their leaders to Versailles
and cried: 'When I say *I wish,* I must be obeyed.' But to no

avail, for the Parlement was supported by everyone who disliked the Jesuits: according to Voltaire, practically the entire nation.

Thus Louis XIV, who died in the middle of this unsettled controversy, left behind very serious problems for his successors. The very success of his measures in his vigorous days created the problems that beset his declining years. As the architect of the French state, he had constructed a framework of government which gave protection, law, and order to the largest organized political unit in Europe. He set twenty million people on an accelerating economic, social, and intellectual evolution, which made them ever more difficult to govern, in spite of the ever-increasing complexity of the machinery of government. The over-ambitious foreign policy made matters worse, but the essential problem would still have existed without it: how to control from the centre a mounting array of institutions of government, themselves at grips with, and too often in the grip of, an ever more restive society. It is now necessary to see how the main social groups were evolving under Louis XIV and his successors.

France: Society in the Eighteenth Century

Nobility

The economic stagnation, punctuated by slumps, which characterized much of the seventeenth century and the first thirty years of the eighteenth, had a depressing effect on the nobility, except that minority of the *noblesse d'épée*, which cornered the sinecures in Church and State, along with that other minority, the *noblesse de robe*, who cornered most of the jobs. The remainder, the old-fashioned provincial nobility, who continued the traditional way of life in château and manor house, assembling perhaps for the winter season in the local capital, be it Rennes, Aix, or Dijon; who contented themselves with living off their rents and seigneurial dues, contemplating their family trees, sending off their sons to find honourable deaths in the king's service or onerous lives in the less sought-after bishoprics, even, in many cases, following the plough, hardly distinguishable from peasants – this important layer of society was in no way pleased with the progress of the Ancien Régime. The army reforms of Le Tellier and Louvois had undermined their military independence, Colbert and his Intendants were cutting down their political power, the upward thrust of the *robins* was eroding their social prestige, while the hard-faced bourgeoisie were foreclosing on their properties. 'The title of *gentilhomme compagnard*', said the Marquis de Mirabeau (one of the exceptions who were making their estates pay), 'has become practically ridiculous among us.... The name of provincial is an insult, and people of fashion are offended when one asks them from which province their family comes, as if to be Dauphinois or Poitevin was not to be French.'[1]

In the Beauvais area there was a regular turnover of estates throughout the Ancien Régime, as ruined gentlemen sold out to their bourgeois creditors: lawyers, usually, or merchants. All over France were nobles who had gone on playing the feudal knight too long in a period of relentless commerce. They and their forefathers had spent too much time in the saddle from the Wars of Religion onwards, and too little at their accounts; while archaic estate-management or plain extravagance completed their ruin. The accounts of the Comte de Tavannes in Burgundy show that, for his château at Beaumont in the early years of this period, he was spending 953 livres a year, while his income was only 483 livres. When Louis XIV called the nobility to the colours as his vassals, or demanded a tax in lieu, some of them wrote heart-rending excuses. 'Are you not really convinced that it is out of my power?' wrote Jean de Carvoisin to the authorities in 1692, who had been taxed at 200 livres. 'Must you know more about it? I have glory enough, and recognition of what I owe to my birth, to keep quiet about the state I am in for such a mediocre sum. If I could manage to borrow it, I would prefer never to talk about it. But where do I find a lender? and when do I pay it back?'[2]

The foreclosing bourgeois bought lands, lordships, and offices; and soon their descendants replenished the ranks of the nobility. Some even completed the cycle by eventually crashing themselves, as did Nicolas Tristan of the Beauvaisis in 1762, whose bourgeois ancestor had put the family on the road to nobility over a century and a half previously. And when the nobility of the *bailliage* of Beauvais met together in 1789, of the fifty-eight who were there in person, only ten came from families who had been gentlemen in the days of Henry IV, about twenty came from outside the area, while as many as twenty-seven were descendants of Beauvais cloth merchants of the seventeenth century.

Thus the provincial nobility maintained itself all through the Ancien Régime, even when bankruptcies were common, by steady recruitment from below. But many avoided the pitfalls, and adapted themselves to the modern world by managing their estates in a bourgeois manner, especially in the last quarter of the eighteenth century. A study of the districts round Toulouse, Bordeaux, and Rennes has shown the nobles there to have been by no means in a state of bucolic decay. They were producing for the market, keeping careful accounts, appropriating common land, clearing the waste, and so on. They were also collecting feudal dues from their tenants in a much more rigorous way; but as these represented only a fraction of their total income (about eight per cent round Toulouse, and five per cent near Bordeaux), this pressure on tenants seems more like commercial exploitation than the 'feudal reaction' it used to be called.

Whatever their economic circumstances, the provincial nobility were a conservative force in French life, in the sense that they clung firmly to their privileges in the face of the expanding State – whether their social prerogatives as members of the Second Estate, or their local rights as inhabitants of a province, especially in those districts where they could use the Provincial Estates as a bulwark against central interference. Their privileges united them with the great nobility of the Court; but otherwise they had little in common. When Louis XIV eliminated clientage, and assembled the magnates round him at Versailles, he drove a wedge between the Court and Country nobility which weakened both. 'I should like to pay you a visit', wrote the Comte de Preux to his sister the Marquise d'Esclavelles, 'but to live in Paris I would have to be your valet. We have 10 to 12,000 livres revenue. With that one cuts a poor figure if one is a count or a baron. However, if you visit me, we will be high and powerful seigneurs.'[3]

The Princes of the Blood and the great feudal nobles, whether kow-towing to the king at St Germain, Fontainebleau, and Versailles, or amusing themselves in the salons and gambling houses of Paris, were somewhat more tame than their ancestors of the Frondes. As baroque sweetened into rococo, so the king humbled the mighty by making them hold the sleeve of his night-shirt as he retired to his chamber, or exhausted them by sending them off every year to fight his battles on the frontier. The elaborate ceremonial, which formalized every activity of the monarch from his *lever* to his *coucher*, bathed him in religious awe; and at morning chapel at Versailles the Court sat on the benches with their backs to the altar and their eyes on the king, high up on the balcony.

Thus employed, the Court nobility were absentee landlords, squeezing their tenants to pay their gambling debts, and always on the look-out for well-paid sinecures from their sovereign. It was a way of life inimical to their political judgement and moral sense. Madame de Maintenon, who spent many years at the very centre of it, said: 'I witness every kind of passion, trea-cheries, meannesses, insensate ambitions, disgusting envy, people with hearts full of rage, struggling to ruin each other, a thousand intrigues, often about trifles. The women of today are insupportable, with their immodest garb, their snuff, their wine, their gluttony, their coarseness, their idleness. I dislike it all so much that I cannot bear it.'[4]

As she and Louis grew old together, the moral tone at Ver-sailles coarsened under the leadership of the next generation of rulers. One of these was the Duke of Orléans, about whom his mother wrote in 1712: 'My son is not by nature inclined to drunkenness, but he often keeps very bad company and he imagines it is a kindness to play *the old rascal* with them; he gets totally drunk, and, once taken with wine, he no longer knows what he is saying or what he is doing.'[5] And when he became Regent on Louis' death, the Court took its tone from him. 'Among people of quality', wrote his mother at that stage, 'I do not know a single couple who love one another and are faithful.'[6] And later in 1722 she described how the Marquises de Polignàc and de Sabran would not allow two duchesses (d'Olonne and de Brissac) to place themselves above them at a ball at the Hôtel-de-Ville. 'You want to place yourselves above us in order to show off your fine clothes which came from your father's shop', they said. The Duchesses retorted: 'If we are not from such a good family as you, at least we are not whores like you.' 'Yes, we are whores, and we really want to be, for it amuses us.'[7]

Marriage to the daughter of a *robin* or bourgeois family was a not uncommon way out of ducal indebtedness; acquiring lucrative appointments was another. The Duc d'Aumont did both. He married Le Tellier's daughter, Madeleine (Louvois' sister), and then with her money got himself appointed First Gentleman of the Bedchamber and Governor of the Boulonnais.

Another brother of Madeleine's became Archbishop of Rheims, a very profitable appointment; while Colbert's son acquired perhaps the juiciest plum of them all: the Archbishopric of Rouen, the capital city of Normandy. And as the Ancien Régime progressed, practically the whole of the upper ranks of the clergy were manned by courtiers. Cardinal Dubois, the Regent's chief minister, was Archbishop of Cambrai as well as the head of seven abbeys, receiving from these sources alone (according to Saint-Simon) 325,000 livres a year. The abbot of Saint-Nicolas at Angers (brother of the Marquis de Mostuejouls) drew 50,000 livres a year from his valuable clutch of benefices, consisting of two abbeys, one priory, and a canonry.[8]

Clergy

These ecclesiastical courtiers were rarely seen in their dioceses or abbeys, for appointments and promotions depended not on zeal in the field but on keeping the right people sweet at Versailles. Once, when a provincial lady at a Court ceremony exclaimed, 'Isn't this Paradise here?', a wit replied: 'Oh no! Up there, there aren't so many bishops.'[9] There were assiduous exceptions, of course, such as Nicolas Choart de Buzenval, who followed his two uncles as Bishop of Beauvais (1650–79), reformed the diocese and turned it into a Jansenist stronghold. But as the eighteenth century wore on, the bishops increasingly became simply a branch of the higher nobility who happened to dress in purple. The Archbishopric of Strasbourg, for example, descended from generation to generation, with a cardinal's hat thrown in, from uncle to nephew in the Rohan family, who were much more likely to be found in the salons of Paris or at their château at Saverne than in the cathedral at Strasbourg. Cardinal de Bernis noted in his *Memoirs* that by 1720 it 'was no longer considered well-bred to believe in the gospels'.[10] Episcopal chores were carried out by *grands-vicaires*, though the bishops themselves occasionally gave a hand, as when Grimaldi, the bishop of Le Mans, confirmed 4,750 people at one go in the courtyard of his castle.

The upper clergy was thus an annex to the nobility; but in

one respect it was more powerful than the main body. For the Church was a corporate entity in a way that the nobility as a whole could never be, so long as the Estates-General and the Assembly of Notables ceased to meet. Coming together every five years in the General Assembly of the Clergy to vote, among other things, the *don gratuit* (the clerical contribution to the royal revenues), the First Estate was able on occasion to dictate to the crown. Where would royal absolutism have been if the other two estates had been similarly organized?[11]

Certainly, the nobility never for one second accepted the loss of political power which had been their lot since the Frondes; and before Louis XIV was dead their counter-attack had begun, which ultimately precipitated the Revolution. Under the ageing king, the aristocratic opposition added its nostalgic notes to the chorus of criticism already mentioned. In the writings of the Duc de Saint-Simon, the Duc de Beauvillier and the Duc de Chevreuse, it dreamed of a return to some fictional noble past, before the centralizing machinery manned by the 'vile bourgeoisie' had been invented. They saw France as a federation of provinces, with Governors instead of Intendants, and regular Provincial Estates tempering the power emanating from Versailles. Under the Regency which followed Louis' death, they had their opportunity. The old king's will had restricted the powers of the Regent in favour of the royal bastards, and the Regent, the Duke of Orléans, made a deal with the Parlements, whereby they broke Louis' will; in return, he allowed them to send in Remonstrances again. Thus, for the first time since Louis' first assumption of power, the Parlements had the opportunity of exercising political leverage. The nobility also had a short period of office in the central executive itself. Ministers were replaced by a series of councils, manned by nobles, who now had the chance of enacting the reforms they had dreamed of while in opposition. But dreams they remained. After a few years of amateurish misrule, the councils were replaced by ministers once more, and France was ruled by the methods of Louis XIV for the rest of the eighteenth century. The nobles had clearly demonstrated their unfitness to govern. They lacked the training, the industry, and the drive:

for far too long they had left these matters to the Robe.

Co-operation with the *robins* in making use of Parlements as organs of resistance to monarchy, which was the only hope left for the old nobility, was rendered difficult in the first half of this period by the contempt in which they held their upstart colleagues. Saint-Simon went so far as to write a *Refutation of the Idea of Parlement being the first body of the State*, in which he scorned them as members of the Third Estate, who, though they had bought judicial offices, could never escape from their 'essential baseness'. Already archaic when they were expressed (1716), these views had no future as the *robins* advanced in wealth, prestige, and power. Under Louis XIV, even, the top *robins* of all – those who crossed over to the king and became Intendants and ministers – were acquiring estates, and founding dynasties, soon to be hard to distinguish from those of the *noblesse d'épée* itself.

Colbert and Louvois left about ten million livres each. The former married three daughters to dukes; the latter possessed the *hôtel* Louvois in Paris, and a great property at Saint-Germain-en-Laye, quite apart from the Château of Ancy le Franc in Burgundy, which was built according to the Renaissance design of Primatice, and in addition to the magnificent palace at Meudon, which his widow exchanged with the king for Choisy and 900,000 livres in ready cash. Under Louis XV, the process continued. D'Argenson graduated from being Lieutenant-General of Police into the high office of Keeper of the Seals. Of his two sons, one, the Marquis, became Secretary of State for Foreign Affairs, while the other, the Count, became Secretary of State for War.

These ministerial families fused more and more with the *noblesse d'épée* in Paris and Versailles, though *robin* wives were not presented at Court. There was the same process of inter-marriage and integration lower down the scale, and in such provincial capitals as Bordeaux, Toulouse, Dijon, or Rennes. There the acquisitive gentlemen of the robe were buying up the châteaux of improvident aristocrats, building the town houses and theatres which still adorn such cities, forming literary academies, commissioning statues and paintings, and even writing books, like Bordeaux's most famous *Parlementaire*, Montesquieu. Around Dijon, in the Côte d'Or, it was the *Parlementaires* who were buying up such vineyards as the religious orders let fall, and who were classifying for the first time those now celebrated wines at Gevrey-Chambertin, Vougeot, and the rest.

In manners and morals, though not so strait-laced as they had been in their great Jansenist days, the *Parlementaires* were less frivolous than their colleagues at Court and took the lead in the Parlements in persecuting Protestants and censoring free-thinkers, much to Voltaire's disgust. As the eighteenth century advanced, they became the sword and buckler of conservatism; and, though in their clashes with the crown they talked the advanced language of liberalism, their only concern was to protect property and privilege from attack. The more intimately they co-operated with the nobility of the sword, the more firmly did they close the door to aspiring members of the bourgeoisie. They solidified into a caste which blocked all avenues of advance, and impeded that steady clamber up the social ladder by peasants and bourgeois, which had so invigorated French life.

Bourgeoisie

Though it was the bourgeoisie who organized the dissolution of the main elements of the Ancien Régime in 1789, this class should not be thought of as a coherent body of rising capitalists. In eighteenth-century France, the term 'bourgeois' applies to such a diversity of competing social and economic groups that it becomes a hindrance to understanding unless its wide coverage is realized. At the top of the scale, where their wealth enabled them to build private *hôtels* in Paris, acquire country houses, estates and lordships, and marry their daughters to impoverished gentlemen, the bourgeois are not easy to distinguish from the nobility. The banker, Antoine Crozat, for example, who received the monopoly of trade with Louisiana for fifteen years (1712), and who, along with Bernard, another Paris banker, and Magon, the Saint-Malo shipowner, ran the Guinea Company, which had the royal privilege of transporting

African Negroes to America, lived like a lord in one of the most splendid *hôtels* in Paris, till he actually became a lord – as the Marquis du Châtel. His brother, Pierre, was a patron of the arts of European reputation, whose Dutch and Venetian paintings had a formative influence on Watteau. His grand-daughter, at the age of fifteen, married the Duc de Choiseul, for twelve years Louis XV's chief minister. She became one of the few wives whose morals were above reproach in that ill-famed court; and without her money, Choiseul would probably never have achieved his high office.

What the Crozats were doing in Paris, other bourgeois were doing in the provinces. Marseilles sent four or five ships to the West Indies in 1719: in 1750 she was sending eighty. Joseph Hugues there made a fortune estimated in 1789 to be worth eighteen million livres. At Bordeaux, where the population practically trebled during this period, the merchants were constructing their splendid avenues and squares and town-houses, which are still worth seeing. In Nantes, they took it into their heads to bleach their linen at Saint Domingue, across the Atlantic.

Similar to these princes of banking and overseas trade were those who made fortunes by manipulating the finances of the crown, which was sinking ever deeper into debt. The three Pâris brothers, for example, reputedly the sons of a humble father who kept an inn on the road from Lyons to Grenoble, reaped their first harvest out of victualling the armies in Louis XIV's later wars. The youngest, Pâris Du Verney, penetrated the inner circle of government finance under the Duc de Bourbon, who ruled France after the Regency (1723–26). Du Verney fixed this deal with the aid of Bourbon's mistress, Madame de Prie, herself the daughter of a financier and wife of a marquis. 'I do not believe that a more heavenly creature ever lived', wrote Saint-Simon. 'She possessed something more than beauty,' wrote Duclos; 'her whole person breathed seduction.'[12] Whatever her gifts, Bourbon was her slave, and Du Verney flourished.

Later, after various vicissitudes, including a spell in the Bastille, he rose to even greater financial power through the good offices of another well-endowed daughter of the bourgeoisie, wife of a *Fermier-Général* and mistress of the king: Madame de Pompadour. 'You unite all the arts, all the tastes, all the talents for pleasure', said Voltaire to her.[13] And with the help of her talents Du Verney grasped unofficial control of government finances during the central period of Louis XV's reign. Behind the scenes, he helped to make and break governments; and during the Seven Years' War had an influence on war policy, as well as on appointments in the high command.

If Pâris Du Verney was the king of government finance, there were quite a few princes not far below his level. The *Fermiers-Généraux*, for instance, about forty in number, made in the region of 50,000 livres a year farming the indirect taxes. They formed companies which advanced large sums to the crown and received in return the right to collect the customs duties or salt duties in a certain area. And when the contract was renewed every six years they had to find 300,000 livres as a *pot-de-vin* for the *Contrôleur-Général des Finances*, as well as 4,000 a year for the man-of-straw in whose name the lease was officially signed.

The big bourgeoisie thus made its fortune out of finance and commerce. At this stage there were not many great industrial fortunes; and, though there were huge manufacturing enterprises such as the Van Robais textile works at Abbeville or the royal factories like the Gobelins at Sèvres, most industrial production was still carried out in small workshops. The capitalists, who organized the production in such centres as Amiens, Rouen or Beauvais, buying, for example, the raw wool, seeing it through the various processes of manufacture, and then marketing the finished lengths, were essentially merchants. Industry was lower in status than commerce, as is clear from the large textile city of Beauvais, where weavers who managed to expand into buying and selling did not carry on weaving once they had achieved a footing in commerce – though they still 'finished' the crude woollen cloth which the local peasants had woven, or bleached their linens.

If the bourgeois of Beauvais are any guide, a post in the bureaucracy still conferred high status, as well as providing a modest return on the capital invested. Generally speaking, it was the well-established merchants, not the newly rising ones, who bought themselves an *office* in the local *élection*, or *bailliage*, *grenier de sel*, or *maréchaussée*. The value of all *offices* was tending to fall from the time of the Frondes onwards, this second grade more so than the bigger jobs in the Parlements; and merchants sank only ten or twenty per cent of their capital in them, putting the rest into land, lordships, house-property, and stocks. Every bourgeois (at any rate in Beauvais) aimed to own at least his own vines at the edge of the city, but preferably a country estate to visit during the summer, or a lordship with its feudal dues. The purchase of an *office* and a manor, then, were the signs that a bourgeois had 'arrived', that he could afford the enjoyment of local power and the luxury of local prestige. The next ambition would be the purchase of a post conferring nobility, a social ascent visible in the signature of François Foy, a member of a family who had their fingers in every bourgeois pie in the Beauvais area, and not a few noble ones as well. As an administrator in the *Bureau des Pauvres*, he began by signing himself 'F. Foy', then 'François Foy de Friancourt', and finally 'De Friancourt'.[14] 'If our grandfather Adam had possessed two sous worth of brains', the joke used to run in the eighteenth century, 'he would have bought himself a post as *Secrétaire du Roi*, and then all men would have been gentlemen.'[15]

It is impossible to detail in full the ranks of the bourgeoisie from this point downwards, but mention must be made of the professions, especially the law, whose practitioners were found at every level of the bureaucracy, or in posts with municipal councils, or acting as agents for property-owning magnates, be they nobles, bishops, or religious houses. Adrien Delahante, for instance, son of a surgeon, lived at Crépy-en-Valois, beginning as a notary, then becoming *procureur* in the *Présidial*, *directeur des fermes* for the Duchy of Valois, bailiff for various lordships belonging to the Maréchal d'Estrées, and so on. On his death in 1737 he left a big fortune and two sons: Adrien, who became Master of the Woods and Forests in the Duchy of Valois, and Jacques, who became a *Fermier-Général*.

Along with the lawyers must be mentioned the surgeons and apothecaries, writers and artists, and the masters of those ancient crafts which had not yet succumbed to the putting-out system of mass production run by merchants, but which still ran small establishments according to the rules of the gild. Some of these were very wealthy: for instance, the *orfèvres* (goldsmiths), who traded on the quay in Paris which still bears their name. At this level, also, must be included the middle ranks of the clergy, the *curés* of the towns and cities, who originated mainly from the middle classes. In Beauvais, with its twelve parish churches, seven chapters of canons, not to mention monasteries and convents, the same family names appear on the lists of the clergy as are found among the merchants, town councillors, and local office-holders. It was a comfortable way of making one or two thousand livres a year, not arduous even in a monastery. 'If I am on the road to heaven,' wrote a monk in Angers, 'I find the carriage very comfortable.'[16]

The bourgeoisie was thus a complicated layer of French society, and would appear even more so were there room to describe the various elements of the *petite* bourgeoisie: the smaller masters in the crafts, retail tradesmen, subordinate functionaries in the bureaucracy, and so on. For simplicity's sake, the bourgeoisie can be seen as divided horizontally into the big, medium and small bourgeoisies; but perhaps a more important division is the vertical one between the business half, on the one hand, and the *rentier*, *officier*, professional half, on the other; though complications inevitably arise from those men, and, more commonly, those families who were in both categories. Speaking very broadly, then, one can say that the businessmen were the dynamic elements and the *officiers* were the conservatives. Louis XIV, with the full support of all the bourgeoisie, clamped law and order on French society, stimulating economic growth. Then there came a stage when business took on its own momentum, and the Colbertian bureaucrats, who had hitherto been pushing the economy from behind, now became a weight on its back. During the eighteenth century, especially during the boom conditions between 1730 and 1770, and even more during the depressed period after that, the winds of economic liberalism blew in from the great ports, and stirred up the whole of French business. Private enterprise demanded the dismantling of mercantilism and the reform of government. This could only be achieved by the elimination of the privileged of every description who hindered economic progress, whether they were clerics whose half-empty monasteries occupied the best sites in the centre of so many French towns, or the monopolistic gild-masters whose antiquated regulations delayed the full flowering of capitalism, or that vast army of functionaries who cluttered up the customs and excise, and the courts of law.

Though there were other strains and stresses, this was the main tension in the bourgeoisie, between business and privilege, between what has been called a 'rising' and a 'falling' bourgeoisie.[17] And the latter, prevented from rising into the caste-ridden nobility, worried by the fall in the value of their *offices*, threatened by the economic power of upstart merchants, and haunted by the vast powers which the State would have to assume in order to rationalize the Ancien Régime, was the class which carried through the Revolution, once the nobility had given sedition its first impetus.

Peasants

At the point where the bourgeoisie shades off into the peasantry, classification becomes difficult, for a minority of the peasantry, in possessions, income, and style of life, were hardly distinguishable from the bourgeoisie, and, in fact, have been styled the 'rural bourgeoisie'. For present purposes, they will be included among the rural classes.

The peasantry owned about a third of the land in France as a whole, though the proportions varied from province to province, and village to village. In Normandy, Brittany, and Poitou, for instance, they held a fifth; in the south, about half. According to an enquiry carried out in the *Élection* of Beauvais in 1717, on the instructions of the Intendant of Paris, the peasants held about forty per cent of the land, the bourgeoisie about thirteen per cent, the Church and the nobility about twenty-two per cent each.[18] The term 'owned' must be qualified. In practice, the peasant had his land in full hereditary possession (except for a minority of *mainmortables* in eastern provinces, in whose case the property could revert to the lord on failure of heirs, among other restrictions). On the other hand, from the strictly legal point of view, the peasant still held his land from his lord and still had to pay quit-rent (variously called *cens*, *champart*, etc.) to the lord, as well as heavy fines when the land changed hands (called *lods et ventes*). Moreover, the lord had various rights over the peasant which could be extremely oppressive. Day to day law suits were tried in the lord's court; he possessed the hunting and fishing rights, could charge road and river tolls, controlled weights and measures, decided when the harvest or the grape-picking should begin; and, what the peasantry found most oppressive of all, had the monopoly of the wine-press, the mill, the oil-mill, the oven, and the market.

In addition, of course, the peasant paid dues to the State and the Church. He paid the *taille*, the *capitation*, and, later, the *vingtième* to the king, as well as the various excises like the *gabelle*. Moreover, he had to draw lots for military service, carry out compulsory road work and help with military transport, while to the Church he paid his tithe – a tenth of his produce.

The peasantry were not, any more than the bourgeoisie or nobility, a homogeneous class, but were a hierarchy of subgroups. In the Beauvaisis, where the social structure has been minutely studied, a village of a few hundred inhabitants consisted of one or two *laboureurs* or *gros fermiers*; five or six medium *laboureurs*; twenty or so smaller peasants owning a small parcel of land, renting some more, and doing industrial work of some kind; and twenty to fifty families of *manœuvriers*, in that area often wool or linen weavers.

To begin at the top, the *laboureur* possessed at least two horses and a plough; in other words, he could plough – hence his name. On an average, he owned about twenty-five acres and leased another farm of about the same size; and he probably would not possess more than eight cattle, five pigs, and thirty sheep. Some of the poorer *laboureurs* took on a second occupation such as butchery or haulage. On the other hand, a minority of them grew quite wealthy by becoming *gros fermiers*; that is to say, by leasing properties of 200, 300, or 400 acres from noble or ecclesiastical landowners. An even smaller number grew extremely rich by becoming *receveurs de seigneuries* as well; that is to say, agents collecting feudal dues for a lord, or tithes for an abbey: or, in districts where the Church was lord, both at the same time. Nicolas Caron of Coudray-Saint-Germer, near Beauvais, left seventy acres when he died in 1672. Sixty-eight years later, his grandson, both *receveur* and *fermier* of the Abbey of Saint-Germer, owned over 250 acres, apart from what he leased. This upward thrust continued, and at the Revolution, the Caron family were in the position to buy the Abbey farm – and they possess it still.

While such wealthy *laboureurs* might easily be confused with the bourgeoisie, the poorer ones are difficult to sift from the medium-level peasants – called *haricotiers* in the Beauvais area and some other districts. The better off families in this group owned perhaps ten acres and rented ten more. Possessing no horses, they perhaps owned a mule, three or four cattle, two or three pigs, and ten or so sheep. Only in good years could they feed their families; while a mediocre or a bad harvest brought indebtedness or starvation. For half the year they had to make ends meet by weaving, tailoring, carpentering and so on. Roughly on the same level as these were the *vignerons*, who usually worked very small parcels of land.

Not counting the paupers and vagabonds (who have left scant records) the poorest people in the village were the *manœuvriers*, possessing, or perhaps sharing with another family, a one-roomed cottage with a loft, a little garden, and maybe two and a half acres of land, and leasing about the same amount. They owned no livestock except a starved cow grazed along the edges of the lanes, four or five chickens, perhaps a pig, and usually three or four sheep. In the Beauvaisis and other northern areas, when a peasant leased land additional to his own, he rented it (*fermage*); but in the centre and south, roughly the area where cattle were used for draught purposes, share-cropping (*métayage*) was general, the tenant giving half or a third of his harvest to the landlord. In Burgundy, so devastated and depopulated by the Spanish War of Louis XIV's minority, share-cropping was the rule at first, while it was necessary to colonize it with peasants who possessed no cash; but as the area prospered they changed over to *fermage*, from about 1750.

If these middling peasants, such as *haricotiers* and *vignerons*, could not live off the produce of their land, except in very good years, how much more necessary was it for the *manœuvriers*, with little or no land, to find work outside. They were the biggest social group in the village. In Pisseleu, near Beauvais, where they have been counted, they amounted to sixty-four per cent of the population.[19] They formed the rural proletariat, a general, and often mobile, labour force, hedging and ditching, carting, harvesting, grape-picking, hay-making, threshing, and generally performing the menial tasks for the *laboureurs*, and the social grades above that. It was a rare *manœuvrier* who was not in debt to a *laboureur* who had ploughed his lot for him, lent him seed, wood, and so on; and the *manœuvrier* paid his debts by hard work.

In some areas, seasonal migration took place: for many farmers would not have managed without temporary reinforcements of labour at crucial points in the year. The proletariat of Burgundy moved into Brie for the grain-harvest, back to Burgundy for the grape-harvest, and then further afield transporting wine. In Picardy the second occupation of the peasants was spinning and weaving.

The bare plain of Picardy – eighty per cent of it given over to grain in most places, with hardly any wastes, or meadows, or woods, or common-land, over-populated and under-productive – presented a terrible challenge to the lower orders. They were caught in the vicious circle of having to sow every possible square foot of land with grain. This made it impossible to keep animals, except a few sheep on the common and fallow, and so they had no manure for their already thankless soil, and nothing to fall back on or sell in a bad harvest. In this precarious sort of husbandry the *manœuvriers* could not have lived without the textile industry.

Equally, as a source of cheap labour, working in the villages, out of reach of gild regulations and Colbert's inspectors, this class was a boon to manufacturers all over France, whether the silk masters of Lyons, the stocking merchants in Languedoc, the linen-drapers of Saint-Quentin employing labour all over Flanders, Artois, Hainault, and Cambrésis, or, biggest of all, the great woollen clothiers of Amiens, Reims, Rouen, or Beauvais, employing vast armies of peasants across the north and west of France. A small number of peasants maintained an appearance of being self-employed manufacturers: that is, they bought their own raw material, wove their cloth on their own loom and then sold it to a merchant. But such brave spirits were very much at the mercy of the market. Take Louis Caillotin, for instance, who died in Luchy in 1681, leaving five acres of land, one cow, five sheep, and four hens, as well as an unfinished length of cloth on his loom. His assets as a weaver of serge, together with his livestock and next harvest, did not add up to the 200 livres he owed to a big wool merchant in Beauvais.[20] It only required one of those slumps which were so frequent before 1740 to reduce such producers to the level of the majority of the rural textile hands: wage-earners, pure and simple.

In the towns and cities, thronging with paupers, domestic servants, industrial workers and general labourers, the same precarious existence on the edge of starvation was the rule till the middle of the eighteenth century. The urban industrial workers were theoretically master-men who had gone through a form of apprenticeship, but, increasingly as the Ancien Régime proceeded, the gilds became controlled by little groups of rich masters who monopolized the positions of power and limited entry to their own children. The general mass of gildsmen was steadily reduced to the level of wage-earners, strictly controlled by their masters, the municipalities and the government inspectors, who together dictated the wages and hours and conditions of labour. When the price of bread was steady and wages were good, workers could subsist. They were in penury when bread doubled or wages were cut. In Beauvais the price of bread trebled in 1649, 1651, 1661–62, 1725; it quadrupled in 1693–94 and 1710; and as these periods of dearth were usually accompanied by industrial depression, the lower classes were confronted by this inordinate cost of living at a time of low wages or unemployment.

In his diary, Le Caron, business agent for the diocese, thus describes their plight in April 1694:

One sees nothing any more at Beauvais but an infinite number of paupers, languishing from hunger and want, and dying in the squares and streets, in the towns and in the country, from lack of bread and from dearth. Having no occupation and work, they have no money to buy bread, and thus they are dying miserably of hunger.... Most of the poor, to prolong their lives a bit and to appease their hunger a little, for lack of bread eat unclean and tainted things, such as cats, the flesh of skinned horses thrown into the gutters, the blood from slaughtered bulls and cows which flows into the stream, offal, guts, intestines and other such things.... Another group of poor eat plants and roots which they boil in water, such as nettles and other similar plants, and all that adulterates the human body ... Some, impelled by hunger, steal and rob, and others go and dig up broad beans and spring corn in order to eat them.[21]

In cases where bodies were not so weak from hunger and minds so entirely preoccupied with the search for food, riots frequently occurred. In the terrible winter of 1709 crowds began to pillage the shops at the Porte Saint-Martin in Paris, and Marshal Boufflers and the Duc de Gramont only succeeded in pacifying them by throwing them money and promising to inform the king. 'The fear of lack of bread has agitated the people into a fury,' wrote Desmaretz, nephew of Colbert and now *Contrôleur Général des Finances*, the same year. 'They have taken up arms in order to carry off corn forcibly; there have been riots in Rouen, Paris and in nearly all the provinces; they have been waging a kind of war which has only ceased while they were busy with the harvest.'[22]

The reigns of Louis XIV and XV were punctuated by riots of this sort, in the countryside as well as the town, especially when wartime taxation, conscription, and requisitioning clamped extra fetters on a peasantry already desperate from hunger or fear of hunger. In 1662, 6,000 rebels rose in the Boulonnais; 600 were killed, wounded or taken prisoner; and of the 3,000 arrested, 1,200 were tried, of whom all the able-bodied men over twenty were broken on the wheel or hanged, except the 400 best specimens, who were sent to man the oars on the king's galleys. In 1664 Béarn was aflame; in 1670, the Vivarais; in 1674, the Bordeaux area; while in 1675 about 20,000 Breton peasants rose up, forcing the gentry to place themselves at their head and demanding self-government for Britanny. Ten thousand soldiers were sent to winter quarters there that winter and proceeded to their terrible chastisement. 'The trees are beginning to bend over the main roads with the weight we have put on them,'[23] wrote the Governor, the Duc de Chaulnes. The revolt was suppressed, but the pillaging troops probably did more damage than the rioters themselves.

Catastrophes of this kind were a regular feature of the Ancien Régime till the better times began in about 1740. Till then the mass of the peasantry were little better than the beasts of the fields. 'We have seen with our own eyes', wrote a missionary from Saint Quentin to Vincent de Paul, organizer of relief during the Frondes, 'herds wandering through the fields, not herds of animals, but of men and women, searching like pigs for roots in the earth.'[24] To La Bruyère the peasants seemed like 'wild animals' also, who were to be seen 'scattered about the countryside, black, livid, and all burnt by the sun, clinging to their earth which they rummaged in and turned over with invincible stubbornness. They have a kind of articulate voice, and, when they get up on their feet, they display a human face, and indeed are men. They withdraw by night into lairs where they live on black bread, water and roots.'[25] In the Beauvais area, where the lives of the peasants have been examined so thoroughly and described so vividly, there is ample evidence to corroborate La Bruyère's remarks.

Here, the peasants were able to consume about forty-eight per cent of their crops, the rest going in royal taxes (twenty per cent), tithes (eight per cent), seigneurial dues (four per cent), seed and other farming expenses (twenty per cent).[26] Taking this into account, a peasant needed to cultivate at least twenty-five acres in a good year and fifty acres in a mediocre one, in order to produce what was then the modest daily ration of four kilograms of bread a day for a family of six. Since three quarters of the population had nothing like this amount of land, they must have lived in constant hunger, even when they were free from famine. And, as has already been mentioned, bad harvests were a regular hazard. Two in succession usually led to a third, if only because most of the seed corn had already been eaten. Disease and malnutrition would then cause the trebling or quadrupling of the normal number of deaths, putting ten to twenty per cent of the people into their graves. It was the death-rate of the adults which quadrupled: the normal infant death-rate was in any case thirty-five per cent, so that it was mathematically impossible for that to treble. But these crises did more than decimate the present population: they ensured a reduced population twenty-five years hence. For when the death-rate was at its height, the marriage-rate dipped towards zero; and judging by the two-thirds drop in births nine months later, so did conceptions. In the crisis of 1693–94, over the year as a whole, the village of Auneuil had twenty births instead of the usual forty; Meru had thirty-four instead of sixty; Mouy had thirty-nine in place of the normal ninety. Thus every few years there was an 'empty generation', a gap in the ranks both of parents and producers; and French population oscillated between twenty millions and thirteen millions. It is not surprising that economic stagnation was so frequent; nor is it strange that so much peasant land fell into the hands of the bourgeoisie (urban or 'rural') in this period.

France: The Collapse of the Ancien Régime

Boom and Slump

It now remains to outline the process whereby the social and political system of France under the Ancien Régime evolved into a mixture too ebullient for the old Monarchy to contain, producing problems too difficult for the most elaborate state in Europe to solve.

Behind all other developments lay economic growth. In the 1740s France entered into a new period of history: the sickly seventeenth century was finally over, and gone were the depressed prices and stunted trade, the slumps and the famines. Till 1776 the economy prospered as never before, with industrial production doubling, trade tripling and colonial trade quintupling. Prices steadily rose, stimulating new investment in every branch of the economy. Farming profits soared and rents rose, as grain, wine, wood, and wool fetched higher prices, turning the rural population into an expanding market for merchants and manufacturers. And inching prosperity steadily forward was the under-tow of rising population.

Between 1715 and 1789 it rose from roughly eighteen million to about twenty-six million, the biggest part of this rise coming after the mid century. Although such demographic changes are still something of a mystery, an important factor in France was undoubtedly the absence (after about 1740) of those famines which had periodically wiped out a third of the population, as well as seriously reducing marriages and conceptions. There were no 'empty generations' after 1750. The children who were born in these years and who grew into manhood under Louis XVI were the first in the modern era to have no first-hand knowledge of periodic famine and permanent near-starvation. The psychological effects of this can only be guessed at; but there is no doubt at all about their swelling numbers and their widening expectations as they began to press against the confines of the existing institutions. All the more galling, when it came, was the economic depression which set in after about 1776. This generation would never be content, as its ancestors had been, meekly to rummage in the kennel for offal, or grub in the woods for roots. Its sights were raised much higher, and it was made of sterner stuff.

Nobles

The most important effect of the boom conditions was to increase the income, and thus the political and social weight, of the chief rent- and profit-takers: the nobility, the financiers, and the businessmen. As Barnave wrote during the Revolution (1791), 'a new distribution of wealth brings about a new distribution of power'.[1] In the second half of the eighteenth century the nobility carried out a veritable counter-revolution, but no longer by using the methods of the Frondes. There was no question, now, of their taking to horse at the head of their dependants in order to hamper the Monarchy. Instead, in the most civilized manner possible, they insinuated themselves into all the places of power, and were in a position to capture the State rather than frustrate it. In this resurgence, Sword and Robe worked hand in glove. Inter-marriage and joint action made them scarcely distinguishable in the political sphere, as they pulled all the levers of power at Court and in the country. They more or less monopolized the higher posts in the armed forces and the Church. They packed the benches of the Parlements and the Provincial Estates. By 1789 they dominated those instruments which Louis XIV had created to subdue them: the ministries at Versailles and the Intendances in the provinces.

Moreover, they were coming closer together in manner of life. The Sword was going into business: collecting feudal dues more efficiently and exploiting their timber, coal and iron. The Robe was beginning to enjoy the aristocratic *douceur de vivre*. 'A young magistrate', wrote a contemporary, L. S. Mercier, 'fears nothing so much as to be known for what he really is.

He talks horses, theatre, women, racing, battles. He blushes to admit a knowledge of his profession.'[2] The nobles were united by riches and by politics, and they co-operated to oppose reform or (what was the same thing) the reduction of their privileges. On the other hand, there were rifts beneath the surface which in the end prevented full co-operation, and which, perhaps, chiefly account for their ultimate political ineptitude: such a contrast to their smoothly operating counterpart across the Channel, whose power in the state they envied so much. Jealousies and suspicions, snobberies, and rivalries abounded. The Sword had all the prestige, but the Robe did most of the work. Of Louis XVI's thirty-six ministers, thirty-five were noble; but only three came from old feudal families, while twenty-six came from the Robe. The magistrates of the provincial Parlements objected to the pretensions of the Paris Parlement to represent the nation at large. 'The provincial parlements', wrote a leading *Parlementaire* from Normandy, 'are always discontented with the tone of superiority of that of Paris.'[3] Moreover, a further gap was widening between all of these, on the one hand, and the impoverished provincial nobility, on the other: like the gentry of Beauce who proverbially stayed in bed while their breeches were being mended, or those seven nobles of Poitou who appeared at the elections of 1789 dressed as peasants.[4]

The Bourgeoisie and Clergy

Thus, the united front which the nobility presented to all royal attempts at reform was so full of cracks that it collapsed before the onslaught of the bourgeoisie. This class, whose advance in the modern era had been due to the piece-meal accumulation of the properties of noble and peasant, was deeply affected by the changes of the late eighteenth century. The boom conditions widened the gulf between the businessmen and the office-holders. The former grew rich, and thus more conscious of all the obstacles that prevented them from growing richer, more impatient of all the irrationalities of the Ancien Régime. They wanted to see the *laissez-faire* policies of the Physiocrats put into force, but at every turn they found their enterprise blocked by privileges: tax anomalies, gild regulations, municipal restrictions, provincial customs barriers, Church rights, noble immunities, Colbertian inspectors, and all the other jacks-in-office. The office-holders, on the other hand, depended for their existence on the very preservation of these same privileges; and in the eighteenth century they were not only under attack from reformers, but were also declining in income and hopes. Rising prices were not kind to their inelastic sources of income; the resurgence of the nobility was blocking their ascent up the social ladder; the boom conditions were rendering office a less attractive field for investment; and, the measure of all this, the value of *offices* was in steady decline.

Part of the trouble was the royal policy of creating new *offices*, not because they had a genuine job to do, but in order to sell them and raise the wind. The city of Angers possessed fifty-three courts of justice, some of them competing fiercely with one another. 'People seeking justice', wrote Joly de Fleury in 1763, 'sometimes have to spend two or three years going to court at great expense in order to find out which court it is they have the misfortune to plead their case in.'[5] The market for *offices* was flooded and their value cheapened. The value of the office of president in the Parlement of Grenoble, for example, fell from 110,000 livres in 1665 to 60,000 livres in 1764;[6] and the whole gamut of *offices*, right to the most humble, fell likewise. The professional bourgeoisie were not merely failing to rise, they were sinking; and they took all the more badly the social barriers which cut them off from the nobility, and the indignities to which they were liable to be subjected. Barnave, later a leading member of the National Assembly in the Revolution, never forgot how his mother was turned out of a box in the theatre at Grenoble by the Governor of Dauphiné – using four fusiliers for the job. Madame Roland resented for life being given a place in the kitchen in the château of Fontenay and not the dining-room. 'The old régime drove us to it (Revolution)', said Danton later, 'by giving us a good education without opening any opportunity for our talents.'[7]

Similar resentments were nourished by their cousins in that vast professional body, the lower clergy – the 60,000 or so *curés* and *vicaires* whose influence was so strong in the formation of public opinion among the masses. Drawn from the middle ranks of society, they opposed the upper clergy, exclusively noble. Scraping a living on a tiny stipend, they resented the idleness of their superiors, who enjoyed most of the tithes. Steadily Gallican they opposed the hierarchy, increasingly Ultramontane; steadfastly Jansenist they hated the Jesuits; restlessly *Richériste* they challenged the bishops with their near-absolute powers of discipline. Prelates could imprison Jansenists, for example, by *lettres de cachet*; according to Arthur Young, blanks of these could be bought, on which only the victim's name had to be inscribed. And if the clergy believed in democracy in the Church, it is not surprising that their flocks favoured equality in the State.

Lower Classes

To the lower classes fell a proportion of the growing prosperity of the third quarter of the eighteenth century, lifting them precariously above the famine level. But this experience only served to exasperate their resentments when depression again stifled the economy in the late 1770s. As Arthur Young frequently observed, French agriculture was out of date. Except in Flanders, fallow was the rule, sometimes every two, sometimes every three years. Some regions, especially in the mountains, produced a crop only once every six or seven years. Some estates (often belonging to nobles) were left completely uncultivated. 'In this thirty-seven miles of country, lying between the great rivers Garonne, Dordogne, and Charente, and consequently in one of the best parts of France for markets', wrote Arthur Young, 'the quantity of waste land is surprising: it is the predominant feature the whole way. Much of these wastes belonged to the Prince de Soubise, who would not sell any part of them. Thus it is whenever you stumble on a Grand Seigneur, even one that was worth millions, you are sure to find his property desert.'[8] Too few fields were put down to grass, resulting in a shortage of livestock; and thus a lack of manure, with its consequence of low yields. The number of mouths to feed rose steadily in the eighteenth century – but farming failed to increase its output in proportion.

Hunger, and fear of hunger, played a dramatic part in the violent episodes of 1789, but the peasantry were by no means of one mind over agricultural reform. Enclosure of the commons was supported by the lords, who, by the right of *triage*, received a third of the enclosed land, and demanded by the landless and semi-landless peasants, who hoped to gain plots of land thereby. It was opposed by the *laboureurs*, who, with their flocks and herds, depended so much on free pasture. For the most part this last group had their way. The changeover from communal to individualistic methods of farming was delayed, and the mass of the peasantry continued their precarious existence just above starvation level as a semi-agrarian, semi-industrial proletariat.

At the same time, their burden of dues grew heavier. The crown, pursuing extravagantly unsuccessful foreign ventures and sinking ever deeper into debt, levied higher taxes, the bulk of which fell on the peasants, since the rest of society was powerful enough to pass the load downwards. Moreover, the lords enforced their rights and collected their dues with increased efficiency, while the Church was no less business-like in the exaction of its tithes. To the peasants these seemed more burdensome and less just than the taxes they paid to the king; and when the last straw came in the form of the harvest failure of 1788, it was against their local oppressors that the peasants rose.

The peasant outrages of 1789 should not be regarded simply as attacks on the feudal system, for the Church and the nobility often employed bourgeois agents to collect their dues, and many lordships, in any case, were owned by members of the middle class, not nobles. The hostility was rather that of the exploited countryside against the blood-sucking town – a feeling that comes out in some of the *cahiers*, the lists of grievances that were prepared for discussion in the Estates-General. One of these, from Autun, talks of the smallholders as 'bent over the earth which they water with their sweat, from the rising almost to the setting of the sun, and from which they bring forth by the labour of their hands that produce, that abundance, which is enjoyed by the citizens of the towns'.[9]

The towns, of course, returned the hostility, for all ranks there favoured measures which could not avoid being prejudicial to the peasants: controlled prices and controlled conditions of sale for farm produce. Not that urban society was agreed on anything else. There was, firstly, the age-old struggle between master-craftsmen and their journeymen, in which the masters could usually rely on the town council, and, if necessary, the king's troops to enforce their will. Secondly, there was the struggle between these and the great merchant capitalists, whose output was based on mass-production by rural labour. Except in the luxury industries the craftsmen were fighting a losing battle both against economic trends and against economic opinion. As modernization left them behind, so they clung the more frantically to their out-of-date privileges and restrictive practices. The depression that began in the late 1770s, with its bankruptcies and unemployment, made incendiary material out of respectable craftsmen. The slump of 1788 set them aflame.

The Enlightenment

The prosperity of the eighteenth century promoted the evolution of French society and encouraged new hopes. The recession at the end aroused old fears. Both made the people ever more difficult to govern. The progress made by French thought had the same consequences, though the writers of the Enlightenment did not advocate rebellion. It is a logical error to suppose that, since Robespierre and Napoleon had read them, the *philosophes* were prophets of terror and tyranny. These misrepresentations, together with some others (such as that they were shallow optimists, soulless rationalists, with a naïve belief in the inevitability of progress), have been due to misunderstanding, or to the tendency of later thinkers to deduce exaggerated consequences from their moderate propositions, or simply to sheer prejudice.

The ideas of the Enlightenment were part of those expanding circles of ripples set in motion by the concepts which Descartes, Newton, and Locke dropped into European thought; and eighteenth-century French thinkers played the biggest part in Europe in advancing the frontiers of knowledge round its whole circumference. Great gains were achieved in mathematics, physics, chemistry, biology, and medicine; but, more to the purpose here, also in the human sciences such as economics, sociology, geography, and history. Newton's methods taught the students of society, as Voltaire wrote in 1741, to 'examine, weigh, calculate, and measure, but never conjecture'.[10] Every aspect of human life was investigated, using the scientific method: the accumulation of facts by observation and experiment, the formulation of general laws, the avoidance of resorting to final causes or mysterious essences, the refusal to construct abstract systems out of touch with reality. They gave up armchair speculation about Man, and turned to empirical observation of men as they existed, not in Society, but in different societies scattered over the face of the earth or throughout the length and breadth of history. Far from being philosophers ruminating in a vacuum, they were practical men: publicists who exposed particular evils, men of action who devised workable reforms. 'Our motto is:' wrote Diderot to Voltaire in 1762, 'No quarter for the superstitious, for the fanatical, for the ignorant, for the foolish, for the wicked and for the tyrants.'[11] The *philosophes* were informed, warm-hearted, tolerant, and humane; they fought obscurantism, bigotry, prejudice, and injustice. They believed that the world could be made a better place to live in, and that the sum of human happiness could be increased. They favoured equality before the law, humane punishments, the career open to the talents, proportional taxation, universal education.

They believed that men were the product of their societies, that their enjoyment of liberty and property depended on the rule of law. 'Just as men have given up their natural independence to live under political laws,' wrote Montesquieu, 'so have they given up their natural community of possessions in order to live under civil laws. The former laws gave them liberty; the latter, property.'[12] A comparative study of societies, they thought, would yield general sociological laws, in accordance with which societies could be changed and men's lot improved. In works such as Montesquieu's *De l'Esprit des Lois* (1748), Condillac's *Essai sur l'Origine des Connaissances Humaines* (1746), Diderot and d'Alembert's *Encyclopédie* (1751 onwards), Voltaire's *Dictionnaire Philosophique* (1764), Rousseau's *Contrat Social* and *Emile* (1762), the men of the Enlightenment broadcast their conviction that compassion and knowledge were more appropriate to the human condition than Christian resignation or reliance on Providence. In the place of the old criteria by which men had evaluted human affairs – whether the Scriptures or the Church, ancient laws or immemorial customs – they put forward, with the exception of one group, the yardstick of utility.

The exceptions were the economists, known as Physiocrats, who believed that societies, like the rest of nature, moved according to unchangeable, unbreakable, natural laws, instituted by the Supreme Being – the best laws possible. The founder of the school, Dr François Quesnay (physician to Madame de Pompadour and Louis XV) publicized his ideas in articles in the *Encyclopédie* and in his book *Tableau Economique* (1758). He believed that agriculture was the sole source of wealth, and that industry and commerce merely modified and distributed the products of the land, which alone would create new values. Thus the landed proprietors were the foundation of the economy. The cultivators came next, while the rest of society were a 'sterile class'. Landed property and the free use of it were natural rights guaranteed by the immutable law: hence the Physiocrats favoured reforms which cleared away all obstacles in the way of the individual pursuing his own interest – *laisser faire, laisser passer*. Thus they wished to liberate agriculture from seigneurial dues, common pasture, internal and external customs duties; and since lands alone created wealth, they said, land should pay the taxes. All this would have involved the destruction of private privileges as well as of the

Colbertian state – as one of their leaders, Turgot, found to his cost when he became *Contrôleur-Général* (1774–76) and tried to institute reforms.

All the *philosophes*, whether they were natural law devotees or not, judged everything by its impact on society. 'In order for something to be regarded as a good by the whole society,' wrote Vauvenargues, 'it must tend to the advantage of the whole society; and in order for it to be regarded as an evil, it must tend to its ruin: that is the great characteristic of moral good and evil.'[13] Such a remark, of course, can hardly be said to be philosophically unimpeachable; but for the most part the *philosophes* were not philosophers. They were more like 'little streams', to use Voltaire's phrase about himself, 'which are clear because they are not very deep'. They were men with an audience. They were out 'to change the general way of thinking', as Diderot expressed it in the *Encyclopédie*.[14] And they had a measure of success – though Voltaire had doubts about the effect of the *Encyclopédie*. 'Twenty folio volumes will never make a revolution', he wrote: 'it's the small, portable books at thirty *sous* that are dangerous. If the Gospel had cost 1,200 sesterces, the Christian religion would never have been established.'[15] But in spite of its size (seventeen volumes of text and eleven of plates) and its price (1,200 livres), it sold widely. By 1768, there were at least sixty copies in Dijon, for example; and in the following year Voltaire wrote: 'The trade in ideas has become prodigious. There are no good houses in Paris or in foreign countries, no château which does not have its library.'[16]

He was underestimating, for the new ideas spread beyond the walls of private libraries. They were broadcast in the endless discussions that took place in the fashionable salons, presided over by such hostesses as Madame de Graffigny, Madame du Deffand, and Madame Geoffrin, who brought high society and the intellectuals together on equal terms. 'A point of morals', said a character in one of Rousseau's books, 'would not be better discussed in a society of philosophers than in that of a pretty woman of Paris.'[17] The new thoughts were disseminated also by the public libraries that were accumulating in Paris and all the provincial cities. They were debated in the academies and reading societies that were springing up everywhere: at Orléans in 1725, Montauban in 1730, Clermont-Ferrand in 1747. The Bordeaux Academy heard a number of scientific papers read by Montesquieu, who founded a prize for anatomy there in 1717. In Dijon ninety-three members of the academy also belonged to twenty other academies in other parts of France, as well as to sixteen others in foreign countries.[18] It was the prize offered by the Dijon Academy in 1750 for the best essay on *Whether the revival of the sciences and the arts has assisted in the purification of morals* that got Rousseau started as a writer. And Aix-en-Provence had the fortune in 1786 to be left one of the richest libraries in Europe by the Marquis de Méjanes.

Though the mass of Frenchmen went on thinking as before, a powerful minority was converted by methods such as these to Enlightened views. The *Académie Française* elected Voltaire to membership (1746). It became good form to conduct experiments and demonstrate to astonished guests the fascinating properties of electricity. Ladies of the Court presented additions to Buffon's collection of animals and plants in order to get a mention in his *Histoire Naturelle*.[19] Intendants tried to put Physiocratic principles into action. To the plaudits of the audience, fashionable ladies suckled their young in their box at the Opera, because Rousseau recommended that babies should be fed by their mothers. As the century proceeded, the new ideas spilled deeper into the middle ranks of the bourgeoisie. At Beauvais in the seventeenth and early eighteenth centuries, the bourgeoisie had no consciousness that they formed a class, nor any fellow feeling with other bourgeois beyond the confines of the city walls. They possessed few books beyond *La Vie des Saints* and *Le Parfait Négociant*,[20] their political consciousness never rose above parochial quarrels between different families or gilds, or between the merchants and the *officiers*, or the town-council and the bishopric, or between the courts of the *bailliage* and the *élection*. For the States-General of 1614 they could not agree on a *cahier*, but sent two, one from the merchants and one from the *officiers*, each containing little but pettifogging, local complaints. Things were different when next the Estates-General met (1789), for in the last decades of the Ancien Régime the bourgeoisie had become politically emancipated, and could think as a class and on a national scale. The Enlightenment had taught them to pool their local greeds and grievances into a common fund of principle; and it imparted to them the political energy which is generated when materialistic ambitions are dressed up in the language of ideals.

Not that there was any question of revolution or any serious alteration of the Ancien Régime. Montesquieu and Voltaire were ardent admirers of Great Britain, but they did not advocate the importation of British institutions into France. 'Human laws', wrote Montesquieu, 'must be so fitted for the people for whom they are made, that it is a great chance if those of one nation can suit another.'[21] The Monarchy had a central place in all their thinking. 'It alone', went the article on *Political Economy* in the *Encyclopédie*, 'has discovered the real means of enabling us to enjoy all the possible happiness and liberty and all the advantages which man in society can enjoy on the earth.'[22] Montesquieu favoured stronger Parlements, Clergy, and Nobility in order to temper despotism; Voltaire denounced all privileged groups for blocking the reforms attempted by a benevolent crown. The *philosophes* not only disagreed with one another, they contradicted themselves – or appeared to. Out of the depth and complexity of Rousseau's rhetoric, men have found arguments in favour of despotism and democracy, socialism and private property, civilization and the primitive life, hedonism and puritanism. The Enlightenment was many-sided. It did not advocate any one doctrine – and certainly not the doctrines of democracy or rebellion. 'The progress of enlightenment is limited', went the *Encyclopédie*, 'it hardly reaches the suburbs; the people there are too stupid. The amount of riff-raff is always about the same ... The multitude is ignorant and doltish.'[23] The responsibility for stirring up mutinous sentiments and teaching rebellious arguments rests far more with the *Richériste* clergy (as has been shown) and with the Parlements, as will now be explained.

Louis XV

The economic, social, and intellectual development of France was making institutional change imperative as society outgrew its seventeenth-century framework. Plans for reform already existed; the ministers were available, willing, and able to carry them through; the kings wished to see them implemented: but the opposition to them was so powerful that neither Louis XV nor Louis XVI had the force of character to carry out the surgical operations necessary to save the Ancien Régime.

The law of averages was bound, sooner rather than later, to throw up monarchs who were less than adequately endowed to direct the kind of régime that Louis XIV had created. 'Absolute monarchical government is excellent under a good King,' wrote the Marquis D'Argenson in his *Journal* (1751), 'but who will guarantee that we shall always have an Henri Quatre? Experience and nature prove that we shall get ten bad ones to one good.'[24] Louis XV was likeable, good-looking, and affectionate, but lacking in firmness and industry, and, bored by the daily tedium of government, he was too easily swayed into unwise decisions by people he was fond of. During his youth, after the Regency (1715–23) and the rule of a Prince of the Blood, the Duc de Bourbon (1723–26), he left things entirely in the hands of his old tutor, Cardinal Fleury, who provided the best period of government that France enjoyed in the eighteenth century (1726–43). The peace and prosperity of Fleury's rule was a blessing for France, but a curse for the king's character. 'He has long formed his scheme of life', wrote D'Argenson in 1730, ' – amusing himself while he leaves the Cardinal to govern, knowing his probity and capacity; but when he goes he intends to shoulder the burden himself. We shall see if he keeps his word.'[25] According to Cardinal de Tencin, a prominent Council member after Fleury's departure, he did not. Tencin's sister described (1743) how her brother had tried to rouse the king from his 'torpor in regard to public affairs. . . . What happens in the kingdom appears no concern of his,' she wrote. 'In the Council he displays complete indifference and accepts everything that is suggested, his apathy leading him to follow the line of least resistance.'[26]

For the rest of his reign he went through the motions of being his own prime minister; but his two great passions, hunting and women, left him insufficient time and energy for the slavery involved. 'His sole vice was women,' wrote the Duc de Croy, 'but he thought that if he repented at death and received the sacraments, it was a trifle.'[27] In this respect he was a typical product of his age. 'Of twenty gentlemen at court', wrote the Paris lawyer Barbier in his *Journal*, 'fifteen do not live with their wives, and have mistresses. It is the same in Paris. So it is ridiculous to ask that the King, who is the master, should be worse off than his subjects and his royal predecessors.'[28] Unfortunately for France, Louis' position was not the same as that of his subjects. For he was responsible for the appointment of men and the choice of measures to govern the country; and too often these decisions were taken in a mistress's bedroom – a council chamber unlikely to encourage firmness of purpose, clarity of judgement, or appreciation of the national interest.

Ministers came and went; wise policies were tried and abandoned, foolish ones incompetently pursued, sometimes two contradictory ones simultaneously. 'His vanity is inconceivable but he cannot give it scope, for he is rightly aware of his incapacity. Though jealous of his authority he is weakly submissive to his ministers. He displays the most repulsive indifference to every sort of business and all kinds of people. His vanity makes him think it is enough to maintain his authority that from time to time he dismisses ministers in whom he has shown the fullest confidence by always following their advice.'[29] Thus wrote the Duc de Choiseul, who gave France a short period of forceful government from 1758 to 1770. He had risen to office partly through his friendship with Madame de Pompadour, and he fell partly through the enmity of Madame du Barry. His indigation with the king was intense. 'His character', he wrote, 'resembled soft wax on which the most diverse objects leave their trace.' Deep traces were left by Madame de Pompadour, who was his official mistress from 1745 to 1751, but who dominated his mind till her death in

1764; and by Madame du Barry, who was his mistress from 1769 till his death in 1774. In between these two, the private brothel of teenagers which he assembled in some houses in a quiet part of the town of Versailles called the Deer Park probably did not have much influence over high policy.

Foreign Affairs

Such constitutional arrangements were bound to produce a fumbling foreign policy, in which unsuccessful attempts were made to pursue aims in Vienna or Warsaw or St Petersburg which had little relevance to France's real interests. The War of Austrian Succession (1740–48) produced at Fontenoy (1745) France's last great military success before the Revolution, but little else of any consequence except an increased royal debt. The Diplomatic Revolution and the Seven Years' War saw French foreign policy groping about in central Europe, pursuing such archaic aims as attempting to get the Prince de Conti made King of Poland, concentrating on the wrong enemy in the wrong war. Had Prussia been defeated, France's ally Austria would have regained Silesia, and thus the greater profit. As it was, the Seven Years' War brought the shame of Rossbach (1757), where Frederick the Great proved how visionary were Bourbon hopes of European domination, and the loss of an empire in America and India, where Great Britain proved that she was now France's main enemy. Choiseul was one of the few who appreciated the situation. 'England is and always will be the enemy of your power and your State,' he wrote to the king. 'Her commercial greed, her arrogance and her envy of your power should warn you that many years must pass before we can make a lasting peace.'[30]

Inside France, one result of these foreign failures was to sap confidence in the régime. Those close to the king were only too aware of the spinelessness of their leader. 'The king', wrote the Abbé de Bernis, protégé of Madame de Pompadour and Minister of Foreign Affairs before Choiseul, 'is not at all anxious about our anxieties, or embarrassed by our embarrassments. There is no precedent of someone taking such a big risk with the same indifference as if he were playing a game of quadrille.'[31] But worse than this, the wars made ever more insoluble the key problem of the Ancien Régime: the bankruptcy of the crown.

Opposition to Reform

There was only one way to pay the crown's debts and to give the government a fair slice of the growing prosperity of the country, and that was to reform the tax-collecting system in such a way that taxes were paid in proportion to income. A rational system of this kind would have required the abolition of privileges. And since these were always stoutly defended by the Parlements, financial reform was impossible without judicial reform. This became the main theme of French politics from the Peace of Paris (1763) to the Revolution: repeated attempts at reform by wise administrators repeatedly frustrated by the privileged corporations: the Provincial Estates, the Assembly of the Clergy, the Assembly of Notables, the Provincial Parlements, and, leading them all, the Parlement of Paris. The tragedy of the Monarchy was that in these confrontations the privileged gained all the victories and the crown got all the blame. The king had enough power to do harm but not enough to do good. He ruled, not by the consent of the governed, but by the sufferance of the privileged; and in order to improve the lot of the former he had to reduce the power of the latter. Thus, to carry out reforms, he had to exert more power.

It was easy (so low was the prestige of the crown in the second half of the eighteenth century) for the Parlements to label this tyranny and to persuade the bourgeoisie that they were right; at least, until the very eve of the Revolution. Public relations was one of the many fields in which the Bourbon Monarchy failed.[32] The public image of the crown was built up from such elements as the futilities of Versailles, the failures of French arms, and the collection of taxes at the point of the sword. The public knew nothing of the blueprints for reform that Enlightened administrators had ready in the drawers of their desks. And so the paradox evolved that those who favoured progress and liberty could only achieve them by methods which appeared to be tyrannical; while those who defended liberty against this tyranny were the most selfish, obscurantist, and oppressive section of society.

To solve the post-war financial crisis, *Contrôleur-Général* Bertin issued new tax decrees in 1763, by which the *vingtième*, a war-time tax paid by all ranks, was continued in peace time. Plans were also announced for the reassessment of incomes. The Parlement of Paris published a remonstrance asserting that the crown had violated French law; the Parlement of Toulouse arrested the Governor of Languedoc; the Parlement of Grenoble tried to arrest the Governor of Dauphiné, but his troops protected him. The king gave way: Bertin was dismissed, the Governors replaced, the tax-decrees rescinded (1764). Writing from Nice the following year, Tobias Smollett pointed out the 'many marks of relaxation in the reins of the French government', and added that all the Parlements 'seem bent on asserting their rights and independence, in the face of the king's prerogative, and even at the expense of his power and authority'.[33]

Brittany, obstreperous as ever, took a leading part in this campaign. During the Seven Years' War, the Governor planned to give this backward province a road-system by introducing the *corvée royale*, the method used elsewhere in France whereby peasants worked on the roads for a number of days each year. The Estates of Brittany refused to countenance this invasion of their rights, and in so doing were supported by the Parlement at Rennes. The king arrested La Chalotais, the leader of the Parlement, and tried him before a special tribunal. The rest of the Parlements of France made a joint protest, and, in so doing, introduced a new and revolutionary concept into the battle. They claimed that, in the absence of the Estates-General, they represented the nation, and that there was one Parlement of France of which each separate Parlement was a 'class'. 'By the fundamental laws of the Monarchy the Parlement of France,' decreed the Parlement of Rouen, for example, 'the one and only public, legal and necessary council of the Sovereign, is essentially ONE, like the Sovereign whose council and organ it is, and like the political constitution of the State, of which it is the custodian and depositary.'[34]

For once the king gave back as good as he got. Early in 1766 his soldiers occupied the Palais de Justice and the ageing roué read the Parlement of Paris a speech saying:

I will not allow an association to be formed in my kingdom that would pervert the natural ties of duty and obligation into a confederation of resistance, nor an imaginary body to be introduced into the Monarchy to disturb its harmony. The magistracy does not form a body, nor an order separate from the three orders of the kingdom. The magistrates are my officers, charged with the truly royal duty of rendering justice to my subjects.... In my person only does the sovereign power rest.... To me alone belongs legislative power without dependence or division.[35]

He said a good deal more to the like effect; but he was not capable of holding back the mounting pretensions of the Parlements as they continued to educate the rest of the nation in the theory and practice of resistance to Monarchy.

By 1770 the deficit was so serious that Louis moved from words to action, and for the last few years of his reign screwed up enough courage to appoint reforming ministers and to see their measures through. In 1771 Chancellor Maupeou abolished the Parlements and created a new set of courts in their place. The gigantic area served by the Parlement of Paris was cut up and divided among six of these new courts. Judges were to be appointed and paid by the crown, instead of by the old system whereby they had bought their places and recouped by charging fees to the litigants. A start was made on reforming the entire judicial system, streamlining the antiquated procedure, disentangling the chaos of overlapping jurisdictions, and so on. The brain behind this was Maupeou's assistant, C. F. Lebrun, later a leading revolutionary, and Third Consul in 1799, who completed his reforms under Napoleon.

With the Parlementary obstructionists out of the way, the *Contrôleur-Général*, the Abbé de Terray, began the assault on the chief bastion of privilege, the fiscal system, with the object of redistributing the tax load in accordance with real income. He increased the yield of the *vingtième* and the *capitation* by initiating a new assessment of income in place of the old tax-rolls.

The squeals of the privileged were deafening. The king was traduced as a tyrant and a robber. Words such as 'natural rights', 'the constitution', 'the nation', and 'citizen' were bandied about. Parlementary supporters were rallied into a so-called Patriot Party; and as their ancestors had done in the Frondes, the Parlementary leaders brought the mob into action on the streets of the capital.

Louis XVI

Whether continuous doses of the Terray-Maupeou-Lebrun medicine could have saved the Ancien Régime will never be known, for with the death of Louis XV their régime ended. It is characteristic of the sorry plight of the Monarchy which the new king inherited that the only method available to him of appearing as a benevolent father of his people was to deal them a crippling blow. Louis XVI dismissed his grandfather's ministers and revived the old Parlements. The speech of Séguier at this 'august ceremony' did not augur well for the new reign. 'It can only add a new sanction to the immutable law of property and to the wise rule of irremovability in public offices,' he told the king. 'The first is founded on the unanimous consent of all Estates, the second has always been recognized by your august predecessors.'[36]

The young man who took this fatal step was timid, kindly, and anxious to please. He was a gluttonous eater, a skilful locksmith, a frigid husband, a conscientious father, an upright member of society. Unfortunately, his good intentions were nullified by his lack of drive. He had not the will-power to over-ride the opposition to measures which he thought were right; he too easily succumbed to the various pressure-groups at Versailles, not least that led by his headstrong wife, Marie Antoinette. When her brother Joseph II of Austria visited her in 1777, he was not impressed by the way the government was run. 'The court at Versailles is different; here rules an aristo-cratic despotism,' he wrote. '... The King is but an absolute lord in order to succeed from one slavery into another. He can change his ministers, but he can never become master of his business.... Petty intrigues are treated with the greatest care and attention, but important affairs, those which concern the state, are completely neglected.'[37] Caught in the contradictions of the Ancien Régime, Louis XVI backed reform and the opposition to reform at one and the same time.

Attempts at Reform

He chose as his *Contrôleur-Général* the Intendant of Limoges, Anne-Robert Jacques Turgot: aristocrat, Physiocrat, and free-thinker. Though an Enlightened reformer, he had joined the king's service by the usual corrupt methods. At the age of twenty-six, and after only a year's experience as a Councillor, he had bought a post as Master of Requests (the usual jumping-off ground for an Intendant) for 100,000 livres – though the regulations required six years' service as a Councillor, and thirty-one years of age at least.[38] The new minister had plans for modernizing the government and the economy on Physiocratic lines. His Six Edicts (1776) included measures to free the internal grain trade, abolish the gilds and convert the *corvée* into a money tax paid by all landowners. The Parlement of Paris refused to register such an attack on privilege, and issued a remonstrance full of phrases about 'the first rule of justice' and 'the fundamental rule of natural right', and condemning this 'project produced by an inadmissible system of equality, whose first effect would be to confound all orders in the state by imposing on them the uniform burden of a land tax'.[39] The king's will collapsed before this outcry and Turgot was dismissed (1776).

The point of no return in the downfall of the Ancien Régime had now been passed. The ministers who followed either made the financial position worse by leaving alone the constitutional issue of privilege, or exacerbated the constitutional struggle by attempting financial reform. In the meantime, the War of American Independence, in which France joined from 1778 to 1783, made a critical situation desperate. In giving military support to rebels against a legitimate Monarchy, Louis XVI taught France a lesson in resistance, by identifying it with patriotism. Moreover, the American colonists gave heart to all those whose feeling of alienation from the régime was pushing them in the direction of violence. They did not so much produce new ideals – for the radicalism which they preached was the common possession of all Europe since the republican tradition of seventeenth-century England had been circulated in the works of Locke and the writers of the Enlightenment. 'The most distinctive work of the Revolution', as R. R. Palmer has said, 'was in finding a method, and furnishing a model, for putting these ideas into practical effect.'[40] What the Americans did was to show the world how the people as a whole could set up a new form of government, as it were, from scratch, by means of electing representatives to a constituent assembly. Here was a model for those who repudiated both divine-right Monarchy and its enemy, the traditional institutions of the corporative State.

The American revolutionary war had a further consequence in France: it added a vast load to the royal debt. Turgot was succeeded by the Swiss banker, Necker, who financed the war by heavy borrowing. This method of dealing with the deficit by adding to it could have had no long-term prospect of success. Even worse was his *Compte Rendu* of 1781, which, by claiming that no debt existed, encouraged the king's opponents in their objections to paying more taxes.

Calonne, in charge from 1783 to 1787, introduced measures similar to Turgot's, including a new land tax to be paid by all classes and to be supervised by new provincial assemblies representing all landowners, noble, clerical or not. Side-stepping the Parlements, he got the king to call (for the first time since 1626) an Assembly of Notables, which turned down his proposals. Calonne was replaced by Brienne, who had been his chief opponent but who now adopted his programme, and spent a fruitless year exchanging abuse with the Parlements. His tougher colleague, Lamoignon, Keeper of the Seals, then repeated Maupeou's coup of 1771. His May Edicts (1788) took away from the Parlements their powers of verifying laws and taxes, and gave them to a new Plenary Court.

The Revolt of the Nobles

The resulting outcry has been termed by French historians the
révolte nobilaire. The Assembly of the Clergy not only voted
one of its lowest *dons gratuits* ever, but also added its Remonstrance against the crown's treatment of the Parlements. In all
the Parlementary towns, the magistrates brought the mob out on
to the streets. In Brittany, the Estates and the Parlement co-
operated to oppose the judicial reforms. One argument they
used was that such changes broke the terms of the original sixteenth-century union of Brittany with the crown of France.
Eventually, the Intendant had to flee to Paris. In Béarn, the
nobility reinstated the Parlement at Pau by force. In Franche-
Comté the Estates met for the first time since 1678; in Provence,
for the first time since 1639. At Grenoble, in Dauphiné, the
citizens refused to let their dismissed *Parlementaires* leave the
city, and the Lieutenant-Governor's troops were bombarded
with tiles and stones in the Rue Neuve. A general assembly of
deputies from the province, which met in the Tennis Court at
the château at Vizille ten miles away, resolved that the king
should be asked to 're-establish the Parlement of Dauphiné and
the other tribunals, to summon the States-General of the kingdom, and to assemble also the Estates of that province'.[41] The
Estates of Dauphiné had not met since they were suppressed by
Richelieu in 1628.

France seemed to be breaking up into her constituent parts;
and Versailles grew less and less able to control affairs, as
Intendants and Governors ceased to obey orders, or, if they
obeyed, failed to get obedience from their subordinates. Very
soon the king retreated once more. In July 1788 the States-
General was summoned to meet in May 1789. In August
Brienne and Lamoignon resigned. Necker returned to office,
repealed the May Edicts and recalled the Parlements. In September the Paris Parlement returned to the capital, registered
the Edict calling the States-General, and at the same time took
that fateful decision as to its composition which turned the
nobles' revolt into the Revolution proper.

The Revolution

The question was whether the three Estates, the Clergy, the Nobility, and the Third Estate, should meet and vote separately, or whether they should vote in common. If they voted together, the Third Estate would have a majority over the other two; if they voted separately, the Clergy and Nobility would be able to exercise a veto over the measures of the Third. When the Estates had last met in 1614, separate voting had been the rule, and the privileged orders had been in a position to block the ambitions of the Third, which represented the vast majority of the nation. In 1788 the Parlement ruled that the Estates would meet 'in accordance with the forms observed in 1614'. At once the mysterious spell which the nobility had been able to cast over the bourgeoisie and the rest was broken, for the claim of the Parlements to be defending the liberties of the nation against encroaching despotism was revealed to be patently false. The consequences unfolded themselves rapidly in the winter and spring of 1788–89, as the elections took place. The leaders of the bourgeoisie and of the lower clergy turned against the privileged orders all the arts of sedition that they had learned from the privileged themselves. At the same time, famine and unemployment made their contribution to the crisis by stirring into action the peasants and workers. 'A change has come over the public dispute,' wrote Mallet du Pan in January 1789, 'the king, despotism and the constitution are secondary questions: the main thing is a war between the Third Estate and the other two orders.'[42]

The year 1789 rapidly brought matters to a head, and in the course of a few months the pent-up grievances of a century burst upon the Monarchy. Louis XVI was called upon to choose between the fears and hopes, greeds and ideals, which had accumulated since the days of Louis XIV. He chose to support the old order. As Marie Antoinette put it: 'The nobility will destroy us, but it seems to me that we cannot save ourselves without it.'[43] When the moment came, the king threw in his lot with the privileged, and Church, Nobility, and Monarchy all went down together, and with them the Ancien Régime.

Russia: From Grand Duchy to World Empire

Main Trends

When Descartes wrote in 1648 that the smallest piece of the Palatinate was worth more than all the Empire of the Tartars or the Muscovites, he was expressing in a somewhat exaggerated form the small impact that Russia made on European affairs at the beginning of this period. It was the same ten years later (1657) when Louis XIV wrote a letter to Tsar Michael. He had already been dead and buried for twelve years. A century later, however, the situation was very different. The Seven Years' War revealed Russia as a great power, somewhat hesitant still in military matters, but capable of terrorizing the smaller states of western Europe, and immovably now a full member of the European states system. Frederick the Great, whose capital had been briefly occupied by Russian troops, was only too well aware of Russian potential. 'All future rulers of Prussia', he wrote, 'must cultivate the friendship of these barbarians.'

The century and a half of the Ancien Régime brought in Russia the hastening and completion of a hitherto long and slow historical process, the chief elements of which were as follows. Firstly, it was a process of the ingathering of Russian lands by an originally insignificant Principality of Muscovy, adding neighbouring principalities one by one to this nucleus; and then rolling back the Mongols, the Poles, the Lithuanians, the Turks, and the Swedes, who had carved up the area in medieval and early modern times. Secondly, it was a process of autocratic centralization without which the above history of mastication and digestion would have been impossible: indeed, the diner would have become the meal. Thirdly, as a means to both the reconquest of neighbours and the making of the absolute state, it was a process of adoption by Russia of the arts and sciences of western Europe. And, fourthly, largely as a result of the first three developments, it was the hardening of a social structure based on lord and serf. These four developments brought Russia into the first rank of the world powers by the end of the Ancien Régime, and enabled her to survive unscathed the French Revolution and the Napoleonic invasion. But it was also thanks to two of them, the autocratic form of government and the rigid social structure, that Russia fell behind again in the nineteenth century, when liberal institutions and rapid industrialization enabled the smaller powers of the West to treat the Russian giant as an equal, almost till our own day.

Early Growth of Muscovy

By the middle of the seventeenth century, these four processes were already long-established characteristics of Russian history. Territorial expansion, to take the first, had been going on since the late Middle Ages. The reign of Vasilii II (1425–62) began the revival. His son, Ivan III (1462–1505), and grandson, Vasilii III (1505–33) added forty thousand square miles to the fifteen thousand he left, including in particular the Republic of Novgorod, an enormous acquisition which brought Muscovy as far as the Urals, the Arctic Ocean, and within mouth-watering distance of the Baltic. In this period, too, Muscovy broke the power of the Mongols of the Golden Horde, and Ivan IV (the Terrible), who ruled from 1547 to 1584, took Kazan from them (1552) and then Astrakhan (1556), gaining control over the entire length of the River Volga as far as the Caspian Sea. As a result of these conquests, Ivan (the first Muscovite ruler generally to call himself 'Tsar') was able to increase the trade with Persia and the East, and begin that penetration of the Siberian spaces which brought the Russians to the Pacific.

The Time of Troubles

These gains were seriously jeopardized in the period after Ivan's death, known as the Time of Troubles (1584–1613), three decades in which Muscovy suffered in quick succession all the teething troubles so familiar to the other European monarchies in their period of emergence. Among these were Ivan's son Fedor, listless and childless; Fedor's wife's brother, Boris Godunov, who usurped the throne; revolts by the great magnates (boyars) against royal centralization; a resurgence by the Mongols, who reached the walls of Moscow (1591); a series of bad harvests causing famine, slump and peasant revolts; pretenders claiming to be the rightful tsar, supported in part by rebellious Don Cossacks; and, to cap it all, Swedish and Polish invasions. The Swedes took Novgorod, the Poles occupied Moscow (1610), while Sigismund, the Polish king, became tsar. The up-shot was a powerful counter-movement; in part a Russian revival against the foreigner; in part a Greek Orthodox crusade against the Catholic usurper; in part a revolt of provincial nobility against the boyars of Moscow. The foreigners were expelled and a National Assembly (Zemsky Sobar) elected sixteen-year-old Michael Romanov as tsar. He was the nephew of Fedor, the last legitimate tsar; the son of Filaret, virtual ruler of Russia and soon to be Patriarch of the Russian Church; a member of one of the highest of the boyar families; and the first of the dynasty which ruled Russia till the Revolution.

The Romanovs

Under the first three Romanovs, Michael (1613–45), Alexei Mikhailovich (1645–76), and Fedor II (1676–82), Muscovy resumed once more her old tradition of defensive, outward probing, though in somewhat gingerly fashion owing to the internal ravages caused by the Time of Troubles. The Swedes were pushed out of Novgorod (1617) and the Poles out of Smolensk (1654). Here Russia's frontiers with her neighbours were clear enough to be drawn on maps and incorporated in treaties. No such precision was possible to the south, in the steppe-lands of the Cossacks. These loosely organized wanderers do not fit easily into any of the normal socio-economic categories. They were a mixture of outlaws and refugees from Muscovy, Poland, Lithuania, and Turkey, together with various

Tartar remnants, part settled, part nomad, half military colonists protecting Europe against the Infidel, half mounted bandits taking tribute from all comers. In this period, the Ukrainian Cossacks tried to play off Poland, Turkey, and Russia one against the other in the hope of creating an independent Cossack state. Moscow was determined to prevent this, as well as another possibility: the incorporation of the Cossacks into Poland or Turkey. In the end she succeeded. The Ukraine was split down the middle, and the Cossacks to the east of the River Dnieper were absorbed into the Russian state, though retaining for most of the Ancien Régime their special rights and liberties. Poland was forced to recognize this in the armistice of Andrusovo (1667), and in the permanent settlement signed with John Sobieski in 1686. In addition, Russia also gained the west-bank city of Kiev.

The treaty of 1686 was part of a larger and more significant arrangement. Poland made these concessions in return for Muscovy's adherence to the Holy League, which John Sobieski was organizing along with the Pope, Venice, and the Emperor. His purpose was a crusade against the Turks, and Russia's contribution was her first confrontations with Turkey: Prince V. V. Golitsin's two Crimean campaigns of 1687 and 1689, in the first of which the fifteen-year-old Peter the Great served as a bombardier. This thrust to the south was big with consequence for Russia, as she inevitably found that one territorial advance to defend existing frontiers required a second thrust to defend that, and then a third, and so on. The treaty of 1686 marks the moment when Russia crossed over permanently into the orbit of European power-politics, and also the start of that policy of wearing down the Turks which lasted into the twentieth century.

Further east, the Cossacks of the Don, who had risen during the Time of Troubles, broke out again in bloody rebellion in 1670 under the leadership of Stenka Razin, who was believed to possess magical powers. After raiding the lower Volga, he was joined on his march on Moscow by hordes of serfs rising against harsh landlords, indigenous peoples resisting the Muscovite state machine, religious dissidents from official Orthodoxy as well as groups of those wandering masses of vagabonds, bandits and refugees who constantly moved about the empty Russian spaces. Like other revolts later in the Ancien Régime, Stenka Razin's was frightening in its early, barbarous enthusiasm, but quickly collapsed before regular troops. Razin was taken to Moscow (1671) and torn limb from limb; though he was never forgotten in the folk-lore and folk-songs of the Russian masses. As well as doling out savage punishments, the governments of the tsars continued their policy of getting some shape into the open frontier regions by persuading Russians and foreigners to develop estates there; and by inducing Cossack leaders to enter the Russian military service in return for land and the privilege of turning lesser Cossacks virtually into their serfs.

In Siberia the same policy was pursued as settlement pushed slowly eastwards in the wake of explorers, hunters and trappers. In 1648 the town of Okhotsk was founded on the Pacific coast. In 1689 a border treaty was signed with China, keeping the Russians out of the Amur valley. In these negotiations, China was represented by two Jesuits, one Spanish and one French.

Peter the Great

This account has already taken us into the reign of Peter the Great, in those early years (1682–89) when Muscovy was ruled by his sister Sophie as Regent. In 1689, when Peter was sixteen, the faction of magnates who supported him overthrew the faction that backed Sophie; and, as Peter began to take up the reins of government in the 1690s, the outward pressure of Russia in all directions began to take on a new intensity. Unlike his forebears in the Romanov line, Peter was a forceful leader, a tireless worker, and a brutal slave-driver. 'I have not spared and I do not spare my life for fatherland and people,' he wrote.[1] Utterly restless, he was constantly on the move from one corner of Russia to another, when he was not exploring western Europe. He could not even endure a banquet without getting up from time to time and running into another room to stretch his legs. Nearly seven feet tall, he was massive in proportion.

He was violent and coarse, a hurricane of activity, playing havoc wherever he raged. He could kill a man with a blow of his fist; and he once ruined the hair-do of Frederick the Great's mother when she was ten years old, by picking her up by the ears to kiss her. He ate like a horse, dispensing with knives and forks, a habit which, along with his belching and farting, made him appear somewhat uncouth at the more refined tables in the West.

As Peter began to send out his never-ending streams of decrees, the wheels of Russian life moved into a higher gear; and the advances that Russia made under his rule must be seen as deriving from the energy he transmitted, unless one is satisfied with the explanation that Russian growth was a self-propelled activity in accordance with some historical destiny. Unfortunately for this view, had Peter not existed, it is only too easy to imagine a second Time of Troubles and a successful attack by neighbours. Peter was right when he wrote towards the end of his reign (1723): 'Our people are like children who never set about their ABC if they are not compelled to it by the master.'[2]

Peter spent his life compelling the Russians to drive their frontiers outwards on all points of the compass. Between 1689 and 1725, only one year, 1724, was completely peaceful; and, among the rest, only thirteen months of peace are to be found. He sent his armies and navies, his embassies and spies, his trade missions and exploration teams in all directions at once. Crisis was permanent and he was constantly on the alert. He acted feverishly and hurriedly. He flung out here and there without sufficient preparation of his own forces or complete enough intelligence of the dispositions of the enemy. His programme of conquests was less like the plans of human reason than the instinctive thrusts of an enraged beast which was often badly mauled. He made up his foreign policy as he went along, and played it by ear with the devotion of an amateur.

His warlike thrusts were against three seas: the Black Sea, the Caspian, and the Baltic; and his motives were primarily commercial. He began with two blows, one after the other, at the Black Sea. His first attack on Azov at the mouth of the

Don failed (1695); his second, with the aid of galleys hurriedly built further upstream at Voronezh, succeeded (1696). Azov was annexed, the naval base of Taganrog founded, a Black Sea fleet laid down. Turkey agreed (1700) that Russia should finally give up her payments of tribute to the Tartars of the Crimea. No sooner had Peter signed peace with Turkey than he was pulled by his alliances with Denmark and Poland into his biggest task of all: a twenty-year fight to the finish with Sweden, hitherto the greatest power in the Baltic.

The Great Northern War

The Great Northern War (1700–21) dominated Peter's reign, and practically all the innovations that he brought to Russian life were in aid of his chief ambition: to grasp and hold a place on the Baltic Sea by defeating Sweden. He began with disaster. He besieged the Swedish-held port of Narva with about 40,000 men – insufficiently prepared for battle in all respects, as he admitted twenty-four years later. The King of Sweden, the eighteen-year-old dare-devil Charles XII, attacked the Russians under cover of a violent snow storm and utterly destroyed them. The Swedes took nearly a third of the Russian siege-train, all their artillery (for what it was worth), and 160 senior officers, including ten generals. Peter wept like a child, but Charles turned aside from his Russian invasion in order to attack Augustus the Strong of Saxony and Poland. This gave Peter a seven-year breathing space in which to create armed forces appropriate to eighteenth-century warfare. In doing so, Peter borrowed freely from Swedish expertise. 'I know the Swedes will long continue to be victorious,' he said, 'but in time they will teach us to beat them.'[3] In 1707 Charles made his thrust into Russia; but, instead of making straight for Moscow, he veered south into the Ukraine in order to get help from Ivan Mazepa, the Hetman of the Cossacks, who were by no means content with their union with Russia. Peter followed each of Charles's moves, placing himself between the Swedes and Moscow, till in 1709 at Poltava he wiped out Charles's army. It was only 22,000 strong, but it was the finest fighting force in Europe, though exhausted by now and short of ammunition.

This 'unexpected victory', as Peter called it, was one of the decisive battles of history, as the rest of Europe quickly noticed. 'It is commonly said that the Tsar will be formidable to all Europe,' said Leibniz in Vienna, 'that he will be a kind of northern Turk.'[4] Poltava spelt the doom of Sweden as the greatest power in the north, but not before twelve more hard years of campaigning were over. Russia conquered Karelia, Ingria, Estonia, and Livonia, dislodging Sweden from her last strongholds in north Germany as well as defeating her at the naval battle of Hango (1714). The Treaty of Nystadt (1721) guaranteed Russia her Baltic conquests, giving her a long stretch of coastline from Viborg round to Riga. It was a break-out into the main currents of European life of immeasurable consequence for Russian development. The words of Count Golovkin's oration during the official celebrations of the treaty were fulsome, as befits such occasions, but true nevertheless. 'By your tireless labours, and under your guidance,' he said to the Tsar, 'we have been led from the shades of ignorance to the stage of glory before the world. We have been so to speak, led from nothing to life, and we have rejoined the company of political nations.'[5]

The South and the East

But the Baltic by no means monopolized Peter's almost super-human energies. The Turks declared war in 1710, urged on by France and by Charles XII, who had taken refuge there after Poltava. And so, in the middle of his Swedish campaigns, Peter had to rush through an inadequately prepared offensive down the River Pruth, hoping for support from Balkan Christians whom he called on to rise against 'the descendants of the heathen Mahomet'. However, he had been badly advised by his intelligence services; and, surrounded by unexpected hordes of Turks and Tartars, he had to buy peace by giving up Azov and his precious coastal settlement (1711). Further east, after the Treaty of Nystadt, he conquered Derbent, Baku and Resht, and the whole west and south coasts of the Caspian Sea from Persia (1722–24), with the object of keeping the decaying Persian kingdom out of Turkish hands and of diverting its silk trade through the waterways of Russia. Further east still, he sent a force to explore Khiva and Bokhara in the Oxus Valley, to be followed by an incursion into India (1714–17). Unfortunately, his men were trapped and murdered, though these geographical sorties enabled him to send a reliable map of the Caspian to the French Academy, of which he had become a member during his trip to Paris in 1717. Beyond that, he sent expeditions into Siberia, founding Omsk in 1717. And, finally, he began the conquest of the Kamchatka Peninsula; and just before he died, sent off the expedition led by the Danish sea-captain, Vitus Behring, which charted the Straits known by his name.

Peter decreed in 1722 that he should name his own successor, but when the moment of death came (1725) he was too ill to pronounce a name. In the ensuing uncertainty, the crown was tossed about like a ball between alternate factions of aristocrats in the Court and Guards, to the accompaniment of coups d'état, forged wills, assassinations, and cruel sessions in the torture chamber. During the reigns of Catherine I (1725–27), Peter's widow; Peter II (1727–30), his grandson; Anne (1730–40), his niece; Ivan VI (1740–41), the grandson of Anne's sister; Elizabeth (1741–62), Peter's daughter; and Peter III (1762), his grandson; effective power was in the hands of a succession of cabals, since the wearers of the crown were too infantile, puerile, or pleasure-bent to take charge.

The War of the Polish Succession

In spite of the confusion at Court, however, Russia's power in the world advanced in this period, borne up by the shock waves resulting from Peter's explosive reign. There was activity all round the circumference of Russia, but the main sectors of aggression in the eighteenth century were west and south, where Russia was thrusting into Poland and Turkey in alliance with Austria; and also playing a leading role in European diplomacy. Poland, with its elective monarchy and rival groups of nobles each possessing the veto, was a comparatively easy victim, though Russia's problem was not so much to beat the Poles as to outwit France and Turkey, who also had fingers in this pie. In 1733, when Augustus II of Poland died, the French managed to get their candidate elected as the new king. This was Louis XV's father-in-law, Stanislas Leszcynski. The Austro-Russian candidate was the son of Augustus II – Frederick Augustus of Saxony – and it did not take long for invading Russian troops to persuade another group of Polish nobles to choose him as their king (Augustus III). Moreover, they were able to maintain him on the throne until Stanislas threw in the towel (1736), being very feebly supported by France. In addition, it was in this war that Russian troops fought in western Europe for the first time. When the 13,000-strong corps reached Prince Eugen at Heidelberg in 1735, he found them, he said, 'a beautifully trained and disciplined body of infantry, whose condition was astonishing after so exhausting a march'.[6]

Before this was over, Russia attacked Turkey (1735–39), who objected to Russian interference in Polish affairs. The war party in St Petersburg decided that this was the right moment to finish Turkey off, and so fulfil Russia's religious and national mission: the liberation of Orthodox and Slav brothers from Turkish oppression. Much effort was put into the campaigns in the Black Sea area, and 100,000 men were lost; but in the end (1739), Russia gained only a defortified Azov, and the right to trade on the Black Sea – so long as it was in Turkish ships.

The Seven Years' War

During the great European War of the Austrian Succession (1740–48) Russian foreign policy dithered, partly because of her war with Sweden (1741–42), partly because she had diplomatic obligations to states fighting on each side, and partly because of the in-fighting at Court between the pro-French and the pro-Austrian groups. Ultimately a Russian army did march (1748), but it was on hire to Great Britain, and in any case saw no action. At the negotiations of Aix-la-Chapelle, therefore, Russia was appropriately excluded. In the Seven Years' War (1756–63), Russia's role was very different. Her diplomacy was one of the chief threads in the tangle of causes that led to the outbreak of hostilities, and her armies exercised a decisive influence over the outcome. Year after year, Russian armies poured through East Prussia, occupied Königsberg, beating Frederick's armies at Zorndorf (1758) and Kunersdorf (1759), and, along with the Austrians, occupying Berlin for a few days in 1760. Frederick the Great was rescued from destruction in the nick of time by the death of the Empress Elizabeth (1762) and the accession of Peter III, who immediately withdrew from the war against his idol.

Catherine the Great

The last Russian ruler in this period, Catherine II (1762–96), was brought to the throne, like her predecessors, by a palace revolution; but, unlike them, she possessed sufficient political skill to avoid becoming the tool of the aristocratic groups which backed her. The fact that she usurped the throne while the reigning monarch, Peter III, was still alive, that her victim was shortly butchered by his gaoler, that the murderer was the brother of her lover, and that the dethroned tsar was her husband, all perfectly fitted in with Russian customs. She had made her plans long before. 'Be assured', she told Sir Charles Hanbury-Williams, the British ambassador (1756), 'that I shall never play the King of Sweden's easy-going and feeble part, and that I shall perish or reign.'[7] And reign she did. A later British ambassador, Sir James Harris, told how she was 'rigidly obeyed'. 'Her character extends throughout her whole administration', he wrote in 1778.[8] Moreover, she did not allow high policy to be deflected from its proper course by her succession of lovers, even though she had a very warm heart. 'If in my youth I had been allotted a husband I could love I would have remained eternally faithful to him,' she once wrote to Gregory Potemkin, the lover with the greatest political influence. 'The trouble is simply that my heart cannot be content even for an hour without love.'[9] As Alexander Pushkin later wrote: 'Many were called and many chosen.' At least twenty-one of her lovers have been identified, of whom ten became installed as official favourites, including Gregory Orlov ('the most beautiful man of his time', she called him) whose coup d'état brought her to the throne; Potemkin, who was, she wrote, 'as beautiful as the day, gay as a lark, shining like a star'; and Platon Zubov, who began his tour of duty in 1789, when he was twenty-two and she was sixty. The English minister, Edward Finch, was right when he wrote that there was 'not one bit of nun's flesh about her'.[10]

Russian foreign policy during her reign was only partly determined by the necessity of pleasing favourites and factions at Court. It resulted mainly from her own lust for the world renown which successful armed aggression brought to rulers under the Ancien Régime. At the same time, it was a continuation of the exploits of Ivan the Terrible and Peter the Great. Of course, for Voltaire and the other western intellectuals who were eating out of her hand and pocketing her presents, she dressed up her aggressions in the language of the Enlightenment; for, as well as tender passions, she also enjoyed intellectual speculation, and the plaudits of the *philosophes* were important to her. Thus, for western consumption, she could project her drive to secure the Black Sea ports as ridding Europe of the heathen Turks. And in Poland, where she did all she could to preserve the impotence of the crown, so as to paralyse the State as an independent force, she always supported opposition nobles and lent aid to Orthodox and Protestant dissidents against official Catholicism. To her palpitating fans in western Europe, she appeared as the defender of religious toleration and the champion of Polish liberties. 'All who cultivate literature and think, in whatever part of Europe they live,' wrote Grimm to her in 1764, 'have regarded themselves as your subjects.'[11]

The Turkish Wars

To Poles and Turks, it was old-fashioned Russian expansionism. Turkey was unfortunate enough to lie in the way of

Russian commercial ambitions. A port on the Black Sea, so went a Russian memorandum, would turn Russia into 'a commercial centre between Asia and Europe'; it would 'make many other peoples and lands its involuntary tributaries and draw to it an important part of Indian and American treasure'.[12] Beyond that, Catherine had dreams of expelling the Turks out of Europe and setting up a Russian ruler in Constantinople. 'It is true that we have war,' she wrote to Voltaire at the start of her first Turkish War (1768–74), 'but Russia has been engaged in this pastime many times and emerges from each war more flourishing than she was before.'[13] The Baltic fleet sailed round to the eastern Mediterranean and destroyed most of the Turkish fleet at Scio and Chesme (1770); a successful drive against the Crimean Tartars was carried out, and Russian armies penetrated beyond the Danube in their march towards Constantinople. The loss of lives and material was staggering, though Catherine treated it with a certain insouciance. 'Cross off Philippopolis, please, from the number of cities,' she wrote to Voltaire; 'it has been turned to ashes this spring by Turkish troops.'[14] The acquisitions which the very favourable Treaty of Kuchuk-Kainardzhi (1774) gave her more than compensated. The Tartars of the Crimea became independent of Turkey, and Russia's possession of Azov was confirmed. In addition, further stretches of Black Sea coast were gained; and the Russian merchant fleet gained the right to navigate freely on the Black Sea as well as pass through the Bosphorous and the Dardanelles.

This was a triumphant outcome, though not entirely satisfactory. There was the problem of the Crimea, 'the pimple on Russia's nose', as Potemkin called it. 'Without the possession of the Crimea', wrote the economist A. K. Storch, 'trade on the Black Sea would have stayed for ever in its childhood.'[15] For several years it was subjected to subversion by Russian agents, and then peacefully annexed in 1783. In a further war against Turkey (1787–92), the victories won by the genius of Alexander Suvorov brought further acquisitions ceded by Turkey in the Treaty of Jassy (1792): Ochakov and the Black Sea territory between the Dniester and the Bug.

Poland

Catherine's gains at Poland's expense were even more shattering for the defeated country. Firstly, in 1763, Russian troops invaded the Duchy of Courland, a fief of Poland, with ice-free ports, which was henceforth treated as Russian territory. Secondly, after the death of Augustus III (1763), the Polish nobles were forced to elect yet another Russian nominee as king: Catherine's former lover, Count Stanislas Poniatowski. Thirdly, when this monarch tried to give the Polish central government some semblance of effectiveness (by introducing hereditary kingship and reducing the ways in which the nobility could hamstring the crown), Russia intervened and in a Russo-Polish treaty the unworkable Polish constitution was placed under Russian guarantee 'for all time to come' (1768). Fourthly, came the notorious three partitions of Poland (1772, 1793 and 1795), whereby, as a result of annexations by Russia in league with Prussia and Austria, Poland almost disappeared from the map. Through the wasting disease of its constitution, one of the largest states in Europe had become one of the weakest.

When she died in 1796, Catherine had extended the Russian Empire by a matter of 200,000 square miles and added some seven million subjects. Russia was firmly established on the Black Sea and the Baltic; and the fertile black-earth region of the steppes was being peopled and cultivated. The economic, social, and cultural results of this acquisition of world-power status unfolded in the nineteenth and twentieth centuries. It is time now to see what internal developments had made the achievements possible.

Russia: The Growth of Autocracy

Origins of Autocracy

In 1787 Joseph II of Austria, who saw much of Catherine the Great's work at first hand, said to the French ambassador to Russia: 'Everything seems easy when one wastes money and human lives. We in Germany or France could not attempt what they dare do here without hindrance. The Lord commands; hordes of slaves obey. They are paid little or nothing; they are badly fed; they do not dare to protest, and I know that in these years fifty thousand persons were destroyed in these new [southern] provinces by the toil and the emanations from the morasses, without their being lamented, even without anyone mentioning it.'[1] He was referring to the most striking internal characteristic of Russia: the autocratic power of the tsars, already well established when this period begins. No other European ruler was so free from restraint by law or custom, institutions or social groups. 'The Tsar is honoured like an earthly god,' wrote Petrus Valckenier, the Dutch diplomat in 1677;[2] and the probability is that this ruthless despotism on the ruler's side and slavish obedience on the people's have their origin mainly in the process of warlike expansion just outlined. When medieval Russia was reduced to a collection of principalities cowering in the northern forests in awe of the Asiatic invaders, only absolute power could have raised the princes of Muscovy above their rivals, and given them the concentration of power necessary to hit back at the Tartars. Possibly, also, the rulers of Muscovy took the unlimited authority of the Tartar khans as their model, and thus (not for the last time) borrowed from their enemies; and certainly the Orthodox Church of 'Holy Russia' regarded Moscow as the third Rome and preached the divinely appointed authority of the lay power. Thus, in late medieval and early modern times, the autocracy was well founded, and the subsequent struggle for survival against Poles, Swedes, and Turks only served to enhance it. When this period began, the Russian constitution was like the government of a vast army, in which the legislature was the tsar's word of command, the executive his staff officers, and the judiciary the knout.

Lack of Corporative Resistance

Apart from the Church, Russia had evolved none of those checks on royal power which restrained the most ambitious of western rulers. Because of economic backwardness, there was only a vestigial bourgeoisie and no cities with chartered rights such as dotted the West. At the time when the agrarian masses of western Europe were gradually emancipating themselves from servile status, the peasants of Russia were increasingly having the shackles of serfdom clamped upon them. Moreover, the nobility had not managed to create national or even local Estates capable of standing up to the tsars; while, as will be shown, the tsars had succeeded in making practically all land-holding dependent on service to the crown: little sub-infeudation or clientage could develop.

Russia was too vast, too poor and too thinly populated: the concentration into settled communities was slow. Russians from the tsar down to the lowest slave were constantly on the move, either on orders from above or in flight from them. The long frontier on the empty lands to the south and east encouraged despotism. By allowing potential forces of resistance to escape, it deflated the opposition. When oppression became unbearable, it was easier for a Russian to become a bandit or a refugee than to stand fast and organize political resistance. The only two institutions which might possibly have played a parliamentary role were in decay at the start of the Ancien Régime. The powers of the Boyar Duma (the Council of the Magnates) had been smashed during Ivan the Terrible's reign of terror, and in the seventeenth century its work was increasingly being done by bureaucratic institutions created by the Romanovs. The Zemsky Sobor (the Assembly of the Land), the rough equivalent of the Estates-General of the West, had played a vigorous part in the national revival during and after the Time of Troubles (1584–1613) and had chosen Michael Romanov as tsar. However, as the Romanov power grew in the seventeenth century, so the Assembly's activities were restricted, and it was not called again after 1653.

Another check to royal power also disappeared under the early Romanovs. This was the system of *mestnichestvo*, whereby the boyars were arranged according to their ancestry in a complicated hierarchy of ranks, making it a dishonour for a given boyar to accept a post in any part of the tsar's service if it was inferior to a post occupied by a boyar of lower birth. This limitation on the freedom of the tsar to appoint his officers according to his own wishes was very much eroded by the early Romanovs, and then abolished in 1682 when the genealogical record-books were ceremoniously burnt.

The Great Schism

As in many western monarchies, another stepping-stone to autocracy was the subjection of the Church, a process easier in Russia as most ecclesiastical posts were manned not by nobles but by commoners. The breaking of clerical power involved three changes: first, the severing of the national church from subordination to an international ecclesiastical authority; second, the reform of its ceremonies and beliefs; and, third, the subjection of its administration to the State, and the secularization of its property. The first change had occurred in the fifteenth and sixteenth centuries, when the fall of Constantinople to the Turks (1453) severed Muscovy's attachment to the Byzantine Church, leading to the creation in 1589 of the Patriarchate of Moscow. The second and third changes took place in the later seventeenth century, when the Church became so divided over reform that it was too weak to resist the encroachments of the state. At the centre of both controversies was Nikon, the proud and authoritarian Patriarch of Moscow from 1652 till his deposition in 1666. He ruthlessly enforced the innovations but steadfastly opposed the state.

The Great Schism is the first example in this period of a recurring phenomenon in Russian history: a convulsive reaction to western influences. Old Muscovy began to smart to the acid of western culture in the seventeenth century, when it began to trickle over the borders in two distinct streams, one caused by the Polish wars, the other by the incorporation of the eastern Ukraine and Kiev. From Poland flowed western, Roman, Renaissance, and Counter-Reformation ideas due to the success of the Jesuits in establishing the Uniate Church there in 1595; from Kiev, southern, Greek, Orthodox, reforming scholarship. Nikon used Kiev to defeat Rome. The old Church of Muscovy had grown decadent. Its clergy were ignorant, its writings and ceremonies deviated from original Greek Orthodoxy as revealed by the most up-to-date seventeenth-century research. Only a Church revitalized after the manner of Kiev, thought Nikon, could defend the nation against Roman Catholicism and other insidious forms of western culture. 'I am a Russian,' he said, 'and the son of a Russian, but my faith and convictions are Greek.'[3]

His reforms included corrections of inaccuracies in the Muscovite translations of the scriptures and service-books, the use of three fingers instead of two to make the sign of the cross, the reduction from twelve to four of the number of genuflections to be made during a certain prayer, and other seemingly external details of a somewhat elaborate and rather mechanical ritual. But, to the mass of Russians, these ceremonies were essentials, not incidentals. They had not drawn the western distinction between matter and spirit, and they believed that their salvation was jeopardized if they departed one iota from the customary forms of worship, or even from the observances of daily life, such as growing a beard, wearing the long cloak, or saying a prayer and making the sign of the cross upon entering or leaving a house. The opposition to the reforms was thus widespread, some preferring execution or suicide, many choosing exile. The Old Believers, as they called themselves, were led by the archpriest Avvakum, who feared the disintegration of the Muscovite way of life under the influence of what he called western 'science' and 'geometry'. Nikon harried them without mercy, and so did successive tsars. Avvakum was burnt at the stake (1681) and his followers were harshly persecuted. Between 1672 and 1691, possibly 20,000 Old Believers burned themselves to death rather than submit. A rent was torn in Russian life which could never be repaired.

The Schism split the Church in at least three ways: the westernizers, the official reformers, and the Old Believers. And it rendered the Church helpless against successive moves to turn it into a department of state. Its rights had already been reduced by certain clauses in the Code of 1649, a body of law produced by the Zemsky Sobor. The Church was forbidden to increase its landed possessions. Its judicial powers were curtailed, and the clergy were made subject to a new government department, the Monastery Bureau. Nikon, who entertained ambitious ideas upon the superiority of Patriarchs to Tsars, called this 'the devil's law'. By 1658 Tsar Alexis, who in youth had deferred to him, could no longer stomach his overbearing pretensions, and Nikon resigned in a huff. After an eight-year tussle, the Church Council of 1666–67 (the same which expelled the Old Believers from the Church) deposed Nikon and declared the precedence of the temporal power over the spiritual. It was a theoretical formulation to which Peter the Great and his successors gave much practical effect.

Peter the Great and the Compulsory 'Service-State'

By the time of Peter's accession in 1682, then, though there might be palace contests about who should be the power behind the throne, or even about who should occupy it, there was no one to question the autocratic power of the semi-sacred tsar. His decrees were carried into effect by the hosts of bureaucrats and soldiers which earlier monarchs had steadily accumulated to carry on the struggle against Tartars, boyars and patriarchs. By violence and guile, the tsars had rooted out any semblance of feudal independence in the great landed magnates. Ivan the Great became notorious for the forcible transfer of boyar families from one end of the country to the other, for his ruthless confiscation of their estates and their transfer to lesser men. It

became established that each owner of an hereditary estate
(*votchina*) had to serve the tsar. If not, his land with its serfs was
annexed to the crown, and then transferred to another man as a
pomestye, that is, an estate granted on condition of service to
the tsar. The princes and boyars of early Muscovy had so
rivalled one another, and been so cut off from the middle and
lesser landowners, that they offered but sporadic, if bitter,
resistance to the tsars; and by the mid seventeenth century the
rulers of Russia had accomplished in fact what proved in most
other monarchies to be only a pipe dream: the reduction of the
nobility into docile servants of the crown. 'In our state of Muscovy', went a late-seventeenth-century decree, 'the serving men
of every grade serve ... by service from land ... and no one
owns land for nothing.'[4]

This compulsory service state was brought to its peak of
development by Peter the Great, under whose powerful blows
all the features of the autocracy so far mentioned were hammered into more perfect shape. His Army Regulations of 1716
put it in this way: 'His Majesty is an absolute monarch who
is not responsible to anyone in the world for his deeds; but he
has the right and power to govern his realm and his lands, as a
Christian sovereign, according to his will and wisdom.'[5]

The Armed Forces

To begin with the *raison d'être* of all the other reforms, Peter
increased and modernized the armed forces. Previous tsars had
gone to war mainly with two sorts of army: on the one hand,
the regulars, consisting principally of the *Streltsy*, registered
Cossacks and other units officered by foreigners; and, on the
other, the militia, that is, nobles at the head of their tenants and
their own supply trains, performing the services they owed to
the tsar in return for the land they held. The *Streltsy*, mainly
artisans, stationed in the suburbs of the capital, were a political
liability in Peter's youth, when they could topple the throne
itself. The militia was an untrained rabble. 'The infantry are
armed with bad muskets and do not know how to use them',
wrote Ivan Pososhkov in an official report (1701). '... for every

one foreigner killed there are three, four and even more Russians killed. As for the cavalry, we are ashamed to look at them ourselves, let alone show them to the foreigner: sickly, ancient horses, blunt sabres, puny, badly dressed men who do not know how to wield their weapons. There are some noblemen who do not know how to charge an arquebus, let alone hit their target. They care nothing about killing the enemy, but think only how to return to their homes.'[6]

Peter disbanded the *Streltsy* and made the Guards the nucleus of a new regular army. The Guards, into which the militia was incorporated, were formed out of the units which Peter had built up as a boy, when he and his friends played soldiers – with increasing realism as they grew up. Recruitment and training were vastly improved, for the disaster of Narva (1700) revealed the inadequacy of the existing volunteers and drafted riff-raff. Apart from foreign experts, the officer class was formed out of the sons of the nobility, who were registered at the age of ten, called up at fifteen for training in the Guards, and then posted for life to a regiment. Evasion of service by a landowner led, if detected, to the loss of his property, and by a law of 1722 to 'public disgrace', a state of civil death in which he could be robbed or murdered with impunity. Beginning in 1705, the rank and file were provided by regular levies of conscripts from the burghers and peasants, at the rate of one recruit for every twenty-six households – or fifty or eighty, according to Peter's requirements. A depot was set up in the chief town of each recruiting district, and there the cannon-fodder of Peter's insatiable armies were trained and held in reserve. These soldiers were called 'immortals', for every loss of a man had to be immediately made good by another conscript from his recruiting district. Twenty-five years' service in the ranks of Peter's victorious but frugally equipped armies was a ghastly fate to befall the Russian masses, who went to desperate lengths to avoid call-up, some having to be dragged to the depot in chains. In spite of the practice, from 1712 onwards, of burning a cross on each recruit's left hand, and in spite of the unspeakably cruel punishments they risked, they deserted in droves. A self-mutilated man, if caught, might have to run the gauntlet three times of 500 soldiers armed with whips. Nevertheless, Peter had increased the regular army more than five-fold by the end of his reign, having over 200,000 men under arms, trained on western lines, not counting 100,000 Cossacks, and numerous colonial troops on the eastern borders.

An even more revolutionary innovation was the creation of a navy, from the modest beginnings with the galleys at Voronezh to the Baltic fleet which defeated the Swedes at Hango and alarmed the British admiralty. All the raw materials for timbers and masts, anchors and sails, were lavishly provided out of Russia's natural resources; but the design and construction of ships as well as the training of the men were heavily dependent on foreign help. Dutch, French, and British naval experts were attracted by the offer of rich rewards, while unenthusiastic sons of the nobility were dispatched to learn the ropes in the shipyards of London, Amsterdam and Venice. By the end of his reign, the Baltic fleet had forty-eight ships of the line and nearly 800 galleys, though the Russian sailors at this stage scarcely felt at home on the sea.

Revenue

Most of the other transformations that Peter brought about in Russian life stemmed from the necessity of recruiting the men for these forces and raising the revenue for financing the wars they fought. Three quarters of the taxes collected were spent in this way. The directives that poured out of Peter's headquarters, wherever they happened to be – whether they ordered new taxes, reorganized central and local government, further subjected the Church, dealt with mass education or economic planning – all were designed in some way to intensify the call-up of men and money, or to improve the nation's capacity to produce them.

Peter experimented continuously with taxation procedures, and succeeded in greatly raising the total revenue, and in making the direct tax the most important single source: fifty-three per cent of the total instead of about thirty-three per cent under his predecessors. The government's total demands were apportioned by the revenue officers among the districts, after which it was up to the towns and villages concerned to produce the amount required. The government thus dealt with communities, not individuals. Before Peter, the basis of the tax had been at first usually the ploughland, and then (from the 1640s) households; and the elected assessors in town and village had apportioned it roughly in accordance with ability to pay. Both methods of assessment, however, discouraged agriculture; in addition the household tax brought a falling return. Revenue did not keep pace with population growth because the people were forming themselves into larger households, some even by joining a number of dwellings together and nailing up all the doors except one. In a decree of 1718 Peter replaced it with the 'soul-tax': a levy on all males 'not omitting old men and the latest babies' (except, of course, those of the nobility and gentry and clergy). A census of all males every twenty years or so (called a Revision) ensured that no one escaped: indeed, groups such as slaves, who had hitherto been beneath the dignity of tax-paying, were swept into the net. In between Revisions, taxes were paid on the basis of the last one, the gaps left by the dead souls of those in flight being made up by neighbours. This put the communities constantly on the alert, and it became increasingly difficult for serfs to take flight. This was the beauty of the system from the point of view of the government and the landlords: it pinned down the peasants in their villages and kept them at the job of providing sustenance for their noble masters, who, in their turn, were serving the tsar. It also practically trebled the revenue.

In contrast with this simplicity, the indirect taxes became ever more varied; and almost anyone with an ingenious idea for raising funds would be given an office in Moscow and told to get on with it. Taxes were levied on horse-collars, hats and boots, hot baths, inns and beehives. Moustaches and beards paid rates according to the status of the wearer: a rich merchant paid 100 roubles a year, while a bearded peasant went tax-free so long as he stayed at home, though he had to pay one kopeck each time he entered or left a city. The State also profited from a number of monopolies which it created and then farmed out, such as those on tobacco, vodka, playing cards, dice and chess-sets, rhubarb, and codliver oil.

Every aspect of Russian life was touched by Peter's continual drive to raise revenue. As Klyuchevsky put it, 'in financial matters Peter was like a coachman who whips on his emaciated horse while pulling constantly at the reins'.[7] His mercantilist policies, for example, aimed at raising money either directly by state trading, or indirectly by fostering prosperity in order to raise the taxable capacity of the community. Similarly, his policy towards the Church was not without its financial motives, though other considerations were present also. When the Patriarch Adrian died in 1700, Peter left the post vacant. The next year he transferred to the Monastery Bureau the control of the vast estates of the churches and monasteries, which henceforth enjoyed only a proportion of their revenues. The remainder was supposed to go to carry out the poor law relief and educational duties which the Church had been neglecting; but, in fact, the State pocketed between one and two hundred thousand roubles a year of it.

The Church

In 1721 any political independence that remained in the Church was snuffed out by the Church Statute, which abolished the Patriarchate and placed the Church under the Most Holy Directing Synod, a government department manned by priests but supervised by a Chief Procurator, an army officer. There was no longer any possibility of a Nikon arising to oppose the tsar's wishes, and the Church became hardly distinguishable from the rest of the bureaucracy. Monasteries were reformed, some were dissolved; and by a decree of 1723 vacancies created by the death of monks were to be filled by old soldiers. Discipline was tightened over the whole Church, which like the rest of society became semi-militarized. The regulations in the Church Statute for building a seminary, for example, laid down that 'all periods [for going to bed, rising, praying, and studying] must be indicated by a little bell, whereby the seminarists at the sound of the bell like the soldiers at the sound of the drum can set about their duties.'[8] A clergy so conditioned, it was thought, would toe the line more readily and not get involved in seditious activities, like the many clergy who had been trying to sabotage Peter's westernizing policies. Under the new methods of Church government, so ran another clause in the Church Statute, 'there is no reason to fear rebellions and confusion that grow out of the control of the Church by an individual.... When the people learn that Church administration is established by decrees of the monarch and decisions of the Senate, it will remain docile and will lose all hope that the clergy will support rebellious movements'.[9]

Administrative Reforms

In order to improve the efficiency of the collection of taxes and the recruitment of troops, Peter made a number of changes in the administration, some hastily improvised, others very carefully planned. When the reign was over, however, though many details were new, the essentials of the centralized bureaucracy he inherited were still there. Under the early Romanovs the central political direction came from the tsar, advised partly by the Boyar Duma, which was fading away, and more commonly by newer groups of Court leaders such as the Private Chancery or the Council. The tsar's orders were carried into effect by forty or so Departments (*Prikazy*) in Moscow, some of which supervised every activity in a given area (such as the *Prikazy* for the Ukraine, Kazan, and Siberia), others a given problem everywhere, such as the Admiralty *Prikaz* which controlled the fleet, or the Apothecaries' *Prikaz* which ran some chemists' shops. Below this level, local government was directed by a number of military Governors (*Voevoda*) appointed by the tsar. These had complete control over every aspect of life in the town or district they ruled. It was an apparently complicated, but essentially simple, system of government by persons acting arbitrarily rather than by institutions governing according to known regulations; and it possessed all the characteristics which such constitutions tend to develop: inefficiency, corruption, and ruthless oppression of the public.

In the field of local government, Peter began by trying to persuade, and then to compel, Russian towns and rural districts to develop self-governing institutions on the lines of what he had observed in western Europe. His object was to place the localities beyond the reach of the rapacious *Voevoda*. By the law of 1699, the townsmen were to elect representatives called *Burgmestery*; but, owing to the lack of suitably educated personnel and even the absence of desire for self-government, these officers soon became the tax-collecting agents of Moscow: part of the bureaucratic system, rather than supervisors of it. Similarly, an attempt in 1702 to get the local nobility to choose men to overlook the agents of Moscow came to nothing; not surprisingly, perhaps, since any noble worth employing was no longer in his locality, but already doing his compulsory service in the bureaucracy itself. A final attempt was made in 1724, when towns were ordered to divide their inhabitants into three groups: the first gild (of the better off), the second gild (of the small traders), and the common people. The two gilds were to elect a municipal council from members of the first gild which would do more than collect taxes: it would govern the town. However, as Peter said, 'English freedom' did not suit the Russians; and two years after his death the councils were placed under the control of the local Governors, and the powers of the central bureaucracy flowed back once more, submerging these islands of self-rule.

More elaborately, Peter made two attempts to reform the government of the provinces. His aim was decentralization: to settle his armies in the provinces, and let the provinces collect the taxes and spend them there and then on recruitment, billeting, and so on, thus avoiding the wasteful detour via the inefficient *Prikazy* far away in the capital. In 1708 Russia was divided into eight Provinces (increased by 1719 to twelve), each under a Governor (*Gubernator*) with full powers. These Provinces were subdivided into Districts (*Uezd*). A further wave of changes was decreed in 1718, according to which a new subdivision, the Counties (*Provintsiia*) was interposed between the Province and the District, to be headed by officers called *Voevoda*, a title recently abolished and now revived. And around the framework of Province-County-District, the care-fully worked out Decree of 1718 articulated a complex hier-archy of local government institutions, borrowed almost entirely from the national enemy, Sweden.

So much for local government. At the centre, Peter created the Senate (1711), a nine-man committee which at first was to take his place while he was away on the Pruth campaign, but which soon evolved into the chief executor of his wishes and the central supervisor of the whole provincial organization, especi-ally the tax-collecting side. It thus finally made redundant the old Boyar Duma. To keep it under his eye, Peter appointed an Inspector-General (1715); then from 1721, Guards officers in rotation kept it up to the mark; and, finally, in 1722, the office of Procurator-General was created to dominate the Senate. The holder of this office was the most powerful man in the empire after the tsar.

To keep an eye on the probity of the bureaucrats, the office of *Oberfiscal* was created (1711), held by a powerful magistrate assisted by a secret army of *Fiscals* operating at all levels of the central and local administration. His job consisted of 'supervis-ing secretly the administration of public affairs, in collecting information concerning inequitable judicial decisions, misappro-priation of public funds, and other matters'.[10] The *Fiscals* were an energetic and conscientious body of men who found corrup-tion everywhere, the more so perhaps as they stood to gain from the fines imposed on the convicted. The problem was how to check on the ethical standards of these enforcers of fiscal purity. As Procurator-General Yaguzhinsky said to Peter, 'we all steal, the sole difference is that some do it on a bigger scale and in a more conspicuous manner than others'.[11] *Oberfiscal* Alexis Nesterov was an assiduous informer against corruption, even succeeding in sending Prince Mathew Gagarin, the Gover-nor of Siberia, to the gallows. Unfortunately, he himself was discovered taking bribes as well, and broken on the wheel.

A further change in the central administration was the crea-tion (from 1718) of nine Colleges to begin with, to replace the old *Prikazy*. Already, the new Provinces and Counties had absorbed the work of several of the *Prikazy*; and now the remainder were abolished or subsumed under the new scheme, which was also based on the Swedish model. The Colleges were supposed to replace medieval confusion with Enlightened rationality. Unlike the *Prikazy*, they were based on a logical division of labour. One College of Justice, for example, combined the fragments of responsibility hitherto shared by seven *Prikazy*. Moreover, the Colleges, consisting of ten members under a president, were to proceed by consultation, and reach decisions by majority vote, thus reducing the chances of corruption. Irregularities, it was thought, would be more difficult to conceal in a group than in the individualistic *Prikaz* system. And, finally, each College was responsible for a given activity over the whole empire: Commerce, Admiralty, Mines and Manufactures, and so on. The Colleges were a westernizing influence on Russia. Not only were they set up in westernized St Petersburg, instead of old Moscow: of the nine, seven were given titles borrowed from western languages.

The Table of Ranks

To man the mushrooming offices in central and local government, Peter coerced the nobility into performing to the full their hereditary obligation of service to the tsar. Their naval and military duties have already been mentioned. Peter saw to it that the forces received two thirds of the nobles, and the civil service one third. The whole service system was steadily regulated. In 1711 the Senate was given the duty of keeping the nobles' records and seeing that no one escaped; and in 1722 a new officer was appointed, the *Herold-Meister*, who was attached to the Senate. At the same time, the Table of Ranks was published. This divided the nobility into two principal sorts, military (army and navy) and civil (court and administration), each arranged in a ladder of promotion consisting of fourteen ranks. Those who reached commissioned rank in the forces and rank eight in the bureaucracy were granted hereditary nobility. They became the Russian nobility, or, to use the title that became usual in the eighteenth century, the *dvorianstvo*.

Under the rapidly expanding military and civil administration of Peter, the career open to the talents was a reality. The old nobility resented the upstarts, of course, and still managed to rise faster up the Table than they did, but they never managed to convert the nobility into a closed caste. The tsar strengthened himself by steadily diluting the aristocracy, and under Peter the time was long past when nobles, through *mestnichestvo*, could dictate to the crown what jobs they would take.

Since Peter's time, arguments have raged about the extent and value of his achievements. Did he single-handed drag Russia into modern times, or was he merely the agent of destiny? Did his changes benefit Russia, or did they bring her irreparable harm? Frederick the Great, in 1746, marvelled at his achievement in 'creating soldiers and ministers out of a nation of wild men, in fact even trying to make philosophers out of them'.[12] An aristocratic critic of autocracy and modernity, Prince Michael Shcherbatov, writing at the end of the eighteenth century, asked the question: 'In how many years, in the most favourable conditions, could Russia by herself, without the autocracy of Peter the Great, have attained her present level of education and glory?'[13] His calculation was: not till a hundred years later. If Peter's military and political reforms did give Russia a great heave forward, they were, on the ground, far from conforming to what they were supposed to be on paper, or in Peter's ideals. If he left the State machine bigger, more complex, more effective than he found it, he also elaborated the opportunities for the ancient public vices of old Muscovy to assert themselves.

A German diplomat, G. Weber, who lived in Russia from 1714 to 1720, described the 'mismanagement of the Provincial Commissioners, Chancellors, and Clerks, who are intrusted with the Collection of Taxes. These Cormorants no sooner enter upon their offices, but they make it their sole Study how to build their Fortunes upon the Ruin of the Country People, and he that came among them having hardly Clothes to his Back, is often known in four or five Years time, to have scraped so much together, as to be able to build large Stone-Houses, when at the same Time the poor Subjects are forced to run away

from their Cottages.'[14] In 1724 the Prussian ambassador wrote
home to his king: 'There are no words strong enough to give
Your Royal Majesty an adequate idea of the unbearable negligence and confusion with which the most important affairs of
all are dealt with in this very place, so that foreign and native
Ministers no longer know where to go or turn.'[15]

Eighteenth Century

At the centre, under Catherine I, Anne, and Elizabeth, the
Senate and the Colleges soon became the playthings of cabals
formed by wealthy landowners or good-looking Guardsmen. In
the Colleges, the presidents dominated business, and succeeded
in evading the control supposed to be exercised by the majority.
In the provinces, soon after Peter's death, a considerable pruning of his Swedish- and German-type functionaries took place.
A law of 1728 restored the old bureaucratic tutelage, by giving
plenary powers to the Governors of the Provinces and the *Voevoda* of the Counties. Discipline slackened and institutions
relaxed their controls, leaving the field free at all levels for the
arbitrary reign of individuals who terrorized the public, and who
were themselves in constant fear of their superiors. 'After all
the pains which had been taken to bring this country into its
present shape,' wrote Daniel Finch, the British ambassador in
1741, '... I must confess that I can yet see it in no other light
than as a rough model of something meant to be perfected here-
after, in which the several parts do neither fit nor join, nor are
well glued together.'[16]

The main theme of Russian constitutional and social history
between Peter the Great and Catherine the Great is the loosening of the grip of the State on the nobles and the tightening of
the grip of the nobles on the serfs. The lack of a fixed law of
succession rendered the throne almost elective, if that word can
be stretched to include conspiracies and assassinations. In addition, the absence of political ability in the emperors and
empresses (till Catherine II elected herself into power) also
increased the power of the nobles. The autocracy survived only
because the nobles were divided. The great aristocrats of the

Court and the Guards differed from the mass of the nobility and, even more important, rivalled one another. The Outs resented the Ins; and the bureaucrats clashed with the armed forces.

The accession of Anne illustrates the situation. It was managed by a small group of the Supreme Privy Council, a new organ formed in 1726, which had effectively exercised the powers of the crown under Catherine I and rendered the Senate practically redundant. In 1730, led by Prince D. M. Golitsin, who had read John Locke, it attempted to limit the autocracy. Before she was offered the throne Anne was made to sign a document called the *Conditions*, in which were listed the decisions which Anne must not take without consulting the Supreme Privy Council. Since the list included the making of war and peace, and the levying of taxes and all the other chief attributes of the executive arm, the Empress was to be effectively in the pocket of a small oligarchy. Anne signed and ascended the throne; and then with the help of a rival group of aristocrats, as well as of representatives of the nobility at large, she repudiated her concessions and then ceremonially tore up the *Conditions* before her assembled supporters. The petitions sent in by the lower and provincial nobility showed that they much preferred autocracy to oligarchy.

The uncertainty at the centre, a recurrent situation between 1725 and 1762, meant that whoever controlled the executive depended on the acquiescence of the nobility at large, who not only filled the upper ranks of the armed forces and civil service, but also, as land- and serf-owners, collected the taxes from the vast mass of the population, as well as controlling their destinies in general. In these circumstances, the *dvoriane* (the nobility) increased their powers and privileges. For example, from 1730 they became responsible to the State for the collection of the poll-tax from their serfs. In 1731 a Military Academy was established in St Petersburg for the sons of nobles, who received their commissions on passing out, and were thus spared the tedium of starting their careers in the ranks. In 1736 compulsory service in the army, navy, and bureaucracy was reduced from life to twenty-five years; and in a family where there were two or more males, one was excused service so that he could manage the family estates. In addition, the nobility during these years gained valuable economic privileges, and a surer control over the lives and property of their serfs. And, finally, under Peter III (1762), they achieved their cherished ambition. Service ceased to be compulsory, and, except in wartime, nobles could resign at will (though in some grades of the civil service they needed the approval of their superiors). They also received permission to travel abroad and to enter the service of foreign rulers. They had thus already taken the first steps in what has been called their 'Golden Age'.

Catherine the Great

Whether that term is justified as a description of Catherine II's reign, and, if it is, what it means exactly, are only two of the uncertainties in the reign of that baffling monarch, for there is no doubt at all that she ruled as well as reigned, and that under her rule the powers of the State over the Russian people were effectively enlarged. If it is admitted that she was a despot, was she an Enlightened despot in any sense of that term? Here the mystery deepens as one tries to discern a pattern in the things she said, or see a theme in the steps she took; or, equally puzzling, as one tries to reconcile her utterances with her actions. She was certainly well read in the writings of the Enlightenment, and knew Montesquieu, Beccaria, and Blackstone, as well as the Cameralists and Physiocrats. She was adept at their style of discourse. 'It is nothing to give a little to one's neighbour when one has a superfluity,' she once wrote to Voltaire; 'but it is immortality to be the champion of the human race, the defender of oppressed innocence.'[17]

Her *Instructions*, which she wrote for the guidance of the Legislative Commission of 1767–68, was a hotch-potch of Enlightened projects for the greater happiness of the Russian people. 'I have acted like the crow of the fable', she wrote to Frederick the Great, 'who made itself a garment of peacock feathers.'[18] But which was she in fact – the peacock or the crow? And how does she explain the fact that the Commission was soon dismissed without passing a single clause of the much-publicized recodification of Russian law? Her attempts to reform central and local government, her subjection of the Church, her liberalization of business – from monopolies and other restrictions – certainly deserved the plaudits of the Enlightened; but where is the Enlightenment in the increased enserfment of the peasantry that marked her reign, or her persecution of Alexander Radishchev, or her ragings against the French Revolution? 'Instinctively', she wrote in 1791, 'I feel the greatest contempt for all popular movements.'[19]

Was the secretary to the British embassy, Henry Shirley, right when he reported from St Petersburg to London that 'the Empress's intentions, at first, were to show what pains she took to render Her subjects happy, but as these intentions did not proceed from principles of the purest nature, Her actions like false pearls have more éclat but less value than the genuine one'?[20] Some of her statements could likewise be accused of falsity, such as the following extract from one of her letters to Voltaire: 'Our taxes are now so modest that there is not a peasant in Russia who cannot eat chicken when it pleases him, and for some time there have been provinces where they prefer geese to chickens.'[21] This seems to justify Alexander Pushkin's later condemnation of the 'repulsive buffoonery in her relations with the philosophers of her century'.[22] In other words, is the correct interpretation that she was bogus from the start, and that her Enlightened hand-outs were window-dressing to hide a sordid reality?

Or was she a naïve beginner who made the not unusual mistake in Enlightened times in thinking that Russian society, being so backward, was especially suitable for Enlightened despotism to work on: a blank sheet, in fact, on which she could imprint rational institutions with a few strokes of the pen. The English visitor, the Rev. John Brown, put it in these words (1765): 'The Russian empire hath (in many parts of it) so far emerged from barbarism as to be sensible of its own defects; and yet hath not so strongly, or universally, received any discordant institutions or impressions, which may not be gradually rooted out, or melted into the general plan of civilization.'[23] In other words, did she begin as a genuine devotee of humanity who later became disillusioned by the practical difficulties in the way of creating universal happiness by royal decree?

Neither of these two simple explanations, that she was a fraudulent image-projector or a disillusioned political innocent, will do by itself. They are not consistent with everything we know about Catherine: how she, the daughter of an impoverished German aristocrat, was brought by her mother to St Petersburg at the age of fifteen to become the bride of the Grand Duke Peter (1745); how she survived the indifference of her husband and the suspicions of the Empress Elizabeth; how she formed a following in the Guards and engineered a coup d'état over her husband's dead body; but also how, unlike her predecessors since Peter the Great, she did not become the prisoner of those who had raised her. She managed instead, by the use of the most prodigious state-craft, to extricate herself from the Court factions, to elevate herself above the mundane political in-fighting, to find herself voted 'the Great and All-Wise Mother of the Fatherland' by the Legislative Commission (1767), to lead Russia through one of its most triumphant epochs, and to die safely in her bed. Certainly, she used propaganda whenever possible; and, without doubt, she grew more cynical with experience. But these are only two threads in the complicated texture of her statesmanship which was mainly concerned with the day-to-day confrontation with political realities. In the struggles between the Ins and Outs at Court, between the great aristocrats of Moscow and St Petersburg and the provincial nobility, between the armed forces and the civil service, between Russia and the conquered nationalities, between the serfs and the rest (to name only some of her problems) she needed brain-power of electronic subtlety to know which interests to conciliate and which to crush. Add to this the fact that she was playing on a world stage, and one realizes that any given words of hers might express cherished ideals or be simply dust thrown in the eyes of the observer; and that any given deed could be a move in one or more of a number of different games. 'Believe me,' she once wrote to the British ambassador, Sir Robert Gunning, 'I have not based my hopes for success on any *one* mode of action. There are moments when it is not necessary to be too precise.'[24]

With the proviso, then, that any general view of Catherine II's reign can be only an approximation to the truth, it does seem clear that she reversed the trend of eighteenth-century Russian history, and returned to the methods of Peter the Great: that is, she resumed control of the State machine, and the State machine enlarged its power over the Russian people. And this is not inconsistent with the period being the Golden Age of the nobility.

Catherine had no doubts about the necessity of absolute rule. 'The Sovereign is absolute', she wrote in Paragraph 9 of her *Instructions* of 1767; 'for there is no other Authority but that which centres in his single Person, that can act with a Vigour proportionate to the Extent of such a vast Dominion.'[25] And though, like Montesquieu, she talked of 'intermediate Powers' forming 'the essential Part of monarchical Government', she did not mean what he meant. She was thinking of the bureaucracy, not his independent Parlements manned by nobles acting as a counter-weight to the monarch. Her 'intermediate Powers, subordinate and depending, proceed from the supreme Power; as in the very Nature of the Thing the Sovereign is the source of all imperial and civil Power'.[26]

Church and Aristocracy

Continuing the policy of her predecessors, she stamped out any remaining traces of insubordination in the Church. It was still very wealthy, some of the monasteries owning more peasants than all but the richest lay landlords. At the Revision of 1747, for example, the monastery of Trinity–St Sergei (the biggest proprietor of serfs in the country) owned about 106,000 male peasants; Trinity–St Alexander Nevsky had 25,464, and the Convent of the Assumption about 24,000.[27] Catherine, by a decree of 1764, ordered the nationalization of all ecclesiastical property, which was henceforth to be administered by a government department, the College of Economy. The upper clergy and monks were to be paid by the State; about half the monasteries were dissolved; thus, about two million Church peasants became State peasants. These were now available to Catherine for distribution as gifts to favourites and politicians – a transfer which reduced them into serfdom. Abroad, she publicized these moves as the triumph of Enlightenment over superstition; at home, she was careful to arrange an elaborate and fully religious coronation service, and always took pains to preserve her image as a devoted daughter of Orthodoxy. Either way, her prestige mounted.

Similarly, she seems to have had a struggle with some of the group of aristocrats who had brought her to power. One of these, Nikita Panin, who condemned the reign of Elizabeth because government then was not by 'the authority of state institutions' but by 'the power of persons', produced a scheme for a new Council to advise the monarch on high policy (1762). This has been interpreted as a scheme to subordinate the Empress to oligarchic control, not unlike Prince D. M. Golitsin's attempt at the accession of Anne. Catherine temporized for nearly six years, and, when such a Council was appointed in 1768 (at the start of the war with Turkey), she was strong enough to ensure that its nine members had purely advisory powers. On the other hand, the fact that Nikita Panin remained Catherine's chief adviser on foreign affairs down to 1780 could be taken to show that there was no struggle between them.

Legislative Commission

Her decision to call the Legislative Commission, however, looks very like an attempt to broaden the basis of her power. As a French diplomat said: 'This princess realizes only too well her utter dependence upon the grandees.... The opinion obtains that in order to shake off the yoke the Empress has assembled the Estates so that she may sound out public opinion.'[28] The official reason for the Commission was the re-codification of Russian law, which had remained unreformed since the Code of 1649, an epoch when the insights of the Age of Reason were not yet available to legislators. From what many of the delegates said, reform was long overdue in the administration of both civil and criminal law, which suffered from the vices of long-drawn-out trials, inadequate police, and the necessity of bribing officials at all levels. 'The *dvoriane* and people of every rank of Pskov county', went the Instruction from that county in the Province of Novgorod, 'suffer extreme ravages from brigands, thieves, robbers and other kinds of criminals, which stops very many of the *dvorianstvo* from living on their estates, for the protection of their lives from wicked torments.'[29] Catherine was confident (at least in her public utterances) that such problems could be solved. 'God forbid', she said in her *Instructions*, 'that after the completion of the legislation any other nation on earth shall enjoy greater justice and, therefore, greater well-being.'[30]

As for the Commission, there were plenty of precedents for assemblies of this kind, though not for Catherine's *Instructions* for it. She devoted two years hard reading and writing to it – a longer period than the Commission's meetings, which ran from July 1767 to December 1768. Its composition was also new. After gerrymandering with at least seven different electoral schemes, Catherine and her ministers eventually produced one which provided for representatives of the various departments of the central government, and of the following social groups: the nobility, the inhabitants of the towns, several different kinds of semi-free peasants, the Cossacks, and the native tribesmen. The chief groups excluded were the clergy (represented by one member of the Synod), about three quarters of the peasants, and all the private serfs. Another novelty was that, unlike all previous assemblies, which had been dominated or monopolized by the nobility, the Commission contained 207 urban representatives, and only 160 representatives from the nobility. This ratio was fully in accord with Catherine's oft-expressed desire to foster the growth of a middle class on western lines; though it does not indicate the predominance of the conquering bourgeoisie, as some historians have thought. For the proceedings of the Commission were dominated by the nobility; who were, in fact, numerically superior (228 in all) since the governments, some towns, peasant and tribal groups chose nobles to represent them.

Catherine brought the deliberations of this non-legislating

law-making body to a fairly swift end in 1768, officially because of the Turkish war, but really, in all probability, for other reasons. The *dvoriane* had revealed themselves to be lacking in the knowledge, ability, and experience required to draft regulations for the government of a vast empire. The quality of the discussions, moreover, had not been a good advertisement in western Europe for Russia's cultural level. 'To give Your Lordship a right idea of this choice collection of men, and their operations,' wrote the British diplomat, Henry Shirley to Lord Weymouth, 'permit me to suppose a certain number of the most ignorant of our petty merchants and shopkeepers in Great Britain and Ireland gathered as the several deputies of those nations in America, who either are subjects, or under the protection of His Majesty, and a few gentlemen unacquainted with the general principles, which constitute the basis of good government: this would be perhaps too favourable a copy of the original.'[31]

In addition, the Commission had taken the lid off a number of controversial issues, one airing of which was quite sufficient for a ruler intent upon establishing her own domination. Sharp conflicts were revealed between nobles, anxious to preserve their privileges (especially their monopoly of serf-ownership), and middle-class men desirous of securing exemption from public service and of acquiring the right to purchase serfs for their factories. The nobles wanted to make it next to impossible for upstarts to achieve noble rank by means of the Table of Ranks; the bourgeoisie wanted to make it illegal for nobles or peasants to set up in business. Rumblings of discontent were also heard from delegates from the Baltic provinces, the Ukraine, and other conquered areas, who feared the extinction of their national rights and peculiarities in a general scheme of Russification. And a handful of delegates even referred to the advantages to be derived from the emancipation of the serfs.

Possibly the chief reason for the quick closing of the Commission was that it had achieved what may have been its main purpose in Catherine's eyes: the consolidation of her power. She had called on the provinces and the bourgeoisie to redress the balance of the Court and the Guards; and the ensuing discussions had anatomized her empire before her very eyes. Though it passed no bills, the Commission allowed many important interests to let off steam; and its work formed the basis of subsequent legislation, in Catherine's reign and in the nineteenth century. It showed the Empress the balance of forces in the State, revealed which interests had to be cultivated, which demands satisfied, which grievances could be ignored, and which reforms had to be shelved. By 1768, as Shirley wrote, the crown was 'firmly on her head'. The Commission gave her the knowledge to keep it there.

Administration of the Provinces and Cities

Some of this knowledge was put to practical use in the Law on the Administration of the Provinces, which was promulgated in 1775. This reform of local government, which was partly based on a study of the Baltic provinces, as well as on Catherine's reading of 'Sir Blackstone' in French translation, had been rendered urgent by changes that had occurred in provincial life during the eighteenth century. With the advance of the frontiers, the growth of population, the settlement of the steppes, and, above all, the progressive emancipation of the nobility from life-long service to the state, there had developed a much more animated provincial life, whose needs were inadequately served by the administrative system left by Peter the Great. Most decisions had to be taken by the Colleges in St Petersburg and Moscow, whose bureaucrats were submerged in paper work. In 1767, for example, the College of Finance had its accounts six million roubles in arrears, and 16,000 matters awaiting decision were piled up on its pending-trays.[32] The capital was out of touch with provincial realities. Even when the provincial nobles were not forced to journey as far as St Petersburg to settle their affairs, the alternative was a trek to the provincial capital, almost as arduous. Peter's system was now too centralized, and his provinces were too large and too few. In addition, chaos and sloth were encouraged by the lack of specialization of function in the various agencies of government, where administration, police, finance, criminal cases and civil suits were all dealt with by the same office. Apart from that, the discussions of the Commission had revealed the desire of the nobility for a share in local affairs, particularly at District level – at the extremities of the tentacles of the bureaucracy, where its many failings were most patent. Probably the Pugachev revolt (1773) finally convinced Catherine of the necessity of reform, revealing as it did how thin on the ground were the forces of law and order.

Briefly, the Law of 1775 made the following chief changes. First, the number of provinces was increased from the fifteen of 1762 to fifty by the end of the reign. Secondly, most of the comprehensive powers exercised by the Colleges in the capital were transferred to the Governors of the Provinces – a big step in decentralization. Thirdly, these powers were split up at provincial and district level, where henceforth administration, finance, and justice were dealt with by separate boards. In addition, the judicial system was re-arranged, providing for the separation of criminal from civil justice, and for three distinct hierarchies of courts for the nobility, the town-dwellers, and the peasants. Fourthly, at district level, a measure of self-government was introduced, whereby the members of the boards were elected locally – except for the presidents, who were still to be bureaucrats.

This framework, which survived in many respects till 1917, was much more responsive to Russian needs than the slow turning wheels of the old Colleges, most of which were one by one wound up during the 1780s. Day-to-day decisions in local government were henceforth taken locally, in the light of the local situation and with the help of the local inhabitants. But this was far from genuine self-government: in fact, the long arm of St Petersburg was considerably strengthened. The elected nobles were given lower ranks, smaller salaries, and inferior powers than the service nobility of the State machine; and, if the nobles were lowly, one could hardly expect much status for the elected representatives of the townsmen and peasants. All had to be obedient servants of the provincial Governors, who, as a contemporary remarked, 'bent and twisted them like pliant willows'.[33] The Governors, in their turn, were appointed from the inner circle of Catherine's advisers, and were responsible to the Procurator-General, the most powerful man in Russia after the Empress. Thus the power of the crown over Russian life was greater and more detailed than ever.

This was also true in the cities where, with the Charter of the Cities (1785), Catherine pursued her policy of trying to inject some life into the anaemic bourgeoisie. The inhabitants of each town were told to form themselves into six corporations – property-owners, merchants, and so on down the scale to unskilled labourers. Those belonging to the first corporation were allowed to drive about the town in a coach drawn by two horses. Those in the second could use a kalash with two horses; while the third corporation was limited to one-horse transport.[34] The six corporations were to elect a municipal council which was to choose a six-man committee (one from each grade) to run urban affairs. But even where these elections and choosings took place (which was not everywhere) urban self-government failed to put down roots, and the cities continued under the tutelage of the (mainly noble) bureaucrats.

A further enhancement of autocratic power came in the 1780s with the Russification of the conquered areas of the Baltic, the Ukraine, and Siberia, hitherto governed according to their own laws and customs. Already, in 1764, Catherine had told the Procurator-General, Prince Viazemsky, that these provinces 'should be easily reduced to a condition where they can be Russified and no longer, like wolves, look for the woods. This can be achieved without effort if reasonable men are put in charge.'[35] In the Ukraine, the Hetman was replaced by a commission under General Rumiantsev in 1764; and then, in 1781, the area was divided into three Provinces, in which the administrative system of the Law of 1775 replaced the institutions of the Cossacks. This pill was sweetened for their leaders by the prospect of jobs and salaries in the imperial service, by the translation of their Cossack titles into the language of the Table of Ranks, and by the introduction of the poll-tax, which turned the cultivators of the soil into serfs (1783). A similar fate was meted out to the Baltic provinces, to Finland, and to Siberia, and ultimately to the segments of Poland gained by the three partitions. By the end of Catherine's reign, the characteristic

institutions of Great Russia prevailed everywhere: the autocracy of the crown, the bureaucracy of the nobility, and the
serfdom of the masses.

Service Nobility

While the nobles and serfs will be examined more fully later,
mention must be made here of the relations of these two classes
to the autocracy. The *dvorianstvo* had welcomed Peter III's
Proclamation of 1762, emancipating them from compulsory service to the State. 'I cannot describe', wrote one of their number,
A. T. Bolotov, 'what unimaginable joy that document produced
in the hearts of all the *dvoriane* of our beloved fatherland. All
very nearly jumped for joy.'[36] Such high jinks were premature,
however, for a glance at the small print of the Proclamation
reveals the unmistakable implication that nobles were still expected to serve voluntarily and to educate their children to do
so. 'We hope', concludes the Proclamation, 'that the whole
noble Russian *dvorianstvo,* appreciative of our generosity to
them and their descendants, will be inspired by their most
dutiful loyalty to Us and zeal, not to absent or hide themselves
from service, but to enter it with pride and enthusiasm.'[37]

And, in fact, they continued to serve under Catherine II.
Though she confirmed their right to serve voluntarily, service
remained as good as compulsory while it remained the only road
to power, patronage, status, and royal smiles. Even the Charter
of the Nobility (1785), which set down the nobles' privileges in
black and white, and represented an advance, as far as the rights
of the individual against the State were concerned, laid down in
Clause 20 that 'at every time necessary to the Russian Autocracy, when the service of the *dvorianstvo* is necessary and
needful to the general good, then each noble *dvorianin* is bound
at the first summons from the Autocratic Authority to spare
neither labour nor life itself for the service of the State'.[38] The
same Charter allowed the nobles to form corporations in their
provinces and districts, and to elect provincial and district
assemblies to meet every three years. But these assemblies had
nothing like the powers of western Estates. They dealt only in

local matters affecting the nobility, about which they could petition the Governor through the proper channels; and, of course, there was no national assembly. Moreover, nobles who had not seen service and reached commissioned rank were excluded from voting or holding office.

To the end of our period, then, the nobles were kept firmly in their place as cogs in the State machine impelled by the big wheels in St Petersburg. There was, however, one very large gap in the powers of the crown, for the nobles were as absolute in their control over their serfs as they were abject in their submission to the State. The enserfment of the millions was the price the tsars paid for the co-operation of the nobles. And, as the Commission of 1767 showed, Catherine was powerless to take away this consolation prize, even had she wanted. The Autocrat of all the Russias had less authority that the limited monarch of Great Britain when it was a question of protecting the meanest of her subjects.

Russia: The Influence of the West

THE achievement of the tsars in acquiring effective control over an area as big as the rest of Europe put together would have been impossible without the aid of techniques borrowed from the rest of Europe. Russia was the first under-developed society to experience the disturbing effects of western economic and intellectual penetration, and already under the Ancien Régime the cleavage was appearing between traditionalists who wished to have no part of the West, and modernists who accepted the paradox that Russia could only fend off the West by adopting the West's techniques.

Early Western Influences

Muscovy began to catch intoxicating whiffs of the more advanced West the moment she began to drive back her western invaders. The defeat of the Poles, and the annexation of Kiev and the Ukraine let in new religious ideas which split the Russian Church with the Great Schism. By that time there were many foreign experts of all kinds in Russia, usually called in by the tsars or leading aristocrats. Moscow churches were built by Italian architects. The armaments works at Tula were founded by a Dutch merchant (1632). The army was drilled on western lines (as far as it was drilled at all). It was led by German and Swedish officers and N.C.O.s, and armed with weapons made either abroad or in Russia by foreign specialists. The first Russian merchant ship was launched on the Caspian by Dutch designers. What few doctors and apothecaries there were came from abroad; and it was foreigners who translated western books on history, geography, and medicine. Broadly speaking, by the mid seventeenth century, Russia was beginning to imbibe medieval western scholasticism – at a time when the West was inaugurating the Scientific Revolution. Tsar

Alexei Mikhailovich (1645–76) surrounded himself with western music, theatre, clothes, and so on; and the three leading statesmen of the years immediately before Peter the Great were all western-orientated: A. L. Ordin-Nashchokin, Artamon Matveev, and Prince Vasili Golitsin. Possibly eighty-five to ninety per cent of the top service nobility were of non-Russian stock.

Another channel for the influx of western ideas was opened by the increasing trade with the West, especially with Great Britain and Holland. From the 1660s there was a regular letter and packet post with the West. In 1706 it went via Smolensk, Vilna, Königsberg, and Berlin, reaching Amsterdam on Thursdays. At twelve on Fridays, it started back by the same route. Other western links were forged by embassies: the first permanent one being set up in Russia by Gustavus Adolphus during the Thirty Years' War. In the second half of the seventeenth century, the Danes and the Dutch established representatives; and so did the Great Elector in 1675. Other powers, such as the Emperor or the King of England, sent plenipotentiaries when necessary. Likewise, between 1656 and 1689, Russia sent five temporary embassies to Italy and four to France.

At the time of Peter's birth (1672) there were probably 18,000 foreigners in Russia, most of them in Moscow. Since 1652 they had been made to live in a special suburb known as the German Settlement, with their own schools, churches, and social life. Tsar Alexei Mikhailovich, who made this provision, was fully prepared to make use of western expertise, but he did not want Russian life sullied with heretical ideas. However, his attempts to have his cake and eat it did not work, especially as it was in the German Settlement that Peter the Great made his early friendships.

Peter the Great

It was Peter who turned this trickle of westernization into a flood. Some nineteenth-century westernizers exaggerated when they said, as Chaadayev did in 1837: 'Peter the Great found only a blank page when he came to power, and with a strong hand he wrote on it the words *Europe* and *Occident*: from that time on we were part of Europe and of the Occident.'[1] Had the page been blank, Peter could hardly have been westernized himself as a youth. Without earlier Russian contact with the West, there would have been no English sailing boat in the barn at Izmailovo for Peter to learn to sail on. On the other hand, there is no doubt that Peter revolutionized the situation. He westernized the civil and military institutions of Russia, as well as the nobles who manned them, and irreversibly brought Russia into full participation in European military, diplomatic, economic, and cultural life. At the end of his reign, for example, he had over twenty permanent embassies in foreign capitals (including Pekin), and there were almost the same number of foreign representatives in St Petersburg.

The Great Embassy

Typically, he began by going to the West himself to see things at first hand. He probably became convinced of the necessity of the Great Embassy during the operations against the Turks at Azov, when Russian inadequacies in ships and sailors were glaringly revealed. 'He therefore sent', as he later wrote, 'a large number of high-ranking people to Holland and other states to learn shipbuilding and sailing. And what was still more wonderful: as if the monarch were ashamed to lag behind his subjects in these skills, he undertook the journey to Holland himself.'[2] But technical education was not the only motive for the mission. Azov had already taught him that Russia would need the help of a western coalition to defeat Turkey. He wrote to the Emperor, the kings of England and Denmark, the Pope, Holland, Brandenburg, and Venice, saying that the aim of the embassy was 'the confirmation of old friendship and love, concerns which were common to all Christendom, the weakening of the enemy of the Cross – of the Sultan of Turkey, the Crimean Khan and all the Moslem hordes – and the permanent increase of the Christian rulers'. The Great Embassy set out in March 1697, under the leadership of Peter's Swiss friend, Francis Lefort. Peter travelled incognito as 'Peter Mikhailov'.

It was the first peaceful visit of a Russian ruler abroad since Princess Olga travelled to Constantinople in the tenth century.

Unlike the usual Grand Tour of the Ancien Régime, Peter's Embassy spent more time in shipyards and gun-shops than in art galleries and tailors' shops; and the souvenirs he took back with him were not so much pictures and statues as tools and the men to use them. He engaged more than a thousand craftsmen at Amsterdam alone. He saw the Baltic coast at Riga, went via Königsberg and Berlin for fairly long stays in Holland and England, and then home through Vienna and Poland (1698).

The West was not always favourably impressed by the behaviour of Peter's party. In Deptford, on the Thames, they stayed in John Evelyn's house, especially redecorated for them on the orders of William III. Unfortunately, they caused £350 worth of damage to the furnishings and utterly ruined the lawn. One of Evelyn's servants said: 'There is a house full of people and right nasty.'[3] Peter lacked the delicacy for a full appreciation of western refinement; but, on the other hand, he was deeply impressed by the advanced state of western technology, and he spent the rest of his reign putting his empire through a compulsory course in westernization. Consignments of Russian nobles were despatched to study abroad, and hordes of foreign technicians were imported to man the top posts in the administration and the armed forces.

Economic Policy

One of Peter's concerns was to put into practice the western economic doctrines of mercantilism. His almost continual wars and the consequent expansion of the armed forces demanded the forcible exploitation of Russia's own resources, in order to overcome the lack of foreign exchange and to fatten the taxable capacity of his subjects. As Peter once wrote, 'our State of Russia is richer than other countries in metals and minerals, which till this time have never been used'.[4] And the reason why they had not been used and why Russia lacked a vigorous commercial and industrial middle class was probably less to do with the existence of serfdom or with the whims of the Russian soul than with the parsimonious manner in which nature had endowed the country in comparison with the West. The soil was unproductive, the weather harsh, and travelling arduous; iron deposits lay in the Urals, hundreds of miles from coal and from the centres of population. Without the State, Russia would have remained under-developed; but Peter's efforts, though far from achieving the self-sufficiency he aimed at, put Russia on a course of economic growth which by the end of the eighteenth century, brought her up to a level of development comparable with that of the rest of Europe.

The new College of Mines and Manufactures organized capital, labour, and raw materials for the new iron foundries, armaments works, and cloth factories – for all of which the state was the biggest customer. Sometimes State enterprises, once established, were sold at bargain prices to merchants or nobles. In other cases, the State induced entrepreneurs to set up in business privately by lending capital, granting exemptions from taxation and military service, and drafting thousands of State-peasants to become their semi-slave working force. By a decree of 1721 manufacturers were even allowed to buy populated villages and to use the serfs in their establishments: a privilege hitherto reserved to the nobility, and one of which the manufacturers seemingly took little advantage.[5]

To ease the flow of goods, rivers were dredged, canals dug, ports constructed, and ships launched; and the gigantic task of linking the Caspian with the Baltic was completed only seven years after Peter's death. In St Petersburg a completely new city was constructed on a marsh (1703) at the western end of the State on the Baltic: a project to which serfs in their thousands had to contribute their roubles and their lives. To the dismay of traditionalists, and in spite of its absurdly long distance from the centre of the empire, Peter moved his capital there; and by a mixture of State compulsion and economic incentives he succeeded in making it Russia's chief port, and in turning the Baltic into the main highway to the West.

In these ways, Peter laid the foundations of Russia's future industrial development: and, though these enterprises were mainly Russian-owned, they were very heavily dependent on westerners for managerial and engineering leadership, as well as skilled craftsmanship. Neither must the extent of the industrial advance be exaggerated. At the end of Peter's reign, for example, the army was still dependent on Yorkshire clothiers for the cloth for its uniforms. Only three per cent of the population were town-dwellers. Russia was still overwhelmingly agricultural, and farming was still in its medieval coma. Most peasants stuck to the immemorially old ways to grow sufficient for their own consumption; while even noble agricultural entrepreneurs, farming commercially for urban markets, were only, economically speaking, peasants writ large.

Education

As well as trying to push the economy in new directions, Peter also tried to westernize the Russian mind; for what little education existed in seventeenth-century Russia was provided by the Church and was mainly theological in content. He set up a School of Navigation and Mathematics in Moscow modelled on the Royal Mathematical School at Christ's Hospital in England. He founded schools of artillery and medicine, as well as nearly fifty mathematical schools in provincial towns. In 1724 he set up the Academy of Science from plans drawn up by Leibniz for the 'study of languages, likewise of other sciences and notable arts, and for the translation of books' – as the foundation decree puts it.[6] It was the beginning of a secular system of higher education, even though at first both professors and students had to be imported from Germany. In 1717 the tsar ordered the translation of a German manual of social deportment called *The Honourable Mirror of Youth,* which attempted to persuade the smarter young nobles, among other refinements, not to get drunk in the daytime, and not to spit in the middle of a group of people, but to one side instead. In 1718 he issued a decree detailing the rules for the conduct of social gatherings in private houses. Women were ordered to join these parties, and to come out from their harem-like seclusion. Clothes came in for a great deal of imperial attention. A decree of 1701 ordered men to wear a jacket in the French or Saxon style, a waistcoat, breeches, gaiters, boots, and caps in the German style; while women were told to wear bonnets, petticoats, skirts, and shoes in the German style. Censors posted at the town gate could tear illegal dress to pieces; while merchants who handled traditional attire could be knouted and sent to forced labour.

These forceful assaults on the body and mind were typical of Peter's methods. In one generation he was trying to hammer into the Russian mentality features which western Europe had acquired only after centuries of weathering. As Chaadayev wrote in 1837, 'the most marked trait of our physiognomy is the absence of spontaneity in our social development'.[7] That was exactly Peter's experience. 'Even if it is good and necessary,' he wrote, 'yet be it novel and our people will do nothing about it unless they are compelled.'[8] Even the laws of the market seemed to have no power. Business initiative had to be kicked from behind, and the joys of profit-making instilled by the knout. In 1712, when the State built some cloth factories for an association of merchants, the decree said: 'If they do not want to do this of their own free will then they must be forced; grant them facilities to defray the cost of the factory so that they may take pleasure in trading.'[9] In other words, Peter pursued western ends with eastern means, and in the outcome his empire lacked some crucial western features. It did not possess a highly diversified social structure, nor a dynamic middle class, nor an independent-minded nobility with national institutions capable of resisting the autocracy. Instead, in spite of all the westernization, Russian characteristics were as firmly entrenched as ever: the arbitrary despotism, the service nobility, and the enserfed cultivators of the soil.

This patchy result was in accord with Peter's wishes, for he was not an idolizer of all things western. Like other Russian rulers before and since, he wrongly believed that he could pick and choose; and legend has it that he once said: 'We need Europe for a few decades; later on we must turn our back on it.'[10] In 1717 he paid a second visit to the West, this time to the France of the Regency which was still suffering from the effects of the War of Spanish Succession. He was less impressed this time. 'It is good', he said, 'to take over arts and sciences from the French: for the rest, however, Paris stinks.'[11] But the experience of all developing countries has shown how difficult it is for rulers to borrow selected products from advanced societies without being also contaminated by the stink. Within a generation after Peter's death, as the Enlightenment began to rub off on to a few Russian minds, complaints were heard that Russia's westernization had not gone far enough: that the masses were still serfs, for example. These were only whispers, but they were a beginning. And while Peter was still alive, the opposite complaints, that westernization had already gone too far, were already an uproar.

Resistance to Westernization

At every stage Peter had to do battle with the traditionalism of old Muscovy. An incident that occurred at the very start of his reign illustrates the size of his self-appointed task of bringing Russia into the Age of Reason. In 1689 A. I. Bezobrazov, member of an old family of serving nobles, was about to set out for a distant post on behalf of the Regent Sophia, when she was overthrown by the coup that brought Peter to the throne. Fearing that his interests might suffer in his absence, he hired a sorcerer to cast a spell over the new administration so that it would favour him. Before long, the police discovered this in a round-up of Moscow wizards; but, far from laughing off this quaint traffic with the occult powers, the authorities took it seriously as an act of treason. Bezobrazov was tortured, sentenced to death, and to the confiscation of all his property.[12] As one of Peter's economic advisers, Ivan Pososhkov, once said: 'The Tsar pulls uphill alone with the strength of ten, but millions pull downhill.'[13]

Among the millions were the Old Believers, large numbers of the lower clergy as well as their untutored flocks, who were all deeply shocked at the impiety of being dragged into the Age of Reason. Fortunately for Peter, many of them were convinced that the end of the world was at hand, and that Antichrist was shortly to be dealt with by divine intervention. This led to passive resignation, and perhaps helps to account for the success

of Peter's brutal methods.[14] But there was much active opposition, too, from the masses driven desperate by taxation and
conscription, from old boyar families ousted from office by
Peter's upstart service nobles, and from country nobles unable
to see any virtue in the long war against Sweden or the building
of St Petersburg, or the imitation of the western style of life.
Their unwilling leader, and unwitting object of all their hopes,
was Peter's unfortunate eldest son, Alexei. 'It is well known to
everyone', Peter wrote to him in 1716, 'that you detest the work
I do for my people without any consideration for my health,
and that after I am gone you will be its destroyer.'[15] Two years
later Alexei was tortured and knouted to death, along with his
friends. It would have required the slaughter of millions to
eradicate the die-hard suspicions which flourished throughout
the eighteenth century: only a very thin upper crust of Russian
society was westernized and thus alienated from the mass. 'We
became citizens of the world,' wrote Karamzin in 1811, 'but
ceased in certain respects to be citizens of Russia. The fault is
Peter's.'[16]

Eighteenth-Century Economic Growth

As citizens of the world after Peter's death, the Russians had
their share of the rising level of economic activity which characterized the Europe of the Ancien Régime. Population rose at a
faster rate than anywhere else in Europe, including Britain. It
rose from the fourteen million of the first Revision of 1724 to
the twenty-nine million of the Revision of 1796, with an additional seven million added accruing from Catherine II's annexations, bringing the grand total at her death to thirty-six million.
Russia thus had the highest population in Europe; but the
composition of this total was significantly different from that of
the more advanced nations of the West in being overwhelmingly rural. Only 4·1 per cent of Russians were urban, compared with 20·5 per cent of the French, and 32 per cent of the
British.

Russian overseas commerce grew steadily, though there is
much guesswork about the figures. Exports rose from 4·2

million roubles in 1726 to 12·8 million roubles in 1762, and then to an annual average of 62 million roubles in the period 1812–15. Imports rose from 2·1 million roubles in 1726, to 8·2 in 1762, and 39·1 in 1812–15. The main exports were flax and hemp, pig-iron, rough linen cloth, timber, ropes, sail-cloth, bristles, hides and furs. In addition, grain exports began to mount in Catherine's reign, as the fertile steppe was painfully ploughed and colonized, and as Russian possessions and privileges on the Black Sea expanded, from the Treaty of Kuchuk-Kainardzhi (1774) onwards. The principal imports were luxury goods, with the exception of Yorkshire woollen cloth for the troops. In other words, the utilitarian products of ordinary Russians were traded against the trinkets required by the westernized nobility: silks and cottons, wines and spirits, and rhubarb, tea, coffee, sugar, and fruits. Moreover, almost all the trade was in foreign hands, British mainly, then Dutch, and German. Britain bought as much Russian merchandise in an average year as any other two nations, and paid more cash to Russia than all the other European nations combined. This was the ready money the Russians needed to pay for the luxuries of the fashionable: mostly German products in the first half of the century, mainly French under Catherine. In the trading operations themselves the Russians were purely passive. In 1750 the Senate complained about the 'deplorable condition of the Russian merchantry'.[17] Similar remarks were made at the meetings of the Legislative Commission (1767). Attempts by Russian merchants under Anne to trade in Russian bottoms with Russian crews came to grief when most of the ships ran ashore in sight of Kronstadt.

Internally, also, Russian business life grew, moderately fast between 1725 and 1762, more rapidly under Catherine II. Among the causes was the increase in population, widening the market and boosting man-power. But the activities of the State were probably the chief driving force: the wars, the mushrooming bureaucracy, and, in the second half of the century, the increasing liberalization of economic life, partly under the influence of Physiocratic ideas. A *ukase* of 1753 abolished all internal customs duties. Catherine II went further: in this respect, a true daughter of the Enlightenment. When in 1763 the Senate put forward a proposal for a monopoly in playing cards, she shouted, 'To the devil with monopolies.' She immediately began a programme of abolishing such economic privileges, ultimately abolishing them all in the manifesto of 1775, which made industry free to all ranks – except serfs, and except vodka distilling, still a noble monopoly.

Russia's industrial growth in the eighteenth century, though undoubted, is difficult to measure, partly because of the loose way in which contemporary statisticians used the word '*fabrika*' to cover anything from a workshop to a large factory. If one takes a rough average of the estimates of recent Soviet historians, it appears that there were between 100 and 200 factories at the end of Peter's reign, and about 2,000 at the end of Catherine's, with the curve rising most sharply in the 1760s.[18] Growth in the iron and copper industries of the Urals was most spectacular. In 1716 there were four enterprises there, in mid century about fifty, in 1762 over 100. By 1800 pig-iron output was the highest in the world. And these giant enterprises, owned partly by nobles, and partly by merchants, and in either case heavily dependent on serf and state-peasant labour, only account for a proportion of Russia's industrial growth. The major part of manufactures were produced by the *kustar* industrial system, that is, by peasants making goods for the village markets. Their products were mainly the cheaper wares of everyday use, but there were also highly skilled craftsmen working with silks and precious metals.

Agricultural output also soared, as the export figures show, but not because of improved methods. The colonization of the Ukraine and the fertile steppe lands down to the Black Sea brought more (and more productive) land under cultivation. These grass lands were exploited mainly by noble entrepreneurs farming commercially with serf labour for the export trade. Total production was therefore boosted without any perceptible improvement in the yield per acre. The majority of Russian farming stayed locked in the grip of archaic and wasteful customs, techniques, and tools. Most peasants could barely keep a few animals alive; and the few beasts who emerged half-starved from the long Russian winter often had to be kept alive with straw from the roofs. In the older areas, the three-field system worked by serf labour was the most common method. The newly opened lands had not yet evolved even to this level of sophistication, but were cultivated by the primitive field-grass husbandry, whereby a field was cropped to exhaustion for several years and then allowed to go back to grass while another field was cleared.

Little improvement in productivity was likely under a régime in which the lords' strips were intermingled with those of the serfs, and in which the nobles' ideas about farming were shackled to the same out-of-date prejudices as those of the peasant. Practically the only method of improving output that the average noble could think of was to make the serfs work harder; while the serfs, for their part, with no property and no rights, had no incentive to increase production. Advanced thinkers in touch with western experience realized that bettering of the peasants' lot was one of the keys to more profitable agriculture. Catherine was ahead of her people on this subject. 'Agriculture can never flourish there,' she wrote in the *Instructions* for the Legislative Commission, 'where no Persons have any Property of their own.' And then she emphasized, '*Every Man will take more Care of his own Property, than of that which belongs to another; and will not exert his utmost Endeavours upon that, which he has Reason to fear another may deprive him of.*'[19] But, as discussions in the Commission showed, and articles in the publications of the *Free Economic Society for the Encouragement of Agriculture and Good Husbandry* amply illustrated, the vast majority of the nobility were so deeply prejudiced against any reduction in their powers over their tenants that any change in this direction by government action was unthinkable. In vain did writers with western experience point out the virtues of the free market. 'In England', wrote S. E. Desnicky in 1780, 'there are no longer any legal hindrances to agriculture, the cultivated land is completely in the commercial sector, with the result that there are no obstacles to buying it for anyone who wants to. The result is that practically all England has been transformed into a tilled field.'[20] But radicals of this kidney were voices crying in a real wilderness: an area of Russian life not for many years to be touched by western ideas.

Education

The probability is that Russians were incapable of sophisticated economic behaviour because of their educational backwardness. Apart from foreign scholars and a few Russians who had studied abroad, the generality of the *dvorianstvo* received only a very rudimentary schooling, while the mass of the people were steeped in ignorance. The middle years of the eighteenth century saw plenty of paper schemes, and many pious hopes were expressed in government circles, but in practice not much advance was made on the very rough outline of public education sketched by Peter the Great. In 1731 the Military Academy was founded, purely for the preparation of young *dvoriane* for the armed forces and civil service. At the same time, some extension of the education of the other ranks was provided in the expanding garrison schools. Another landmark was the foundation in 1755 of Moscow University, along with two gymnasia, one for nobles, and one for the common people (excluding serfs). These were part of the ambitious schemes of the westernized administrator Ivan Shuvalov, designed to drag Russia into the eighteenth century. N. N. Popovsky, lecturing at the new university, thus attempted to stir the intellectual ambitions of his students: 'You can soon show that nature has endowed you with minds no worse than those on which other nations pride themselves; assure the world that it is a late beginning in the sciences, rather than the lack of ability, which has kept Russia from joining the ranks of the enlightened nations.'[21] Enthusiasts of this sort were making a start, but standards remained low, and attendance thin till the next century. The Faculty of Law had only one student in 1765, likewise the Faculty of Medicine in 1768. Shuvalov also founded the Academy of Arts (1757), but the Court and nobility continued to be heavily dependent upon Italian and French architects, painters, and sculptors for as long as the Ancien Régime lasted. The

Winter Palace, for example, and other fine buildings in St Petersburg, were the work of the Italian, Bartholomew Rastrelli.

Catherine II was not impressed by the educational level of her adopted people, from the Court downwards. 'Never had a people before its eyes more objects of fanaticism,' she wrote about the inhabitants of Moscow, 'more wonder-working images ... more churches, more of the clerical crew, more convents, more devout hypocrites, more beggars, more thieves.'[22] She appointed Ivan Betsky as president of the Academy of Arts, and director of the St Petersburg Military Academy. He had been brought up in the salons of the West, and proposed Rousseauite schemes for using the schoolroom to turn out a 'new breed of humanity'. In practice, his achievements did not advance far beyond the setting up of the Moscow Orphanage (1763), the St Petersburg Orphanage (1772), the Smolny Convent at St Petersburg for daughters of the *dvorianstvo* (1764), and a second girls' school for commoners (except serfs) in 1765. After his retirement in 1780 Catherine II employed Fedor Yankovich de Mirievo, a graduate of Vienna University who had taken part in the Austrian educational reforms of 1774. His Statute of Popular Schools was approved by the Empress in 1786. This planned a network of schools in district and provincial capitals: elementary schools with a two-year course and high schools with a four-year course. A count made just after the Empress's death found forty-nine high schools in action, containing 7,001 pupils, and 239 elementary schools, with 15,209 pupils.

These figures, together with others on soldiers' schools, church schools and so on, suggest that there was more general education available to Russians at the end of this period than at the beginning. But what its quality was like, or how far down it penetrated into the ranks of the people, are questions very difficult to answer. Publishing-figures suggest progress. In 1762, for example, ninety-five titles were published, including five periodicals; in 1788, 439 titles came out, including nineteen periodicals. As for the education of the top nobility, that tended still to be provided outside the public sector. The *haut-monde* were usually educated privately, and received their grounding in things western at first hand, either in Russia from imported tutors, teachers and dancing-masters, or in the capitals of western Europe themselves. By the last quarter of the eighteenth century such people became difficult to distinguish from the denizens of Versailles. With their snuff-boxes and lace-cuffs, their coaches and cuisine, their rococo drawing rooms and Enlightened morals, even in their language, they were more French than Russian. 'Our forefathers', said a St Petersburg journal in 1783, 'called it *education* when they taught their children the Psalms and how to count on the abacus; after this they would give their enlightened son a book of hours printed in Kiev.... This *education* can hardly be called education, for the duties of the citizen and Natural Law were unknown to the youngsters.'[23]

The main body of the nobility were not so easily uprooted from Russian traditionalism, and they resisted the sell-out to western culture just as their fathers and grandfathers had criticized Peter the Great. 'There is no one among them', wrote Edward Finch, the British ambassador in 1741, 'who would not wish St Petersburg at the bottom of the sea.... Besides, they are persuaded that it would be much better for Russia in general to have nothing more to do with the affairs of Europe than it formerly had, but confine itself to the defence of its own ancient territories strictly called so.'[24] Hostility to an alien Court was one of the ingredients in the growing national consciousness, a pride already visible in Michael Lomonosov, scientist and poet, and greatest intellectual product of eighteenth-century Russia. He did much to develop the Russian language, which had, according to him, 'the majesty of Spanish, the vivacity of French, the firmness of German, the delicacy of Italian, and the richness and concise imagery of Greek and Latin'.[25]

The same emotions fostered liberalism in many a noble who suffered under the arbitrary acts of the autocracy. Equally, liberalism was fostered directly by contact with the West. The most outstanding example in this period was Alexander Radishchev, graduate of the university of Leipzig and devotee of the *philosophes*. His *Journal from St Petersburg to Moscow*, published in 1790, chipped away at the pillars of Catherine's

Russia: the autocracy, the bureaucracy, and the serfdom. He wrote,

A stream that is barred in its course becomes more powerful in proportion to the opposition it meets. Once it has burst the dam, nothing can stem its flood. Such are our brothers whom we keep enchained. They are waiting for a favourable chance and time. The alarum bell rings. And the destructive force of bestiality breaks loose with terrifying speed.[26]

Catherine said the work was 'manifestly revolutionary', and its author 'infected and full of the French madness'. She exiled him to Siberia; but, as the nineteenth century was to prove, this was no way to stamp out liberalism. Rulers of under-developed countries who import the technologies of more advanced societies do so at their peril.

Russia: Lord and Serf

Nobility

Russian society was hammered into its eighteenth-century shape, in common with the rest of Russian life, by the actions of the State. The tsars had one by one crushed the over-mighty boyars, and created the serving *dvorianstvo* in their place. By the mid seventeenth century, of the twenty-three wealthiest serving landowners, only nine were descendants of old princely families; while the remainder were untitled serving-men, mainly kinsmen and favourites of the one boyar family that went up instead of down, the Romanovs. These nobles had received their estates from the crown. Between 1682 and 1711 alone, 1,366,000 acres of arable land and 43,500 peasant households were handed over as royal bounty in this way: a practice which continued throughout the Ancien Régime. Catherine II gave away 800,000 peasants to private landowners. Her son Paul gave 2,000 to a man who dedicated a poem to him.

At the same time as creating the serving nobility, the tsars had much reduced the holdings of hereditary lands (*votchinas*); and most land had been turned into service estates (*pomestyes*), granted temporarily to men who served the tsar on condition of that service. By the time of Peter the Great, when *votchin-niki* were all serving and *pomestyes* were not returned to the tsar but inherited by the family of the serving man, there was little difference between the two, a change that was legally recognized by a decree of 1714. Hereditary landowning thus approximated to what it was in the west of Europe, except that (apart from Church land) all land was held on condition of service to the autocracy. Peter the Great exacted his full quota of service, and by the Table of Ranks (1722) made service the basis of a social status.

Between Peter's death (1725) and the accession of Catherine

II (1762) the nobility gained in power in relation to the State. Among the privileges they acquired were, first, the reduction of their compulsory service from life to twenty-five years (1736), and then their emancipation from it (1762). Under Catherine II, they were allowed a not very heady draught of provincial and district self-government, drowned as it was with a big dash of autocratic-bureaucratic resurgence. The high point in their Golden Age came in 1785 with the issue of the Charter of the Nobility, which confirmed their old privileges and conferred some new ones. The *dvoriane* were granted the right to resign from service (a limited privilege in practice), to travel abroad, and to serve foreign princes. They could not be deprived of their nobility or property except when found guilty of certain crimes, such as breaking an oath, brigandage, or theft. And they could be tried only by their peers, and were exempt from corporal punishment – at least until they had been degraded. The estates of those who were degraded and deprived in this way were no longer to be confiscated by the crown but passed on to the heirs. Nobles were free to sell estates they had bought, but the disposal of their hereditary estates was still tied up with restrictions. They were exempt from the poll-tax and the billeting of troops. In addition to these advantages, the Charter confirmed the economic position of the *dvorianstvo* as the most favoured social group. They could own populated villages, for example, buy urban houses, exploit the minerals and timber of their estates, set up industrial enterprises, maintain fairs, and sell their own produce wholesale, at home or abroad.

To these real bread-and-butter privileges, the Charter added some toys, in the form of district and provincial assemblies, with certain powers of self-government, but no real teeth. Catherine did not allow the nobility to form a national estate, capable of resisting the crown. She constantly frustrated their desire to become a closed, hereditary caste, and maintained the principle, enshrined in Peter's Table of Ranks, of automatic ennoblement at the appropriate grades in the service. 'Birth here', wrote an English observer late in the century, 'gives but little claim to preference or consideration; both are regulated by the degree of rank acquired by service.'[1] Though the career open to the talents was thus maintained, however, Russia would have been singular among eighteenth-century countries if titled rank had not given the nobles a head start in the race for promotion. Patronage eased the career of A. T. Bolotov, for example, who was enrolled in the army while still a minor, because his father knew a field-marshal.[2] And favouritism received official support under Catherine II when the decree of 1765 announced that nobles were to be promoted with 'an advantage over non-*dvoriane* according to their quality'.[3]

The whole life of a noble was shaped by the necessity of serving the tsar, a duty difficult to evade as the clerks in the *Herold-Meister*'s office at St Petersburg kept tabs on him from the day he was registered as a small boy till the time he retired as an old man. From 1714 onwards Peter forced the nobility to undergo elementary schooling in arithmetic and geometry before joining the service – on pain of being forbidden to marry. Without his teacher's certificate, the noble could not get his marriage licence. And even when he married, the noble had little opportunity to put down roots in any locality, at least, not till late in the eighteenth century, as the service had him constantly on the move. 'Noble families', wrote Michael Shcherbatov, 'were often so scattered in the service that often one did not come again in contact with one's relatives during one's whole lifetime.'[4] But long before this point in his life, a noble was likely to have been moved about as a child, as his father, also in the service, was transferred from one posting to another. Education was also a very peripatetic business. A. T. Bolotov began school at Pskov at the age of six, where he learned an Epistle of St Paul to the Corinthians almost by heart (1744). His father was then posted to Estonia and later elsewhere, and by the time he joined his regiment in Livonia at the age of seventeen, young Bolotov had studied under a serf-tutor on the family estates, under a German-speaking N.C.O. in Estonia, and in a private school for nobles in Courland, as well as in two different boarding schools in St Petersburg.[5]

Bolotov had received special permission to extend his education. Normally, a young noble joined a regiment at the age of fifteen and served a few years in the ranks: an apprenticeship

Peter the Great had insisted upon. The better-off nobles performed this chore in one of the three Guards regiments, mounting guard, doing fatigues, and drawing ordinary rations. One of
these regiments, the Dragoons, had as many as 300 princes in
its ranks in Peter's day. After this basic training, the young
noble received his commission, the well-connected in the
Guards, the others in more hum-drum units. They used every
kind of ruse to avoid these hardships, many receiving help from
friends or relatives in the bureaucracy. 'An unlimited number
of slothful gallants,' wrote Pososhkov in Peter's reign, 'each of
whom would have been capable of chasing five of the enemy,
but who have secured lucrative positions, live peacefully and
increase their wealth. Others escape service by judicious bribery
or by feigning illness or holy imbecility.'[6] After much com-
plaining, they got their way under Anne, and by passing
through her Military Academy (1731) they were able to get
their commissions without serving in the ranks. Sailors went
through the Naval Academy to officer the fleet; civil servants
mainly learned their jobs in a government office.

The great mass of the nobility were glad to secure a very
modest command in a line regiment, or a humble job at a provincial government desk, for only a minority belonged to the
aristocratic connections who officered the Guards and achieved
the highest political appointments. In eighteenth-century Russia, it was possible for a noble family to become very poor
indeed, as for generation after generation the family stubbornly
followed the custom of dividing the father's property among all
the children. Laws even had to be passed making it illegal for
a *dvorianin* to sell himself into slavery. On the other hand, with
luck at Court, it was possible to become immensely rich very
quickly. Alexander Menshikov acquired vast estates and thousands of serfs as chief adviser and intimate friend of Peter the
Great. His father had been a stable hand, but he himself was
raised to the rank of prince (1707) – the last to be so honoured
till Paul's reign (1796–1801). He was not the last to make a
fortune at Court, however, and many others followed in his
path, notably the Orlovs and Potemkins of Catherine II's reign.

A computation made in 1777 showed that the vast majority of

landlords (83 per cent) owned less than a hundred serfs. Only 16·2 per cent had over 100, 51·8 per cent between 10 and 100, and 32 per cent below 10. On the basis of these figures, perhaps, an upper, middle, and lower class of nobles can be distinguished, with the first owning about 80 per cent of the serfs. By the end of the Ancien Régime some of the aristocrats were immensely wealthy. Count N. P. Sheremetev, for instance, owned 185,610 serfs, and Count Vorontsov 54,703. At the bottom of the scale, on the other hand, were many rustic nobles scarcely distinguishable from peasants. In 1771 a delegate from some provincial nobles told the Senate that over 200 young nobles in his area, who wanted to join the royal service, could not do so as they lacked the necessary boots and clothes. The social backwardness of noble life in the provinces till late in the century extended up to the most powerful families, who tended to regard themselves as only camping out when they left Moscow or St Petersburg. Even Prince D. M. Golitsin's manor house (according to an inventory taken in 1731) consisted of only two rooms, with some ikons and pictures on the walls.[7]

Serfs

Rich or poor, the nobles depended for their income on the labour of their serfs – always in short supply in comparison with land. 'I don't need land,' wrote A. I. Bezobrazov in 1681 to a steward who had just bought him some in the south, 'I need peasants.'[8] And it was chiefly because of their dearth that the cultivators of the soil had deteriorated from the peasant proprietors they had mostly been in the late Middle Ages to the serfs they had nearly all become by 1650. This process of degradation was due partly to the fall in peasant incomes, partly to the action of landlords, but mainly, it seems, to the pressures of the evolving centralized autocracy. As has been shown, each of the rulers of Muscovy gave away large tracts of state land to serving nobles, or to the Church, thus converting 'black' peasants (more or less independent farmers paying a quit-rent to the State) into renters of private land. In 1500 'black' peasants formed the majority of the cultivators; in 1700 they formed seven per cent. In these two centuries, peasant incomes and size of holdings fell, as a result of economic crises and political catastrophes, accompanied by mounting State taxes and landlords' exactions. The changes in taxation culminating in Peter the Great's poll-tax have already been mentioned. The increases in rents can be illustrated by the amount of work peasants were made to do on the lord's demesnes. This seems to have been one day per week in the fifteenth century, and three days and more by 1700.

His economic plight placed many a peasant in the power of his landlord by making him his debtor, and thus giving the lord the legal means of tying the peasant to the estate. An alternative for the peasant was flight, either to another lord, or to the empty regions on the moving frontier, or to a life of banditry. All these possibilities prompted landlords to seek means, legal and extra-legal, of pinning their tenants down. And one of the greatest worries of the middle and lower landlords was how to prevent their tenants being enticed away by the magnates, and, when they were, how to get them back again.

In all of this the tsars, bent on a policy, as we have seen, of raising up the *dvoriane* and casting down the boyars, made flight more difficult and recapture more easy by a series of laws whose motive was the support of the nobility, but whose main result was the immobilizing, and thus the enserfment, of the peasantry. These enactments culminated in the Code of 1649, which remained the basis of Russian law into the nineteenth century. Its many pronouncements on peasants and peasant flight had the following five main effects on enserfment. First, it abolished the time limit beyond which a lord could not claim the return of a fugitive tenant or one enticed away by another lord. Earlier legislation had allowed a lord only five years for the recovery of a fugitive. In 1642 this was extended to ten years for peasants in flight, and fifteen years for those who had been poached by a rival lord. Now the Code vastly increased the lord's power by giving him an infinite time to recapture his men. Secondly, previous laws tying the peasant to his estate had applied only to the head of the family. The

Code of 1649 extended the ban on movement to the sons, brothers and nephews who lived with him. Thirdly, lords gained the right to move peasants about from one *votchina* to another, or from one *pomestye* to another – though not, of course, from a *pomestye* to a *votchina*, for that would have contradicted the main purpose of the 1649 laws on peasantry: it would have deprived a service estate of its labour. To give an example of the sort of transfers that were possible, if a lord (his son, nephew or steward) murdered another lord's peasant, he had to replace him with the best of his own peasant families.

Fourthly, peasants were deprived of the right to full ownership of property, the law taking the line that the peasant's goods ultimately belonged to his lord. Fifthly, the peasant was denied legal existence. He had long been under his lord's jurisdiction for offences committed on the estate. Now, in a dispute outside the estate, he was to be represented by his lord, except in cases of murder, theft, highway robbery or the possession of stolen goods. Nothing in the Code of 1649, or in subsequent legislation, defined the precise relationship between a serf and his lord (though the question was debated in the 1767 Commission); and, even had the serf been given any legal rights against his lord, he had no means of enforcing them. The Code made it illegal for the serf to bring complaints against his lord, except in cases of treason or misconduct with a female serf. Thus, from 1649 the serf was at the mercy of his lord, who not only pressed his legal claims to the hilt, but also extended his dominion in extra-legal ways which the autocracy was unwilling, or unable, to check. The way was open for the victory of brute force. Because he had stolen five-and-a-half gallons of wine from the steward, a late-seventeenth-century serf had this sentence pronounced against him: 'The offender is to be mercilessly beaten with the knout until there is scarcely any breath left in his body.'[9]

The enserfment of the peasantry with the help of the state continued from 1649 right through the Ancien Régime, either as the result of enactments for that purpose, or as an indirect consequence of laws made for other reasons. The process can only be sketched here. Peter the Great's contribution was to make the lord responsible for the military call-up and for the poll-tax. In 1731 the lords were made the agents of the State for actually collecting the tax. A law of 1724 prevented serfs from travelling from their estates to engage in trade without their lords' written consent endorsed by a public official. After 1744 they needed printed passports in addition. An enactment of 1737 prevented a serf from buying land or a business except in the name of his lord. A decree of 1760 allowed lords to deport recalcitrant serfs to Siberia, so long as they were forty-five or under, and accompanied by their wives, restrictions which were easy to evade. Ivan Turgenev's mother sent two of her serfs to Siberia on one occasion for not bowing to her when she passed by. This law, like the British shipments of convicts to America or Australia, was, from the government's point of view, a good way of colonizing Siberia, though the long journey, mostly on foot, is said to have caused a seventy-five per cent wastage rate.

Under Catherine II, whatever Enlightened hopes she may have entertained, the trend continued. By her time, the extra-legal or illegal sale of serfs was generally accepted, with or without land, with or without the rest of their families. The status of the serf had changed. Just as the *pomestye* had been converted into a heritable private property, so had the serf ceased to be attached to the land and become tied instead to the person of his lord. Bondsmen became the small change in the payment of dowries or the settlement of gambling debts. In mid century male serfs without land fetched about thirty roubles, the cheapest ones bringing in as little as three or five roubles. By the end of the century, the price had risen to 100 or 200 roubles, or more. Special talent commanded more, of course: a pretty young female serf might cost 500 roubles. Count N. P. Sheremetev emancipated the actress Parasha in order to make her his wife.[10] Prince Potemkin paid 40,000 roubles for a fifty-piece serf orchestra.

Catherine limited the sale of serfs only by forbidding the use of the hammer at public auctions. In 1765 she allowed lords to sentence serfs to hard labour with the Admiralty. This punishment, along with the deportation to Siberia, enables one to form an idea of the quality of the serfs' everyday existence; for they often ran away to Siberia, and volunteered for the galleys. A further twist to the screw was given by Catherine with her decree of 1767 forbidding all complaints by serfs against their lords on pain of knouting and penal servitude for life. Russian serf-owners, wrote the Empress to Diderot, were 'free to do in their estates whatever seemed best to them, except to give the death penalty, which is prohibited to them'.[11] Such a limitation may have satisfied her mentor in Enlightenment, but it was little consolation to a serf who happened to die as the result of prolonged whipping. On the whole, the autocracy did not come down very hard on nobles caught ill-treating their serfs. The wife of a certain Captain Kashinev, for example, once gave a serf such 'an unendurable punishing' that he hanged himself. She was condemned to six weeks' penance in a nunnery.[12]

By the end of the Ancien Régime, about half of the peasants were serfs in the strict sense used in the last few paragraphs, that is, bondsmen of nobles. The other half consisted of about thirty varieties of social groups, all with different origins and histories, who were gradually assimilated during the period into the category of State peasants, managed by the Treasury, whose standard of life and legal rights were a little better than those of the private serfs. In this group were the remnants of the once predominant 'black' peasants, as well as the Church peasants (after the secularization of 1764) and numerous other groups. Among the last were tiny groups of land holders who paid no dues, no taxes, and performed no military service: for instance, the descendants of Ivan Susanin, who had lost his life saving the future Tsar Michael Romanov from capture by the Poles during the Time of Troubles; and the progeny of Ivan Riaboev, who discovered mineral waters in 1714, which did Peter the Great some good. Similar to the State peasants were some other categories of non-private peasants: for example, court peasants, peasants attached to factories and mines, postal peasants, falconers (about a thousand strong in the 1780s), stable peasants, and so on.

All these peasants who were not owned by noble landlords

had the advantage that the State could do something to mitigate their sufferings. On the other hand, they were always in danger of losing their superior position by being handed over as royal gifts to favourites, a transfer to which Catherine II was particularly prone. Moreover, she increased the number of private serfs in another way: when the conquered provinces were forced to accept Russia's administrative system in the 1780s, the cultivators of the soil there were Russified into serfdom at the same time. And, as we have seen, the autocracy of Catherine steadily abdicated responsibility for the serfs, relinquishing them to the arbitrary mercies of their lords.

Life on the Estates

The landlord's principal concern was to squeeze as much produce out of his estates, and therefore as much work out of his tenants, as possible. Most lords, during most of the Ancien Régime, had the same economic outlook as their peasants: that is to say, they were subsistence farmers, even when subsistence grandly consisted of the steady transport of cartloads and sledloads of provender from the countryside to the mansions of Moscow and St Petersburg. Commercial agriculture was exceptional until the last two decades of the eighteenth century, when southern landlords began to specialize in production for export through the newly acquired Black Sea ports. Large numbers of landlords (especially the aristocrats) were absentees. They were performing their service to the tsar, or were congregated in the capital to avoid the brigands, or the boredom, that made provincial life unattractive. Gradually through the eighteenth century, though, the provinces became more populated, especially under Catherine II, when the release from compulsory service and the decentralization of government encouraged nobles to move out from Moscow and St Petersburg and begin to form that local life which forms the familiar background to so much of nineteenth-century Russian literature.

Whether physically present or not, Russian landlords did not develop the absentee mentality, but, either directly themselves, or indirectly through their stewards, took an intimate interest in estate-management, the source of their necessities and luxuries. This consisted principally in organizing the labour of the peasants among whose strips the lord's own demesne was scattered, and alongside whose animals the live-stock of the manor-house grazed. The peasants paid rent for their strips either in the form of _barshchina_ (labour services) or _obrok_ (a quit-rent in cash or kind) or a mixture of the two. _Barshchina_ tended to predominate in fertile areas with good access to communications and markets, where the landlord would reserve, perhaps, half the estate for himself and operate as a large-scale agrarian entrepreneur – though such a phrase flatters a mode of production dependent on peasant labour and draught-animals, and peasant equipment and know-how. The tenants were divided into small groups for the allotment of tasks and the payment of dues. Each group (called a _tiaglo_) consisted of at least a married couple, though the size of each working unit could vary, as children became old enough to join (at fifteen, sixteen, or seventeen) and as adults became old enough to retire (at fifty for women, sixty to sixty-five for men). Each _tiaglo_ tended to work about three days a week on the lord's strips, and the rest of the week on their own. Hours of work were about fourteen to sixteen in summer and eleven to thirteen in winter. Owing to the fact that the numbers making up each _tiaglo_ varied through the years, the peasants' strips had to be redistributed from time to time so as to ensure that each _tiaglo_ had an amount of land roughly corresponding with the number of its members. There was not much encouragement here for more scientific methods, in spite of the pleas of one or two improving landlords in the Free Economic Society. A serf who spent the first half of the week working land belonging to his lord, and the second cultivating strips shortly to be taken away from him, lacked the incentive to improve.

The _obrok_ system of payment was usually operated on infertile soils which produced no surplus for the market, or on fertile soils which were too far from markets or ports for any surplus to be sold. In these areas, the landlords did not exploit a seigneurial reserve; but all the land was divided among the tenants, who raised the money (or produce) to pay their rent from their strips or by doing odd jobs. Though landlords said they disliked *obrok*, circumstances often forced their hand. On some ungrateful soils almost any means of keeping peasants working and eating was welcome. 'When there is no work in the fields for the women, girls, and children,' wrote P. I. Rychkov for the benefit of his colleagues in the Free Economic Society, 'while in the woods there are nuts, mushrooms, hops, and other useful things, make them go out gathering without letting the favourable moment pass, and thus make a profit for the master.'[13]

The work done by *obrok*-paying serfs was often industrial, and they formed the backbone of the *kustar* industry (see p. 296). Landlords as a rule did not mind their tenants making themselves useful as craftsmen in this way; but often *obrok* involved allowing serfs to work away from the estate, sometimes in far distant towns or industrial regions, frequently for months on end. For this, the serfs required passports. Often they were sent off in a party with someone in charge, and always thoroughly questioned on their return, especially as to the amount of wages they had earned, so that the lord received his due share. Writing to the Free Economic Society about the peasants in his province of Vologda in 1766, A. V. Oloshev said that 'many of them go to Moscow or St Petersburg, and, in order to provide for the subsistence of their families and pay their *obrok* and poll-tax, they do peddling and other jobs, useless to society, but sometimes lucrative for the peasants and for them alone'.[14] The majority of the population of most towns probably consisted of peasants with passports, in the curious economic position of working as wage-earners in order to pay their feudal dues. Landlords disliked the system because it tended to upset the outlook of the serfs, who were never the same again once they had been to the city, and never again quite fitted into the system of 'silent obedience' which was supposed to be their role.

The steward (usually a serf) ran the estate and collected the dues with the help of a hierarchy of serf officials appointed by the lord, or elected by the community (the *mir*) with his approval. His 'right-hand man' (as A. T. Bolotov called him) was the *starosta*, the mediator between steward and peasants, who reported to the steward every evening on the details of the day's work and took his orders for the morrow. Below him were other officials, treasurers, and clerks; and in direct charge of the daily farming tasks were foremen: centurions in charge of 100 or 200 serfs, and tithing-men commanding groups of ten. One of the steward's jobs was to take away the serf's seed-corn from him at harvest in case he sold it. This was then kept in the manor grange till it was time to give it back again at seed-time. 'The negligence of these lazy, good-for-nothings', wrote A. T. Bolotov in 1770, 'is so great that they never calculate for how long their grain will be enough to feed them; they sell their last bushels without thinking of the future, and eat their money or get drunk with it.'[15]

The steward not only supervised the farming, and reported serfs who did not work hard enough so that they could be punished, he also minutely policed the everyday life of the inhabitants of the *mir*, punishing misdemeanours, authorizing minor expenditure, putting down drunkenness, keeping out strangers, seeing that everyone went to church on Sundays (unless they were required for *barshchina*). The village morals were a vital concern of the steward. Adultery was 'cruelly punished', wrote Bolotov, 'because of its being often the cause of the ruination of families, of disputes and lasting hatreds between close relatives'.[16] Everything was done to prevent the break-up of the 'big families', the basic working groups. Equally, everything was tried to add to the labour force. The lord might order marriages between peasant girls of twenty and boys of twelve or thirteen: the steward had the job of making the necessary arrangements. On the Sheremetev estates fines were imposed on serf-spinsters from the age of seventeen upwards.[17]

The landlord had usually done his spell in the armed forces or the bureaucracy, and tended to run his estate like a barracks. The workers on the estate, wrote F. Udolov, must be made 'to understand that it is not for their own profit that they devote themselves to agriculture and other work suitable to their condition. . . . They must take as a model the soldiers who face danger and even sacrifice their lives for the fatherland, carrying out everything they are ordered to do and following the wishes of those who command them.'[18] Some veteran *dvorianin* went so far as to punctuate the working day with the roll of drums and the sound of bugles. It was generally agreed in noble circles that strict discipline was the only medicine for 'the morals and character of our lower orders', as Bolotov wrote in 1770. 'The only way,' he felt, 'or almost, to be sure [of success] was to punish without pity, and without regard to persons, the first to commit an infringement. This is necessary to sow fear among the others and make oneself obeyed. The news will spread fear among the peasants and make them prudent in future.'[19]

Most landlords adopted the method of punishing the steward harshly for any mistakes, and making him pay personally for any losses that occurred on the estate. Baron Stroganov ordered in 1752, for instance, that in cases where peasants took flight, the steward was to be knouted and made to pay the expenses of getting them back. Prince Kurakin sent instructions to his estates in Rostov in 1794 that, if a steward was found drunk, he was to be fined 500 roubles for the first offence, and suffer corporal punishment before the assembled *mir* for the second. Meanwhile, the stewards in their turn took it out of their subordinates; and ultimately the dead weight of fine and punishment fell on the mass of the serfs, who bore the brunt with resignation for years on end, till desperation drove them to suicide, flight, or bloody insurrection.

Not all serfs worked in agriculture, for not all estates were given over to farming. A minority of nobles became industrial entrepreneurs, turning their manors into centres of cotton and silk production, or distilling, sugar-refining, potash and salt-petre making. This phenomenon usually occurred in the infertile centre and north-west in the last decades of the century, as farming there began to feel the competition of the rich soils of the south. Serfs of such lords performed their *barshchina* on the factory floor. Some lords, instead of starting factories, hired their serfs to industrialists who had. In these cases, the serfs would be driven in herds from village to industrial centre, sometimes hundreds of miles away.

In addition, many State peasants became forced industrial workers also. Under Peter the Great's industrializing programme, both State enterprises and those owned by merchants were manned by thousands of State peasants, as well as criminals, paupers, and vagabonds. Known as 'assigned peasants', they became the hereditary serfs of their new proprietors. In 1734 the policy was further developed by a decree which stated, among other things, that anyone starting an iron mill could get 100 to 150 families of State peasants assigned to him for each blast-furnace he operated. The mining and metallurgical industries of the Urals were the most voracious recipients of assigned peasants, whose numbers there were swelled by peasants in flight, and by Old Believers, who resembled persecuted religious minorities elsewhere in Europe in being especially honest and energetic workers. In 1767 about ninety-one per cent of industrial workers were forced; in 1804, about seventy-three per cent. The remainder were free workers earning wages; and many of these were only apparently free, being serfs away from home earning the wherewithal to pay their *obrok*. The total number of male workers in the Urals rose from 31,383 in 1719 to 312,218 in 1796. Full-time workers lived in barracks at the plant or on plots of land near by. Part-time workers often had to travel long distances. Some, according to a report made in 1762 to Catherine II, travelled from home a distance of over 250 miles three times a year.

Besides the peasants in the fields, factories, and mines, there were swarms of people on the move: peasants in flight from oppressive masters, or wandering in search of food, soldiers on the run, escaped convicts, Bashkirs and other nomadic tribes, Cossacks and Old Believers. In seventeenth-century Russia, nowhere was safe from brigands, who infested the roads and invaded the towns. Even in St Petersburg, as late as 1737, a decree was published ordering a permanent picket to be posted of one officer, one corporal, and eight men, to put down brigandage in the city. By the mid eighteenth century, the towns were reasonably safe, but in the depths of the country landlords rarely felt secure. When the brigands came out of the woods, nobles often had to take to them. On rivers and highways, merchants travelled in convoy and took military precautions overnight.

Rebellions

Riots and rebellions were frequent among these itinerant marauders, either as they collided with one another, or as they fought back against the agents of the autocracy who were constantly trying to pin them down. To an Englishman writing in 1764 Russia appeared 'as one great mass of combustibles with incendiaries placed in every corner'.[20] The Cossacks of the frontier regions of the Don, the Volga, and the Ural were especially inflammable. But even in Moscow province itself, between 1764 and 1769, thirty lords were slain by their peasants, and five others had attempts made on their lives. Such isolated outbreaks, fairly easy to suppress, formed the general pattern throughout the Ancien Régime. Large-scale rebellions were difficult to achieve in the vast, empty spaces with their poor communications. Moreover, the enemies of the autocracy were too diverse and divided amongst themselves to make common action frequent. Townsmen had different grievances from peasants; Bashkirs and other colonial peoples did not easily join with Russian serfs fighting the same enemy; while religious differences hindered joint action between Old Believers and Orthodox Christians, and between Moslems and them both.

Occasionally, however, enough elements combined to produce rebellions that made the authorities fear that the Time of Troubles was back again. With each uprising, the autocracy was shaken to its foundations; but on each occasion, the rebels, lacking a bourgeoisie at their head, were defeated and decimated. The first, led by Stenka Razin, has already been mentioned. The second, led by Kondraty Bulavin (in 1707–8), the Hetman of the Don Cossacks, was serious because it coincided with an anti-Russian rebellion of the Bashkirs along the Volga, and set the Russian serfs in revolt against their masters. The revolt was suppressed by regular troops, and Bulavin committed suicide.

The third, and most serious, was the famous Pugachev

rebellion of 1773–75, a time when all the permanent, everyday grievances of the masses were intensified by disappointment at the failure of the Legislative Commission to emancipate the serfs (as rumour had promised), and by the belief that the rightful tsar, Peter III, was still alive; in fact, was none other than Pugachev himself. Emelian Pugachev, a Don Cossack who had fought in the Russian army in the Seven Years' War and had then turned frontier outlaw wanted by the police, started the rebellion among the Yaik Cossacks in 1773. Calling himself Peter III, he issued cunningly-worded manifestoes which drew in vast but diverse support. 'First comes God,' he proclaimed, 'and then come I, your mighty sovereign.'[21] He began with eighty followers, but soon had as many as twenty or thirty thousand partisans under his command. And he not only drew strength from the discontents of the frontier: he also set in flame the factory workers of the Urals and the peasants of the central region. He promised a return to the old religion; 'the old cross and prayers, heads and beards'. At the same time he offered land and freedom from bondage. 'Those who hitherto were gentry in their lands and estates, these opponents of our rule and perturbators of the empire and ruiners of the peasants,' he ordered, '—seize them, punish them, hang them, treat in the same way as they, having no Christian feelings in them, oppressed you, the peasants.'[22]

He captured Kazan (except the Kremlin there) in 1774, and threatened Moscow; and it took generals and regiments released from the Turkish war to suppress him. He was taken to Moscow in an iron cage, broken on the wheel, beheaded, dismembered and burnt (1775). The Yaik Cossacks were reorganized and renamed the Ural Cossacks; the River Yaik had its name changed to the River Ural; Pugachev's house was burnt to the ground; his village was moved across to the other side of the Don. Everything possible, in fact, was done to obliterate the stain; but neither landlords nor serfs could ever again forget the social revolution that almost took place.

Brigandage and rebellion were not the only escape routes from servitude, however. A tiny minority managed to climb a rung or two on the social ladder to join the middle class. Some *obrok* payers, for example, managed to rise out of the ranks of the industrial workers or village craftsmen to become owners of commercial or industrial enterprises. Such serfs were extremely profitable to their lords, paying their *obrok* sometimes in thousands of roubles a year. The great serf-owning magnates such as the Sheremetevs and the Orlovs did well out of the enterprise of their serfs. In Moscow and St Petersburg, where each house had to have a plaque with the owner's name on it, some streets were entirely made up of houses bearing their names. In fact, they were premises operated by their serfs in their masters' names, serfs being by law incapable of owning property.

Count Sheremetev also owned the industrial centre of Ivanovo, a collection of manufacturing villages in the province of Vladimir, where not only the workers, but also most of the owners were his serfs. Linen spinning and weaving made Ivanovo an important textile producer by the early eighteenth century, selling its wares as far afield as St Petersburg and Astrakhan. In the second half of the century colour-printing made it even more like the Manchester of Russia. One of the Sheremetev serfs was E. I. Grachev, who in 1781 had a factory of 312 looms, besides which he owned over 8,000 acres of land, 180 male serfs, and 200 female. In 1795 he purchased his liberty. To get it, he paid Count Sheremetev 135,000 roubles, and gave him his two factories with their land and peasants, worth about 100,000 roubles. But that did not prevent him from surviving as an industrialist whose family rose in the social scale in the nineteenth century.[23]

As well as serfs, State peasants who were energetic and clever enough could also prosper, as did Nikita Demidov (1656–1725), who began as a gunsmith in Tula. With Peter the Great's help, he evolved into a giant armaments manufacturer in the Urals, employing thousands of workers and making, it was said in 1725, 100,000 roubles a year, by which time he had entered the nobility.

By such means did the tiny Russian bourgeoisie spring up. It was a delicate plant, which took to Russian soil reluctantly, in spite of the imperative decrees of Peter the Great, and the more subtle encouragements of Catherine, both of whom recognized the seriousness of this gap in the Russian social make-up when compared with the West. But the middle classes had too much against them. Geographically, they had a tougher row to hoe than their western brothers. Psychologically, the arbitrary power of lord over serf, and of tsar over all, did not inspire business confidence. 'All manner of Industry and Desire of Gain is extinguished among the Boors,' wrote G. Weber, a German diplomat who lived in Russia from 1714 to 1720, 'and if by Chance one happens privately to get a small Sum, he hides it out of Fear of his Lord under a Dunghill, where it lies dead to him.'[24] Economically, the middle classes had to compete with highly privileged nobles and especially pampered foreigners, as well as firmly entrenched bureaucrats running industry and commerce as State activities. Socially, they could rise, but only by becoming cogs in the State machine. Politically, they refused to cut teeth. The Code of 1649 tied 'city people' permanently to their towns, disobedience being punished by the knout and exile to Siberia. A decree of 1658 imposed the death penalty on illegally mobile burghers. Both Peter the Great and Catherine the Great tried to get them to stand on their own feet in local government – while at the same time making sure that the heel of the bureaucracy was still on their necks. It is not surprising that their efforts failed.

Conclusion

In a way, their refusal to flourish was the revenge of the bourgeoisie on the despotism served by nobles, just as a peasant level of agriculture was the serfs' revenge against the landlords. Russia made great political and economic progress under the Ancien Régime, but a limit was reached at the end of the eighteenth century. Aggression and oppression, the methods of the Romanovs, had brought Russia on to equal terms with the great powers of Europe; but at a cost which caused her to fall behind again in the nineteenth century. In the grip of autocracy, bureaucracy, and serfdom, Russia could not go forward at the pace of western states with middle classes, freer institutions, and industrial revolutions. Though her great cultural flowering was about to come, Russia had many years to wait before the full potential of her gigantic size could be exploited. What can be said in favour of the Romanovs is that their rule had incubated the economic and intellectual forces which would one day bring this about. As Prince Adam Tsartoryski, a Polish exile who settled in Russia in 1795, said: 'The prosperous reign of Catherine had confirmed the Russians in their servility, though a few rays of European civilization had begun to penetrate.'[25] Already, the tide of economic development was flowing which would one day wear away the foundations of Russia's archaic social system. And already there were nobles who could say, as N. I. Turgenev said in 1860: 'From my childhood I felt a pronounced repulsion for serfdom; I instinctively sensed all the injustices in it.'[26] But perhaps the judgement of Alexander Herzen on Catherine the Great is nearer the mark – as a verdict on the whole of our period. 'The Winter Palace,' he wrote in the Foreword of his edition of Catherine's Memoirs (1859), 'with its military and administrative machinery, was a world of its own. Like a ship floating on the surface of the ocean, it had no real connection with the inhabitants of the deep, beyond that of eating them. It was the *State for the State*.'[27]

Prussia: The Great Elector

A Corporative State

At the beginning of the Ancien Régime, Prussia did not exist as a state. She was merely a chance collection of ingredients that were capable by an immense effort of being compounded into one. And had not the effort been made, there is little doubt that this little clutch of separate provinces which together formed Brandenburg-Prussia would have been swallowed up one by one by marauding neighbours. Nothing connected these territories except the ruling house of Hohenzollern, which, as a lucky prize-winner in the births, deaths, and marriages lottery of the previous century, happened to be sovereign in each one. They were dotted about the north European plain from the Rhine in the west to the Niemen in the east, with spaces between them greater than their own dimensions. Apart from the Elector himself, nothing worked in favour of unity. Geography had not provided them with natural frontiers, economic development had not made them into a prosperous going concern, history handed down no common traditions on which to found patriotism; while, from the point of view of defence, these territories were a nightmare to their sovereigns all through the Ancien Régime. What nature failed to bestow on Prussia had to be supplied by the moral force of her rulers; and genetics happened to throw up three remarkable Hohenzollerns with the genius and the will-power more than equal to the task. For their effort in pulling together these territories, in order to preserve Brandenburg-Prussia as a small German principality, generated enough energy to make her very soon the strongest State in north Germany, and, by the end of this period, a power of European status. This result was achieved by clamping on the Prussian people a bureaucratic absolutism unique in Europe; and by eliciting (or imprinting) traits of national character which have made Prussianism one of the shaping forces of modern world history.

The foundations of the new State, as well as the scaffolding for the superstructure, were the achievement of the first of these great rulers, the Elector Frederick William, known already in his life-time as the Great Elector (1640–88). He created a standing army, destroyed the control over revenues exercised by the nobles in their provincial Estates, sketched out the main features of a bureaucracy, and transformed Prussia's role in foreign affairs. He brought an end to the victimization which had been Prussia's fate as the passive plaything of the great powers, and by vigorous activity managed to wring some profit out of the international struggle.

The Great Elector's inheritance, which was large by German standards, consisted, firstly, of the Brandenburg Mark (the central block of territory on which the electorate was based); secondly, the Duchy of Cleves and the counties of Mark and Ravensburg in the west (inherited by the Hohenzollerns on the death of the last duke in 1609); thirdly, the Duchy of East Prussia in the east (a fief of Poland inherited in 1618); and, fourthly, the Duchy of Pomerania on the Baltic coast on either side of the river Oder (inherited in 1637). Unfortunately for the Hohenzollerns, Pomerania was occupied by the Swedes in 1637, and claimed by them at Westphalia (1648) as a '*Satisfaktion*' for helping the Protestant cause in the Thirty Years' War. For the time being, the Great Elector had to rest content with Eastern Pomerania (the poorer share) and accept as compensation the three secularized bishoprics of Halberstadt, Minden, and Cammin, and the ultimate possession (achieved in 1666) of the archbishopric of Magdeburg. He owed this compensation to French diplomacy, which favoured the build-up of Prussia as a counterweight to Austria.

The mere possession of the second largest area of land in the Empire, however, was as likely to lead to political weakness as strength, for the 'Prussian States' (as they legally termed themselves as late as 1794) had several serious disadvantages. In the first place, each state was a separate entity, with its own institutions, interests, and traditions. The same ruler might be Elector of Brandenburg, Count of Mark and Ravensburg, Duke of Pomerania, and Prince of Halberstadt and Minden, but the subjects of each of these provinces regarded the subjects of the others as foreigners, saw no point in fighting their battles, and had no intention of taxing themselves in order to contribute to their defence.

In the second place, as well as being unable to get joint action, the Hohenzollerns, in each of their different manifestations, were severely limited by parliamentary institutions which had steadily gained ground on them during the sixteenth and seventeenth centuries. In the Brandenburg Mark, for instance, the Estates not only had the right to consent to taxation; they also appointed the officials to collect and spend it. They also controlled appointments in the Church; and, jointly with the Elector, managed the recruiting, training, provisioning and employment of the armed forces. Moreover, the Elector had to follow their wishes in the formation of alliances with foreign powers. In East Prussia (a fief of the King of Poland), the Estates, by using the Elector of Brandenburg and the King of Poland as levers against one another, had probably achieved even greater independence. And each province, from East Prussia across to Cleves, insisted on its *Indigenatsrecht*, that is, the limitation of civil and military offices to native-born provincials. It was a valuable privilege, as the Estates of East Prussia declared in 1657: it was 'the whole country's but, above all, the indigenous nobility's greatest benefice'.[1] Each territory had its *Regierung*, its government, with judicial and political powers similar to those of the provincial Parlements in France; and they all had their hierarchies of judicial, financial, and administrative functionaries, all tied up in the networks of patronage operated by the landed magnates, as much beyond the Elector's control as were the *officiers* in the kingdom of France.

In the third place, the Elector was weak in each of his provinces because (except in his Rhenish lands) the noble landowners, the Junkers, had managed to monopolize social and economic power. The economic developments of the previous two centuries had ruined the once prosperous towns, and transformed the once independent peasantry into a serf labour-force toiling on large landed-estates which grew agricultural produce for the markets of western Europe (made profitable by the sixteenth-century Price Revolution). Like all magnates east of the Elbe, the Junkers were not western-style receivers of rents and feudal dues, but large-scale entrepreneurs, who at the same time as exploiting the labour of the communities in their possession also controlled their police and justice, installed their schoolmasters and appointed their clergy. The Reformation, moreover, had added to their power, for, as in England, the secularization of the Church had benefited not the prince but the landowners. The Elector, as a result of these developments, could not call upon the clergy or the commons to act as counterweights to the overwhelming power of his Junker antagonists.

The fourth source of weakness was the foreign situation. The Great Elector inherited a land in 1640 which was overrun alternately by the Swedish and Imperial forces fighting in the Thirty Years' War, and sometimes by both at the same time. Moreover, his outlying provinces to the east and west entangled him in what were the two chief areas of international conflict at the start of the Ancien Régime. Cleves and Mark were involved in the struggle for the lower Rhine waged between France and Holland, on the one hand, and the Austrian and Spanish Habsburgs, on the other; while East Prussia was a pawn in the Baltic contest between Sweden and Poland. In the savage international order of the emerging absolutist states, it was no longer possible for a small state to eke out a passive political existence in the interstices left by the great powers. Rulers had to go forward or backward: there was no staying in the same place, as the Great Elector's father had tried to do. The inertia which characterized the behaviour of George William (1619–40) in the Thirty Years' War had placed the future of Brandenburg in jeopardy. But in order to put right this fourth, external, weakness, she required a ruler who could first solve the other three, internal, problems. And in the Great Elector, the Hohenzollern line uncharacteristically produced the man who could do it.

The Great Elector

The explanation of the political ability and moral force which the Great Elector possessed, and of the purposes to which they were put, probably lay partly in his recent ancestry and partly in his early upbringing. His grandfather, John Sigismund, turned Calvinist in 1613, in order to get Dutch and Palatinate backing for his claims to the Jülich-Cleves inheritance. His father, George William, married Elisabeth Charlotte of the Palatinate: sister of the Winter King, and grand-daughter of William the Silent, the hero of the Dutch revolt. Thus the Great Elector had blood flowing in his veins from the two most gifted Calvinist fighting families in western Europe. Moreover, he received an excellent education in Holland, at the University of Leyden and in the stimulating household of Prince Frederick Henry (whose daughter he later married).

In the most advanced state in Europe, he received the most up-to-date grounding it was possible to have in commerce, shipping, colonization, drainage, and canal-building, as well as in the organizing and training of troops (especially infantry) and in the building and capture of fortresses. From the same source, he drank the strong waters of Calvinism, the energizer of rational economic and political enterprise, which gave to those who believed in it the certainty that they were in receipt of God's grace as a chosen instrument. It was a religious outlook usually associated with republican resistance, but it took on an extra power as the ideology of a prince, especially when it was fortified (as it was in this case) with the precepts of the *raison d'état* tradition coming down from Machiavelli. According to this latter doctrine, a ruler has the duty to devote his all in the service of the state, including, if need be, his moral rectitude. This union of fighting puritanism and ruthless exploitation of every possibility, which Calvinism and *raison d'état* gave to the Great Elector, combined with the attitude of submission to earthly authority and of taking worldly things as they came, which Lutheranism had taught his subjects, proved ideal for the creation of the Prussia of the Ancien Régime. All the subsequent Hohenzollerns inherited this gift of transmuting what, to a superficial glance, might seem to be knavery, into deeds of the highest nobility; for they were imbued with the conviction that they were serving something higher than themselves, even if, as in Frederick the Great's case, the belief that he was the first servant of the State was deduced not from Christian but from Enlightened premises.

The rational application of means to ends was not the only philosophy that the Great Elector picked up in Holland (or that some of his subjects learned from Huguenot refugees). His character (and theirs) had also built into it those austere virtues that the Dutch and French Calvinists had absorbed from their reading of the Stoics: simplicity of life, avoidance of luxury and waste, fulfilment of one's duty to God and the community, and, above all, constancy, firmness, and perseverance in the trials of life.

Thus armed, the Great Elector inherited his electorate prostrated by the Thirty Years' War (1640). As we have seen, he succeeded in extricating Brandenburg from this catastrophe with some profit by the Treaties of Westphalia (1648). These early years taught him the necessity of creating his own army in place of the provincial militias and mercenary rabble which the colonel-contractors had supplied hitherto. 'Alliances, certainly, are good,' he wrote subsequently (1667), 'but one's own forces, on which one can more surely rely, are better still; and a ruler gets no consideration if he has no resources and folk of his own, for it has been these, since the time I therefore maintained them, that have made me, thank God, "considerabel".'[2] But an army required an increase in revenue, and the Estates possessed the power of the purse. The Estates, therefore, had to be subdued.

The Estates of Brandenburg

The crucial victory in this struggle was won over the Estates of Brandenburg, which, in a series of confrontations between 1649 and 1653, could see no reason why they should dip into their pockets for the defence of Cleves or Pomerania. The struggle ended with an agreement, the Recess of 1653, which looked like a victory for the Junkers. By it, the Elector promised to preserve the Junkers' rights of jurisdiction over their peasants, their right to imprison peasants who complained wantonly, their privilege of buying out peasants' land (if the noble who did this had no estate of his own), and of dispossessing peasants judged guilty of serious crimes. Another clause had the effect of fastening serfdom (*Leibeigenschaft*) on larger numbers of peasants, who henceforth could be removed from their land at the will of the lord, were liable to unlimited labour services, and were tied to the soil, along with all the members of their families. Other clauses ensured that nobles' land should not be acquired by non-nobles; that nobles could export their corn, cattle, wool, and so on free of duty, and import duty free all the food, wine, salt, mill-stones and so on that they required for their own use.

Apart from yielding these powerful economic and social advantages which the Junkers had over the rest of society, and which outlasted the Ancien Régime, the Great Elector also made a number of political concessions in this Recess (about consulting the Estates over policy and appointments and so on) which had no permanent value to the Junkers at all. The reason for this was the way in which he used the grant which the Estates voted him in return for these privileges: a sum of 530,000 thalers, payable in instalments over the following six years. With it he raised a peace-time army which was never again disbanded. It enabled him before long to make two crucial breaks with the past: in foreign affairs, to initiate that inexorableness of purpose and sinuosity of method which were to take Prussia to world power; at home, to collect further taxes without the consent of the Estates – the essential pre-condition of building the all-Prussian state. Both innovations occurred during the War of the North between Sweden and Poland (1655–60).

Foreign Policy

The Great Elector joined first one side and then the other, his army seeing successful action in the battle for Warsaw (1656). At the Peace of Oliva (1660) both sides rewarded his nimble footwork by recognizing his possession of East Prussia in full sovereignty, and no longer as a fief of Poland. At home, he expanded his army to 22,000 men, and paid for it (in spite of the Estates' refusal) by collecting three times as much revenue as before, arbitrarily – on the plea that the necessities of defence knew no law. After this, he never looked back. He had an army, and with it the means of enforcing his wishes, not only on Brandenburg, but also on Pomerania, Magdeburg, Halberstadt, and Minden, and to a certain extent on East Prussia and the Rhineland as well. Abroad, it enabled him to intervene actively in the great European struggle between the Emperor and Louis XIV, and their allies. With great dexterity, he transferred his weight from one end of the see-saw to the other, aiming at preserving the balance of power, and hoping by fair means or foul to wrest Western Pomerania from Sweden. In this respect he was unsuccessful; for, although he conquered the territory twice, defeated the Swedish army impressively at Fehrbellin (1675), and captured Stettin (1677), the diplomatic arm of Louis XIV was long enough at this stage to ensure that Sweden kept Western Pomerania whenever the question arose at peace conferences. Nevertheless, at the Great Elector's death in 1688, Brandenburg-Prussia had a standing army of over 30,000 men, and, from the point of view of the great powers, was a state worth hiring.

Growth of Absolutism

To achieve this remarkable success, he had to set in motion the principal components of the machinery of the all-Prussian state. In the 1650s, when he began, public life was practically non-existent except at the provincial and local level. There were only three common institutions: himself, the army, and the Privy Council. This last was a small committee to deal with interprovincial matters, which had been in existence, on and off, since 1604. Out of it now began to unfold the central departments for the direction of all-Prussian affairs, as the Great

Elector set in motion his great enterprise. The primary task was the collection of revenue.

Apart from subsidies paid by his various allies (amounting to less than ten per cent of the total), there were two main sources of income, which shared the financial burden about equally: the royal domains and the taxes. The Elector was more fortunate than the kings of France or England in possessing substantial lands of his own, containing, perhaps, a quarter or a third of the whole peasantry. The income from them was collected by royal bailiffs, partly from rents of estates leased to farmers, partly from the direct exploitation of corn and cattle production, brewing, mining, and timber-working, and partly in the form of miscellaneous tolls, taxes, and monopolies to which the crown had the right. In order to make this department as productive as possible, the Great Elector reformed it, first of all (1651) at provincial level, by re-casting the Domains Chambers in each province, to which the district bailiffs were responsible. The Domains Chambers were extricated from the Junker-dominated provincial governments (*Regierungen*), and placed under the control of Berlin, where he planned a central Chamber (the *Hofkammer*) formed out of a group of Privy Councillors. This came into being just after his death.

The domains, under their Central and Provincial Chambers, took care of about half the revenue of Prussia. The other half was provided by taxation. Here the Great Elector inherited the Contribution, a direct land and poll tax, which fell on the peasants and burghers. The nobles were exempt, and the town patricians managed to avoid paying their full share. In general, the Contribution was out of date, and not assessed on the growing sectors of the economy. In its place, the Great Elector wanted the Excise (a Dutch idea) – a tax on beer, wine, spirits, salt, cattle, artisans, and so on. The general run of burghers favoured this sales-tax, because it would force the aldermen and nobles to contribute. The Estates vigorously opposed it for the same reason. In the end, as a compromise, the Excise was introduced in the towns (voluntarily in 1667, compulsorily in 1680), while the villages still paid their Contribution. These town and country taxes remained the basis of military finance for the rest of the Ancien Régime, the former being particularly useful to the monarchs, for, first, it enabled them to extract their fair share of the mounting commercial prosperity; and, second, it rendered them independent of the Estates whose organs now entered into their long decline.

These two taxes were at first collected by the old authorities, the town councils and the Estates; but gradually the Great Elector introduced a separate hierarchy of bureaucrats which either absorbed the old or pushed them rudely aside. These new men were the War Commissars, very similar to the *Commissaires* (or Intendants) of France. Their job was to maintain the standing army. Some were placed alongside the contracting colonels to ensure that they acted as part of a nationalized organization and not as units of private enterprise as in the past. Others collected the Excise and the Contribution in the localities, the former coming to be known as *Steuerräte* and the latter as *Landräte*. These were responsible in each province to Provincial War Commissars, who in their turn came under the General War Commissar in Berlin.

Thus, by the end of his reign, the Great Elector had constructed the main framework of two bureaucratic pyramids. For the domains, he had the Hofkammer in Berlin controlling the Domain Chambers in the provinces, which in their turn ruled over the bailiffs in the localities. For taxation, there was the General War Commissar in Berlin, who supervised the Provincial War Commissars, who controlled the *Steuerräte*, collecting the Excise in the towns, and the *Landräte*, collecting the Contribution in the country. The ultimate object was the creation of as large an army as possible, which could protect the growing state from interference from without, and coerce any community which resisted the way things were going within. Force was required to bring the outlying provinces into line: East Prussia and Cleves-Mark.

The Great Elector's sovereignty over East Prussia may have been recognized by the Treaty of Oliva (1660), but it was not by the East Prussian Estates, especially the volatile citizens of Königsberg, a city three times the size of Berlin. A long and hard struggle ensued in the 1660s and 1670s, in which the East

Prussians tried to get help from the King of Poland; and the Great Elector managed to subordinate them to his bureaucratic apparatus in the end only by occupying the province with his army, imprisoning one leader without trial for life, and executing another. Even so, the Berlin government did not succeed in introducing the Excise there till as late as 1716. In Cleves and Mark, the Excise never was established, in spite of nine separate attempts by the Great Elector. For these provinces on the Rhine and Ruhr were quite unlike Germany east of the Elbe in social structure and economic development. Here the nobles paid taxes, and the peasants were free and took some part in local government, as did the vigorous urban communities. They resisted the invasion of the agents of Berlin, every inch of the way, right through the Ancien Régime. 'Muddle-headed fools,' Frederick the Great later called them irritably, 'conceived when their fathers are drunk, without either natural or acquired talents.'[3] The Great Elector had only a limited success with them. By the Recesses of 1660 and 1661 they gave up their right to negotiate with foreign powers, to exclude Electoral troops, and to appoint and dismiss all officials. On the other hand, the Estates retained the privileges of assembling whenever they wished, and of voting their own taxes. Cleves and Mark thus remained little islands of something approaching constitutional monarchy in an otherwise absolute state.

Economic Policy

As well as throwing his tax-collecting net as wide as possible, the Great Elector did all he could to raise the prosperity of his subjects, so that he could tax them even further. In nothing was he more under the influence of the Netherlands than in his economic policy. He constructed a canal from the Oder to the Elbe via the River Spree and Berlin, in order to divert the Silesian traffic away from Stettin, still in Swedish hands. He built a tiny fleet on the Baltic. He sent off colonial expeditions, formed an East India Company and an American Company, bought a trading post in the West Indies, and founded Great Fredericksburg on the coast of West Africa. More important, he colonized his own lands. To people his sparsely settled corner of north-east Europe, he used the inducements of religious freedom and financial help to bring in Lutheran refugees from the Palatinate, Calvinists from Saxony, and, above all, Huguenots from France, especially after the revocation of the Edict of Nantes. Twenty thousand of them had settled in Brandenburg by 1700. To make the utmost use of the skills of these immigrants, companies were formed with the help of the War Commissars to manufacture textiles, glassware, iron, copper, and brass goods, candles, soap, paper, and other utilitarian and luxury products. As a protection to these new enterprises, the import of many foreign manufactured goods was forbidden, as well as the export of raw wool, leather, skins, furs, and other important raw materials. This was normal mercantilist practice, but a peculiar Prussian form of industrial control was the sharp separation of town and country so as to facilitate the collection of the Excise. Industry was forbidden in the villages, townsmen found it very difficult to acquire land, and the Elector's Excise men were waiting at all the town gates to control the movement of goods and men. Of course, complete success did not crown all these attempts at economic planning. The colonial companies were wound up before long; Brandenburg never achieved self-sufficiency in manufactured goods, and remained overwhelmingly an exporter of primary products. Nevertheless, the Domains Chambers and the War Commissars lifted the economy out of the mire where the Thirty Years' War had left it. The Great Elector's revenues, for example, rose from one million thalers at the start of his reign to over three million at the end.

Conclusion

Thus Prussia's modern history as a series of revolutions carried out from above had begun. But to appreciate exactly how far the process had gone, it is important to notice that much of the old world still remained. The erosion of local patriotism, for example, took time. As late as 1678, the East Prussian nobility yearned for the restoration of their 'still unforgotten blissfulness, liberty, and peaceful tranquillity'. They wished to be left alone with East Prussian affairs. 'Why should they let themselves be exploited to death,' they added, 'since the Roman Empire is, after all, not of the slightest concern to them.'[4] Moreover, the power of the Junkers in society had been bent, not broken. There was no attempt (as in France) to replace them by members of the bourgeoisie. On the contrary, the *Steuerräte* were steadily taking over municipal government and reducing urban life in all its detail to State tutelage. By contrast, the arm of the State did not reach very deeply into the countryside. The *Landrat* at the head of the county may have been appointed by Berlin, but he had previously been elected by his fellow nobles. He was more like an English Justice of the Peace than a French Intendant. Moreover, the Junkers held all the leading positions in the army and bureaucracy. Instead of being pushed aside by the rising state, they were being transformed into a service nobility – or, rather, a proportion of them were. Their relations and friends went on as before. In the Army, the Elector's power of appointment descended no lower than the rank of colonel. In the villages, the Junkers were undisturbed in the government of their manorial subjects. And in each province, the whole machinery of private justice was dominated by them through their control of the *Regierungen*.

Nevertheless, by the time he died (in the year of the 1688 Revolution in England) the Great Elector had laid down the hull of the absolutist Prussian state. Even though there was much tackle yet to be fitted by his successors, the main timbers were secure : a standing army unified under the orders of the sovereign, a regular income beyond the reach of the Estates, a staff of functionaries to collect it, spend it, and increase it, and a foreign policy unfettered by the prejudices of provincial Diets. The Great Elector could well regard himself as 'considerabel'.

Prussia: Frederick I and Frederick William I

Frederick I

The Great Elector's son Frederick (1688–1713) has tended to be regarded as a freak in the Hohenzollern line during the Ancien Régime. 'All in all', wrote Frederick the Great, 'he was great in small matters, and small in great. And his misfortune willed it that he had his place in history between a father and a son whose superior talents eclipsed him.'[1] Frederick may have been undersized, ill-favoured, and weak-kneed, while they were massive and masterful; or spendthrift while they saved; yet he made his distinct contribution to the building of the Prussian state.

Under him, the evolution of the all-Prussian public administration continued on the lines laid down by the Great Elector. During the first decade of the reign (1688–97), high policy benefited from the vigorous leadership of a career bureaucrat who became virtual prime minister, Eberhard von Danckelman. And during this period the central departments continued to crystallize out of the Privy Council. Unfortunately, he aroused the jealousy of the old-style aristocrats who fawned on the Elector's Hanoverian wife, Sophie Charlotte, and through their intrigues he was dismissed, imprisoned for ten years, and made to surrender all his property. From 1698 to 1711, the government was in the hands of a flattering incompetent, Count von Wartenberg, whose influence over Frederick gave his reign that tone by which it is usually remembered.

The daily government of Prussia began to adopt the form which became standard in the eighteenth century. Frederick abandoned the practice of consulting ministers in the Privy Council, or in some sub-committee of it, and, like Frederick William I and Frederick the Great after him, took his decisions in the privacy of his cabinet; although, in complete contrast to their practice, it was not Frederick who made decisions but Wartenberg. Similarly, the policy of Frederick, like that of the other Hohenzollerns in this period, was to raise the might of the Elector in the State, and the prestige of the State in Europe, though the means adopted were in complete contrast to theirs. Like many an heir of a self-made entrepreneur, Frederick squandered his father's savings in the pursuit of outward magnificence. Instead of planning his spending according to his income, he managed his accounts the other way round, and ran himself into debt aping the style of life of his wealthier neighbours. Not content with the modest Dutch taste of the Great Elector's Berlin, he bought himself a Louvre and a Versailles in the Berliner Schloss and the Palace of Charlottenburg. Puritan domesticity gave way to baroque splendour in all its forms. Taking his cue from Louis XIV, the most successful monarch of his day, he decided that winning battles was only one of the ingredients in the recipe for success in the international power-struggle. He introduced elaborate court ceremonial, acquired pictures and jewellery, silver and porcelain. He sent his architect, Andreas Schlüter, on a tour of Italy in order to polish up his baroque (1696). He founded the University of Halle (1694), the Academy of Arts, and the Academy of Sciences. He gave jobs to Philip Spener and August Hermann Francke whose Pietism made such a profound impression on the Prussian national character. He encouraged Christian Thomasius and Christian Wolff, who spread the ideas of the Enlightenment; he employed Samuel von Pufendorf and Veit Ludwig von Seckendorf, historians and political theorists; while he and Sophie Charlotte showered favours on the greatest German thinker of the age, Gottfried Wilhelm von Leibniz.

The greatest prize in the race for prestige was the title of King, which he gained by renewing in 1700 his father's treaty of alliance with the Emperor. Prussia was to provide 8,000 troops for the War of the Spanish Succession, in return for a subsidy of 100,000 thalers and the Emperor's permission to call himself 'King in Prussia'. In Königsberg, the following year (out of deference to Austria, since Prussia was outside the Holy Roman Empire) he crowned himself as Frederick I. His chase after that bauble has been criticized on the grounds that it led to the misapplication of Prussia's resources in foreign affairs, by forcing her to fight the battles of Austria, Britain, and Holland in the western War of the Spanish Succession (1702–13), thus preventing her from intervening more profitably in the Great Northern War (1700–1721), in which she might have levered Western Pomerania from Sweden or West Prussia from Poland. Certainly, the Duke of Marlborough forced Frederick to fight in the West (and the Prussian troops distinguished themselves, as at Blenheim, for example), and this involved standing idly by on occasion while Russian and other northern powers devastated Prussian territory at their convenience. On the side of Frederick and Wartenberg it has been argued that the true interest of Prussia lay in helping to defeat the attempts of Louis XIV to achieve the mastery of Europe; and that, if Frederick William I finally gained Stettin and much of Western Pomerania in 1720, part of the explanation of this success was that France was no longer strong enough to stop him.

In any case, under Frederick I, Prussia lacked the resources for an independent foreign policy. He was swaggering with an army and a court suitable to a European power, on the income of an impoverished German principality: an extravagance made all the more devastating by the tendency of Wartenberg and his friends to line their own pockets as well. Frederick's glamour was purchased with weakness at home and abroad. In Prussia ready cash had to be raised by living off the future: by running into debt, by mortgaging the Excise, by leasing out the Domains on easy rents for long terms. Abroad, subsidies were doled out by Austria, Holland, and Britain, in return for which Prussia surrendered her freedom of movement. There was no future in such policies, as Crown Prince Frederick William realized while still a young man. And he made it his life's work to construct some foundations for the glittering, but rickety edifice he inherited in 1713.

Frederick William I

Frederick William I (1713–40) brought Prussia back to the path

roughed out by his grandfather and namesake, the Great
Elector. The complex Soldier-King, brutal, prudish, and coarse,
hooked on tobacco and beer, and hag-ridden with religious
anxieties, never spared himself in his neurotic determination to
prevent, as he once said, 'the old stories of my father from
awakening again'.[2] From the age of fifteen he regularly sat in
on his father's cabinet meetings, held several times a week; and,
while still a youth, served with Marlborough and prince Eugen
in the Low Countries. Like his grandfather, he was deeply
impressed by the Puritan sobriety and business-like rationality
of the Dutch way of life. The scandalous extravagances of his
father's ministers affronted his cheese-paring instincts, and the
pawn-like role of Prussian in the international power game
humiliated his pride. Moreover, his campaigning experience
with the allies convinced him that his state could only be preserved by untiring efforts to achieve two principal results: a
State treasure, and an army which could compensate for
Prussia's helplessness by the sheer quality of its men and
training.

By this time, his obsessive concern with his duty was already
second nature to him thanks to the pedagogic methods of one
of his Huguenot tutors, who shocked him into effort by convincing him that his lack of academic progress might be a
sign that God had predestined him to eternal damnation. He
became certain that the rise of Brandenburg-Prussia was a sign
of God's grace on the work of the Hohenzollerns; and when he
was converted to Pietism in 1711 his selfless devotion to his
kingdom was further intensified by the teachings of that movement: that the proof of genuine rebirth is in the striving to
bring about God's kingdom – to achieve success for the community, that is, not, as in Calvinism, for oneself. God had
placed him on the throne, he wrote in 1722, 'not to be idle, but
to work, and to rule his land well'.[3]

His Economies

Already before his accession, he had managed to get Wartenberg
and his fellow leeches prised off the body-politic (1710–11);

and a tremor ran through the rest of the office-holders when he became king in 1713. Everyone felt at once that there was a new hand on the helm. 'The king applies himself in an extraordinary way to everything,' wrote Lintelo, the Dutch ambassador, 'reads everything through before signing it, and he has told me himself that he wants to have no peace till he has put everything on a good footing.'[4] The day after his father's death, he said to the members of the government: 'My father found pleasure in splendid buildings, great quantities of jewels, gold, and furniture, and outward magnificence – allow me to have my amusement also, and that consists chiefly in a quantity of good troops.'[5] And the army – the only economy they were about to make (the War of the Spanish Succession having just ended) – was the only item of expenditure he did not curtail. All other costs were lopped without mercy. At Court, the salary bill was reduced from 157,647 thaler a year to a few thousands. Thirty-seven *castrati*, violonists, cellists, singers, and composers lost their jobs; and so did many others, including the servant who, as a reward for 'preparing the chocolate', was drawing fodder for four horses. The cooking staff was decimated: a needful reform, as more than one Berlin hotel had been serving meals provided by the royal kitchens. The royal stables were reduced from 600 horses to 120; the dead king's widow pared down to one servant and one maid. Ministers who had hitherto drawn feed for twenty to thirty horses were now cut back to six; while most of the other courtiers and functionaries had their forage cut out altogether. 'My father', said the new King, 'provided so much forage so that everybody could follow him into the country, and I cancel it, so that everyone stays in Berlin.'[6]

The fortunate ones who kept their jobs had their salaries slashed. Whether generals, ministers, or menials, everyone had to trim his manner of life after the example of the king himself. Bishop Ursinus had his stipend of 4,000 thaler halved, while his three sons, his son-in-law, and his brother-in-law all lost their places at Court. Out of his father's twenty-four royally furnished châteaux and pleasure-houses, Frederick William kept on only Wusterhausen (his own estate when he was Crown

Prince), Potsdam, Charlottenburg, Oranienburg, and Köpenick. The remainder he ordered to be sold or leased. The Berliner Schloss was used to house the bureaucrats of the central departments. Under it, deep in the earth, he built a strong room to contain the coins he minted out of his father's precious gold and silver objects. Here was the start of the Prussian treasure – no longer the king's, but the State's. As much as any feature of Prussianism, it singled out Prussia from the generality of European states – which tended to have a National Debt in lieu.

The Army

The purpose of all this pruning was to expand the army. The new Table of Ranks issued in 1713 overturned Frederick I's conceptions of social status, and set the tone for the next two centuries. A Field-Marshall was graded above a Lord Chamberlain, and so on down the line: the military was declared to be superior to the civil. Frederick William called the army 'the basis of his temporal bliss', on which rested 'his true interest as well as security, but equally his glory and prestige'.[7] And this is not a surprising philosophy in a ruler whose total existence up to his accession (1688–1713) had been threatened amidst continuous European wars. 'Fritz,' he later said to the twelve-year-old future Frederick the Great, 'think about what I tell you, always maintain a good and large army, you can have no better friend and you cannot maintain yourself without one. Our neighbours want nothing better than to overthrow us, I know their aims, and you will yet get to know them as well, believe me, don't pay attention to vanities, but stick to reality, always think highly of a good army and money, out of which the glory and security of a prince is made.'[8]

In the first year of his reign, Frederick William increased the infantry by 8,000 men, and the cavalry by over 1,000; in the course of his reign, he raised the total numbers from 39,000 to over 80,000. In 1740, the year of his death, Prussia had the third or fourth strongest army in Europe, whereas Prussia was only the tenth in size and only the thirteenth in population. And in the course of the eighteenth century, the army took up two-thirds of the State revenues, that is, more than the total raised by taxation. At the end of the Ancien Régime, von Schrötter, a soldier turned minister, pointed out Prussia's peculiarity as being 'not a country with an army, but an army with a country which served as headquarters and food magazine'.[9]

Meticulous over the tiniest detail, Frederick William was as much concerned with the quality of the recruits, the state of their kit, and the level of their training as he was with sheer numbers. Even as Crown Prince at his hunting lodge at Wusterhausen he had formed his own battalion of tall troops which he and his friend, Prince Leopold of Anhalt-Dessau, drilled to perfection, using the lessons they had learned with Marlborough in the Malplaquet campaign. The exercises and tactics of these grenadiers now became the model for the whole army: the 'Potsdam University'. The King wrote the first full Infantry Regulations himself (1714), and the endless drilling and manoeuvring they enforced eventually produced the army that astonished Europe under Frederick the Great, with its unique powers of manoeuvre and its rapid and accurate fire. The manning of the units was also revised. The old, the small, and the weak were weeded out, and replaced by tall and hefty youths. Recruiting became an obsession and an industry. As many native Prussians were roped in as possible without ruining the agriculture and industry that provided the revenues – though, at times, Frederick William came dangerously near to killing the goose that laid the golden eggs.

Prussians were declared in an edict of 1714 to owe life-long service: 'the young men in accordance with their natural birth and almighty God's own order and command' were 'duty-bound and obliged to serve with goods and blood'.[10] The Junkers, to whose power the growing royal army was essentially a menace, were called up to be the officers. The Domains Chambers and the *Landräte* had the duty of keeping careful records of the nobility in their areas, and of dispatching suitable sons of the Junkers to the capital each year, where they were trained in the Berlin *Kadettenhaus*, or later in others set up in Potsdam, Stolpe, and Kulm, or perhaps in a regiment.

Nobles were forbidden to study in universities and schools abroad: for Prussianization could only properly be carried out in native educational establishments. This 'will have the advantage', wrote Frederick William in 1722 for the benefit of his son, 'that the whole nobility will be brought up from youth onwards in your service and will know no lord other than God and the King in Prussia'.[11]

Gradually, the Junker families acquiesced. Instead of opposing the army as a foreign body in the State, they accepted it as the natural career for a Junker, especially as the pay to be earned in the higher ranks became a significant compensation for the depressed economic situation of landowners since the Thirty Years' War. The king sent noble officers to serve in other provinces than their own, so as to foster new, all-Prussian loyalties. He himself always wore an officers' coat. Between cadet and colonel, no badges of rank were worn: they were all one, in a separate new caste, the officer-corps, which, as the king made clear in the Table of Ranks, and at every other possible opportunity, conferred the top social status in the land.

Frederick William also formed the character of his officers in his own punctual, punctilious, puritan image. They were made responsible for the training, equipment, and management of the men, even in peacetime, instead of leaving such mundane matters, as hitherto, to the N.C.O.s. They were made to give up their unruly, cavalier mode of life: gambling, duelling, chasing booty, or women – these were hardly signs of God's favour. Frederick William warned his son against mistresses, operas, plays, ballets, and masquerades. 'My dear successor', he wrote, 'rest well assured that all fortunate rulers, who have God before their eyes and have no mistresses (whores rather they should be called) and live a godly life – God will pour on them all worldly and spiritual blessings.'[12] But God could also withdraw his favour; and this is what he deeply feared. 'God gives heart to the army', he wrote, 'and takes it away from soldiers as well.'[13]

Every unit had a padre, even in peace time: one usually trained in the Pietism of Halle University, and normally assured of a substantial benefice on retirement (where he could spread a favourable image of the army among his flock). Every commander sent up annual reports on the officers in his unit, and these dossiers (*Conduitenlisten*) contained information on all aspects of an officer's conduct, including his private life. In time, the behaviour of the officer corps was transformed into the conscientious, regular, frugal, punctual, and obedient Prussian mode of life, which in its turn was transferred to the civilian sphere as well.

The rank and file of the army were recruited by the colonels and captains, who were given a certain sum of money to keep their units up to strength in men and equipment. These men terrorized their neighbourhoods, and the rest of Germany, too – for forceful recruiting was not confined to the native sons of Prussia, but extended into neighbouring states, whether they liked it or not. Some did – the Dukes of Mecklenburg, for example, who supplied streams of their luckless subjects for the Prussian army. Sometimes the foreign element rose as high as two thirds of the total, for Frederick William found that there was a limit to the number of Prussians he could drag away from their normal pursuits without jeopardizing the economy. And so, in order to have more money available for foreign recruiting, regimental and company commanders gradually formed the habit of enrolling their own serfs in their units (or the serfs of friends or relations) and then letting them go home on leave for nine or ten months of the year. With the pay thus saved, these officers could then hire more foreigners.

This brilliant scheme for joining the benefits of a militia to the virtues of a regular army was made official by Frederick William in 1733 with the establishment of the canton-system. Prussia was divided into regimental cantons. These were districts containing 5,000 hearths from which an infantry regiment would call up its recruits. In the case of cavalry regiments, the cantons consisted of 1,800 hearths. Regimental cantons in their turn were divided into company and squadron cantons. Here the captain was the local tyrant. He registered the serf boys at the age of ten, and then frequently inspected them on their estates till they were called to the colours. And then, after one-and-a-half to two years' training, they were sent back on leave to their agricultural toil for most of each year, except for the summer manoeuvres and inspections in April and May. It was an inspired compromise between the otherwise competing demands of agriculture and recruiting. And the serfs had to be used in the forces, because the king insisted on each unit having a core of natives to see that the foreigners did not desert – though they did in their thousands. In a similar fashion, the colonels and captains made a profit on their foreigners. They economized on their pay by allowing them on leave in the towns as *Freiwächter*, where they took jobs as artisans, or labourers, or even hawkers. Here again was a useful compromise, this time between the army and industry. Only in such ways did Prussia manage to support such a uniquely vast army in proportion to her population.

The Administration

The financial requirements of the army were the 'fly-wheel of the State machine', as Otto Hintze called it;[14] and Frederick William applied himself to the problems of raising revenue with the same obsessive interest in detail that he showed as commander-in-chief. His aim was to rescue the crown from the money-lenders at home, and to cut the political strings with which foreign subsidies bound Prussian freedom of action abroad. His method was to fill in the myriad details to the outline of an administrative system left by his predecessors, and with it to galvanize the whole society into tireless, conscientious activity. The bureaucracy was to be disciplined like the army. 'One must serve the king with life and limb,' he wrote in 1714, 'with goods and chattels, with honour and conscience and surrender everything except salvation. The latter is reserved for God. But everything else must be mine.'[15]

Of the two central financial departments left by the Great Elector, the office of General War Commissar had been reorganized on collegiate lines as the General War Commissariat under Frederick I (1712); while the Hofkammer was expanded into the General Finance Directory by Frederick William the following year. For the first ten years of Frederick William's reign, these two carried on as before. That is, the General War Commissariat supervised the military taxation, which was made up of the Excise in the towns and the Contribution in the country, collected for the Provincial War Commissariats by their local *Steuerräte* and *Landräte*. Meanwhile, the General Finance Directory controlled the royal domains (and all the other sources of crown income) by means of the Provincial Domains Chambers and local bailiffs. Year by year their organization became more fully articulated and their bite on Prussian life deeper. Steadily, they gained ground in their running fight with what was left of the antique functionaries of the provincial Estates. Any disputes in which they were involved were withdrawn from the ordinary courts (headed in each province by the *Regierungen*), and a separate body of public law was built up to deal with cases involving the State (the exact opposite of what happened in England). But the Domains Chambers and the War Commissariats more and more frequently also clashed with one another.

There was a conflict between Excise and Domains officials in Minden, for example, over which of the two could include the breweries in their field. Elsewhere they took one another to court over saltworks. In general, it was a conflict between town and country interests, since the War Commissariats and the Domains Chambers, as well as collecting revenue, put into motion the mercantile system. They were thus the driving force behind Prussian economic enterprise; and the Excisemen wanted cheap food and a good price for industrial goods, while the Domains people saw things the other way round. By 1723 the irascible monarch had lost patience with their quarrels. 'As if they belonged to different lords with different interests,' he wrote, '... each supports out of our money lawyers and advocates to litigate against each other, in other words against us.'[16] His solution was to join the two systems into one, centrally, provincially, and locally. 'Since we could no longer bear this state of affairs,' he wrote, 'we resolved to abolish both colleges and we order you to declare this to them in our name. In their places we will establish a *General-Ober-Finanz-Kriegs-und-Domainen-Direktorium*.' The General Directory, as it is usually called, had a president (the king), five vice-presidents (or ministers), and fourteen councillors.

The classical bureaucratic absolutism of the Prussian Ancien Régime was thus completed. The Soldier-King expected unreflecting obedience. 'I have command over my army', he said, 'and should I not have command over a thousand damned pen-pushers?'[17] He once threatened to brand the whole Medical College if they did not succeed in protecting Prussia from the plague that was raging in Hamburg. On another occasion he said of some civil servants: 'They shall dance to my music or the devil take me. Like the Tzar I will hang and roast and treat them as rebels.'[18] And he did, in fact, hang an embezzling councillor, and display the corpse for a few weeks in front of the War and Domain's Chambers building in Königsberg. He wanted his ideal bureaucrat to be, as he wrote, 'an intelligent, assiduous, and alert person who after God values nothing higher than his king's pleasure and serves him out of love and for the sake of honour rather than money and who in his conduct solely seeks and constantly bears in mind his king's service and interests, who, moreover, abhors all intrigues and emotional deterrents'.[19]

Every office and every board had its *Règlement*: its detailed code of instructions laying down exactly what was to be done in the most minute detail. Individual initiative was superfluous, for any problem not taken care of in the *Règlement* had to be passed up to higher authority. The *Règlement* of the General Directory was written by Frederick William himself. Article II, Paragraph 17 reads: 'The General Directory shall meet at seven in summer, at eight in the winter.' Paragraph 19 says: 'If the ministers can dispose of the affairs in an hour they are free to adjourn. But if they cannot finish in the morning they must remain together without interruption until 6-00 p.m. or until they finish all affairs. If they meet after 2-00 p.m. we order our Marshall that he shall bring them food and drink and in such a manner that half may eat while the other half works.' And Paragraph 21 orders that: 'If one of the ministers or councillors comes an hour late without our written permission, 100 ducats shall be deducted from his pay.'[20] Moreover, in their meeting room, he kept them over-mindful of their duty by having a life-size portrait of himself hung behind his empty, presidential, chair.

'Kabinett' Government

For he was not there in person. The King of Prussia did not discuss policy with his ministers as other European monarchs did. He ruled *'aus dem Kabinett'* – though it was as unlike English cabinet government as it was possible to be. Frederick William did not consult his ministers, or ask for their advice. He asked for information, or received requests; and then he issued orders. The whole administration of the State was dependent on the shuffling of papers up and down the hierarchies; and matters were no different at the culminating peak. Frederick William was rarely in Berlin. He preferred Wusterhausen or Potsdam; or he was out in the provinces on one of his inspections. Moreover, he was probably aware that his own ungovernable temper and apoplectic mode of discourse rendered him an unsound committee-man. Instead, he sat in his cabinet, read the documents that were handed to him by one of his secretaries, and then gave his commands – by means of marginal comments or written orders.

Here was a complete contrast to his father's custom of leaving things to his prime ministers, Danckelman, or Wartenberg. Frederick William warned his son of the importance of doing his own budgeting, and fixing his bureaucrats' salaries 'so that the whole world knows that they come from you and not from others'. In this way, he said, 'it will bring all the civil servants in Berlin and in the provinces right under your control, so that they must all depend on your favour and not on your ministers or favourites.'[21] But the king was not content simply to issue orders: he was constantly on the look-out in towns and villages to see how they were being obeyed. Wearing ordinary old clothes, he visited cottages and workshops to see things for himself. To a cobbler making a pair of army boots, he said: 'If you can work for my soldiers, you can do it for me as well.'[22] In Potsdam, at six o'clock one March morning, as he was taking a stroll, he turned the drowsy postmaster out of bed and set him about his duties with blows from his walking-stick.

The Church

The General Directory was not the only central department to which Frederick William sent orders from his cabinet. A second department was the Ministry of Justice, which was essentially what was left of the old Privy Council. Under its purview came religious, education, and judicial affairs. As was to be expected, the Monarchy, while tolerantly welcoming refugees of all faiths in order to colonize the untenanted fields, at the same time increased its grip on the Protestant churches. Both Pietism and Enlightenment had the effect of bringing Lutherans and Calvinists closer together, an approximation aided both by Frederick I and Frederick William, though they both failed in their efforts to unite the two. Under Frederick William, the provincial consistories which governed the churches were made subordinate to Berlin, visitations became more frequent and more searching, and, in general, every detail of church life was brought under closer royal scrutiny. Frederick William was among other things desirous of ensuring that the clergy preached appropriate submissiveness to earthly authority in their sermons.

Education

Similarly, he took a great interest in primary education, ordering in 1717 that all children should go to school from the age of five to twelve in order to receive religious instruction and to learn the three R's. Of higher education, and of the kind of cultural manifestations which had received so much encouragement in the previous reign, he was not so enamoured. As Frederick the Great later said, 'under Frederick I, Berlin was the Athens of the North; under Frederick William, she became the Sparta'.[23] During his reign the University of Halle became overwhelmingly Pietist in outlook; and the Enlightened philosopher, Christian Wolff, was dismissed in 1723 and given forty-eight hours to get out of the country. The Pietists had convinced the king that Wolff's ideas could be used to justify desertion from the army. And until Frederick the Great came along and reversed everything, the Pietists dominated higher education. Generations of army officers, civil servants, clergy, writers, and other professional men imbibed the spirit of frugal living, modest dress, self discipline, and hard work for the community. If Calvinism was the religion of the capitalist entrepreneur, Pietism was the faith of the bureaucrat. Moreover, if Pietism was less interested in metaphysical speculation than in creating God's kingdom on earth, it turned out to be not so very different in practice from the Enlightenment. Between the two of them, they produced an élite in Prussian society which was the perfect instrument of Enlightened Absolutism. Moreover, in complete contrast to the gentlemanly amateurism on which English public men prided themselves, they were thoroughly grounded in Cameralism, an academic discipline in which Frederick William created two chairs in 1727, one at Halle, the other at Frankfurt on the Oder. It was a combination of law, economics, and administration: a degree course tailor-made to train the men who sat in the General Directory, and in the War and Domains Chambers.

Justice

In judicial affairs, the Ministry of Justice was less effective in imposing its will than in religious and educational matters. This was the area in which the powers of the Estates, exercised through the provincial *Regierungen*, dragged on the longest. Samuel Cocceji was made supreme minister of justice in 1738, with the task of imposing in this field the all-Prussian uniformity and centralization that was fully evolving in all the others. His three main tasks were, first, to impose a central supreme court on top of the *Regierungen*; secondly, to develop uniform procedures; and, thirdly, to compile a common body of law. As Frederick the Great said, 'it was enough to be rich to win one's case and to be poor to lose it'.[24] The old provincial officials (like the *officiers* of France) fought a rearguard action every inch of the way, and Cocceji only gradually achieved success in his first two aims under Frederick the Great. His uniform body of law had to wait till 1794 before taking effect.

Foreign Affairs

As well as the General Directory and the Ministry of Justice, there was a third main central department which received orders from the king in his cabinet. This was the Foreign Office, through which the Soldier-King conducted his peaceful foreign policy. He was too unsubtle, and too religious, a man to succeed in international affairs, especially as he could not bear to risk his precious army on the battle-field. 'My dear successor', he wrote in his Testament, 'I entreat you for God's sake not to begin an unjust war and not to be an aggressor; for God forbids unjust wars.'[25] His only warlike acts were in the closing stages of the Great Northern War (1700–1721), when he joined Peter the Great in order to be in at the kill when Sweden was finally defeated. He occupied Stettin, and took Stralsund; and in the peace treaty (1720) received Stettin (and thus the mouth of the Oder) along with the eastern part of Swedish Pomerania. By this date, France was no longer strong enough to prevent Prussia from securing the outlet to the Baltic for which she had struggled for so long. After that, Frederick William played an undistinguished and unsuccessful role in the Machiavellian diplomatic manoeuvrings that occupied the great powers till the outbreak of the War of the Austrian Succession in 1740. He shifted his weight from the Emperor's side to that of France, and then back again. 'He who can maintain the balance in the world can always profit by it,' he said.

He showed little profit – except an intact army, 80,000 strong, a war treasury of eight million thalers, and a revenue which he had raised from 3,655,000 thalers in 1714 to 7,000,000 in 1740. If he did not fully appreciate the power of his state in European affairs, this was quickly proved by his successor in the first months of his reign (1740), when he launched his onslaught on Silesia. Prussia was no longer a client state, but a

European power; and, as Frederick the Great said of his father, 'his work made mine possible'.[26] But the real ordeal – when Prussia was tested almost to destruction point – was the Seven Years' War (1756–63), in which she 'did and suffered', as Christian von Westphalien said, 'what very probably no other state in Europe would have possessed either courage or perhaps patience enough to endure and do'.[27] That Prussia came through owed not a little to the solidity of the military and civil edifice Frederick William built, reinforced as it was by the steel of the Prussian character which his idiosyncratic work and example did so much to temper.

Prussia: Absolutism and Prussianism

The Junkers

The work of the Great Elector, Frederick I, and Frederick William I in creating the all-Prussian monarchy could not help but etch deep marks on the behaviour of the Prussian people; and this was the period when that characteristic amalgam of social structure, style of life, and attitude of mind known as 'Prussianism' began to make its appearance. Not that this was purely the creation of these rulers, deliberate or otherwise. For the Prussians were not entirely putty in the hands of their rulers, and their way of life was shaped as much by resisting absolutism in some fields as by yielding to it in others. The Junkers, for example, may have lost the political power they used to wield as feudal barons at the head of their vassals, or as law-makers meeting in their Estates; and they may, instead, have been enrolled into the new State army and bureaucracy. Nevertheless, as a *quid pro quo*, they had increased their social and economic power over the rest of society. And even their political power was not lost for ever. Under Frederick the Great (as will be seen) and especially under his successors, they asserted themselves once more as a political force, this time in their new role as top bureaucrats and generals. And whatever happened to the nobles affected the fate of the subordinate ranks of society, the burghers and peasants.

The success of the Hohenzollerns in subordinating the nobility to the Monarchy (if only temporarily) was partly due to the devastation and depopulation of the Thirty Years' War, which brought an end (for the time being) to the boom which the great landowners east of the Elbe had enjoyed since the late Middle Ages. During this long period of prosperity, the nobles had risen in economic and political power, on the one hand, impoverishing the burghers and enserfing the peasants, and, on the other, turning the princes into constitutional monarchs.

Their wealth came from the export of grain, timber, and other primary products to the markets of western Europe, where the Price Revolution was expanding demand. And, as is usually the case when the production of goods is organized for distant markets, the producers of the goods themselves were reduced by the organizers to the level of a property-less proletariat – a similar fate (only worse) to that which befell the textile-making smallholders of Picardy (see p. 215). In Prussia the system of production known as *Gutsherrschaft* evolved. Here the peasants lost their land and their civil rights to the land-lords, who operated as a combination of large-scale agricul-tural entrepreneurs, feudal seigneurs, and local chiefs of police. The same wave of prosperity which raised them economically well above the townsmen and serfs also lifted them politically above the monarchs. For this was the period when the Junkers established their corporative state, or *Ständestaat*; that is, their system of government in which the prince was forced to share his power with Junkers, legislating in their Diets, and governing in their *Regierungen*.

These two trends of the early modern era, the growth of the *Ständestaat* system of government and the *Gutsherrschaft* system of production, suffered opposite fates during the Thirty Years' War and under the great Hohenzollern rulers. The first was reversed, and the second was intensified. The Thirty Years' War hit the Junkers hard enough to enable the Great Elector and his successors to take away their influence in politics, but not hard enough for the kings to be able to affect their predominance in society. Not that the Hohenzollerns were intent upon the social and economic levelling of the landlords; for, although they wished to wipe out their military and political power *outside* the royal system, they wished to employ their martial and administrative talents to the full *inside* the royal system. Thus the Junkers received the support of the State in preserving their practical exemption from taxation, their seigneurial power over their serfs, their self-government in the counties under the leadership of their chosen represent-atives, the *Landräte*, and their monopoly of the leading posi-tions in the army and bureaucracy.

In this early period, in other words, the policy of the Hohenzollerns towards the nobles was ambivalent, if not confused; and it did not develop a firm outline till about halfway through the reign of King Frederick William I. Till that point, the atmosphere was that of centralizing monarchs taming recalcitrant barons by employing men from the middle classes. Under the Great Elector, this provided considerable opportunities for movement up the social scale. Three of his generals, for example, Derfflinger, Hennigs, and Lüdcke, were sons of peasants, and yet could dine at the Elector's table. And Frederick William I, in his early years, was notorious for his determination to establish the superiority of the crown over the nobility 'like a rock of bronze'. The haughty independent-mindedness of families like the Bismarcks and the Schulenburgs made his blood boil. 'Spiteful and disobedient people', he called them.[1] He lost no opportunity, in these early days, of enlarging the royal domain by picking up whatever noble estates he could lay his hands on. He made it a rule, as late as 1732, that estates on the domain should not be leased to nobles and officers, but that the whole administration of them should be in the hands of members of the bourgeoisie.

Shortly after this date, however, royal policy began to favour the nobility. This new approach was based on the realization that the attack on the nobles' bread and butter must stop if they were to fulfil their tasks as leaders of the army and the civil service. The next king, Frederick the Great (1740–86), encouraged the nobility from inclination as well as from policy. They were no longer in his eyes a class for the king to fear. 'In Prussia there are no factions or rebellions to fear,' he wrote in 1752, 'the sovereign needs to govern only mildly and only be on his guard against a few indebted and dissatisfied nobles or canons or monks in Silesia.'[2] Accordingly he instructed his bureaucrats to favour the nobility in legal contests between the latter and the royal domain. 'For what is a small loss to me is a great profit to the nobleman, whose sons defend the land and whose breed is so good that they deserve to be preserved by all possible means.'[3] Frederick had learned to value his nobles in the battles of the War of the Austrian Succession. 'On such days', he wrote in 1752, '... one learns to appreciate the worth of good officers; then one learns to love them.'[4] He also preferred them as bureaucrats. Of all the twenty ministers he appointed to the General Directory during his reign (1740–86), only one was a commoner. This was Friedrich Gottlieb Michaelis, son of a pharmacist, who served for two years only, and in the lowest ministerial post, that of Postmaster General. On the other hand Frederick was never able to fill the civil service with nobles of ancient lineage. The shortage of educated Junkers with administrative talents and industrious habits forced him still to rely on the services of commoners trained in the law and Cameralism, or experienced in business life. Thus the ratio of nobles to commoners did not greatly change. Frederick simply saw to it that nobles got easy promotion. Count von Münchow, for example, became Minister for Silesia at the age of thirty-three. Blue blood enjoyed exemption from the examinations which were supposed to be mandatory from 1770; and a long line of ancestors could take the place of long years of seniority as a qualification for advancement. In this way, the cream of society coagulated at the top of the armed forces and the civil service.

This equivocal policy of the Hohenzollerns, who now struck at the Junkers, now soothed them, or welcomed them with open arms, was mirrored by the attitude of the Junkers themselves towards the absolutist state. While stubbornly resisting royal attacks on the political powers of their Diets and *Regierungen*, they were nevertheless, in the depression of the Thirty Years' War and after, often glad for their younger sons to find jobs in the administrative boards and military commands created by the Hohenzollerns, even if there they worked alongside careerist commoners. Under the Great Elector and Frederick I, the Junkers still felt that the best people should hold themselves aloof from the royal service, and concentrate on running their manors and filling the traditional offices of the Diets and *Regierungen*. But as the expanding army and bureaucracy of Frederick William I created more and more entrancing opportunities (at the same time as it made the antique provincial organs of government less and less meaningful), so the nobility began to stream, and then to flood, into the royal service. Under Frederick the Great, the transformation was complete. No mode of life could compare in prestige with working for the King of Prussia. In 1739 the thirty-four generals were all nobles, and of the 211 staff-officers only eleven were commoners. By 1804 the infantry had only two commoners out of all the 422 staff-officers and generals, while the cavalry had four non-nobles out of 276. In a count taken of the adult nobles of Brandenburg Mark in 1800, sixty-eight per cent were in the army or had retired from it. The corresponding figure for East Prussia was sixty per cent.

Militarization of Prussian Life

This happy marriage of monarchy and aristocracy (with the king wearing the breeches till the death of Frederick the Great) established the tone of Prussian life for a century and more. To put it simply, it militarized the community. Prussia had been created as a state by the army. The bureaucracy had been created to serve the needs of the army. The upper classes now dominated both, and their soldierly code of conduct became the value system of the whole society, and ultimately of all Germany. How could it be otherwise when such a large proportion of the nobles were brought up from boyhood in the *Kadettenhaus*, rose to the rank of captain, major, or colonel by the age of fifty, and in retirement still officered the militia in time of war? Even off duty, or on leave, or in retirement, the regimental style of life went on, for the Junkers had long been accustomed to exacting instant obedience from their serfs. In fact, it was because they were such good serf-drivers that the Hohenzollerns especially valued them as against members of the bourgeoisie.

On the manor the landlords had absolute powers over their serfs (except those of life and death), and during the Ancien Régime managed to frustrate what little efforts the crown made to protect the peasants. In fact, so necessary were the nobles to the army, that the effect of the Hohenzollerns was to reinforce Junker power in the localities rather than reduce it. As a modern authority, Gerhard Ritter, has said, 'the Prussian sovereigns compensated their landed nobility for the loss of their political rights, as it were, by supporting their position as patrimonial lords'.[5] As Frederick the Great said in 1752, 'the preservation of the nobility [was] an object of policy of the Kings of Prussia; [for] the noble class were the foundations and pillars of the state'.[6] Each lord (and more than half the land was under private *Gutsherrschaft*) was the sole employer, police-chief, and judge, as well as manager of the village school and patron of the parish church. Moreover, the affairs of the county were managed by the *Landrat*, a fellow landlord, chosen by his neighbours, even though also appointed by the king. Thus all orders from the king through the bureaucrats of Berlin and the provincial capitals reached the citizens of the counties only through the mediation of the *Landräte*, who were not pure bureaucrats, but local representatives. The result was that, in their relations with their tenants, the Junkers were as good as undisturbed by royal orders, however imbued with the humanitarian views of Pietism or Enlightenment they might be.

These local tyrants, boorish, unlettered, and beer-swilling (especially in the first half of the period) were harsh task-masters over their tenants. Von Luben, a high official, reported, to the King in 1710:

They plague them with heavy Egyptian services with manifold corn and other carrying duties, harsh punishments and other dues to such an extent that they remain poverty-stricken; one cannot squeeze the contribution and other taxes out of them, or they run away; if they do so they are fetched back and things go worse with them; the people are punished and treated cruelly.... They cannot obtain justice at the governments and regional and local courts because the nobles sit in them, and these have an interest on account of their own estates and peasants, and do not want to prejudge their own cases.[7]

And these same lords, during the summer manoeuvres and inspections, were officers in the army commanding these same serfs as conscripts. Seigneurial authority was thus reinforced by military command, and vice versa, swelling the self-import-ance of the Junkers, and deepening the humiliation of the peasants. As in civilian life, the arm of the State did not reach deep enough into the armed forces to protect the rankers from exploitation by their officers. Just as the civil administration of the Hohenzollerns was riddled with gaps where feudal power still ruled, so did the nationalized army still contain vast pockets of private enterprise. A captain bought his company from his predecessor. The State paid him fixed allowances for the up-keep of his unit and its equipment, out of which, by careful management, by running his command like a business concern (*Kompaniewirtschaft*, it was called), the captain aimed to make his fortune. Besides his monthly pay, the captain received fixed allotments for his horses, for medicine, for horse-medicine, weapons, recruiting, and so on, all of which could be made to yield a profit. On top of these were other perquisites. The peasants living in the canton had to provide forage and other supplies: the captain fixed his own prices for these. In the cavalry remounting could bring in cash. The oldest officer of a troop had the privilege of selling old horses and buying new ones (in the Ukraine, Moldavia, and so on) on a commercial basis. In the garrison towns, the commander fixed the price of everyday commodities; the officers gave their men leave to work as artisans and labourers, and then pocketed a portion of their wages. The commander of a canton could exploit the legal helplessness of the inhabitants placed in his charge by illegally taking fees to grant marriage-licences; a practice which led to peasant immorality, it was often complained. Another profitable side-line was to accept a bribe from a father who wished to keep his son out of the army – and then to call him up just the same. And the higher the rank, the lusher became the financial possibilities. General Bogislav Friedrich von Tauentzien was one who (in the words of Frederick the Great himself) 'had nothing from his home and attained a fortune of at least 150,000 Thaler' – purely through military service.[8]

The incorporation of the Junkers into the officer class tended to turn the manor into a parade-ground; but the militarization of Prussian life went further than this. As has been shown, the civil service with its ranks and *règlements* was not only modelled on the army and designed primarily as a convenience for the army: it was also expected by Frederick William I and

Frederick the Great to behave with the clockwork precision of the army. And if day-to-day civil administration was turned into a drill, its military character was further intensified by the Hohenzollern habit of filling the bureaucracy with ex-soldiers. 'Officers understand how to obey and how to get obedience,' wrote Frederick in 1752, 'and if one hands over any matter to them for checking, they carry it out themselves, and with greater dependability than the others.'[9] Ex-officers were appointed Forestmasters, Postmasters, Councillors on the War and Domains Chambers, members of provincial *Regierungen*, even members of the General Directory, or Ministers, like Friedrich Wilhelm von Grumbkow, first a general at the age of thirty-three and then one of Frederick William's most important ministers.

Army officers were particularly influential in the counties, where they often held the post of *Landrat* – a kind of militarized Justice of the Peace. As the king's chief representative in the county, he was responsible for law and order, road upkeep and poor relief (often coming to the same thing), tax-collecting and military administration. He saw to it that selected nobles' sons were sent off to the *Kadettenhaus*, and that the correct number of peasants' sons were enrolled, trained, and then called to the colours under the canton system. He was responsible for rounding up deserters; for allotting the army horses among the villages for the summer grazing; for collecting the forage-tax which the peasants paid instead during the winter months; for placing ex-soldiers in suitable employment. He was especially busy when the army marched through his county. He had to organize billets, grazing, forage, baggage-transport with the required number of horses, carts, and peasants.

The towns were also in the army's grip. Even if the *Steuerrat* was not a noble ex-officer (which he sometimes was) but had climbed up the bureaucracy the hard way, nevertheless the chief officials he worked with usually were. In contrast to the *Landrat*, the *Steuerrat* was no independent local worthy, but a thoroughgoing bureaucrat; and, as against the counties, the towns had lost all vestiges of self-government and were fully meshed in with the State machine. The function of the towns was to supply food, drink, billets, stables, forage, jobs, manufactured goods, and above all excise income – all in aid of the troops. The garrison commander had full powers over retail trade; the municipal committees were usually presided over by army officers; the parson was usually a former regimental padre; the rank-and-file functionaries were often time-expired N.C.O.s. Out of eighteen new employees appointed by the Excise, for example, between 21 June and 21 July 1776, there were ten invalided soldiers and three N.C.O.s. Between 21 December 1776, and 31 July 1777, a total of twenty-five new men were engaged. Of course, four were nobles and nine were ex-soldiers.[10]

Thus from the top of society to the bottom the military was superior to the civil. In mixed judicial commissions, the president was always a soldier. If an officer belonged to a provincial *Regierung*, he was automatically given the chair. In wartime, officers were protected from all legal processes. If the king wanted a trusted investigator to carry out a secret inspection of any area of the civil administration, like the tsars of Russia, he usually had recourse to an officer. Not only jobs, but sine-cures as well were reserved for the military. There were in Prussia, for example, about 800 prebends in cathedral chapters available, each worth about 2,000 thaler a year – the salary of a minister of the crown. The chapters nominated to half of these; while the other half were in the king's gift. He filled them with retired officers.

Middle Classes

After the first half of the Ancien Régime, then, the nobility began to identify themselves with the higher ranks of the army and bureaucracy; and the kings, in their turn, began to treat them as the apple of their eye. The consequence was that in the second half of the period, the burghers (like the bourgeoisie of France and the middle classes in Britain) increasingly felt their advancement blocked by the dead weight of privilege above them. This had not always been so, for in the early years of the Ancien Régime, when the Hohenzollerns still handled the great landlords with caution, if not hostility, the middle classes were welcomed into the royal service, promoted, and even ennobled. Though the Great Elector preferred loyal and able nobles for his highest appointments, these were at times in short supply. He (and his successors) always preferred commoners for the secretarial work in the *Kabinett*; and during his reign and Frederick I's there was a steady recruitment of burghers into the army and all branches of the civil service. Assiduous commoners trained in the law could reach the highest rungs of royal employment. Such was the career of Paul von Fuchs, for example, who was a professor of law before becoming one of the Great Elector's chief advisers. Frederick I's chief minister, Eberhard von Danckelmann, was originally a commoner who had made skilful use of his opportunities as royal tutor. Another source of middle-class talent was business. The richest man in Berlin after King Frederick William I was his minister, Johann Andreas Kraut, a merchant banker.

Indeed, under Frederick William I, the influence of commoners in the royal service reached its peak. Like Louis XIV and Peter the Great, he opposed the notion that the high-born had the hereditary right to high office: he preferred to make and break his servants himself. And, although under him the top employments went to nobles (for example, they had a virtual monopoly of appointments in the army from the rank of captain upwards), nevertheless, the career was more open to middle-class talents in his reign than it ever was to be again till the downfall of the monarchy after the First World War. Under Frederick II, as has been mentioned, the burghers were increasingly kept out of the chief employments, even though they were still recruited in about the same numbers. In Silesia, for example, noble understudies in government offices received a permanent position after four to five years' training, whereas bourgeois apprentices had to wait fifteen to twenty years before being established. Frederick was particularly averse to having commoners in commissioned ranks in the army, even though he was to open the gates during the desperate dangers of the Seven Years' War. 'Most of them think in an inferior way,' wrote Frederick in his *Testament* of 1768, 'and are bad officers.'[11] On the other hand, commoner N.C.O.s could be commissioned as officers as a reward for exceptional service in battle. Moreover, sons of bourgeois parents who had acquired noble land (*Rittergüter*) could expect ennoblement after ten years' service as captains in the artillery or in a garrison. But this again was exceptional: for nobles were forbidden to sell their land to commoners. In the same way, exceptionally fortunate bureaucrats of burgher origin could be ennobled if they managed to acquire *Rittergüter* – even better, if they acquired a noble wife as well. Such was the happy experience of Samuel von Marschall, merchant's son, then councillor in Frederick the Great's *Kabinett*, then minister – and husband, first, of a von Schwerin, and, then, of a von Münchow. And what distinguished the Prussian middle class sharply from the French or British was the difficulty of acquiring nobility by sheer purchase. 'Nobility must only be acquired by the sword or bravery or other distinguished conduct and service,' wrote Frederick the Great. 'I will not have any other vassals except those who are capable of performing useful service for me at all times in the army.'[12]

Thus, although one or two spectacularly able or lucky burghers broke through to the top, there was for the majority of the bourgeoisie a clearly marked ceiling to their social and political ambitions. In this respect, the frozen social scene of Prussia differed sharply from the bubbling activity in Britain or France. It was more like the rest of Germany, where, as Madame de Staël wrote, 'everyone is in his rank, in his place, as it were, at his post'.[13] As has been mentioned, nobles were forbidden to sell noble land to burghers without royal permission. By a law of 1762, burghers who had managed to acquire noble land were forbidden to sell it to other commoners. A law of 1775 laid it down that a commoner could not inherit noble land if there was a noble heir still living.

By the same token, nobles were not allowed to set up in trade in towns. The crown was afraid that some of them might devote themselves to commerce at the expense of their proper trade of war, and thus (as Frederick put it) 'be taken away from their *métier d'honneur*'.[14] Behind this policy of insulating the classes one from the other, there were two important motives. The first was to preserve the nobles in possession of their estates and their serfs, so that they could serve the State, especially in the army. 'This body of men,' wrote Frederick in 1768, 'supplies officers to the army and subjects for all the great employments of the State. I have supported them in the possession of their lands and have put obstacles in the way of commoners to make it difficult for them to buy noble properties. Here are my reasons: if commoners possess lands, they will open the way for themselves to all employments.'[15] Instead, they had to be content with the lower ranks. Sons of the wealthier burghers, for example, having passed their university examinations, might expect to become judges in municipal or manor courts after serving eighteen months or two years in a junior capacity in a municipal court or in a provincial *Regierung*, and passing a further examination. A career in the administration was just as controlled by examinations and apprenticeships as it was in the judiciary. Candidates for posts as Councillors on provincial War and Domains Chambers, or for jobs as *Steuerräte* or *Landräte*, had to put in several years with one of the Chambers as well as pass an examination in the theory and practice of administration. Less ambitious burghers had to be content with jobs under the town councils, which had been brought thoroughly under the State administration. Those with lower sights still entered the Church, a career in which, unlike the army, administration or judiciary, there was absolutely no competition from the nobility; but in which, on the other hand, pay was low and prospects poor. There were too many applicants for too few jobs, and many clergymen had to fill in many frustrating years of tutoring, school-mastering, or writing till they landed a benefice, perhaps at the age of forty. And the other professions were even less enticing: for Prussian social and economic life had not evolved far enough in the direction of capitalism to provide much work for lawyers, or doctors, or surgeons.

The Economy

If the first reason for keeping the bourgeoisie in their place was the protection of the Junkers, the second was the collection of the Excise. This tax on commerce and industry would have been extremely difficult to collect had not merchants and artisans been cooped up in their towns. For this reason, artisans were forbidden to work up raw materials in the villages, for here the Excise did not apply. Only a small number of essential craftsmen were permitted in country districts: wheelwrights, blacksmiths, or carpenters. All the rest were herded inside the town wall or palisade; and all movement in or out was closely controlled by the Excisemen at the gates, who levied their duties on the goods, and inspected the passes of the human beings. No travel was possible without full documentation.

Within the towns, bureaucratic control was at its most perfect. The town officials had been reduced to the status of creatures of the *Steuerräte*: and below this level the gilds were also absorbed into the State system between 1732 and 1735, with a view to putting an end to their independent outlook, traditional modes of production, and repeated failure to keep their workmen in order. State control penetrated deep, and every item of municipal expenditure above ten thaler required government approval. Very little room was left for personal initiative, and as a result private enterprise failed to flower. Prussia was so organized by the Hohenzollerns that any energy or intelligence that appeared in the middle classes was attracted into the magnetic field of the army and bureaucracy. As a penalty, the economy exacted a heavy price from the Prussian kings. They had to provide the drive behind any business progress, supplying capital, markets, and know-how. Frederick William I, for example, created the woollen industry, mainly with army uniforms in mind. He established a warehouse (the *Lagerhaus*) in Berlin to provide wool at a steady price for the weavers. Shortly afterwards, he opened a State-run factory for making army cloth; and before long he had orphans spinning in their schools, paupers in their workhouses, and soldiers in their barracks. Under Frederick the Great the economic activities of the bureaucracy expanded, even though, wherever he could achieve it, the king preferred privately operated to nationalized manufacturing. In coal and metal mining (so vital to the armaments industry) the role of the State varied from place to place. In the Ruhr, the Royal Mining Office (founded in 1768) closely supervised a number of small, privately owned mines. And Berlin was represented in the Ruhr by Baron von Stein, later the reformer of Prussia after the collapse before Napoleon. In newly conquered Silesia, on the other hand, the Mining Office, under the local leadership of Friedrich Wilhelm von Reden, created large-scale nationalized mines and ironworks. Indeed, the wool and metal industries would never have quickened into life so early in Prussia had not the universities and the War and Domains Chambers trained such highly skilled, enterprising, and dedicated public servants, who alone were able to provide the funds, the skilled labour, the latest ideas, and the newest inventions – such as Boulton and Watt steam-engines imported from Britain.

The biggest contribution made by the crown to Prussian industrial growth, perhaps, was to provide the market. Not all industries, however, could be so comfortably feather-bedded in this respect as the woollen and metallurgical industries were by the armed forces. The luxury industries which Frederick's officials tried to foist on the Prussian economy were frail growths for a number of reasons. The silk brocades of Prussia could not outdo those of Lyons in price or quality; the clock and watch makers established in the village of Friedrichsthal near Oranienburg could not compete with the Swiss; nor could Berlin porcelain shift Meissen from its dominating position on the European market. But probably the chief reason for their lack of success was that the State machinery which created them also condemned them to having no home market. For how could the price-controlled, wage-controlled shopkeepers and artisans, Excised at every turn, be expected to accumulate the savings to buy such luxuries? And how much the less could the labourers and conscripts, hawkers and paupers, who formed the bottom half of the urban population?

Peasants

The peasants, perhaps, were the least capable of all, paying as
they did roughly forty per cent of their income in Contribution,
and forty per cent to their lord. In 1756 a peasant in one of the
counties of Pomerania is recorded as having paid eighteen thaler
in Contribution and Forage-money out of a holding which
brought him twenty-two thaler a year at the most. Even in their
minuscule trading operations, the peasants could hope for little
profit, for their output was marketed under State control. The
price of farm produce was calculated by the authorities in such
a way that it was not so low as to make it impossible for the
peasant to pay his taxes, and not so high as to be beyond the
allowance which the army paid to the troops for their food and
drink. Thus, far from being a market for luxury goods, the
peasants could hardly afford their basic necessities.

The peasant was the beast of burden who carried on his back
the main weight of Prussia's thrust towards the status of a great
power, for even at the end of the eighteenth century the population was overwhelmingly rural. Frederick the Great called
them that 'class of people who deserve the greatest regard, who
make the greatest contribution to easing the burdens of the
state; who furnish the whole state with food and necessities,
supply the army with a big proportion of its recruits, and provide all the other classes of subjects with an increase of new
townsmen'.[16] The rise of Prussia depended on the toil of villagers in the fields and meadows, and their sacrifice on the
field of battle, as well as their steady mulcting through the
Contribution. Everything depended on the peasants' willingness to till and drill, to pay his taxes – and keep quiet. And, on
the whole, throughout the Ancien Régime, they did so. 'The
peasants are indeed human beings,' wrote a clergyman in
1684, 'but somewhat more churlish and uncouth than the
others. ... When they eat they do not use a fork, but they dip
their five fingers into the pot.' And he added: 'The peasants
have that in common with the stockfish: these are best when
beaten well and soft. The dear peasants too are well-behaved

when fully burdened with work; then they remain well under control and timid.'[17] That was part of the secret of Prussian political stability under the Ancien Régime. King and noble conspired to keep the mass of the population in a state of economic and social subjection well below the level at which they would have leisure and presumption enough to make political activity thinkable.

Since Prussia stretched across northern Europe from the Rhineland over to Poland, there were wide variations in the lot of the village masses. Broadly speaking, the further east they lived, the more abject was their situation. In Cleves-Mark, where *Gutsherrschaft* did not establish itself, the lord of the manor was similar to a French or British landowner, keeping only a small domain for himself, and living on the rents received for all the rest. Only a minority of the peasants were personally tied to the lord. Most were freeholders or leaseholders, personally free, even if owing certain traditional services. They worked on the lord's domain, for instance, two or three days a week. Towards the Elbe in Magdeburg and Halberstadt, the landlord had the right to a cow or a horse on the peasant's death. Beyond the Elbe in the Brandenburg Mark, the peasant had to have his lord's permission to marry. In the east in general, the lord was practically absolute on his estates. The serfs were bound to the domain. Some could choose their heirs, others had to leave their strips of land to whichever of their children the lord designated. All paid dues and services which grew more onerous as the *Gutsherrschaft* system became widely established. Serf children (except for one boy and girl per family) had to work in the lord's household. As adults, they required the lord's permission to learn a trade, to marry, or take on a small-holding. Serfs could not leave the manor. If they did, the lord could pursue them, and it was illegal for other lords to harbour them. Broadly speaking, they worked for the lord six days a week. And working alongside them in the fields, in the forests, down the mines, and in the metal shops, was another class of people: landless day-labourers (*Instleute*) who were halfway between free peasants and serfs. In East Prussia, they formed the most numerous social group.

The Kings of Prussia had little success in improving the lot of the peasants, except on the royal domain, where the lease-holders, being bourgeois, did not put up such a stubborn fight as the nobles against change. On the Junker estates, the crown had to acquiesce in the degradation of the serfs' conditions of existence, and also in the dedication of the landlords to out-moded methods of production. There was no agrarian revolu-tion in Prussia, either in the sense of the wholesale adoption of new crops and rotations developed in Holland and Britain, or in the sense of enclosing the peasants' land, as happened in Britain. In the question of enclosure, the crown was very interested, and frequently intervened to stop it. From 1709 edicts were issued throughout the eighteenth century for the '*Konservation*' of the peasants' land, that is, to save it from being absorbed into the direct possession of the landlord, whether he was a Junker, a church, a monastery, or a domain leaseholder. This legislation was not concerned with peasants as individuals: that is, it did not prevent lords turning parti-cular peasants out of their holdings. It was concerned with the peasantry as a class, and laid down that when a lord moved a peasant out of his land he had to replace him with another, so that the total number of peasants and of peasant-holdings did not diminish. The Hohenzollerns were determined to pre-serve this social group, without whose efforts the whole Prus-sian adventure would have met disaster. For these were the men who grew the grain, paid the Contribution, repaired the roads, maintained the fortresses, provided grazing for army horses, supplied oats, hay, and straw at below-market prices, lent relay-horses for the baggage-trains, and, above all, pro-duced hefty sons for the regiments. 'We shall see to it that anyone who drives one of our subjects out of his land through irresponsible procedures,' wrote Frederick the Great, 'will be punished not differently from anyone who longed to drive any of our soldiers out of the rank and file.'[18]

For the peasants were not only at the beck and call of their landlords, they were also at the tender mercies of the recruit-ing officers, especially after Frederick I joined in the War of the Spanish Succession, and Frederick William I began that build-up of the forces which never ceased under the Ancien Régime. In the early years of the Sergeant-King, forceful recruiting struck terror throughout the peasantry, so ghastly was life-long service in the Prussian rank and file. To keep out of uniform they went to any lengths: self-mutilation, suicide, or selling all they had in order to buy off the recruiting officer. Sometimes whole villages fled, leaving the fields uncultivated. And it was because the army was threatening its own extinction by turning Prussia into a desert that Frederick William officially recognized the canton system in 1733, whereby the serf could carry the musket and till the soil at one and the same time.

By this system, recruiting was carried out by the captains in the company cantons till 1763, when the responsibility was transferred to regimental headquarters in regimental cantons. Suitable future soldiers were enrolled at the age of ten, but left at home on the farm where they had to wear a red necktie (or some other outward sign of their military destiny) and also submit to inspection from the local officers from time to time. The young peasant was then called to the colours for his basic training of one and a half to two years, and then sent back home as a soldier on leave (*Urlauber*). Serfs became common soldiers, free peasants tended to become N.C.O.s – all under the landlords as officers. Once back in his village (except in war-time) the recruit carried on the life of a peasant, apart from the two or three months of the year when the spring and summer manoeuvres took place. While on the farm, the *Urlauber* was not allowed to forget that he was a soldier. He had to wear a regimental coat, or cap, or necktie during the week in the fields, and full uniform on Sundays at church. (These were not difficult to buy second-hand, since all soldiers were allowed to sell their old uniform once a year.) Frederick William I, mindful of every detail, changed the comfortable seventeenth-century uniform into something tighter and more close-fitting – a symbol of strength and discipline. He was afraid, otherwise, that his soldiers 'would become peasants again'.

Elaborate precautions were taken to reduce desertions. In Pomerania, for example, every community had to appoint a night-watchman to prevent soldiers or peasants from absconding; peasants had to be on the alert day and night to recapture deserters; and a soldier or *Urlauber* could ask anyone for his pass, and arrest anyone without satisfactory papers. When the alarm-bell rang for a desertion, everyone had to lend a hand. Peasants had to put their farm-horses at the officers' disposal, and perhaps have them ruined in the chase. Careless villages were heavily fined. If they could not produce the fine, the two leading villagers might be condemned to cart stone for two months at a near-by fortress. A captured deserter could expect the gibbet, or a flogging, and the confiscation of all his property.

Discipline was severe, whether on the parade ground or on the manor, for under the canton system, the commander in the one case was the seigneur in the other. The whip and the cane were frequently employed, the object being (in the words of Frederick the Great) to give the common soldier 'more dread of the officer than of the enemy'.[19] It is not surprising to learn that the suicide rate went up significantly at inspection time in April and May, and that four times as many soldiers as civilians tried to put an end to their days. Even discounting these severities, however, there is no doubt that the interpenetration of military and agrarian life played havoc with the latter. Output could not help being adversely affected when both landlord and tenants might be drafted to manoeuvres at crucial moments in the farming year; or when everyone had to down tools to pursue a deserter, or drop everything in order to provide men, horses, and carts whenever a troop of artillery or a baggage-train happened to pass through the district. Neither was it much consolation to the peasant to be compensated for these vexations out of the War Chest: for this money was furnished by the Contribution, and so the peasant was being reimbursed with his own money.

The size of the military load carried by the peasants depended upon the proportion of foreigners to natives in the army, and this varied. Under Frederick William I, two thirds of the army were native Prussians; by 1742 this figure was down to one third; from the 1750s onwards it tended to be half. The Hohenzollerns were faced with the dilemma: whether to sacrifice the economy to military efficiency or vice versa. Too many natives in the army led to a fall in production; on the other hand, the quota of natives could not be allowed to fall below a third for they were required to see that the foreign conscripts did not run away in mid campaign. In garrison towns, unreliable recruits might be made to sleep in the billets of married N.C.O.s, who would be made responsible for their continued appearance on parade. For it was in the towns that the foreigners were quartered; and here they had a determining influence on the urban economy, both as a market for the towns' produce, and as a source of labour for their industries. Berlin's population, for instance, rose to 100,000 under Frederick William I, of which 20,000 were soldiers. Army pay was so low (it was not raised again after 1713) that soldiers were forced to find work in the town. Their officers did not mind allowing them leave (and thus saving their pay); and in this way the *Freiwächter* system grew up in the towns, similar to the *Urlauber* system in the villages, whereby the soldiers spent the greater part of the year working in industry.

The militarization of life by the mid eighteenth century, then, reached down to the lowest levels of society in town and village; and extended upwards to the Junkers, now fully enrolled in the Hohenzollern absolutism. It culminated in the king who was also Commander-in-chief, whether he was sleeping on his camp-bed in the palace at Potsdam, or signing *Kabinett* orders dressed in his army uniform. This was the army which was shortly to become the model for all Europe. In 1753 the Venetian ambassador to Vienna, Andrea Tron, wrote back to his government: 'All these innovations which ... practically every nation in Europe is making now in every aspect of the said [military] profession are all made in imitation of what the King of Prussia does, saying that to those who have knowledge of these matters the Prussian troops are the best regulated and the best disciplined in Europe.'[20] But what Frederick the Great did with this warlike instrument, and what it did to him must be the subject of the next chapter.

Prussia: Frederick the Great

Upbringing

The Prussian state which Frederick the Great thrust upwards to the status of a great power in the first year of his reign was formed in most of its detail by Frederick William I. Similarly, the personal qualities of the new king owed much to the hard training to which his brutal and neurotic father submitted him as a child and youth. Frederick William's pedagogic programme for his son, which he elaborated with typical thoroughness and detail, was more suitable as a breaking-in course for a wild animal than as an upbringing for a sensitive and gifted boy. Frederick, whose natural inclinations were towards the arts, and to the philosophy of the Enlightenment, reacted against a régime, worked out minute by minute, which had him out of bed at the crack of dawn, clapped him into a grenadier's uniform, forced him to trail round all day inspecting troops and domain properties, and to listen all evening to the coarse jestings of the king and his cronies in the so-called Tobacco-Parliament. At the age of sixteen Frederick was already writing his first poetry and signing himself 'Frédéric le philosophe'. He preferred his mother's salon or the pleasures of the library to his father's barrack-room binges or the joys of the hunt. Frederick William warned him against 'effeminate, lascivious, womanly occupations which were highly indecent for a man';[1] but the louder he raged, the more unbending and self-enclosed grew the boy. And as Frederick's silent endurance and firmness of purpose developed in his resistance to his father, so did his father's wrath swell at never knowing 'what goes on in this little head'. As the estrangement widened, Frederick William's demented mistrust of his son, as well as his bullying attitude, took on the appearance of mental disease. His suspicions of Doris Ritter, for example, seem pathological.

She was the sixteen-year-old daughter of a Potsdam head-master, and in all innocence she accepted presents from the young Crown Prince who admired her voice. Frederick William had her publicly flogged, and then locked up in a work-house.

The quarrel grew fiercer than a difference of tastes or a clash of temperaments, however, for it developed political overtones. Frederick frequented the circle of friends who attended his mother's social functions, and she despised the king's philistinism. For Sophia Dorothea cultivated the arts, and adopted the modish ideas of the Enlightenment. She attracted the support of those aristocratic families whose rich pickings at the Court of Frederick I had been so rudely revoked by Frederick William, and whose resistance to his centralizing policies made them the party of the opposition. Foreign, as well as home, affairs were involved, for the Queen was the sister of the Elector of Hanover who was also George II of Britain. Her faction favoured an alliance with Britain and France, and a British marriage for Frederick and his sister. The king was convinced, on the contrary, that Prussia's best interests could only be served by a union with the Emperor.

The rift between father and son was thus psychological, philosophical, and political. The king suspected that the Crown Prince wished to destroy his life's work; Frederick regarded his father's kingdom as a prison from which he longed to escape. Crisis point was reached in 1730 when Frederick in fact plotted to escape to exile in France or Britain. The king discovered the plan, and condemned to death his confidant, a young Prussian officer named Katte. Locked up in the fortress at Küstrin, Frederick had to witness his friend's execution, which the ferocious king arranged immediately in front of his window. Grenadiers forced him to look by holding his head in the right direction till he fainted away. After this climax in their mutual loathing (in which the king possibly considered executing his son, though it is not certain) a kind of armistice was arranged between them which lasted till the end of the king's reign (1740). For the contest had not only toughened Frederick's iron will: it had also taught him all the arts of deception and diplomacy.

He went through the motions of penitence and reform, while his father ostensibly conceded forgiveness and reconciliation. Frederick took a post in Küstrin under the War and Domains Chamber; then he became colonel of a regiment stationed at Neuruppin (1732); then he married a bride who was chosen by his father and related to the Emperor (1733). The king, for his part, allowed Frederick his own establishment in the rebuilt castle at Rheinsberg. Here, from 1736–40, he assembled friends of his choosing, and read philosophy, history, poetry, mathematics, and science, poring over his books from four in the morning, and often still making notes at two o'clock in the night. These were the happiest years of his life. Rheinsberg was the university where he graduated not only as a ruler and commander-in-chief, but also as a *philosophe* fit to exchange ideas with the greatest minds of the European Enlightenment.

Character and Ideas

He was fully trained, in other words, to strike the swift and reckless blows which have earned him the admiration and detestation of mankind. He became king in August 1740. In December, with the rape of Silesia, he crashed his way on to the world stage. Although only twenty-eight, he was old in the ways of the world, a philosopher turned man of action, a poet and musician as well as an administrator and warrior, a cynic who despised his rival rulers as well as the people he governed, but who yet was prepared to make any personal sacrifice in the interests of the state he had inherited. 'His special failing is his contempt for mankind,' wrote the Marquis de Valori, who was French ambassador to Berlin during Frederick's first ten years.[2] 'If I except the Queen of Hungary and the King of Sardinia, all the other princes of Europe are merely illustrious imbeciles,' he wrote himself later.[3] 'The great mass of the people and the common herd of the nobility', he wrote on another occasion, 'remain what nature made them, namely evil animals.'[4] Yet this misanthrope had the most profound reverence for the destiny of Prussia and the most self-effacing sense of duty towards it. 'There is only one good,' he said, 'which is that of the state in general.'⁵ 'A well-conducted government', he wrote in a famous passage, 'must have a system as coherent as a system of philosophy, so that finance, policy and the army are co-ordinated to the same end, namely the consolidation of the state and the increase of its power. Such a system can only emanate from a single brain, that of the sovereign. Idleness, pleasure-seeking, and imbecility are the causes which keep princes from the noble task of securing the happiness of their people. The sovereign is the first servant of the State.'⁶

No servant ever bent his back for a master with greater devotion or for longer hours. Whether sitting at his desk at Potsdam, or striding through newly planted villages in Pomerania, or in the saddle at the head of his troops, this little coffee-swilling despot, with his huge dark-blue eyes and soft, captivating voice, exhausted himself into a premature old age in the service of his abstract employer. Perhaps his most characteristic quality was his stoical fortitude in the face of danger. 'He who cannot withstand misfortune', he wrote, 'is not worthy of fortune.'⁷ He did not believe in God, but he worshipped Prussia. 'All religions, when one looks into them', he said, 'rest on a system of fable more or less absurd.'⁸ On the other hand, he believed that the universe was arranged according to the principles of reason, and his rule of life was the rational application of means to ends, all in the cause of Prussian greatness. And whatever evil is perpetrated by those who erect the State into a deity, whether against the individuals in the State or against neighbouring powers, it is as well to be clear about Frederick's motives. He was not pursuing his own glory, nor that of the Hohenzollerns. He was genuinely seeking the greatness of Prussia – whatever crimes he may have committed in her name.

The elevation of the State into an ethical absolute is fraught with moral danger, and monarchs like Frederick, with their heads in the clouds of abstract speculation, grow oblivious to the havoc their feet are creating on the ground. And, although he wrote a book called *The Antimachiavel* (while still Crown Prince) in which he said, 'I have always regarded *The Prince* as one of the most dangerous books in the world,'⁹ yet as king he acted fully in accordance with the principles of *raison d'état*.

'Our task', he wrote of kings in his *Histoire de mon temps* (composed in the middle of his invasion of Silesia), 'is to watch over the happiness of our peoples. When we find they are endangered by an alliance it is our duty to break it, the sovereign thereby sacrificing himself for their welfare.... It is better that the sovereign should break his word than that the people should perish.'[10]

War of the Austrian Succession

The practical results of this philosophy were made manifest in 1740, when, within a few sensational months of his accession, he revolutionized the European situation and transformed Prussia from a second-class state into a major power. The Emperor Charles VI unexpectedly died on October 20th at the age of fifty-five, leaving only a daughter, Maria Theresa, as heiress to the loose collection of territories which made up Austria, and which hitherto had never had a female ruler. Although these territories, and the powers of Europe, had accepted Charles's so-called Pragmatic Sanction which guaranteed his daughter's succession, other claimants were not slow to come forward to exploit the legal niceties of this unprecedented situation. Even rulers who were prepared to accept Maria Theresa as Queen in the Habsburg lands were not prepared to vote for her husband as Holy Roman Emperor. Moreover, Maria Theresa's weakness in the early weeks of her reign was suddenly increased by the death of the Empress Anne of Russia, leaving a disputed succession to a two-month-old heir. Thus Austria was deprived for the time being of Russian help. She presented a temptation which Frederick could not resist.

The House of Hohenzollern had long entertained claims to parts of Silesia, but these cut little ice with the rationalist in Potsdam. It was not Frederick's style to be impressed by historical traditions or the accident of hereditary succession. For him, Silesia was simply necessary, on political, geographical, and economic grounds, to make Prussia a great power: to end, in his words, her 'hybrid situation, between electorate and kingdom'.[11] Silesia's resources would enrich Prussia. Her population was already half that of Prussia; her wealth eventually brought in an income equal to half that of Frederick's royal domain. Moreover, Silesia would help to knit together the sprawling Hohenzollern territories and reduce their vulnerability. In addition, in the confused diplomatic situation in the Empire and in Europe as a whole, a blow struck now could gain more than centuries of negotiations. 'Ambition,' explained Frederick himself in 1740, 'the wish to make a name for myself, turned the scales, and war was resolved upon.'[12]

The rape of Silesia began in December 1740. 'Farewell, Gentlemen', said Frederick to the officers of the great army he had inherited from his father, 'to the rendezvous of fame, whither I shall follow you without delay.'[13] At the same time, he wrote to his uncle, George II of Britain, 'I have been compelled to send my troops into the Duchy in order to prevent others seizing it, to my great disadvantage and to the prejudice of the just claims which my House has always had to the larger part of that country. I have no other purpose than the preservation and the real benefit of the House of Austria.'[14] Frederick's campaign became part of the European War of the Austrian Succession (1740–8) as the coalitions polarized about France, on the one side, and Austria and Britain on the other. The Prussian army won its first battle of the eighteenth century at Mollwitz (1741) and Silesia was easily conquered from the hard-pressed Habsbugs. Thereafter, till 1745, Frederick signed truces, re-opened hostilities, and won further battles, just as it suited him – even if, at times, it meant leaving his French ally in the lurch. His purpose was to hang on to Silesia, and at the same time to prevent either France or Austria destroying the other. The rest of Europe fought on till 1748, when the Treaty of Aix-la-Chapelle confirmed Prussia's possession of Silesia. Frederick had proved to his own and the Prussians' satisfaction that 'negotiations without arms produce as little impression as musical scores without instruments'.[15]

He had also raised the enmities within the European states-system to a new level of intensity. 'If you must go to war', he wrote in 1752, 'fall on your enemy like thunder and lightning.'[16] Like Napoleon later on, Frederick had the advantage over other generals in being both Commander-in-chief and Head of State. As against the stately, defensive manoeuvring of eighteenth-century warfare, he launched vigorous assaults; and his aim was to destroy the enemy's army rather than capture his ground. His armies made up for their modest size by the perfection of their drill and the intensity of their fire-power. Their speed of loading and firing enabled him to deploy his men in three lines instead of four, thus increasing the length of his front and cutting down the chances of being outflanked. Moreover, he himself was at his most brilliant when directing a battle. No contemporary general could match the dexterity of his mind or the fortitude of his spirit. Moreover, none of them had his advantage of being able to negotiate for a separate peace, or in other ways exploit the ever-changing diplomatic situation.

Seven Years' War

His very success now committed him to a life of standing permanently on watch. 'We have drawn upon ourselves the envy of Europe by the acquisition of Silesia,' he wrote, 'and it has put all our neighbours on the alert; there is not one who does not distrust us.'[17] Prussia had been the sole substantial gainer at Aix-la-Chapelle; and the other powers spent the years of peace between 1748 and 1756 refurbishing their armed forces and re-negotiating their alliances in preparation for a second war which each hoped would be more profitable than the first. The chief outcome of the diplomatic manoeuvring as far as Prussia was concerned was, first, the celebrated diplomatic revolution, by which Austria and France ended their centuries-long enmity to form an alliance; and, secondly, the build-up of a scheme by Russia and Austria to dismember Prussia. By 1756 Frederick was convinced that a coalition of Austria, Russia, Saxony, and other powers was about to attack him. He struck first, and thus brought into being the hostile alliance which had hitherto been mainly a product of his imagining. 'It is true', he wrote, 'that the King begins hostilities; but since this term is often confused with aggression, and since the Court of Vienna is always seeking to incriminate Prussia, the meaning must be explained. By aggression one understands any action opposed to the meaning of a treaty of peace. A League for offensive purposes, incitement to war against a third power, the plan of invading the territories of another prince, a sudden invasion: all these things are aggressions. Whoever anticipates them may commit hostilities but he is not the aggressor.'[18] But even if one accepts Frederick's explanation that his attack on Saxony in 1756 was only a form of defence, it still remains true that what he was defending was the booty gained by his invasion of Silesia in 1740. That was aggression by his own definition, or anybody else's.

His troops conquered Saxony fairly swiftly, but not quickly enough to leave time to attack Bohemia in the same campaigning season. He thus lost the advantage of surprise, and instead gave the grand alliance of Austria, Russia, Sweden, France, and the Circles of the Empire time enough to prepare a massive assault on him on three main fronts. In 1757 the French army, assisted by troops of the Circles, thrust into western Germany; the Austrians into Silesia; the Russians into East Prussia. The Prussians seemed about to be overwhelmed, till at the end of the year Frederick won two of his greatest victories. At Rossbach, his 22,000 Prussians defeated 43,000 French and Imperialists; and, at Leuthen, 30,000 Prussians beat 80,000 Austrians.

The rest of the Seven Years' War as far as Prussia was concerned consisted mainly of manoeuvrings and sieges. Frederick's enemies closed in on him on all sides; he struck back wherever possible. As Gerhard Ritter has described it, he was like a surrounded lion 'who falls now on one pursuer now on another with unexpected leaps, and keeps dealing out more and more frightful blows with his paw in the hope that their courage will finally fail, that their aggressive spirit will be exhausted'.[19] That Prussia survived was due, in the first place, to the British, who paid Frederick an annual subsidy from 1758 onwards, and also relieved him of French pressure by forming an army in west Germany under Prince Ferdinand of Brunswick, consisting of British, Hanoverians, Hessians, and Brunswickers – the army with which Pitt hoped to conquer Canada – on the Elbe. And Prussian survival was due, in the second place, to the magnificent

Prussian army and its ubiquitous commander. Napoleon thought it was Frederick rather than the army.

In the bloodiest warfare of the eighteenth century, with much of his country in enemy hands, Frederick was often in despair and ready to make use of the eighteen opium pills he carried on him in a little gold box. Fortunately, his unbreakable stoicism supervened and outlasted the determination of his foes. 'In these disastrous times', he wrote, 'one must fortify oneself with iron resolutions and a heart of brass.'[20] In 1758 he beat the Russians at Zorndorf. 'The Russians fought like devils,' wrote the British ambassador who was there. 'The King's firmness of mind saved all.'[21] In 1759 a massive Austro-Russian army beat him at Kunersdorf, where he had two horses shot from under him and a snuff-box in his pocket flattened by a bullet. 'I think all is lost', he wrote. 'I shall not survive the ruin of my country.'[22] Berlin only escaped conquest because of the failure of his enemies to follow up their advantage. The surrender of a Prussian army to the Austrians at Maxen, with the subsequent loss of most of Saxony, deepened the gloom of 1759, which was only slightly relieved by Ferdinand's victory over the French at Minden, and by the decision of the new French Foreign Minister, Choiseul, to reduce his effort in Germany in order to concentrate on colonial warfare. In 1760 Frederick beat the Austrians at Leignitz and Torgau, without, however, delivering Prussia from her overall critical situation. 'I burn on a low fire,' he wrote. 'I am like a body in process of mutilation which loses a limb every day.'[23]

Ruin seemed inevitable in 1761 as Pitt resigned and the new British government began to taper off its help. Frederick was only saved from destruction by the fortunate death of the Empress Elizabeth in 1762. 'We have just learned that the Messalina of the North is dead and that her successor is well disposed towards us,' he wrote in some relief.[24] Peter III, in fact, idolized Frederick. He immediately called off the Russian attacks, and offered to hand back East Prussia, and even to help reconquer Silesia. Shorn of French and Russian help, Maria Theresa could not go on alone, and so Austria and Prussia signed the Treaty of Hubertusburg in 1763, restoring the pre-war situation. At the same time France and Britain signed the Peace of Paris.

Later Foreign Policy

In these testing years of the Seven Years' War, Prussia had now proved beyond doubt that she was a major power. The little state that in the War of the Spanish Succession had been gratified to be hired by the great contestants had now withstood the combined onslaughts of three major powers and two minor ones. The reckless gamble of 1740 had condemned Prussia to twenty-three years of ordeals, some of them almost past enduring. She had survived; but the necessity of remaining permanently on the *qui vive* was not over in 1763. For the remainder of his reign, Frederick was condemned to ceaseless diplomatic and military activity designed to head off Austrian attempts at revenge. He allied with Catherine II for this purpose, from 1764 onwards, and supported her schemes for maintaining Poland in a state of anarchic impotence. In 1772 he went further, and joined Russia and Austria in the first partition of Poland, gaining West Prussia. We may accept Horace Walpole's condemnation of these powers as 'the most impudent association of robbers that ever existed', but the only alternative for Frederick was to sit back and watch Russia establish herself in the territory between East Prussia and the rest of his state.

Within Germany itself, he was the leader of the opposition to Austrian advance. When the Elector of Bavaria died without heirs in 1777 and Austria made attempts to lay hands on part of his inheritance, Frederick made an alliance with Saxony and invaded Bohemia (1778). This so-called War of Bavarian Succession (1778–9) saw Frederick's last and least glorious campaign. Very little more than skirmishing and foraging took place; but Frederick's diplomatic isolation of Austria was successful, and she had to abandon her Bavarian claims. Similarly, in 1785, when Austria was attempting to give away the Austrian Netherlands in exchange for Bavaria, Frederick organized a League of Saxony, Hanover, and more than a dozen other German states (the *Fürstenbund*) to prevent her.

As well as being constantly on the alert in Germany and Europe against Austrian reprisals, Frederick also had to heal the wounds his aggression had inflicted on his own people. When he returned to Berlin after the Seven Years' War, he was a prematurely aged man, though only just over fifty. He was a grey-haired figure of skin and bone in his worn-out old uniform, bent crooked with gout, with a hard look on his face. He rejected the suggestion of a drive through the city in a state-coach, and reached the Schloss by the side-streets. The next day a deputation of *Landräte* came to see him to congratulate him, and present petitions. But he rudely interrupted their spokesman's address, and said: 'Be quiet and let me speak to you. Have you got pencils? Well, take a note of this: write down how much rye, how much seed, how many horses, oxen, and cows you most seriously need in your counties. Work this out properly and come and see me again the day after tomorrow.'[25] With this typically stern and flinty paternalism, the first servant of Prussia began his work of reparation.

There was no question of leaving recovery to private initiative. 'The prince is to the society he governs what the head is to the body,' he wrote in his *Essai sur les formes de gouvernement et sur les devoirs des souverains* (1771): 'he must see, think, act for the whole community.'[26] Frederick dedicated his entire self to the endless drudgery which he exacted from himself as Head of State; and he expected similar devotion from his bureaucracy and army, the nerves and sinews of the body-politic. He made few changes in the superb administrative system left to him by his father, but raised it to ever higher levels of activity. His military demands, and his mercantile programme, especially, forced the civil service to impinge on Prussian life in ever increasing detail; while his mounting expectations caused him to curse them in ever more mocking language. 'Out of 100 councillors', he wrote to the West Prussian War and Domains Chamber in 1774, 'one can always have 99 hanged with a clear conscience, for if there is one honest man amongst them, it is a lot.'[27] And on the only occasion when members of the General Directory dared to be critical of his post-war economic reforms, he replied in a *Kabinett* Order: 'I am astonished at the impertinent report you send me. I excuse the ministers because of their ignorance, but the malice and corruption of the writer of it must be punished as an example, otherwise I shall never bring the rascals under control.'[28] Privy Councillor Erhard Ursinus was thereupon imprisoned in the fortress at Spandau.

Prussia was governed by one man, for only Frederick saw the whole situation. He sat in his *Kabinett* in Potsdam writing out his Orders, and the movements of his pen were the heart-beats of the State. Even a peasant's marriage-licence, or a craftsman's permit was worded as if it had been issued by the king in person. Every evening the courier from Berlin reached Frederick's residence, Sans Souci. Five secretaries arranged the documents in order, ready to place them before the king in the morning. 'He began his work early in the morning with foreign affairs', wrote Mencken, one of his secretaries; 'he had already read the deciphered dispatches of his ambassadors and now he dictated to his secretary an answer to every dispatch, whether important or not, from the first letter to the last, often several pages. Thereupon he dictated to another secretary answers to all letters on domestic affairs, to reports of the chambers on accounting and finance, and to the reports of the military inspectors of the army. Some of these he had already decreed by marginal notes. While this was being done, another secretary prepared a brief extract of all the less important letters and petitions from private persons. This was then placed before the king who decreed each item in a few words.'[29] The secretaries then retired to write fair copies of the letters, which they brought back for the king's signature in the late afternoon. He worked hard, decided swiftly, postponed nothing. 'His superiority of talent,' wrote Sir Andrew Mitchell, the British ambassador, 'the readiness and fertility of his invention, fill me with confidence.'[30]

Uncluttered by family life, undistracted by Court ceremonial, he always worked overtime. His whole year was worked out in detail, hour by hour. He saw the ministers of the General Directory only two or three times annually. In between, he plied them with paper, and expected quick dispatch. 'If everybody does his duty and works diligently', he wrote, 'all current business can be disposed of in three hours during the morning.

However, the whole day will not be long enough to get through with the work in hand, if members of the board tell each other stories, read the newspapers, go for a walk or keep themselves busy with other matters which have nothing to do with the functions of the board.'³¹ And as a contribution to this efficiency, he cut out the free lunch that Frederick William used to lay on for his top bureaucrats.

Economic Policy

The constant task of the king and his civil service was the stimulation of the economy, and especially the repair of the serious damage it had suffered during the wars. Frederick intensified his father's mercantilist manipulation of economic life. 'The basis of commerce and industry', he wrote in 1752, 'is to prevent money leaving the country by making at home all the things we used to buy abroad.'³² Stimulus for any economic progress could only come from the State, for this was practically the sole possessor of the capital, provided the majority of the market, and had more or less the monopoly of what talent and enterprise was available in Prussian society. All the usual devices of mercantilism were employed by Frederick the Great with Prussian thoroughness, and adhered to stubbornly throughout his reign – a time when other states were moving in the Physiocratic direction of free trade. He founded overseas trading companies, such as the Russia Company and the Levant Company, though these did not succeed in freeing Prussia from dependence on Dutch and British merchants. The Overseas Trading Corporation (*Seehandlungsgesellschaft*) was granted the monopoly of trade in salt and wax in the Baltic countries (1772). A State marine insurance company was started to take this business away from Hamburg. Internally, he freed trade by reducing internal tolls and by draining rivers, linking them with canals, building port installations, and so on. The Oder, for instance, after the conquest of Silesia under Prussian rule for its full length, was much improved as a highway, enabling the industrial riches of the new province in textiles and minerals to be better exploited. To ease credit, a State bank was set up in

Berlin with branches in Breslau, Königsberg, Magdeburg, Stettin, Elbing, Frankfurt-on-Oder, Emden, and Cleves. The capital was provided by the king. Moreover, he used various devices to found new industries: granting monopolies, lending buildings, finding experts, and, of course, lending capital. Frederick's expenditure in this field averaged three million thaler a year. And the result was considerable industrial development, and, especially, diversification. Prussia now took her place among the economically advanced states like France and Britain, though still behind them in output. A favourable balance of trade was at last achieved, and, above all, an increase in revenue.

The civil service also expended much money and effort on agriculture. Ministry experts showed peasants the latest crops and methods: turnips, potatoes, crop-rotation, animal breeding, manuring, and so on. They had more success on the farms of the royal domain than on the Junker land, where the serfs in their depressed social position were hardly accessible to government influence. More effective, perhaps, in encouraging farming was the State's policy of stabilizing grain prices by setting up depots of grain at scattered points throughout the land to serve as a reserve in case of war. By heavy buying in good years, and massive selling in bad, these magazines kept the grain market steady, assuring level prices for industrial workers and soldiers, and a steady market for the farmers. On top of this, the State did much to colonize the countryside with foreigners. Swamps were drained and wastes cleared, to be settled with immigrants attracted to Prussia by financial grants and social privileges. In this field Frederick did not have the outside help that his predecessors had enjoyed. Their immigration policies had been greatly assisted by religious persecution in other parts of Europe. Frederick was denied this luck, but nevertheless beat their record: partly because of his own Enlightened indifference to the religion of his subjects. 'It matters not to the State what metaphysical opinions dominate men's minds,' he wrote in 1768; 'enough that everyone behaves as a good citizen and patriot.'[33] He gave Jesuits asylum in Silesia, when they were being expelled from Roman Catholic states; though he did not encourage Austrian priests, of course. 'If Turks and heathens came and wanted to populate the country,' he said, 'we would build them mosques and churches.'[34] During his whole reign, 300,000 foreigners moved in and 900 new villages were founded. It was a better method than armed aggression of adding a new province to the State.

The general outcome of Frederick's economic policies can best be summarized with the aid of a few statistics. The total area of Prussia rose from 118,926 square kilometres in 1740 to 194,891 square kilometres in 1786. The population rose from two-and-a-half millions to five millions. And the people were a more precious acquisition than the territory. 'The first principle which presents itself', wrote Frederick in his *Political Testament* of 1768, 'the most general and the most true, is that the real strength of a state consists of the number of its subjects.'[35] One consequence was to enable him to raise the army from its 83,000 of 1740 to its 200,000 of 1786. Moreover, the balance of trade changed from being 500,000 thaler on the wrong side in 1740 to three million on the right side in 1786. The total crown revenue moved from seven million to nineteen million thaler; the State treasure from eight million to fifty-one million thaler. There was thus no cause for the Prussian crown to call a States-General.

The *Aufklärung*, or Enlightenment

Most of Frederick's energy went into the task of increasing the numbers and affluence of his subjects, so that they would provide men and money for the army. He was an intellectual himself, but he despised the common run of mankind too much to be a fully Enlightened ruler. He paid attention to the welfare of the people only in so far as that contributed to the welfare of the State; and the only sense in which he was a true ruler of the Age of Reason was his strict adherence to the principle of *raison d'état*. It was in this spirit that he promulgated a detailed scheme of elementary education in 1763. All children between five and thirteen were ordered to go to school from eight till eleven o'clock in the mornings and from one to four in the afternoons, except Wednesdays and Saturdays. This was the winter programme: in summer, school was to be held on mornings only. There were to be no holidays, and on Sundays the children were to work at their catechism. Teachers were to be the products of the seminary in Berlin where they were to be taught 'the cultivation of silk and pedagogy'. In fact, through lack of teachers and the inability of poor parents to pay the fees or spare their offspring from breadwinning, the spread of universal education was slow and painful, and much remained to be done after Frederick's death. Moreover, what primary education there was never rose above the status of poor relation to industry and the churches, and its content was mainly limited to the production of industrious and well-behaved citizens. On the other hand, there was great enthusiasm for private education among middle-class parents, anxious for their children to reach university and rise in the bureaucracy. By the end of the Ancien Régime, the Prussians were possibly the best-schooled and most conscientious people in Europe. But there was over-production in this field, and Prussian towns were filling up with discontented young graduates who were burning with enthusiasm for the ideals of the *Aufklärung*, but seething with indignation at a social system which offered such modest and ill-paid careers. Such were the young men who became the writers and readers on which the great literary revival of the late eighteenth century was based.

This younger generation of Lessing, Herder, Goethe, Schiller, and Kant, which produced the greatest intellectual outburst in Germany since the Reformation, meant little to Old Fritz, who was a devotee of the Enlightenment of France. Frederick regarded German as a 'semi-barbarous' tongue, and wrote a treatise with the title *De la Littérature Allemande, des défauts qu'on peut lui reprocher, quelles sont les causes, et par quels moyens on peut les corriger*. 'I have read no German book since my youth,' he once said, 'I speak German like a coachman, and now I am an old fellow of fifty-six years and have no more time for it.'[36] Not that his French was perfect, but he much preferred the clarity and polish, the wit and bite, of French writing to the deeper and more mysterious chords struck by the *Sturm und Drang*. This is one sense in which he was Enlightened; and though there were gaps in his knowledge and his mind was studded with prejudices, he was unusually learned for a monarch. The Prince de Ligne, himself a cultivated man, thus described Frederick's conversation: 'The King's encyclopaedic range enchanted me. The arts, war, medicine, literature, religion, ethics, history and legislation were discussed.'[37] He revived the Prussian Academy, and made the French scientist, Maupertuis, president. He bought five copies of the books he wanted to read for his identical libraries at Potsdam, Sans Souci, Charlottenburg, Berlin, and Breslau. Typically, though, he kept a firm distance between the intellectuals and political power. 'It is for the *philosophers* to be the teachers of the universe and the masters of princes,' he said in 1740; but added: 'They must instruct the world by argument, and we by example. They must discover, and we practise.'[38] He wrote endlessly, and his published *Works* and *Political Correspondence* run into scores of large volumes. His symphonies are sometimes played today, and well over 100 of his sonatas and concertos for the flute have survived.

If he outpaced his fellow monarchs in intellectual matters and despised them as politicians, he nevertheless followed the common herd of Ancien Régime rulers in one respect. From Louis XIV onwards they all built their baroque and rococo palaces as a form of display, like peacocks in season, as an exhibition of their wealth and power (sometimes as a substitute for them). Frederick the Great was no exception. He added a new wing to Charlottenburg. He put up the Opera House, the Church of St Hedwig, and other imposing edifices in Berlin. He built his new rococo residence of Sans Souci, and rebuilt the palace at Potsdam. He was determined to show the world that Prussians could do other things than brew beer and march in line.

Weaknesses of Prussianism

These great successes so far described must be mainly attributed to the moral force of the king and the conscientious application of his officers and officials. But there was a price to pay; and this was paid partly by the Prussian people in their collapse before

Napoleon, and more fully by the Germans as a whole in more recent times. One significant development under Frederick was the growth of the power of the army and bureaucracy in the State, and the growing predominance of the nobility within them. Of course, the resurgence of the nobility in the second half of the eighteenth century is a European phenomenon, but it was particularly sinister in Prussia. For under the Hohenzollerns there were no longer any representative institutions to keep the aristocrats in line – there was hardly, in fact, any movement demanding such institutions, so drugged were the people by the Hohenzollerns' success.

The Bureaucracy

The civil service of Frederick the Great's time was no longer the eager stripling of Frederick William I's day, responsive to every nuance of the royal wishes. It was middle-aged and stiff in the joints, overwhelmed with work and benumbed with routine. Age and experience had endowed it with set habits and a mind of its own. Especially in Berlin, in the General Directory, it could become a hindrance to Frederick's wishes, either because the proper channels were silting up with slowly moving paper, or because the bureaucrats were forming their own policies, independently of the king, sometimes in opposition to him. The lumbering General Directory enraged Frederick, for example, by being unable to inform him how many pounds of coffee were annually consumed in Prussia. Ministers would frustrate him by feeding him with false information. Count von Hoym, the Silesian minister, once added 20,000 to a population return, because he knew how greatly the king enjoyed high population figures. Provincial Chambers learned all the tricks of passive disobedience. When Frederick abolished all fees in the public service, except for petty 'service charges', the War and Domains Chambers of Silesia carried on collecting the old fees – though they changed their name in the records to 'service charges'.

The General Directory became so swamped with business that collegial procedure had to be abandoned to allow individual ministers to specialize in certain fields, and to correspond individually with the king on them. Count von Schulenburg, for example, ran Department III, that is, Cleves, Mark, Moers, Geldern, Ostfriesland, Halberstadt, Minden, Ravensburg, Tecklenburg, Lingen, and Magdeburg. But, in addition, he was also in charge of the Stamp Department, Forestry, Government Construction and Monopoly, the Overseas Trading Corporation (*Seehandlung*), the Prussian Bank, the Tobacco Monopoly, and the Mint. He could get through the business only by having twenty-five private secretaries working permanently in his own household, and leaving considerable freedom to his subordinates.

With each of the other three ministers specializing (though not quite on the scale of the arch-pluralist Schulenburg), the General Directory, from the 1770s onwards, abandoned its role as the central co-ordinating committee for all-Prussian affairs. A great deal of business never came up before it at all, as Frederick channelled work elsewhere in an attempt to compensate for its clumsiness. He himself often dealt direct with the presidents of the seventeen provincial War and Domains Chambers, where collegial methods still operated, and where Prussian home government was essentially carried on. Similarly, he by-passed the General Directory by creating new departments at the centre. Newly acquired Silesia was given a separate minister, resident in Breslau (1742). In 1768 the Ministry of Mines was created; in 1770 the Ministry of Forests – each with no more than a nominal connection with the General Directory. The *Régie* was created in 1766 in the teeth of their opposition. By it, Frederick handed over the collection of the Customs and Excise to a French tax-farmer, de Launay, assisted by about 200 Frenchmen. They received extremely high salaries, as well as five per cent of any revenue they collected above a certain minimum. The regular Prussian bureaucrats angrily counterattacked this foreign body in their midst, but it took them twenty years before they succeeded in getting it abolished (1786).

Resurgence of the Nobility

This divide-and-rule technique which Frederick used to ginger up his central administration was supplemented in the provinces by a different approach. Here, like the emperors of Russia, he encouraged the revival of the local power of the Junkers, as a counterweight to his own bureaucrats. In the first place, the nobility in their county assemblies were encouraged to discuss their problems, and their suggestions were fed through to Berlin by the *Landräte*. Secondly, the *Landschaften* (or rural credit associations) increased noble involvement in politics in a similar way. Beginning in Silesia in 1770, these were associations of landowners for providing mortgages on easy terms for nobles whose fortunes had been damaged in the Seven Years' War and the economic crisis which followed. These loans were backed by the joint liability of the province, and subsidized out of the royal treasure. The noble deputies who were elected by the county assemblies to manage these *Landschaften* were not content only to discuss rates of interest when they met, or even crop-rotation and stock-breeding. They became the means by which the squires could make Berlin aware of their political demands. It was as if the old Estates had come to life again.

The third example of the revival of noble power in the localities is provided by the legal reforms of Samuel Cocceji, who began his task under Frederick William I (see p. 349), but who had to postpone really effective action till 1746 onwards. His reform of the procedure and personnel in the local courts (up to the *Regierung* in each province) and his incorporation of these into an all-Prussian judicial system (with a final court of appeal at Berlin) extinguished the independence of the last remaining body of officials of pre-absolutist Prussia. From now on, judges ceased to be an almost independent corporation of self-appointed *officiers*, living on fees and perquisites, and took their place as properly trained, appointed, and salaried members of the bureaucracy. But if Cocceji's reforms obliterated the last traces of the traditional Prussian *Ständestaat* (and introduced a much fairer system of justice), they also entrenched the nobility more securely in the new absolutism. An end was called to the process (begun under Frederick William I) whereby the War and Domains Chambers, as instruments of centralization, had taken the *Regierungen*'s judicial business. Cocceji's reshaped *Regierungen* could now, as part of the royal service, be given more work. They were allowed to handle all cases in which noblemen were involved, for example, without interference from the bureaucrats, even if the crown were a party. Moreover, the nobles secured the higher positions in the judicial hierarchy; and at the bottom, of course, there was no interference by the State with the rights of Junkers to run their manor courts as of old.

The revival of noble power in the localities, and the fragmentation of government business at Berlin, were only two of the methods which Frederick employed to counter the obstructionism, deliberate or otherwise, of the sprawling bureaucracy. In addition, like his father, he went on regular tours of inspection, during which even senior administrators were capable of getting a black eye, and army officers guilty of negligence sometimes preferred suicide to facing the king's anger. But Frederick could not see everything for himself, and he had to rely on information supplied to him by the Fiscals – sometimes, even, by petty local informers, or by juniors spying on their seniors. In 1755, for example, he wanted to know how diligently Massow, the Minister for Silesia, was carrying out his orders. He accordingly arranged to send a copy of them to the President of the Breslau Chamber, Massow's subordinate, who was to report back in secret to the king.

None of these devices, however, could halt or disguise the trend of events – the inexorable resurgence of the Junkers. This development was different from the noble revival in England, where the nobility and gentry first reduced the power of the State over society before taking over the running of it themselves; and from the French situation, where the *noblesse* in the Parlements, the provincial estates, the Church, and other traditional institutions, succeeded in blocking the extension of a reforming State-machine. In Prussia, the Hohenzollerns had succeeded in replacing the *Ständestaat* with royal absolutism, and had managed to eliminate the power of the Estates, the *Regierungen* and other local institutions through which the Junkers had carried on their old resistance to a centralizing monarch. But by the end of Frederick's reign, the Junkers were again in a position to resist the Crown, not by opposing the machinery of the State (as in France and Britain), but by challenging the power of the King to operate it. With the nobility in control of the leading posts in the army, the administration, and the judiciary, Prussia was ripe for conversion into a limited monarchy – limited, not by traditional representative institutions, but by the State machine which the Monarchy itself had assembled.

Decline of the Prussian Army

With their control of public affairs, the Junkers could effectively block any serious moves in the direction of Enlightenment; and, hampered by this strait-jacket of conservatism, Prussian life languished. The reforms which might have prevented the ignominious collapse before Napoleon could not be made. In the first place, the army retained its position as the top priority of the nation's endeavours. Frederick protected its pre-eminence in the State as carefully as his father had, and frequently reminded civil servants of their inferior status. In 1774, for example, when the West Prussian Chamber suggested moving the garrison from Marienwerder elsewhere because of the housing shortage, Frederick wrote: 'You are all fools. If you think that, in the interests of a councillor who is actually a thief and an accomplice of cheats, that for such a fellow I shall move a single dragoon, you are quite mistaken.'[39] Unfortunately, the army became too puffed up by this kind of adulation and too intoxicated by memories of its own past brilliance to make the effort to keep up with the times. During the last decades of the Ancien Régime, the army of Frederick the Great fell behind that of Louis XVI in equipment and training. Moreover, its morale sank as the proportion of foreigners was stepped up to a half – an increase which brought in its train more brutal discipline in order to keep down desertions. And when the test came, after the French Revolution, the Prussian serf-soldier was no match for the emancipated French patriot. His pay had not changed since 1713; neither had his obligation to the horrors of life-long service. 'How was affection for the profession of soldier to be expected,' wrote the more humane King Frederick William III in 1797, '[when his situation was] so pitiful and wretched?'[40] Nor was morale high in the ranks of the officers, which, owing to the prejudice against native burghers, were filled with noble foreigners.

Rigid Social Structure

In the second place (and because of the army), no change could be permitted in the social structure, frozen almost into immobility by the rigidly maintained apartheid between nobles, burghers, and peasants. It was impossible to change the noble-serf relationship without finding some way of recruiting soldiers other than the canton system, in which noble-officers commanded serf-privates for two months of the year, and worked on the land growing food for the rest. The position of the serfs deteriorated, in fact, during the second half of the century, with the wider spread of commercialized farming (*Gutsherrschaft*) and with the increased buying and selling of estates. As cogs in a now capitalist machine, they lost what little human dignity they had possessed in the more traditional days, when serfs belonged to the same noble family for generations at a time. 'Since the noble has for the most part given up his ancestors' venerable principle of being a father to his serfs and exchanged it for the role of a usurer and estate-broker,' reported a *Landrat* in 1799, 'so the position of the peasantry has worsened from year to year.'[41] Moreover, it was impossible to end the social isolation of the middle classes without finding a method of collecting revenue (for the army) other than the Excise, which separated town and country with town-walls and passport-controls; and without changing a promotion system in all the public services except the churches, which reserved all the higher posts for the nobility.

The Economy

In the third place, the requirements of the army (with their attendant fiscal and social consequences) held back economic growth. Undoubtedly, the Hohenzollern mercantilist measures sparked off Prussian industrialization earlier than would have been the case had it been left to private enterprise. But, as the Ancien Régime came to an end, the network of controls became a hindrance to progress, for Frederick had his eye on revenue and power politics rather than on economic growth as such. The Excise, besides being a dead weight on enterprise, kept industry and commerce walled up in towns where they were hamstrung by gild regulations enforced by civil servants. Moreover, the sharp separation of town and country frustrated just that kind of industrial growth which was most flourishing in Britain and France, and which may have been an essential precondition for the Industrial Revolution. This was the putting-out system for the mass production of every-day goods by cheap rural labour, beyond the control of the gilds. And another essential condition for industrial progress was also lacking: a buoyant home market. The State collected such a large slice of business profits that the mass of the people were too abject to create the rising demand which a thriving economy requires. Certainly, they could not buy the products of the porcelain, silk, and other luxury trades, which the State had artificially inseminated with royal capital in order to prevent the export of bullion, or to ruin the hated Saxons. As Sir James Harris, the British ambassador, wrote in 1776 (the year of the publication of *The Wealth of Nations*):

The King of Prussia never can be taught to believe that a large treasure laying dormant in his coffers impoverishes his kingdom; that riches increase by circulation; that trade cannot subsist without reciprocal profit; that monopolies and exclusive grants put a stop to emulation and, of course, to industry; and, in short, that the real wealth of a sovereign consists in the ease and affluence of his subjects.[42]

People Untrained in Politics

In the fourth place, Frederick's system stultified the political education of the Prussian people. Political wisdom cannot be expected to grow in a community where the method of government requires unthinking obedience to orders from above rather than the free collaboration of the people. 'The Prussian Monarchy', wrote another British ambassador, Hugh Elliot, towards the end of the reign, 'reminds me of a vast prison in the centre of which appears the great keeper, occupied in the care of his captives.'[43] 'From time immemorial', wrote Count von Gneisenau after the débâcle before Napoleon, 'every effort has been made to make men useful to the State machine ... but far less has been done to make them free and noble and independent so that they believe that they are a part of the whole and that they possess a value in themselves.'[44] The most ominous gap in Prussian society was the lack of a strong, confident, and ambitious bourgeoisie. Taking the political sting out of the middle classes was perhaps the most ingenious ruse of the whole Hohenzollern system. So benumbed were they by the problem of creeping rank by rank up the civil service, so denatured by the necessity of getting good reports in their *Konduiten-Listen*, and so mesmerized by their philosopher-king's incredible success abroad, that they never criticized the system. They were frustrated and angry, of course, especially the clever graduates with only humble, low-paid jobs to look forward to, but they attacked the nobility not the State. And their hostility found expression, not in political activity, but in the emotional outpourings of the *Sturm und Drang*. And when the French Revolution came, Prussian intellectuals congratulated the French on now being able to establish a form of government as Enlightened as the one they possessed in Prussia, where there was no need for revolution because there was no tyranny.

Lack of political training was not confined to the bourgeoisie, however. Even at the top, Frederick expected subservience not initiative; and when he died he left behind yes-men not statesmen. Moreover, his policy of snubbing the General Directory and distributing central authority among a variety of institutions entailed great risks. Only the king and the secretaries of the *Kabinett* could ensure co-ordination, for only they saw the whole picture. But, as has been shown, even the super-efficient Frederick was incapable of managing the vast complex that Prussia had now become. And a state which depended so much on the tireless industry of a genius was destined for trouble under a monarch who was a normal human being. As Mirabeau wrote at the time, 'if ever a foolish prince ascends this throne, we shall see the formidable giant suddenly collapse and Prussia will fall like Sweden'.[45] Whether or not Frederick's successors, Frederick William II (1786–97) and Frederick William III (1797–1804), were foolish princes is a question beyond the scope of this book. Suffice it to say that their modest talents were insufficient to stem the tide of noble resurgence. The taking of major political decisions slipped from their hands, into those of the ministers or the *Kabinett* secretaries. Moreover, in the Prussian General Code of 1791 (revised in 1794), which was the final outcome of the work of Cocceji in unifying and codifying the law, the privileges of the nobility as 'the first estate in the State' were spelled out in all their detail. Under the Section entitled *Privileges of the Nobility*, for example, Article 35 said: 'The nobleman has an especial right to places of honour in the state for which he has made himself fit.'[46] And the same Code also guaranteed rights to the bureaucracy which made it a new estate of the realm. For example, it gave them the 'qualified legal right', to quote Professor Rosenberg, 'to permanent tenure and the unqualified right to due process of law in case of questionable conduct'.[47] And since, during the last years of Frederick the Great, the chiefs of the bureaucracy through the examination system had captured control of recruitment to the civil service and promotion within it, the noble bureaucrats were, in effect, after Frederick's death, in control of the absolute powers of the State: accountable to none, neither the king nor the people. In other words, as Professor Kraus of Königsberg University wrote in 1799, Prussia was a 'thinly veiled aristocracy' not an 'unlimited monarchy'. And 'this aristocracy', he added, 'rules the country in undisguised form as a bureaucracy'.[48]

Thus the end of the Ancien Régime saw Prussia in decline, locked in a social and political system which rendered her incapable of repairing her crumbling foundations. For twenty years after Frederick's death her faults accumulated till she bit the dust before the French at Jena (1806). It took a crisis of this magnitude to make Prussia accept the reforms of Stein and Hardenberg. They were able in the years after Jena to uproot only some of the vices which had sprouted under the Ancien Régime and which had jeopardized Prussian power. The remainder were left to grow, for they were regarded as virtues.

Austria: The Rise of the Austrian Monarchy, 1620-1740

The End of the Holy Roman Empire

'When the Empire began to sink', said Leibniz, 'God awakened a new power in Austria.'[1] This will be the main theme of this chapter, except for the aspect of divine intervention, which does not come within the historian's competence, although it was a living reality in the minds of the pious Habsburgs with whom we are concerned. The year 1648 marks the failure of the last of a long series of attempts by the Habsburgs to achieve great-power status as rulers of the Holy Roman Empire of the German Nation. By 1789 they had achieved their ambition at last, but in a totally different guise: as rulers of the Austrian Monarchy. And this metamorphosis received official recognition during the humiliating wars against Napoleon. In 1804 the Habsburg Monarch took the title of 'Emperor of Austria'. In 1806 the Holy Roman Empire was scrapped. And these two events symbolise the course which Austrian history took during the Ancien Régime.

The Treaties of Westphalia which ended the Thirty Years' War (1618-48) enshrined the double aspect of the Habsburgs' failure as Holy Roman Emperors. In the political field, the Emperor had failed to subdue the princes and other Estates of Germany; in the religious sphere, the Emperor as leader of the Counter-Reformation had failed to vanquish the German Protestants. Henceforth, the Habsburgs continued to pursue the same two ends – absolutism in government and regimentation in religion – but in a more restricted sphere. Instead of squandering their strength in the hopelessly large all-German field of action, they concentrated on their more manageable hereditary territories. In Germany the imperial institutions staggered on like figures in a dream. The princes still met to elect their

Emperor. The Diet still assembled in the Rathaus at Regensburg to settle all-German problems. In fact, it sat permanently from 1663 onwards, a congress of diplomats endlessly discussing, and rarely settling, a long agenda of trivial disputes. But such imperial ghosts no longer embodied the living German reality. As Johan de Witt, the chief minister of Holland, expressed it in 1664, 'the German Empire was not a live body, but a puppet whose limbs were worked by brass wires'.[2] The flesh and blood Germany was to be found either in the powerful principalities such as Saxony, Bavaria, or Brandenburg – the socalled 'armed estates' with their own military forces; or in the various Circles into which the smaller communities grouped themselves to defend Germany from Turkey in the east and France in the west. And with these living entities the Emperor had relations which were much more like foreign diplomacy than internal government. As rulers, they henceforth had their being only in what for the sake of convenience is called 'Austria': and it is as such that they will be treated in this chapter. Before Westphalia, they had used their Austrian resources to back imperial dreams; after it, they channelled imperial prestige (such as it was) into Austrian purposes.

The Austrian Monarchy

Not that the Austrian Monarchy was any more united in 1648 than the German Empire itself. It consisted of three main parts: first, the Habsburg hereditary lands; second, the lands of the Bohemian Crown; and, third, the lands of the Hungarian Crown. Moreover, each of these three parts was a loose collection of smaller units. The hereditary territories included Austria-above-the-Enns based on Linz, Austria-below-the-Enns with its capital at Vienna, as well as the various *Länder* of socalled Inner Austria: Styria based on Graz, Carinthia on Klagenfurt, and Carniola on Laibach (Ljubljana) – among others. In addition the Habsburgs owned Tyrol and Vorarlberg, along with territories in south-west Germany such as Freiburg-im-Breisgau – all of which had their headquarters at Innsbruck. During the previous century these territories had all been split up among different branches of the Habsburg family, and it was not till 1665 (when Tyrol joined the main body) that they all had the same man – Leopold I – as ruler. Even so, Leopold still had multiple manifestations: he was a duke in Austria, a count in Tyrol, a lord in Freiburg, and so on.

He was also a man of many parts when he was wearing his Bohemian Crown. He was King of Bohemia with his capital at Prague; and Margrave of Moravia with his capital at Olmütz (Olomouc). A third possession of the Bohemian Crown was Silesia, with its capital at Breslau. And the situation was similar in Hungary where the Magyar nobles (like the Bohemian) had elected Habsburgs as their kings since 1526. The wearers of the Crown of St Stephen ruled Hungary, Transylvania, Croatia, Slavonia, and Dalmatia; but in 1648 a third of this area had been occupied by the Turks for over a century, while Transylvania had managed to make itself into a principality independent of the Habsburgs – even signing the Treaties of Westphalia as a sovereign state. Thus only about a quarter of Hungary was effectively ruled by the Habsburgs: though it was to be through the reconquest of this Danubian area that Austria first raised herself to the status of a great power.

Along with their rows of titles (which would take too many pages of this book simply to list) the Habsburgs ruled many different races: Germans, Czechs, Slovaks, Magyars, Croats, Serbs, and so on. Nor is this the whole story, for in the eighteenth century they acquired the southern Netherlands, and Lombardy and other Italian provinces – thus adding Belgians and Italians to their responsibilities. It is not surprising that European diplomats were under some difficulty in finding a suitable way to refer to the ruler of this constitutional and racial hotch-potch. To call him the 'Emperor' was strictly correct, but even that title referred to only one of his German roles. In any case, between 1740 and 1745, a Habsburg was not chosen to wear the imperial crown, and Maria Theresa had to refer to herself as 'Queen of Hungary'. The titles which diplomats commonly used from about 1700 onward were the 'Austrian Monarchy' and the 'House of Austria' – names which fittingly suggest how little in common these lands and peoples possessed apart from their ruler.

It was not until the middle of the seventeenth century that the House of Austria seriously began the attempt to form a unified state out of their many provinces. On his death in 1564, for example, the Emperor Ferdinand I had shared them all out like private property among his three sons. The Europe of the Ancien Régime, however, was too dangerous a place for this archaic attitude to survive, and the Habsburgs were forced into a policy of centralized absolutism, following in the wake of their chief European rivals, France and Prussia. It was a late start: too late, in fact. The British diplomat and poet, Matthew Prior, noticed this Austrian habit of being behind the times when he attended the peace conference at Rijswijk (1697). He wrote that 'the *augustissima casa* never yet had done something at the time when it should have been done'.[3] And for all their efforts in the eighteenth and nineteenth centuries, the most august House never did succeed in making up for lost time.

Central Government

The chief central institutions at work in Vienna when this period opened resembled household offices rather than government departments, and were moreover not entirely disentangled from the other institutions which served the Habsburg Monarch in his other guise as Holy Roman Emperor. There was, firstly, the Treasury (*Hofkammer*), which fixed the budget, apportioned the taxation requirements among the monarchies and duchies, collected the revenue accruing from the royal domain and from regalian rights over gold and silver mines, mints, trading monopolies, taxes on Jews, indirect taxes, and so on. Secondly, the Supreme War Council (*Hofkriegsrat*) formed the high command, planning the defence against the Turks, and provisioning the armed forces, as well as conducting diplomacy with the powers of eastern Europe. Thirdly, there was the Privy Council (*Geheime Rat*), which advised on high policy. By our period, it was about sixty strong and mainly decorative; and Leopold I replaced it with the Privy Conference (*Geheime*

Konferenz) in 1669, a more manageable body of four or five.
Even so, it did not form the embryo of later all-Austrian administration as the Privy Council did in Prussia. This role was
played by the fourth department, the Court Chancellery (*Hof-
kanzlei*). This had begun as a humble office for drafting documents and recording minutes, but in the seventeenth century
it grew into the chief agent of centralization in the Austrian
Monarchy. Its bourgeois members, trained in the law, developed
a detailed knowledge of the whole Habsburg dominion, and
achieved a grip on over-all administration beyond the powers
of the aristocrats in the other offices: even if this did not amount
to much, in comparison with developments in France and
Prussia. The Austrian Chancellery grew in importance especially after its separation from the Imperial Chancellery in 1620;
and the decline of the latter and the rise of the former are the
constitutional tokens of the fact that the Habsburgs had shifted
their weight from their imperial to their Austrian foot. Under
the Ancien Régime, the Chancellery swallowed practically all
aspects of central government except finance and war.

These central institutions were characteristically slow, lumbering, and ineffective. Right through the Ancien Régime, their
efforts seemed fated to be too little and too late. Whether waging
war, collecting taxes, or stimulating business enterprise, Vienna
was rarely on top of the job, and the situation these institutions
were purporting to control seemed always one jump ahead.
Armies in the field won astonishing victories in spite of Viennese
planning. Revenues trickled in, small in size and usually in
arrears, in defiance of central budgeting. Indeed, Habsburg in-
solvency was chronic. Leopold I's election as Emperor in 1658
had to be financed with Spanish money. During the siege of
Vienna in 1683 the Saxon army was allowed daily rations for
24,000 men, though its total strength was only 9,000. Saxon
private soldiers thus had plenty of beer and meat for sale. Habsburg warfare was always heavily dependent upon foreign subsidies, whether from the Pope, the Dutch, or the British. In 1704
the Duke of Marlborough had to engage his private fortune with
the Viennese bankers before they would lend the Monarchy
enough money to pay arrears in wages. His fellow commander,

Prince Eugen, was constantly hamstrung in the field because of dilatory staff work back in Vienna. 'If the people who run this country are not traitors,' he wrote in 1703, 'then assuredly they are the biggest asses I have ever seen in my life. Addressing them is like speaking to a brick wall.'[4]

Corporative State

One reason why the central administrators seemed like asses was the tenuousness of their grip on internal affairs. The Monarchy was not simply a loose confederation of separate lands which happened to owe allegiance to the same man. This allegiance itself was weakened by the circumstance that every one of these lands was a *Ständestaat*, a state in which the ruler had to share power with the Estates. Wherever he turned, the Habsburg Monarch was cut off from direct contact with the mass of his subjects by institutions manned by the nobility; while, at the same time, his bureaucrats and soldiers had to work and fight alongside their bureaucrats and soldiers in a dual system of government. The Crown and the Estates struggled against one another throughout this period. During the early seventeenth century religion had been the bone of contention, and in nearly all the Diets and town councils of the Monarchy the Protestant nobility and middle class had defended their traditional privileges and ultra-modern churches against a Crown inspired by the Counter-Reformation to adopt the latest statecraft in order to defend the old religion. After the Treaties of Westphalia (1648) had assured religious victory for the Habsburgs in Austria (if not in the Empire), the struggle took on a different form, as the Monarchy tried to increase its hold on the provinces, with a view to rolling back the Turks, the French, and later the Prussians. In this conflict, which continued beyond the end of the Ancien Régime, the Monarchy's half of the administration tended to be the progressive force. The half belonging to the Estates stood guard over tradition, defending the existing social structure and economic system, blocking the attempts of the Monarchy to innovate. And though the Monarchy, crippled as it was by archaism, might be able to defeat the even more traditional Turks, it could not hope to compete seriously with such modernizing states as Russia, France, and Prussia, where the rulers were bringing about internal cohesion through dynamic central institutions. One observer from the France of Louis XIV expressed his horror in 1667, when Leopold I was about to call a meeting of the Hungarian Diet. 'There is no prudence at all in committing the person of the Emperor to the discretion of an insolent populace and to the power of an assembled Diet which regards itself as equal, if not superior, to the master.'[5]

Of course, he was referring to the toughest institution the Habsburgs ever tried to break, but the Estates in all the *Länder* were powerful adversaries as well. Their composition varied. In Lower Austria, for instance, the Diet consisted of fifteen prelates, the Rector of the University of Vienna, 225 princes, counts, and viscounts, 115 knights, with one bourgeois vote to represent the city of Vienna and eighteen towns and markets. In Styria, sixteen towns and twenty market-places had to share one voice in the Diet. The only town represented on the Bohemian Diet was Prague. In Hungary, the Diet had two Houses, the Upper for the magnates, the Lower for the nobles. Elsewhere there were usually three chambers: for the clergy, the nobles, and the knights. Thus the third Estate was usually known in Austria as the 'Fourth Estate'.

The half century before the Treaties of Westphalia had seen a fierce struggle between the Habsburgs and their Diets; for the Monarchy led the crusade for the Counter-Reformation, while the nobility and bourgeoisie became riddled with Protestantism. At every opportunity, the nobility exploited the military and financial weakness of the Emperor, as well as the rivalries between different branches of the Habsburg family, to secure self-government and freedom of worship, and to spread the contract theories of government which Protestants were working out in France, the Netherlands, and Great Britain. On occasion (for example, in 1608), the Estates of the separate provinces even met together to form an ephemeral Estates-General. Armed resistance to the Crown was not uncommon, not only in Transylvania, Hungary, and Bohemia, but in Austria proper. In

Bohemia, where the stern Protestantism of the nobility and bourgeoisie was reinforced by nationalistic resistance to Viennese rule, the revolt of the Estates led to the Thirty Years' War.

Bohemia

It also led to the turn of the tide, and gave the Monarchy its first victories in this long struggle with the Estates. The Czech nobility were defeated at the battle of the White Mountain (1620), and the military superiority of the Emperor Ferdinand II (1619–37) enabled him to make sweeping social, religious, and political changes. He worked on the assumption that, by revolting, the Bohemians and Moravians had forfeited their rights, and that he was free to work out a new constitution for them from scratch. Twenty-seven of the rebel leaders were executed, and many more nobles and townsmen lost their property. About half the total number of landed estates changed hands, and possibly 150,000 Czechs went into exile. Certainly, the names are known of 322 nobles, 1,780 intellectuals, clerics, and artists, 8,486 peasants and craftsmen who moved into Saxony. Of the old aristocracy, only eight families remained (such as the Kinskys, the Waldsteins, and the Kaunitzes). The forfeited land was sold at knock-down prices to Austrians and Czechs who had backed the Emperor, as well as to many foreign officers fighting in the Emperor's armies: Germans, Italians, Spaniards, French, English, Scottish, and Irish.

This clean sweep of the upper class was accompanied in Bohemia by the changes in government propounded in the Renewed Constitution of 1627 (with a similar arrangement for Moravia in 1628). The Crown ceased to be elective and became hereditary in the House of Habsburg. The Diet was reconstituted, and its powers much reduced. Though it could still debate the budget proposals sent down from the Treasury in Vienna, it no longer administered the country through its permanent committees alone, but had to accept supervision from royal bureaucrats. Moreover, the central government of Bohemia was transferred to Vienna in the Bohemian Chancellery there.

Similarly, urban self-government ceased as the town councils lost their property and had to submit to the control of nobles or civil servants.

Counter-Reformation

At the same time, the powerful apparatus of the Counter-Reformation was introduced, led by the Jesuits and other militant orders. They took over the parishes, the schools, the universities, and the press, and conducted a vigorous campaign of reconversion to the Catholic and Habsburg outlook on life. From 1651 Reformation Commissions were set up, which made lists of non-Catholics, gave them six weeks' instruction, and then offered them the choice between conversion and exile. By these means, and others, Protestantism was harried to the level of an underground movement.

Similar steps were taken, or had already been taken in the hereditary lands. In Upper, Lower, and Inner Austria, Protestants were offered the choice between conversion and exile, and out of the area covered by the present boundaries of Austria probably 100,000 Protestants took the latter course. Austrian loss of talented manpower was the gain of such cities as Regensburg. Nuremberg, Augsburg, Ulm, and other more distant parts. While some Austrian villages were completely depopulated, the records show that in some south German villages in the late seventeenth century half of those baptized were of Austrian origin. One brilliant exile was Georg von Derfflinger, who emigrated from a village near Linz to become the field-marshal who reorganized the Brandenburg army for the Great Elector. In Austria, much land changed hands under the crusading Emperors Ferdinand II (1619–37) and Ferdinand III (1637–57); and the back of the Protestant resistance was broken not only in the Estates, but also in the city councils. Vienna was transformed as a result. Forfeited town houses and vineyards belonging to Protestant merchants were acquired by Catholic nobles and religious houses; and on this land the medieval buildings were demolished and a new Vienna began to arise: aristocratic, baroque, and Roman Catholic.

Thus in the early years of the Ancien Régime the Monarchy had made significant gains in Austria and Bohemia. First, the power of Protestantism was broken, and generations of Austrians could now be indoctrinated with the values of the Counter-Reformation by an enthusiastic Church backed by a generous State. An incense curtain dropped round the country, insulating the educated classes from the new scientific and political ideas which were disturbing western Europe in the last years of the seventeenth century and the whole of the eighteenth. Secondly, the resistance of the Estates had been crippled, and the Diets and town councils, churches and universities had been repeopled with men who were not inclined to threaten the religious and political unity of the new monarchy that the Habsburgs were trying to create. Moreover, they all had to work alongside the officials of the new bureaucratic framework that was steadily being assembled. And, in addition, the Monarchy had emerged from the Thirty Years' War with the valuable asset of a standing army: nine regiments of foot, and ten of horse.

The overall result was that the nobility in any of the provinces were unlikely to carry their opposition to Vienna to the lengths of trying to take their province out of the Monarchy altogether – though this was not impossible, as will be seen. In Bohemia, however much the new, Germanized landowners might object to the creeping encroachments of the State, they were in no position to make common cause with the mass of Czech peasants and craftsmen. On the other hand, the provinces had not been as fully integrated as they had been in France, and were about to be in Prussia. The crucial battle over taxation had yet to be fought and won. The Diets still possessed the power of the purse; and to a great extent it was their provincial administrative machinery which still collected the direct taxes, spent much of them, ran the law courts, controlled the police, hired, trained, and provisioned the armed forces. To be sure, they were supervised in this work by civil servants appointed by the Crown, but even these were often provincial men with provincial loyalties. And at the local level, in the districts, life went on practically without benefit of civil servants. Trained bureaucratic talent was too thin on the ground for the Monarchy to be able to supersede the traditional officeholders completely. The chief representatives of the Crown in each province, for example, the *Landmarschall* in Lower Austria, the *Landesoffizier* in Bohemia, or the *Oberhauptman* in Silesia, tended to be local magnates. Moreover, when the monarch's chief man in the province was also president of the local Diet, absolute monarchy had still some way to go. As the French traveller Casimir Freschot observed on passing through Bohemia in the early eighteenth century: 'Might one not say that the aristocracy hinders as much as it can the service of His Majesty, which certainly does not appear to be any too firm.'[6] And if Habsburg rule was none too firm in Bohemia, how much more tottery was it in the third section of the Monarchy, Hungary, where few of the steps towards absolutism so far mentioned had yet been taken.

Foreign Affairs

The reduction of the territories of the Hungarian Crown to obedience to Vienna could not begin while Turkey occupied about a third of the area, and Louis XIV financed rebellions in the rest. In other words, Hungary was an aspect of foreign affairs, and an account of her internal development will not be intelligible till a word has been said about Austria's international situation.

During the period covered by this book, Austria's powers were almost as fully stretched by vast responsibilities and ambitions as they had been in the days of the Emperor Charles V. In his dual capacity as Holy Roman Emperor and Austrian Monarch, Leopold I (1658–1711) had interests running over the length and breadth of Europe, and he seldom had the luxury of fighting on one front at a time. His principal opponents were Louis XIV in the west, against whom he defended the Rhine; and Turkey in the east, who threatened to advance yet further up the Danube. In addition, he hoped to inherit the Spanish empire after the death of Charles II, and thus unite once more the Habsburg family possessions. This archaic daydream caused him to hanker after the Spanish Netherlands (Belgium) and large tracts of Italy, as well as the Spanish peninsula itself. Unfortunately, Louis XIV was even more deeply involved in Spanish ambitions than Leopold. Their mothers were sisters, daughters of Philip III, their wives were half-sisters, daughters of Philip IV; but in each case the French king was connected to the elder princess.

Leopold was actually in Spain pursuing his theological studies when he became heir to the Austrian Monarchy. As a younger son of Ferdinand III, he was intended for the Church, but had to abandon what would probably have been a more congenial career when his elder brother died. With an Austrian Habsburg father and a Spanish Habsburg mother, he had all the family physiognomy in exaggerated form: 'the long narrow face', to quote a recent study, 'the large (and in all portraits somewhat tired-looking) eyes, the long, slightly hooked nose, and, above all the "Habsburg lip" – a protruding lower lip – and the long, jutting, pointed chin'.[7] Sensitive, withdrawn, and indecisive, he was not cut out for government, still less for war, though he did not spare himself in the cause of duty. His chief loves were books, ballets, operas, and oratorios; and besides playing the spinet he composed at least seventy-nine religious and 155 secular works. As a ruler, he followed the advice that Charles V had bequeathed to the Habsburg family: 'trust no one, listen to everyone, decide alone'; though he listened to priests more than laymen. 'One cannot overstate what power beyond the realm of conscience the fathers exercise at this court', reported the Venetian ambassador in 1678. 'It surpasses by far the influence of the ministers.'[8] But if Jesuits and Capuchins and Franciscans did preponderate among his advisers (and he sent 700 letters to the Bishop of Vienna alone between 1670 and 1685), nevertheless, no favourite ruled. He made his own decisions, even though he did take a very long time over them. And as he struggled inside his conscience to reach a belated choice between the contrary counsels proffered by the factions at Court, he was supported by a mystical belief in God's providence which gave him an inner calm often mistaken for lack of application to business. 'He promises everything, issues peremptory orders', wrote Prince Eugen in anger on one occasion, '... but nothing happens.'[9]

The chief of his many problems was whether to defend Habsburg and German interests in the west, or pursue Austrian ambitions in the east: a dilemma made all the more painful by the fact that both the Turks and the French were entering on a period of vigorous aggression, and, what is more, were co-operating together. If he faced the one, he was sure of a stab in the back from the other; while he lacked the resources to tackle both at the same time. During the early part of his reign, he gave most of his attention to the Turks, and was forced to accept the humiliations of French gains of Habsburg and Imperial territory on the Rhine and in the Netherlands. It was only after 1697 that he was able to play a vigorous part in halting Louis XIV.

The Ottoman Empire

The Ottoman Empire had already entered upon its protracted decline. In the long run it was to be no match for the growing states of the West, with their scientific outlook, capitalist economy, bureaucratic administration, modern technology, and advanced methods of raising revenues and recruiting, equipping, and drilling armies. On the other hand, Turkey was capable from time to time of staging alarming revivals. The reign of Leopold I was such a time. Mehmed IV, who became Sultan in 1648, left politics in the hands of his mother, along with the Chief Black Eunuch and the other wire-pullers of the Serail, while he concentrated on his toys and games, as a boy, and on his horses and hounds, as a man. From 1656 onwards, the real rulers of Turkey were a dynasty of Grand Viziers of the Köprülü family. Presiding over the Divan (the central council), they staged a ruthless clean-up of the administration at home, and embarked on a series of aggressions abroad. Western diplomats recognized the new power situation by adopting the habit of referring to Turkey as the 'Sublime Porte': for this was the name of the Grand Vizier's palace near the Serail at Constantinople. From it the swarming armies and navies of

Turkey received orders to advance against Russia, Poland, Venice, and Hungary.

Reconquest of Hungary

In Hungary, the untamed Magyar baronage was ready to use any means available to rid their country of Turks and Austrians. Haughty and headstrong, they were ungovernable at the best of times: the most intractable subjects, perhaps, confronting any European monarchy. But in the conditions of the mid seventeenth century, chaos reigned. In the first place, it was impossible for the Habsburgs to set up stable conditions of government while Transylvania was striking out as an independent state, Austrian-occupied Hungary was longing to throw off the Germans, and the rest of the country was lying under the ruinous occupation of the Turks. In the second place, the identification of the Monarchy with the Counter-Reformation added to its difficulties, for many of the nobility (especially the lesser ones) were Calvinists whose consciences were nonconformist to a high degree; while the German colonists in the mining towns were Lutherans. As late as 1681, the Lower House of the Diet contained seventeen Calvinists and forty-five Lutherans out of a total of 144 deputies. While the third stimulant to anarchy was French diplomacy and hard cash, ever present to keep Habsburg troops away from the West.

The chief sufferers were the brutally exploited Hungarian people, their country reduced to the status of a no-man's land. The Turks raided the countryside for slaves – though sometimes they were prepared to return them for a ransom. In September 1652, for example, the Turkish garrison at Eger ravaged as far as Tokay, picking up more than 100 Hungarians, who fetched 200,000 golden florins in ransom, as well as five nobles whose price was 40,000 thaler a head. On the other hand, the atrocities of the German armies sent to liberate the Magyars were just as hideous. A protest of 1662 accused them of cutting children in pieces, and of throwing them in the fire. Here perhaps was the main origin of that implacability which turned Hungary into the Ireland or the Catalonia of the Habsburg

Monarchy. 'The Hungarians nurse such a hatred against the Germans', reported General Montecuccoli, their would-be liberator from the Turks, 'that they even hate any Hungarian who appears to be well disposed to them.'[10]

The story of the reconquest of the lower Danube begins with György II Rákóczi, the Prince of Transylvania (1648–60), who attempted to transform his principality into a powerful state by turning the Rumanian dependencies of Turkey, Moldavia and Wallachia, into his vassals; and by joining in the War of the North (1655–60) in the hopes of winning the throne of Poland. Determined to suppress this over-ambitious subordinate, the Grand Vizier Mehmed Köprülü (1656–61) invaded Transylvania and replaced Rákóczi with a more pliant tool, Prince Mihály Apafi, an ardent Calvinist who ruled from 1661–90. When the Austrians tried to oppose this move, the next Grand Vizier, the young and accomplished Ahmed Köprülü (1661–76), launched two campaigns against Vienna, the second of which was brilliantly defeated by Montecuccoli at St Gotthard (1664). Much to the irritation of the Hungarian magnates, Leopold failed to use this opportunity to roll back the Turks towards Constantinople. In order to free himself for action in the west, he signed the truce of Vasvár with Turkey (1664) not only recognizing Apafy in Transylvania, but also handing back border-fortresses captured from the Turks in 1663.

Siege of Vienna

For the next twenty years, with Turkey fighting elsewhere, Leopold attempted to do in Hungary what his predecessors had done in Bohemia: to turn it into a catholic and obedient province of the Austrian Monarchy. He tried terror and persecution till 1681, and then persuasion and constitutionalism, but to no avail. He could not bring the noble families to heel. As fast as one group of ringleaders were executed, others would emerge or invade from neighbouring states, sustained by French or Turkish help. Finally, in 1683, the ambitious Grand Vizier Kara Mustafa (1676–83) decided that his reign needed the *éclat* and the booty which only the conquest of Vienna could bring. He recognized the Magyar rebel, Imre Thököly, as King of Hungary and vassal of Turkey, and commanded his vast Turkish armies to advance up the Danube valley. At the same time, he ordered his vassals in Transylvania, Moldavia, and Wallachia, and even the Tartars of the Crimean Khan, to take part in what was to be the last Moslem thrust at the Christian west.

Sultan Mehmed IV took time off from hunting to lead the main Turkish army as far as Belgrade, after which Kara Mustafa himself pushed on towards Vienna. The Austrian army, which since Montecuccoli's death was commanded by Duke Charles of Lorraine, the Emperor's brother-in-law, was only 40,000 and could not do more than delay the advance of the Turkish horde of 200,000 men. By early July, the Grand Vizier was at the gates of the capital, calling upon the defenders to surrender. 'Accept Islam, and live in peace under the Sultan', he commanded in a document handed to the Viennese. 'Or deliver up the fortress, and live in peace under the Sultan as Christians; and if any man prefer let him depart peaceably, taking his goods with him! But if you resist, then death or spoliation or slavery shall be the fate of you all!'[11] Unfortunately for the Sultan, he now made the fatal mistake of grossly over-estimating the difficulty of capturing the city. Instead of storming it at once (a tactic which might have succeeded), he deployed his men, with their 25,000 tents and 50,000 carts, in a crescent about the west of Vienna, stretching from Grinzing round to Schönbrunn, intending to starve it out. The Court had already left, and Leopold I sat out the siege of Vienna well upstream at Passau.

Meanwhile, the relieving force was being assembled on the wooded heights of the Wiener Wald to the north of Vienna. Imperial and papal diplomacy had secured valuable help, in spite of the efforts of Louis XIV's agents to prevent it. The alliance between Leopold and John III Sobieski, King of Poland, had already been signed earlier, at the time when it was not clear whether the Grand Vizier would attack Vienna or Cracow. Troops were also sent by the Swabian and Franconian Circles, as well as by the Electors of Bavaria and Saxony, who both fought in person. On September 12th, when the Viennese were practically exhausted by two months of heavy bombardment and short rations, the international army crashed down the slopes of the Kahlenberg on to the unwitting Turks and defeated them. 'We came, we saw, and God conquered', wrote Sobieski to the Pope that day, grossly understating the role of Charles of Lorraine.[12] The Turks had to beat a hurried retreat into Hungary, leaving behind vast treasures for the allies to squabble over, as well as the corpses of all the women of the Grand Vizier's harem, his Christian slaves, and the animals from his menagerie – all of which Kara Mustafa ordered to be slain. The Grand Vizier himself was later ceremonially strangled in Belgrade on the Sultan's orders: a purge organized by the Chief Black Eunuch. But Mehmed IV also was overthrown not long after (1685), in spite of selling off his horses and hounds to appease his angry subjects. The Turkish government was thus in no fit state to resist the onslaughts which the Habsburgs were now in a position to launch.

The year 1683 was the turning point in the rise of the Austrian Monarchy, which henceforth began to impinge on European affairs with a new vigour. During the next fifteen years, the armies of Leopold not only reconquered practically the whole of Hungary, but also took an active part against France in the War of the League of Augsburg (1688–97), thus fighting on two fronts for the first time. The international army which had saved Vienna immediately dispersed, for the King of Poland and the German princes were only concerned with defending Christian Europe, not with helping Leopold conquer a kingdom for himself. There was foreign help, to be sure. Venice declared war on Turkey in 1684, and Russia in 1686, but these states fought separate campaigns. Austria now fought alone in Hungary, and thus enjoyed the enormous advantage of a unified command in place of the tetchy counsels of self-important princes. Especially important was the appointment of Prince Eugen as commander-in-chief in 1697. This short and ill-shaped exile from the court of Louis XIV now entered upon his glorious career as the modernizer of the Austrian army and the hammer of the Turks and French.

By this stage the Turks had been defeated at Mohacs (1687), driven out of Belgrade (1688), and compelled to abandon Transylvania (1691), but were now making a powerful counter-attack. Prince Eugen received orders from the irresolute Supreme War Council to 'act with extreme caution and ... forgo all risks and avoid engaging the enemy unless he has overwhelming strength and is practically certain of being completely victorious'.[13] He did nothing of the sort. He boldly attacked a Turkish army far superior in numbers to his own, and in a few hours at Zenta (1697) annihilated it, winning the whole war. The Turks lost 20,000 killed and 10,000 drowned, and left behind booty which included 9,000 wagons, 60,000 camels, 1,500 cattle, and 700 horses. By the Treaty of Carlowitz (1699), Turkey ceded Transylvania and the whole of Hungary (apart from the Bánát of Temesvár) and most of Slavonia and Croatia. Leopold was now in a good position to make the Hungarians 'wear Bohemian breeches'.

Hungarian Institutions

The Hungarians were descended from the free and equal community of mounted warriors who had moved over to the middle Danube from the Pontic steppes in the tenth century. Now settled on the land and submitting to a king, they nevertheless had not forgotten their pristine privileges, such as their personal freedom, their exemption from taxation, their right to elect a dynasty to rule over them, and to be consulted in their Diet about any proposed changes. By our period the Hungarian 'nation' which possessed these rights consisted of about 30,000 noble families. The mass of the population, mostly serfs, but including poor, so-called 'sandalled' nobles, and the inhabitants, mostly German, of the Royal Free Boroughs on Crown land, were excluded from these privileges. Moreover, within the 'nation' itself two clear groups were evident: the magnates and the ordinary nobles, the former about 200–300 strong.

In the Diet the magnates sat in the Upper House along with the great officers of the Crown and the prelates. In the Lower House sat the representatives of the nobles, two from each county, along with a few urban deputies. Since the aristocracy and the nobility possessed roughly half of the noble land each, the former were immensely wealthy, possessing latifundios of 50–100 thousand acres and more. The greatest family of all, the Esterházys, at one time owned seven million Hungarian acres; and at the Diet of 1662 supplied five members of the Upper House. George Szelepcsényi, the Archbishop of Esztergom, brought to Vienna for safe-keeping during the Turkish attack of 1683 cash worth 70–80,000 florins, and plate and other treasures worth 400,000 florins, which when melted down got the impecunious high command in Vienna out of its financial straits. The Habsburgs cultivated the good will of such magnates, giving them important executive posts in Hungary, encouraging them to build palaces in Vienna, and relying on their support in the Diet, much like the Hanoverians with their Lords Spiritual and Temporal. They had even, with the help of Cardinal Pázmány (a Calvinist noble turned Jesuit) brought many of them back into the Catholic Church. The Batthyánys, the Pálffys, the Esterházys, the Rákóczis, the Károlyis, and others, along with their serfs, were all Catholics by Leopold's time. Thus the Habsburgs had the makings of a party in Hungary. But even if they had managed to gain a Walpolian control over the Diet (which was never remotely likely), or called it only rarely (as they did in the seventeenth century), or by-passed it altogether (as they were inclined to do in the eighteenth century) – Hungary would have still remained one of the most limited monarchies in Europe, because of the county Diets.

Effective internal government was operated by the counties in a system of local autonomy unique in Europe. Here the nobility elected deputies to each county Diet, which passed local legislation and elected executive officers, including the chief one, the Föispán. The 'sandalled' nobility could not sit in the county Diet, but had votes in the elections to it which they sold like any freeholder or potwalloper. If the aristocrats made the decisions in Pozsony (Pressburg), Buda, or Vienna, the nobility dominated the counties, the real centres of resistance to Habsburg absolutism. Living in their small country houses, in close touch with the common people, the ordinary nobility were the carriers of Magyar tradition, wearing Magyar dress, speaking the Magyar tongue, tenacious of their Calvinism, and implacable in the defence of their liberties.

With the help of the magnates (and especially because of rivalries between them), Leopold I managed, in the wake of the retreating Turks, to bring Hungary into a semblance of submission to Vienna, but, because of the nobles, never succeeded in integrating her into the Habsburg absolutism. The tormented history of his attempts has already been touched on. When Ahmed Köprülü launched his two thrusts up the Danube in 1663 and 1664, the Hungarians had proclaimed the Insurrection, the traditional feudal levy in which each noble paraded under arms with a tenth of his tenants. Led by Count Miklós Zrinyi (an ardent nationalist poet), they harassed the Turks, though it was Montecuccoli with his mainly German army who really stopped them at St Gotthard (1664). The Hungarian leaders regarded the lenient treaty of Vasvár as a betrayal, and broke out in a badly organized rebellion, this time under the leadership of Zrinyi's brother Péter. Leopold decided on terror, and occupied Hungary with German troops. Four leaders were beheaded (1670); hundreds of nobles were arrested and had their property confiscated; while others fled into exile to plot revenge. In the rear of the Austrian troops came the Jesuits to take over the parishes from which the Protestant clergy were removed at the point of the sword. Forty pastors were condemned to row in the galleys at Naples, till they were rescued by Admiral de Ruyter and given asylum in Holland.

The reign of terror was a failure, leading merely to more violent Magyar conspiracies, such as the rising in 1678 led by the handsome young Imre Thököly. And so, in 1681 Leopold changed course completely, and summoned the Diet to meet at Sopron Ödenburg). Here the Magyars received back their traditional rights of self-government. They chose their own head of state, the palatine; the Hungarian Treasury was made independent of Vienna; the persecution of Protestants was called off; the Diet was to meet every three years. And this *volte-face* occurred just in time to ensure that most Hungarians did not join the Turks in their attack on Vienna in 1683, although Imre Thököly, furthering his own ambitions, did.

With the Turks defeated and in retreat, however, Leopold switched courses again, and at the Diet of Pozsony (Pressburg, or Bratislava) in 1687 forced the Hungarians to declare their Crown hereditary in the male Habsburg line (and no longer elective unless the male line ran out). Moreover, they had to abandon their right of resistance (*jus resistendi*) to the king: a right granted by the King of Hungary in the Golden Bull of 1222. Leopold's generals, bishops, and administrators now embarked on a despotic campaign to eliminate the Magyar rebels, harry the Protestants, and clamp the fetters of Viennese centralism on Hungarian local institutions. But the truculent Magyars responded with perennial conspiracy and rebellion. The atrocities committed by the retreating Turks were matched by the barbarities of the liberating Austrians. It is said that peasants sold their children into slavery in order to meet the exactions of the Emperor's soldiers. Moreover, the Viennese policy of cutting up the proud and ancient Magyar kingdom drove men desperate. Leopold's aim was to plant pro-Habsburg men into all positions of wealth and power in order to make a Bohemia out of Hungary. Transylvania was governed direct from Vienna (1697). The whole length of the frontier with Turkey was militarized under the Supreme War Council and deliberately settled with non-Magyar colonists, including about 200,000 Orthodox Serbs. And the government commission appointed to re-allot the territory re-conquered from the Turks slipped vast estates to a few pro-Habsburg aristocrats, and made implacable enemies of the disappointed claimants. Finally, the outbreak of the War of the Spanish Succession (1702–14) and with it the increased supplies of French gold brought about the last gigantic uprising of the Ancien Régime (1703). This was no mere aristocratic plot, but a spontaneous protest of men of every class and creed, who roped in the young Ferencz II Rákóczi as their reluctant leader. As the French were thrusting at Austria through Bavaria, the Magyars dreamed of 'French and Hungarian soldiers meeting in the streets of Vienna.... Everything here is quite desperate,' reported the Dutch ambassador in Vienna. 'The Monarchy is on its last legs and will go down in a general military collapse unless there is some miraculous intervention of the Almighty.'[14] In the event, Austria was rescued by the defeat of the French at Blenheim (1704). Denied French backing, the Magyar rebellion subsided into guerilla warfare and terrorism which lasted till 1711 – by which time more damage had been inflicted on Hungary, probably, than during the 150 years of Turkish occupation.

By this time Leopold was dead (1705) and so was his successor, Joseph (1705–11). The new Emperor, Charles VI (1711–40), favoured reconciliation. 'The Hungarians must be relieved of the belief that they are under German domination', he said.[15] The peace of Szatmár (1711) confirmed the constitutional position of 1687, but offered an amnesty to the rebels, and promised to deal with Hungarian complaints at a Diet. The long struggle for independence was for the moment over, and for the rest of the Ancien Régime the Magyars had to abandon hopes of playing an independent role in European power politics, and reconcile themselves to a semi-colonial status within the Austrian Monarchy. But thanks to the central and local Diets Hungary remained a colony, and avoided being integrated as a province. Austria had swallowed her, but she was never able to digest her.

The Spanish Succession

Having thrown the Turks back from Vienna almost as far as Belgrade, and transformed the capital from an outpost on a dangerous frontier into the heart of a secure civilization, the Habsburgs were free to turn their attention to the west, and to contemplate the seductive possibilities that the approaching demise of Charles II of Spain was dangling before the rest of the great powers.

Charles's various wills aimed at keeping the Spanish inheritance intact. Leopold I and Louis XIV (through their Spanish mothers and wives) would each have liked the whole empire; but, as each was opposed to the other taking all, and as the rest of Europe was not prepared to stomach Spain joined whole to either France or Austria, both Leopold and Louis showed willingness from time to time to divide the Spanish empire up between them. However, Austria's inflexibility was more than anything responsible for the fact that no generally accepted scheme of partition had been agreed upon when the Spanish king died, and that war was more or less inevitable when Charles II bequeathed his entire empire to the French candidate, and Louis XIV accepted it (1700).

In the War of the Spanish Succession, Austrian troops fighting in the Grand Alliance against France enhanced the reputation of the Monarchy by victories in Bavaria (where Prince Eugen and Marlborough jointly saved Vienna at Blenheim in 1704); in Piedmont (where Eugen's defeat of the French at Turin in 1706 forced them to withdraw from north Italy); and on the Rhine and in the Netherlands. At the same time, a sizeable army was pinned down in Hungary by the Rákóczi rebellion. In view of all these responsibilities, the only armament that Leopold could afford to send to the Spanish theatre of operations was his son, the Archduke Charles, whom he reluctantly allowed to go there as King Charles III. In 1704 the British fleet shipped him, via Windsor, to Portugal, and then landed him in Catalonia (1705). Though he twice entered Madrid, he was secure only in Aragon, Catalonia, and Valencia, where the rebellious populace accepted his support for their traditional repudiation of Madrid, and where he could be supplied by British ships.

This latter support was snatched away from 1710 onwards, however, for a Tory government bent on peace was formed in London. Moreover, the war aims of the Grand Alliance were suddenly revolutionized by the death of the new Emperor, Joseph I. This vigorous and handsome young man, who got more pleasure out of life than the average Habsburg, and who served the Monarchy well by backing the reforms of Prince Eugen, was carried away unexpectedly by small-pox in 1711. The self-styled Charles III of Spain now became the Emperor Charles VI; and the allies, whose aims certainly did not include the revival of the empire of Charles V, abandoned the Catalans to their fate. In the peace settlement, which the allies signed with France at Utrecht (1713), and in which Austria and the Empire belatedly acquiesced at Rastatt and Baden (1714), Austria showed a handsome profit. She gained the Spanish Netherlands (Belgium), Milan, Naples, and Sardinia. This was not enough for Charles VI, however and it was too much for Philip V, the new, Bourbon, King of Spain. They continued to grapple in Italy and Sardinia for several years, till the other powers managed to persuade them that the partition of the Spanish Empire was there to stay. By an agreement signed in 1720, Charles VI, among other concessions, recognized Philip V as King of Spain, and Philip recognized the cession of Belgium to Austria. Moreover, Charles VI received Sicily from Savoy, giving up Sardinia in return. The War of the Spanish Succession was really over.

War Against Turkey

The gains of Utrecht brought Austria greater revenues, and enabled her to inflict further damage on the Turks in the war which now broke out (1716–18). The Ottoman Empire, making yet another fresh spurt, had driven the Venetians out of the Morea, a threat that Charles VI could not ignore in view of his new possessions in Italy. Moreover, the Austrian military machine, re-energized by the reforms which Prince Eugen had carried out since he became President of the Supreme War Council (1703), was adequate to the task. It was a drilled and disciplined professional force, with regular pay, uniform dress and equipment, adequate supplies and barracks, rational schemes of promotion – and all the other improvements necessary to bring Austria belatedly into line with the other advanced states of the Continent. It was, at last, worthy of the prince himself, now in his fifties, but still tough and wiry, his mind cool quicksilver in the heat of the battle. At Peterwardein (1716) he took five hours to scatter the main Ottoman army, killing 6,000 Turks, including the Grand Vizier, and capturing his sumptuous tent, which took 500 men to pitch. The next year he recaptured Belgrade, defeating a Turkish army five times the size of his own – the greatest victory of his career. And by

the ensuing Treaty of Passarowitz (1718), the Austrian possessions in the Balkans stretched as far as they ever would under
the Ancien Régime. The Emperor gained the Bánát of Temesvár (that is, the rest of Hungary), the north part of Serbia,
including Belgrade, and sections of Bosnia and Wallachia.

Charles VI

Eugen now became celebrated as the 'noble knight' in folk
song, and received effusive letters of thanks from the Emperor,
but he was reaching the end of his virtual premiership in the
Austrian government. Unfortunately for the Monarchy, Charles
VI now listened to rival cliques of advisers, especially the
Spanish *camerilla* he had brought back with him from Catalonia. He had abandoned his Spanish pretensions with the
utmost reluctance. After all, he had been King of Spain in his
own eyes since the age of sixteen, and he brought back much
that was Spanish from his ten-year reign there. Spanish priests
and politicians had great influence at Court, encouraging his
dreams of castles in Spain, and duplicating in Vienna the
elaborate court ritual of Madrid. Charles was in any case cold
and haughty, but the 'Spanish reverence', the deep genuflexion
with which he and his family had to be saluted, distanced him
further from his subjects. A mediocre mystic, he lacked grandeur of his own. 'He was endowed with the qualities which
make a good citizen,' wrote Frederick the Great. '. . . He had
been brought up to obey, not to command.'[16] The baroque
ceremonial at the Hofburg aimed to elevate him above his
essential ordinariness, and succeeded in keeping him out of
touch with reality. He was convinced that he had a special
relationship with the Queen of Heaven, but this did not inhibit
him from taking a mistress here on earth. He trusted in God,
but did not keep his powder dry. He was surrounded by a
Court of 2,000 persons in paid employment and 30,000 more
who were hangers-on in hope of a place. Among the extravagances which the Monarchy could ill afford was the annual
provision of two casks of Tokay for soaking the bread that fed
the imperial parrots, and fifteen hogsheads of wine in which to

bathe them. Charles adored the opera, and played the cembalo himself. He practised horsemanship in the Spanish Riding School, and followed a year-long schedule of hunting. In April it was the turn of herons at Laxenburg; during the summer and early autumn, it was stags at the Favorita Palace, followed by ten days in October in the Burgenland after hares and pheasants. Back at the Hofburg for the winter, Charles chased wild boar, or whatever else could be beaten up in the vicinity of Vienna. The hunt ceased only in Lent, which the pious Habsburg observed with full rigour, along with all the other festivals of the year. 'I have led a pious life here in Lent which has not left me free for a quarter of an hour,' wrote the French ambassador to Cardinal de Polignac in Rome. '... Only a Capuchin with the most robust health could endure this life during Lent. In order to give your Eminence some idea, I have spent altogether between Palm Sunday and Easter Wednesday, 100 hours at church with the Emperor.'[17]

Counter-Reformation

Charles VI's piety may have seemed excessive and old-fashioned to an aristocrat from the court of Louis XV, but it suited the mood of Austria during the first half of the Ancien Régime. After the devastations of the Thirty Years' War, the victory (inside Austria) of Catholicism over heresy, and the defeat of the heathen Turks, Austria experienced a renaissance – but it took the form of the Counter-Reformation artificially prolonged right into the era of the Enlightenment. Church and State and society had to be rebuilt, morally and physically; and the religious orders, the Emperor, and the aristocracy led the resurgence by building churches and monasteries, chancelleries and town-halls, palaces and country-houses, all in the baroque manner, which foreign artists and craftsmen first brought over the Alps from Italy, and which native artists in the era of Charles VI developed into a distinct style indelibly stamped on the territories of the House of Austria, whether Czech, Magyar, or German. From the time when Leopold I began the fairly modest remodelling of the still medieval Hradcany Palace in

Prague and the Hofburg in Vienna to the splendid period under Charles VI when J. B. Fischer von Erlach, Johann Lukas von Hildebrandt, and Jacob Prandtauer were constructing their sumptuous palaces and monasteries, architecture's main purpose, along with that of the attendant arts of painting, sculpture, gardening, and music, was to inspire the people with awe at the glory of God and the mightiness of the prince. Voluptuous curves and rich colours, theatrical lighting and histrionic sculpture, the crowded frescoes high in the cupola, and the stately ceremony down below, all conspired to enhance the majesty of the ruling powers of Heaven and earth, and to arouse admiration and submission in the subjects. The baroque buildings of Austria are monuments to the drive for orthodoxy and absolutism which characterized the Monarchy during these reigns. 'For this is the sole and supreme motive behind distinguished and stately buildings', wrote Prince Karl Eusebius von Liechtenstein towards the end of the seventeenth century; 'the immortal name and fame and eternal memory that the structure will leave behind.'[18]

This Austrian emphasis on the irrational side of man's nature (while elsewhere the Scientific Revolution and the Enlightenment dominated the intellectual scene) is evident also in the other great art that Vienna made its own, music. The imperial Court gave the lead in staging operas, ballets, and oratorios, while the pattern was repeated in palaces, churches, and monasteries up and down the country. Over 400 Italian operas were produced under Leopold I, and it was typical that Johann Philipp von Schönborn, Bishop of Würzburg, should take with him on a visit to Vienna a whole ship loaded with musicians and instruments. In music, as in architecture, it was mainly Italian composers and performers (especially Venetians) who began a tradition which later made Vienna a musical centre of European renown.

Artistic advance was achieved at the expenes of science, reason, and material progress: for publicity on behalf of the Catholic Monarchy was also propaganda against Jews, Protestants, and any deviations from the philosophical line of the Counter-Reformation. The spirit of doubt and criticism, of experiment and free enquiry was killed by the expulsion of the Jews by Leopold I (1669–70), by the successive purges of the Protestants, and by the stranglehold on intellectual life which the Church achieved through its censorship of the press, and its control of the universities, schools, and pulpits. Abraham a Sancta Clara, for instance, the monk from the Viennese monastery of the Barefoot Friars of St Augustine who became the city's most popular preacher and was appointed court preacher by Leopold (1677), was hardly on the side of Enlightenment. 'Nowhere among all the people does one find such stubborn and faithless persons as the miserable Jews', he told his doting congregation; 'they are the scum of the godless and faithless.'[19] And though the Jews were allowed back into Vienna later in Leopold's reign, they had to live in special dwellings, pay extra taxes, and wear a yellow badge. Charles VI was equally illiberal. Bohemian Protestants were persecuted with torture and the galleys. Protestants were expelled from Upper Austria and Inner Austria between 1723 and 1725, some peasants fleeing as far afield as Georgia in America. Austrian troops helped the neighbouring Archbishop of Salzburg when he drove out the Protestants from his territories in 1722 and 1723.

The result of this obscurantism (indeed, one of its purposes) was to insulate Austria from the invigorating influences of the Enlightenment, and to impede her material progress and social evolution. 'I don't find that learned men abound here,' wrote Lady Mary Wortley Montagu, 'there is indeed a prodigious number of alchemists at Vienna; the philosopher's stone is the great object of zeal and science.'[20] And in this intellectual quarantine the majority of the Austrians were not ideologically equipped to move ahead. 'They are so religious that they don't want to tinker with God's work', wrote Wilhelm von Schröder, Fellow of the London Royal Society and economic adviser to Leopold I. 'They want to keep things as it has pleased God to give them. This is the great ignorance which makes them sullen and negligent when it comes to work for their own good.'[21] However arguable the connections may be between the Reformation and the rise of capitalism, there is no doubt that the

Counter-Reformation helped to hold it down in Austria. The spirit of enterprise was stifled by the propaganda of the Church against any interference with the existing social order. Poverty, so Abraham a Sancta Clara used to argue, was a double blessing from God, giving the poor man the opportunity of reaching Heaven through his sufferings, and the rich man through his charity.

Economic Backwardness

Of course, there were plenty of other causes of Austria's lack of economic growth besides sermons. She was located by geography in a commercial back-water in the east while the main trade of Europe had moved to the Atlantic in the west. She had ports at Fiume and Trieste, but bad communications with them, and no fleet. Unnavigable rivers and non-existent roads hampered trade everywhere; while bad transport was worsened by the tariff barriers which the Diets erected between the various provinces. With the Monarchy thus chopped up into small local regions, there was little prospect to offer industrial entrepreneurs aiming at a national or international sale. And, even if there had been an Austrian common market, industry was so effectively controlled by the gilds, whose purpose was to share out the local market between members, maintain traditional methods, and keep out newcomers, that enterprising men could not have taken great advantage of it. In addition, Austria was short of labour. Besides the depopulation of the Thirty Years' War, she suffered from the self-inflicted wounds of exiled Protestants and Jews. And this was manpower difficult to replace because of the rigidly maintained social structure. The serfs were tied to the manor and forced to work many days a week for the lord: restrictions which did not encourage the growth of urban life or craftsmanship. Besides, the towns were everywhere on the decline, falling into the power of the aristocrats, who took over their wealth, dominated their government, and stunted their growth. Social mobility became restricted, except for a few very able clerics or bureaucrats. The gap between lord and serf was too wide and there was little in

between to bridge it. Besides, class lines were hardened by
racial and religious differences. The gulf between the Czech
peasantry and their German lords, for example, was too wide to
cross. While in Hungary, where business was run by German
or Greek colonists, the towns acted as a damp-course preventing Magyar peasants from rising in the world.

All these factors limited the evolution of Austrian commerce
and industry, and were the basic cause of Habsburg financial
weakness. Two comparisons will show the position. Charles VI
ruled a population more than two-and-a-half times as big as
that ruled by George II of Britain, but enjoyed only half his
revenues. Similarly, Charles could barely raise 100,000 soldiers
out of his twenty-five million subjects, whereas Frederick William I of Prussia could muster 80,000 highly trained men out
of a population of two and a half millions. Both Leopold I
and Charles VI had been told more than once by their Cameralist advisers that poor subjects make poor sovereigns. 'The
prince must first help his subjects to a good livelihood', wrote
Schröder, 'if he wants to take something from them.'[22]

Mercantilism

Apart from Schröder, there were two other immigrant theorists
in Leopold I's reign who were ready with mercantilist advice:
Johann Joachim Becher, the best economist of the three, and
Philipp Wilhelm von Hörnigk, the most widely read, in his
resoundingly entitled work *Österreich über alles, wenn es nur
will (Austria above all, if she but wills)*. Their works formed
a body of economic doctrine dipped into by Austrian monarchs
throughout the Ancien Régime; and, if no economic miracle
ensued, the fault was in the practice rather than the theory.
Though a College of Commerce was set up by Leopold I, to
stimulate the economy, and other similar bodies followed in
Charles VI's reign, these rulers had a very limited success in
their attempts to develop banking, manufacturing, and commerce. Factories making high-grade porcelain, glass, and textiles were set up on the royal domain, for example, in the teeth
of gild resistance. On the southern fringe of the Monarchy, the

Eastern Company was founded in 1719, which, after starting a candle and a hosiery factory at Fiume, and buying up a woollen cloth factory at Linz, went into liquidation for lack of capital and markets. Similarly, on the northern coast, Charles VI chartered the Ostend Company in 1723 for commerce with the East and West Indies, and then abandoned it eight years later, mainly at the behest of Britain and Holland who objected to the competition. The mercantilism of this period is a sorry tale of short-lived and fragile enterprises, winding up through lack of capital, shortage of manufactured goods, absence of civil servants with business knowledge, as well as the short-sighted desire of the Crown for a quick profit, and, above all, the lack of an adventurous bourgeoisie. The Habsburgs were trying to have their cake and eat it. They longed for modern business growth, but stultified it by sponsoring the philosophy of the Counter-Reformation, shoring up the traditional social system, and doing little to break the power of such conservative institutions as gilds and Diets.

The Administration

Essentially, the power of the Austrian Monarchy was still too weak to effect detailed changes in Austrian life, although some steps in the direction of absolutism were taken in the reign of Charles VI. The provinces had lost any independent voice in all-Austrian affairs, and high policy was made in Vienna. Even there, however, there was insufficient unity of direction. The provinces were administered by separate boards: the Austrian, Bohemian, and Hungarian Chancelleries, as well as the Netherlandic Council for Belgium, and the 'Spanish Council' for the Italian provinces: the name is yet another sign of Charles's reluctance to abandon his Spanish aspirations. These, and other central organs such as the Treasury and the Supreme War Council, were supervised by the Privy Conference. But the Emperor was feeble in his overall control. For one thing, he was a bad judge of character: witness his fatuous remark on the death of Prince Eugen in 1735: 'Now, see, everything will be better organized.'[23] Neither did he possess the force of character to co-ordinate his competing committees. He corresponded with them by means of Bartenstein, a very able civil servant; but high policy very much depended on which of the rival Court factions possessed the royal ear at any given moment. Too often he could not choose between contending interests, and took refuge in postponing decisions. His daughter Maria Theresa must have had him partly in mind when she observed that 'many of my forebears have been accused of all too dilatory deliberation or indecision in the affairs of State and of their country'.[24]

While sluggishness and lack of team-work characterized the central government, the provinces, through their Diets, still retained the financial and other prerequisites for self-government. The Italian provinces ticked over as before, and so did Belgium. Prince Eugen, who was Governor of Milan from 1706 to 1716, and of the Netherlands from 1716 to 1724, never saw Milan after 1707, and never visited Belgium as Governor-General at all. In Hungary the central and county Diets maintained their grip on Magyar affairs. At the Diet of Pozsony (1712–15), called as promised at the time of the Treaty of Szatmár (1711), Charles VI swore to respect the Hungarian rights. He was angling for support for the Pragmatic Sanction. On the other hand, the nobles gave up one fundamental right. In place of the feudal *Insurrection*, they voted for a standing army to be paid for out of Hungarian taxation (of the peasants, of course). This represented a real gain for Vienna, as those troops were incorporated into the Austrian army under German officers. Finally, in Bohemia and the hereditary Austrian lands, some inroads were made on the administrative power of the Diets, but their crucial taxation rights had not been broken.

The Pragmatic Sanction

Charles VI's contribution to Austrian statebuilding was of a different character. He put most of his effort into gaining European recognition for the Pragmatic Sanction (1713): a private Habsburg family agreement, at first, and then a publicly proclaimed constitutional law, whereby the Habsburg Monarchy was to descend undivided to Charles's eldest son, and, if there were no son, then to his eldest daughter (and not to the daughters of his deceased elder brother, Joseph I). Unfortunately, his only son died in 1716, and in spite of the pilgrimage he made with the Empress to Mariazell, and in spite of laying before Our Lady of Austria a silver statue of the Christ child of the same weight as the dead son, he was not vouchsafed another son. Instead, Maria Theresa (born in 1717) now became sole heiress, forcing him to redouble his efforts to avoid a disputed succession on his death. He spent the 1720s and 1730s persuading the Diets of the Monarchy, the princes of the Empire, and the powers of Europe, to guarantee this arrangement, though making important concessions in return. Inside Austria, these concessions, which mainly consisted of a recognition of the powers of the Diets in the provinces, prevented Charles from taking any steps in the direction of absolutism – which Prince Eugen recommended as a better alternative. It prevented him, in other words, from building up the army and treasure which Frederick William I of Prussia was at that time concentrating on; for these could only have been achieved at the expense of the Estates.

Similarly, he had to make sacrifices in Europe in order to gain support for the Pragmatic Sanction. Fortunately, there is no need to risk the vertigo which a detailed scrutiny of the gyrations of European diplomacy in this period would bring. In brief, the pursuit of guarantors for the succession helped to force Austria to give up the Ostend Company, and to allow Spanish troops into Parma and Piacenza (1731). Moreover, it was an important factor in dragging Austria into the War of the Polish Succession (1733–38). Fighting for the Saxon candidate in alliance with Russia, Austria lost most of her possessions in Italy, and scarcely succeeded in defending the Rhine against France. Prince Eugen, who was in command here, was no longer his old self, over seventy, as he was, with a hacking cough and a tendency to drop off in the afternoons. In the peace treaty (1738) France in effect gained Lorraine from Charles's son-in-law, Francis Stephen; though in Italy Charles fared better than his lost battles warranted. He gave up Naples and Sicily to the Spanish prince, Don Carlos, and got Parma and Piacenza in exchange, as well as Tuscany for Francis Stephen, while France guaranteed the Pragmatic Sanction.

Finally, his alliance with Russia also led him into the disastrous war with Turkey (1736–39). The Ottoman Empire was now rejuvenated and aggressive once more, after making peace with Persia, and carrying out military reforms under the guidance of an ex-colleague of Eugen's, the French adventurer, Count Bonneval – or Bonneval Pasha, as he now was. Eugen himself was dead, and his armies now lost battle after battle in a disgraceful manner. The victories of the Turks led to a swift turnover in Austrian commanders. In 1737 General Doxat, who lost the town of Nish, was beheaded, while his Commander-in-Chief, Field-Marshal Seckendorf, was dismissed and placed under house arrest pending trial. The next year Count Königsegg, his successor, was dismissed, not only from his army command, but also from the Presidency of the Supreme War Council. His successor, Field-Marshal Oliver Wallis, was not optimistic when he took over in the spring of 1739. 'The first of my predecessors in this post is in prison,' he wrote, 'the second has been demoted to the status of a palace eunuch; it only remains for me to have my head cut off at the end of the campaign.'[25] He exaggerated, however, for when Belgrade had fallen, he and Count Neipperg, who negotiated the surrender, were only gaoled for the rest of the reign. And after all the defeats came a further twist of the knife: the victories of Charles's allies, the Russians, in what is now Rumania. This unpleasant foretaste of Austro-Russian rivalry in the Balkans led Austria to sue for peace, and by the Treaty of Belgrade (1739), Austria lost all the gains of Passarowitz, except the Bánát of Temesvár.

Conclusion

The pathetic performance of the Austrian armies in these two wars demonstrated to all the world, and especially to Crown Prince Frederick of Prussia, that all was not well inside the Monarchy. In brief, she had fallen behind her neighbours in the modernization of her system of government, especially under Charles VI. In the seventeenth century she made her mark even with old-fashioned institutions; for her rivals, France, Russia, and Prussia, were not then so far ahead in the drive for absolutism; while her chief enemy, Turkey, was more backward still. In this period the Habsburgs succeeded in resurrecting the power of their House in a new guise: as Austrian Monarchs instead of Holy Roman Emperors. Out of the debris of the Thirty Years' War a new power arose in Europe, which threw back the Turks, subjected the hereditary lands, the Kingdom of Bohemia and the Kingdom of Hungary, to all-Austrian rule, and indoctrinated it with Counter-Reformation piety and baroque culture. At the same time Austria powerfully contributed to the defeat of French aims of European hegemony, and gained valuable territory in Italy and the Netherlands.

However, in the eighteenth century, the size of this far-flung monarchy, and the immoderate nature of its ambitions, now revealed serious weaknesses. In two important fields, France, Russia, and Prussia had gone far ahead: in the reduction of the Church, and in the integration of the provinces. The weakness of his state in these two areas was the root cause of Charles VI's poverty and poor showing in European politics, of his cap-in-hand negotiations over the Pragmatic Sanctions and his disastrous military defeats. The Austrian bureaucracy could not get its hands on what taxable wealth there was, let alone increase it by enlightened paternalism. The Church and the Estates defended tradition, and impeded the spread of that social mobility and intellectual flexibility which were the preconditions of modernization. At no point was the Crown in direct touch with the mass of the subjects. In addition, the inertia of the provinces was encouraged by the disharmony at Vienna. All-Austrian progress was impossible with the Chancelleries all pulling in different directions, as Maria Theresa discovered when she succeeded. 'I see very well', she said, 'that with us everything happens far too slowly. This will always be our ruin, and no one ever hurries himself to carry out the most urgent tasks of all.'[26] And it was she who sat in the driver's

seat when her horseless-carriage of a state had to face the
Rolls-Royce which Frederick the Great set in motion in December 1740.

Austria: Maria Theresa, 1740–80

Loss of Silesia

In 1740, when Charles VI's unexpected death suddenly un-
loaded the responsibilities of the Monarchy on to the shoulders
of Maria Theresa, she was twenty-three and surrounded by the
dithering old ministers of her father's reign. There was Philipp
Ludwig Sinzendorf, the Chancellor, for example, aged sixty-
nine, and Count Gundaker Starhemberg, aged seventy-seven,
who had been at the head of the Treasury for thirty-seven
years. She was, as she later said, 'without money, without
credit, without an army, without knowledge or experience, and
also without advice, because each of the counsellors wanted
first of all to wait and see how matters would turn out'.[1] Frederick's invasion of Silesia was soon followed by the formation
of a European coalition which aimed at breaking up the
Austrian Monarchy, and sharing out the pieces. Prussia was to
have Lower Silesia; Saxony was to get Upper Silesia, Moravia,
and Lower Austria; Bavaria was to receive Bohemia and Upper
Austria as well as the title of Holy Roman Emperor; Spain was
to regain her Italian possessions; while France, misguided by
anachronistic thinking into inspiring this affair, was to gain
Belgium, and enjoy the ruin of the Habsburgs whom she still
regarded as France's deadly enemies.

When the news of the alliance reached Vienna, Sinzendorf
and Starhemberg 'both fell back into their chairs like dead
men', according to the British Ambassador.[2] Maria Theresa
had to make her own decisions, as her putative dominions, so
carefully cemented together by the Pragmatic Sanction, fell
apart like a tenement in an earthquake. While Frederick II
took Silesia, Charles Albert of Bavaria invaded Upper Austria
with French help, and got himself elected ruler by the Diet at
Linz. Shortly after, in Prague, the Estates elected him King

of Bohemia; while in 1742 he was elected Emperor Charles VII. In her desperate plight she threw herself on the mercy of the normally peevish nobility of Hungary, by appearing in person at the Diet of Pozsony with her child Joseph in her arms (1741). Her youth, charm, and vulnerability seem to have worked a miracle on the chivalrous emotions of the Magyars, especially as she backed these fugitive qualities with solid guarantees for Hungary's independent form of government. With acclamation the assembled Estates offered their lives and their blood, with the promise of about 100,000 men. This gesture saved the Austrian Monarchy. The Queen of Hungary, as she now was called, later acknowledged that it was to the Hungarians that 'she was indebted for her existence on the throne of her ancestors'.[3] It was not so much the troops that saved the day, for the promised number were never supplied. It was the moral effect of the gesture on the rest of the Monarchy and on Europe. It enabled the House of Habsburg to survive the War of the Austrian Succession (1740–48), suffering only the loss of Silesia to Prussia, and of Parma, Piacenza, and Guastalla to Don Philip of Spain.

Maria Theresa

Frederick II admired the mettle of his dauntless adversary. 'She has done credit to her throne and to her whole sex,' he said.[4] Maria Theresa had practically none of the family physical characteristics. Moreover, though she was dignified and devoted to high ideals, she was at the same time warm-hearted and human. She did not keep her subjects at bay with the traditional Habsburg *hauteur*, but charmed and captured them with her easy friendliness and artless spontaneity. As well as a Queen she was a devoted wife and mother, and during the first two decades of her reign, when she waged two European wars and revolutionized the system of government, she brought sixteen children into the world. She was made by nature to be the motherly head of a large family, and she brought up her children and ruled her subjects by instinct rather than science. Her statesmanship depended not on political philosophy or long-term planning, but on day-to-day decision-making whose wisdom derived from her sound judgement of men, and shrewd political sense, guided by principle not expediency. 'I do not belong to myself but only to the public,' she said. And again: 'However much I love my family and my children, so much that I would not spare myself effort, trouble, anxiety, or work, yet I would have preferred to them the country's general good if I had been persuaded in my conscience that I could further it or that the well-being of my subjects required it, seeing that I am the general and chief mother of my country.'[5]

Kaunitz

One of the ministers she picked and then stood by, in spite of the opposition his fresh ideas aroused among the old-fashioned, was Kaunitz, who was made Chancellor in 1753, and who guided Austrian foreign policy for the rest of the reign and the next. This eccentric Bohemian aristocrat combined a breath-taking vanity with a clarity of vision into world realities un-equalled in European diplomacy. According to Frederick the Great, he was 'a solemn, arrogant, mouthing, brow-beating kind of man, with a clear intellect twisted by perversities of temper, especially by a self-conceit and arrogance which are boundless';[6] yet already at the peace conference at Aix-la-Chapelle he had drawn the conclusions that were to revolu-tionize Austrian foreign policy as well as the European scene. Henceforth, he had concluded, Prussia, not France, was the main enemy, and the prime object of Austrian policy should be the reconquest of Silesia. This was also Maria Theresa's hope, which she refused to abandon, not out of ambition or passion for aggrandizement, but, as she wrote to him when he was ambassador in Paris, 'because I grow ever more and more convinced that the welfare of my house depends on it and that this loss is the source of our predicament in the Empire as well as in the north'.[7] And the way to regain Silesia, he taught her, was not an alliance with the maritime powers, who were not interested in Silesia, but only in the defence of their own interests against France.

Diplomatic Revolution

The celebrated reversal of alliances, that is, the formation of the seemingly overwhelming coalition of Austria, France, Russia, Sweden, and the Circles of the Empire against Prussia, was the rather over-ripe fruit of Kaunitz's diplomacy. Unfortunately, the Seven Years' War (1756–63) was a failure. The alliance of giants lumbered along with no common purpose. Kaunitz's diplomacy had been too clever, and the allies soon realized that they were sacrificing themselves mainly for the benefit of Austria. Moreover, the dilatory manoeuvring of the Austrian command could not compare with the audacity and endurance of Frederick the Great; nor could their fumbling bureaucracy match the efficiency of his streamlined state. By the Treaty of Hubertusburg (1763), Maria Theresa had once more to counter-sign the loss of Silesia.

Reforms in the Central Government

It was clear from her performance in these two wars that Austria's armed forces, civil service, economy, and general way of life badly needed modernization; and the internal history of Austria under Maria Theresa is a crescendo of reforms, leading to the frantic reign of Joseph II. In this respect, as in most others, her reign falls into two periods: before and after 1765, the year when her husband, Francis Stephen, died, and Joseph II succeeded him as Emperor in Germany and co-regent in Austria. Francis had been too docile a creature to have any influence on affairs. 'The Empress and my children constitute the Imperial family', he once said: 'I am only a private individual.'[8] During his lifetime, when Maria Theresa was in charge, piecemeal pragmatism was the policy; after his death, Joseph more and more introduced the radical programme of the Enlightenment. The chief motives were external security and public welfare, though these had different priorities in different minds. For most of Maria Theresa's ministers, the guns came before the butter, though it must be said that the

Empress herself was much more genuinely concerned with humanity than the self-advertizing Enlightened absolutists, her contemporaries. 'Our own welfare is inseparably connected together with that of our subjects,' she wrote in a government instruction in 1761, '... hence then the augmentation of the sovereign's power and income must be sought in no other way than by furthering the common welfare and enrichment and by making no distinction between the interests of the sovereign and that of the Estates.'[9] The method of achieving these goals was the perfecting of the machinery of centralized absolutism. 'We work together', she wrote to the co-regent in 1771, 'and are proud to make this system general, since we unite all the branches and by this means organize everything much more simply. We want all the ministers we employ to think and work in the same manner. In that way costs will be reduced.'[10]

The pre-1765 reforms were first introduced by Haugwitz, and then modified by Kaunitz. Count Friedrich Wilhelm Haugwitz, the son of a Saxon general, was head of the administration in that part of Silesia which Austria had been able to keep, and was thus able to admire the bureaucratic improvements that Frederick the Great introduced in the part he had won. His ideas for giving Austrian government an overhaul (which he submitted on the Empress's invitation) were very much influenced by Prussian models. In brief, he proposed increasing the standing army to a size that would require five times the normal revenue; and to achieve this he suggested ways of breaking the financial and military powers of the Estates. The rest of Maria Theresa's ministers saw red. These aristocrats, after all, worked in Vienna, not primarily for the health of the Monarchy as a whole, but to guard the interests of Bohemia, or Upper Austria, or whatever province their property was situated in. Maria Theresa, on the contrary, backed Haugwitz completely. 'Any one who will not obey,' she said, 'let him be, only such people will never more appear before my eyes here.'[11]

Haugwitz's solution to the financial problem was the ten-year tax scheme (1748), whereby each Diet in Austria and Bohemia voted taxes for ten years instead of the usual one. At the same time, their military contributions in kind (such as the provisions of horses, forage, daily rations, and so on), were to be commuted to a cash payment. Moreover, both the financial and the military administration were to be taken over by civil servants from the standing committees of the Diets. And, finally, nobles and clergy would pay taxes for the first time, based on a new land survey. The peasants would pay a similar income tax in place of their poll-tax – only at twice the rate paid by the nobles and clergy.

This radical upheaval of old customs had to be negotiated with each of the Diets. The Estates of Styria, Carniola, Gorizia, and Gradisca took three years before conceding. Carinthia in the end had to be forced into line by royal decree. Bohemia and Moravia gave in more quickly. The nobles there were not in a strong moral position – hanging their heads somewhat after recently paying homage to Charles Albert of Bavaria as their king. Besides, they could hardly oppose military reform with Frederick the Great on their border in Silesia.

The Bohemians resented much more bitterly another part of Haugwitz's reforms: the merging of the Bohemian and Austrian Chancelleries into one common institution, the *Directorium* (1749). The Harrachs and Kinskys and other Bohemian aristocrats at Court put up a stiff opposition, but Maria Theresa was firm, glad to see the barriers down between at least two of her kingdoms. The Bohemians, on the other hand (as well as Czech historians since), regarded this step as a much more serious inroad on their independence, even, than Ferdinand II's reframing of their constitution after the Battle of the White Mountain (1620). Haugwitz looked upon the new Directory (over which he presided) as the Austrian equivalent of the Prussian General Directory. Some functions were subtracted from it, and others added. Foreign affairs had already been separated in 1742 when the State Chancellery (*Staatskanzlei*) was set up. This was the organ over which Kaunitz presided from 1753 onwards. The other important task separated from the central administration was the judiciary, when the Supreme Office of Justice (*Oberste Justizstelle*) was erected in 1748 to function as a Supreme Court and Ministry of Justice. This separation of justice from administration would enable the sovereign, wrote Maria Theresa, to 'further a just and God-pleasing procedure between lords and subjects, and to watch carefully that the poor, and especially the subjects [serfs], are not oppressed by the rich, and especially by the lords'.[12] At the same time she began a reform of the legal code.

While the Directory lost responsibility for justice and foreign affairs, it gained the Treasury (1749) and the Universal Directory of Commerce (1753), as well as other departments. Indeed, it took on so many tasks that it became top-heavy; and it will be best to follow its fate before turning to the infrastructure that Haugwitz created at provincial and local levels. The Directory aroused so many enemies, and performed so disappointingly in the Seven Years' War, that Kaunitz took over internal administration as well as foreign affairs, considering that the Directory had ruined the effect of his skilful diplomacy in bringing about the reversal of alliances. In 1761 he renamed it the United Bohemian and Austrian Chancellery; withdrew finance from its purview once more, giving it to the Treasury and the Audit Office (*Hofrechnungskammer*); and also taking commerce away and giving it to the Council of Commerce. Thus, at this stage, there were six main central departments: the United Chancellery, the State Chancellery, the Supreme Office of Justice, the Treasury, Audit Office, and the Supreme War Council. Above all these, Kaunitz created the State Council (*Staatsrat*) in 1760, which took the place of the Privy Conference as chief advisory body to the Crown. Consisting of the State Chancellor together with three aristocrats and three knights, the Council of State gave opinions on internal administration and legislation, a kind of parliament of top bureaucrats. It became the day-to-day motor of the State machine, with the result that Maria Theresa's Austria was a bureaucratic absolutism, rather than a personal one on Prussian lines.

Provincial and Local Government

More revolutionary than the changes that Haugwitz and Kaunitz made in the central government were the corresponding reforms they made at provincial and local level. Essentially, their overall effect was to provide bureaucratic machinery to take over the financial and military tasks taken away from the Diets by the ten-year tax scheme. In each *Land* an administrative board was set up (called a 'Representative and Chamber' at first, but usually a *Gubernium* from 1763 onwards) which worked under the Directory (later the United Chancellery) collecting revenue, and recruiting and equipping troops. For the latter task they set in motion a conscription scheme similar to the Prussian Canton system; and gradually they took on further tasks, such as price control, and the protection of serfs from the excesses of their lords. Provincial justice was kept separate from the *Gubernia*, being still under the traditional chief courts of the provinces, and now supervised by the new Supreme Office of Justice in Vienna.

Beneath the *Gubernium*, at local level, each province was divided into districts headed by a civil servant called the District Chief (*Kreishauptmann*), who was responsible partly to the Diet, and partly to the *Gubernium*. Beginning in 1748, a network of these local officers was strung out all over the provinces of Austria and Bohemia. At first, when trained men were in short supply, the *Kreishauptmann* tended to be a local landowner, something like an English Justice of the Peace; but, as bureaucrats trained in Cameralism gradually became available (and this became compulsory after 1776), they took on the appearance of French Intendants, or a combination of Prussian *Steuerräte* and *Landräte* (there being no Prussian separation of town and country in Austria). At the same time the more the State increased its active intervention into the workings of society (as will be seen) the more numerous the tasks the District Chiefs performed. They became concerned with police, roads, schools, hospitals, poor law, churches, trade, and so on. By the same token they became more and more servants of the crown, and less and less agents of the Diets.

Of course, the Diets, and the other provincial and local institutions, did not take the creation of the bureaucratic state lying down, especially when it was used to improve the welfare of the peasants. But the State turned a deaf ear to their complaints – which were particularly loud in Bohemia. Kaunitz, himself a Bohemian noble, wrote in 1763:

Other sovereigns try more and more to restrict the nobility, because the true strength of the State consists of the biggest section of the people, that is, of the common man; and he deserves the chief consideration, whereas he is more oppressed in Bohemia than in the Austrian provinces. Instead of thinking of some means of putting right this evil, Your Majesty's own servants will advise the exact opposite, and propose, at the same time, a form of government which stands opposed to the supreme power, to the prejudice of the sovereign.[13]

Maria Theresa's method of dealing with obstructionism was firm but subtle. She abolished nothing, but left Diets, permanent committees, town councils, gilds, manorial courts and other institutions standing where she found them, with the idea that in time they would become ghostly shells, emptied of real significance as the bureaucrats gradually took over their work. Typical of the fusion of old and new was the way in which the chief officer of the *Gubernium* in each province became, in 1765, the President also of the provincial Diet. And as the Diets lost their duties, many nobles stayed away from the meetings. This exodus made it easier for the crown to manage the remainder with the judicious distribution of titles and honours.

The crown thus steadily advanced at the expense of the nobility – much more so than in Prussia, where the Junkers were treated with great consideration since they were vital to the army and civil service. In Austria, on the contrary, the nobles were too wealthy to be so dependent on State employment, and so the State could afford to hit them hard, or at least brush them aside. And the reforms in higher education (which will be touched on later) enabled the Monarchy to replace tradition-bound noble amateurs with enlightened professionals. By 1768 Kaunitz could say, 'the most serious difficulties are already overcome. Proposals for improvements will no longer as hitherto be regarded with contempt, or even as crimes, and the prejudice against all innovations is lessening day by day. Above all we no longer live in deep ignorance of what happens abroad, but instead our eagerness increases to turn useful foreign discoveries and equipment into our own'.[14]

The Church

One useful discovery which Kaunitz and others picked up from their scrutiny of foreign inventions was the importance of reducing the power of the Church, already achieved in Britain, Russia, Prussia, and France. In Austria, on the contrary, the Thirty Years' War and the late flowering of the Counter-Reformation had enabled the Church to maintain and extend its sway in areas of life considered by the philosophers of absolutism to be purely the concern of the State. The Church ran hospitals, for example, organized poor relief and other welfare services. It paralysed intellectual life by its grip on schools and universities, pulpit, and press. It possessed vast wealth and manpower, too much of which was excluded from productive economic activity. It enjoyed taxation and other privileges at home, and was in part subject to orders from abroad. Its courts gave it judicial authority over large areas of the citizen's public and private life. Like the Diets, in other words, it interposed barriers between the monarch and his subjects, and stood in the way of the absolutist ideal: of the State as a community of individuals, equal at least in their submission to the prince.

It was Kaunitz and Joseph II who cast covetous eyes on the Church, and not Maria Theresa, who was a pious Catholic of the traditional Habsburg kind. For her the salvation of the House of Austria in the War of Austrian Succession, for example, was a miracle wrought by the Almighty. 'I ascribe this by no means to my virtue but exclusively to God's Grace' was a typical sentiment of hers.[15] Thus the policy of striking at the Church for political or economic reasons was contrary to her deepest beliefs. So was the Enlightened notion of toleration, which for her smacked of indifference and expediency. In her view to persecute the Jews was pleasing to God. She drove them out of Bohemia in 1745; and in 1777 she wrote: 'In future no Jew shall be allowed to remain in Vienna without my special permission. I know of no greater plague than this race, which on account of its deceit, usury, and hoarding of money is driving my subjects to beggary.'[16] Similarly, to encourage the Protestants simply because they were good for trade seemed to her immoral. 'Without a ruling religion?', she asked Joseph who favoured toleration. 'Tolerance and indifference are just the very means to undermine everything.'[17]

Thus she opposed very strongly the mounting campaign of Kaunitz and Joseph to lop off all branches of ecclesiastical activity not directly concerned with salvation, and allowed herself only with the greatest reluctance to be persuaded that some such measures were essential to the power of the crown and thus the safety of the State. During her reign Jansenists pushed out Jesuits as the leading exponents of Catholic piety in Vienna; and one of these, Gerhard von Swieten, was her personal physician and chief adviser over education. Of Dutch Protestant origin, he helped to develop a Catholic outlook which was more rational and less indulgent than that of the Jesuits, and at the same time was not incompatible with the Enlightenment. Particularly influential, also, were the ideas of Bishop Nicolaus von Hontheim as expressed in his treatise *On the state of the Church and the Legitimate Power of the Roman Pontiff*, which he published in 1763 under the pen-name of 'Febronius'. Catholicism and the Enlightenment could come together in the views of Febronianism that the Church ought to be governed by the successors of all the apostles, not merely by the successors of St Peter; and that it ought to limit its activities to the spiritual sphere.

As a result, and especially after 1765, when Maria Theresa was a despondent old widow and no match for the dialectical skill of her erudite son, twin campaigns against the Church were mounted: first, to cut its links with Rome, secondly, to decrease its power and increase its social utility in the Austrian Monarchy. In 1765 a special commission, the *Giunta Economale*, was set up in Milan to strip the Church of its economic privileges. The Secret Instruction issued to it in 1768, and then applied generally in the Monarchy, laid down the general principle that every ecclesiastical activity not specifically entrusted by Jesus to the apostles was the responsibility of the crown. The clergy became taxed without papal approval; monasteries were dissolved; church courts came under the supervision of the judiciary; church property had to submit to inspection by civil servants. Similarly, church holidays were reduced in number so as to increase working hours; and the State limited the founding of new monasteries, and the purchase of land by existing ones; while the law laid down twenty-four as the minimum age for vow-taking, and removed the right of sanctuary from St Stephen's Cathedral and the *Schottenkirche* in Vienna. Even the religious monopoly of the Church was abolished, as Protestants ceased to be hounded out of the country, and could take degrees at the University of Vienna (1778). As for Rome, the sovereign's permission became necessary for the publication of papal orders; and also of bishops' orders, if they resided outside the Monarchy, such as the Archbishop of Salzburg and the Bishop of Passau. Moreover, the Roman heads of religious orders such as the Jesuits, Franciscans, Capuchins, and so on, were forbidden to conduct visitations of Austrian monasteries. While, in 1773, when the Pope suppressed the Jesuit order, Maria Theresa reluctantly complied. In Austria Jesuit property was seized by the crown to form a fund for the reform of education. 'I am very sorry for them but there is nothing to be done,' she wrote. 'Every month I feel weaker and more depressed.'[18]

Education

The reform of the educational system was part of the same campaign, in the sense that the object was to secularize and modernize it, and make it more socially useful. 'The school is and remains a political matter,' so Maria Theresa is said to have remarked.[19] 'The education of the young of both sexes', ran the General Education Regulation of 1774, 'is the most important basis for the prosperity of the people.'[20] The universities were removed from the control of the Jesuits to become state institutions where up-to-date knowledge in the physical and social sciences could be imparted, in German instead of Latin. The University of Vienna was modernized by Gerhard von Swieten, beginning with the Medical Faculty in 1749. In 1752 a lectureship in German Eloquence was founded, and filled by a Slovene called Johann Siegmund Valentin Popowitsch. Most significant for the development of the Austrian State-machine was the instruction given in law and politics. In 1754 the Chair of Natural Law was founded and given to Karl Anton von Martini; while in 1763 Joseph von Sonnenfels was appointed Professor of Political Sciences (*Polizei-und Kammeralwissenschaften*). Through their hands, and the hands of like-minded colleagues, passed several generations of future bureaucrats, grounded in the latest empirical knowledge and imbued with the generous ideals of the Catholic Enlightenment.

Schools as well as universities were reformed, again with a view to increasing the output of economically useful citizens, and to shaping the Austrian mind to fit comfortably into the absolutist régime. Kaunitz gave his idea of the education of the masses in a memorandum to Maria Theresa. 'One must give them a horror of theft, lying, drunkenness, ingratitude, and all the vices that the laws do not punish . . . ,' he said. 'One must inspire them with a love of the Prince as their common father, and of their country as the mother who nurses them, with submission to their station in society, with fidelity and obedience. One must finally give them the highest idea of the reward which, in this world or the next, awaits those who make the supreme sacrifice in the service of their sovereign.'[21] Gradually the Jesuits were removed from their dominating position in secondary education, and, after their dissolution and the formation of the Education Fund, the way was clear for wholesale reform. It took the form of the General Education Regulation brought out by the Abbé Felbiger in 1774: a complete scheme for primary and secondary education, including technical and grammar schools, as well as training colleges for teachers. It was perhaps the most elaborate and enlightened educational system in Europe. And by the end of Maria Theresa's reign (1780) there were in the hereditary lands fifteen training colleges, eighty-three high schools, forty-seven girls' schools and 3,848 elementary schools, training over 200,000 children.

The Economy

Thus the bureaucratic machine created by Haugwitz and
Kaunitz enabled the Monarchy to intervene effectively in
Austrian society and to begin to shape it to desired ends. The
economy also received much attention from civil servants, with
the object of overcoming those obstacles to economic growth
which private business was so far too puny to surmount: the
lack of roads, canals, ports, and ships; the internal tariff barriers; the powers of the gilds and seigneurs; the shortage of
skilled manpower and capital; the absence of the spirit of
enterprise; the loss of Silesia, the Monarchy's most advanced
province. Maria Theresa's reign began with a more systematic
adoption of the advice of the seventeenth-century Mercantilist
writers such as Schröder, Hörnigk, and Becher, which had
hitherto received only piecemeal and not very successful application. It continued (during the co-regency) with a steady
evolution in the direction of the Physiocrat ideals. As has been
shown, the Council of Commerce, an independent central
organ of economic control, had been established by Kaunitz,
but this was modified later, and a great deal of economic planning was operated through the ordinary administrative pyramid
of Chancellery – *Gubernium* – *Kreishauptmann*.

In outline, the measures adopted were as follows. Austria
and Bohemia were united into a common market, and a high
tariff wall was placed round the whole Monarchy. Transport
was improved; for example, the *Karolinenstrasse* was built, a
highway linking Hungary to Fiume, to serve the lands conquered from Turkey, which had been carefully colonized with
Germans. Great hopes were entertained for Trieste and Fiume
as international ports, the idea being to raise Austria to the
status of a maritime power and a trading nation – instead of a
country that was simply traded with. Unfortunately, the money
spent there did not pay off, though it irritated the Venetians.
Joseph II, who inspected the area in the 1760s, sent back dismal
reports. 'With the greatest expense, Trieste does not have a
secure port', he wrote to his mother; 'it makes a show of houses,

especially in the new city, but does not have merchants of importance, has little money and a miserable trade. Many ships
flying the Imperial flag, constructed in the days of enthusiasm,
now rot in the harbour, shattered by the north-east wind.'[22]
Efforts to make use of the Danube also foundered. In the 1770s,
a ship owned by an aristocratic banker pioneered the Turkish
market. Loaded with metal goods, cloth, glass, and porcelain,
it ultimately reached the Black Sea, after navigating the arduous
lower Danube and overcoming the obstacles placed by un-
friendly Turkish officials. It had few successors.

One of the troubles was that Austrian industrial products
were never sufficiently competitive in price and quality with
those of France or Britain, in spite of much government
encouragement. The State lent capital and equipment to entrepreneurs, provided they were aiming at the national or international market. It also exempted them from the restrictive
regulations of the gilds, which tended to keep out new men
and new methods. Other stimulants were the supply of cheap
labour and raw materials as well as patents of monopoly, and
exemptions from military service and the billeting of troops.
In addition, the officials laid down norms for quality and price,
established schools of spinning and weaving, and issued pamphlets such as von Justi's *A Clear Lesson in the Cultivation of
Silkworms and the Production of Silk for the Imperial Royal
Hereditary Lands* (1754).[23]

After the loss of Silesia, Bohemia became the most indus-
trialized area, especially in the German hill and forest section.
Bourgeois textile entrepreneurs developed the putting-out system, while aristocrats such as the Kinskys and Waldsteins employed their own serfs in workshops on Russian lines. The
area round Vienna was also productive, especially for china,
while Linz possessed the biggest textile factory in the Monarchy, and Styria was important for mining, iron-works, saltworks, and gunpowder production. Compared with these areas,
the Tyrol (as ever, resistant to Viennese pressures) was backward, and so was Carinthia, the poorest province of all, where
sixty-eight per cent of the peasants were unmarried. Everywhere,
though, the response of Austrian enterprise was disappointing in

comparison with the amount of bureaucratic energy expended; and one of the chief causes of this was the backward state of agriculture and the depressed condition of the serfs.

The Serfs

This was a problem familiar to the authorities at least since the reign of Leopold I. 'Without the labour of the peasant', wrote Becher, 'the artisan would have nothing to manufacture, and without those two the merchant would have nothing to trade. Consequently, the peasant is the foundation not only of the nobility, but of the civil estate and its society.'[24] In those days, however, the nobility could be as cross-grained as it wished in the defence of privilege; but now the reforms of Maria Theresa had given the crown adequate bureaucratic means of carrying out its will. It is difficult to generalize in this sphere, as the conditions of the peasantry varied by custom from place to place. Whether they were all serfs or not has been a matter of controversy, the answer depending on the definition of that term. In general, the peasants were tied to the manor, and could not leave without the lord's permission and the payment of a fee (*Abfahrtgeld*). They were subject to the lord's court in civil cases, and in criminal cases as well on large estates, though the death sentence was not supposed to be imposed without government permission. They had to grind their corn at his mill, buy their liquor from his still, and follow his banner in wartime. The lord decided which marriage-partner they should have, and what job they should take. For the cultivation of the soil, the peasants could rent or buy either of the two kinds of fields, those on the lord's demesne (*domestikal*), and those on the village land (*rustikal*); but the lord retained the reversionary right, and peasants could not mortgage, sell, or divide properties without his permission. Payment consisted of forced labour (*Robot*): farm work, hunting, driving, spinning and weaving, and so on. There were two kinds of *Robot*, limited and unlimited, and the amounts performed varied from province to province – from three to six days a week. In addition, there were dues to be paid in kind, as well as fines on inheritance, and tithes to the Church, and taxes to the State. Agriculture was backward: three-field husbandry, or four- or five-field husbandry was usual, while in the Alps field-grass farming predominated, consisting of regular alternation of land between tillage and grazing. And below the level of this social class were the landless labourers, and the poor and vagabonds – these last were known as *Schubspersonen*, that is, people to be pushed on to the next village.

The motives behind Maria Theresa's measures for improving the condition of the peasantry were mixed. Humanitarian considerations certainly moved the Empress and some of her civil servants; but these in themselves would not have justified what amounted to an attack on the nobility's power and pocket had there not been clear political and economic advantages for the state in view. Joseph II's philosophy of peasant protection was not unlike the thinking behind the fattening of pigs by a farmer. The general scheme was to drag out the serf from under the power of the lord, and place him under the protection of the State, that is, of the new civil service of United Chancellery, *Gubernium* and *Kreishauptmann*. This, it was believed, would make for more productive agriculture, loosen up the social system so as to provide labour for industry, and allow the state to cut itself a bigger slice of the peasant's income than the lord.

The theory that agriculture based on serfdom was unproductive was now a commonplace among the advanced thinkers of Europe. 'Poor peasant, poor kingdom; poor kingdom, poor king', as François Quesnay, the French Physiocrat, put it.[25] Or, as von Justi, the German Cameralist, said in his *Foundations of the Power and Happiness of States* (1760): 'As long as the peasants do not have complete property rights, they lack the most noble motive, the most effective incentive to cultivate their land to the best of their ability, for they must always fear that they or their children will be evicted.'[26] On the other hand, peasant protection could go too far and risk two possible dangers. The nobles might mutiny against this attack on their property, and the peasants might get ideas above their station and riot for even bigger concessions.

Treading carefully on this very thin ice, Maria Theresa's ministers began their reform, which took the form of, first, fixing legal limits to the serf's obligations and the lord's powers, where none existed; secondly, enforcing limits where they did exist but had been hitherto ignored; and, thirdly, reducing the obligations and the powers. In 1753 the privilege of granting permission to marry was taken away from the lord. In 1769 the lord was forbidden to punish peasants without the permission of the *Kreishauptmann*, and the peasant was given permission to bring complaints against his lord. In 1772, however, in case peasants put too strong an interpretation on this right, the law was altered, and very severe penalties awaited peasants who showed 'stubbornness, obstinacy, disorder, wickedness, wantonness, or would even dare to take part in mob gatherings and uprisings'.[27]

The most difficult reform for the crown to achieve was the limitation of the *Robot*. Joseph believed that the less the serf did for his lord the more he could do for his prince. Fact-finding commissions were sent out to make official records (*Urbaria*) of exactly what obligations peasants owed. At the same time negotiations with the provincial Diets led to reductions. In 1771 a maximum of three days a week was declared in Silesia; in 1772 two days a week with draught animals was fixed for Lower Austria. Negotiations with the Estates of Styria at Graz were long and arduous. When asked to limit the *Robot* to two days a week like Lower Austria, the Diet's committee called the request 'an unjustified interference by the sovereign with the age-old privileges of the Estates, and an equally unjustified degradation of the value of individual demesnes'.[28] In the end, after ten years of arguing, they agreed to three days a week.

In Bohemia famine and pestilence were making reform urgent. During the crisis of 1770 to 1772 Joseph travelled among the fever-ridden hamlets, tasted the peasants' bad bread, and anonymously gave large amounts out of his own pocket for relief. But the nobles were so obstructive in their negotiations with the crown, and the peasants had been given such extravagant expectations by the fact-finding commissioners, that a violent rebellion broke out in 1775 – the year after the defeat of Pugachev. As an official reported back to Vienna,

> several thousands having at the start refused the *Robot* under the false pretext that the Court had exempted them, but that the lords were preventing this from being carried out; their number being soon augmented by the co-operation of so many unfortunate people in this kingdom who have suffered exceedingly for several years from calamities of war and famine – they are now committing enormous excesses, pillaging châteaux ... leaving their fields without sowing them ... and since Hussites and other sectaries scattered about and hidden till now in the kingdom have joined the rebels, they have already sacked churches, broken the altars and images of saints, carried off the sacred vessels and thrown the consecrated wafers onto the ground.[29]

Joseph was forced to set his troops on the very people he hoped to help. He drowned the rebellion in blood; but at the same time he issued over the heads of the Estates at Prague the *Robot Patent* of 1775, limiting week-work to a maximum of three days. But it was not enough. Peasant reforms under the Ancien Régime never were. At the end of Maria Theresa's reign, the French traveller, Riesbeck, recorded how the Czech peasants had 'an indescribable detestation against everything German'.[30]

As in Prussia, more could be done for peasants on the royal domain than on noble estates, and Councillor Raab, in particular, took some path-finding measures in commuting *Robot* owed to the Crown to money payments, and in breaking up estates into small parcels for sale to peasants on easy terms. At the same time, the new civil service did all it could by education and propaganda to improve the peasant's agriculture and general well-being. Pamphlets were issued, such as the one entitled *How to Plant Pumpkins which in View of the Rising Price of Grain Can Serve as Food for the Poor*. Nor, under this maternal government, were peasant morals neglected. A decree of 1753 for Lower Austria said, for example: 'For the abolition of excessive gaiety and the sinful life, especially among the young peasant folk, which stem partly from unrestrained nightly meetings, partly from dances held until late

into the night, and partly also from the immodest garments
worn by some women in parts of the country, it is ordered that
these late meetings cease completely, and that dances shall not
last longer than nine o'clock in winter and ten o'clock in
summer.'[31] In 1771, moreover, peasant wedding-feasts were
cut down from three days to one.

Hungary

The reforms so far mentioned in this chapter – the revolution
in government and the intervention of the Monarchy into
religious, economic, and social life – have concerned only
Austria and Bohemia, for Hungary continued to be a special
case. Here, there was only one area where the Viennese
bureaucracy could freely practise the precepts of Enlightened
rationality: the military border with Turkey. Ignoring the
Hungarian Diet (and thus acting unconstitutionally), the Monarchy colonized these advance areas with veterans of the Seven
Years' War and other German immigrants – a piece of social
engineering which in a decade laid out there a smiling pattern
of small farms occupied by peasant proprietors. In Hungary
proper, however, not as much could be achieved, for the powers
of the central and county Diets, far from being broken, had
been confirmed, even enlarged, on that dramatic occasion in
1741 when the Magyars came to the rescue of the Habsburg
Monarchy. In that historic hour, Maria Theresa had agreed
that the exemption of noble land from taxation was a fundamental and unalterable law. After that she called only two
further Diets (in 1751 and 1764) and found it impossible to
persuade them to agree to two vital changes she had made in
Austria-Bohemia: the taxation of the nobility and the improvement of the lot of the serfs. At one meeting of the Upper
House, the suggestion that the obligation of the peasants should
be limited by law was received with 'uproarious laughter'.
Indeed, any proposal to limit their traditional privileges was
stigmatized as an invasion of the rights of the nation – some
westernized magnates even using arguments about 'intermediate powers' they had picked up from Montesquieu. Thus the

Haugwitz-Kaunitz reforms in government – the ten-year tax system, the union of Chancelleries, the network of *Gubernia* and *Kreishauptmänner* – could not be extended to Hungary.

There, even if the central Diet ceased to meet, local life was firmly in the control of the country Diets and their elected officials. These lesser nobles (like the country gentry of England and the provincial nobility of France) were far from awe-struck by the ministers of the Crown. And there was no need for these head-strong gentry to look up their Montesquieu: passive resistance to Viennese orders was sufficient to make them unworkable in the villages. Indeed, they were not beyond sabotaging unpleasant regulations by the simple process of dismissing all their officials. In view of this, the Hungarian peasants probably did not get the full benefit of the *Urbarium* which Maria Theresa issued by decree in 1767, after she had given up hope of having it enacted by the Diet. By it, the peasant's *Robot* was limited to one day a week with draught animals, or two without. In addition, he was legally free to leave his holding so long as he had paid all his dues. Observers agree that some improvement in peasant welfare occurred as a result of Maria Theresa's efforts; but the French traveller Riesbeck in the last years of her reign thought the Magyar lower orders were barbarians. He classed them with Indians and Negroes, considering that their manners had been completely destroyed by oppression, misery and lack of education. He remarked on 'the grinding poverty which in Hungary makes such a nauseating contrast with the prodigality of the great'.[32] That was just the point: serious improvements were unlikely to be made as long as peasants were regarded as not being part of the 'nation'. 'God himself has differentiated between us,' wrote a Magyar at that time, 'assigning to the peasant labour and need, to the lord, abundance and a merry life.'[33]

Nor could Hungarians expect improvements while their economy was not included as a full member of the Habsburg mercantile community. On the contrary, Hungary was exploited by the Austro-Bohemian part of the Monarchy, rather as Ireland and the American Colonies were milked in the British old colonial system. Since Hungary refused to pay her proper share of taxation (only a quarter, when in view of her size and population it should have been half), Vienna excluded her from the benefits of the Austro-Bohemian market, condemning her to remain in an underdeveloped condition in which she could never hope to produce her fair share of revenue. Tariff regulations, and the whole policy of mercantilism operated by the Council of Commerce, with its loans and other special aids to new enterprises, was biased in favour of Austro-Bohemia, where most of Maria Theresa's ministers and bureaucrats were landowners, and where, after all, the bulk of her revenues originated.

Of course, Hungarian backwardness was not solely due to Austrian policy. The Turkish occupation, the wars of liberation, the rebellions and the pacifications, must share the blame. And so must the antiquated Magyar outlook on economic activity, which left industry to the German colonists, and commerce to the Greeks and Serbs, and caused unwillingness to provide the capital necessary to drain the swamps, build the roads, and canalize and embank the rivers. In these circumstances, it was impossible to market agricultural surpluses – though these were unlikely to be great in a community which had not advanced beyond the two- and three-field rotation, or even the more primitive practice of scratching up a different patch of grassland each year. If Magyar farm produce was going to reach the market, it had to be able to walk there, and so their only appreciable trade was in cattle, horses, sheep, and pigs on the hoof.

Hungary then remained unhappily excluded from the Austro-Bohemian political and economic system, much as the Empress wanted to woo Magyar affection. She regarded them as 'fundamentally a good people with whom one can do anything if one takes them the right way'.[34] And the ones she took the right way were the magnates. There were 108 families of these, owning about a third of the land, some, like the Esterházys and the Batthyánys, being immensely wealthy. She encouraged them to build palaces in Vienna, and she gave them honours, titles, and posts in the army, the diplomatic service, the Court and government. Here they spoke, not Hungarian, but French

and German, and forgot their Magyardom in the rococo deli-
cacies of the cosmopolitan capital. They used to have their
portraits done in intimate and lifelike pastels by Angelica
Kauffman, hear operas by Gluck, listen to the Esterházy
orchestra conducted by Haydn, or attend a performance by
the child-wonder Mozart. They married into western families,
and sent their children to the Theresianum – the aristocratic
academy which Maria Theresa founded in Vienna. Nor were
the lesser nobles neglected. Every year each county sent two
noble youths to join the Royal Hungarian Bodyguard, which
she also had founded. After five years at Court, many were
seduced into a pro-Habsburg outlook; but some imbibed the
radical ideas of the Enlightenment, which on their return
home further fortified Magyar ungovernability. Acculturation
to the Habsburg way of life, then, may have softened their
rough Magyar manners, but it did not seduce them from their
ultimate loyalty to Hungary. The Austro-Hungarian dualism
was already firmly established.

Foreign Policy

In the minds of Kaunitz and Joseph, all the internal changes
so far described were designed ultimately to make larger
revenues and more powerful armies available for the pursuit of
an aggressive foreign policy. Their diplomatic and military
forays during the co-regency (1765–80) caused Maria Theresa
deep distress. Prince Albert of Saxony recorded in his *Mémoires* how Joseph's methods upset his mother, 'who could not
absolutely hide his faults from herself, [and] suffered especially to notice in him a violence and hardness of character
whose consequences she feared'.[35] Maria Theresa was out of
sympathy with the cynical statecraft of the eighteenth century,
and could not follow the slick rationalizations of self-styled
Enlightened rulers, nor help loathing what she called 'the
irreligion, the decay of morals, the jargon of the day which I
can scarcely understand'.[36] She was entirely against the moves
which led to the partition of Poland (1772). Joseph and Kaunitz
were as much to blame as Frederick II and Catherine II, if not

more. It was an Austrian step which started the avalanche. In 1769 Joseph used one of the Ancien Régime's favourite proced-ures for the conduct of international relations: archival warfare. The Austrians searched their records and dug up an old claim to the county of Zips, which they promptly annexed. By 1772 Joseph was quite clear that 'in the event of a total destruction of Poland we must get a good morsel'.[37] This morsel was Galicia. Maria Theresa opposed the policy, but had to acquiesce in the end. 'She carved territory from Poland with one hand', said the French Ambassador unfairly, 'and used her handker-chief with the other.'[38]

Two years yater she unsuccessfully opposed the policy of par-titioning Turkey, whèn Joseph annexed Bukovina as Austria's compensation for the gains Russia made at the Treaty of Kuchuk-Kainardzhi. She was similarly browbeaten into the War of the Bavarian Succession (1778–79). The idea of annex-ing Bavaria had been at least at the back of Habsburg minds for centuries, and when, late in 1777, the Elector Maximilian Joseph died without legitimate heirs, Joseph wrote to Kaunitz: 'Since we have no time for detailed discussion I am in favour of immediate occupation of Lower Bavaria. I advise you to say nothing to Her Majesty in order not to spoil to-day's cere-mony.'[39] (It was New Year's Day). Austrian troops invaded Bavaria in spite of Maria Theresa's protests. 'I am not opposed to the settlement of these affairs by negotiation,' she said, 'but never by force of arms, a method which would rightly turn everyone against us from the start.'[40] She was right. The opposition was organized by Frederick II, whose troops in-vaded Bohemia to take part in this actionless war. Austria had to abandon her Bavarian claims and be content with the face-saving tip of the Inn Quarter, a triangle of land between the ecclesiastical states of Passau and Salzburg. 'It is a trifle', wrote Joseph on inspecting the prize; 'yet it is good so far as it goes and is most conveniently situated for Upper Austria.' And, giving neat statistical form to the motives behind his foreign policy, he added: 'There are about 80,000 souls and the yield is perhaps half a million florins.'[41]

By the following November (1780) the restraining hand of

Maria Theresa was removed, for she was dead. She had been (to quote a recent historian) 'the most radiant figure in the portrait gallery of the 18th Century'.[42] She had saved the Monarchy from dissolution in its most critical hour; and, if she had failed to solve the Hungarian problem, and made few changes in Milan and Belgium, her administrative reforms in Austria-Bohemia provided solid foundations for social and economic advance which survived till 1918. She had won the crucial victory over the nobles, and had given the crown the possibility of fostering the middle and lower classes, a favour they could hardly have expected from the Estates. Near the end of her reign, Councillor von Greiner, a government financial expert, wrote: 'What found more opposition than the Haugwitz tax system? Were not all ministers, even the most experienced and intelligent, willing to stake their lives on a bet that the country would not be able to carry this exorbitant burden for six years? Now almost thirty years have passed and the country carries not only the Haugwitz contributions but nearly twice as much.'[43]

At this stage, however, Maria Theresa was old and full of misgivings about Joseph II, especially his ecclesiastical policy, which she thought displeasing to God, and his foreign policy, which reminded her too painfully of her old demon, Frederick the Great. She saw the danger to Austria's future in her son's encouragement of Russia's ambitions in Poland and the Balkans. She opposed the aggression in Bavaria, which had driven the Princes and Circles of Germany to abandon Habsburg leadership and turn to a rival power, Prussia. And she died in deep anxiety for the future of her children, especially Marie-Antoinette, the wife of the doomed King of France, and Joseph II, married to a high-minded but deductive philosophy of government which lifted him dangerously out of touch with political realities on the ground.

Austria: Joseph II, 1780–90

Joseph II

'As soon as Joseph stands alone at the rudder, a revolution will take place by which the present inhabitants will be made already unrecognizable in the next generation.'[1] So wrote Riesbeck, the French traveller in Austria during the last years of Maria Theresa. And he was right. Joseph II tried to pack into the brief decade of his reign all the blessings of centralized absolutism which the century from Louis XIV to Frederick the Great had produced, as well as other improvements which would require the French Revolution itself to carry into effect. He failed, of course, and wrote for his epitaph these words: 'Here lies a prince who despite his best intentions could realize nothing of his plans.'[2] On the other hand, he did make the next generation unrecognizable. Indeed, the fall-out from his explosive reign caused mutations in society which have affected Austrian history ever since.

Joseph II was the Enlightenment enthroned, with all its idealism and all its ingenuousness. 'Since I have ascended the throne, and wear the first diadem in the world,' he wrote to his representative in Rome in 1781, 'I have made philosophy the legislator of my empire.'[3] This philosopher-king kept himself abreast of the latest ideas of European scholarship, especially in the fields of politics and economics, and was intellectually well-endowed to master them. 'He possesses the most solid, profound and best-informed mind I ever met,' wrote Catherine the Great after entertaining him in Russia. 'To catch him out one would have to get up very early.'[4] But he proved in his life the perilous insufficiency of mere intellect in the conduct of affairs when it lacks the kind of instinct which anchored his mother so firmly in human reality. He saw himself as the incarnation of reason and virtue, selflessly burning himself out in the war against error, vice, superstition, traditionalism, and all the other enemies of human progress. On the other hand, he appeared to his subjects as a bleak, hard-driving, sharp-tongued, over-bearing know-all. Having early lost a well-loved wife and child, he was bitter and impatient, irritable and highly-strung. He was deaf to criticism of his measures, and blind to their effect on his people. So convinced was he of the correctness of his own judgement and the sincerity of his own idealism, he could not understand how his subjects could fail to appreciate that he was doing them good, even if it was against their wishes. He wrote in 1787:

Since my accession to the throne I have ever been anxious to conquer the prejudices against my station, and have taken pains to gain the confidence of my people; I have several times since given proof, that the welfare of my subjects is my passion; that to satisfy it, I shun neither labour, nor trouble, nor even vexations, and reflect well on the means which are likely to promote my views; and yet in my reforms, I everywhere find opposition from people, of whom I least expected it.[5]

Enlightened Absolutism

These reforms were a further intensification of the efforts of the previous reign. Under Maria Theresa, till 1765, changes had been tentative and pragmatic. After that date, pragmatism had been sharpened by theory. Joseph now threw pragmatism overboard and put his faith in philosophy alone. In brief, his ambition was to further extend the apparatus of centralized absolutism, and with it sweep the Monarchy clean of the diverse bric-à-brac with which the tides of history had littered it. His Enlightened bureaucrats would eliminate all the peculiarities of language, religion, local government, social class, custom and habit which no longer passed the test of reason, and equalize all in their obedience to the all-providing State. Only in this way, he was convinced, could the Austrian Monarchy exploit her vast resources to the full, and so regain her dominating position in Europe – his ultimate object. As he wrote during the morning after his indulgence in the War of the Bavarian Succession – cold-sober in his disillusionment:

I recognize above all that our situation has greatly deteriorated after the last war through the excessive burden of debt, that our provinces are impoverished, and cannot afford to maintain the present military establishment, and that only the improvement of our agriculture, industry, trade, and finance will make possible the upkeep and expansion of our military forces to meet future eventualities.[6]

Joseph had been taught by his reading of the *philosophes* and his knowledge of Austrian history that these improvements were unlikely to come about except on orders from above. Like Frederick the Great, he believed political authority was not a gift from God, but a trust from the people; that the Monarch was the first servant of the State, and that its welfare was his first duty. He deduced from such Lockeian premises a power far more absolute than Louis XIV could claim as God's representative on earth. In the seventeenth century, when the State was the Monarch, and absolute power was also personal glory, despotism was limited by the checks that even kings had to place on sheer egotism. In the eighteenth century, when the State was separated from the Monarch, and raised above him in importance, there was no theoretical limit to absolutism, for kings could do for the State what modesty would have forbidden them to do for themselves, even to the extent of breaking the moral law. There is no tyrant so oppressive as the ruler who sacrifices himself – risks, perhaps, his very salvation – in the service of his people. Joseph believed all this; and also in a further set of doctrines which buttressed absolutism. He believed in the natural law which governed human relations just as it did the physical world. A ruler who did not enforce it with absolute ruthlessness would be as absurd as an engineer who built a bridge not in accordance with the laws of physics. It was nature that was the tyrant, not the king.

Just as the Monarch obeyed the law of nature, so, thought Joseph, must his servants obey him. 'Subordination is the sole motive force in the State here,' wrote the French traveller, Riesbeck. 'I have not so far been able to detect here a spark of the Englishman's love of freedom or the feeling of honour which distinguishes our countrymen.'[7] The Austrian bureaucrats, trained in the school of the Enlightenment, were expected to give immediate effect to the thousands of long edicts which issued from Joseph's office at the average rate of two a day. In a circular of 1781, he ordered that civil servants 'must not act purely as useless copyists, not simply devote their backsides to sitting and their hands to signing for the State,' but 'must sacrifice the powers of their souls, their reason, their wills, and their whole strength to such work, and thus without considering the hours, the days, the manner, try zealously to keep it in good condition'.[8] He expected the same self-sacrifice that he himself gave to the full. 'Anyone who serves or wishes to serve the State,' went an order of 1784, 'must completely forget himself, and no secondary matters, such as his own affairs or personal diversion, should distract him from his principal occupation.'[9] Only the bracing provided by a disciplined public service, he believed, could make up for the lack of an all-Austrian patriotism – an emotion so difficult to arouse in such a diverse confederation of languages, nations, races, and creeds. 'Our Monarchy is large, complex, and made up of different lands put together,' he wrote as a youth. 'If everyone joined hands with warm hearts and good will, I could still foresee happy results, and I don't doubt that we can achieve it, if we genuinely want it, and determinedly insist upon it.'[10]

Reforms in Government

The changes he put through in the administration of Austria-Bohemia were designed to give it greater unity, uniformity, simplicity, and economy: in a word, to streamline it for its task of reshaping Austrian society. The central, provincial, and local governments were pruned of superfluous offices. Salaries were cut and higher productivity demanded. Ministers and bureaucrats were expected to take their cue from the austere Emperor himself, who drank no wine and slept on straw. In Vienna the Council of State was reduced to four members; while the Treasury was merged with the United Chancellery (as it had been in Haugwitz's original reforms). Internal affairs were thus concentrated in one supreme office, now reorganized into

thirteen departments. Similarly, at Pressburg, the Transylvanian
Chancellery was merged with that of Hungary. At provincial
level, neighbouring *Gubernia* were joined together, reducing
their total number from twelve to six. By this scheme, for example, Upper and Lower Austria were joined, as were Silesia
and Moravia, and Styria, Carinthia, and Carniola. In their turn
the provincial governments made further inroads into what was
left of the traditional institutions. From 1783 the permanent
committees of the Diets were suspended, and their work transferred to the civil service. The Diets had to remain content with
having two of their representatives sit as councillors on the
provincial *Gubernia*. Likewise, municipal self-rule, where it
existed, was eliminated, as special bureaucrats were deputed to
supervise the choice of magistrates, and inspect their work.

To ensure loyalty and efficiency, the servants of the State were
closely supervised by one another. Dossiers were kept on all
bureaucrats, recording the extent of their zeal during office
hours as well as their peccadilloes after them. On top of this,
the police were given the task of spying on the administration
at all levels, and reporting misconduct to Vienna. Originally, the
police had functioned as the long arm of the benevolent State,
their job being to protect the citizen from ill-treatment by the
traditional organs of manor, Diet, or municipality. Now, they
took on the task of protecting the State from its own servants.
By the end of the reign, however, when rebellion against
Joseph's measures was threatening everywhere, they had been
turned into a secret organization seeking out sedition wherever
it might hide. The man behind this ominous change was
Count Pergen, president of the *Gubernium* of Lower Austria,
who from 1786 onwards began to reshape the police in secret,
and to issue instructions that were not made public even to the
other ministers. In the Secret Instruction of 1786, the police
were ordered 'unobtrusively to investigate what the general
public is saying about the Emperor and his government, how
public opinion is developing in this respect, whether among
the upper or the lower classes there are any malcontents or perhaps even agitators (*Aufwickler*) coming to the fore; all of
which is to be consistently reported to headquarters according

to the prescribed procedure'.[11] In 1789 the police were with-drawn from the purview of the Court Chancellery, and set up under Pergen as an independent Ministry of Police. Thus, during the disturbances which marked the end of his reign, the Enlightened monarch was employing a department which operated outside the publicly declared laws of the realm and denied to suspects the protection of the ordinary machinery of justice.

The Church

These changes in the bureaucracy and police enabled the Emperor to manipulate Austrian society more effectively: to modernize it, to stir it into economic activity, to enrich it, to enable it to produce higher revenues. In the main, his policies towards the Church, the law, education and social welfare, the emancipation of the serfs, and the promotion of economic growth, amounted to a speeding up of trends he had initiated during the co-regency. In the first place he revolutionized religious life. The Patent of Toleration (1781) gave civil equality and freedom of worship to Lutherans, Calvinists, and Orthodox Christians, though their services had to be discreet, and their churches without steeples, bells, or porches giving on to a main street. Joseph's motives were mainly economic. 'I stand for freedom of belief,' he wrote, 'in so far as I am prepared to accept everyone's services in secular matters, regardless of denomination. Let everyone who is qualified occupy himself in agriculture or industry; I am prepared to grant the right of citizenship to anyone who is qualified, who can be of use to us, and who can further industrial activity in our country.'[12] In the same year he launched his attack on such monks and nuns who could not prove their social utility. 'It is necessary I should remove certain things out of the domain of religion which never did belong to it,' he wrote. 'As I myself detest superstition and the Sadducean doctrines, I will free my people of them; with this in view, I will dismiss the monks, I will suppress their monasteries, and will subject them to the bishops of their dioceses.'[13] All monasteries not engaged in charitable or educational work, which, as Joseph wrote, 'professing a mode of life purely contemplative, do not render any visible service or utility to the public or to their neighbours',[14] were dissolved. Their buildings were sold cheap as factories, warehouses, or residences; and in some cases their archives were sold as waste-paper. On the proceeds was founded the *Religionsfond*, with which Joseph financed his wholesale rationalization of church organization.

Bishops living abroad lost their jurisdiction, and so Passau and Salzburg no longer exercised authority in Austria. New dioceses were created at Linz, St Pölten, Laibach, Königgrätz, and Budweis. New parishes were marked out, new churches built and superfluous ones closed in a grandiose reshaping of the parish system which aimed at a situation where no one would be more than an hour's walk from church, and which gave the Austrian Church its present lineaments. In Moravia 180 new benefices with the cure of souls were founded; in Lower Austria, 263; in Hungary, over 1,000.

It would be a mistake to infer from this missionary work that Joseph II was a religious enthusiast. On the contrary, he re-garded his clergy (who were now paid by the State) less as agents for getting his subjects into heaven than as public officials charged with the duty of turning their parishioners into law-abiding, patriotic, and highly productive citizens. All the new posts were filled with clergy of a Jansenist or Enlightened turn of mind; and to ensure a good supply of these he removed their education from the institutions run by bishops and abbots, and concentrated it in state-controlled General Seminaries set up in each province. Here the ordinands, both regular and secular, were taught to value practical learning above pious ignorance, and service to society above slavery to superstition. 'Religion is the most effective instrument to further moral conditions. Secular legislation will be insufficient on several points if not supported by the bond of religion and its "punishments",' wrote Joseph von Sonnenfels. '. . . Therefrom it follows that it is the concern of the sovereign as secular authority that his subjects should be well instructed in religious matters.'[16]

From such a philosophy came Joseph's detailed interference

in worship and other aspects of religious life that earned him the sobriquet of 'my cousin the sacristan' from Frederick the Great. He cut the number of holidays, processions, and pilgrimages, as a waste of valuable man-hours. He regulated church music, limited the number of candles on the altar, controlled the dressing up of images in the side chapels. He introduced civil marriage, opened Catholic cemeteries to Protestants, Jews, and suicides; and ordered corpses to be buried in sacks in place of coffins. 'At the burial of the body', he decreed, 'no other intention can exist than to expedite its putrefaction. Nothing is less suited for this purpose than burial in coffins.'

Naturally, this meddling in ecclesiastical affairs was not taken kindly in Rome, but Joseph turned a deaf ear to papal protests. As far as the Court of Rome was concerned, he once wrote, he was prepared 'through filial obedience to ask its consent, at the start, to the arrangements that one wishes to make, but to assure it at the same time that, if it does not agree, one will not stop having carried out whatever one finds convenient for the well-being of the State'.[17] In effect, the well-being of the Josephinian State required the adoption of Louis XIV's Gallican position of 1682: that is, the lines of communication between Rome and the Austrian Church had to pass through the imperial government. The Pope, for his part, took this amiss. 'We are, Most Beloved Son in Christ, not minded to indulge with Your Majesty in the sort of quarrel which agitated the Middle Ages', he chided. '... Our spirit is far from such conflicts ... We therefore burn with desire ... to discuss with you, on a most friendly footing, as father with son, this and other subjects of innovation which had plunged us into deepest grief.'[18] He even made the journey to Vienna – the first papal feet to tread on German soil since 1414 – but to no avail.

Education

Joseph's policy of turning the Church into a department of State performing useful social functions was part of a wider plan for the conquest of the Austrian mind and its adaptation to State purposes. The system of education was another part; and

here the Emperor continued the educational policy of the previous reign, if in a more utilitarian and parsimonious manner.
Naturally, he was opposed to the traditional ideas of what
schools were for. 'Parents believe they have reached their goal
and made their son a great statesman when he takes part in the
Mass, tells his beads, makes his confession every fortnight,
reads only what the limited intellect of his priest permits', he
wrote. 'Everybody says: What a charming young man and
how well brought up! Yes, indeed, if the State were a cloister
and our neighbours were monks.'[19] He was also against knowledge for its own sake, and did not encourage pure science or
the fine arts. His ideal was a practical training without frills. He
saw to it that admissions to universities exactly fitted vacancies
in the civil service. He economized wherever possible. 'In my
view,' he said, 'the professors are too well paid.' He relegated
all universities except those of Vienna, Pest, Louvain, and
Pavia to the rank of high-school. Thus Mozart was far from
being the only victim of his cheeseparing.

Secret Police

The State's attempt at thought-control did not cease, however,
when pupils left their school or university. It was turned into a
life-long surveillance through the secret police and the censorship of literature. It must not be supposed that a free press was
part of the Enlightenment as seen by Joseph II or other Viennese intellectuals, for that would be to confuse it with liberalism. 'In regard to the *mores* as well as the religion and the
political opinions of the citizen,' wrote Sonnenfels in his
Grundsätze der Polizeiwissenschaft, 'nothing is more apt to
check vice than the curtailment of the freedom to write and to
read writings of a kind that run counter to religion, state, *mores*,
and righteous ways of thinking. It is the function of censorship
to prevent the spread of erroneous, obnoxious, and dangerous
opinions.'[20] Under the Emperor, the censorship followed the
same evolution from early liberalism to eventual reaction as
the police – as, indeed, the whole Josephinian experiment.
When he succeeded, the censorship was strict: even the papal

Index was banned, so as to prevent Austrians from learning the titles of unsuitable books. In 1781, however, the bite was taken out of the press laws as far as the Enlightenment was concerned. In these years the rules were operated so as to favour those who attacked the privileges of the nobility and clergy, for Joseph deliberately sought the co-operation of middle-class intellectuals – journalists, university lecturers, and civil servants – in his struggle with traditional institutions. Soon, the market became flooded with writings using arguments from natural law to ridicule the inequalities and injustices of Austrian society. These advanced speculations struck sympathetic chords in the hearts of a wide public; and it became a habit – indeed, an addiction from which the Austrian bourgeoisie were never to recover – to submit the Ancien Régime to scrutiny under the light of reason. 'It is his heart which ennobles a man', wrote Mozart, the victim of aristocratic snubs. 'I may not be a Count, but I have more honour within myself than many a Count.'[21] Similar thoughts crossed the minds of masses of commoners besides musicians: cobblers, upholsterers, cooks, and even peasants.

By calling in the aid of middle-class intellectuals, Joseph had unwittingly beckoned what in Austria was called the Fourth Estate into the political arena for the first time since the days of Luther. It was a dangerous proceeding, for, as his policies turned sour in the late 1780s, and he began his retreat from his earlier generous views by calling on the secret police and censorship, so did he learn that the artillery of the Enlightenment could as easily be trained on the power of kings as it could on the privileges of the nobility and clergy. Opponents of absolute rule could find plenty of ammunition in the writings of the very men whom the Emperor had preferred to high academic or State office. Karl Anton von Martini, who was Professor of Natural Law at the University of Vienna and intellectual aide to the Emperor, used to teach that a monarch derived his authority from the community, which has conferred its powers on him by a 'contract of submission'. But by so doing the people do not surrender their innate rights. He wrote:

The subjects retain their innate rights as well as those social rights which they have obtained through the contract of submission, by which each individual has promised society and society has promised each individual to promote their mutual welfare. The contract of submission does not confer on the ruler any more power than is necessary for the attainments of the social purpose. He cannot transcend this limitation of his power without violating the rights of his subjects.[22]

Thus Joseph now had two distinct enemies in the field against him, each talking the same language, but in support of quite different interests. It was a common phenomenon in Europe at the time. On the one hand were arrayed the nobility and clergy defending the institutions of the past; on the other were massing the people at last demanding a more egalitarian society in the future. Both demanded a limited monarchy, and towards the end of his reign he had to choose between them. Like other monarchs when faced with the issue, he chose tradition; for the events of 1789 in France were a terrible warning to governments which permitted free speculation. 'The unsuitable material presented in various newspapers,' reported Count Pergen in 1790, 'which are so cheap that even the lowest classes are buying them, is having a very mischievous effect on their readers, induces them to draw ominous analogies, and stirs a rebellious mood.'[23] And by the time of Joseph's death that year, the censors had once more got a stranglehold on the Austrian press.

Judicial Reform

These sinister shifts which marked the end of his reign must not be allowed to obscure the genuine attempts he made earlier to eliminate the crying injustices of Austrian society. He carried much further, for example, the attempts made in his mother's reign to improve judicial procedure and rationalize the laws. The Order of Civil Procedure (1781) greatly enlarged the powers of the State to supervise, and set aside if need be, the judgements of the traditional manor, municipal, and ecclesiastical courts, and thus to protect the many against the powerful.

Though the primary courts were left untouched, appeal courts were provided at *Kreis* and *Gubernium* level, the whole system being watched over by the Supreme Office of Justice at Vienna. High standards were demanded from the State judges, who had to pass stiff examinations. Moreover, the feudal courts had to employ properly qualified judges, or else the lord had to become qualified himself. At the same time, work continued on the Civil Code, the first volume of which came out in 1786. Criminal law and procedure were also reformed, in accordance with the latest Beccarian ideas, in the Penal Code of 1781, and the Code of Criminal Procedure of 1788. By these measures, class distinctions before the law were abolished; and state employees, clerics, and university graduates also had their special legal privileges taken away. Accused persons were given greater protection and better opportunities for appeal; and the death penalty was abolished, except in court-martial proceedings. Joseph considered death too mild a punishment, and also a waste of labour. He preferred flogging, followed by productive hard labour, such as towing ships up the Danube.

The Serfs

The protecting hand of the State also reached out to improve the legal and economic situation of the peasants. Firstly, the Patent to Abolish Serfdom (*Leibeigenschaftsaufhebungspatent*) of 1781 was issued with a preface declaring that 'it will have the most useful influence on the betterment of industry and agriculture, and that reason and humanity alike require this change'.[24] As a result of this measure serfs could marry whomever they liked without getting the lord's permission, or paying him a fine. Moreover, they could leave the manor, settle wherever they liked, and take up whatever job suited them. Secondly, the Land Purchase Patent of the same year (*Grundeinkaufungspatent*) gave government encouragement to the purchase of their strips by peasants, and legal security to those who did so. Thirdly, the Patent Concerning Subjects (*Untertanspatent*, 1781) provided effective machinery and free legal advice to enable a peasant to appeal from his lord's court to that of the

State. Fourthly, the Penal Patent (*Strafpatent*, 1781) limited the lord's right to punish his tenants. He needed government approval before he could inflict imprisonment of more than eight days, for example.

None of these reforms was so revolutionary or caused so much social upheaval as the fifth change that Joseph attempted: the abolition of the *Robot*. To begin with, he speeded up the process started by Raab, under Maria Theresa, of breaking up feudal relations on lands owned by the crown, or forfeited by the Jesuits or by dissolved monasteries, or belonging to municipal corporations. On these estates, *Robot* was abolished, and the demesne lands were divided among the peasants, who were also made full owners of the lands they cultivated. All through the 1780s, a special commission painstakingly laboured at this task, and, though hampered by the shortage of surveyors, obstructed by lay and ecclesiastical landlords, and undermined by a suspicious peasantry, they succeeded in turning thousands of serfs into freeholders or leaseholders of farms, to which they could now devote all their time and labour. To Joseph, however, this was merely a pilot scheme leading to what in his eyes was the real reform: the abolition of *Robot* on all private estates as part of a wholesale rationalization of the tax structure.

The revenues of the Austrian Monarchy were produced by a system as irrational and wasteful as in any other eighteenth-century state. It had four main faults. First, the expense of collecting revenue was extravagant out of all proportion to the amount that reached the Treasury. Second, taxes were levied roughly in inverse proportion to ability to pay. This was true of provinces as well as social groups: Hungary, for example, paid far less than her fair share, while the lower classes everywhere bore the brunt of the burden, since the nobility and clergy had long since secured exemptions. This had the result, thirdly, of discouraging economic growth; and, fourthly, of maintaining the government permanently on the brink of bankruptcy. Joseph's Physiocratic solution was a single land-tax assessed on gross income. 'It is the task of the financial administration,' he wrote in the days of the co-regency, 'to collect the taxes as cheaply, exactly and correctly as possible, without imposing excessive burdens on the lower classes. Burdens should be evenly distributed, and nobles, peasants and burghers should pay according to their means. If there are some individuals who enjoy certain privileges, they should be treated like the others; and the same is due in justice to those who bear a disproportionate burden.'[25]

In order to achieve this, means had to be measured: that is, a census of the population and register of landed property had to be made. The former, already begun under Maria Theresa, was speeded up; the latter was started in 1785, using professional surveyors reinforced by army officers, and ultimately by teams of peasants, to carry out the survey. Then, in 1789, the new law was promulgated. As its name implies, the Tax and Agrarian Regulation (*Steuer- und Urbarialregulierung*) covered taxes paid to the state and dues paid to the lord. Only a proportion of all peasants (perhaps a fifth) were involved: that is, rustical peasants paying more than two gulden a year in tax. The small rusticals, as well as the dominical peasants and all cottagers and labourers came outside its benefits. Henceforth, the peasants concerned were to secure the great advantage of paying out only thirty per cent of their gross income in taxes and dues, instead of about seventy per cent as in the past. This thirty-per cent comprised 12 2/9ths to the State and 17 7/9ths to the lord and church, the latter figure in lieu of all seigneurial obligations, including tithe and *Robot*.

This revolutionary measure was to have been imposed in November 1789; a most unfortunate moment, when the ideas of the French Revolution were already sweeping across Europe like an epidemic, when all the Emperor's other plans were failing, and when he himself had only a few months yet to live. He had the pain of seeing this promising attempt at social engineering opposed by lord and peasant alike. The nobles stonewalled on their properties, and passed remonstrances in their Diets. They could see their world collapsing in chaos; they were certain that the interference of the State between lord and peasant would make social discipline impossible. The Diet of Moravia objected to the new limitations on their right to punish peasants 'since it is certain that all classes of men and the brutal masses of peasants in particular cannot always be brought to obedience by good treatment, since it is also known that the extreme insubordination of the rural populations is provoked by the numerous formalities nowadays required, and since in a word a few blows inflicted on the spot have more effect than severer penalties that may be too delayed'.[26] On top of that, it was feared, the abolition of *Robot* could only lead to the landlords' bankruptcy. 'Our desperation will know no limits,' voted the Estates of Styria. 'Terrible evil will come over us, we shall be bereft of all we have, our property will disappear, and we shall stand before the eyes of the world as unreliable debtors.'[27]

The peasants, in their turn, were far from grateful. Those who remained outside the scope of the new law resented being left at the mercy of their lords. Those whose *Robot* and tithe were abolished objected to paying money dues instead. All were badly informed and suspicious, both of the government's intentions and of the willingness of the property-owners to carry them out. In 1789 and 1790 they began to withdraw their labour, set fire to manor-houses, assault their lords; and, as Joseph lay on his death-bed, his troops were once more on the march against his own subjects.

In forcing his people to submit to this welfare programme at the point of the sword, Joseph illustrates the ambivalence to be found at the core of the thought of the Ancien Régime, the clash of Enlightenment with absolutism. With Joseph, as with other eighteenth-century governments, it is impossible to say in what proportion concern for the people was mixed in his mind with support for the State, how far he was motivated by humanitarianism and how far by power politics. The French traveller, Riesbeck, wrote that 'he loves the people and knows their worth'.[28] And in his drive for the emancipation of the peasants, he was certainly mindful of the happiness that increased prosperity would bring them. (He would not have been a pupil of the *philosophes* otherwise.) On the other hand, he had his eyes mainly on improving their capacity to pay taxes. And the way to achieve this (as the Cameralists and Physiocrats taught) was to extract the rural masses from the tentacles of the seigneurial system and the traditional Church, give them land and the freedom to exploit it, security of tenure and confidence in the future – all guaranteed by the royal courts. Thus liberated, the peasants would expand their agricultural output as the motives of rational self-interest came into play; or, alternatively, would be free to migrate to the towns and there stimulate the expansion of industry.

The Economy

Joseph's general economic policy was a mixture of pragmatic decisions to meet particular cases and a theoretical belief in using the powers of the State to clear away any artificial obstacles to the working of the natural economic order. 'For industry, for commerce,' he wrote, 'nothing is more necessary than liberty, nothing more harmful than privileges and monopolies.'[29] In practice, this led to protective tariffs at the frontiers, and economic liberalism within. In the former case, for example, measures in 1784 prohibited the import into Austria of goods that could be produced at home. In the latter case, the gilds lost their restrictive controls over industrial progress; and large-scale industry was given its head, unfettered by State supervision or financial aid. The outcome was an impressive rise in industrial production, especially in Bohemia and the suburbs of Vienna. Other signs of economic expansion were the rise of population (exclusive of Lombardy and Belgium) from 18,700,000 in 1780 to over 21,000,000 in 1790; and the rise in revenue from under sixty-six million florins to over eighty-seven million. Or, to take perhaps the most significant statistics, the increase in the army from 108,000 to 300,000.

Lombardy

The changes so far described concern only the Austro-Bohemian territories of the Monarchy. It remains to see how successful Joseph was in imposing this revolution-from-above on his non-German lands: Lombardy, Belgium, and Hungary, all of which had been left by Maria Theresa in full enjoyment of their traditional institutions of self-government. In Lombardy power was in the hands of privileged oligarchies, such as the Council of Sixty of the city of Milan, and the Senate of the Duchy of Lombardy. Although serfdom did not exist, there were many reforms that Joseph wished to carry out, including the modernization of the Church, the reform of the law and judicial system, and, above all, the improvement of the revenue by reducing the tax-exemptions of the privileged. In these aims he had the support of the younger generation of the upper class in Milan, who believed that, in view of the deeply entrenched position of the privileged, concerned only to preserve their power, Enlightened reform could be carried out in Lombardy only by a strong Monarchy. This group included Cesare Beccaria, whose plans for the abolition of torture were blocked by the Senate of the Duchy; and the economist, Pietro Verri, who once wrote: 'Whenever old disorders have been eradicated speedily and with success, it will be seen that it was the work of a single enlightened person against many private interests.'[30] Joseph II, the single enlightened person, discovered in Lombardy, as elsewhere, that social and economic reforms were impossible without constitutional change. He therefore introduced new courts of law, divided the Duchy into new administrative districts manned by Intendants responsible to Vienna, and in 1786 abolished the heckling Senate and Council of Sixty.

Belgium

In Belgium, where the traditional machinery of government had been left to idle under Charles VI and Maria Theresa, modernization was much more difficult. The ten provinces were quite separate from one another, each governed according to its venerable constitution – such as the charter of the chief province, Brabant, known as the *Joyeuse Entrée* and granted by the duke in 1355. Within each province, the characteristic privileged groups of a bygone era kept Belgian life in a state of self-satisfied stagnation: clergy, nobility, university, town councils, gilds, and so on. And Joseph, the sole link between these separate units, could introduce no improvements without treading on the toes of hundreds of proud and recalcitrant office-holders.

Not that this deterred him: he was accustomed, after all, to taking on nobles, clergy, and burghers – and peasants as well, if need be. Legislating simply by royal decree, he began to export to Belgium the same programme of modernization that he was giving to Austria and Bohemia. He dissolved monasteries, tolerated Protestants, inspected the University of Louvain, abolished torture, attacked the gilds, and, in 1781, began the wholesale creation of a rational judicial and administrative system, which depended on Vienna and side-stepped the manors, town-councils, and provincial Estates. The aristocrats and city-fathers of Belgium, who enjoyed perhaps the lightest tax-burden in Europe (outside Poland), began to fear for their property and privileges. They refused taxes, voted remonstrances, and planned resistance; and by the autumn of 1789 Belgium was aflame with riots and demonstrations, and each province separately issued its own declaration of independence.

Hungary

In Belgium the Austrian Monarchy was somewhat taken by surprise by the violence of the revulsion; in Hungary, long experience had prepared them for the worst. So as to avoid taking the oath which recognized Hungary's independent form of government, Joseph refused the coronation ceremony, and showed what he thought of Magyar autonomy by transferring the Crown of St Stephen from Budapest to Vienna (1784). He had no intention of following the conciliatory policy of Maria Theresa, but envisaged extending to the Magyars the full Josephinian programme of modernization, if necessary using force. The Toleration Patent, the Patent to Abolish Serfdom, the reform and reorganization of the Church – all applied in Hungary. In 1784 the census began, and Joseph sent a battalion to bring the Magyar county authorities into obedience, so suspicious were they of the counting of heads. But the experience convinced the Emperor that reform was practically impossible while it depended on the *Föispáns* and the other county officers for implementation. Just as in Maria Theresa's day, they could quietly sabotage any measure they did not like at the local level. He therefore began to dismantle these traditional forms of government and to replace them with the hierarchy of authorities that the Haugwitz-Kaunitz reforms had clamped on Austria-Bohemia. In Vienna the United Hungarian-Transylvanian Chancellery became the apex of the new administrative pyramid. Hungary, Croatia, and Transylvania were joined together in one huge *Gubernium* divided into Districts. The national Diet and the county Diets were suppressed; the elected county officials lost their authority. In their place Austrian bureaucrats took charge in the new Districts (1785). The boundaries of these were marked out according to population density, and did not follow the outlines of the old counties – for Enlightened rulers cared little for historical tradition, and not much more for geography.

Thus bureaucratically armed, Joseph ordered the land surveyors to go to work (1786) and provide the evidence for a taxation system based on ability to pay. The aristocracy and nobility simmered with indignation; while further measures stoked up their fury, such as the introduction of conscription in place of the feudal levy, and the replacement of their private courts of justice with a network of new courts of first instance and courts of appeal, all run by Austrian judges and following Austrian procedure. Linguistic reform added nationalistic fuel to the flames. German replaced Latin as the language of government, and ousted Magyar as the vehicle of education. By 1789 the Emperor, whose persistence was merely stiffened by acts of defiance, had brought Hungary once more to the brink of armed revolt, this time encouraged by the diplomacy of Prussia, which had now replaced France as the sharpest thorn in the side of the Austrian Monarchy. It was, in the end, the collapse of Joseph's foreign adventures which brought these accumulated discontents to a head, and it is to these that we must now turn.

Foreign Policy

Joseph's foreign policy was characterized by territorial greed tempered by diplomatic naïvety and military incapacity: a continuation of his fumblings during his mother's reign. In support of his aggressive designs against Turkey in the Balkans, and against Prussia in Germany and Europe, he relied on the continuation of the friendship of France, and on the new alliance with Russia (1781). Both failed him. Between 1781 and 1784, he made several provocative moves against Holland in order to open the River Scheldt to shipping other than Dutch (to which it was confined by the Treaties of Westphalia, 1648). Largely through French unhelpfulness, he had to abandon the attempt. Similarly, Russian indifference and French opposition forced him to abandon his plan for exchanging Belgium for Bavaria. As in 1779, Prussia led the opposition inside Germany, and succeeded in creating a League of Princes (the *Fürstenbund*) pledged to oppose Austrian ambitions (1785). Joseph was particularly disappointed in Russian behaviour, as he had two years earlier given her great diplomatic support to secure the Crimea from Turkey (1783). But he was taken in by Catherine's bluff right to the disastrous end. She managed to convince him that Russian forces were powerful enough to defeat Turkey without Austrian help; and in 1788, in order to stop Russia grabbing all the booty, he declared war on a somewhat rejuvenated Turkey when he was not really ready. The dismal campaign of 1788 once more revealed the Emperor as a hopeless general; his bad health in 1789 fortunately allowed Field-Marshal Loudon to recover some ground. Nevertheless, when Joseph died in 1790, the war had become a tragic failure. It not only killed his extravagant foreign ambitions, however. It also compelled the abandonment of practically the whole of his internal programme.

Rebellion and Retreat

All Joseph's chickens came home to roost at once, for the years

1789 and 1790 were far from favourable years for revolutioniz-
ing an empire from above. It was a time of bad harvests and
economic depression. It was a time of conscription, billeting,
requisitioning, war taxation, belt-tightening, and military defeat.
It was, above all, a time when the events in France were em-
boldening the oppressed of Europe and unnerving all those in
authority. In consequence, Joseph's castles in the air were
demolished by himself and his successor, or blown up by his
opponents. Practically the whole of his double programme had
to be jettisoned. On the one hand, that is, the attempt to
emancipate the masses at the expense of the clergy, nobility, and
urban patricians; and, on the other, the bid to unify the diverse
and scattered peoples of the Monarchy with common and
uniform institutions, inspired by an all-Austrian patriotism.

To take the former first, it was clear by 1789 that the peasants
and burghers, whom Joseph in his Enlightenment had carried a
modest stage forward in the direction of social equality, had
advanced their expectations far beyond what he envisaged, or
what he was politically capable of achieving in the teeth of noble
opposition. In Bohemia the peasants, according to an English
observer, were 'loud in their praise of the Men of their own
rank in France'.[31] In Vienna the workers stormed the bakers'
shops, and staged an anti-war demonstration before the palace
gates. The Editor of *Wiener Zeitung* wrote in a letter: 'In
France a light is beginning to shine which will benefit the
whole of humanity. Necker has persuaded the King to leave
the throne of despotism, and to set an unprecedented example
which is of such a nature that all countries will have to follow
it sooner or later.'[32] The Tyroleans rebelled against military
conscription, and forced Joseph to cancel it. In Carinthia in
1788, and Vorarlberg and Tyrol in 1789, conservative revolts
broke out among the peasants who were shocked by Joseph's
rationalist attack on Church ceremonies, statues, and superstitions.

All sections of Austrian society were thus against him: those
he had tried to help, and those at whose expense the help had
been offered. There seemed no alternative (especially in his
weak physical condition) to accepting the advice of the great

aristocrats – and retreat. 'The nobility is justifiably dissatisfied,' wrote Count Pergen, the Minister of Police, in 1790.[33] Joseph gave the secret police the go-ahead signal; re-imposed the censorship; consulted conservative magnates instead of Enlightened civil servants; personally gave a dressing-down to some professors from the University of Vienna for teaching ideas at variance with Catholic dogma; and postponed the enforcement of his new law on taxation and *Robot*. But it was not till after his death (February, 1790) that the real retreat was conducted by his brother, Leopold II.

As he had so well been proving as Grand Duke of Tuscany, Leopold was as Enlightened as his brother. But he was also a practical politician at the same time, with a gift, which Joseph lacked, of being able to divine the amount which the desirable has to concede to the possible. Once in Vienna he cancelled the merger of administration and finance, and made the Treasury independent once more. He restored the tithes and abandoned the General Seminaries. He cancelled the single land-tax and restored the *Robot*: the peasants had to wait till 1848 for their emancipation. For their part, the nobles were deeply relieved at this frank recognition that the Monarchy could not afford to throw them to the wolves. In the Estates of Lower Austria 'tears of unlimited awe and of sublime thankfulness ran down the cheeks of the whole numerous assembly'.[34] And in case these were tears which one might doubt ever ran, they were recorded in the minutes.

The retreat was sounded also in the second campaign – the attempt to unify the Monarchy. In Lombardy Leopold restored the Senate and Council of Sixty. In Belgium he offered a full restoration of the powers of the Estates; but they, on the contrary, stuck to their independence. In Hungary Joseph ordered the return of the Crown of St Stephen, promised a Diet, and cancelled all his decrees except those granting toleration, the reorganization of the Church, and the abolition of serfdom. On the day he died, Buda was already celebrating these concessions: the crowd was busy removing German flags from public buildings and burning them in the streets. And Leopold, on his accession, ordered practically a complete return to the

pre-Josephinian situation. Spontaneously, the Diets took over
the administration again, some of them passing resolutions laced
with French Revolutionary phraseology. The Diet of Pest resolved, for example: 'By the social contract which creates the
state, sovereignty lies in the hands of the people; Mother
Nature has written this maxim in all hearts, and no right-
minded Ruler could bring it into doubt.'[35] Thus spoke the
Magyar nobility: perhaps four per cent of the population.
What the real people thought about the abandonment of
Joseph's endeavours on their behalf may be gathered from the
words of the 'Decretum of the Peasants', a document which
was distributed in central Hungary in 1790. The lords, it said,

want to consider our blood like that of dogs and pigs so as to mis-
treat, beat and kill us as they please. They say they have bought us
out of their pockets, like pigs, and can therefore kill us as pigs. They
want to force the king to yield them this power over us.... Are we
pigs? Do we not have human blood, too?...Are the armies that
faithfully serve the king not composed of our sons?...Do we not
deserve for all this that each of us should own a small piece of the
country's soil?...Let us advance ... raise up our sticks, pitchforks
and axes against the cruel, parasitic, time-stealing, country-ruining,
king-robbing lords.[36]

Conclusion

It had been one of Joseph's life purposes to create an Austria
in which such blood-curdling class-hatred would be unthinkable; but his life was too short for such an enterprise. Even as
the French Revolution broke out, he was a finished man,
plagued with varicose veins, erysipelas, weak lungs, and a bad
stomach. 'The Emperor is at death's door,' wrote Thomas Jefferson in June, 1789, 'blazing up a little, like an expiring taper, but
certainly to extinguish soon.'[37] But even if he had not died the
following year, at the early age of forty-eight, it is still difficult
to see how he could have ridden the seas that threatened to
overwhelm the Monarchy, except by heaving-to as Leopold did.
Thus his failure appears inevitable. For one thing, he used the
wrong methods. He took the second step before he had taken

the first, as Frederick the Great said. He was despotic, and had no conception of inviting the co-operation of the subjects whose good was his goal. 'It is best to inform the public of one's intentions at once, and, after deciding, to listen to nothing to the contrary and to persist inviolably in the execution of what one will have found good,' he once wrote.[38] He was also too theoretical. He climbed the steps of logical deduction till his head was in the clouds. Moreover, he underestimated the imperviousness to outside pressure of the institutions, the customs, the mentality, in which history can imperceptibly imprison a society; and overestimated the capacity of government to effect change, at least in his day. Leopold had a much more vivid perception of the sheer inertia of things as they are. 'It is useless to do people good by force,' he wrote, 'if they are not convinced of its usefulness. Through force one can estrange hearts and souls, but never change opinions, and one gains nothing of permanence by these methods.'[39]

Joseph was also ill-prepared for the contrariness of political life, for the tendency, for example, of government measures to produce the opposite result from what was planned. His subjects were so scandalized by the new burial regulations, whose only motive was public health, that he had to rescind them. 'Since they display so great an interest in their bodies even after their death, without realizing that they are then nothing but stinking cadavers,' he wrote, 'His Majesty no longer cares how they bury themselves in the future.'[40] Another case in point was his insistence on German as the language of government and education. 'Anybody can easily imagine', he wrote, 'what an advantage it will be to the general welfare when the same official language rules over the whole Empire. As a result, bonds of brotherly love will tie together all the parts of the Monarchy. The French, English, and Russians serve as a proof of this.'[41] In the event, his Germanization programme made Czechs, Magyars, and other nationalities more aware of their own languages, and contributed no little to the cultural renaissance and nationalistic revival which the subject peoples were to achieve in the following half-century. And if Joseph stimulated the nationalism which would one day break up the Monarchy

as a union of diverse peoples, he also called into life the liberalism which would finish it as an absolute form of government.
He had brought Austria out of Baroque obscurantism into progressive Enlightenment. He had introduced religious toleration,
subdued the Church, modernized education, and trained clerics
and bureaucrats imbued with his own ideals. He had abolished
serfdom, and he had given the peasants the protection of the
law, as well as the vision of an Austria made up of small
farmers working for themselves, and paying taxes according to
income. He had set the Monarchy on the road to industrialization, economic growth, and social change.

He had set Austria in motion, in other words. But, on the
other hand, he also bequeathed the means to resist change. The
army, the civil service, the clergy, the censorship, the secret
police – as well as a certain measure of all-Austrian patriotism –
made a strait-jacket which enabled Austria to survive Napoleon,
and avoid falling apart for another hundred years. And he had
created these instruments in order to bring to an end the monopoly of wealth, power, and status enjoyed by a small minority,
and to spread the benefits of modern civilization to the people
at large. Typically, for example, he opened the *Prater* and the
Augarten, hitherto aristocratic preserves, as public parks for
the people of Vienna. And on the gates of the latter he had the
following words inscribed: 'This amusement place is dedicated
to all people by their well-wisher.'[42] He undoubtedly worked
for all his people; but sheer good wishes have only a precarious
existence in public life. And in the panic of 1789 and 1790, the
nobility was able to reassert itself and force the Monarchy into
collaboration. Together they proved a formidable combination.

Britain: Mixed Monarchy

The Rise of Britain

The middle of the seventeenth century saw Britain, like France, agitated by rebellion, though much more seriously. The king, Charles I, had been executed (1649) and the country was being governed by a committee. After a decade of republican trials and errors, the Monarchy was restored (1660) to remain, though much modified, till the present day. At that stage Britain was of no account in the world, except as a client of other powers. '*England* could hardly breathe after her past ills', wrote Louis XIV in a survey of European politics (1661), 'and only tried to strengthen the government under a newly re-established king who was, moreover, well-inclined towards France.'[1] Yet when the eighteenth century closed, Britain was the greatest power in the world, and, already on the escalator of industrialization, about to become greater still. This remarkable upswing in the fortunes of Britain was due to her political evolution and economic growth, both in their separate spheres and in their interaction one upon the other. But to say that mixed monarchy and private enterprise were the basis of British power is one thing; to decide which is the chicken and which the egg is another. It is difficult to imagine one without the other; but in the interests of clarity they must be extricated one from the other.

Weakness of the State

The British form of government went off at a tangent to that of the rest of Europe in this period, but these changes cannot be easily made clear without a preliminary glance at the peculiarities of the political system which the men of 1650 inherited. Matters took the turn they did because the crown of England, in comparison with the monarchies on the Continent, was in some respects unusually weak, and in others exceptionally strong.

In the first place, the power of the crown over the citizen was limited in a number of ways by the common law. Agents of the executive could be tried in the ordinary courts of law for acts carried out in the course of their duties. The chief agents of the crown could be arraigned before the highest court of the land, Parliament, as Charles I's chief minister, Strafford, was in 1641. Citizens were protected from arbitrary power by the writ of *Habeas Corpus*, which ordered prison governors to produce the prisoner for regular trial. The king, in his turn, had methods of frustrating this procedure, and it later had to be improved by parliamentary enactment (for example, in 1679), yet in it Englishmen had a unique buckler against executive power. Similarly, in trial by jury citizens had some protection against attempts of the State to twist justice for political ends. Charles II was foiled in his legal attack on his almost revolutionary opponent, Lord Shaftesbury, by the action of the grand jury of Middlesex, which saved Shaftesbury's life by deciding that there was no case to answer against him.

These safeguards, which were embedded in the common and statute law of England, held to be superior to the crown itself, were often evaded in practical use by aggressive royal agents, and even attacked on a theoretical level by the unfortunate early Stuarts. The most serious threat to their survival was the creation of special tribunals, off-shoots of the Royal Council, such as the Star Chamber. Nevertheless, these liberties came unscathed through the power build-up of the Tudors and early Stuarts, and survived to shape the character of modern Britain. They endured partly because of the reverence which surrounded the supposedly immemorial traditions on which they were based; partly because of the tenacity with which they were defended by the common lawyers and their courts; but mainly because of the protection which they were afforded by Parliament.

The High Court of Parliament was the second of the chief sources of weakness in the English Monarchy. It consisted of the king and two Houses: the House of Lords, in which sat the peers and the bishops; and the House of Commons, in which sat the Members of Parliament. Thus, membership of the upper House was determined by inheritance or crown appointment; that of the lower by some form of election (to be described later) by the people at large. Already, by the beginning of the modern era, Parliament was the highest court of justice, and was, in addition, alone capable of changing the law or authorizing taxation. By the start of our period it was not only claiming to tell the king what ministers he ought to appoint and what measures he ought to pursue, but went so far as to levy war against Charles I, defeat him in battle and execute him. By 1650 this embodiment of the judiciary and legislature had become more than a check on the executive. It was the executive itself.

The aggressiveness of this victory appears astounding when viewed alongside the fate of the Estates in most other countries of Europe, where kings were eliminating their powers or snuffing out their very existence; or where, if this was not the case, the Estates were stagnating in passive reaction. The causes of the success of the Estates of England are too complex to be elaborated fully here. Broadly speaking, Parliament gained in power, first, because the Tudors used it to make, unmake, and remake the English Reformation; and, secondly, because the economic and intellectual changes of the sixteenth century enormously enhanced the wealth and the pretensions of the classes who sat in it. Thus Parliament's muscles developed through the exercise given it both by the king, on the one hand, and by his eventual enemies, the nobility and gentry, on the other. The Monarch used it to gain support against the Pope and other Catholic powers. The landed classes used it because modes of political action which would have been normal on the Continent (brigandage, perhaps, or warfare based on feudal services or clientage) had been rendered futile in England by the vigorous rule of the Tudors.

The Tudor period (1485–1603) in this, as in so many ways, marks a turning point in English history, when Parliament replaced the battlefield as the arena in which king and nobility settled their differences. Kings became less worried about what fighting strength their vassals could bring into the field than about what voting support their Privy Councillors could whip up in the House of Commons. If noblemen leapt into the saddle, it was not in order to take to the hills, but to canvass their part of the county. On both sides more attention was paid to polishing speeches than sharpening swords. And if they came to blows again in the Civil Wars (1642-49), that was due to unusual incompetence on the one side, extraordinary ambition on the other, and mismanagement on both: teething troubles of a new technique in politics.

The third respect in which English kings were comparatively weak in relation to their subjects was the small size of the establishment of the executive power. Few monarchies commanded a smaller armed force, headed a more tenuous bureaucracy or disposed of a poorer revenue. To a great extent the reasons were geographical. The surrounding seas had long provided excellent internal communications, resulting in early unification. The same waters protected England from foreign invasion. Unlike many a Continental state, England was thus not in constant danger of falling apart into separate provinces, or being cut in pieces by an aggressive neighbour. It was not the result of national character, nor of God 'revealing himself first to His Englishmen' (to use Milton's words). It was simply a piece of luck that England could afford the luxury of being lightly administered. While Continental States could not survive outside the iron-lung of absolute rule, Englishmen could stretch themselves under a bureaucratic framework as light as gossamer.

Not that the Tudors and early Stuarts did not try to emulate their Continental cousins. The king and his Council sent out streams of orders telling people what wages to pay their workers, what crops to grow in their fields, what prices to charge for bread, how to deal with unemployment, how to get to Heaven, what kind of hat to wear; but to little avail, for the executors of these orders were not middle-class civil servants trained in administrative techniques and imbued with the ideology of service to the State, but Lords-Lieutenant and Justices of the Peace: in other words, substantial local landowners, unpaid and unyielding. ''Tis in the power of the Gentry of England', wrote Daniel Defoe in 1703, 'to reform the whole Kingdom without either Laws, Proclamations, or Informers; and without their concurrence all the Laws, Proclamations and Declarations in the world will have no Effect; the Rigour of the Laws consists in their Executive Power.'[2] In other words, the men who ran local government were the same sort of people as sat in Parliament, and English monarchs could effect little in the teeth of their opposition. Moreover, the crown could do little to by-pass their inertia. That would have required a bureaucracy backed by troops – impossible without money, and Parliament held the purse-strings. The House of Commons would vote supplies for little except a patriotic war; and, England's geographical position being what it was, these supplies were spent mostly on sailors and ships – hardly suitable instruments for a would-be despot.

These three sources of weakness, the strength of the law, the power of Parliament, and the smallness of the establishment, had the following results. The king could achieve nothing that was against the wishes or consciences of the powerful interests in the country. When these differed from him, he could not bend them into submission, but they could frustrate his designs. And when they differed as much as they did under James I and Charles I, Civil War resulted, leading to frustration for both sides and weakness for England. On the other hand, when they agreed, as they did under the Tudors (who had the gift of nosing out the nation's aspirations) or under the Hanoverians (who, in view of the revolution of 1688, had to do what they were told, however unwillingly), then the State flourished. For it was in these periods that came into play those other ways in which the English monarchy differed from the Continental: the ways in which it was especially strong.

Strength of the State

The strength of the executive power when fully deployed derived from the unity which England early achieved as a small island. Long before our period, England was already one judicial area, with one uniform system of law. To an increasing degree she was an economic unit, and what obstacles there were to the growth of the national market were physical ones erected by nature, not customs posts set up by privileged sub-regions. Economic growth was fostered by a strong State, under what the contemporary Thomas Wilson called the 'supreme and awfull authority which the Prince hath over all subjects great and mean, noe man, not the greatest in the whole land, haveing more authority than the meanest but as he deriveth it from the Prince by Commission'.[3] Moreover, under the comparative security provided by the Tudors, during whose reign feudal banditry was at last suppressed, foreign powers successfully defied, and the Church turned into a department of State, there developed also a psychological unity – the spirit of nationalism. This emotion – now the dynamic of politics the world over – appeared early in England. Ahead of other peoples, the English set up their country as their chief object of worship, which seduced them from all other loyalties, whether earthly or heavenly, and sanctified all their deeds, whether right or wrong.

When crown and people were working in broad agreement, as they were in the sixteenth and eighteenth centuries, then nationalism gave a direction and force to England's policy abroad that were out of proportion to her small size. Englishmen were unambiguously first and foremost subjects of the crown. There was no question of other allegiances: to a feudal lord, perhaps, or a province, or a city, or even to a church. And, even in the distracted seventeenth century, the parliamentary opponents of the crown thought on nationalistic lines. Their activities were not a break-away movement, but a take-over bid; and the unity of England was one of the reasons why they succeeded where the Frondeurs failed. Nationalism aids revolutionaries as well as governments.

Seventeenth Century

The seventeenth century, however, until 1688 was primarily a period when State and society were at cross-purposes, and when the weakness of the executive was more in evidence than its strength. This is true just as much of the republic which Oliver Cromwell set up as of the Stuart Monarchy it replaced. Cromwell's weakness was that he represented only one of several groups that had opposed Charles I. Even before the fighting began in 1642 this composite opposition began to break up. As the rebel command leaned for support on groups lower and lower down the social scale, with religious and political opinions correspondingly more radical, so they shed support on their right: the moderate Anglicans, and then the Presbyterians. Ultimately, Cromwell stirred up on his left the Levellers, a movement led by John Lilburne with strong support in the City of London crowd and the army rank and file. The programme of these shopkeepers, craftsmen, and yeomen, with its demand for law reform, the abolition of tithes, and the vote for all males, except servants and paupers, was too revolutionary for the generals to stomach. 'You have no other way to deal with these men but to break them in pieces', said Cromwell. '... If you do not break them they will break you.'[4] And when he suppressed them by force, he knocked away his supports on the left and became further isolated. His opinion on the most disturbing political question of that time – what sort of Church should England have – was that of a minority; and he held power simply because he commanded the army. He believed in Independency and toleration: in a Calvinist church consisting of a very loose union of independent congregations and freedom of worship for most other Christians. As military dictator, however, he was in the contradictory position of imposing Independency by central direction and enforcing toleration by persecution. In his isolated eminence, he gradually accumulated in opposition to himself not only those who had supported Charles I, but most of those who had opposed him as well; and it was not long after his death that the Monarchy was restored by one of his generals, George Monck, in 1660.

The restored Monarchy was limited in some crucial respects. Henceforth, the royal power was subject to the law, as made by Parliament, and as judged by the common law courts – not as issuing from the royal breast and enforced in the Star Chamber. Moreover, the king now depended for most of his income on Parliamentary grants. Thus it was extremely difficult for Charles II (1660–85) and James II (1685–88) to emulate Louis XIV and create an absolutism based on a bureaucracy and an army.

But it was not impossible, and the shaping of the peculiar constitutional features which Britain possessed during the Ancien Régime was not yet inevitable. Certainly, neither of these kings took it for granted, and, by making full use of what room for manoeuvre was left for them by the Restoration Settlement, they almost succeeded in bringing Britain into line with France. Charles had the political skill to succeed, but not the industry; James had the sense of mission, but it blinded him to practical realities. Under their rule, State and society once more parted company, though they did not fly to the extremes of 1642–60. Under Charles the opposition made noisy attempts to pass the Exclusion Bill, setting aside the legitimate heir to the throne, James, Duke of York, because of his Roman Catholicism. They failed, and their leader, the Earl of Shaftesbury, had to flee abroad for his life. Under James the king twisted the law in order to pack the administration and the armed forces with his Roman Catholic followers. He blundered, and the almost universal opposition, with the help of William of Orange, forced him to abdicate in the Revolution of 1688.

The Revolution of 1688

After 1688, and for most of the Ancien Régime, violent clashes between those who ran the State and those who made the running in society no longer hindered British progress. The violence subsided at once, though the clashes continued till 1716 in the form of the fiercest party warfare and the keenest electioneering ever known in English history. Public life in these decades was shaken by the death-rattles of the old and crude methods of settling political differences, and the birth-pangs of a new and more subtle system. In the 1690s, clashes of interest, disputes over policy, and animosities between persons began to be polarized (as will be later explained) between two parties, the Whigs and the Tories, which had originally appeared on the scene during the Exclusion crisis of Charles II's reign. This split was not confined to the small world of the London politicians, but divided towns and villages throughout the land. The Triennial Act of 1694 made for more frequent elections – twelve, for example, between 1689 and 1715, a record in English history, as J. H. Plumb has shown. At the same time, for a variety of reasons, the number of voters had increased. 'An electorate, therefore,' says J. H. Plumb, 'for the first time in English history, had come into being.'[5] Until the techniques of managing this new phenomenon had been worked out, and until the Protestant Succession of the Hanoverian dynasty had been safely carried through, the political peace which the Revolution of 1688 made possible could not be fully actualized.

The political stability of the eighteenth century was brought into being, as Plumb has shown, by certain long-term 'tidal' movements in the economy, the social structure, and the general outlook of the English people; but it also depended very much on the wisdom of the ruling élite (especially Sir Robert Walpole) in exploiting the possibilities made available to them by the Revolution of 1688. The governing families of Hanoverian England were wise in the ways of political men; and their expertise consisted very much in applying to eighteenth-century politics the lessons they had learned from seventeenth-century strife. Characteristics acquired during the Civil War and the Revolution were inherited by the eighteenth century, when politicians knew in their bones how to settle political quarrels without resort to violence. This peace was also due to the arrangements made at the Revolution and their subsequent evolution, which produced constitutional machinery with enough negative feedback in it to ensure that crown and people were brought into concord. Disputes in the royal Closet, discussions in the Cabinet and debates in Parliament replaced the armed conflicts, the treason trials and the hangings of the previous era. In the mid seventeenth century, the Marquis of Newcastle, at the head of his tenants, rode out to fight in the

Civil War. In the mid eighteenth century, the Duke of New-castle, in a similar equestrian exercise, would have been leading his faithful to the hustings. Political success now depended on choosing the right issue, not the right battlefield, over which to fight.

The enactments of 1688 and succeeding years so reduced the powers of the executive that henceforth it was impossible for any king to become a tyrant whether he used the methods of Charles I or Cromwell, Charles II or James II; and whether he aimed to impose economic planning, military discipline or religious order. First, by the Bill of Rights (1689), the crown was settled on William and Mary, followed by Anne; and later on the Hanoverians, by the Act of Settlement (1701), excluding many nearer claimants because they were Roman Catholics. Thus Divine Right came to an end, and the succession to the throne now depended no longer on laws laid up in Heaven but on rules laid down in black and white. Secondly, the so-called Toleration Act ended the persecution of most religious dissenters. Thirdly, the judges were now placed out of reach of executive interference, and accused persons granted more safeguards. Fourthly, the king was forbidden to raise an army without parliamentary consent. Fifthly, the censorship of the press ended with the non-renewal of the Licensing Act. And, sixthly, Parliament became a regular and unavoidable presence on the political scene.

This last restriction on the executive (and the guarantee of the continuance of all the rest) was brought about partly by the Bill of Rights (which ordered that 'parliaments ought to be held frequently'); partly by the Triennial Act of 1694 (which ordered that no parliament and no intermission between parliaments should last longer than three years); but most of all by the post-Revolutionary methods of financing government. Only a small part of the crown's total needs (that is, the Civil List, sufficient for normal peace-time administration) was granted for life. The remainder (and this constantly increased with the wars that rarely ceased after 1689) was voted and audited by Act of Parliament. 'It was taken up as a general maxim', wrote Bishop Burnet at the time, 'that a revenue for a certain and short term was the best security that the nation could have for frequent parliaments.'[6]

Government in the Eighteenth Century

For the remainder of the Ancien Régime, then, although the king was still the head of the executive and appointed his ministers and pursued his policies, there was no escape from a meeting of Parliament at least once a year. If policy required a change in the law, only Parliament could effect that. But in the eighteenth century this was a rare requirement. Everyone agreed that the government should confine itself at home to day-to-day administrative tasks necessary to keep things ticking over. There was hardly any such thing as a 'home policy', no place for government as Continental absolute monarchies practised it, or as we conceive it today. Government for the Hanoverians was mainly a question of foreign and imperial policy; and between the English Revolution of 1688 and the French Revolution of 1789 Britain followed the most spirited and aggressive programme in her history. Here lay the importance of Parliament, which had to vote the supplies for raising the soldiers and sailors, and for subsidising Continental allies. Thus, kings from William III onwards could only appoint such men and adopt such measures as would gain a majority in the House of Commons – now the more important of the two, as it alone could initiate money bills and represented, if only to a small extent, the nation at large.

The king arrived at his decisions and issued his instructions in consultation with individual ministers in his Closet. In addition, his chief ministers, no longer the Privy Council (now grown too large) but a committee of it called the Cabinet, considered problems that the king submitted to them, and gave him their advice on them. William III, Anne, and George I in his early years often presided at Cabinet meetings; but after 1717 this ceased, and the leading minister (usually the First Lord of the Treasury) led discussions and reported results to the king. This minister ultimately came to be called the Prime Minister, though for most of the eighteenth century this was a term of abuse, smacking of Richelieu and Mazarin and all things French. The questions which the Cabinet discussed were usually such as might face some difficulty in getting through the House of Commons. In general, the Cabinet acted as a filter between king and Parliament, intermediaries whose job it was to make each side modify its proposals in the interests of harmony. Their job was least difficult (though never for a moment easy) when the king appointed men of whom Parliament approved. Such ministries were long-lasting and able to get things done, outstanding examples being Walpole's (1722-42), Pelham's (1747-54), North's (1770-82) and Pitt's (1784-1801). But if the king chose ministers who were unpopular in Parliament (as George III's first appointment, Bute, was), or if Parliament forced the king to accept men he hated (for example, the Fox-North coalition of 1783), then such ministries were short-lived, for in such periods, king and Parliament only frustrated one another. The elder Pitt's ministry, which ran the Seven Years' War, seems like an exception; but then he was exceptional, and so were the times. Unwillingly George II simply had to bow before Pitt's immense popularity and ability.

How did ministers bring Crown and Parliament into harmony? With the former, techniques depended on the wearer. William III (1689-1702) ran his own affairs. Anne (1702-14) had her views, but lacked the intellectual endowment to govern a state, or to overcome the tactics of clever politicians playing on her prejudices. George I (1714-27) and George II (1727-60) were headstrong, self-opinionated, and obstinate, but ultimately manageable, whether by cajolery, bullying, deception, or even reason. Walpole used to get Queen Caroline to plant ideas in George II's head so skilfully that the strutting little man thought they were his own. After her death (1738) he was not so easy to handle, crotchety and harried by piles as he was. In 1746 Henry Pelham had to go so far as to get his colleagues to resign in a body in order to make the king give up consulting Carteret, who was not a member of the government, and whose policies did not stand a chance of winning House of Commons approval. Young George III (1760-1820) was a more difficult problem. With the modest intellectual powers that he inherited from his parents and the obstinate will that he developed for himself, with his pathetic devotion to duty and his crippling inability to see beyond the end of his nose, he was much to blame for the political strife that marked the first half of his reign. Later, old age and madness rendered him more tractable.

Parliament

Over the post-Revolution period as a whole, the Cabinet steadily gained on the Crown. At the start, the king, William III, governed the country; at the end, the Prime Minister, William Pitt, essentially did that work. Ministerial responsibility had been achieved by 1717, that is, as Clayton Roberts has put it, 'all those laws, customs, conventions, and practices that serve to make ministers of the king rather than the king himself responsible for the acts of the government, and that serve to make those ministers accountable to Parliament rather than to the king'.[7] This double development, like so much else, depended upon the growth of the party system, and the discovery of the techniques of manipulating it by managers – or 'undertakers' as they were then called. 'In the first place', says Clayton Roberts, 'party distinctions led men to refuse to serve in a Cabinet if their opponents also sat there, a practice which forced the monarch to choose between groups of men, rather than to play them off against each other. Secondly, party loyalties made it possible for the undertakers to retain support in the House of Commons even though they accepted preferment at Court.'[8] The methods by which undertakers secured Parliamentary support will be more readily understood when a word has been said about the composition of that body. The members of the lower House were elected roughly every three years till the Septennial Act (1716), and then every six or seven, by constituencies which were either counties or boroughs. In the counties the forty-shilling freeholders had the vote; while in the boroughs there were great variations, from small towns, where the M.P. was chosen by a score or a hundred freemen, to large cities where, perhaps, the mass of the people (except paupers) had the vote. In Bury St Edmunds the thirty-seven members of the Corporation chose the members; in Nottingham, about 2,000 freemen and forty-shilling freeholders. In Boroughbridge the owners of about seventy properties held under an ancient tenure called 'burgage-tenure' took part in the election. Here the Duke of Newcastle spent much time and money buying up these properties piece by piece until he had the majority, making Boroughbridge a constituency, in effect, with one elector.

In the counties the elections were arranged by the nobility and gentry meeting in one or other of the country houses or in an inn in the local market town. Once their wishes became known, the forty-shilling freeholders knew how to cast their votes – such were the pressures that the landed classes could exert, as landlords of farmers, as employers of labour, and as customers of tradesmen, on voters not yet protected by the secret ballot. A county M.P. could behave with great independence in the House of Commons; and so, indeed, could some of the representatives of the most corrupt little boroughs. Where an M.P. had done his own bribing and was, so to speak, the owner-occupier of the seat, he was in a position to act with the utmost purity in Parliament and vote with an independence of mind denied to the nominees of a modern political party. About half the members of the lower House come into this category, and will be here henceforth referred to as the Country Gentry.

The freedom of the rest of the M.P.s was limited to a greater or lesser extent by engagements which the members had entered into, either in the constituencies during the election, or in the corridors of Westminster subsequently. To take the constituencies first, except in those boroughs ('open boroughs') where the electorate was so large as to be unmanageable, the borough constituencies were subject to the influences of the great magnates, sometimes so powerful as to amount to ownership, as the Pitts owned Old Sarum, or the Marlboroughs Woodstock, or the Duke of Newcastle what he called 'my own two boroughs': Aldborough and Boroughbridge in Yorkshire. The methods of influencing were so varied and subtle as to make modern electioneering seem simple and mechanical by comparison. In Taunton in 1781, for example, plans for winning the election included giving £500 'to encourage the further progress' of the 'newly established silk manufacture', £300 for 'preserving the woolen manufacture now on its decline in the town', twenty-nine shillings each for '250 poor persons who now have a right to vote', a public dinner after the election, and a piece of plate for the mayor – about £105.[9] In 1705 the mayor of Colchester suddenly increased the electorate and the voting strength of his own side, by swearing in a hundred outsiders as freemen, not publicly in the Town Hall, but 'in the Night-Time, in Alehouses and Taverns, without the Town Clerk'.[10] In 1721 the Earl of Bristol gave the Corporation of Bury St Edmunds 'a dinner of twenty nine dishes (warm)' which 'cost above five and twenty pounds, besides my own beef and mutton, veal and venison'.[11]

In the counties, too, electioneering had to be assiduous. The Duke of Marlborough, to please 'several freeholders in Oxfordshire' in preparation for the famous contested election there in 1754, wrote to the government for a pardon for Ann Grant, 'a poor woman in Oxford gaol under sentence of transportation for stealing a shift and an old cloak'.[12] Members who became elected under the auspices of great men such as these were usually expected to vote as their patron directed once they reached the House of Commons. In 1775, for example, the Earl of Sandwich was looking for a candidate for his borough of Huntingdon, and he made known 'the conditions on which alone I can take him by the hand, namely, the *thinking and acting as I do in all American points and supporting the present administration in their whole system*'.[13] This is the way in which leading politicians formed their parties: groups of five, ten, or twenty strong who formed the units of Hanoverian political warfare.

The most important patron was the king himself – or in other words the government of the day. In Harwich, for example, so many of the voters were employed in the customs service, the post office and the admiralty, that it was practically a government 'pocket borough'. Besides this kind of influence, the government advanced money to their supporters so that they could try their chances in non-government boroughs. Thus Lord North told George III in 1782 that he had issued £2,000 to support the Duke of Chandos and Sir Richard Worsley in Hampshire; £4,000 to 'Lord Onslow to enable him to maintain the Contest' for the county of Surrey; and that he had spent £6,000 in Bristol, where 'there were *two* elections, both contested', and £8,000 in Westminster, where 'the expense of both candidates fell on the Crown'.[14]

Members elected in these ways were thus not free agents when it came to speaking and voting in the House of Commons. And their freedom might be further restricted by a second method: the exercise of patronage at Westminster itself. They might accept a post and thus become 'placemen'. The government disposed of large numbers of 'places' in the armed forces, the Civil Service, the colonies, the Church of England, and the Royal Household. It also had lucrative contracts on offer for victualling the fleet, clothing the army, or handling the government's financial business. All of this bounty tended to have a magical effect on the political behaviour of those M.P.s who received a piece of it, either for themselves or for friends or relations.

About half the House of Commons were independent Country Gentry, then, and about half were linked up with some 'connection' or other – either with one of the small parties led by great noblemen, or with the government's own 'party', the placemen. A ministry was made up of a coalition of one or two parties. Its regular voting strength consisted of the 100 to 200 placemen, along with the supporters of the magnates who formed the coalition. The opposition was led by those magnates not in office. Their regular voting strength consisted of their own parties, as well as (for much of the time) the placemen of the Prince of Wales, who had his own small establishment, and who was usually not on speaking terms with the king. The opposition leaders were thus at a disadvantage in not having the 100 or so government placemen on their side. On the other hand, if they could not grant places and contracts, they could at least promise them if they became ministers in the future, and in this way they might collect the votes of members prepared to take a sporting chance.

The task of both ministers and opposition was to woo the independent Country Gentry, about half of whom tended to support the government of the day, while the other half consisted of nature's dissenters. Hanoverian politicians may seem corrupt to twentieth-century eyes; and we may deplore 'the great Chain of political Self-Interest', which, according to an early eighteenth-century critic, 'extended from the *lowest Cobbler* in a *Borough*, to the *King's first Minister*'.[15] Nevertheless the House of Commons was far from being corrupt enough to give Prime Ministers automatic majorities. In addition to the placemen and the parties, a Prime Minister needed the votes of a good proportion of the Country Gentry – which money could not buy. Only wise measures, put over by skilled debaters, could ensure the favour of these stiff-necked guardians of public morality, individual liberty, national prestige, the Church of England, the landed interest, and low taxation – 'men', as one of them put it in 1781, 'neither to be frowned into servility nor huzzard into faction'.[16] The most highly skilled political managers of the century were powerless without their confidence, and no one was more aware of this dependence than Walpole and North, who were in turn forced to resign by their defection in 1742 and 1782. Managing Parliament was even more difficult than managing the king, and for that reason those Prime Ministers who stayed in power for any length of time owed their success to their wisdom in following the precedent set by Sir Robert Walpole in not taking a peerage. Though the vast majority of their Cabinet colleagues sat in the House of Lords, Walpole, Pelham, North, and Pitt knew that their place of work was the front bench of the House of Commons. It was drudgery that few were fully equal to. George III himself wrote: 'That Lord North should feel a little languid on the Approach of the Meeting of Parliament is not surprising, it is far from being a pleasant Sensation even to me.'[17]

Thus the corrupt and the uncorrupt had their function to perform in eighteenth-century politics. The Country Gentry, on the one hand, prevented Parliament from becoming merely the rubber-stamp of the king and his ministers; 'influence', on the other, provided the cement which bound together the nucleus of the government side. A balance was maintained between tyranny and anarchy. The presence of the independent members saved the crown from growing out of touch with public opinion; the joint action of the bribed avoided the danger of all measures, good or bad, being obstructed by a Parliament of individualists. Moreover, Prime Ministers needed 'influence' all the more because they did not possess that great lever which their modern successors have: disciplined parties, national in scale.

Political Parties

The names 'Whig' and 'Tory' were frequently used in the eighteenth century, but mainly with the purpose, not uncommon in political nomenclature, of confusing the hearer rather than enlightening him, and of obscuring the issue rather than clarifying it. Modern readers would probably be less bamboozled if historians of the Hanoverian period stopped using these terms – just as today we would view the world more realistically if we dropped the adjectives 'left-wing' and 'right-wing'.

At the start of the period covered by this book, on the other hand, 'Whig' and 'Tory', though terms of abuse, denoted something fairly precise. The Tories were the supporters of Charles II who were whipped together by Danby in his pioneer efforts at parliamentary management; the Whigs were the diverse group that Shaftesbury drilled into a united force in the opposition. The Tories built their philosophy of Church and king on the pamphleteer Sir Robert Filmer, whose *Patriarchia, or the Natural Power of Kings asserted against the Unnatural Liberty of the People* was first published in 1679, though written before the Civil War. The Whigs propagated their views in favour of Parliament and Toleration in the pamphlets of the philosopher John Locke, whose *Two Treatises of Government* were first published after the Revolution of 1688, but were probably written as tracts in support of the Exclusion campaign (1679–81).

Under Charles II and James II, then, the ideological content in the two names was reasonably clear; but the view becomes blurred in the linguistic anarchy that set in for some years after 1688. The Revolution was the joint effort of both parties; but its success took a great deal of the wind out of both their sails. It was not easy for Tories to go on preaching Divine Hereditary Right when they had just helped to chase the rightful king across the Channel; nor was it politic for Whigs now in office to continue to proclaim the virtues of resistance. For the Whigs, who had opposed the Stuarts, now had their own William III, and some of them now supported monarchy. Some, however, remained in opposition, for they were resisters, not simply of Stuarts, but of kings in general. With them in the opposition were many of the Tories, who had now lost their legitimate monarch – but not all. Some Tories still voted with the Court, for they had backed Charles II, not because he was a Stuart, but because he was a king. During the 1690s, however, two recognizable parties emerged from the fog, as the Whigs came to represent, broadly speaking, the Court point of view, and the re-constituted Tory party began to support the interests of the Country. And the struggle between the two of them remained intense right up to 1716, while there was still a possibility of restoring the Stuarts, and politicians still had to make choices which could lead to office and power for the winners, and ruin and exile for those who backed the losers.

After the Hanoverian Succession (1714), the terms become less obscure, but also less relevant. All members of the House of Commons, except about 150 Country Gentry, called themselves 'Whigs', including the leaders of all the governments and all the oppositions. 'The chief struggle now', wrote Lord Hervey, 'lay not between the Jacobites and Hanoverians, or Tories and Whigs, but between Whigs and Whigs, who, conquerors in the common cause, were now split into civil contest among themselves, and had no considerable opponents but one another.'[18] The Whig mob which supported Shaftesbury against Charles II was very like the Tory mob which backed

Bolingbroke against Walpole, or the Patriot crowd which supported Pitt against George II, or the Radical movement which bore up Wilkes in his struggle with George III. The social position and political outlook of Hanoverian Whigs were so similar to those of the Restoration Tories, that historians of England under the Ancien Régime would probably do well to follow the advice of Bolingbroke, who wrote in 1721: 'Let the very Names of *Whig* and *Tory* be for ever buried in Oblivion.'[19]

Court and Country

A more helpful division is that between Court and Country. These two concepts form useful guidelines, especially as they lead back into the early seventeenth century and forward towards our own day. On the Court side were the king and all those who controlled the chief institutions through which the power of the State was deployed: the Royal Household, the ministries, the armed forces, the Church, the 'City'. On the Country side were the elements of society who, for one reason or another, resisted the activities of the Court: gentlemen who objected to the interference of the Court in the way they ran their local communities as Justices of the Peace; provincial business men envious of the privileges of the 'City'; dissenters from the doctrines and worship of the Church of England; and the freemen of the City of London, a powerful body of radicals almost permanently at odds with the financial magnates of the 'City', and thus usually in opposition to the Court.

The seventeenth century was a century of revolution in England because the division between state and society coincided with the division between Court and Country. In other words, the dynamic elements in society, whether economic, social or ideological, were on the side of the Country. The Civil War and the Revolution of 1688 changed the distribution of forces. The Court was much enlarged (in fact, was captured) by the leading elements in society. Thus for much of the ensuing Ancien Régime, although a Court-Country polarization persists, there is no conflict between State and society, because society's leaders are on the Court side, and thus head the institutions of the State. With the Prime Minister and the Cabinet mediating between king and Parliament, and relieving tension between them, the eighteenth century constitution ensured that the State did what society wanted. On the Country side were those who objected to the way things were going. Some were conservatives who were losing: such as Jacobites and Tories, rendered archaic by political change, or squires, yeomen and craftsmen made bankrupt by economic progress. Others resisted the Court from a radical point of view: not because they were losing, but because they had everything to gain – members of the middle and lower classes whom economic progress was calling into political life. The discontents of all the Country elements were voiced in Parliament by the Tories and the opposition Country Gentry, and fully exploited by opposition leaders such as Bolingbroke, Pulteney, the Elder Pitt, Wilkes, and Charles James Fox. All Prime Ministers had to pay careful attention to their prejudices if they wished to stay in power.

If the Country groups were a menace to governments, they were not, till the 1780s, a threat to the State. For a century after the Revolution of 1688, State and society were in tolerable harmony, and Britain exploited to the full those peculiar strengths and weaknesses mentioned at the beginning of this chapter. Government was strong abroad and weak at home. Abroad, Britain overtook Holland as the leading commercial nation and replaced France as the greatest European power. At home, with the power of the State at its minimal, society was able to enlarge the rights of the individual, and was free to perform its greatest creative act – the Industrial Revolution.

Britain: Social Evolution and World Power

Social Structure

In many respects, English society was very similar to French society already described. There was an enormous difference in wealth between the few great landlords at the top (with perhaps twenty or thirty thousand acres bringing in £20,000 or £30,000 a year), and the great mass of landless labourers at the bottom living permanently on the brink of starvation. And, as in France, the gap between these two was filled with a rich diversity of social groups, a hierarchy which stretched from the bottom to the top with barely perceptible differences between one rank and the next. And even more than in France, probably, movement up and down this scale was growing easier as economic progress loosened up the medieval order. This easier social mobility was viewed with great apprehension by many who believed, with Shakespeare, that 'degree, priority and place' were as divinely ordered as the movements of the planets in the heavens.[1] 'Take but degree away,' he wrote just before the start of this period, 'untune that string, and hark, what discord follows.'[2]

Though statistical proof is lacking, the evidence seems to show that England was a little further than France along the road to economic evolution, though still a little behind Holland. Certainly, Englishmen thought they were wealthier than Frenchmen. Gregory King, pioneer statistician, assistant to the Royal Cosmographer, then Secretary to the Commissioners of the Public Accounts, calculated the average annual income in the year 1688 to be £8 1s 4d in Holland, £7 18s in England and £6 3s in France. Nearly a century later, in 1776, Adam Smith had the same impression: that Holland, in proportion to size and population, was 'by far the richest in Europe', while England was 'perhaps the second richest'.[3] Economists of the time were quite clear about the connection between commercial development and social mobility. Charles Davenant, for example, when the Act of Union with Scotland (1707) was under discussion, was quite sure that bringing Scotland into the English trading system would give the Scots 'such great Wealth as shall exempt 'em from the bondage they now ly under to their great Lords and Heads of Clans. ... They have the Example of England before their eyes,' he added, 'where the Nobility and Gentry had almost the same power over their Tenants, as is now exercis'd in Scotland, 'till our Commons became inrich'd by foreign Traffick.'[4]

From the late Middle Ages onwards, villeinage had become copyhold, fiefs had become freehold, and the abolition of the Court of Wards in 1660 finally snuffed out knight service, liberating land from dues and services to the crown, and confirming landholders as landowners. Feudal relations were thus a thing of the past, but they were not the only medieval bonds that were looser in England than in France and elsewhere. The enclosure movement was steadily withdrawing agriculture from the dead hand of manorial custom; while the power of the gilds over commerce and industry was shrinking to a ceremonial, drained of economic reality – at a time when mercantilists such as Colbert were breathing new life into Continental gilds or creating them where they had never before existed. Moreover, since the Reformation had turned the Church into a department of state and its property into a plaything of the laity, the hold of the clergy over society was reduced to a shadow of its medieval self. 'If there were only one religion in England,' wrote Voltaire, 'one would have to fear despotism; if there were two, they would cut each other's throats; but they have thirty, and live happy and in peace.'[5] Whether he was a member of the Church of England or one of the dissenting sects the average Englishman made up his own mind instead of accepting orders from above; and a society where private judgement held sway was bound to diverge more and more from those Continental nations where the Counter-Reformation was coming to the aid of the State in renewing intellectual discipline. The contrast between England and France here is striking. From 1660 to

1689 English Dissenters were persecuted, but they were not harried out of the land. Only a few years after the Revocation of the Edict of Nantes (1685) English non-conformity was given freedom of worship by the Toleration Act (1689). It is true that for the rest of the Ancien Régime they were treated as second-class citizens and not allowed into politics; but that had the effect of focusing their talents on business, and turning them into leaders of the Industrial Revolution.

And one final respect in which discipline was much slacker in England than in France has already been stressed. State paternalism was impossible after the Civil War and the Revolution of 1688; and governments had to limit themselves to regulating external trade. Inside the tariff walls the economy was a paradise for free enterprise. Moreover, the absence of State control had a further result. In England there was no bureaucracy and army to soak up the talented members of society. Instead of looking to the royal service as the means of satisfying their aspirations, ambitious middle-class men in England, unlike their counterparts almost everywhere on the Continent, put their savings, their energies and their brains into business. Enterprise that was wasted in Europe, in war and the satisfaction of princely vanities, was more profitably devoted in England to raising the *per capita* output of worldly goods and services.

Nobility and Gentry

There were important differences, too, between the English nobility and that on the Continent. In the first place they were not cut off from the rest of society by special privileges such as being exempt from taxation, or coming under a special body of law, or having certain employments, like the upper ranks of the army, exclusively reserved for them. English landowners were a long way from enjoying the pleasures of paying no taxes. They at least paid their fair share, along with the rest of society, and far more than their share up to 1715, when the land-tax was more often than not at four shillings in the pound. The legal privileges of English peers were small by

Continental standards. The smallest tradesman could secure redress from the greatest nobleman in the land. Some French bourgeois, on hearing this from an Englishman, were scandalized. 'C'est peu de chose d'être noble chez vous!' they said, '– ce n'est pas naturel tout cela.'[6].

Even if the privileges of English peers had been greater, the effect would have been less evident than on the Continent, owing to their small numbers. Until towards the end of this period, there were under 200 peers, while the *noblesse* in France numbered over 200,000. In other words, the real social and economic equivalent of the *noblesse* was not the peerage, but the nobility and gentry together. 'Nobility,' wrote James Harrington in 1656, 'in which style ... I shall understand the *Gentry* also, as the French do by the word *Noblesse*.'[7]

Thus, no insuperable barrier separated an English lord from the rest of the nation. He was not in a closed caste, but mixed freely with the ranks below, whether he was Lord John Sackville playing cricket for Kent under the captaincy of Rumney, his head gardener, or the Duke of Bridgwater supervising the cutting of the canal from his coalmines to Manchester, or the Duke of Newcastle getting drunk with freeholders in Sussex inns in order to canvass their votes. Arthur Young noted the difference when he was entertained at the Duc de la Rochefoucauld's at La Roche-Guyon in 1788:

At an English nobleman's there would have been three or four farmers asked to meet me, who would have dined with the family amongst ladies of the first rank. I do not exaggerate when I say that I have had this at least a hundred times in the first houses of our islands. It is, however, a thing that in the present state of manners in France would not be met with from Calais to Bayonne, except by chance in the house of some great lord that had been much in England.[8]

The reason was partly that so many English noblemen were of recent creation – not of ancient race with names going back into the mists of time, but Tudor and Stuart upstarts who had managed to jump on to the right bandwagons. The Duke of

Bedford, one of the leading politicians of George III's reign and perhaps the richest landowner, was descended from a medieval trading family that supported the Tudors and received the lands of several dissolved monasteries as a reward. Created barons by Henry VIII, earls by Edward VI, and dukes by William III, they did well out of their political services; but perhaps even better out of their speculative building in Bloomsbury or their trade with China, carried on in the duke's own ships. For every Bedford that reached the top, there were dozens of others who rose only as high as the gentry, after being lawyers, or brewers, merchants, or sugar-planters. The countryside round London, especially, was littered with their country houses, but they were to be found all over the kingdom. 'It was no extraordinary thing,' Daniel Defoe was told at Bradford-on-Avon, 'to have clothiers in that country worth from ten thousand to forty thousand pounds a man, and many of the great families, who now pass for gentry in these counties, have been originally raised from, and built up by this truly noble manufacture.'[9]

This comparatively easy ascent helped to blur the distinction between the upper class and the rest, but so did the movement downwards, operating in two main ways. First, the children of peers were commoners, hardly distinguishable from the gentry; and owing to the English practice of entailing the bulk of the family property on to the eldest son, the younger sons of both nobility and gentry had to make their own way in the world. Whether they acquired benefices in the Church, commissions in the army, or were apprenticed to a profession or even a business – they mixed with, and sometimes married into, the middle classes. Secondly, the nobility and gentry engaged in commerce and industry themselves, for, according to the English system of values, there was nothing derogatory about it, as there was in France.

For many of them business was the natural corollary to exploiting their landed estates. Lord Ashburnham had an iron-foundry in Sussex, and coal and lead mines in Wales. The Earl of Shrewsbury had a blast furnace near Sheffield. The Earl of Derby had a cotton factory at Preston. The Earl of Devonshire mined copper; the Duke of Rutland, lead; the Marquis of Rockingham, coal. Sir Nigel Greasley cut a canal to take his coals to Newcastle-under-Lyme; while John Fuller, a Sussex landowner, made cannon for the crowned heads of Europe. 'A Furnace is a fickle mistress and must be honoured and her favours not to be depended on,' he wrote to the King of Naples in 1754 to explain the late delivery of some ordnance. 'I have known her produce twelve tons per week, and sometimes but nine tons, nay, sometimes but eight, the excellency of a Founder is to honour her dispositions but never to force her inclinations.'[10]

Business was nevertheless only a sideline compared with agriculture and the development of the estate. Like the French nobility (but unlike the aristocrats of eastern Europe), the English landed magnates were not agricultural entrepreneurs, directly exploiting their estates for the market, but were mainly receivers of rents. They tried to avoid having too much capital tied up in farming stock, and preferred to let their lands to farmers who could provide their own working capital. On the other hand, unlike the French, they paid little attention to getting in what remained of feudal dues from their tenants, and were much more interested in putting their relations with the farmers on to a contractual basis, leasing their lands at market rents. When times were bad and prices low, as they were during the good harvests of the 1730s and 1740s, the landlords spent money on capital projects such as drainage, marling, improved farm buildings, or enclosures, and even turned a blind eye to arrears of rent – in order not to lose their tenants. When times were good, as they were in the last decades of the century, they did the same, not simply to keep tenants, but to raise rents. Capital spent on enclosure of the open-fields and waste, together with such new roads and buildings as these occasioned, enabled rents to be raised to such a degree that they represented a return of fifteen to twenty per cent on the outlay. It was difficult to beat such an investment on the Stock Exchange. And in addition these injections of capital turned English agriculture into the envy of Europe. 'Since Lewes, we have been crossing the most beautiful countryside in Europe,' wrote the Comte de

Mirabeau on 30 August 1784, 'from the variety of the sites, and from the greenness, beauty and opulence of the landscape, the cleanliness and rural elegance of each property.'[11]

This, then, was the part played by the great landlords in the agriculture of the period. They were not agricultural tycoons, nor were they feudal seigneurs: they were good landlords to lease-hold tenants. Magnates who experimented in new techniques themselves, such as the Earls of Egremont at Petworth, the Dukes of Bedford at Woburn, the Cokes at Holkham or the Townshends at Raynham, were the exception. Generally, the advances were made by the smaller owner-occupiers and the tenant-farmers, trying out new crops, new rotations, and, most important of all, mixing stock-breeding with the cultivation of the soil. Some of these techniques were described by an observer in 1750, who recorded the great improvements he noticed in Norfolk and Suffolk 'ever since they learned the way of sowing and houghing Turnips in their open, common, sandy Fields, which has not only proved a Preparation to their succeeding crops of Barley, but such Turnip-Crops give them a vast Profit besides, by feeding their horned Beasts with them to the Degree of Fatting; so as to fit them in a compleat manner for a Smithfield market, where Thousands of them are sold in a Year, and by their cooling, Fat Dung and fertile Urine, that their Runts, Oxen or cows leave behind them in the Land, they so dress and prepare their dry husky hungry warm sandy grounds, as to cause them to retain more plentiful crops of barley of late years than they had formerly'.[12]

The nobility and gentry, then, as the owners of three-quarters of the land, the basis of England's greatest industry, employing perhaps two thirds of the population and earning two thirds of the national income, dominated the economy. Even when the share of agriculture in the economy had dropped to about a third (as it had by the end of the eighteenth century) they were still on top, for they had money invested in every kind of financial, commercial, and industrial operation, and seats on the boards of City companies, as well as on those in Bristol and Liverpool, Glasgow and Birmingham, Manchester and Leeds. More important still, their broad acres gave them social and political power. They controlled all the governing institutions, whether central or local, military or civil, spiritual or temporal, executive, legislative or judicial. Wherever one looks, it is impossible to escape them, whether it is in the Royal Household or the King's Cabinet, the House of Lords or the House of Commons, the army or the navy. They were bishops, deans, canons and chaplains; they were Lords Lieutenant, officers in the militia and Justices of the Peace, and even at times mayors of boroughs. Their subscriptions launched epic poems and translations from classics; their homes brought business to architects, sculptors and painters; their custom maintained orchestras and opera-companies; their libraries sheltered philosophers, historians and scientists. The destiny of Great Britain was in their hands, and judging by the outcome they were capable hands.

And well they knew it. Their glowing pride and thrusting confidence are evident in everything they did and wrote. 'The far greater part of the globe is overspread with barbarism or slavery,' wrote Edward Gibbon: 'in the civilized world, the most numerous class is condemned to ignorance or poverty; and the double fortune of my birth in a free and enlightened country, in an honourable and wealthy family, is the lucky chance of a unit against millions.'[13] Throughout the Ancien Régime, there was the conviction, amounting almost to a certainty, that the English gentry were an object of special concern to God, or at least to the Supreme Being. They would all have said Amen to the prayer of John Ward, M.P., who asked: 'O Lord, thou knowest I have mine estates in the City of London and likewise that I have lately purchased an estate in fee simple in the County of Essex. I beseech Thee to preserve the two counties of Middlesex and Essex from fire and earthquake. And as I have a mortgage in Hertfordshire, I beg Thee likewise to have an eye of compassion on that county. For the rest of the counties: Thou mayest deal with them as Thou art pleased.'[14]

However, fortune did not favour all the gentry equally, and so they must not be pictured as one united family. Indeed, it was the clash of interest between the successful and the unsuccessful that helped to shape the political history of the period, making and breaking ministries, overthrowing régimes and dynasties, and giving birth to fruitful political ideas. Broadly speaking, they can be divided into two groups. On the one hand, there was a small group of perhaps 1,200 nobility and wealthy gentry with incomes at the end of the eighteenth century of £3,000 a year up to about £50,000 a year. On the other, there was a larger group of perhaps 20,000 lower gentry and squires with incomes ranging from below £3,000 down to £300 a year. From the start of this period till almost the end the greater landowners were gaining land at the expense of the lesser gentry, and of the yeomen below them.

The process began with the Civil War among those Royalists who had their property sequestrated and who paid a heavy fine to get it back. (Those who had their land confiscated mostly succeeded in getting their hands on it again by 1660.) Such gentry entered our period deeply in debt, with their estates denuded, their timber sold, and generally in no fit condition to survive the economic hazards and heavy taxation of the next fifty years. They continued to feel the effects of the Civil War, as Sir John Culpepper, one of their number, expressed it, 'as men do sometimes old bruises or the sins of their youth very long after'.[15] The estate of Sir William Palmer in Bedfordshire was not finally sold up till 1713. Some lasted longer, but in their weak financial position these lesser gentry were very susceptible to the hard knocks dealt by unwise marriages, heavy gambling, improvident building, or simply incompetent management. In 1700 Sir William Chaytor, whose estate was near Darlington in Durham, was thrown into the Fleet Prison in London, along with his servant George, for debt. 'I wish thou hadst seen what a day George and I had yesterday,' he wrote to his wife from his gaol, 'he mending my old drawers and I mending my old breetches and setting buttons on my ruff coat which was almost worn to pieces in riding up.'[16] Lady Chaytor pawned all her belongings, but to no avail, and Sir William died in prison in 1721.

Misfortunes of this kind did not dispose the lesser gentry to those peers and gentlemen who prospered at their expense. The county squires particularly hated the Court and the 'City', picturing them as an unsavoury alliance for waging unnecessary wars, financed by unfair taxation, purely for the sake of lining their own pockets. Their resentments were expressed by Squire Western in *Tom Jones*: 'the lords ... I heate the very name of *themmun*'. They formed the core of the Country interest which supported Shaftesbury and the Whigs against Charles II and Danby, aided Bolingbroke and the Tories against William III and Marlborough, and urged on Pitt and the Patriots against George II and Walpole.

Till the second half of the eighteenth century, economic conditions were unkind to landowners who had nothing else to fall back on: but those who had – those who combined estate-ownership with business or politics, or both – prospered exceedingly. They belonged to the category of nobility and wealthy gentry, already mentioned, who bought up the estates of ruined squires and freeholders, as one by one they came on to the market. Great landed property gave them political power, which in its turn gave them advantages in business, and thus the wherewithal to purchase more landed property. The Earl of Nottingham made about forty or fifty thousand pounds out of three periods in office as Secretary of State between 1688 and 1716, emoluments which enabled him to buy the land and build the house at Burley at a cost of £80,000. The Duke of Chandos rebuilt his home, Cannons, as a magnificent palace, out of the profits of the office of Paymaster (1705–12). Sir Robert Walpole began a modest £2,000 a year Norfolk squire, but his twenty-one years as First Lord of the Treasury brought him incalculable profits. After his death his pictures alone were sold to Catherine II of Russia for £40,000. Henry Fox, first Lord Holland, made his fortune as Paymaster from 1757 to 1765. His two sons received a rich inheritance, even after their father's estate had paid off their debts, to the tune of about £200,000.

In 1726, according to their latest historian, 'a quarter of the peerage held government or court office, and most other places were in the hands of their relatives and dependants'.[17] In such a manner had the hard-faced men who did so well out of the

Civil War and the Restoration, the Revolution of 1688 and the Protestant Succession of 1714 consolidated their position in politics and society. True, they had risked their all at times, but their gambles had paid off. By the system of strict settlement, which practically all parents adopted in this period, the heirs became, in effect, life tenants of the property, and were prevented by legal arrangements from dispersing it. They were forced to hand it on intact to their heirs. The inheritance laws thus held estates together; while the economic forces were adding property unto those who had the most already, building acre by acre the foundations of that remarkable solidity and stability which marked English society almost to the end of the Ancien Régime.

During the same period the upper classes set the tone for the rest of society, and from them the middle and lower classes took their values. These were a gamey mixture of coarseness and refinement, debauchery and decorum, vulgarity and taste. 'I am one of that Rank of men called Country Squires,' wrote Sir George Savile, 'and can not deny but that I have a Passion for my Doggs (but neither in Kind or Degree I protest at all like That which I have for a fine Woman).'[18] Billingsgate curses and Latin tags mingled in their conversation; they grew stupefied guzzling the finest claret, and then relieved themselves in the chamberpot in the Chippendale sideboard. The obituary which appeared in the *Ipswich Journal* in 1788 of one of the gentry of Essex would probably have fitted many. 'His morals were rather of the relaxed kind,' it went, 'but as his gratifications were always manly, and even benevolent, they may certainly be excused in these licentious times.'[19]

In their manners and morals the nobility and gentry were not so very different from the French, if a little less polished. On the other hand, they set an example of liberal-mindedness and tolerance which was all their own. They were realistic and practical, and their way of governing fostered a society which was flexible without being anarchic, and a people who were ordered without being submissive. Above all, they did not recoil from commerce as though it were a nasty smell under their noses. They were not ashamed to see that their wives and daughters were taught book-keeping; and they felt no disgrace in drawing their dividends. The middle and lower classes were thus not diverted from their proper tasks by the snobberies which beset many a Continental community.

Middle Classes

Moreover, the middle-class Englishman (as has been shown) was free from a further limitation. It was not the height of his ambition to abandon business at the earliest opportunity and invest his all in a local-government post. Neither was he hamstrung at every turn in his business life by a network of regulations, whether enforced by the gilds, or by the State, or both. But these differences apart, English business and professional life was sufficiently similar to the French to make it unnecessary to dwell on it in detail here. Bristol, Liverpool, and Glasgow expanded like Nantes, Bordeaux, and Marseilles. Shipbuilding flourished, and English merchantmen rivalled the French across the Atlantic in the West Indies and mainland America, eastwards in the Indies and on the continent of India, and in the length and breadth of the Mediterranean. As in France, mercantile initiative called into life and growth a vast array of industries; and these, like the French, were run in every kind of way to be found in the history of industrial organization. Independent craftsmanship was found among the cutlers of Sheffield, or among the silversmiths, the watchmakers, and telescope manufacturers of London. The putting-out system was found everywhere, whether it was serge-making round Exeter, worsted-weaving round Norwich, or the production of coarser woollens round Halifax, or of linens and fustians round Manchester. Just as in France, the workers walked weekly into Leicester with the stockings they had knitted, or into Birmingham with the nails they had cut. And, finally, there were factory-type concentrations, whether it was at the royal arsenal at Chatham, whose building-yards, employing hundreds of men, seemed to Defoe to be 'like a well-ordered city'; or at Thomas Lombe's silk works in Derby, where, by the 1720s, machinery driven by water-power was giving employment to several hundred hands. Equally, commerce and industry, as well as agriculture, spawned their complex hierarchies of professional men; lawyers and accountants, bankers and estate-managers, doctors and surgeons, architects and painters, schoolmasters and clergy.

Much as English business resembled the French, however, there was a further difference which almost cancels out the similarities. English business was so much more successful, and occupied a proportionately bigger place in the life of the nation. France remained overwhelmingly agricultural, long after the Ancien Régime had ended, whereas in England the freeholders and tenant-farmers were turning even farming into an industry, where enclosure was the equivalent of the factory system, and where output shot up in the eighteenth century just as it did in commerce and industry. 'Our Merchants are Princes,' shouted Daniel Defoe[20]; and, on another occasion, 'the true-bred Merchant is the most intelligent Man in the World'.[21] The story of their success can only be sketched here with the help of a few statistics. In the 1660s total exports in a year were worth about four million pounds; in the 1760s they were worth well over fourteen million. In the 1660s there was an unfavourable balance of trade of about three million pounds; by the 1760s this had been turned into a favourable balance of well over three million. Not that eighteenth-century trade statistics should be taken too literally: they leave out of account invisible exports such as the foreign earnings of the growing merchant fleet, and the invisible imports of the smugglers, for example, and of the young gentlemen on the Grand Tour. In the two years after the Peace of Paris (1763) 40,000 English travellers are said to have passed through Calais. The lion's share of this commercial boom belonged to the America and West Indies trade, in which, for example, exports increased five-fold between 1700 and 1760, and imports four-fold.

A similar tale is told by the growth of British shipping – from 323,000 tons in 1702 to 496,000 tons in 1763 – and by the growth of the ports. Between 1700 and 1750 Bristol's population rose from 48,000 to 100,000, Liverpool's from 6,000 to 35,000. Similarly, industrial production rose. Exports of cloth nearly doubled between 1660 and 1700. The output of coal – used in a variety of industries from brewing to brick-making, and soap-boiling to metal-working – trebled between the 1680s and the 1780s. In every trade, entrepreneurs as bold as brass were making headway. 'I am studying to outdo all England,' wrote Sam Hill, the Yorkshire clothier.[22] 'I hope to ... ASTONISH THE WORLD ALL AT ONCE, for I hate piddleing you know,' wrote Josiah Wedgwood, the Staffordshire potter.[23] And if we had the statistics of the inventions brought in by such as these – whether in labour-saving devices, or in industrial management, or in marketing techniques – they would confirm the impression of astonishing vitality. Lacking these, we must rely on contemporary impressions. 'Few countries are equal, perhaps none excel, the British in the number of contrivances of their Machines to abridge labour', wrote the Rev. Josiah Tucker in 1757. '... at Birmingham, Wolverhampton, Sheffield and other manufacturing Places, almost every Master Manufacturer hath a new Invention of his own, and is daily improving on those of others.' He concluded that it was 'a specimen of practical mechanics scarce to be paralleled in any part of the world'.[24]

Economic Growth

How is this extraordinary upsurge of energy to be explained? A full account is beyond our capacity in the present state of knowledge. We are too ignorant both of individual psychology and social science. We cannot penetrate fully into the processes which made Britain the workshop of the world, any more than we can explain why Josiah Wedgwood should be fired with the ambition to become 'Vase Maker General to the Universe'.[25] We can only suggest a few of the factors which would form part of a full explanation, and they would include much that has been said in this chapter already. Geographically, Britain was an island, in a favourable trading position, about the right size for early unification. Politically, the Tudor and Stuart periods had produced a suitable combination of order, security and freedom, within which the socially and intellectually important elements in the nation could shake themselves free from medieval constraints. In the mid seventeenth century England climbed out of the boglands of under-development and began to coast freely over the plateau of the Age of Reason, where empiricism, utilitarianism and free-enterprise provided a motive-power such as the world had never before seen.

One significant British characteristic in the era was the propensity, not only to adopt innovations, but to go out and steal the inventions of others. The techniques of intensive farming were learned from the Dutch, as were the advanced designs in ship-building and all the subtleties of banking, stocks and shares, and high finance. The Huguenots fleeing from Louis XIV were welcomed with open arms, and so were their technical skills. Spitalfields velvets and satins certainly owed their quality to Huguenot know-how, and glass at Bristol and Stourbridge probably did likewise. Henry de Portal, whose paper-mill at Laverstoke in Hampshire included the Bank of England among its customers, was a refugee from the Dragonnades at Bordeaux; while Louis Crommelin, who established the Irish linen industry, had fled from St Quentin in Picardy. Manchester manufacturers made printed cottons in imitation of the products of India. The Lombe silk factory at Derby was based on the secrets of mechanical silk-throwing stolen in Leghorn; the 'Dutch Loom', which enabled one Lancashire weaver to produce as much ribbon as four had done before, came from Leyden. Midland iron manufacturers sent Andrew Yarranton to Saxony to discover how to make tin-plate; John Wilson, the Ainsworth textile manufacturer, spent a good deal of money in the Middle East trying to get the secrets of 'Turkey red'.

But undoubtedly the most important foreign borrowings were William III from Holland and George I from Hanover; while the chief invention of all, constitutional monarchy, was discovered at home. The British constitution had the virtue that the State could intervene or refrain from intervening as the business community desired; at the same time, the social system ensured that there was no split between the nobility and gentry who ran things, on the one hand, and the business community, on the other. From the economic point of view, they were all one: summed up in Defoe's couplet:

'Fate has but little Distinction set
Betwixt the Counter and the Coronet.'[26]

In France Versailles clashed with Paris, and both were far distant from the business centres of Nantes, Bordeaux, and Marseilles; in England the City of London was right next-door to the City of Westminster, and when London's gates were chopped up and sold as souvenirs in 1760 a genuine fusion of interests was symbolized. The English landed classes were remarkable for their ability to think of the interests of the whole nation, instead of that of the land only, or of individual provinces, as was the case elsewhere. Moreover, they were forced to consider the merchant community for less idealistic reasons. The merchants had their lobbies in Parliament, where the East India interest (say) or the West India interest could affect governmental majorities. And the government was dependent on the business community in the 'City' for raising its loans and handling its financial business.

Financial Revolution

The skill with which the leaders of society managed British policy was probably the most important ingredient in any explanation of British economic growth. Private enterprise may have provided the motive power of the economy, but the State constructed the highway on which it ran. In other words, we must not look for the blind working out of unconscious economic forces: we must pay attention to deliberate acts of government. The Industrial Revolution could not have occurred without the work of men: whether comparatively obscure, behind-the-scenes reformers like Sir George Downing, who was Secretary to the Treasury Commissioners under Charles II, or more famous statesmen like Walpole, Chatham, or Pitt. To the chief results of their work, we must now turn.

First, the statesmen carried out during the first fifty years of this period a series of financial reforms without which Britain would never have achieved world power in the eighteenth century. As a result, the 'City' became the headquarters of world finance, and British limited monarchs had far more revenue to play with than the most despotic of Continental kings. It has been calculated that by the 1780s the people of Britain were paying taxes at the rate of thirty-five shillings per head, while the French paid twenty-one shillings, the Austrians twelve shillings, the Russians six shillings, the Prussians six shillings, and the Poles one shilling.[27] British governments drew their revenue mainly from Customs, Excise, and the Land Tax; that is, the fiscal system was based broadly: on both land and business, producer and consumer. Moreover, tax farming ceased, and the Customs duties after 1671 and the Excise after 1683 were handled, like the Land Tax, by commissioners appointed by the crown. The whole fiscal system was steadily overhauled during the last decades of the seventeenth century; but the chief cause of its vigorous health was the fact that all taxes depended on Act of Parliament, that, increasingly after the Restoration, and regularly after the Revolution, they were appropriated by Parliament for specific purposes. This guarantee enabled governments to borrow in anticipation of the revenue, and thus to use savings which were mobilized by a growing banking system run by scriveners, goldsmiths, and other merchants. From 1693 the National Debt can be said to start: the formation of a perpetual debt, whose principal was not repaid but whose interest was provided from duties specifically allotted by Act of Parliament. And the creation of the Bank of England in 1694 and the re-coinage of 1696 completed what has been called a 'financial revolution'.[28]

In most Continental states, revenue was dragged with the utmost difficulty out of most unwilling subjects. British taxpayers had no qualms about showering their savings on a government which was safely under their control. No other state could so effectively mobilize its resources and bring them to bear in world affairs. It is the chief reason for the two other British successes under the Ancien Régime. It enabled Britain to sweep aside the Dutch, the Spanish, and the French, to become the chief commercial and colonial state. It gave her the strength also to defeat France and her allies time and time again, and to become the greatest world power; and that at a time when the English population was only about a third of the French.

Commercial Revolution

Secondly, then, the politicians fostered commercial growth. The attacking note was sounded after the Restoration. 'What we want,' said the Duke of Albemarle, 'is more of the trade the Dutch now have.'[29] An attempt to achieve this was made by armed aggression in the second Dutch War (1665-67); though without much success except for the capture of New Amsterdam, which had its name changed to New York. Much more effective was a series of measures known as the Navigation System, originating under the Commonwealth in the Navigation Act of 1651, and being given more teeth in, among others, the Navigation Act of 1660. By it, the chief imports had to come to England either in ships which were English-owned and three-quarters English-manned, or in ships belonging to the countries where the goods originated. These products were 'enumerated' in the statutes: naval stores from the Baltic; fruits, oils, and wines from the Mediterranean; sugar, cotton, tobacco, and dyes from the colonies. Similarly, by the Staple Act (1663), the colonies had to buy practically all their European goods in England and import them in English ships.

As these measures began to bite, the Dutch lost their old position of being the chief market for British exports, the chief source of British imports, and the chief supplier of shipping services. By 1716, for example, Exeter clothiers were selling serge direct to Spain and Germany instead of to Amsterdam middlemen; and before long English merchants were importing Russian hemp direct from Archangel instead of via Dutch intermediaries. The growth of British tonnage and port installations has already been referred to. Britain became, in other words, a world *entrepôt* with a vast fleet. The double aims of 'Profit and Power', as the rich East India merchant, Sir Josiah Child, called them in the seventeenth century, were pursued right through the eighteenth century. 'Our trade,' said Pitt who led Britain successfully through the Seven Years' War, 'depends upon a proper exertion of our naval strength: that trade and maritime force depend upon each other ... that riches, which are the true resources of the country, depend upon commerce.'[30]

This was part of the British version of mercantilism, the universal economic philosophy of the Ancien Régime throughout most of its course. And as well as fostering shipping and controlling colonial trade, governments pursued tariff policies which were similarly aimed at stimulating business activity. The goal was to secure a favourable trade balance by encouraging exports and discouraging imports; but the benefits expected from this were a good deal more subtle than a simple inflow of bullion. Tariffs were steadily modified in order to stimulate home industries and thus create employment. From the late seventeenth century onwards, and especially during Walpole's period of office (1721–42), duties were abolished on exports of English products such as manufactured goods and corn and on the import of raw materials required by British industry. Conversely, duties on the import of manufactured goods were increased, while the export of English raw materials such as wool was discouraged. And, more positively, bounties were paid to encourage the export of grain and to stimulate the home production of such manufactures as silk and sail-cloth.

It must be stressed that the English version of mercantilism did not involve the clamping on to the economy of a detailed system of tutelage as was usually the case on the Continent. In England, the State simply provided a favourable environment in which private initiative could work out its own salvation. But even this was attacked by Adam Smith (1776) and his nineteenth-century followers. Nevertheless, historians today are convinced that State action was an essential ingredient in the commercial revolution – the indispensable preliminary to the Industrial Revolution which began at the end of the century.

Imperialism and World Power

The third great achievement of successive governments from 1650 onwards was to give aid and comfort to mercantile enterprise by a series of diplomatic forays and aggressive wars. Already by the mid seventeenth century the eventual domination of world trade by Britain was being worked out in the imagination of certain writers; while the overthrow of the Stuarts produced governments more responsive to their recommendations. The first problem, as has been shown, was to oust the Dutch. 'If England were once brought to a Navigation as cheap as this Country [Holland],' wrote Downing, the architect of the Navigation System, 'good night, Amsterdam.'[31] British foreign policy later ensured that it was goodnight Madrid and goodnight Paris as well.

The Interregnum governments pointed the way. In 1650 the first Board of Trade was set up; in 1651 the Navigation Act was passed. Between 1651 and 1660 over 200 ships were added to the navy; merchant ships began to sail under protection of armed convoys; the government resumed control over the colonies across the Atlantic whose links with the home country during the Civil War had loosened; the East India Company was reconstituted and given a new charter (1657). A war with Holland (1652–54) forced her to accept the Navigation Acts; a treaty with Denmark gave English merchants access to the Baltic; a treaty with Portugal (1654) enabled the British to replace the Dutch as the carriers of the trade of the Portuguese empire; a war with Spain resulted in the annexation of Jamaica (1655).

After the Restoration (1660), the forward policy continued. New York was captured from the Dutch (1664); the territory later to become North and South Carolina was granted by Charles II to eight lord proprietors (1663); Pennsylvania was granted to William Penn (1681); the Royal West Africa Company received its charter to convey slaves across the Atlantic from bases on the west coast of Africa; the East India Company received Bombay from the king (1668) and founded Calcutta (1687). Nearer home, Scotland and Ireland were brought into subjection. The Scots gave up their own parliament for a joint Parliament of Great Britain (Treaty of Union, 1707) and were rewarded by being allowed the benefits of the Navigation system. A period of fruitful co-operation followed. To Ireland, on the other hand, the Commonwealth, the Restoration and the Revolution brought rebellion and repression, civil conflict and international war; and the ultimate clamping down on the dispossessed Irish Catholic peasantry of the rule of an absentee, English, Protestant ascendancy. Ireland was excluded from the Navigation system, paralysed economically and forcibly turned into a colonial slum.

With the Revolution of 1688 'Profit and Power' were pursued more aggressively than ever. British foreign policy was never single-minded, of course, and the maintenance of the balance of power in Europe in order to defend the Church of England and the constitutional monarchy in a dangerous world of Roman Catholic and despotic powers was the prime consideration. But British shipping – in the Mediterranean, the Baltic, and the Atlantic – was also threatened by these same powers, and so the interests of commerce were never far from the minds of Secretaries of State, especially when they defended their policies in Parliament. The wars were at first European, with colonial aggression as a side-show; but during the War of Spanish Succession (1702–13) and subsequent eighteenth-century conflicts, imperialistic advance came to be seen as the end and European battles only as the means. British gains at the Treaty of Utrecht (1713) signified the trend. Across the Atlantic, Britain gained Newfoundland and Nova Scotia in the north, and the *asiento*, the monopoly of importing slaves into the Spanish colonies, in the south. In Europe, she gained Minorca and Gibraltar, guaranteeing her naval power in the Mediterranean; and made France demolish the fortifications at Dunkirk, the port from which privateers had damaged British shipping in the Channel.

In the eighteenth century all British ministers were mindful of the importance of commerce, whether like Walpole they fostered it by maintaining peace, or like Pitt by waging war. In the War of Austrian Succession (1740–48) and the Seven Years' War (1756–63), Britain fought in America, the West Indies, Africa, India, and the Philippines (apart from Europe); and, by the Treaty of Paris (1763), had become the greatest colonial and sea-going power. So secure was British domination in America, in fact, that the colonists developed sufficient self-confidence to wish to break out of the shell of British economic and political control. Their successful War of American Independence (1776–83) lost to Britain her thirteen colonies there; but already the moves were being made to establish what later came to be called 'the second British Empire'. This consisted mainly in a shift to the east, and the gradual setting up of a world network of trading posts and naval bases. The East India Company extended its sway into India, and in 1788 established itself in addition at Penang in the Malay Peninsular. In the Pacific Captain Cook made his three voyages of exploration to Australia and New Zealand (1768–80), and in 1787 the first shipment of convicts arrived to settle New South Wales.

Such were the energetic results of the successful partnership between State and society in the Britain of the Ancien Régime. 'The splendour of this Monarchy,' wrote Jonas Hanway, 'is supported by commerce and commerce by naval strength.'[32] If further evidence is required, one has only to recall the victorious wars that Britain waged against Revolutionary and Napoleonic France in the years immediately after the period covered by this book (1793–1815). And if that is insufficient, one can point out that Britain, at the same time, was incubating two movements that would later change the world: liberal democracy and the Industrial Revolution, both of which will be referred to in the next chapter.

Conclusion

I N the realms of government and society, the principal achievements of the Ancien Régime which were of moment for the future were the bureaucratic state, the Industrial Revolution, and the beginnings of liberal democracy. Progress in these varied from state to state, and depended greatly on how far change had gone in the structure of society itself. It depended, for example, on how far Estates had been turned into classes; how far the corporative state had been turned into the nation state; how far the lumpy texture of the old order had been ground into the fine sand of mass society; how far the horizontal barriers between the different levels of the hierarchies, and the vertical barriers between regions and provinces, had been dissolved to create a community of individuals all legally equal in their relation to the State; how far social mobility had eaten away at the frontiers of privilege. The future was to be with the nation states which succeeded in making two crucial improvements. In the first place, they had to develop bureaucratic machinery capable of effectively impinging on society. And in the second place, they had to foster societies composed of politically equal citizens who had the means of effectively influencing the decisions of the State, and who, if socially arranged in classes, were nevertheless galvanized by social mobility.

Much has been said in the preceding chapters about the fortunes of the bureaucratic state, but little space has been devoted to the other major developments, industrialization and democracy. The bureaucratic state was mainly a Continental product, which Britain has had reluctantly to copy during the nineteenth and twentieth centuries. Industrialization and democracy, on the other hand, were largely pioneered in Britain before being exported the world over. All three ideally required the breakdown of the corporative ordering of society.

On the Continent the absolute monarchs, while making big in-roads on the political power of the privileged classes, were unwilling or unable to undermine their social and economic power. They all wished to increase their revenues, of course, and so they landed themselves in the paradoxical position of attempting to achieve economic growth while supporting a social hierarchy which obstructed it. The only way for them to shift the privileged groups was to invite the political co-operation of the middle and lower classes; but this was going too far for eighteenth-century monarchs, however Enlightened they were in their desire for social welfare, and however absolutist they were in their opposition to the nobility. On the Continent the breakthrough had to come violently, when the bour-geoisie, peasants, and workers forced their co-operation on Louis XVI in 1789. As J. H. Hexter has so vividly expressed it, 'the middle class in Europe did not enter the Promised Land gently and gradually, by a sort of imperceptible oozing "develop-ment". It arrived in a holocaust, spattered with its own blood and the blood of its enemies.'[1]

In England, social mobility, political equality, and industrial-ization came more peacefully, even though they owed some of their victories to the chastening effect which Parisian violence had on the privileged classes. The monarchy in England had gone through a period of modest, but sufficient, absolutism before our period began. The leaders of the hierarchical society had then succeeded in capturing and muffling the State, but not before the State, helped by economic growth, had gone far to lower the barriers within the hierarchies, and produce a society of classes with mobility between them. Thus, under the Ancien Régime, England prospered greatly. The State re-sponded effectively to the demands of society, like a man satisfyingly in tune with the drives of his unconscious. But prosperity itself proved seditious, and produced two forces – the Radical movement and the Industrial Revolution – which overthrew the Ancien Régime as effectively, if not so suddenly, as the Revolution in France.

The Radical Movement

The accelerating pace of economic development in Britain affected all classes of society, not simply the landowners and merchant houses, but all the myriad grades below: yeoman-farmers, shopkeepers, craftsmen, and labourers – all the masses whose labour produced the goods and services on which Britain's prosperity was based. Economic growth and social improvement stirred these classes into political life; and one of the chief legacies which the Ancien Régime left to later times was the radical movement, dedicated to the task of gaining political power for the common man.

We are not here concerned with the labouring poor, as they were called (a third, or perhaps half of the nation), for they were still below that level of subsistence at which political consciousness awakens. Whether they were cottagers with an acre and a cow, or squatters possessing nothing but a shack on the common, bread-winning was a full-time occupation for them, their wives and their children. Like the peasants of Picardy, they hedged and ditched for the farmers, and worked at one or other of the manufactures that produced goods by means of the putting-out system. Living on the edge of starvation as they did, they were constantly applying for Poor Law relief, though this burden on the rates was lightened every five years or so by one of those fevers which thinned the ranks of the poor. In 1736, for example, a 'Distemperature in the Air', according to Dr Deering at Nottingham 'swept away a great number (but mostly Children)'[1]; while in Yorkshire, according to Dr Hillary, 'many of the little country towns and villages were almost stripped of their poor people'.[3]

Poverty drove many on to the roads to seek work elsewhere (be it coal-mining in Newcastle or copper-mining in Cornwall), or to become thieves and vagabonds, or to fill the slums of London and the provincial cities as coal-heavers or rag-pickers, chimney-sweeps, or ballad-sellers. Johann Archenholtz, a visitor from Germany, thought it 'wonderful that the crowds of poor wretches who continually fill the streets of the metropolis, excited by the luxurious and effeminate life of the great, have not some time or another entered into a general conspiracy to plunder them'.[4] But political action was beyond their comprehension till very late in the Ancien Régime. At the time of the Civil War, for example, it was said that the mass of the people 'care not what government they live under, so as they may plough and go to market'.[5] Later, John Locke observed that the labourer's share of the national income 'being seldom more than a bare subsistence, never allows that body of men time or opportunity to raise their thoughts above that, or struggle with the richer for theirs (as one common interest) unless when some common and great distress, uniting them in one universal ferment, makes them forget respect, and emboldens them to carve to their wants with armed force'.[6] In other words, the lower classes' nearest approach to political action was rioting over some particular wrong: over the wages of coal-heavers at the London docks, or over the introduction of machinery in industry or enclosure in agriculture, or over toll gates or Methodist preachers, or over the price of mackerel in Norwich or the price of bread anywhere.

Political activity, then, was limited to the upper half of the population, and even there it was generally confined to nobility and gentry and middle classes. The way in which they divided up the political arena between them into two parts, Court and Country, has already been touched on. But right at the beginning of this period and right at the end, the Country interest brought into violent political life another stratum of society which may be called for convenience' sake the 'lower middle classes' – a layer extending from impoverished country squires and modest wholesale merchants down through small freehold farmers to copyholders, shopkeepers, and craftsmen, as well as their attendant cohorts of lawyers, clergy, and so on. The thoughts and feelings of these lowly people are rarely heard 'live' by the historian, for, except for these two occasions, the noise made by the upper classes is too deafening.

The first occasion was the Civil War, when, as is the way with revolutions, the political centre of gravity moved gradually to the left, till Cromwell was relying for support on this stratum of society, whether they were the rank and file of the New

Model Army, or the apprentices and tradesmen of the City, or members of extremist Protestant congregations. Until they were forcibly suppressed, these groups formed a hot-house of political and social thought. Practically every reform that has been tried in subsequent European history was mooted by one or other of these idealists: the democratization of the Church, freedom of speech, freedom of the press, aid to widows and orphans, law reforms, prison reforms, the communal ownership of property. For a time they were organized into a political force by John Lilburne, who led the Levellers, a party embracing both the City radicals and the Army rank and file. The way to Utopia was to be via Parliamentary reform, as outlined in their manifesto *The Agreement of the People*, which demanded biennial elections, equal electoral districts, and the extension of the franchise to all males, except wage-earners and paupers (that is, except the bottom half of the nation mentioned above). They debated their proposals with Cromwell and his generals at Putney in 1647. 'I think', said Colonel Rainborough, 'that the poorest he that is in England hath a life to live, as the greatest he; and therefore truly, sir, I think it's clear, that every man that is to live under a government ought first by his own consent to put himself under that government.'[7]

Such radicalism was too extreme for Cromwell, and when, after the execution of the king (1649), the Levellers renewed their agitation, he decided to suppress them. 'If you do not break them,' he said, 'they will break you.'[8] Like the Frondeurs in Paris, the English upper classes learned their lesson: that it was a highly dangerous game to allow mechanics and husbandmen to intervene in their internal conflicts. After the Restoration, with the armies disbanded and the Dissenting congregations persecuted, the lower middle classes had few opportunities for political expression, except as clients of the great. From time to time they were roused into action by politicians in support of the Country interest. They rioted during elections now and then, in boroughs with a wide suffrage; but their main field of action was the City of London mob. Here, the radicals supported leaders of the opposition in Parliament, such as Shaftesbury under Charles II, or Bolingbroke and then Pitt under the first two Georges. It is not until the first twenty years of George III's reign that we find them going into action once again on their own account.

This second period of radical agitation was connected with another civil war: the revolt of the American Colonies. The accession of George III (1760) brought to the throne a young man who has aptly been described as a 'conscientious bull in a china shop'. Though he had no intention of overturning the constitution and becoming a dictator, his more active intervention in the choice of ministers and the direction of policy was a spanner in the works of that political management that had operated so smoothly under Walpole, Henry Pelham, and the Duke of Newcastle. Inadequate ministers were appointed who pursued calamitous policies just at a time when problems were unusually acute, with unrest in England, Ireland and America stirring in the aftermath of the Seven Years' War. The ensuing crisis was so profound that the nature of the Country opposition changed, and with it the nature of British politics. The radical elements ceased to be deferential clients of the Country leaders. Instead of trailing in the rear of the movement, they advanced to its head; with the result that the Country interest ceased to be backward-looking, stationary and suspicious of change, and became forward-looking, progressive and clamant for reform. One of the most dynamic forces in subsequent British politics, the Radical movement, was indestructibly created.

As in France, Austria, and elsewhere, the opposition to the régime always consisted of conservative and radical elements. Before 1688 and after 1780, the radical side predominated; but for most of the Ancien Régime the Country party was reactionary. The stability of this hundred years, as has been shown, was due to the fact that the dynamic elements in society controlled the state. The static elements thus constituted the opposition; and typical Country attitudes were to be against centralized government in Whitehall and high finance in the City; to oppose Continental entanglements, standing armies, and high taxation. They felt that the only way to ensure that the Court pursued the real interests of the nation was to bring it more firmly under the control of the nations' representatives: that is, to expel all placemen from Parliament, to abolish waste in high places, to eliminate corruption from government departments, to have more frequent elections, to give more weight in Parliament to the counties, where the unsullied Country Gentry predominated. 'The knights of the shire', as Chatham put it in 1770, 'approach nearest to the constitutional representation of the country, because they represent the soil.'[9] The Country Gentlemen wished to break the monopoly that the great aristocrats had achieved in politics; and here they had full support from the middle ranks of business in the City of London. 'As to your nobility', said William Beckford, Alderman and Member of Parliament, in 1761, 'about 200 men of quality, what are they to the body of the nation? Why, Sir, they are subalterns.... They receive more from the public than they pay to it.'[10]

Such were the Country views of gentry and merchants as they joined hands with freeholders and craftsmen to oppose the governments of George III during the critical years which began in the middle 1760s. Few of them intended to produce what had ultimately emerged by the middle 1780s, when the crisis for the time being was over: the Radical movement, dedicated to parliamentary reform. What led to the change was the realization that George III and his ministers not only made a series of disastrous mistakes, but were also supported in them by steady parliamentary majorities. Corruption had gone too far for Country medicine: only Radical surgery could save the body politic.

George III, on coming to the throne, replaced the national hero, Pitt, by a Scottish favourite, Bute, negotiated the unpopular Treaty of Paris (1763), and arrested John Wilkes, an unscrupulous demagogue on the make, for criticisms published in his periodical, the *North Briton* (1763). The government's subsequent persecution of Wilkes smacked sufficiently of extraordinary, un-British, even illegal, use of the executive arm, that the opposition grandees could not resist the temptation to use Wilkes as a stick with which to beat the government – helping him at the same time to project himself as a hero to the London mob. In 1768 and 1769, government and Parliament raised popular anger to a new pitch by expelling Wilkes three times from the House of Commons, even though each time he had been elected by a majority of the voters in the County of Middlesex. The 1770s saw the multifarious enemies of George III and his men sharpening their polemical weapons for a full-scale attack upon the established order of things.

They were assisted by the Irish in their revolt against British mercantile regulations which broke out at this time. Henry Grattan, their leader, reminded his compatriots in 1779 of the 'right vested in the subject to resist by force of arms, notwithstanding their oath of allegiance, any authority attempting to impose acts of power as laws, whether that authority be one man or a host, the second James or the British Parliament'.[11] But more than this, they were inspired by the American Declaration of Independence (1776) and its successful defence on the field of battle (1776–83). English radicals looked on the American rebels as allies in a common struggle. 'I do not like this War', wrote Richard Hayes, a yeoman farmer of Kent in his diary. 'This unnatural War', he called it, 'against our best allies or friends the Americans.'[12]

By this time, the politicians in the opposition in Parliament had lost control of the movement, for the fiery spirits were inclined to view the Rockingham Whigs, and other opposition magnates, as little better than the men on George III's side. Ministers were not the only ones who were devotees to corrupt ways. After all, members of the Marquess of Rockingham's group were direct descendants of the supporters of Sir Robert Walpole, who was regarded at the time as having practically invented corruption. 'The R. party', wrote the reforming Reverend William Mason, '(who were brought up under Mr Pelham, who was a sort of usher in the Orford school, and taught the same grammar, and whom the Duke of Newcastle followed as far as he was able to spell) are precisely of the same opinion. They have shewn it in all their manoeuvres concerning our association, and have, by so doing, lost every shadow of interest which they had in this country.'[13] In the Association Movement (1779–80), the last and most serious outbreak of English Radical activity in the period covered by this book, the politicians only tagged on behind a bandwagon driven by extra-parliamentary committees. These were led in London by supporters of John Wilkes, and in the provinces by the gentlemen and freeholders of Yorkshire organized by the Reverend Christopher Wyvill.

Principle and expediency formed a partnership in Wyvill and Wilkes. Wyvill was an idealist who served the Radical cause 'from a detestation of corruption, that execrable principle of government; from indignation at direct and open invasions of our rights; and from an honest zeal to defend public liberty', as he put it.[14] Wilkes roused the masses in order to raise the wind. 'I owe money in France,' he had written in 1768, 'am an outlaw in England, hated by the King, the Parliament, and the bench of bishops.... I must raise a dust or starve in gaol.'[15] Between them, they inaugurated a new era in British politics, at the end of which the power to appoint ministers had been stripped from the Monarchy and given, not to the nobility and gentry, but to the people at large. In 1780, the peak year of agitation, fresh political demands were urged and new political methods adopted, both of which were to become everyday affairs in the nineteenth century. In March deputies from twelve counties and four towns formed the Plan of Association to campaign for 'economical reform', the addition of a hundred county members to Parliament, and annual elections. In April the House of Commons passed Dunning's famous, if at that time innocuous, resolution, that 'the influence of the crown has increased, is increasing, and ought to be diminished'. In the country at large, new techniques of agitation were employed: public meetings were held, resolutions passed, and petitions sent; pamphlets were distributed, and pledges were demanded from parliamentary candidates; political Clubs and Corresponding Societies were formed. In other words, a nationwide, extra-parliamentary campaign was waged among the electorate and the general public beyond that. It was a model for the future.

By the summer of 1780, however, the peak of enthusiasm was passed. Country gentry began to have second thoughts when London Radicals moved further to the left, and campaigned for universal male suffrage, election by ballot, and so on. And the heart went out of them when a drunken mob led by an anti-Catholic fanatic, Lord George Gordon, pillaged their way through London for several days until they were dispersed by the soldiery. Reforming fervour cooled in 1782, when North resigned, and 1783, when the American War came to an end. The *coup de grâce* was given by the outbreak of the French Revolution, after which reform seemed not only like treason against the crown, but also disloyalty to the nation. This period ends with the radical leaders in gaol; but radical ideals were less easy to suppress. As Charles James Fox had said in 1783: 'The reform if ever it is effected must be the result of the call of the people; and whenever the voice of the people on the subject is declared, it must prevail.'[16]

The Industrial Revolution

'I could write you volumes', said Thomas Jefferson in a letter home from England towards the end of the Ancien Régime, 'on the improvements which I find made, and making here, in the arts. One deserves particular notice ... the application of steam as an agent for working grist mills.'[17] He was describing the beginnings of the Industrial Revolution, one of the two chief events which ended the period covered by this book. What began in Britain in the last two decades of the eighteenth century was as revolutionary as the events that Jefferson also witnessed in France in 1789. For the first time it became possible to raise mankind above the precarious subsistence level which the mass of men had endured for the whole of human history. It was as if in Britain a few men had managed to scale a cliff on to a new level of possibilities from which they could never be dislodged. A new epoch in human life opened as the methods were found of rapidly improving the material conditions of life – or, as economists put it, of creating sustained increases in *per capita* real income.

The reasons why the Industrial Revolution took place at all, and why it occurred first in Britain, are the subject of a continuing debate. The explanation may be that it is a national

characteristic of the British to be specially gifted in this direction. Or, perhaps, that industrialization is a natural stage in
economic evolution, and that what we should look for are, not
its causes, but the obstacles that had been hitherto holding it
back, and the reasons why they were now at last removed. There
are other possibilities, equally difficult to prove: that, for
example, one new factor (such as cheap money) set things in
motion; or, perhaps, that a unique, simultaneous coincidence
of a lot of old factors did the trick. What seems beyond doubt
is that an increasing pressure of demand for increased output
built up in eighteenth-century Europe, that it pressed more
heavily on the more advanced economies, and that, of these,
Britain was the most responsive to it, and was also in a situation where the only possible way of responding was to concentrate production in factories using machinery – since any
expansion of the existing methods of production was no longer
possible.

This increase in demand was brought about in several ways.
Firstly, in Europe itself, there was a rise in population, felt
most strongly in Britain, where the rate of increase was highest.
Europe also experienced improved harvests, increased urbani-
zation and a generally rising real income per head in the second
half of the eighteenth century. Here again Britain fared better,
and most European travellers felt that the standard of life of the
poorest classes was higher in England than elsewhere. The
economic consequences of this were clear to the much-travelled
Arthur Young, who recorded of the Dordogne area in France,
for example, that 'all the country girls and women, are without
shoes or stockings; and the ploughmen at their work have
neither sabots nor feet to their stockings. This is a poverty that
strikes at the root of national prosperity; a large consumption
among the poor being of more consequence than among the
rich.' Cottages with no glass to the windows made him ask:
'Can a country be likely to thrive where the great object is to
spare manufactures?'[18]

Another cause of this growing pressure of demand in Europe
was the emergence of the European states, with their growing
bureaucracies and police-forces creating law and order over

greater areas, and their development of land and water transport, steadily widening the market and reducing costs. But here again, Britain was in a favoured position, geographical endowment and political advance having given her economic unity far beyond the Continent, where internal tariffs and political barriers still hampered the circulation of goods.

In the second place, there was a steadily increasing demand from outside Europe, as America, Africa, and Asia were progressively settled and exploited. Here again Britain felt the pressure most. A century of aggressive tariff and naval policies had enabled her to out-trade the Dutch, the Spanish, and the French in the world's markets. This evolution in maritime trade, and the accompanying elaboration of finance and credit institutions, gave Britain more exposed nerve-ends in more parts of the world than any of her nearest rivals, as well as a swifter responsiveness to the incoming signals.

Moreover, the type of goods which the factories and machines were created to make were just those whose demand was felt most strongly in Britain; that is to say, moderately cheap, mass-produced, standardized articles. In traditional societies the demand is either for luxury goods made by highly skilled artists for the aristocracy, or for the immemorial produce of village craftsmen for the peasants. Thus, an increase in demand for violins, say, at the court of a German princeling, or for the various styles of peasant costume that differed from district to district, say, in Brittany, was hardly likely to call factories into existence. Western European merchants, on the other hand, trading in the rest of the world, required quantity not quality: masses of cheap printed cottons or stamped metal products. This kind of product was also what was in demand in England. There, the social structure had evolved furthest beyond that of the traditional society, and the diverse social ranks that filled the gap between noble and peasant produced a pattern of consumption that encouraged the making of everyday goods on a mass-scale: 'useful and necessary household Goods', as Defoe put it in 1728. He was well aware that the mass of the people were 'the Life of our whole Commerce, and all by their Multitude: Their Numbers are not Hundreds or Thousands, or

Hundreds of Thousands, but Millions: 'tis by their Multitude, I say, that all the Wheels of Trade are set on Foot'.[19]

The pressure of the European and the extra-European demand was felt in all the advanced economies of Western Europe, in France, the Netherlands, parts of Germany, but most of all in Britain; and Britain was the only economy to respond to it by initiating the Industrial Revolution. In other words, Britain, in the first place, was not able to supply the increasing demand by expanding the traditional modes of production. Her only alternative was the use of machines in factories. And, in the second place, Britain was able to adopt this revolutionary alternative, for reasons which will be shortly mentioned.

Firstly, then, Britain could not expand the putting-out system. On the Continent, there were regions as yet unindustrialized, containing reserves of peasant labour not hitherto tapped by manufacturers. By comparison, Britain had already run dry, and there were complaints of a labour shortage all through the eighteenth century. Nor could employers get more work out of their existing labour-force by offering financial incentives. The modern worker as we know him (or, perhaps as we used to know him), psychologically conditioned to respond with harder work or longer hours to offers of increased earnings, and to fit in, in other ways as well, with the laws of economics, had not yet been created under the Ancien Régime. British workers in that period opted for leisure once they had earned their keep; and, if four working days a week could achieve this, then they would spend the other three in the tavern. If an employer raised their piece-rates, their output would fall, for they would then be able to afford an even longer week-end. 'When wages are good', wrote Defoe, 'they won't work any more than from hand to mouth: or if they do work they spend it in riot and luxury.'[20] The consequence was that British employers badly needed machines to make up for the shortage of labour, and factories where the labour-force could be disciplined, or, at least, the juvenile part of it.

Thus, Britain could respond to the pressure of rising demand only by recourse to revolutionary methods; and we must now, secondly, examine the circumstances which made her able to meet the challenge in this way. Probably the most important factor was the growth of freedom and security since the Civil War. As has been stressed already, this was the most striking difference between Britain and the Continent. In the absence of gild and State controls, the forces of the market were free to reward enterprise and punish the lack of it; while, in Europe, State subsidies and urban privileges often masked laxity and feather-bedded incompetence. After the political, religious and intellectual turmoil of the seventeenth century, English society was flexible and innovating, less hidebound by tradition and more open to change. Its values encouraged enterprise: the aristocracy poured no inhibiting scorn on business, nor the clergy any anathemas, and successful merchants, and even manufacturers, could gain social acceptance. The nobility, as we have seen, could adapt themselves to agricultural experiments; the middle classes in all their diversity could adapt themselves to anything. William Cotesworth of Gateshead on the Tyne imported indigo, cochineal, and other dyes from the Atlantic and the Mediterranean, flax and whale-fins from Rotterdam, wine and dried fruit from Bordeaux, wheat and other grains from London, besides trading in tea, sugar, chocolate, and tobacco. In addition, he sold grindstones in Sweden and America, was a large coal owner and salt producer, and ran a business called the English Sword Blade Company, using German labour.

Skill was fostered at all levels: among financiers, farmers, merchants, and manufacturers, above all among mechanics. Britain must have been richer in technical skill than other countries, since even when the Continent began to emulate the British example, their progress was slow, and decades behind, and always at first dependent on the importation of British technicians. In addition, Britain was rich in the key raw materials: coal and iron in close proximity to one another at home; cotton and other necessary imports readily available through her world trading system. Capital was also available in plenty. The rate of interest was low, and the growth of banking and credit institutions ensured the invigorating flow of savings; while the political and social system encouraged the plough-back of profits, and not their diversion into the purchase of titles of nobility or jobs in the bureaucracy. On the other hand, the high rate of investment, which used to have a high place in the estimation of historians as the trigger of British industrialization, is now no longer regarded as being so crucial. Some Continental rulers such as Louis XIV and Frederick the Great poured capital into business without stimulating their subjects into causing an industrial 'take-off'. In the British textile industry, on the other hand, where the most important innovations were made, capital requirements were modest. A forty-spindle spinning-jenny, for example, cost about six pounds in 1792: about two weeks' wages of the forty women it replaced.[21]

Finally, the innovations that took place in the textile industry to meet expanding demand were of such a kind that they had repercussions throughout the economy. Machines had been introduced in previous centuries and factories had been set up – but without causing any chain-reaction. On the other hand, the improvements initiated in Georgian Derbyshire and Lancashire set off a process which has never stopped. Firstly, the cotton-spinning inventions (especially Arkwright's Water-Frame [1769] and Crompton's Mule [1779]) not only replaced hand-labour, and ultimately put it out of business, they also required power. This led to concentration in factories using first water-power, and then steam. The textile industry was complex, with the result that mechanization in spinning soon led to mechanization in weaving and other departments. Thirdly, it was also a large industry, so that textile changes resounded throughout the economy. In other words, it had the necessary characteristics to begin that mutual interaction between industries, that counter-point of change whose crescendo was the world's first Industrial Revolution.

Notes

CHAPTER I

1. Dietrich Gerhard, 'Regionalismus und ständisches Wesen als ein Grundthema europäischer Geschichte', *Alte und Neue Welt in Vergleichender Geschichtsbetrachtung* (Göttingen, 1962), p. 38.
2. Alasdaire MacIntyre, *New Statesman*, 3 Jan. 1969, p. 18.
3. Francis Haskell, *Patrons and Painters* (1963), p. 246, n. 3.
4. F. H. Hinsley, *Power and the Pursuit of Peace* (Cambridge, 1963), p. 30.
5. Hinsley, p. 163.
6. Friedrich Meinecke, *Machiavellism* (English trans. 1957), p. 288.
7. Hinsley, p. 177.
8. ibid., p. 182.
9. Vicente Rodríguez Casado, *De La Monarquía Española del Barroco* (Seville, 1955), p. 33.
10. Alexis de Tocqueville, *L'Ancien Régime* (English trans. Oxford, 1947), p. 226.
11. Dietrich Gerhard, 'Amtsträger zwischen Krongewalt und Ständen – ein Europäisches Problem', *Alteuropa und die Moderne Gesellschaft, Festschrift für Otto Brunner* (Göttingen, 1963), p. 236.
12. Harold Perkin, *The Origins of Modern English Society, 1780–1880* (1969), p. 40.
13. Boris Porchnev, *Les Soulèvements populaires en France de 1623 à 1648* (French trans. from Russian, Paris, 1963), p. 548.
14. E. Lousse, *La Société d'ancien régime, organisation et représentation corporatives*, vol. 1 (Louvain, 1943), p. 133.
15. Jaime Vicens Vives, 'Estructura Administrativa Estatal en los Siglos XVI y XVII', *Rapports, XIe Congrès International des Sciences Historiques* (Göteborg–Stockholm–Uppsala, 1960), vol. IV, p. 1.
16. Boris Porchnev, 'Les Rapports politiques de l'Europe occidentale et de l'Europe orientale à l'époque de la Guerre de Trente Ans', *Rapports, XIe Congrès International des Sciences Historiques* (Göteborg–Stockholm–Uppsala, 1960), vol. IV, p. 160.

17. Gerhard Oestreich, 'Zur Heeresverfassung der deutschen Territorien von 1500 bis 1800', *Forschungen zu Staat und Verfassung, Festgabe für Fritz Hartung* (Berlin, 1958), p. 432.

18. Lavender Cassels, *The Struggle for the Ottoman Empire, 1717–1740* (1966), pp. 36–7.

19. Vincente Rodriguez Casado, *La Política y los políticos en el reinado de Carlos III* (Madrid, 1962), p. 49.

20. E. Lousse, p. 326.

21. Michael Roberts, *Essays in Swedish History* (1967), p. 205.

22. Hermann Kellenbenz, 'Probleme der Merkantilismusforschung', *Rapports, XIIe Congrès International des Science Historiques* (Vienna, 1965), p. 182.

23. Roland Mousnier, *La Vénalité des offices sous Henri IV et Louis XIII* (Rouen, 1945), p. 462.

24. Fritz Hartung and Roland Mousnier, 'Quelques Problèmes concernant la monarchie absolue', *Relazioni, X Congresso Internazionale di Scienze Storiche*, vol. IV (Florence, 1955), p. 47, n. 1.

25. F. Valsecchi, *L'Assolutismo illuminato in Austria e in Lombardia*, vol. I, (Bologna, 1931), p. 7.

26. Jaime Vicens Vives, op. cit., p. 3.

27. S. O. Schmidt, 'La politique intérieure du Tsarisme au milieu du XVIIIe siècle', *Annales, économies, sociétés, civilisations*, (Paris, 1966), p. 97.

28. Anatole G. Mazour, *The First Russian Revolution 1825* (Berkeley, 1937), p. 42.

29. Dietrich Gerhard, op. cit., p. 32.

30. Peter Gay, *The Enlightenment: An Interpretation*, vol. I, *The Rise of Modern Paganism* (1967), p. 94.

31. ibid., p. 139.

32. Basil Willey, *The Seventeenth-Century Background* (1934, 7th edition, 1957), pp. 4 and 6.

33. G. E. Mingay, *English Landed Society in the Eighteenth Century* (1968), p. 150.

34. Antonio Ubieto, Juan Reglá, José María Jover and Carlos Seco, *Introducción a la Historia de España* (Barcelona, 2nd edition, 1965), p. 379.

CHAPTER 2

1. Paul Zumthor, *Daily Life in Rembrandt's Holland* (1962), p. 320.

2. C. R. Boxer, *The Dutch Seaborne Empire, 1600–1800* (1965), p. 5.
3. ibid., p. 236.
4. Charles Wilson, *Profit and Power* (1957), p. 41.
5. Boxer, p. 95.
6. J. H. Elliot, *The Revolt of the Catalans* (Cambridge, 1963), p. 538.
7. Charles Wilson, *The Dutch Republic* (1968), p. 22.
8. John H. Murray, *Amsterdam in the Age of Rembrandt* (Norman, Oklahoma, 1967), p. 86.
9. Wilson, *The Dutch Republic*, p. 170.
10. Boxer, p. 168.
11. Paul Hazard, *The European Mind, 1680–1715* (1964), p. 112.
12. Wilson, *The Dutch Republic*, p. 42.
13. J. H. Huizinga, *Dutch Civilisation in the Seventeenth Century and Other Essays* (1968), p. 62.
14. Robert Halsband (ed.), *The Complete Letters of Lady Mary Wortley Montagu*, vol. I, *1708–1720* (Oxford, 1965), p. 249.
15. Boxer, p. 35.
16. Pieter Geyl, *The Netherlands in the Seventeenth Century*, Part II, *1648–1715* (1964), p. 191.
17. Boxer, p. 36.
18. Nesca A. Robb, *William of Orange*, vol. I, *1650–1673* (1962). p. 161.
19. Boxer, p. 62.
20. Huizinga, p. 60.
21. Wilson, *The Dutch Republic*, p. 52.
22. Murray, p. 25.
23. Boxer, p. 120.
24. Geyl, p. 109.
25. ibid., p. 247.
26. Boxer, pp. 170–1.
27. Wilson, op. cit., p. 53.
28. Boxer, p. 89.
29. Geyl, pp. 192, 193.
30. ibid., p. 17.
31. Frederick L. Nussbaum, *The Triumph of Science and Reason, 1660–1685* (New York, 1953), p. 136.
32. ibid., p. 137.
33. Geyl, pp. 32–3.
34. Boxer, p. 84.

35. Pierre Goubert, *Louis XIV et vingt millions de Français* (Paris, 1966), p. 95.
36. Boxer, p. 95.
37. Geyl, p. 22.
38. Wilson, p. 51.
39. Pieter Geyl, *History of the Low Countries, Episodes and Problems* (1964), p. 162.
40. ibid., p. 119.
41. Geyl, *Netherlands*, p. 134.
42. ibid., p. 204.
43. ibid., p. 205.
44. ibid., p. 167.
45. Stephen B. Baxter, *William III* (1966), p. 389.
46. Geyl, *Netherlands*, p. 279.
47. Baxter, p. 388.
48. Boxer, p. 107.
49. ibid., p. 291.
50. ibid., p. 271.
51. Huizinga, p. 100.
52. Charles Wilson, *Economic History and the Historian* (1969), pp. 46–7.
53. Boxer, p. 106.
54. Walter L. Dorn, *Competition for Empire, 1740–1763* (New York, 1940), p. 163.
55. Huizinga, p. 33.
56. Geyl, *History*, p. 170.
57. R. R. Palmer, *The Age of Democratic Revolution, The Challenge* (Princeton, 1959), p. 325.
58. Boxer, p. 38.
59. Palmer, p. 338.

CHAPTER 3

1. J. H. Elliott, *The Revolt of the Catalans* (Cambridge, 1963), p. 504.
2. ibid., p. 215.
3. Martin Hume, *The Court of Philip IV, Spain in Decadence* (1907), p. vii.
4. ibid., p. 446.
5. ibid., p. 385.
6. ibid., p. 53.

7. Antonio Domínguez Ortiz, *La Sociedad Española en el Siglo XVII*, vol. 1, (Madrid, 1963), p. 36.
8. Hume, p. 450.
9. ibid., p. 511.
10. J. O. Lindsay (ed.), *The New Cambridge Modern History*, vol. VII, *The Old Régime 1713–63* (Cambridge, 1957), p. 276.
11. Henry Kamen, *The Spanish Inquisition* (1965), p. 46.
12. Elliott, op. cit., p. 45.
13. ibid., p. 400.
14. ibid., p. 10.
15. ibid., p. 200.
16. ibid., p. 70.
17. Kamen, p. 9.
18. Domínguez Ortiz, op. cit., p. 47.
19. Hume, p. 503.
20. Domínguez Ortiz, op. cit., p. 43.
21. Jaime Vicens Vives (ed.), *Historia Social y Económica de España y América*, vol. IV (Barcelona, 1958), p. 92.
22. Antonio Domínguez Ortiz, *La Sociedad Española en el Siglo XVIII* (Madrid, 1955), p. 145.
23. Vicens Vives (ed.), *Historia Social y Económica*, vol. III (Barcelona, 1957), p. 306.
24. ibid., p. 310.
25. Domínguez Ortiz, *Siglo XVIII*, p. 128.
26. Vicens Vives (ed.), op. cit., p. 246.
27. Domínguez Ortiz, *Siglo XVIII*, p. 153, n. 64.
28. Elliott, op. cit., p. 252.
29. Richard Herr, *The Eighteenth-Century Revolution in Spain* (Princeton, 1958), p. 105.
30. Vicens Vives (ed.), op. cit., p. 271.
31. Domínguez Ortiz, *Siglo XVII*, pp. 37–8.
32. Vicens Vives (ed.), vol. III, p. 332.
33. Antonio Ubieto, Juan Reglá, José María Jover, and Carlos Seco, *Introducción a la Historia de España* (Barcelona, 2nd edition, 1965), p. 291.
34. Domínguez Ortiz, *Siglo XVIII*, p. 204.
35. Domínguez Ortiz, *Siglo XVII*, p. 91.
36. ibid., p. 120.
37. Domínguez Ortiz, *Siglo XVIII*, p. 278.
38. Kamen, p. 136.
39. Vicens Vives (ed.), vol. IV, p. 235.

40. Vicente Rodríguez Casado, *La Política y Los Políticos en el Reinado de Carlos III* (Madrid, 1962), p. 67.
41. John Nada, *Carlos the Bewitched, The last Spanish Habsburg, 1661–1700* (1962), p. 193.
42. Domínguez Ortiz, *Siglo XVII*, p. 219, n. 85.
43. ibid., p. 244.
44. ibid., p. 245.
45. Nada, p. 220.

CHAPTER 4

1. Antonio Domínguez Ortiz, *La Sociedad Española en el Siglo XVIII* (Madrid, 1955), p. 38.
2. Comitato Internationale di Scienze Storiche, *Atti del X Congresso Internazionale, Roma 1955* (Rome, 1957), p. 450.
3. Vicente Rodríguez Casado, *De la Monarquía española del barroco* (Seville, 1955), p. 82.
4. Raymond Carr, *Spain 1808–1939* (Oxford, 1966), p. 42, n. 5.
5. Vicente Rodríguez Casado, *La Política y Los Políticos en el Reinado de Carlos III* (Madrid, 1962), pp. 90–1.
6. Domínguez Ortiz, *Siglo XVIII*, p. 368, n. 4.
7. Jaime Vicens Vives (ed.), *Historia Social y Económica de España y América*, vol. IV (Barcelona, 1958), p. 236.
8. ibid., p. 238.
9. Antonio Ubieto, Juan Reglá, José María Jover, and Carlos Seco, *Introducción a la Historia de España* (Barcelona, 2nd edition, 1965), p. 361.
10. Rodríguez Casado, *Carlos III*, pp. 210–11.
11. Carr, p. 61.
12. Rodríguez Casado, op. cit., p. 40.
13. ibid., p. 112.
14. Vicente Rodríguez Casado, *La Administración Pública en el Reinado de Carlos III* (Oviedo, 1961), p. 51.
15. Carr, p. 62.
16. Domínguez Ortiz, *Siglo XVIII*, p. 93, n. 28.
17. Richard Herr, *The Eighteenth-Century Revolution in Spain* (Princeton, 1958), p. 28.
18. Vicens Vives (ed.), vol. IV, p. 19.
19. ibid., pp. 99–100.
20. Rodríguez Casado, *Carlos III*, p. 42.
21. Ubieto, *et al.*, op. cit., p. 358.
22. Vicente Rodríguez Casado, *Administración*, p. 15.

23. Ubieto, *et al.*, op. cit., p. 354.
24. Carr, p. 32, n. 1.
25. Jaime Vicens Vives, *Aproximación a la historia de España* (3rd edition, Barcelona, 1962), p. 148.

CHAPTER 5

1. Emmanuel Le Roy Ladurie, *Histoire du Languedoc* (2nd edition, Paris, 1967), p. 76.
2. Boris Porchnev, *Les Soulèvements populaires en France de 1623 à 1648* (Paris, 1963), p. 524.
3. ibid., pp. 535–6.
4. Le Roy Ladurie, p. 81.
5. William F. Church (ed.), *The Greatness of Louis XIV, Myth or Reality?* (Boston, 1959), p. 47.
6. ibid., p. 88.
7. Ernest Lavisse, *Histoire de France depuis les origines jusqu'à la Révolution*, vol. 7(1) (Paris, 1905), p. 160
8. F. L. Carsten (ed.), *The New Cambridge Modern History*, vol. V., (Cambridge, 1961), p. 238.
9. Church, p. 47.
10. Pierre Goubert, *Beauvais et le Beauvaisis de 1600 à 1730* (Paris, 1960), p. 13.
11. Lavisse, p. 195.
12. Goubert, p. 197.
13. Philippe Sagnac, *La Formation de la société française moderne*, vol. I (Paris, 1945), p. 35.
14. Roland Mousnier, *La Vénalité des offices sous Henri IV et Louis XIII* (Rouen, 1945), p. 623.
15. Porchnev, p. 559.
16. Robert Mandrou, *La France aux XVIIe et XVIIIe siècles* (Paris, 1967), p. 181.

CHAPTER 6

1. Philippe Sagnac, *La Formation de la société française moderne*, vol. I (Paris, 1945), p. 50.
2. William F. Church (ed.), op. cit. (Boston, 1959), p. 21.
3. G. P. Gooch, *Louis XV, The Monarchy in Decline* (1956), p. 5.
4. Church, p. 87.

5. Gooch, p. 3.
6. Pierre Goubert, *Louis XIV et vingt millions de Français* (Paris, 1966), p. 46.
7. Sagnac, I, p. 51.
8. Church, p. 5.
9. Sagnac, I, p. 51.
10. Gooch, p. 4.
11. Sagnac, I, p. 52.
12. Roland Mousnier, 'État et commissaire, recherches sur la création des intendants de province (1634–1648)' in Richard Dietrich and Gerhard Oestreich (eds.), *Forschungen zu Staat und Verfassung, Festgabe für Fritz Hartung* (Berlin, 1958), p. 327.
13. Roland Mousnier, *Histoire générale des civilisations*, vol. IV (Paris, 1960), p. 266.
14. Boris Porchnev, *Les Soulèvements populaires en France de 1623 à 1648* (Paris, 1963), p. 549.
15. F. L. Carsten (ed.), *The New Cambridge Modern History*, vol. V (Cambridge, 1961), p. 243.
16. Church, p. 41.
17. Victor-L. Tapié, *The Age of Grandeur* (New York, 1960), p. 271, n. 3.
18. ibid., p. 134.
19. Mousnier, *Histoire*, p. 274.
20. Sagnac, I, p. 89.
21. Goubert, op. cit., p. 57.
22. Sagnac, I, p. 97.
23. ibid., p. 93.
24. ibid., p. 144, n. 3.
25. ibid., p. 94.
26. ibid., p. 93.
27. ibid., p. 94.
28. John McManners, *French Ecclesiastical Society under the Ancien Régime* (Manchester, 1960), p. 8.
29. Sagnac, I, p. 191, n. 1.
30. ibid., p. 54, n. 1.
31. Goubert, p. 52.
32. Sagnac, I, p. 54.
33. Goubert, p. 210.
34. Mousnier, *Histoire*, p. 296.
35. Church, p. 18.
36. Paul Hazard, *The European Mind, 1680–1715* (1964), p. 27.

37. Sagnac, I, p. 148.
38. Hazard, p. 188.
39. Sagnac, I, p. 153, n. 1.
40. Gooch, p. 13.
41. Sagnac, I, p. 164.
42. Hazard, p. 84, n. 1.
43. Sagnac, I, p. 168.
44. ibid., p. 169.
45. ibid., p. 221.
46. Georges Pagès, *La Monarchie d'Ancien Régime en France* (Paris, 1932), p. 186.

CHAPTER 7

1. Philippe Sagnac, *La Formation de la société française moderne*, vol. II (Paris, 1946), p. 46.
2. Pierre Goubert, *Beauvais et le Beauvaisis de 1600 à 1730* (Paris, 1960), p. 211.
3. Robert Forster, 'The provincial noble: a re-appraisal', in *American Historical Review*, vol. 68 (1962–63), p. 691.
4. G. P. Gooch, *Louis XV, The Monarchy in Decline* (1956), p. 21.
5. Sagnac, I, p. 173.
6. Sagnac, II, p. 40.
7. ibid., p. 41.
8. John McManners, *French Ecclesiastical Society under the Ancien Régime* (Manchester, 1960), p. 76.
9. Sagnac, I, p. 98.
10. Peter Gay, *The Enlightenment: An Interpretation* (1967), p. 339.
11. Georges Pagès, *La Monarchie d'Ancien Régime en France* (Paris, 1932), p. 166.
12. Gooch, p. 50.
13. ibid., p. 154.
14. Goubert, p. 337, n. 71.
15. Martin Göhring, *Die Amterkäuflichkeit im Ancien Régime* (Berlin, 1938), p. 296.
16. McManners, p. 79.
17. Alfred Cobban, *The Social Interpretation of the French Revolution* (Cambridge, 1964), p. 61.
18. Goubert, p. 157.

19. ibid., p. 159.
20. ibid., p. 163.
21. ibid., p. 303, n. 118.
22. Sagnac, I, p. 218.
23. ibid., p. 142.
24. Boris Porchnev, *Les Soulèvements populaires en France de 1623 à 1648* (Paris, 1963), p. 537.
25. Sagnac, I, p. 138.
26. Goubert, pp. 180–1.

CHAPTER 8

1. Robert Mandrou, *La France aux XVIIe et XVIIIe siècles* (Paris, 1967), p. 193.
2. A. Goodwin (ed.), *The European Nobility in the Eighteenth Century* (1953), p. 27.
3. Goodwin, p. 33.
4. Alfred Cobban, *The Social Interpretation of the French Revolution* (Cambridge, 1946), p. 29.
5. Martin Göhring, *Die Amterkäuflichkeit im Ancien Régime* (Berlin, 1938), p. 328.
6. Cobban, p. 59, n. 2.
7. J. M. Wallace-Hadrill and John McManners (eds.), *France, Government and Society* (1957), p. 182.
8. Arthur Young, *Travels in France and Italy* (1915 edition), p. 59.
9. Cobban, p. 96.
10. Peter Gay, *The Party of Humanity* (1964), p. 23.
11. Peter Gay, *The Enlightenment: An Interpretation* (1967), p. 206.
12. Philippe Sagnac, *La Formation de la société française moderne*, vol. II (Paris, 1946), p. 88, n. 1.
13. Sagnac, vol. II, p. 83.
14. Gay, *Party*, p. 130.
15. ibid., p. 36.
16. Sagnac, II, p. 102, n. 1.
17. ibid., p. 149.
18. Mandrou, p. 168.
19. Roland Mousnier and Ernest Labrousse, *Histoire générale des civilisations*, vol. V (Paris, 1953), p. 11.
20. Pierre Goubert, *Beauvais et le Beauvaisis de 1600 à 1730* (Paris, 1960), p. 346.
21. Mousnier and Labrousse, p. 62.

22. ibid., p. 77.
23. ibid., p. 78.
24. G. P. Gooch, *Louis XV, The Monarchy in Decline* (1956), p. v.
25. ibid., p. 65.
26. ibid., p. 114.
27. ibid., p. 113.
28. ibid., p. 94.
29. ibid., p. 111.
30. ibid., p. 191.
31. Sagnac, II, p. 160.
32. R. R. Palmer, *The Age of Democratic Revolution, The Challenge* (Princeton, New Jersey, 1959), p. 87.
33. Tobias Smollett, *Travels through France and Italy* (1949 edition), p. 276.
34. Palmer, pp. 94–5.
35. ibid., pp. 95–6.
36. Göhring, p. 309, n. 55.
37. Saul K. Padover, *The Revolutionary Emperor: Joseph II of Austria* (2nd edition, 1967), p. 82.
38. Göhring, p. 316.
39. Palmer, p. 451.
40. ibid., p. 214.
41. Gaston Letonnelier, *Histoire du dauphiné* (1958), p. 105.
42. Wallace-Hadrill and McManners, p. 172.
43. Norman Hampson, *A Social History of the French Revolution* (1963), p. 50.

CHAPTER 9

1. B. H. Sumner, *Survey of Russian History* (1961), p. 89.
2. R. Wittram, *Peter der Gross, der Eintritt Russlands in die Neuzeit* (Berlin, 1954), p. 32.
3. G. P. Gooch, *Catherine the Great and other Studies* (1954), p. 205.
4. M. S. Anderson, *Europe in the Eighteenth Century, 1713–1783* (1961), p. 176.
5. Vasili Klyuchevsky, *Peter the Great* (trans. Liliana Archibald) (1965), p. 253.
6. Nicholas Henderson, *Prince Eugen of Savoy* (1964), p. 287.
7. Gooch, p. 10.

8. ibid., p. 96.
9. ibid., p. 44.
10. Michael T. Florinsky, *Russia, A History and an Interpretation* (New York, 1953), vol. I, p. 452.
11. Gooch, p. 78.
12. Georg Sacke, 'Adel und Bürgertum in der Regierungszeit Katherinas II von Russland', *Revue belge de philologie et d'histoire*, vol. XVII (Brussels, 1938), p. 826.
13. L. J. Oliva, *Russia and the West from Peter to Krushchev* (Boston, 1965), p. 35.
14. ibid., p. 35.
15. Sacke, p. 842.

CHAPTER 10

1. Saul K. Padover, *The Revolutionary Emperor: Joseph II of Austria* (2nd edition, 1967), p. 255.
2. R. Wittram, *Peter der Grosse, der Eintritt Russlands in die Neuzeit* (Berlin, 1954), p. 7.
3. B. H. Sumner, *Survey of Russian History* (1961), p. 168.
4. Sumner, p. 81.
5. Michael T. Florinsky, *Russia, a History and an Interpretation* (New York, 1953), vol. I, p. 426.
6. Vasili Klyuchevsky, *Peter the Great* (trans. Liliana Archibald) (1965), p. 89.
7. ibid., p. 179.
8. Wittram, p. 131.
9. Florinsky, p. 414.
10. ibid., p. 372.
11. ibid., p. 384.
12. Friedrich Meinecke, *Machiavellism* (Eng. trans. 1957), p. 331.
13. Klyuchevsky, p. 257.
14. Herbert H. Rowen, *From Absolutism to Revolution, 1648–1848* (New York, 1963), p. 82.
15. Wittram, p. 138.
16. Lionel Kochan, *The Making of Modern Russia* (1962), p. 118.
17. G. P. Gooch, *Catherine the Great and other Studies* (1954), p. 61.
18. Paul Dukes, *Catherine the Great and the Russian Nobility* (Cambridge, 1967), p. 56.
19. Gooch, p. 103.
20. Jerome Blum, *Lord and Peasant in Russia from the Ninth to*

the Nineteenth Century (Princeton, 1961), p. 537.

21. L. Jay Oliva, *Russia and the West from Peter to Krushchev* (Boston, 1965), p. 34.

22. ibid., p. 54.

23. N. Hans, 'Dumaresq, Brown and some early educational projects of Catherine II', *Slavonic and East European Review*, vol. 40 (1961–62), p. 233.

24. Dukes, p. 50.

25. L. Jay Oliva, p. 36.

26. ibid., p. 37.

27. Blum, p. 363.

28. Leo Gershoy, *From Despotism to Revolution, 1763–1789* (New York, 1944), p. 112.

29. Dukes, p. 171.

30. Florinsky, p. 547.

31. Dukes, p. 221.

32. ibid., p. 142.

33. Georg Sacke, 'Adel und Bürgertum in der Regierungszeit Katherinas II von Russland', *Revue belge de philologie et d'histoire*, XVII (Brussels, 1938), p. 835.

34. Nikolai N. Alexeiev, 'Beiträge zur Geschichte des Russischen Absolutismus im 18. Jahrhundert', *Forschungen zur Osteuropäischen Geschichte*, vol. 6 (Berlin, 1958), p. 38.

35. Florinsky, p. 555.

36. Dukes, p. 40.

37. ibid., p. 43.

38. ibid., p. 227.

CHAPTER II

1. L. Jay Oliva, *Russia and the West from Peter to Krushchev* (Boston, 1965), p. 18.

2. R. Wittram, *Peter der Gross, der Eintritt Russlands in die Neuzeit* (Berlin, 1954), p. 66.

3. Vasili Klyuchevsky, *Peter the Great* (trans. Liliana Archibald), (1965), p. 29, n. 1.

4. ibid., p. 133.

5. Roger Portal, 'Manufactures et classes sociales en Russie au XVIIIe siècle', *Revue historique*, CCII (1949), p. 5.

6. L. Jay Oliva, p. 11.

7. ibid., p. 18.

8. Klyuchevsky, p. 134.

9. ibid., p. 145.

10. ibid., p. 263.

11. Wittram, p. 35.

12. Jerome Blum, *Lord and Peasant in Russia from the Ninth to the Nineteenth Century* (Princeton, 1961), pp. 217–18.

13. Klyuchevsky, p. 95.

14. William H. McNeill, *Europe's Steppe Frontier 1500–1800* (Chicago, 1964), pp. 153–4.

15. Wittram, p. 56.

16. L. Jay Oliva, p. 22.

17. ibid., p. 28.

18. Portal, p. 175.

19. Paul Dukes, *Catherine the Great and the Russian Nobility* (Cambridge, 1967), p. 88.

20. Michael Confino, *Domaines et seigneurs en Russie vers la fin du XVIIIe siècle* (Paris, 1963), p. 78, n. 2.

21. Hans Rogger, *National Consciousness in Eighteenth-Century Russia* (Cambridge, Mass, 1960), p. 109.

22. Rogger, p. 18.

23. Marc Raeff, 'Home, School, and Service in the Life of the 18th-Century Russian Nobleman', *Slavonic and East European Review*, vol. XL (1961–62), p. 302.

24. Rogger, p. 13.

25. ibid., p. 103.

26. Herbert H. Rowen, *From Absolutism to Revolution, 1648–1848* (New York, 1963), p. 180.

CHAPTER 12

1. R. R. Palmer, *The Age of Democratic Revolution, The Challenge* (Princeton, 1959), p. 402.

2. Paul Dukes, *Catherine the Great and the Russian Nobility* (Cambridge, 1967), p. 24.

3. ibid., p. 159.

4. L. Jay Oliva, *Russia and the West from Peter to Krushchev* (Boston, 1965), p. 30.

5. Dukes, pp. 28–9.

6. Vasili Klyuchevsky, *Peter the Great* (trans. Liliana Archibald) (1965), p. 95.

7. Dukes, p. 18.

8. Jerome Blum, *Lord and Peasant in Russia from the Ninth to the Nineteenth Century* (Princeton, 1961), p. 266.

9. Klyuchevsky, p. 125.

10. Michel Laren, 'Nobles et paysans en Russie, de l'age d'or du servage à son abolition (1762–1861)', *Annales, économies, sociétés, civilisations* (Paris, Jan-Feb. 1966), p. 123.

11. Blum, p. 441.

12. Nikolai N. Alexeiev, 'Beiträge zur Geschichte des Russischen Absolutismus im 18. Jahrhundert', *Forschungen zur Osteuropäischen Geschichte*, vol. 6 (Berlin, 1958), p. 40.

13. Michael Confino, *Domaines et seigneurs en Russie vers la fin du XVIIIe siècle* (Paris, 1963), p. 146, n. 1.

14. ibid., pp. 204–5.

15. ibid., pp. 56–7.

16. ibid. p. 58.

17. Laren, p. 124.

18. Confino, p. 95.

19. ibid., p. 49.

20. B. H. Sumner, *Survey of Russian History* (1961), p. 149.

21. Alexeiev, p. 61.

22. Sumner, p. 146.

23. Roger Portal, 'Aux Origines d'une bourgeoisie industrielle en Russie', *Revue d'histoire moderne et contemporaine*, vol. VIII (Paris, 1961), pp. 35–60.

24. Herbert H. Rowen, *From Absolutism to Revolution, 1648–1848* (New York, 1963), p. 81.

25. G. P. Gooch, *Catherine the Great and other Studies* (1954), p. 35.

26. Blum, p. 566.

27. L. Jay Oliva, p. 49.

CHAPTER 13

1. Hans Rosenberg, *Bureaucracy, Aristocracy and Autocracy: The Prussian Experience, 1660–1815* (Cambridge, Mass., 1958), p. 53.

2. Carl Hinrichs, *Preussen als Historisches Problem, Gesammelte Abhandlungen* (Herausgegeben von Gerhard Oestreich) (Berlin, 1964), p. 234.

3. G. P. Gooch, *Frederick the Great* (1947), p. 280.

4. Rosenberg, p. 34.

CHAPTER 14

1. Carl Hinrichs, *Preussen als Historisches Problem, Gesammelte Abhandlungen* (Herausgegeben von Gerhard Oestreich) (Berlin, 1964), pp. 256-7.
2. ibid., p. 195.
3. Bruno Gebhardt, *Handbuch der Deutschen Geschichte*, vol. 2 (Stuttgart, 1955), p. 263.
4. Hinrichs, p. 117.
5. ibid., p. 95.
6. ibid., p. 100.
7. Hans Rosenberg, *Bureaucracy, Aristocracy and Autocracy: The Prussian Experience, 1660-1815* (Cambridge, Mass., 1958), p. 38.
8. Hinrichs, p. 191.
9. Rosenberg, p. 40.
10. Otto Büsch, *Militärsystem und Sozialleben im alten Preussen, 1713-1807, Die Anfänge der sozialen Militarisierung der preussisch-deutschen Gesellschaft* (Berlin, 1962), p. 15.
11. Büsch, p. 81, n. 16.
12. Hinrichs, p. 88.
13. ibid., p. 45.
14. Büsch, p. 2.
15. Reinhold August Dorwart, *The Administrative Reforms of Frederick William I of Prussia* (Cambridge, Mass., 1953), p. 36.
16. ibid., p. 168.
17. Hinrichs, p. 162.
18. Rosenberg, p. 89.
19. ibid., p. 93.
20. Dorwart, p. 203.
21. Hinrichs, p. 125.
22. ibid., p. 126.
23. Penfield Roberts, *The Quest for Security, 1715-1740* (1947), p. 63.
24. G. P. Gooch, *Frederick the Great* (London, 1947), p. 318.
25. Gerhard Ritter, *Das Problem des Militarismus in Deutschland* (Bonn, 1955), p. 5.
26. Gooch, p. 131.
27. Hinrichs, p. 63.

CHAPTER 15

1. Hans Rosenberg, *Bureaucracy, Aristocracy and Autocracy: The Prussian Experience, 1660–1815* (Cambridge, Mass., 1958), p. 164.
2. Gerhard Ritter, *Friedrich der Grosse, ein Historisches Profil* (3rd edition, Heidelberg, 1954), p. 198.
3. Otto Büsch, *Militärsystem und Sozialleben im alten Preussen, 1713–1807, Die Anfänge der sozialen Militarisierung der preussisch-deutschen Gesellschaft* (Berlin, 1962), p. 102.
4. ibid., p. 93.
5. ibid., p. 79, n. 3.
6. ibid., p. 79.
7. F. L. Carsten (ed.), *The New Cambridge Modern History*, vol. V (Cambridge, 1961), p. 438.
8. Büsch, p. 133.
9. ibid., p. 139.
10. Henri Brunschwig, *La Crise de l'état prussien à la fin du XVIIIe siècle et la genèse de la mentalité romantique* (Paris, 1947), pp. 147–8.
11. Büsch, p. 104.
12. ibid., p. 94.
13. Brunschwig, p. 60.
14. Büsch, p. 82.
15. Brunschwig, p. 60.
16. Büsch, p. 11.
17. Carsten (ed.), p. 438.
18. Büsch, p. 58.
19. ibid., p. 43.
20. F. Valsecchi, *L'Assolutismo illuminato in Austria e in Lombardia*, vol. I (Bologna, 1931). p. 99.

CHAPTER 16

1. Gerhard Ritter, *Friedrich der Grosse, ein Historisches Profil* (3rd edition, Heidelberg, 1954), p. 37.
2. G. P. Gooch, *Frederick the Great* (1947), p. 125.
3. ibid., p. 287.
4. ibid., p. 190.
5. Henri Brunschwig, *La Crise de l'état prussien à la fin du XVIIIe*

siècle et la genèse de la mentalité romantique (Paris, 1947), p. 17.

6. Gooch, p. 282.
7. Ritter, p. 75.
8. Gooch, p. 280.
9. ibid., p. 272.
10. ibid., pp. 305–6.
11. Ritter, p. 116.
12. ibid., p. 17.
13. Gooch, p. 13.
14. ibid., p. 8.
15. ibid., p. 20.
16. Ralph Flenley, *Modern German History* (1953), p. 66, n. 1.
17. Gooch, p. 26.
18. ibid., p. 39.
19. Ritter, p. 172.
20. Gooch, p. 41.
21. ibid., p. 44.
22. ibid., p. 46.
23. ibid., p. 49.
24. ibid., p. 53.
25. Ritter, p. 157.
26. Brunschwig, p. 17.
27. Ritter, p. 192.
28. ibid., p. 191.
29. Walter L. Dorn, 'The Prussian Bureaucracy in the Eighteenth Century', *Political Science Quarterly*, vol. XLVI (1931), p. 411.
30. Gooch, p. 26.
31. Hans Rosenberg, *Bureaucracy, Aristocracy and Autocracy: The Prussian Experience, 1660–1815* (Cambridge, Mass., 1958), p. 91.
32. Brunschwig, p. 53.
33. Flenley, p. 69.
34. Peter Gay, *The Enlightenment: an Interpretation* (1967), p. 348.
35. Brunschwig, p. 119.
36. Frederick Hertz, *The Development of the German Public Mind*, vol. II (1962), p. 301.
37. Gooch, p. 142.
38. Franco Venturi, 'L'Illuminismo nel Settecento Europeo', *Rapports, Congrès International des Sciences Historiques*, vol. IV (Göteborg–Stockholm–Uppsala, 1960), p. 117.
39. Hertz, pp. 280–1.

40. Otto Büsch, op. cit., p. 46.
41. ibid., p. 155.
42. Leo Gershoy, *From Despotism to Revolution, 1763–1789* (New York, 1944), p. 88.
43. Gooch, p. 104.
44. Gordon A. Craig, *The Politics of the Prussian Army, 1640–1945* (Oxford, 1964), p. 41, n. 3.
45. Gooch, p. 296.
46. R. R. Palmer, *The Age of Democratic Revolution, The Challenge* (Princeton, New Jersey, 1959), p. 511.
47. Rosenberg, pp. 190–1.
48. ibid., p. 201.

CHAPTER 17

1. Therese Schüssel, *Kultur des Barocks in Österreich* (Graz, 1960), p. 24.
2. Pieter Geyl, *The Netherlands in the Seventeenth Century*, Part II, *1648–1715* (1964), p. 62.
3. R. J. Rath (ed.), *Austrian History Yearbook*, vol. I (Rice University, 1965), p. 15.
4. Nicholas Henderson, *Prince Eugen of Savoy* (1964), p. 77.
5. Jean Berenger, 'La Hongrie des Habsburgs au XVIIe siècle. République nobiliaire ou monarchie limitée', *Revue historique*, CCXXXVIII (1967), p. 31.
6. Victor-L. Tapié, *The Age of Grandeur* (New York, 1960), p. 209.
7. Adam Wandruszka, *The House of Habsburg* (1964), p. 131.
8. Robert A. Kann, *A Study in Austrian Intellectual History, From Late Baroque to Romanticism* (1960), p. 23.
9. Henderson, p. 77.
10. Hugo Hantsch, *Die Geschichte Österreichs*, vol. 2 (Graz–Vienna–Cologne, 1962), p. 28.
11. John Stoye, *The Siege of Vienna* (1964), p. 152.
12. Stoye, p. 266.
13. Henderson, p. 40.
14. ibid., p. 89.
15. C. A. Macartney, *Hungary, a short history* (Edinburgh, 1962), p. 93.
16. Lavender Cassels, *The Struggle for the Ottoman Empire, 1717–1740* (1966), p. 22.
17. ibid., p. 21.

18. Hantsch, p. 129.
19. Kann, p. 78.
20. Henderson, p. 243.
21. Kann, p. 121.
22. Edith Murr Link, *The Emancipation of the Austrian Peasant, 1740–1798* (New York, 1949), p. 25.
23. Henderson, p. 289.
24. Wandruszka, p. 148.
25. Cassels, p. 172.
26. Hantsch, p. 139.

CHAPTER 18

1. Adam Wandruszka, *The House of Habsburg* (1964), p. 141.
2. Hugo Hantsch, *Die Geschichte Österreichs*, vol. 2 (Graz–Vienna–Cologne), p. 554.
3. ibid., p. 544.
4. Hugo Hantsch (ed.), *Gestalter der Geschicke Österreichs* (Innsbruck–Vienna–Munich, 1962), p. 241.
5. Wandruszka, p. 148.
6. Leo Gershoy, *From Despotism to Revolution, 1763–1789* (1944), p. 90, n. 22.
7. Hantsch, *Geschichte*, p. 167.
8. G. P. Gooch, *Maria Theresa and other studies* (1951), p. 17.
9. Hantsch, *Geschichte*, p. 182.
10. ibid., p. 214.
11. ibid., p. 156.
12. Edith Murr Link, *The Emancipation of the Austrian Peasant, 1740–1798* (New York, 1949), p. 47.
13. Hantsch, *Geschichte*, p. 182.
14. ibid., p. 197.
15. Wandruszka, p. 147.
16. Robert A. Kann, *A Study in Austrian Intellectual History, From Late Baroque to Romanticism* (1960), p. 158.
17. Hantsch, *Geschichte*, p. 160.
18. Gooch, p. 46.
19. Hantsch, *Geschichte*, p. 185.
20. ibid., p. 227.
21. Link, p. 75.
22. F. Valsecchi, *L'Assolutismo illuminato in Austria e in Lombardia*, vol. I (Bologna, 1931), p. 218.

23. Link, p. 85.
24. ibid., p. 29.
25. Valsecchi, p. 171.
26. Link, p. 103.
27. ibid., p. 48.
28. ibid., p. 54.
29. Valsecchi, p. 66, n. 2.
30. Hantsch, *Geschichte*, p. 560.
31. Link, p. 72.
32. Hantsch, *Geschichte*, p. 230.
33. C. A. Macartney, *Hungary, a short history* (Edinburgh, 1962), p. 113.
34. ibid., p. 97.
35. Valsecchi, p. 75.
36. Gooch, p. 45.
37. ibid., p. 63.
38. ibid., p. 66.
39. ibid., p. 78.
40. ibid., p. 79.
41. ibid., p. 102.
42. G. P. Gooch, *Frederick the Great* (1947), p. 13.
43. Link, p. 42.

CHAPTER 19

1. Hugo Hantsch, *Die Geschichte Österreichs*, vol. 2 (Graz–Vienna–Cologne, 1962), p. 207.
2. Frederick Hertz, *The Development of the German Public Mind*, vol. II (1962), p. 337.
3. Herbert H. Rowen (ed.), *From Absolutism to Revolution: 1648–1848* (New York, 1963), p. 174.
4. G. P. Gooch, *Catherine the Great and other studies* (1954), p. 87.
5. Rowen (ed.), p. 176.
6. A. Goodwin (ed.), *The New Cambridge Modern History*, vol. VIII (Cambridge, 1965), p. 286.
7. Hantsch, p. 559.
8. ibid.
9. F. Valsecchi, *L'Assolutismo illuminato in Austria e in Lombardia*, vol. I (Bologna, 1931), p. 128.
10. Hantsch, p. 208.
11. Ernst Wangermann, *From Joseph II to the Jacobin Trials* (Oxford, 1959), pp. 37–8.

12. A. Goodwin (ed.), p. 290.
13. Rowen (ed.), p. 174.
14. Valsecchi, p. 111.
15. Robert A. Kann, *A Study in Austrian Intellectual History, From Late Baroque to Romanticism* (1960), p. 173.
16. Edith Murr Link, *The Emancipation of the Austrian Peasant, 1740–1798* (New York, 1949), p. 143.
17. Valsecchi, p. 82, n. 2.
18. Saul K. Padover, *The Revolutionary Emperor: Joseph II of Austria* (2nd edition, 1967), p. 170.
19. G. P. Gooch, *Maria Theresa and other studies* (1951), p. 23.
20. Kann, p. 196.
21. Wangermann, p. 12.
22. ibid., p. 20.
23. ibid., p. 48.
24. Link, p. 106.
25. Goodwin (ed.), p. 287.
26. R. R. Palmer, *The Age of Democratic Revolution, The Challenge* (1959), pp. 395–6.
27. Link, p. 141.
28. Hantsch, p. 559.
29. Valsecchi, p. 240.
30. Palmer, p. 105.
31. Wangermann, p. 33.
32. ibid., p. 24.
33. ibid., p. 52, n. 3.
34. Link, p. 163.
35. Palmer, p. 388.
36. ibid., pp. 392–3.
37. Padover, p. 284.
38. William E. Wright, *Serf, Seigneur, and Sovereign, Agrarian Reform in Eighteenth-Century Bohemia* (Minneapolis, 1966), p. 159, n. 10.
39. Hantsch, p. 243.
40. Padover, p. 165.
41. Hantsch, p. 217.
42. Padover, p. 36.

CHAPTER 20

1. F. L. Carsten (ed.), *The New Cambridge Modern History*, vol. V (Cambridge, 1961), p. 2.

2. Harold Perkin, *The Origins of Modern English Society 1780–1880* (1969), p. 41.

3. Charles Wilson, *England's Apprenticeship 1603–1763* (1965), p. 5.

4. Christopher Hill, *The Century of Revolution 1603–1714* (Edinburgh, 1961), p. 132–3.

5. J. H. Plumb, *The Growth of Political Stability in England 1675–1725* (1967), p. 29.

6. G. Burnet, *History of His Own Time*, vol. IV (Edinburgh, 1753 edition), p. 61.

7. Clayton Roberts, *The Growth of Responsible Government in Stuart England* (Cambridge, 1966), p. viii.

8. Roberts, p. 440.

9. W. T. Laprade (ed.), *The Parliamentary Papers of John Robinson* (1922), p. 38.

10. *The House of Commons Journals*, vol. XVI, p. 470.

11. S.H.A.H., *The Letter-Books of John Hervey*, vol. II (Wells, 1894), p. 177.

12. *Additional Manuscripts* (British Museum), vol. 32732, f. 601.

13. Laprade, p. 26.

14. Sir John Fortescue (ed.), *The Correspondence of George III* (1927–28), No. 3668.

15. Rev. John Brown, *Estimate of the Manners and Principles of the Times* (7th edition, 1758), vol. I, p. 107.

16. William Cobbett, *The Parliamentary History of England* (1806–1812), vol. XXII, p. 149.

17. Fortescue, No. 3165.

18. R. R. Sedgwick (ed.), John, Lord Hervey, *Memoirs of the Reign of George II*, vol. I (1931), p. 3.

19. Henry St John, Viscount Bolingbroke, *The Craftsman*, No. 40. 24 April 1721.

CHAPTER 21

1. Charles Wilson, *England's Apprenticeship 1603–1763* (1965), p. 5.

2. ibid., p. 6.
3. David S. Landes, *Technological Change and Development in Western Europe, 1750–1914*, in H. J. Habakkuk and M. Postan, *The Cambridge Economic History of Europe*, vol. VI, Part I (Cambridge, 1965), p. 4.
4. *The Scottish Historical Review*, vol. 35 (1956), pp. 146–9.
5. Peter Gay, *The Enlightenment: An Interpretation* (1967), p. 170.
6. G. E. Mingay, *English Landed Society in the Eighteenth Century* (1963), p. 285.
7. Wilson, p. 109.
8. Arthur Young, *Travels in France and Italy* (1915 edition), p. 119.
9. Mingay, pp. 103–4.
10. ibid., pp. 199–200.
11. Philippe Sagnac, *La Formation de la société française moderne*, vol. II (Paris, 1946), p. 190, n. 2.
12. Wilson, pp. 248–9.
13. Mingay, p. 287.
14. ibid., p. 117.
15. H. J. Habakkuk, 'Landowners and the Civil War', *Economic History Review*, 2nd Series, vol. XVIII (1965), p. 148.
16. Edward Hughes, *North Country Life in the Eighteenth Century* (1952), pp. 1–2.
17. Mingay, p. 71.
18. ibid., p. 152.
19. ibid., p. 217.
20. Daniel Defoe, *A Plan of the English Commerce* (1729, Oxford, 1927 edition), p. 7.
21. Wilson, p. 275.
22. ibid., p. 296.
23. N. McKendrick, 'Josiah Wedgwood: An Eighteenth-Century Entrepreneur in Salesmanship and Marketing Techniques', *The Economic History Review*, 2nd Series, vol. XII (1959–60), p. 421.
24. Wilson, p. 311.
25. McKendrick, p. 433.
26. Dorothy Marshall, *The English People in the Eighteenth Century* (1956), p. 54.
27. R. R. Palmer, *The Age of Democratic Revolution: The Challenge* (Princeton, New Jersey, 1959), p. 155.
28. Wilson, p. 224.
29. ibid., p. 165.
30. ibid., p. 281.

31. ibid., p. 168.
32. ibid., p. 357.

CHAPTER 22

1. J. H. Hexter, *Reappraisals in History* (1961), p. 116.
2. J. D. Chambers, *The Vale of Trent, 1670–1800* (Cambridge, 1957), p. 25.
3. Chambers, p. 29.
4. L. Radzinowicz, *A History of the English Criminal Law*, vol. I (1948), p. 711.
5. Charles Wilson, op. cit., p. 110.
6. C. B. Macpherson, *The Political Theory of Possessive Individualism* (1962), p. 223.
7. A. S. P. Woodhouse, (ed.), *Puritanism and Liberty. Being the Army Debates (1647–49)* (2nd edition, 1950), p. 53.
8. Christopher Hill, *The Century of Revolution, 1603–1715* (Edinburgh, 1961), pp. 132–3.
9. Ian R. Christie, *Wilkes, Wyvill and Reform* (1962), p. 50.
10. Christie, p. 9.
11. J. Steven Watson, *The Reign of George III, 1760–1815* (Oxford, 1960), p. 389.
12. G. E. Mingay, *English Landed Society in the Eighteenth Century* (1963), p. 261.
13. Christie, p. 104.
14. ibid., p. 72.
15. ibid., p. 26.
16. ibid., p. 178.
17. Robert E. Spiller, *The American in England during the first half century of independence* (New York, 1926), p. 153.
18. Arthur Young, *Travels in France and Italy* (London, 1915 edition), p. 25.
19. David S. Landes, 'Technological Change and Development in Western Europe, 1750–1914', in H. J. Habakkuk and M. Postan, *The Cambridge Economic History of Europe*, vol. VI, Part I (Cambridge, 1965), p. 281.
20. Dorothy George, *English Social Life in the 18th Century* (1923), p. 31.
21. Landes, p. 297.

Select Bibliography

EUROPE

Bibliographies

American Historical Association, *A Guide to Historical Literature* (revised periodically).

Bromley, J. S. and Goodwin, A. (eds), *A Select List of Works on Europe and Europe Overseas, 1715–1815* (Oxford, 1956).

Davies, Alun, *Modern European History 1494–1788, A Select Bibliography* (Historical Association Helps for Students of History No. 68) (1966).

Roach, John (ed.), *A Bibliography of Modern History* (Cambridge, 1968).

General Works

Anderson, M. S., *Europe in the Eighteenth Century, 1713–1783* (1961).

Ashley, Maurice, *The Golden Century, 1598–1715* (1969).

Beloff, Max, *The Age of Absolutism, 1660–1815* (1954).

Carsten, F. L. (ed.), *The New Cambridge Modern History*, vol. V, *The Ascendancy of France, 1648–1688* (Cambridge, 1961).

Clark, G. N., *The Seventeenth Century* (2nd edition, Oxford, 1947). *War and Society in the 17th Century* (Cambridge, 1958).

Cobban, A., (ed.), *The Eighteenth Century* (1969).

Coles, Paul, *The Ottoman Impact on Europe* (1968).

Dorn, Walter L., *Competition for Empire, 1740–1763* (New York, 1940).

Friedrich, Carl J., *The Age of the Baroque, 1610–1660* (New York, 1952).

Gershoy, Leo, *From Despotism to Revolution, 1763–1789* (New York, 1944).

Goodwin, A. (ed.), *The New Cambridge Modern History*, vol. VIII, *The American and French Revolutions, 1763–1793* (Cambridge, 1965).

Hampson, N., *The First European Revolution, 1776–1815* (1969).

Hatton, R., *Europe in the Age of Louis XIV* (1969).

Hinrichs, Carl, 'Staat und Gesellschaft im Barockzeitalter', in *Preussen als Historisches Problem* (Gerhard Oestreich ed.) (Berlin, 1964), pp. 205–226.

Hubatsch, Walter, *Das Zeitalter des Absolutismus, 1600–1789* (Brunswick, 1962).

Lindsay, J. O. (ed.), *The New Cambridge Modern History*, vol. VII, *The Old Régime, 1713–1763* (Cambridge, 1957).

Mann, G. and Nitschke, A. (eds), *Propyläen Weltgeschichte: Eine Universalgeschichte*, vol. VII, *Von der Reformation zur Revolution* (Berlin–Frankfurt–Vienna, 1964).

Molesworth, H. D., *The Princes* (1969).

Mousnier, Roland, *Les XVIe et XVIIe Siècles* (3rd edition, Paris, 1961).

    Labrousse, Ernest, and Bouloiseau, Marc, *Le XVIIIe Siècle (1715–1815)* (Paris, 1953).

Muret, Pierre, *La Prépondérance anglaise (1715–1783)* (Paris, 1937).

Nussbaum, Frederick L., *The Triumph of Science and Reason, 1660–1685* (New York, 1953).

Palmer, R. R., *The Age of Democratic Revolution, The Challenge* (Princeton, 1959).

Pennington, D. H., *Seventeenth-Century Europe* (1970).

Rauch, Georg von, 'Die neuere Geschichte (1500–1815) in der sowjetischen Geschichtsschreibung der Gegenwart', in *Jahrbücher für Geschichte Osteuropas*, Neue Folge, vol. III (1955), pp. 71–83.

Roberts, Penfield, *The Quest for Security, 1715–1740* (New York, 1947).

Rule, John C., *The Early Modern Era, 1648–1770* (Boston, 1966).

Sagnac, Philippe, et Saint Léger, A. de., *La Prépondérance française: Louis XIV (1661–1715)* (3rd edition, Paris, 1949).

    La Fin de l'Ancien Régime et la Révolution Américaine (1763–1789) (Paris, 1952).

Stoye, John, *Europe Unfolding, 1648–1688* (1969).

Trevor-Roper, H. R., *Religion, the Reformation and Social Change, and other essays* (1967).

    The Age of Expansion: Europe 1559–1660 (1968).

Wagner, Fritz, *Europa im Zeitalter des Absolutismus, 1648–1789* (1948).

Wolf, John B., *The Emergence of the Great Powers, 1685–1715* (New York, 1951).

International Relations

Dehio, Ludwig, *The Precarious Balance: The Problem of Power in Europe, 1494–1945* (1963).

Hatton, R. M. and Bromley, S. J. (eds), *William III and Louis XIV* (Liverpool, 1968).

Hinsley, F. H., *Power and the Pursuit of Peace* (Cambridge, 1963).

Livet, G., *La Guerre de Trente Ans* (Paris, 1963).

Porchnev, B. F., 'Les Rapports politiques de l'Europe occidentale et de l'Europe Orientale à l'époque de la Guerre de Trente Ans', in *Rapports, XIe Congrès International des Sciences Historiques*, vol. IV, *Histoire Moderne* (Göteborg–Stockholm–Uppsala, 1960), pp. 136–163.

Rabb, T. K., *The Thirty Years' War* (1964).

Steinberg, S. H., *The Thirty Years' War and the Conflict for European Hegemony, 1600–1660* (1966).

Viner, Jacob, 'Power versus Plenty as objectives of foreign policy in the 17th and 18th centuries', in *World Politics*, vol. I, No. 1 (1948).

Wedgwood, C. V., *The Thirty Years' War* (1938).

Williams, Glyndwr, *The Expansion of Europe in the Eighteenth Century* (1966).

Zeller, Gaston, *Histoire des relations internationales, Les Temps modernes, II, De Louis XIV à 1789* (Paris, 1955).

The 'General Crisis'

Aston, Trevor (ed.), *Crisis in Europe 1560–1660, Essays from 'Past and Present'* (1965).

Merriman, Roger Bigelow, *Six Contemporaneous Revolutions* (Oxford, 1938).

Government

Barker, Ernest, *The Development of the Public Services in Western Europe 1660–1930* (2nd edition, New York, 1945).

Gerhard, Dietrich, 'Amtsträger zwischen Krongewalt und Ständen – Ein Europäisches Problem' in *Alteuropa und die moderne Gesellschaft, Festschrift für Otto Brunner* (Göttingen, 1963), pp. 230–247.

'Problems of Representation and Delegation in the Eighteenth century', in *Ancien Pays et Assemblées d'Etats, études publiées par la Section Belge de la Commission Internationale Pour L'Histoire des Assemblés d'Etats*, vol. XXXVII (Louvain–Paris, 1965), pp. 117–149.

'Regionalismus und ständisches Wesen als ein Grundthema europäischer Geschichte', in *Historische Zeitschrift*, vol. CLXXIV (Berlin, 1952), and reprinted in Gerhard, D., *Alte und Neue Welt in vergleichender Geschichtsbetrachtung* (Göttingen, 1962).

Hartung, Fritz and Mousnier, Roland, 'Quelques problèmes concernant la monarchie absolue', in *Relazioni, X Congresso Internazionale di Scienze Storiche*, vol. IV (Florence, 1955), pp. 1–55.

Haussherr, Hans, *Verwaltungseinheit und Ressorttrennung vom Ende des 17. bis zum Beginn des 19. Jahrhunderts* (Berlin, 1953).

Hintze, Otto, 'Der Commissarius und seine Bedeutung in der allgemeinen Verwaltungsgeschichte' (1910) in his *Staat und Verfassung, Gesammelte Abhandlungen zur allgemeinen Verfassungsgeschichte* (2nd edition, Göttingen, 1962).

Kiernan, V. G., 'Foreign Mercenaries and Absolute Monarchy', in *Past and Present*, No. 11 (1957).

'State and Nation in Western Europe', in *Past and Present*, No. 31 (1965).

Klaveren, Jacob van, 'Die historiche Erscheinung der Korruption in ihrem Zusammenhang mit des Staats- und Gesellschaftsstruktur betrachtet' in *Vierteljahrschrift für Sozial- und Wirtschaftsgeschichte*, vols. XLIV (1957), XLV (1958), XLVI (1959).

'Fiskalismus-Merkantilismus-Korruption. Drei Aspekte der Finanz- und Wirtschaftspolitik während des Ancien Régime', in *Vierteljahrschrift für Sozial- und Wirtschaftsgeschichte*, vol. XLVII (1960), pp. 333–353.

Lubasz, Heinz, *The Development of the Modern State* (1964).

Meinecke, Friedrich, *Machiavellism* (English trans. 1957).

Oestreich, Gerhard, 'Zur Heeresverfassung der deutschen Territorien von 1500 bis 1800', in Richard Dietrich and Gerhard Oestreich (eds.) *Forschungen zu Staat und Verfassung, Festgabe für Fritz Hartung* (Berlin, 1958).

Raumer, K. von, 'Absoluter Staat, korporative Libertät, persönliche Freiheit', in *Historische Zeitschrift*, vol. 183 (Berlin, 1957).

Roberts, Michael, 'The Military Revolution, 1560–1660', in his *Essays in Swedish History* (1967).

Swart, K. W., *The Sale of Offices in the Seventeenth Century* (The Hague, 1949).

Vicens Vives, Jaime, 'Estructura administrativa estatal en los siglos XVI y XVII', in *Rapports, XIe Congrès International des Sciences Historiques*, vol. IV, *Histoire moderne* (Göteborg–Stockholm–Uppsala, 1960), pp. 1–24.

Wittram, Reinhard, 'Formen und Wandlungen des europäischen

Absolutismus' in Runte, Heinrich (ed.), *Glaube und Geschichte: Festschrift für Friedrich Gogarten* (Giessen, 1948), pp. 278–299.

Enlightened Absolutism

Andrews, Stuart, *Enlightened Despotism* (1967).

Bruun, Geoffrey, *The Enlightened Despots* (2nd edition, 1967).

Gagliardo, John G., *Enlightened Despotism* (1968).

Hartung, Fritz, *Enlightened Despotism* (1957).
    and Mousnier, Roland, 'Quelques problèmes concernant la monarchie absolue' (see under *Government*).

Lefebvre, Georges, 'Le Despotisme éclairé', in *Annales historiques de la Révolution Française*, vol. XXI (Paris, 1949), p. 98.

Moraze, C., 'Finances et despotisme: Essai sur les despotes éclairés', in *Annales*, vol. XX (1948), pp. 279–296.

Wines, Roger (ed.), *Enlightened Despotism: Reform or Reaction?* (Boston, 1968).

Economic History

Clough, S. B. and Cole, C. W., *Economic History of Europe* (3rd edition, Boston, 1952).

Coleman, D. C., 'Eli Heckscher and the Idea of Mercantilism', in *Scandinavian Economic History Review*, vol. V (1957), pp. 3-22.

Haussherr, Hans, *Wirtschaftsgeschichte der Neuzeit* (Weimar, 1954).

Heaton, H., *Economic History of Europe* (New York, 1948)

Heckscher, Eli, *Mercantilism* (English trans., 2nd edition, 2 vols, 1956).

Henderson, W. O., *The Industrialisation of Europe, 1780–1914* (1969).

Kellenbenz, Hermann, 'Probleme der Merkantilismusforschung', in *Rapports, XIIe Congrès International des Sciences Historiques* (Vienna, 1965), p. 182.

Klaveren, J. van, 'Die Manufakturen des Ancien Régime', in *Vierteljahrschrift für Sozial- und Wirtschaftsgeschichte*, vol. LI (1964).

Landes, David S., 'Technological Change and Development in Western Europe, 1750–1914' in Habakkuk, H. J. and Postan, M. (eds), *The Cambridge Economic History of Europe*, vol. VI, Part I (Cambridge, 1965), p. 4.

Meuvret, J. 'L'Agriculture en Europe au XVIIième et XVIIIième siècles' in *Relazioni, X Congresso Internazionale di Scienze Storiche*, vol. IV (Florence, 1955), pp. 139–168.

Redlich, F., 'European Aristocracy and Economic Development' in *Explorations in Entrepreneurial History*, vol. VI (1953), pp. 78-93.

Slicher, van Bath, B. H., *The Agrarian History of Western Europe, 500–1850* (1963).

Warrener, D., 'Some controversial issues in the history of agrarian Europe', in *Slavonic and East European Review*, vol. XXXII (1954), pp. 182–184.

Wilson, Charles, *Mercantilism* (1958).

Society

Ariès, Philippe, *L'enfant et la vie familiale sous l'Ancien Régime* (Paris, 1960) (English trans. by R. Baldick: *The Centuries of Childhood*, 1962).

Barber, Bernard and Barber, Elinor G. (eds), *European Social Class: Stability and Change* (New York, 1965).

Betts, R. R., 'La société dans l'Europe centrale et dans l'Europe orientale', in *Revue d'histoire comparée*, No. 2 (1948).

Blum, Jerome, 'The Rise of Serfdom in Eastern Europe', in *American Historical Review*, vol. 62 (1957), pp. 807–836.

Brunner, Otto, *Neue Wege der Sozialgeschichte* (Göttingen, 1956). (Festschrift für), *Alteuropa und die moderne Gesellschaft* (Göttingen, 1963).

Goodwin, A., (ed.), *The European Nobility in the Eighteenth Century* (1953).

Labrousse, Ernest, 'Voies nouvelles vers une histoire de la bourgeoisie occidentale aux XVIIIe et XIXe siècles (1700–1850)', in *Relazioni, X Congresso Internazionale di Scienze Storiche*, vol. IV, *Storia Moderna* (Florence, 1955), pp. 365–396.

Langer, W. L., 'Europe's initial Population Explosion', in *American Historical Review*, vol. 68 (1963).

Lousse, E., *La Société d'ancien régime, organisation et représentation corporatives*, vol. I, *Études Présentées à la Commission Internationale pour l'Histoire des Assemblées d'États* (Louvain, 1943); reviewed by Dhondt, J. in *Revue belge de philologie et d'histoire*, vol. XXVI, pp. 284–292.

Moore, Jr., Barrington. *The Social Origins of Dictatorship and Democracy, Lord and Peasant in the Making of the Modern World* (1967).

Mousnier, Roland, 'Problèmes de Méthode dans l'étude des structures sociales des seizième, dix-septième, dix-huitième siècles', in Konrad Reggen and Stephan Skalweit (eds) *Spiegel der Geschichte. Festgabe für Max Braubach zum 10 April 1964* (Münster, 1964).

'Problèmes de stratification sociale: Actes du Colloque International, 1966' (Paris, 1968).

Les Hiérarchies sociales de 1450 à nos jours (Paris, 1969).

Rudé, G., 'The Study of Popular Disturbances in the "Pre-Industrial" Age', in Historical Studies, Australia and New Zealand (1963).

Culture

Artz, Frederick, B., From the Renaissance to Romanticism, Trends in style in art, literature, and music, 1300–1830 (Chicago, 1962).

Berlin, Isaiah, The Age of Enlightenment (New York, 1956).

Bronowski, J. and Mazlish, Bruce, The Western Intellectual Tradition (1960).

Coates, W. H., White, H. V. and Schapiro, J. S., The Emergence of Liberal Humanism: an Intellectual History of Western Europe, vol. I, From the Italian Renaissance to the French Revolution (New York, 1966).

Cobban, Alfred, In Search of Humanity (1960).

Courtney, C. P., Montesquieu and Burke (Oxford, 1963).

Cragg, G. B., The Church in the Age of Reason, 1648–1789 (1960).

Crocker, Lester (ed.), The Age of Enlightenment (1969).

Dijksterhuis, E. J., The Mechanisation of the World Picture (Oxford, 1961).

Gay, Peter, The Enlightenment: An Interpretation, vol. 1, The Rise of Modern Paganism (1967), vol. 2, The Science of Freedom (1970).

Hall, A. R., From Galileo to Newton, 1630–1720 (1963).
The Scientific Revolution, 1500–1800 (1954).

Hampshire, Stuart, The Age of Reason (New York, 1956).

Hampson, N., History of European Thought, vol. 4, The Enlightenment (1969).

Haskell, Francis, Patrons and Painters (1963).

Hazard, P., The Crisis of the European Mind, 1680–1715 (1953).
European Thought in the Eighteenth Century from Montesquieu to Lessing (1954).

Lively, J. F., The Enlightenment (1966).

Mandrou, R., 'Le Baroque européen Mentalité pathétique et révolution sociale', in Annales, vol. XV (1960), pp. 898–914.

Mazzeo, J. A., Renaissance and Revolution, The Remaking of European Thought (1967).

Venturi, Franco, 'L'Illuminismo nel Settecento Europeo', in Rap-

ports, XIe Congrès International des Sciences Historiques, vol.
IV, *Histoire Moderne* (Göteborg–Stockholm–Uppsala, 1960).
   Settecento Riformatore (Turin, 1970).
   Utopia and Reform in the Enlightenment (Cambridge, 1971).
Vereker, C. H., *Eighteenth-Century Optimism* (Liverpool, 1966).
Wasserman, Earl R., *Aspects of the Eighteenth Century* (1965).
West, J. F., *The Great Intellectual Revolution* (1965).

The Revolutions

Amann, Peter, *The Eighteenth-Century Revolution: French or Western?* (Boston, 1963).
Ford, Franklin L., 'The Revolutionary-Napoleonic Era: How much of a watershed?' in *American Historical Review*, vol. 69 (1964), p. 18.
Godechot, Jacques, *Les Révolutions, 1770–1799* (*Nouvelle Clio*, No. 36) (Paris, 1963).
Hobsbawm, Eric, *The Age of Revolution: Europe from 1789–1848* (1962).
Palmer, R. R., *The Age of the Democratic Revolution*, vol. II (Oxford, 1965).
Rudé, George, *Revolutionary Europe, 1783–1815* (1964).

UNITED PROVINCES

Bibliographies

Algemene Geschiedenis der Nederlanden, 12 vols. (Utrecht, 1949–58), vols 6, 7, and 8.
Kossmann, E. and J., 'Bulletin critique de l'historiographie néerlandaise', published annually in *Revue du Nord. Revue historique trimestriel, le Nord de France–Belgique–Pays Bas* (Lille, 1954 onwards).

General Works

Algemene Geschiedenis der Nederlanden, 12 vols. (Utrecht, 1949–58), vols 6, 7, and 8.
Baxter, Stephen B., *William III* (1966).
Blok, P. J., *History of the People of the Netherlands*, 5 vols. (New York, 1898–1912).
Boxer, C. R., *The Dutch Seaborne Empire, 1600–1800* (1965).
Cobban, Alfred, *Ambassadors and Secret Agents: the Diplomacy of the First Earl of Malmesbury at the Hague* (1954).
Geyl, Pieter, *The Netherlands in the Seventeenth Century*, Part I, *1609–1648* (1961); Part II, *1648–1715* (1964).

History of the Low Countries, Episodes and Problems (1964). *Orange and Stuart, 1641–1672* (1969).

Renier, G. J., *The Dutch Nation. An Historical Study* (1944).

Robb, Nesca A., *William of Orange, a personal portrait*, 2 vols. (1962, 1966).

Vlekke, B. H. M., *The Evolution of the Dutch Nation* (New York, 1945).

Wilson, Charles, *The Dutch Republic and the Civilisation of the Seventeenth Century* (1968).

Economic History

Barbour, Violet, *Capitalism in Amsterdam in the 17th century* (Baltimore, 1950).

Dillen, J. G. van, 'Amsterdam's role in seventeenth-century Dutch politics and its economic background', in J. S. Bromley and E. H. Kossmann (eds), *Britain and the Netherlands*, vol. II (Groningen, 1964).

Hoboken, W. J. van, 'The Dutch West India Company: the Political Background of its Rise and Decline', in J. S. Bromley and E. H. Kossman (eds), *Britain and the Netherlands*, vol. I (1960).

Schöffer, I., 'Did Holland's Golden Age coincide with a period of crisis?', in *Acta Historiae Neerlandica*, vol. I (Leyden, 1966), pp. 82–107.

Wilson, Charles, *Anglo-Dutch Commerce and Finance in the 18th Century* (2nd edition, Cambridge, 1966).

'The Decline of the Netherlands', in Charles Wilson, *Economic History and the Historian, Collected Essays* (1969), pp. 22–47.

Profit and Power. A Study of England and the Dutch Wars (1957).

'Taxation and the Decline of the Empires, an unfashionable theme', in Charles Wilson, *Economic History and the Historian. Collected Essays* (1969).

Society

Huizinga, J. H., *Dutch Civilisation in the 17th Century and other essays* (English trans. Arnold J. Pomerans, 1968).

Murray, John H., *Amsterdam in the Age of Rembrandt* (Norman, Oklahoma, 1967).

Roorda, D. J., 'The ruling classes in Holland in the seventeenth century', in J. S. Bromley and E. H. Kossman (eds), *Britain and the Netherlands*, vol. II (Groningen, 1964).

Zumthur, Paul, *La Vie quotidienne en Holland au temps de Rembrandt* (Paris, 1959), English trans. *Daily life in Rembrandt's Holland* (1962).

Culture

Gelder, Enno van, *The Two Reformations in the 17th Century* (The Hague, 1964).

Gelder, H. E. van, *Guide to Dutch Art* (The Hague, 1961).

Kossmann, E. H., 'The development of Dutch political theory in the seventeenth century', in J. S. Bromley and E. H. Kossmann (eds), *Britain and the Netherlands*, vol. I (1960), pp. 91–110.

SPAIN

Bibliographies

Centro de Estudios Internacionales, Universidad de Barcelona, *Indice histórico español* (1952 onwards) (Quarterly, reviewing books and articles on Spanish history).

Sánchez Alonso, B. (ed.), *Fuentes de la historia española e hispano-americana*, 3 vols (3rd edition, Madrid, 1952).

Vicens Vives, Jaime, Reglá, J., and Nadal, J., 'L'Espagne aux XVIe et XVIIe siècles', in *Revue historique*, vol. CCXX (Paris, 1958), pp. 1–42.

General Works

Bottineau, Y., *L'Art de cours dans l'Espagne de Philippe V* (Bordeaux, 1963).

Bruguera, G. F., *Histoire contemporaine d'Espagne 1789–1930* (Paris, 1953).

Carr, Raymond, *Spain, 1808–1939* (Oxford, 1966).

Chaunu, P., 'Notes sur l'Espagne de Philippe V (1700–1746),' in *Revue d'histoire économique et sociale*, No. 4 (1963).

Dolores Mateos, Maria, *La España de Antiguo Régimen: Salamanca* (Salamanca, 1966).

Domínguez Ortiz, A., *Política y hacienda de Felipe IV* (Madrid, 1960).

Elliott, J. H., *Imperial Spain, 1469–1716* (1963).
  The Revolt of the Catalans (1558–1640) (Cambridge, 1963).
  'The Decline of Spain', in *Past and Present*, No. 20 (1961), pp. 52–75.

Herr, Richard, *The Eighteenth-Century Revolution in Spain* (Princeton, 1958).

Hume, Martin, *The Court of Philip IV. Spain in Decadence* (1st edition, 1907).

Kamen, H., *The War of Succession in Spain, 1700–1715* (1969).

Kendrick, T. D., *Mary of Ágreda* (1967).

Lynch, John, *Spain under the Habsburgs*, vol. 2, *1598–1700* (Oxford, 1969).

Marañón, Gregorio, *El Conde-Duque de Olivares* (Madrid, 1936: 3rd edition, 1952).

Maura, Duque de, *Vida y reinado de Carlos II*, 2 vols. (2nd edition, Madrid, 1954).

Nada, John, *Carlos the Bewitched, The Last Spanish Habsburg, 1661–1700* (1962).

Ubieto, Antonio, Reglá, J., Jover, J. M., and Seco, C., *Introducción a la historia de España* (2nd edition, Barcelona, 1965).

Vicens Vives, Jaime, *Aproximación a la historia de España* (3rd edition, Barcelona, 1962).

Vilar, Pierre, *Spain, A Brief History* (1967) (Trans. of *Histoire d'Espagne*, Paris, 1949).

'Le Temps du Quichotte', *Europe*, vol. XXXIV (Paris, 1956), pp. 3–16.

Wandruszka, Adam, *The House of Habsburg* (1964).

Crown of Aragon

Carrera Pujal, J., *Historia política y económica de Cataluña*, 4 vols. (Barcelona, 1946–7).

Domínguez Ortiz, A., 'The Revolt of Catalonia against Philip IV', in *Past and Present*, No. 29 (1964), p. 105.

Elliott, J. H., *The Revolt of the Catalans (1558–1640)* (Cambridge, 1963).

Vilar, Pierre, *La Catalogne dans l'Espagne moderne*, 3 vols. (Paris, 1962–4).

Voltes Bou, P., *Barcelona durante el gobierno del Archiduque Carlos de Austria (1705–1714)* (Barcelona, 1963).

El Archiduque Carlos de Austria, rey de los Catalanes (Barcelona, 1952).

Government

Christiansen, Eric, *The Origins of Military Power in Spain, 1800–1854* (Oxford, 1967).

Desdevises du Dezart, G., *L'Espagne de l'Ancien Régime*, 3 vols. (Paris, 1897–1904) (new edition in *Revue hispanique*, vols LXIV, 1925, LXX, 1927, LXXIII, 1928).

Kamen, H., 'Melchior de Macanaz and the foundations of Bourbon power in Spain', in *English Historical Review*, vol. 80 (1965), pp. 699–716.

Palacio Atard, V., 'El Despotismo ilustrado español', in *Arbor* (1947).

Perez Bustamente, C., 'El reinado de Fernando VI en el reformismo español del siglo XVIII', in *Revista de la Universidad de Madrid*, vol. III (1954).

Rodríguez Casado, V., *Política interior de Carlos III* (Valladolid, 1950).

De la Monarquía española del barroco (Seville, 1955).

La Administración pública en el reinado de Carlos III (Oviedo, 1961).

La Política y los políticos en el reinado de Carlos III (Madrid, 1962).

'Iglesia y estado en el reinado de Carlos III', *Estudios Americanos*, vol. I (Seville, 1958), pp. 5–57.

'La revolución burgesa del siglo XVIII español', in *Arbor* (1951).

Sánchez Diana, J. M., 'El Despotismo ilustrado de Federico II y su influencia en españa', in *Arbor* (1954).

Valiente, T. F., *Los Validos en la monarquía española del siglo XVIII* (Madrid, 1963).

Society

Bomli, P. W., *La Femme dans l'Espagne du Siècle d'Or* (The Hague, 1950).

Chaunu, P., 'La Société espagnole du Siècle d'Or', in *Annales*, vol. VII (Paris, 1951).

Desdevises du Dezart, G., *L'Espagne de l'Ancien Régime*, 3 vols. (Paris, 1897–1904) (new edition in *Revue hispanique*, vols LXIV, 1925, LXX, 1927, LXXIII, 1928).

Domínguez Ortiz, A., *La Sociedad española en el siglo XVII* (Madrid, 1963).

La Sociedad española en el siglo XVIII (Madrid, 1955).

Kany, C. E., *Life and Manners in Madrid, 1750–1800* (Berkeley, 1932).

Palacio Atard, V., *Fin de la sociedad española del Antiguo Régimen* (Madrid, 1952).

Vicens Vives, Jaime (ed.), *Historia social y económica de España y América*, vols. III and IV (Barcelona, 1957, 1958).

Economic History

Callahan, W. J., 'Crown, nobility and industry in eighteenth-century Spain', in *International Review of Social History*, vol. XI (1966).

Carrera Pujal, J., *Historia de la económica española*, 5 vols. (Barcelona, 1943-4).

Chaunu, H. and P., *Séville et l'Atlantique (1504-1650)*, 12 vols. (Paris, 1955-9).

'Économie atlantique. Économie mondiale', in *Journal of Modern History* (1953-4), pp. 91-104.

Hamilton, Earl J., *American Treasure and the Price Revolution in Spain, 1501-1650* (Cambridge, Mass., 1934).

War and Prices in Spain, 1651-1800 (Cambridge, Mass., 1947).

'The Decline of Spain', in E. M. Carus-Wilson (ed.), *Essays in Economic History* (1954).

'Monetary disorder and Economic decadence in Spain, 1651-1700', in *The Journal of Political Economy* (Chicago, 1953).

'Monetary Inflation in Castile, 1508-1660', in *Economic History*, vol. II (1930-33), pp. 177-212.

'Money and Economic recovery in Spain under the first Bourbon', in *Journal of Modern History*, vol. XV (1943), pp. 192-206.

Kamen, H., 'The Decline of Castile: the last crisis', in *Economic History Review*, 2nd Series, vol. XVII (1964), pp. 63-76.

Klaveren, J. van, *Europäische Wirtschaftsgeschichte Spaniens im 16. und 17. Jahrhundert (Forschungen zur Sozial- und Wirtschaftsgeschichte*, Band 2) (Stuttgart, 1960).

Klein, J., *The Mesta* (Cambridge Mass., 1920).

La Force, Jr., James Clayburn, *The Development of the Spanish Textile Industry, 1750-1800* (Los Angeles, 1965).

McLachlan, J. O., *Trade and Peace with Old Spain, 1667-1750* (Cambridge, 1950).

Vicens Vives, Jaime, *Manual de historia económica de España* (Barcelona, 3rd edition, 1964).

Vilar, P., 'Problems of the Formation of Capitalism', in *Past and Present*, No. 10 (1956).

Review of E. J. Hamilton, in *Annales* (1949), pp. 29-45.

Viñas y Mey, C., *El Problema de la tierra en la España de los siglos XVI-XVII* (Madrid, 1941).

Culture

Herr, Richard, *The Eighteenth-Century Revolution in Spain* (Princeton, 1958).

Kamen, H., *The Spanish Inquisition* (1965).

Klingender, F. D., *Goya and the democratic tradition* (1948).

Sánchez Agesta, Luis, *El Pensamiento político del despotismo ilustrado* (1953).

'Feijóo y el pensamiento politico español', in *R. E. P.*, vol. XII.

Sarrailh, J., *L'Espagne éclairée de la seconde moitié du XVIIIième siècle* (Paris, 1954).

'La Crise spirituelle et économique de l'Espagne à la fin du XVIIIième siècle', in *Journal of Modern History*, vol. XXVII (1955).

FRANCE

Bibliographies

Godechot, Jacques, *Les Révolutions, 1770–1799* (*Nouvelle Clio*, No. 36) (Paris, 1963).

Mandrou, Robert, *La France aux XVIIe et XVIIIe siècles* (*Nouvelle Clio*, No. 33) (Paris, 1967).

Préclin, Edmond, et Tapié, Victor-L., *Le XVIIe siècle* (2nd edition, Paris, 1949).

Le XVIIIe siècle (Paris, 1952).

General Works

Behrens, C. B. A., *The Ancien Régime* (1967).

' "Straight History" and "History in Depth": the experience of writers on eighteenth-century France', in *Historical Journal*, vol. VIII (1965), pp. 117–126.

Cobban, Alfred, *A History of Modern France, vol. I, 1715–1799* (2nd edition, 1961).

Corvisier, A., *L'Armée française de la fin du XVIIe siècle au ministère de Choiseul: Le Soldat*, 2 vols. (Paris, 1964).

Dakin, Douglas, *Turgot and the Ancien Régime in France* (New York, 1965).

Duby, G. and Mandrou, R., *History of French Civilisation* (English trans. J. B. Atkinson, 1966).

Lavisse, Ernest, *Histoire de France depuis les origines jusqu'à la Révolution*, vols 7–10 (Paris, 1905–10).

Lough, John, *An Introduction to Seventeenth-Century France* (1954).

An Introduction to Eighteenth-Century France (1960).

Locke's Travels in France, 1675–1679 (Cambridge, 1953).

Méthivier, Hubert, *L'Ancien Régime* (Paris, 1961).

Mousnier, Roland, *L'Age classique, 1598–1715* (Paris, 1954).

Nef, J. U., *Industry and Government in France and England, 1550–1640* (1940).

Sagnac, Philippe, *La Formation de la société française moderne*, vol. I, *La Société et la monarchie absolue (1661–1715)* (Paris, 1945); vol. II, *La Révolution des idées et des moeurs et le déclin de l'Ancien Régime (1715–1788)* (Paris, 1946).

Tapié, Victor-L., *La France de Louis XIII et de Richelieu* (Paris, 1952).

Temple, Norah, 'French towns during the Ancien Régime', *History*, vol. LI (1966), pp. 16–34.

Tilly, H., *The Vendée* (Cambridge, Mass., 1964).

Tocqueville, A. de, *L'Ancien Régime* (English trans. M. W. Patterson) (Oxford, 1947).

Zeller, Gaston, *Aspects de la politique française sous l'Ancien Régime* (Paris, 1964).

International Relations

André, Louis, *Louis XIV et l'Europe* (Paris, 1950).

Hatton, R. M. and Bromley, J. S. (eds), *William III and Louis XIV* (Liverpool, 1968).

Zeller, Gaston, *Histoire des relations internationales. Les Temps modernes II, de Louis XIV à 1789* (Paris, 1955).

The Frondes

Kossmann, Ernst H., *La Fronde* (Leiden, 1954) (in French).

Mandrou, Robert, *Classes et luttes des classes en France au début du XVIIe siècle* (Florence, 1965).

Mousnier, Roland, 'Quelques raisons de la Fronde. Les causes des journées révolutionnaires parisiennes de 1648' in *XVIIième siècle*, No. 2 (Paris, 1949).

'Recherches sur les soulèvements populaires en France avant la Fronde', in *Revue d'histoire moderne et contemporaine* (Paris, 1958), pp. 81–113.

Porchnev, Boris F., *Les Soulèvements populaires en France de 1623 à 1648* (Paris, 1963); *Die Volksaufstände in Frankreich vor der Fronde, 1623–1648* (Leipzig, 1954) (Trans. from Russian).

Louis XIV

Church, William F. (ed.), *The Greatness of Louis XIV, Myth or Reality?* (Boston, 1959).

Goubert, Pierre, *Louis XIV et vingt millions de Français* (Paris, 1966). Trans. *Louis XIV and Twenty Million Frenchmen* (1969).

Hinrichs, Carl, 'Zur Selbstauffassung Ludwigs XIV in seinen Mémoires', in *Preussen als Historisches Problem, Gesammelte Abhandlungen* (ed. Gerhard Oestreich) (Berlin, 1964), pp. 299–315.

Judge, H. G., *Louis XIV* (1965).

Méthivier, Hubert, *Louis XIV* (Paris, 1950).

Wolf, John B., *Louis XIV* (1968).

Louis XV

Gooch, G. P., *Louis XV, The Monarchy in Decline* (1956).

Méthivier, Hubert, *Le siècle de Louis XV* (Paris, 1966).

Louis XVI

Fay, Bernard, *Louis XVI, or the End of a World* (English trans. P. O'Brien) (1968).

Government

André, Louis, *Michel Le Tellier et Louvois* (Paris, 1942).

Bamford, Paul Walden, *Forests and French Sea Power, 1660–1789* (Oxford, 1956).

Bluche, François, *Les Magistrats du Parlement de Paris au XVIIIe siècle (1715–1771)* (Paris, 1960).

Bordes, M., 'Les Intendants de Louis XV', in *Revue historique,* vol. 223 (1960), pp. 45–62.

Bosher, J. F., *The Single Duty Project: A Study of the Movement for a French Customs Union in the 18th Century* (1964).
    French Finances, 1770–1795: From Business to Bureaucracy (Cambridge, 1970).

Bromley, J. S., 'The Decline of Absolute Monarchy (1683–1774)', in J. M. Wallace-Hadrill and John McManners (eds), *France, Government and Society* (1957).

Cole, C. W., *Colbert and a Century of French Mercantilism* (New York, 1939).

Dakin, Douglas, *Turgot and the Ancien Régime in France* (New York, 1965).

Ellul, J., *Histoire des institutions de l'époque franque à la Révolution*, Part IV (Paris, 1962).

Fréville, H., *L'Intendance de Bretagne (1689–1790)*, 3 vols. (Rennes, 1953).

Göhring, Martin, *Die Amterkäuflichkeit im Ancien Régime* (Berlin, 1938).

Gruder, Vivian R., *The Royal Provincial Intendants: a governing élite in eighteenth-century France* (New York, 1968).

King, James E., *Science and Rationalism in the government of Louis XIV, 1661–1683* (Baltimore, 1949).

Lacour-Gayet, Robert, *Calonne: financier, réformateur, et contre-révolutionaire* (Paris, 1963).

Livet, G., *L'Intendance d'Alsace sous Louis XIV, 1648–1715* (Strasbourg, 1956).

McCloy, S. T., *Government assistance in eighteenth-century France* (Durham, N. C., 1946).

McManners, J., 'The Revolution and its antecedents (1774–1794)', in J. M. Wallace-Hadrill and John McManners (eds), *France, Government and Society* (1957).

Marion, M., *Dictionnaire des institutions de la France aux XVIIe et XVIIIe siècles* (Paris, 1923).

Matthews, G. T., *Royal General Farms in 18th-Century France* (Oxford, 1958).

Mousnier, Roland, *La Vénalité des offices sous Henri IV et Louis XIII* (Rouen, 1945).

'Etat et commissaire. Recherches sur la création des intendants de province (1643–1648)', in *Forschungen zur Staat und Verfassung. Festgabe für Fritz Hartung* (Berlin, 1958).

'Le Conseil du Roi de la mort de Henri IV au gouvernement personnel de Louis XIV', in *Études d'histoire moderne et contemporaine*, vol. I (1947), pp. 29–67.

'L'Evolution des finances publiques en France et en Angleterre pendant les guerres de la Ligue d'Augsbourg et de la Succession d'Espagne', in *Revue historique* (1951), pp. 1–23.

'La Participation des Gouvernés à l'activité des Gouvernants dans la France du 17e et 18e siècles', in *Études suisses d'histoire générale*, vol. XX (1962–63), pp. 200–229.

'L'Evolution des institutions monarchiques en France et ses relations avec l'état social', in *XVIIe siècle*, Nos. 58–59 (Paris, 1963).

Mousnier, R., Bluche, F., Corvisier, A., Goubert, P., and Tapié, V-L., 'Serviteurs du Roi: quelques aspects de la function publique dans la société française du XVIIe siècle', in *XVIIe siècle*, Nos. 42–43 (Paris, 1959).

Pagès, Georges, *La Monarchie d'Ancien Régime en France* (Paris, 1932).

Prestwich, Menna, 'The making of the Absolute Monarchy (1559–1683)', in J. M. Wallace-Hadrill and John McManners (eds), *France, Government and Society* (1957).

Shennan, J. H., *The Parlement of Paris* (1968).

Society

Asher, Eugene L., *The Resistance to the Maritime Classes. The Survival of Feudalism in the France of Colbert* (Berkeley, 1960).

Barber, E. G., *The Bourgeoisie in 18th-Century France* (Princeton, 1955).

Bois, Paul, *Les Paysans de l'Ouest* (Le Mans, 1960).

Davies, Alun, 'The Origins of the French Peasant Revolution of 1789', in *History*, vol. XLIX (1964), p. 24.

Ford, Franklin L., *Robe and Sword* (1953).
    Strasbourg in Transition, 1648–1789 (1958).

Forster, Robert, *The Nobility of Toulouse in the 18th Century: a social and economic study* (Baltimore, 1960).
    'The Provincial Noble: a reappraisal', in *American Historical Journal*, vol. 68 (1962–63), pp. 681–691.

Goubert, Pierre, *Beauvais et le Beauvaisis de 1600 à 1730* (Paris, 1960).
    L'Ancien Régime, vol. I, *La Société* (Paris, 1969).
    'The French peasantry of the Seventeenth century, A regional example', *Past and Present*, No. 10 (1956), p. 55.

Halphen, L. and Doucet, R., *Histoire de la société française* (Paris, 1953).

Kaplow, Jeffry, *Elbeuf during the Revolutionary Period: History and Social Structure* (Baltimore, 1964).

Lefebvre, Georges, *Etudes Orléanaises I. Contribution à l'étude des structures sociales à la fin du XVIIIe siècle* (Paris, 1962).

Le Roy-Ladurie, Emmanuel, *Les Paysans de Languedoc* (Paris, 1966).

Lüthy, Herbert, *La Banque Protestante en France de la Révocation de l'Edit de Nantes à la Révolution*, 2 vols. (Paris, 1959 and 1961) (good review by J. Bouvier, in *Annales*, vol. XIX (Paris, 1963), 779–792).

McManners, John, *French Ecclesiastical Society under the Ancien Régime* (Manchester, 1960).

Meuvret, Jean, 'Les crises de subsistance et la démographie de la France d'Ancien Régime', in *Population* (Paris, 1946), pp. 643–650.

Mongrédien, G., *La vie quotidienne sous Louis XIV* (Paris, 1948).

Rascol, P., *Les Paysans de l'Albigeois à la fin de L'Ancien Régime* (Aurillac, 1961).

Ravitch, N., 'The social origins of French and English Bishops in the Eighteenth Century', in *Historical Journal*, vol. VIII (1965).

Reinhard, M., 'Elite et noblesse dans la seconde moitié du XVIIIe siècle', in *Revue d'histoire moderne et contemporaine* (1956), pp. 5–37.

Roupnel, G., *La Ville et la Campagne en XVIIIe siècle, étude sur les populations du pays dijonnais* (2nd edition, Paris, 1955).

Saint Jacob, Pierre de, *Les Paysans de la Bourgogne du Nord au dernier siècle de l'ancien régime* (Paris, 1960).

Soboul, Albert, *The Parisian Sans-Culottes and the French Revolution, 1793–4* (English trans. G. Lewis, Oxford, 1964).

Williams, G. A., *Artisans and Sans-Culottes. Popular movements in France and England during the Revolutionary Period* (1969).

Economic History

Bamford, P., 'Entrepreneurship in seventeenth and eighteenth century France', in *Explorations in Entrepreneurial History* (1957).

Bloch, Marc, *Les Caractères originaux de l'histoire rurale française* (new edition, Paris, 1952) (English trans.: *French Rural History. An Essay on its basic characteristics*, 1966).

Bourde, André J., *The Influence of England on the French Agronomes, 1750–1789* (Cambridge, 1953).

Grassby, R. B., 'Social status and commercial enterprise under Louis XIV', in *Economic History Review*, 2nd Series, vol. 13 (1960).

Labrousse, Ernest, *La Crise de l'économie française à la fin de l'Ancien Régime et au début de la Révolution* (Paris, 1944).

Scoville, Warren C., *The Persecution of the Huguenots and French Economic Development, 1680–1720* (Berkeley-Los Angeles, 1960).

Taylor, George V., 'Types of capitalism in Eighteenth-Century France', in *English Historical Review*, vol. LXXIX (1964), pp. 478–497.

Various, 'Aspects de l'économie française au XVIIe siècle', in *XVIIe Siècle*, Nos. 70–71 (Paris, 1966).

Culture

Barrière, Pierre, *La Vie intellectuelle en France du XVIe siècle à l'époque contemporaine* (Paris, 1961).

Bien, David D., *The Calas Affair* (Oxford, 1960).

Cobban, Alfred, *In Search of Humanity* (1960).

  Rousseau and the Modern State (1934).

  'The Enlightenment and the French Revolution', in Earl R. Wasserman (ed.), *Aspects of the Eighteenth Century* (1965), pp. 305–315.

Diaz, Furio, *Filosofia e Politica nel Settecento Francese* (Turin, 1962).

Foucault, Michel, *Folie et déraison, Histoire de la folie à l'âge Classique* (Paris, 1961) (English trans. *Madness and Civilisation: a history of insanity in the age of reason*, trans. and abridged by Richard Howard, 1967).

Gay, Peter, *Voltaire's Politics: The Poet as Realist* (1959).

  The Party of Humanity. Studies in the French Enlightenment (1964).

  The Enlightenment: An Interpretation, vol. 1, *The Rise of Modern Paganism* (1967), vol. 2, *The Science of Freedom* (1970).

Gottschalk, Louis, *Lafayette between the American and French Revolutions, 1783–1789* (1950).

Grimsley, Ronald, *Jean D'Alembert, 1717–1783* (Oxford, 1963).

Guehenno, Jean, *Jean-Jacques Rousseau* (Paris, 1962) (English trans. by John and Dorothy Weightman, 2 vols., (1966).

Judge, H. G., 'Church and State under Louis XIV', in *History*, XLV (1960).

Mandrou, Robert, *Introduction à la France moderne. Essai de psychologie historique (1500–1640)* (Paris, 1961).

Mornet, D., *Les Origines intellectuelles de la Révolution* (Paris, 1933).

Mousnier, Roland, 'Comment les Français voyaient la France au XVIIe siècle', in *XVIIe Siècle*, Nos. 25–26 (Paris, 1955).

Orcibal, Jean, *Louis XIV et les Protestants* (Paris, 1951).

Palmer, R. R., *Catholics and Unbelievers in XVIIIth-Century France* (Princeton, 1939).

Poland, Burdette, C., *French Protestantism and the French Revolution* (Princeton, 1957).

Proust, Jacques, *Diderot et L'Encyclopédie* (Paris, 1962).

Rothkrug, Lionel, *Opposition to Louis XIV: the Political and Social Origins of the French Enlightenment* (1965).

Shackleton, R., *Montesquieu: a Critical Biography* (Oxford, 1961).

Smith, D. W., *Helvétius: A Study in Persecution* (Oxford, 1965).

Snyders, George, *La Pédagogie en France aux XVIIe et XVIIIe siècles* (Paris, 1965).

Wilson, Arthur M., *Diderot, The Testing Years 1713–1759* (New York, 1957).

The Revolution

Cobban, Alfred, *Aspects of the French Revolution* (1968).

    Historians and the Causes of the French Revolution (Historical Association Pamphlet, G.2. revised edition, 1958).

    The Social Interpretation of the French Revolution (Cambridge, 1964).

Egret, Jean, *La Pré-Révolution Française, 1787–1789* (Paris, 1962).

Göhring, Martin, *Geschichte der Grossen Revolution* (2 vols., Tübingen, 1950, 1951).

Goodwin, A., *The French Revolution* (1953).

Hampson, N., *A Social History of the French Revolution* (1963).

Lefebvre, Georges, *Quatre-vingt-neuf* (1939). trans. R. R. Palmer, *The Coming of the French Revolution* (1947).

    La Révolution Française (Paris, 1957 edition). trans. Elizabeth M. Evanson, *The French Revolution from its origins to 1793* (1962).

McManners, J., 'The Revolution and its antecedents (1774–1794)', in J. M. Wallace-Hadrill and John McManners, *France, Government and Society* (1957).

Rudé, George, *The Crowd in the French Revolution* (Oxford, 1959). *Revolutionary Europe, 1783–1815* (1964).

Salvemini, Gaetano, *La Rivoluzione francese, 1788–1792* (new edition, Milan, 1962). trans. *The French Revolution* (1954).

Soboul, Albert, *La Révolution Française* (Paris, 1965).

Sydenham, M. J., *The French Revolution* (1965).

RUSSIA

Bibliographies

Black, C. E. (ed.), *Rewriting Russian History: Soviet Interpretations of Russia's Past* (New York, 1956).

Carson, G. B., 'Recent works on the History of Russia in the period from the Tatars to Catherine II', in *Cahiers d'histoire mondiale*, vol. VIII (1964), pp. 548–563.

Curtiss, John S., 'History', in Harold H. Fisher (ed.), *American Research on Russia* (Bloomington, 1959).

Keep, J. L. H., 'Verzeichnis des englischsprachigen Schrifttums (ausser U.S.A.) 1939–1952 zur Geschichte Osteuropas und Südost-europas', in *Forschungen zur osteuropäischen Geschichte*, vol. 5 (Berlin, 1957), pp. 119–162.

Leitsch, W., 'Russische Geschichte von der Wahl Michail Romanovs bis zur Ermorderung Pauls (1613–1801)', Parts 1, 2, 3 and 4, in *Jahrbücher für Osteuropa*, Neue Folge, vols. IX, X, XI (1961–63).

Mazour, Anatole G., *Modern Russian Historiography* (2nd edition, Princeton, 1958).

General Works

Anderson, M. S., *Britain's Discovery of Russia, 1553–1815* (1958).

Charques, R. A., *A Short History of Russia* (1956).

Clarkson, Jesse D., *History of Russia* (New York, 1961).

Dmytryshyn, Basil, *Medieval Russia, A Source Book, 900–1700* (1967).

Florinsky, Michael T., *Russia, A History and an Interpretation*, vol. I (New York, 1953).

Gitermann, Valentin, *Geschichte Russlands*, 3 vols (Zürich, 1944, 1945, 1949).

Klyuchevsky, V. O., *A History of Russia*, 5 vols (New York, 1960). *The Rise of the Romanovs*, trans. and ed. Liliana Archibald, assisted by Mark Scholl (1969).

Kochan, Lionel, *The Making of Modern Russia* (1962).

Loewenson, Leo, 'The Moscow Rising of 1648', in *Slavonic and East European Review*, vol. 27 (1948), pp. 146–156.

Longworth, P., *The Cossacks* (1969).

Nol'de, Boris, *La Formation de l'Empire Russe* (Paris, 1953).

O'Brien, C. Bickford, *Russia under two Tsars, 1682–1689. The Regency of Sophia Alekseevna* (Berkeley, 1952).

Pares, Bernard, *A History of Russia* (3rd edition, 1955).

Polonska-Vasylenko, N. D., *The Settlement of the Southern Ukraine 1750 till 1775* (New York, 1955).

Portal, Roger, *The Slavs* (1969). trans. from French edition of 1965.

Putnam, Peter (ed.), *Seven Britons in Imperial Russia* (Princeton, 1952).

Riasanovsky, N. V., *A History of Russia* (2nd edition, Oxford, 1969).

Schakovskoy, Zinaida, *Precursors of Peter the Great* (1964).

Stökl, Günther, *Russische Geschichte* (Stuttgart, 1962).

Sumner, B. H., *Survey of Russian History* (1961).

Vernadsky, G. V., *A History of Russia* (New Haven, 1961).

The Tsardom of Moscow, 1547–1682 (New Haven, 1969).

Wilson, Francesca, *Muscovy: Russia through Foreign Eyes, 1553–1900* (1970).

International Relations

Gerhard, Dietrich, *England und der Aufstieg Russlands. Zur Frage des Zusammenhanges der europäischen Staaten und ihres Ausgreifens in die aussereuropäische Welt in Politik und Wirtschaft des 19. Jahrhunderts* (Munich–Berlin, 1933).

Kaplan, Herbert, H., *The First Partition of Poland* (New York, 1962).

Lewitter, L. R., 'Poland, the Ukraine and Russia in the seventeenth century', Parts 1 and 2, in *Slavonic and East European Review*, vol. 27 (1948–49).

Longworth, P., *The Art of Victory: The Life and Achievements of Generalissimo Suvorov, 1729–1800* (1965).

McNeill, W. H., *Europe's Steppe Frontier, 1500–1800* (Chicago, 1964).

Madariaga, Isabel de, *Britain, Russia and the Armed Neutrality of 1780. Sir James Harris's Mission to St Petersburg during the American Revolution* (1962).

Mediger, Walter, *Moskaus Weg nach Europa. Der Aufstieg Russlands zum europäischen Machtstaat im Zeitalter Friedrichs des Grossen* (Brunswick, 1952).

O'Brien, C. Bickford, *Muscovy and the Ukraine. From the Pereiaslav Agreement to the Truce of Andrusovo, 1654–1667* (Berkeley, 1963).

Porchnev, Boris, 'Les rapports politiques de l'Europe occidentale et de l'Europe orientale à l'époque de la Guerre de Trente Ans', in *Rapports, XIe Congrès International des Sciences Historiques* (Göteborg–Stockholm–Uppsala, 1960).

Rauch, G. von, 'Moskau und die europäischen Mächte des 17. Jahrhunderts' in *Historische Zeitschrift*, vol. 178 (1954).

Sebes, Joseph, *The Jesuits and the Sino-Russian Treaty of Nerchinsk, 1689* (Rome, 1961).

Sumner, B. H., *Peter the Great and the Ottoman Empire* (Oxford, 1949).

Government

Alexeiev, Nikolai N., 'Beiträge zur Geschichte des russischen Absolutismus in 18. Jahrhundert' (trans. from Russian), in *Forschungen zur Osteuropäischen Geschichte*, vol. 6 (Berlin, 1958), pp. 7–81.

Amburger, E., *Geschichte der Behördenorganisation Russlands von Peter dem Grossen bis 1917* (Leiden, 1966).

Confino, M., 'La Politique de tutelle', in *Revue des études slaves*, vol. XXXVII (1960).

Kaplan, F. I., 'Tatisceva and Kantemiri. Two Eighteenth-Century exponents of a Russian bureaucratic style of thought', in *Jahrbücher für Geschichte Osteuropas* (1965).

Keep, J. L. H., 'The Decline of the Zemsky Sobor', in *Slavonic and East European Review*, vol. 36 (1957), pp. 100–122.

Pipes, R. E., 'The Russian Military Colonies', in *Journal of Modern History*, vol. XXII (1950).

Portal, R., 'Les Bachkirs et le Gouvernement Russe en XVIIIe siècle', in *Revue des études slaves*, vol. 22 (1946).

Raeff, Marc, *Plans for political Reform in Imperial Russia, 1730–1905* (1966).

    'L'État, le gouvernement et la tradition politique en Russie impériale', in *Revue d'histoire moderne et contemporaine* (1959).

    'Staatdienst, Aussenpolitik, Ideologien', in *Jahrbücher für Geschichte Osteuropas*, vol. 7 (1959), pp. 149–181.

    'The Russian Autocracy and its officials', in *Harvard Slavonic Studies, IV: Russian Thought and Politics* (Cambridge, Mass., 1957).

    'State and Nobility in the ideology of M. M. Shcherbatov', in *American Slavic and East European Review*, vol. XIX (1960).

Society

Blum, Jerome, *Lord and Peasant in Russia from the 9th to the 19th Century* (1961).

Confino, M., 'Le Paysan russe jugé par la noblesse au XVIIIe siècle', in *Revue des études slaves*, vol. XXXVIII (1961).

    'Seigneurs et Intendants en Russie aux XVIIIe et XIXe siècles', in *Revue des études slaves*, vol. XLII (1964), pp. 274–291.

    Domaines et Seigneurs en Russie vers la fin du XVIIIe siècle (Paris, 1963).

Dukes, Paul, *Catherine the Great and the Russian Nobility* (Cambridge, 1967).

Eeckaute, Denise, 'Les brigands en Russie du XVIIe au XIXe siècle: mythe ou réalité?' in *Revue d'histoire moderne et contemporaine*, vol. XII (1965), pp. 161–202.

Laran, Michel, 'Nobles et paysans en Russie, de l'age d'or du servage à son abolition (1762–1861)', in *Annales, économies, sociétés, civilisations* (Paris, 1966).

Pascal, R., 'Le paysans dans l'histoire de Russie', in *Revue historique*, vol. CLXXIII (1934).

'La Civilisation paysanne en Russie', in *Revue d'histoire de la philosophie et d'histoire générale de la civilisation* (1937).

'L'Entr'aide paysanne', in *Revue des études slaves*, vol. XX (1942).

Portal, R., 'Aux origines d'une bourgeoisie industrielle en Russie', in *Revue d'histoire moderne et contemporaine*, vol. VIII (1961), pp. 33–60.

'Du servage à la bourgeoisie: la famille Konovolov', in *Revue des études slaves*, vol. XXXVIII (1961), pp. 143–150.

L'Oural au XVIIIe siècle. Étude d'histoire économique et sociale (Paris, 1950).

'Manufactures et classes sociales en Russie au XVIIIe siècle', in *Revue historique*, vol. CCI (1949), pp. 161–185.

Raeff, Marc, 'Home, School and Service in the Life of the 18th-Century Russian Nobleman', in *Slavonic and East European Review*, vol. XL (1962), pp. 295–307.

Origins of the Russian Intelligentsia: the Eighteenth-Century Nobility (New York, 1966).

Robinson, G. T., *Rural Russia under the Old Régime* (1932).

Ruffman, Karl-Heinz, 'Russicher Adel als Sondertypus de europäischen Adelswelt', in *Jahrbücher für Geschichte Osteuropas*, vol. IX (1961), pp. 161–178.

Sacke, G., 'Adel und Bürgertum in der Regierungszeit Katherinas II von Russland', in *Revue Belge de Philologie et d'Histoire*, vol. XVII (1938).

'Adel und Bürgertum in der gesetzgebenden Kommission Katherinas II von Russland', in *Jahrbücher für die Geschichte Osteuropas*, vol. III (1938), pp. 408–417.

Smith, R. E. F., *The Enserfment of the Russian Peasantry* (Cambridge, 1968).

Economic History

Confino, M., 'Maîtres de forge et ouvriers dans les usines metallurgiques de l'Oural aux XVIIIe-XIXe siècles', in *Cahiers du monde russe et soviétique*, vol. 2 (1960).

Fisher, Raymond H., *The Russian Fur Trade, 1550–1700* (Berkeley, 1943).

Kahan, A., 'The Costs of "Westernization" in Russia', in *Slavic Review*, vol. XXV (1966).

Kulischer, J., *Russische Wirtschaftsgeschichte* (German trans., Jena, 1925).

'Die Kapitalistischen Unternehmer in Russland (insbesondere die Bauern als Unternehmer) in Anfangsstadien des Kapitalismus' in *Archiv für Sozialwissenschaft und Sozialpolitik*, vol. LXV (1931).

Lyashchenko, P. I., *History of the National Economy of Russia* (New York, 1949).

Price, Jacob M., *The Tobacco Adventure to Russia: Enterprise, Politics, and Diplomacy in the Quest for a Northern Market for English Colonial Tobacco, 1676–1722* (Philadelphia, 1961).

Warrener, D., 'Some controversial issues in the history of agrarian Europe', in *Slavonic and East European Review*, vol. XXXII (1954), pp. 182–184.

Culture

Billington, James H., *The Icon and the Axe: An Interpretative History of Russia* (New York, 1965).

Blanc, Simone, 'L'Église russe à l'aube du "Siècle des Lumières" ', in *Annales* (1965).

Cherniavsky, Michael, *Tsar and People: Studies in Russian Myths* (1961).

'The Old Believers and the new religion', in *Slavic Review*, vol. XXIV (1966), pp. 1–39.

Hans, N., 'Dumaresq, Brown and some early educational projects of Catherine II', in *Slavonic and East European Review*, vol. 40 (1961–62).

Lang, D. M., *The First Russian Radical: Alexander Radishchev, 1749–1802* (1959).

Laran, M., 'La Première génération de l' "intelligentsia" roturière en Russie', in *Revue d'histoire moderne et contemporaine*, vol. XLIV (1966).

Lewitter, L. R., 'Peter the Great, Poland, and the Westernization of Russia', in *Journal of the History of Ideas*, vol. XIX (Lancaster, Penn., 1958).

McConnell, A., *A Russian Philosophe: Alexander Radishchev, 1749–1802* (The Hague, 1964).

Miliukov, P., *Outlines of Russian Culture*, 3 vols. (Philadelphia, 1942).

Oliva, L. Jay, *Russia and the West from Peter to Krushchev* (Boston, 1965).

Raeff, Marc, *Origins of the Russian Intelligentsia: The Eighteenth-Century Nobility* (New York, 1966).

'State and Nobility in the Ideology of M. M. Shcherbatov', in *American Slavic and East European Review*, vol. XIX (1960).

Rogger, Hans, *National Consciousness in Eighteenth-Century Russia* (Cambridge, Mass., 1960).

Smolitsch, Igor, *Geschichte der russischen Kirche, 1700–1917* (Leiden, 1964).

Tompkins, S. R., *The Russian Mind: from Peter the Great through the Enlightenment* (Norman, Oklahoma, 1953).

Peter the Great

Blanc, Simone, 'A Propos de la politique économique de Pierre le Grand', in *Cahiers du monde russe et soviétique*, vol. III (Paris, 1962).

Cracraft, James, *The Church Reform of Peter the Great* (1971).

Geyer, D., 'Peter und St. Petersburg', in *Jahrbücher für Geschichte Osteuropas* (1962), pp. 181–200.

Klyuchevsky, Vasili, *Peter the Great* (English trans. by Liliana Archibald', (1965).

Oliva, L. J., *Peter the Great* (New York, 1971).

Raeff, Marc, *Peter the Great, Reformer or Revolutionary?* (Boston, 1963).

Sumner, B. H., *Peter the Great and the Emergence of Russia* (1950).
Peter the Great and the Ottoman Empire (Oxford, 1949).

Wittram, Reinhard, *Peter der Grosse, der Eintritt Russlands in die Neuzeit* (Berlin–Göttingen–Heidelberg, 1954).
Peter I, Czar und Kaiser. Zur Geschichte Peters des Grossen in seiner Zeit (Göttingen, 1964).

Mid Eighteenth Century.

Schmidt, S. O., 'La politique intérieure du Tsarisme au milieu du XVIIIe siècle', in *Annales* (1966), pp. 95–110.

Talbot Rice, Tamara, *Elizabeth: Empress of Russia* (1970).

Catherine the Great

Dukes, Paul, *Catherine the Great and the Russian Nobility* (Cambridge, 1967).

Gooch, G. P., *Catherine the Great and Other Studies* (1954).

Papmehl, K. A., 'The Problem of Civil Liberties in the Records of the Great Commission', in *Slavonic and East European Review*, vol. XLII (1964), pp. 274–291.

Portal, R., 'Pougatchev: une révolution manquée', in *Études d'histoire moderne et contemporaine*, vol. I (1947).

Reddaway, W. F. (ed.), *Documents of Catherine the Great: the correspondence with Voltaire and the instruction of 1767 in the English text of 1768* (Cambridge, 1931).

Sacke, G., 'Katherine II im Kampf um Thron und Selbstherrschaft', in *Archiv für Kulturgeschichte*, vol. XXIII (1923), pp. 191–216.
'Zur Charakteristick der gesetzgebenden Kommission Katherinas II von Russland', in *Archiv für Kulturgeschichte*, vol. XXI (1931), pp. 166–191.

Thompson, G. S., *Catherine the Great and the Expansion of Russia* (1947).

PRUSSIA

Bibliographies

Gebhardt, Bruno (ed.), *Handbuch der Deutschen Geschichte*, vol. 2, (16th to 18th Centuries), 8th edition (Stuttgart, 1955).

Skalweit, Stephen, 'Preussen als historisches Problem', in *Jahrbuch für die Geschichte Mittel- und Ostdeutschlands*, vol. III (Tübingen, 1954).

General Works

Barraclough, G., *Factors in German History* (Oxford, 1946).

Bruford, W. H., *Germany in the 18th Century* (1935).

Carsten, F. L., *The Origins of Prussia* (Oxford, 1954).

Dietrich, Richard (ed.), *Preussen, Epochen und Probleme seiner Geschichte* (Berlin, 1964).

Eckhardt, F. W., *Das Zeitalter des Absolutismus. Deutsche Geschichte von 1648 bis 1789* (1950).

Fay, Sidney B., and Epstein, Klaus, *The Rise of Brandenburg-Prussia to 1786* (1937, revised edition, 1964).

Feuchtwanger, E. J., *Prussia: Myth and Reality. The Role of Prussia in German History* (1970).

Flenley, Ralph, *Modern German History* (4th edition, revised Robert Spencer, 1969).

Franz, Günther, *Der Dreissigjährige Krieg und das Deutsche Volk* (Jena, 1943).

Gebhardt, Bruno (ed.), *Handbuch der Deutschen Geschichte*, vol. 2 (8th edition, Stuttgart, 1955).

Hertz, Frederick, *The Development of the German Public Mind*, vol. II (1962).

Hinrichs, Carl, *Preussen als Historisches Problem* (collected essays, ed. Gerhard Oestreich) (Berlin, 1964).

Hintze, Otto, *Die Hohenzollern und ihr Werk* (5th edition, Berlin, 1915).

Holborn, H., *A History of Modern Germany*, vol. II, *1648–1840* (1964).

Kohn, Hans (ed.), *German History. Some New German Views* (1954).

Macartney, C. A. (ed.), *The Habsburg and Hohenzollern Dynasties of the Seventeenth and Eighteenth Centuries* (1970).

Pascal, Roy, *The Growth of Modern Germany* (1946).

Rassow, Peter, *Deutsche Geschichte im Überblick* (Chapter on 18th century by Carl Hinrichs) (Stuttgart, 1962).

Ritter, Gerhard, *Staatskunst und Kriegshandwerk. Das Problem des 'Militarismus' in Deutschland*, vol. 1, *Die altpreussische Tradition (1740–1890)* (Munich, 1954).

   The Corrupting Influence of Power (English trans. of *Die Dämonie der Macht* by F. W. Pick, Hadleigh, 1952).

   Das Problem des Militarismus in Deutschland (Bonn, 1955).

Government

Dorn, Walter L., 'The Prussian Bureaucracy in the Eighteenth Century', in *Political Science Quarterly*, vols XLVI and XLVII (1931 and 1932).

Dorwart, R. A., *The Administrative Reforms of Frederick William I of Prussia* (Cambridge, Mass., 1953).

Hartung, F., 'Studien zur Geschichte der preussischen Verwaltung', in *Abhandlungen der preussischen Akademie* (Berlin, 1942).

   Deutsche Verfassungsgeschichte vom 15. Jahrhundert bis zur Gegenwart (6th edition, Stuttgart, 1954).

Hinrichs, Carl, 'Die preussische Zentralverwaltung in den Anfängen Friedrich Wilhelms', in *Preussen als Historisches Problem*, pp. 138–160.

Hintze, Otto, *Staat und Verfassung* (collected essays, ed. Gerhard Oestreich, 2nd edition, Göttingen, 1962).

   Geist und Epochen der preussischen Geschichte (Leipzig, 1943).

   'Preussens Entwicklung zum Rechtstaat' in *Forschungen zur Brandenburgischen und Preussischen Geschichte*, vol. 32 (1920).

   'Der Österreichische und der preussische Beamtenstaat im 17. und 18. Jahrhundert', in *Staat und Verfassung*, p. 321.

Jablonowski, Horst, 'Der preussische Absolutismus in sowjetrussicher Sicht', in K. Repgen and S. Skalweit (eds) *Spiegel der Ges-

chichte: Festgabe für Max Braubach zum 10. April 1964 (Münster, 1964), pp. 565–580.

Oestreich, Gerhard, 'Zur Heeresverfassung der deutschen Territorien von 1500 bis 1800', in Richard Dietrich and Gerhard Oestreich (eds), *Forschungen zu Staat und Verfassung, Festgabe für Fritz Hartung* (Berlin, 1958).

Parry, Geraint, 'Enlightened Government and its Critics in Eighteenth-Century Germany', *Historical Journal*, vol. VI (1963), pp. 178–192.

Rosenberg, H., *Bureaucracy, Aristocracy and Autocracy: the Prussian Experience, 1660–1815* (1958).

Weil, Herman, *Frederick the Great and Samuel von Cocceji* (Madison, Wisconsin, 1961).

Army

Büsch, Otto, *Militärsystem und Sozialleben im alten Preussen 1713–1807* (Berlin, 1962).

Craig, Gordon A., *The Politics of the Prussian Army, 1640–1945* (1955).

Demeter, Karl, *The German Officer Corps in Society and State, 1650–1945* (1965).

Shanahan, W. O., *Prussian Military Reforms, 1786–1813* (New York, 1945).

Society

Bog, Ingomar, *Die bäuerliche Wirtschaft im Zeitalter des Dreissigjährigen Krieges* (Coburg, 1952).

Büsch, Otto, *Militärsystem und Sozialleben im alten Preussen 1713–1807* (Berlin, 1962).

Carsten, F. L., 'The Origin of the Junkers', in *English Historical Review*, vol. LXII (1947), pp. 145–170.

Czybulka, Gerhard, *Die Lage der ländlichen Klassen Ostdeutschlands im 18. Jahrhundert* (Brunswick, 1949).

Görlitz, Walter, *Die Junker. Adel und Bauer im deutschen Osten* (Glücksburg, 1956).

Rosenberg, H., 'The Rise of the Junkers in Brandenburg-Prussia, 1410–1653', in *American Historical Review*, vol. XLIX (1943–44), pp. 1–22, and 228–242.

Economic History

Bechtel, Heinrich, *Wirtschaftsgeschichte Deutschlands von Beginn des 16. bis zum Ende des 18. Jahrhunderts* (Munich, 1952).

Henderson, W. O., *The State and the Industrial Revolution in Prussia, 1740–1870* (Liverpool, 1958).

Studies in the Economic Policy of Frederick the Great (1963).

Ludloff, R., 'Industrial Development in 16th- and 17th-Century Germany', in *Past and Present*, No. 12 (1957), p. 58.

Lütge, F., *Deutsche Sozial- und Wirtschaftsgeschichte* (2nd edition, Berlin–Göttingen–Heidelberg, 1960).

Terveen, Fritz, *Gesamtstaat und Retablissement: Der Wiederaufbau des nördlichen Ostpreussens unter Friedrich-Wilhelm I, 1714–1740* (Göttingen, 1954).

Culture

Barnard, F. M., *Herder's Social and Political Thought. From Enlightenment to Nationalism* (Oxford, 1965).

Brunschwig, Henri, *La Crise de l'état prussien à la fin du XVIIIe siècle et la genèse de la mentalité romantique* (Paris, 1947).

Hertz, Frederick, *The Development of the German Public Mind*, vol. II (1962).

Hinrichs, Carl, 'Der Hallische Pietismus als politische-soziale Reformbewegung des 18. Jahrhunderts', in *Preussen als Historisches Problem* (collected essays, ed. by Gerhard Oestreich, Berlin, 1964), pp. 171–184.

Oestreich, Gerhard, 'Calvinismus, Neustoizismus und Preussentum, eine Skizze', in *Jahrbuch für die Geschichte Mittel- und Ostdeutschlands*, vol. V (1945), pp. 157–181.

Pascal, Roy, *The German Sturm und Drang* (Manchester, 1953).

Pinson, K. S., *Pietism as a factor in the Rise of German Nationalism* (New York, 1934).

The Great Elector

Carsten, F. L., 'The Great Elector and the Foundation of the Hohenzollern despotism', in *English Historical Review*, vol. LXV (1950), pp. 175–202.

'The Resistance of Cleves and Mark to the despotic policy of the Great Elector', in *English Historical Review*, vol. LXVI (1951), pp. 219–241.

Hartung, Fritz, 'Der preussische Staat und seine westfälischen Provinzen' in *Westfälische Forschungen*, vol. 7 (1954), p. 7.

Hinrichs, Carl, 'Der Grosse Kurfürst 1620–1688', in *Preussen als Historisches Problem*, pp. 227–252.

Schevill, F., *The Great Elector* (Chicago, 1947).

Frederick I

Hinrichs, C., 'König Friedrich I von Preussen', in *Preussen als Historisches Problem*, pp. 253–271.

Frederick William I

Ergang, Robert, *The Potsdam Führer. Frederick-William I, Father of Prussian Militarism* (New York, 1941).

Hinrichs, Carl, 'Der Regierungsantritt Friedrich William I' in *Preussen als Historisches Problem*, pp. 91–137.

　　Friedrich Wilhelm I. König in Preussen. Eine Biographie. Jugend und Aufstieg (Hamburg, 1941).

　　'Friedrich Wilhelm I', in *Preussen als Historisches Problem*, pp. 40–72.

　　'Der Konflikt zwischen Friedrich Wilhelm I und Kronprinz Friedrich', in *Preussen als Historisches Problem*, pp. 185–202.

　　'Das Ahnenerbe Friedrich Wilhelms I', in *Preussen als Historisches Problem*, pp. 73–90.

Skalweit, Stephan, 'Friedrich Wilhelm I und die preussische Historie', in *Jahrbuch für die Geschichte Mittel- und Ostdeutschlands*, vol. VI (Tübingen, 1957), pp. 107–131.

Terveen, Fritz, *Gesamtstaat und Retablissement: Der Wiederaufbau des nördlichen Ostpreussen-unter Friedrich Wilhelm I, 1714–1740* (Göttingen, 1954).

Wagner, G., 'Friedrich Wilhelm I, Tradition und Personlichkeit', in *Historische Zeitschrift*, vol. 181 (1956).

Frederick the Great

Bussmann, W., 'Friedrich der Grosse im Wandel des europäischen Urteils', in *Festschrift für H. Rothfels* (1951).

Gooch, G. P., *Frederick the Great* (1947).

Henderson, W. O., *Studies in the Economic Policy of Frederick the Great* (1963).

Horn, D. B., *Frederick the Great and the Rise of Prussia* (1964).

Ritter, Gerhard, *Friedrich der Grosse. Ein historisches Profil* (3rd edition, Heidelberg, 1953). Trans. with introduction by Peter Paret (1968).

Rothfels, H., 'Friedrich der Grosse und der Staat', *Geschichte in Wissenschaft und Unterricht* (1962).

Skalweit, Stephan, 'Friedrich der Grosse und der Aufstieg Preussens', in *Die Europäer und ihre Geschichte. Epochen und Gestalten im Urteil der Nationen* (Munich, 1961).

Frankreich und Friedrich der Grosse, der Aufstieg Preussens in der öffentlich-Meinung des 'Ancien Régimes' (Bonn, 1952).

Weil, Herman, *Frederick the Great and Samuel von Cocceji* (Madison, Wisconsin, 1961).

AUSTRIA

Bibliographies

Gebhardt, Bruno, *Handbuch der Deutschen Geschichte*, vol. 2 (16th to 18th Centuries) (8th edition, Stuttgart, 1955).

Uhlirz, Karl and Mathilde, *Handbuch der Geschichte Österreichs und seiner Nachbarländer Böhmen und Ungarn*, 4 vols., (Graz–Leipzig–Vienna, 1927–44).

Zöllner, Erich, *Geschichte Österreichs* (3rd edition, Vienna, 1966).

General Works

Duffy, C., *The Wild Goose and the Eagle: a Life of Marshall von Brown, 1705–1757* (1964).

Flenley, Ralph, *Modern German History* (4th edition, revised Robert Spencer, 1969).

Hantsch, Hugo, *Die Geschichte Österreichs*, vol. 2, *1648–1918* (3rd edition, Graz–Vienna–Cologne, 1962).

    Die Nationalitätenfrage im alten Österreich. Das Problem der konstruktiven Reichsgestaltung (Vienna, 1953).

Hertz, Frederick, *The Development of the German Public Mind*, vol. II (1962).

Holborn, H., *A History of Modern Germany*, vol. II, *1648–1840* (1964).

Kann, Robert A., *The Habsburg Empire: A Study in Integration and Disintegration* (New York, 1957).

Lhotsky, Alphons, *Österreichische Historiographie* (Vienna, 1962).

Litschauer, G. F., *Kleine Österreichische Geschichte* (Vienna, 1961).

Macartney, C. A., *The Habsburg Empire, 1790–1918* (1969).

    The Habsburg and Hohenzollern Dynasties of the Seventeenth and Eighteenth Centuries (1970).

Rassow, Peter, *Deutsche Geschichte im Überblick* (The chapter on this period by Carl Hinrichs) (Stuttgart, 1962).

Rath, R. J. (ed.), *Austrian History Yearbook*, vol. I (Austin, Texas, 1965).

Taylor, A. J. P., *The Habsburg Monarchy* (1948).

Wandruszka, Adam, *The House of Habsburg* (1964).

Zöllner, Erich, *Geschichte Österreichs* (3rd edition, Vienna, 1966).

International Relations

Bernard, Paul, P., *Joseph II and Bavaria. Two Eighteenth-Century Attempts at German Unification* (The Hague, 1965).

Braubach, Max, *Versailles und Wien von Ludwig XIV bis Kaunitz* (Bonn, 1952).

Turkey

Barker, Thomas M., *Double Eagle and Crescent: Vienna's Second Turkish Siege and its Historical Setting* (Albany, 1967).

Cassels, Lavender, *The Struggle for the Ottoman Empire, 1717–1740* (1966).

McNeill, William H., *Europe's Steppe Frontier 1500–1800* (Chicago, 1964).

Stoye, John, *The Siege of Vienna* (1964).

Wagner, Georg, *Das Türkenjahr 1664. Eine europäische Bewährung* (Eisenstadt, 1964).

Prince Eugen

Braubach, Max, *Prinz Eugen von Savoyen. Eine Biographie*, 5 vols. (Vienna–Munich, 1963–65).

    Geschichte und Abenteuer: Gestalten um den Prinzen Eugen (Munich, 1950).

Henderson, N., *Prince Eugen of Savoy* (1964).

Sweet, Paul R., 'Prince Eugene of Savoy and Central Europe', in *American Historical Review*, vol. LVII (1951), pp. 47–63.

Wagner, Hans, 'Der Staatsman Prinz Eugen', in *Österreich in Geschichte und Literatur*, vol. VII.

Leopold I, Joseph I, Charles VI

Redlich, O., *Weltmacht des Barock. Österreich in der Zeit Kaiser Leopolds* (4th edition, Vienna, 1961).

    Das Werden einer Grossmacht (1700–1740) (4th edition, Vienna, 1962).

Stoye, John, 'The Emperor Charles VI: The early years of the reign', in *Transactions of the Royal Historical Society*, 5th Series, vol. 12 (1962), pp. 63–64.

Maria Theresa

Arneth, Alfred von, *Geschichte Maria Theresas*, 10 vols. (Vienna, 1863–79).

Crankshaw, Edward, *Maria Theresa* (1969).

Gooch, G. P., *Maria Theresa and other Studies* (1951).

Hantsch, Hugo, *Gestalter der Geschichte Österreichs* (Innsbruck–Vienna–Munich, 1962).

Pick, R., *Empress Maria Theresa: the Earlier Years, 1717–1757* (1966).

Walter, F., *Männer um Maria Theresa* (Vienna, 1951).
    Die Theresianische Staatsreform von 1749 (Vienna, 1951).

Joseph II

Bernard, Paul P., *Joseph II* (1968).
    Joseph II and Bavaria. Two Eighteenth-Century Attempts at German Unification (The Hague, 1965).
    The Origins of Josephinism. Two Studies (Colorado, 1964).

Fejtö, F., *Un Habsburg révolutionnaire. Joseph II* (Paris, 1953) (German trans. *Joseph II. Kaiser und Revolutionär. Ein Lebensbild*, Stuttgart, 1956).

Maass, Ferdinand, *Der Josephinismus (1760–1850)*, 5 vols. (Vienna, 1950–60).

Mitrofanov, P. von, *Joseph II: seine politische und kulturelle Tätigkeit* (German trans. from Russian, Vienna–Leipzig, 1910).

Padover, Saul K., *The Revolutionary Emperor: Joseph II of Austria* (2nd edition, 1967).

Silagi, Denis, *Jacobiner in der Habsburger Monarchie: Ein Beitrag zur Geschichte des aufgeklärten Absolutismus in Österreich* (Vienna, 1962).

Wagner, Hans, 'Die Reise Josephs II nach Frankreich 1777 und die Reformen in Österreich', in *Österreich und Europa. Festgabe für Hugo Hantsch* (Graz–Vienna–Cologne, 1965).

Walter, F., 'Die Organisierung der staatlichen Polizei unter Kaiser Joseph II', in *Mitteilungen des Vereins für Geschichte der Stadt Wein*, vol. VII (1927), pp. 22–53.
    Die Österreichische Zentralverwaltung (1740–1792), 2 vols. (Vienna, 1938, 1951).

Wangermann, Ernst, *From Joseph II to the Jacobin Trials* (Oxford, 1959).

Winter, E., *Der Josephinismus: Die Geschichte des Österreichischen Reformkatholizismus, 1740–1848* (revised edition, Vienna, 1962).

Zöllner, Erich, 'Bemerkungen zum Problem der Bezeihungen zwischen Aufklärung und Josefinismus', in *Österreich und Europa. Festgabe für Hugo Hantsch* (Graz–Vienna–Cologne, 1965).

Leopold II

Wandruszka, Adam, *Leopold II*, 2 vols. (Vienna, 1963–64).

Government

Hellbling, E. C., *Österreichische Verfassungs- und Verwaltungsgeschichte* (Vienna, 1956).

Hintze, Otto, 'Der österreichische und der preussische Beamtenstaat im 17. und 18. Jahrhundert', in Gerhard Oestreich (ed.), *Staat und Verfassung* (2nd edition, Göttingen, 1962).

Müller, P., 'Der aufgeklärte Absolutismus in Österreich', in *International Bulletin of the Historical Sciences*, IX (1937).

Schwartz, Harry F., *The Imperial Privy Council in the Seventeenth Century* (Cambridge, Mass., 1943).

Strakosch, Henry E., *State Absolutism and the Rule of Law (1753–1811)* (Sydney, 1967).

Valsecchi, F., *L'Assolutismo illuminato in Austria e in Lombardia*, 2 vols. (Bologna, 1931, 1934).

Walter, F., 'Die Organisierung der staatlichen Polizei unter Kaiser Joseph II', in *Mitteilungen des Vereins für Geschichte der Stadt Wien*, vol. VII (1927), pp. 22–53.

 Die Theresianische Staatsreform von 1749 (Vienna, 1951).

Wines, Roger, 'The Imperial Circles, Princely Diplomacy and Imperial Reform, 1681–1714', in *Journal of Modern History*, vol. 39 (1967), pp. 1–29.

Economic History

Freudenberger, Herman, *The Waldstein Woolen Mill: Noble Entrepreneurship in Eighteenth-Century Bohemia* (Boston, Mass., 1963).

 'Industrialisation in Bohemia and Moravia in the Eighteenth Century', in *Journal of Central European Affairs*, vol. XIX (1960), pp. 347–356.

 'The Woolen-Goods Industry of the Habsburg Monarchy in the Eighteenth Century', in *Journal of Economic History*, vol. XX (1960), pp. 383–406.

 'Three Mercantilist Proto-Factories', in *Business History Review*, vol. XL (1966).

Halm, Hans, *Habsburgischer Osthandel im 18. Jahrhundert* (Munich, 1954).

Hoffmann, Alfred, *Österreichs Wirtschaft im Zeitalter des Absolutismus. Festschrift für Karl Eder* (Innsbruck, 1959).

Klíma, A., 'Industrial Development in Bohemia, 1648–1781', in *Past and Present*, no. 11 (1957), p. 87.

Society

Brion, M., *Daily Life in the Vienna of Mozart and Schubert* (trans. from French, 1961).

Brunner, Otto, *Adeliges Landleben und Europäischer Geist* (Salzburg, 1949).

Grüll, Georg, *Bauer, Herr und Landesfürst. Sozialrevolutionäre Bestrebungen der oberösterreichischen Bauern von 1650–1848* (Linz, 1963).

Jelnsic, K., 'La noblesse autrichienne', in *Annales*, vol. VIII (Paris, 1956), pp. 355–365.

Link, Edith Murr, *The Emancipation of the Austrian Peasant, 1740–1798* (1949).

Schüneman, K., *Österreichs Bevölkerungspolitik unter Maria Theresa* (Berlin, 1935).

Varga, J., *Typen und Probleme der Bäuerlichen Grundbesitzer in Ungarn, 1767–1849* (Budapest, 1965).

Wright, William E., *Serf, Seigneur, and Sovereign, Agrarian Reform in Eighteenth-Century Bohemia* (Minneapolis, 1966).

Culture

Bernard, Paul B., *The Origins of Josephinism. Two Studies* (Colorado, 1964).

Coreth, Anna, *Pietas Austriaca, Ursprung und Entwicklung barocker Frömmigkeit in Österreich* (Vienna, 1959).

Kann, Robert, A., *A study in Austrian Intellectual History from Late Baroque to Romanticism* (1960).

Maass, Ferdinand, *Der Josephinismus, 1760–1850* (Vienna, 1950–60).

Mecenseffy, Grete, *Geschichte des Protestantismus in Österreich* (Graz–Cologne, 1956).

Schüssel, Therese, *Kultur des Barock in Österreich* (Graz, 1960).

Valjavec, F., *Die Entstehung der politischen Strömungen in Deutschland, 1770–1815* (Munich–Vienna, 1951).

Wagner, Hans, 'Der Höhepunkt der französischen Kultureinflüsse in Österreich in der zweiten Hälfte des 18. Jahrhunderts', in *Österreich in Geschichte und Literatur*, vol. V (1961).

Winter, E., *Der Josephinismus: Die Geschichte des Österreichischen Reformkatholizismus, 1740–1848*, (revised edition, Vienna, 1962).

Zöllner, Erich, 'Bemerkungen zum Problem der Beziehungen zwischen Aufklärung und Josefinismus', in *Österreich und Europa. Festgabe für Hugo Hantsch* (Graz–Vienna–Cologne, 1965).

Bohemia

Betts, R., *Essays in Czech History* (1969).

Denis, E., *La Bohème depuis la Montagne Blanche*, 2 vols. (Paris, 1903).

Freudenberger, Herman (see under *Economic History*).

Kerner, R. J., *Bohemia in the Eighteenth Century* (New York, 1932).

Klíma, A. (see under *Economic History*).

Weinzierl-Fischer, Erika, 'Die Bekämpfung der Hungersnot in Böhmen 1770–1772 durch Maria Theresa und Joseph II', in *Mitteilungen des Österreichischen Staatsarchivs*, vol. 7 (1954).

Wright, William E. (see under *Society*).

Hungary

Berenger, Jean, 'La Hongrie des Habsbourgs au XVIIe siècle. République nobiliaire ou monarchie limitée', in *Revue historique*, vol. CCXXXVIII (1967).

Hollander, A. N. J., 'The Great Hungarian Plain: A European Frontier Area', *Comparative Studies in Society and History*, vol. III (1960–61).

Macartney, C. A., *Hungary, a short history* (Edinburgh, 1962).

McNeill, William H. (see under *Turkey*).

Marczali, H., *Hungary in the 18th Century* (Cambridge, 1910).

Miskolczy, Gyula, *Ungarn in der Habsburger Monarchie* (Vienna–Munich, 1959).

Pach, P., *Die ungarische Agrarenentwicklung im 16–17. Jahrhundert: Abbiegung vom Westeuropäischen Entwicklungsgang* (Budapest, 1964).

Silagi, Denis, *Ungarn und der geheime Mitarbeiterkreis Leopolds II* (Munich, 1961).

Sugar, Peter S., 'Influence of the Enlightenment and the French Revolution in 18th-Century Hungary', in *Journal of Central European Affairs*, vol. XVII (1958), pp. 331–355.

Varga, J. (see under *Society*).

Wagner, Georg (see under *Turkey*).

Croatia

Rothenberg, G. E., *The Austrian Military Border in Croatia, 1522–1747* (Urbana, Illinois, 1960).
    The Military Border in Croatia, 1740–1881. A Study of an Imperial Institution (Chicago, 1963).

Italy

Benedikt, Heinrich, *Kaiseradler über dem Apennin. Die Österreicher in Italien, 1700–1866* (Vienna–Munich, 1964).

Limoli, Donald, 'Pietro Verri, a Lombard Reformer under Enlightened Despotism and the French Revolution', in *Journal of Central European Affairs*, vol. XVIII (1958), p. 260.

Roberts, J. M., 'L'Aristocrazia lombarda nel 18 secolo', in *Occidente*, vol. VIII (1952), pp. 305–325.

Valsecchi, F. (see under *Government*).

Wandruszka, A., 'Österreich und Italien im 18. Jahrhundert', in *Österreich Archiv* (Vienna, 1963).

Belgium

Benedikt, Heinrich, *Als Belgien noch österreichisch war* (Vienna, 1965).

Gilissen, J., *Le Régime représentatif avant 1790 en Belgique* (Brussels, 1952).

BRITAIN

Bibliographies

Buttman, W. A., 'Early Hanoverian England (1714–1760): Some Recent writings', in *Journal of Modern History* (1963).

Chrimes, S. B. and Roots, I. A., *English Constitutional History* (Historical Association *Helps for Students of History* No. 58).

Davies, G. (ed.), *Bibliography of British History: Stuart Period* (1928).

Pargellis, S. M. and Medley, D. J. (eds), *Bibliography of British History: The Eighteenth Century, 1714–1789* (Oxford, 1951).

Vaucher, P., 'L'évolution intérieure de l'Angleterre au XVIIIe siècle: quelques problèmes', in *Revue historique*, vol. CCXXXVI (1966).

General Works

Aylmer, G. E., *The Struggle for the Constitution, 1603–89* (1963).

Baxter, S. B., *William III* (1966).

Briggs, Asa, *The Age of Improvement* (1959).

Browning, A. (ed.), *English Historical Documents*, vol. 8 (1660–1714) (1953).

Christie, Ian, *Myth and Reality in late Eighteenth-Century British Politics, and other Papers* (1970).

Clark, G. N., *The Later Stuarts* (2nd edition, Oxford, 1956).

Dickinson, H. T., *Bolingbroke* (1970).

Green, David, *Queen Anne* (1970).

Hexter, J. H., *Reappraisals in History* (1961).

Hill, Christopher, *The Century of Revolution* (Edinburgh, 1961).

Reformation to Industrial Revolution, a Social and Economic History of Britain, 1530–1780 (1967).

Horn, D. B. and Ransome, M., *English Historical Documents*, vol. 10 (*1714–1783*) (1957).

Kenyon, J. P., *The Stuarts* (1958).

McInnes, Angus, *Robert Harley: Puritan Politician* (1970).

Marshall, Dorothy, *Eighteenth-Century England* (1962).

Michael, W., *Englische Geschichte im 18. Jahrhundert*, 5 vols. (Leipzig, 1920–1955), of which vols 1 and 2 are trans. as *England under George I* (1936, 1939).

Ogg, David, *England in the Reign of Charles II*, 2 vols. (Oxford, 1956).

    England in the Reigns of James II and William III (Oxford, 1955).

Plumb, J. H., *England in the Eighteenth Century* (1950).

    The First Four Georges (1956).

    Sir Robert Walpole, vol. 1, *The Makings of a Statesman* (1956), vol. II *The King's Minister* (1960).

Watson, J. S., *The Reign of George III, 1760–1815* (Oxford, 1960).

Williams, B., *The Whig Supremacy, 1714–1760* (2nd edition, Oxford, 1962).

International Relations

Cobban, Alfred, *Ambassadors and Secret Agents. The Diplomacy of the First Earl of Malmesbury at the Hague* (1954).

Harlow, Vincent T., *The Founding of the Second British Empire, 1763–1793*, vol. 1 (1952), vol. 2 (1964).

Hatton, R. M. and Bromley, J. S. (eds), *William III and Louis XIV: Essays 1680–1720* (Liverpool, 1958).

Horn, D. B., *The British Diplomatic Service, 1689–1789* (Oxford, 1961).

    Great Britain and Europe in the Eighteenth Century (Oxford, 1967).

Jones, J. R., *Britain and Europe in the Seventeenth Century* (1966).

The Civil War

Everitt, A., *The Community of Kent in the Great Rebellion 1640–1660* (Leicester, 1966).

Roots, Ivan, *The Great Rebellion, 1642–60* (1966).

Government

Ashley, Maurice, *The Glorious Revolution of 1688* (1966).

Aylmer, G. E., *The King's Servants, The Civil Service of Charles I, 1625–1642* (1961).

Beattie, J. M., *The English Court in the Reign of George I* (Cambridge, 1967).

Boulton, J. T., *The Language of Politics in the Age of Wilkes and Burke* (1963).

Carswell, John, *The Descent on England* (1969).

Cone, Carl B., *Burke and the Nature of Politics, the Age of the French Revolution* (Kentucky, 1964).

Derry, J. W., *The Regency Crisis and the Whigs, 1788–9* (Cambridge, 1963).

Dickson, P. G. M., *The Financial Revolution in England, 1688–1756* (1967).

Foord, Archibald S., *His Majesty's Opposition 1714–1830* (Oxford, 1964).

Holdsworth, Sir William, *A History of English Law*, vol. 10 (1938).

Holmes, Geoffrey, *British Politics in the Age of Anne* (1967).

and Speck, W. A., *The Divided Society: Party Conflict in England, 1694–1716* (1967).

Jones, J. R., *The First Whigs: the Politics of the Exclusion Crisis 1678–83* (Oxford, 1961).

Keir, Sir David Lindsay, *The Constitutional History of Modern Britain, 1485–1937* (3rd edition, 1948).

Kenyon, J. P., *The Stuart Constitution, 1603–1688* (Cambridge, 1966).

Kramnick, Isaac, *Bolingbroke and his Circle* (Oxford, 1969).

Mitchell, L. G., *Charles James Fox and the Disintegration of the Whig Party, 1782–1794* (Cambridge, 1971).

Namier, Sir L. B., *England in the Age of the American Revolution* (1930).

The Structure of Politics at the Accession of George III (2nd edition, 1957).

Norris, John, *Shelburne and Reform* (1963).

Owen, John B., *The Rise of the Pelhams* (1957).

Pares, R., *King George III and the Politicians* (Oxford, 1953).

Plumb, J. H., *The Growth of Political Stability in England 1675–1725* (1967).

Roberts, Clayton, *The Growth of Responsible Government in Stuart England* (Cambridge, 1966).

Rubini, Dennis, *Court and Country, 1688–1702* (1968).

Thomas, P. D. G., *The House of Commons in the Eighteenth Century* (Oxford, 1971).

Thomson, Mark A., *A Constitutional History of England, 1642 to 1801* (1938).

Western, J. R., *The English Militia in the 18th century, The Story of a Political Issue, 1660–1802* (1965).

Williams, E. N., *The Eighteenth-Century Constitution* (Cambridge, 1960).

Witcombe, D. T., *Charles II and the Cavalier House of Commons, 1663–1674* (Manchester, 1966).

Zagorin, Perez, *The Court and the Country* (1969).

Economic History

Ashton, T. S., *An Economic History of England: the eighteenth century* (2nd edition, 1966).

　　The Industrial Revolution, 1760–1830 (Oxford, 1949).

Chambers, J. D., and Mingay, G. E., *The Agricultural Revolution, 1750–1880* (1966).

Clark, G. N., *The Wealth of England, from 1496–1760* (Oxford, 1946).

Deane, Phyllis, *The First Industrial Revolution* (Cambridge, 1965).

Habakkuk, H. J., 'English Landownership, 1680–1740', in *Economic History Review*, 1st Series, vol. 10 (1939–40).

　　'Landowners and the Civil War', in *Economic History Review*, 2nd Series, vol. 18 (1965).

Hartwell, R. M., *The Causes of the Industrial Revolution in England* (1967).

Henderson, W. O., *Britain and Industrial Europe, 1750–1850* (Leicester, 1966).

Jones, E. L., *Agriculture and Economic Growth in England, 1650–1815* (1968).

Mantoux, Paul, *The Industrial Revolution in the Eighteenth Century* (1928).

Mathias, Peter. *The First Industrial Nation, an economic history of Britain, 1700–1914* (1969).

Nef, J. U., *Industry and Government in France and England, 1540–1640* (Philadelphia, 1940).

Ramsay, G. D., *English Overseas Trade during the Centuries of Emergence* (1937).

Wilson, Charles, *England's Apprenticeship 1603–1763* (1965).

Society

Ashley, Maurice, *Life in Stuart England* (1964).

Bell, H. E. and Ollard, R. L., *Historical Essays, 1600–1750, presented to David Ogg* (1963).

Briggs, Asa, 'Middle-class consciousness in English politics 1780–1846', in *Past and Present*, vol. 9 (1965), p. 65.

Chambers, J. D., *The Vale of Trent, 1670–1800* (Cambridge, 1957).

George, M. D., *England in Transition* (1953).

　　London Life in the Eighteenth Century (1925).

Habakkuk, H. J., 'La disparition du paysan anglais', in *Annales*, vol. XX (Paris, 1965).

Hecht, J. J., *The domestic servant class in eighteenth-century England* (1956).

Hoskins, W. G., *The Midland Peasant* (1957).

Hughes, Edward, *North Country Life in the Eighteenth Century* (1952).

　　North Country Life in the Eighteenth Century, vol. II, *Cumberland and Westmorland, 1700–1830* (Oxford, 1965).

Laslett, Peter, *The World We Have Lost* (1965).

Manning, B., 'The Nobles, the people, and the constitution' in *Past and Present*, vol. 9 (1956), p. 42.

Marshall, Dorothy, *The English People in the Eighteenth Century* (1965).

Mingay, G. E., *English Landed Society in the Eighteenth Century* (1963).

Perkin, Harold, *The Origins of Modern English Society, 1780–1880* (1969).

Ravitch, Norman, 'The Social Origins of French and English bishops in the eighteenth century', in *Historical Journal*, vol. VIII (1965), pp. 309–325.

Speck, W. A., 'Social status in late Stuart England', *Past and Present*, vol. 33 (1966), p. 148.

Stone, Lawrence, *The Crisis of the Aristocracy, 1558–1641* (Oxford, 1965).

　　Social change and revolution in England, 1540–1640 (1965).

　　'Social mobility in England, 1500–1700', in *Past and Present*, vol. 33 (1966), p. 16.

Thompson, E. P., *The Making of the English Working Class* (1963).

Wearmouth, R. F., *Methodism and the Common People of the Eighteenth Century* (1945).

Williams, E. N., *Life in Georgian England* (1962).

Williams, G. A., *Artisans and Sans Culottes, Popular movements in France and England during the Revolutionary period* (1969).

Culture

Best, F. G. A., *Temporal Pillars* (Cambridge, 1964).

Cranston, M., *John Locke* (1957).

Greenleaf, W. H., *Order, Empiricism and Politics: Two Traditions of English Political Thought, 1500–1700* (Oxford, 1964).

Laslett, Peter, 'The English Revolution and Locke's "Two Treatises of Government"', *Cambridge Historical Journal*, vol. XII, p. 40.
    (ed.) John Locke, *Two Treatises of Government* (Cambridge, 1961).

Macpherson, C. B., *The Political Theory of Possessive Individualism* (1962).

Salmon, J. H. M., *The French Religious Wars in English Political Thought* (Oxford, 1959).

Schofield, R. E., *The Lunar Society of Birmingham* (Oxford, 1963).

Skinner, Quentin, 'The ideological context of Hobbes's political thought', in *Historical Journal*, vol. IX (1966), pp. 283–317.

Stewart, John B., *The Moral and Political Philosophy of David Hume* (New York, 1963).

Summerson, J. N., *Architecture in Britain, 1530–1830* (1953).

Sykes, Norman, *Church and State in England in the Eighteenth Century* (1934).

Waterhouse, E. K., *Painting in Britain, 1530–1790* (1953).

Watkins, J. W. N., *Hobbes's System of Ideas* (1965).

Willey, Basil, *The Seventeenth-Century Background* (1934).
    The Eighteenth-Century Background (1949).

The Radical Movement

Black, E. C., *The Association: British Extra-Parliamentary Political Organisation, 1769–1793* (Oxford, 1963).

Butterfield, Herbert, *George III, Lord North, and the People, 1779–1780* (1949).

Christie, Ian R., *Wilkes, Wyvill and Reform* (1962).

Cone, Carl B., *The English Jacobins: Reforms in Late Eighteenth-Century England* (New York, 1968).

Maccoby, S., *English Radicalism, 1762–85* (1955).

Rudé, George, *Wilkes and Liberty: a social study of 1763–1774* (Oxford, 1962).

Sutherland, L. S., *The City of London and the opposition to Government, 1768–74: a study in the rise of Metropolitan Radicalism* (1959).

The American Revolution

Alden, J. R., *The American Revolution, 1775–83* (1954).

Bailey, Bernard, *The Ideological Origins of the American Revolution* (Oxford, 1967).

Beloff, M. (ed.), *The Debate on the American Revolution, 1761–83* (2nd edition, 1960).

Donoghue, B., *British Politics and the American Revolution, The Path to War, 1773–75* (1964).

Gipson, L. H., *The Coming of the Revolution, 1763–75* (1954).

Guttridge, G. A., *English Whiggism and the American Revolution* (Oxford, 1966).

Mackesy, P., *The War for America, 1775–1783* (1964).

Miller, J. C., *Origins of the American Revolution* (Pal. Alto, 1959). *Triumph of Freedom, 1775–83* (Boston, 1948).

Pole, J. R., *Political Representation in England and the Origins of the American Republic* (1966).

Scotland

Campbell, R. H., *Scotland since 1707: the Rise of an Industrial Society* (Oxford, 1965).

Smout, T. C., *A History of the Scottish People, 1560–1830* (1969).

Ireland

Becket, J. C., *The Making of Modern Ireland, 1603–1923* (1966).

Boulton, G. C., *The Passing of the Irish Act of Union* (Oxford, 1966).

Johnston, Edith M., *Great Britain and Ireland, 1760–1800* (1963).

Lyons, F. S., *Ireland since the Famine* (1971).

Acknowledgements

Thanks are due to the following for permission to quote extracts from the works mentioned: to George Allen and Unwin (F. Hertz, *The Development of the German Public Mind*, vol. II, 1962); to Routledge and Kegan Paul (Harold Perkin, *The Origins of Modern English Society, 1780–1880*, 1969; and G. E. Mingay, *English Landed Society in the Eighteenth Century*, 1963; and Norman Hampson, *A Social History of the French Revolution*, 1963); to the Macmillan Company (Michael T. Florinsky, *Russia, a History and an Interpretation*, 1953; and Herbert H. Rowen, *From Absolutism to Revolution, 1648 to 1848*, 1963).

Index

More about Penguins
and Pelicans

Penguinews, which appears every month, contains details of all the new books issued by Penguins as they are published. From time to time it is supplemented by *Penguins in Print*, which is a complete list of all available books published by Penguins. (There are well over three thousand of these.)

A specimen copy of *Penguinews* will be sent to you free on request, and you can become a subscriber for the price of the postage. For a year's issues (including the complete lists) please send 30p if you live in the United Kingdom, or 60p if you live elsewhere. Just write to Dept EP, Penguin Books Ltd, Harmondsworth, Middlesex, enclosing a cheque or postal order, and your name will be added to the mailing list.

Note: *Penguinews* and *Penguins in Print* are not
available in the U.S.A. or Canada

Europe since Napoleon

David Thomson

This history of modern Europe – already a standard work, which has been reprinted eight times – was written in the belief that the pattern of European development since 1789 can only be understood by a study of those all-embracing forces that have affected the whole continent, from Britain to the Balkans.

Thus Dr Thomson emphasizes particularly the overall factors of population growth, industrialization, overseas expansion, democracy and socialism, the impact of nationalism, and the connexion between war and revolution. He considers these, not country by country, but phase by phase, so that the development of European civilization over the past century and a half is unfolded as a continuous whole.

The result is a history whose every detail has a significant contribution to make in depicting the pattern of the past, – a history of which the *Economist* said: 'It is to be hoped that it will be found ... wherever intelligent men and women think and read.'

Not for sale in the U.S.A. or Canada